ORDNANCE SURVEY

STREET ATLAS
Berkshire

Contents

IV *Key to maps*

VI *Administrative boundaries*

1 *Street maps*

154 *Index explanation and abbreviations*

155 *Index of towns, villages and rural localities*

156 *Index of street names*

PHILIP'S

First edition published 1990
Third edition published 1994 by

Ordnance Survey   and   Philip's
Romsey Road   an imprint of Reed Consumer Books Limited
Maybush   Michelin House, 81 Fulham Road, London, SW3 6RB
Southampton SO16 4GU   and Auckland, Melbourne, Singapore and Toronto

ISBN 0-540-05992-7 (Philip's, hardback)
ISBN 0-540-05993-5 (Philip's, softback)
ISBN 0-319-00475-9 (Ordnance Survey, hardback)
ISBN 0-319-00476-7 (Ordnance Survey, softback)

To the best of the Publishers' knowledge, the information in this atlas was correct at the
time of going to press. No responsibility can be accepted for any errors or their
consequences.

The representation in this atlas of a road, track or path is no evidence of the existence of
a right of way.

Printed and bound in Great Britain by
Butler & Tanner Ltd, Frome and London

Key to map symbols

⊛	**British Rail station**
⊖	**London transport station**
🚂	**Private railway station**
⬤	**Bus or coach station**
Ⓗ	**Heliport**
♦	**Police station** (may not be open 24 hours)
✚	**Hospital with casualty facilities** (may not be open 24 hours)
☐	**Post office**
+	**Place of worship**
▮	**Important building**
P	**Parking**
120	**Adjoining page indicator**
═══	**Motorway or dual carriageway**
A27(T)	**Main or through road** (with Department of Transport number)
─┬─	**Gate or obstruction to traffic** (restrictions may not apply at all times or to all vehicles)
– – – – –	**Footpath**
— — —	**Bridleway**
– – –	**Path**
═══	**Track**

The representation in this atlas of a road, track or path is no evidence of the existence of a right of way

Amb Sta	**Ambulance station**	LC	**Level crossing**
Coll	**College**	Liby	**Library**
FB	**Footbridge**	Mus	**Museum**
F Sta	**Fire station**	Sch	**School**
Hospl	**Hospital**	TH	**Town hall**

0	¼	½	¾	1 mile
0	250m	500m	250m	1 Kilometre

The scale of the maps is 3½ inches to 1 mile (1:18103)

The small numbers around the edges of the maps
identify the 1 kilometre National Grid lines

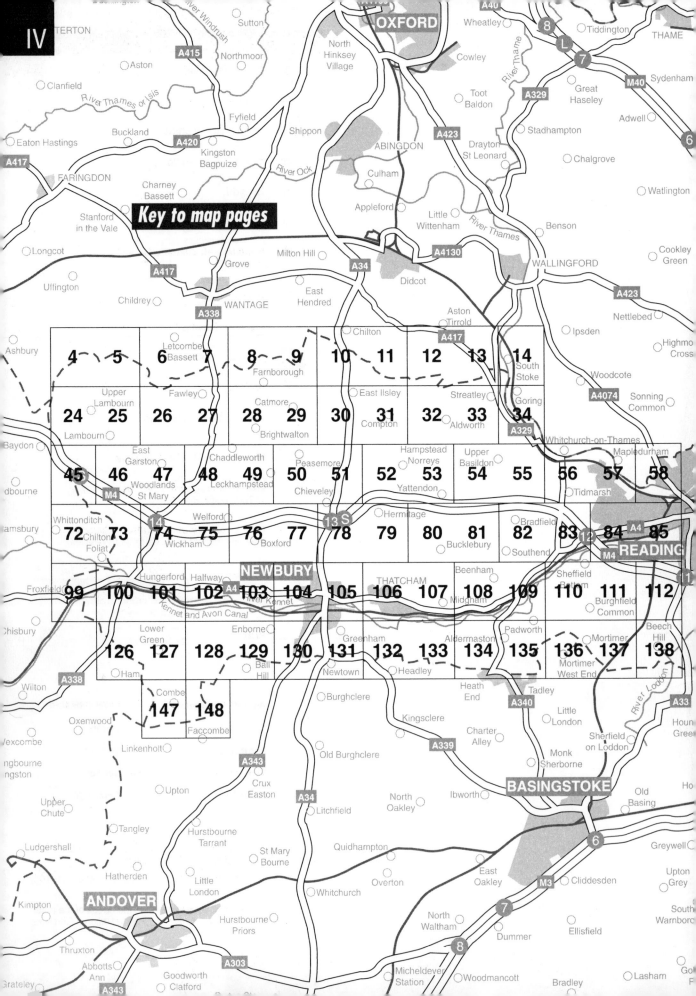

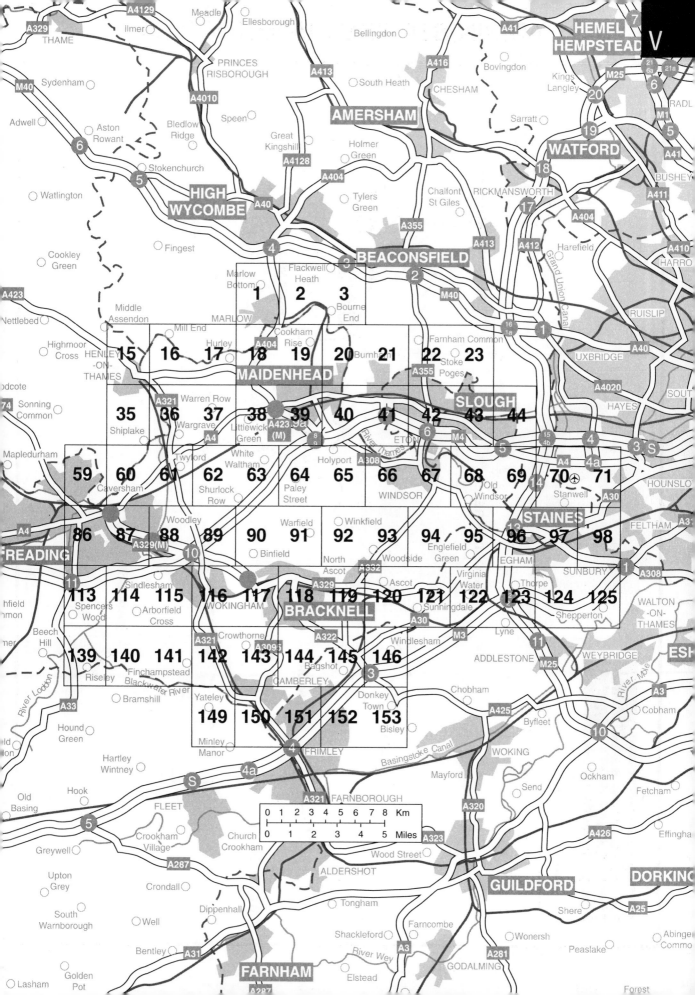

ADMINISTRATIVE BOUNDARIES

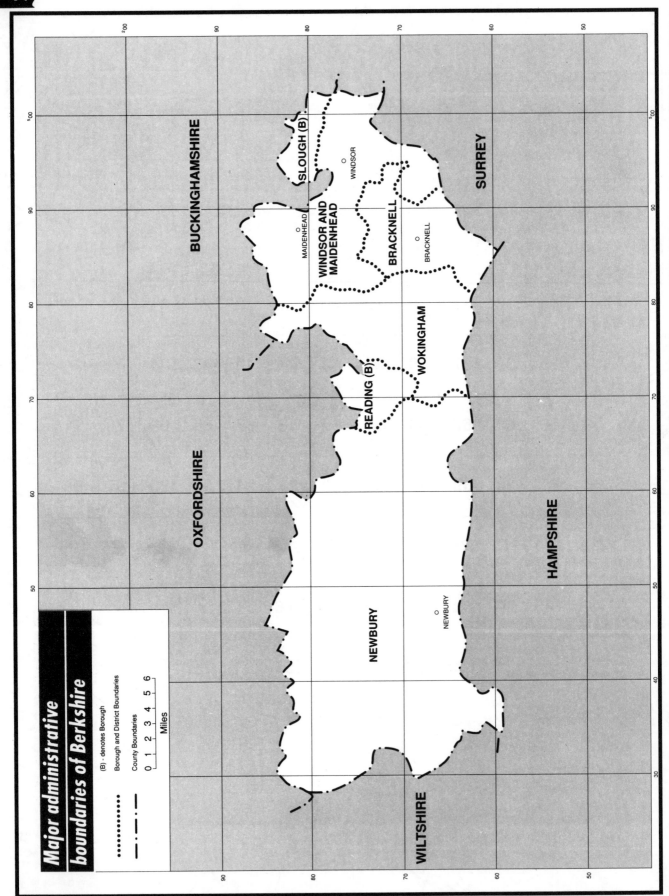

Major administrative boundaries of Berkshire

(B) - denotes Borough

Borough and District Boundaries

········· County Boundaries

0 1 2 3 4 5 6
Miles

BUCKINGHAMSHIRE

SLOUGH (B)

WINDSOR
○ WINDSOR

WINDSOR AND MAIDENHEAD

MAIDENHEAD
○

BRACKNELL

BRACKNELL
○

SURREY

WOKINGHAM

READING (B)

OXFORDSHIRE

NEWBURY

NEWBURY
○

HAMPSHIRE

WILTSHIRE

not continued, see key diagram

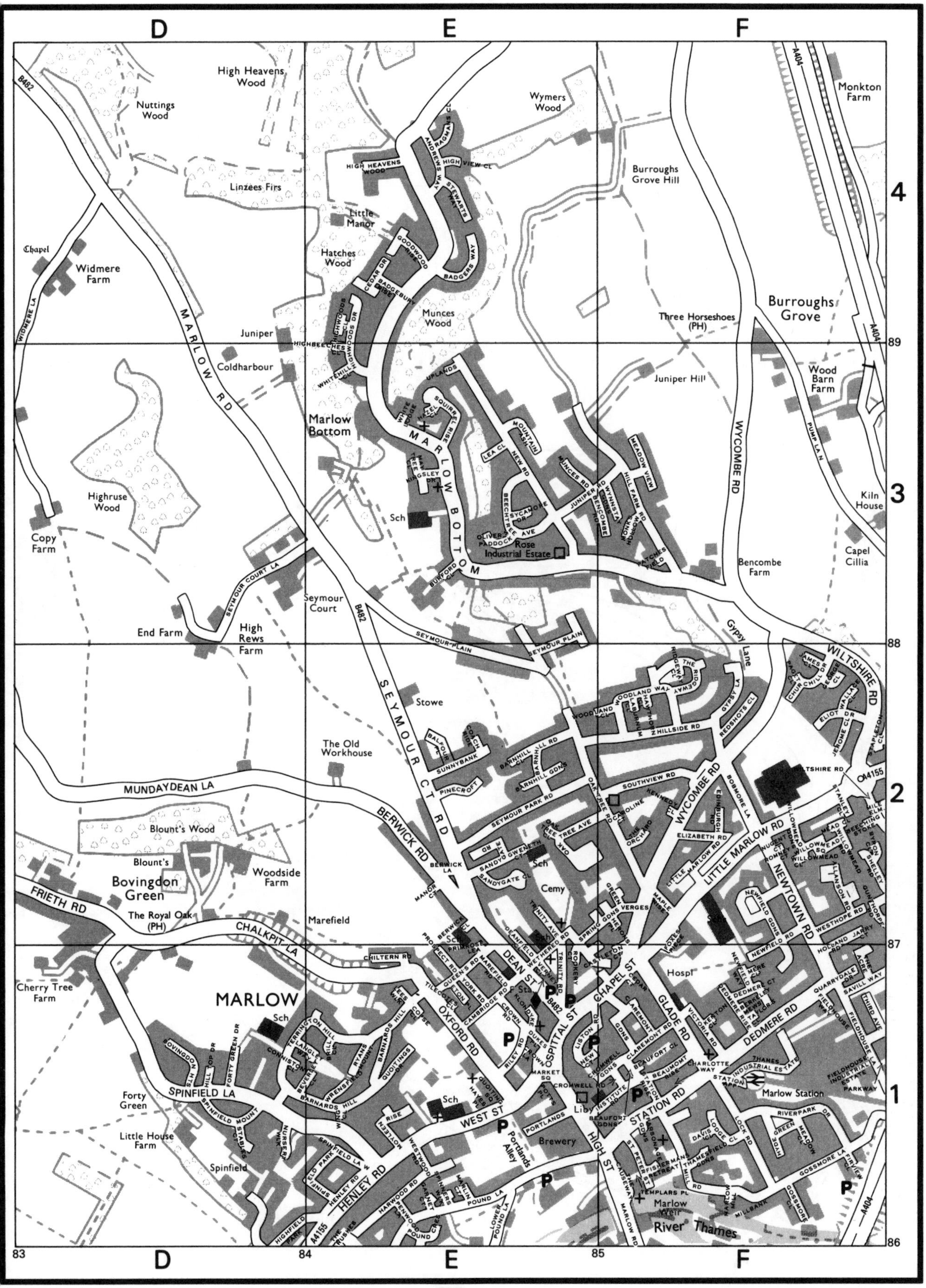

2

18

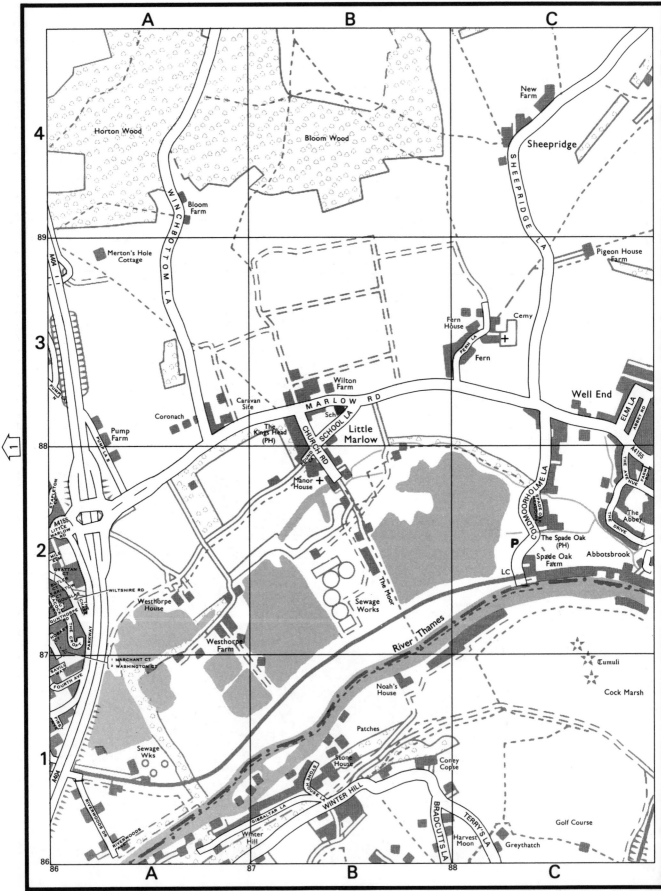

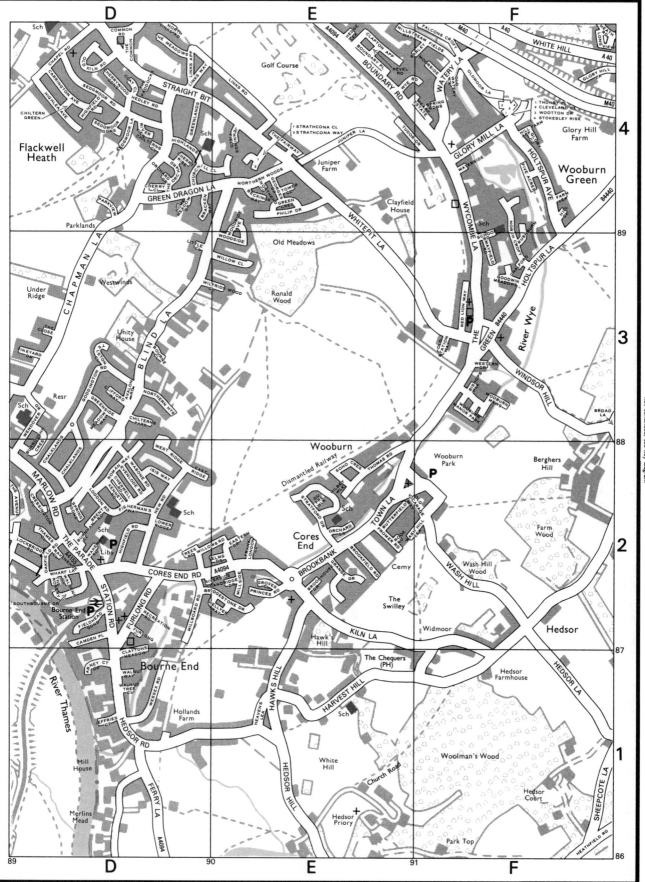

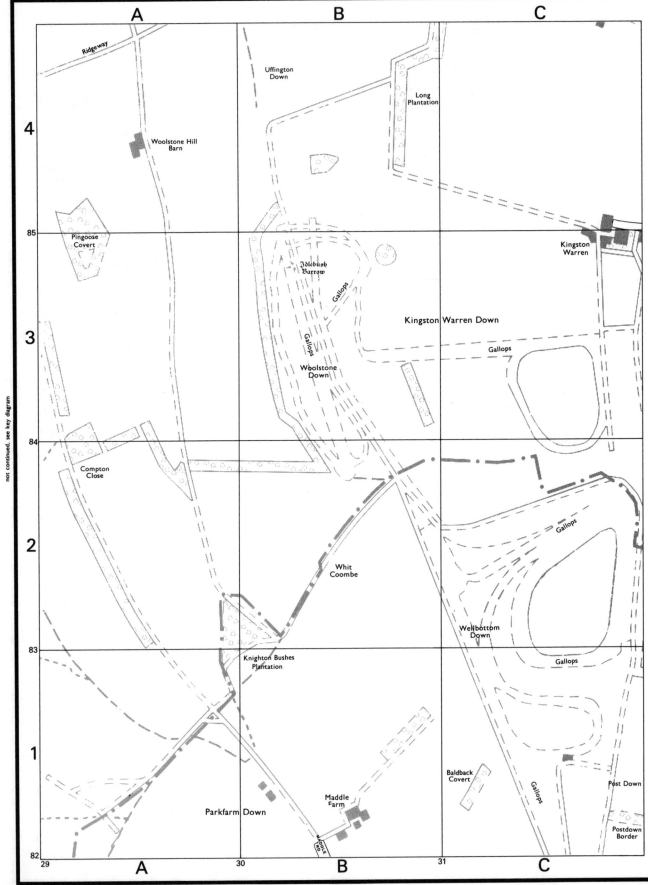

A   B   C

Ridgeway

Uffington
Down

Long
Plantation

4

Woolstone Hill
Barn

85

Pingoose
Covert

Idlebush
Barrow

Kingston
Warren

Gallops

Kingston Warren Down

3

Gallops

Gallops

Woolstone
Down

84

Compton
Close

2

Whit
Coombe

Gallops

Wellbottom
Down

83

Knighton Bushes
Plantation

Gallops

1

Baldback
Covert

Gallops

Post Down

Maddle
Farm

Parkfarm Down

Postdown
Border

82

29   A   30   B   31   C

5

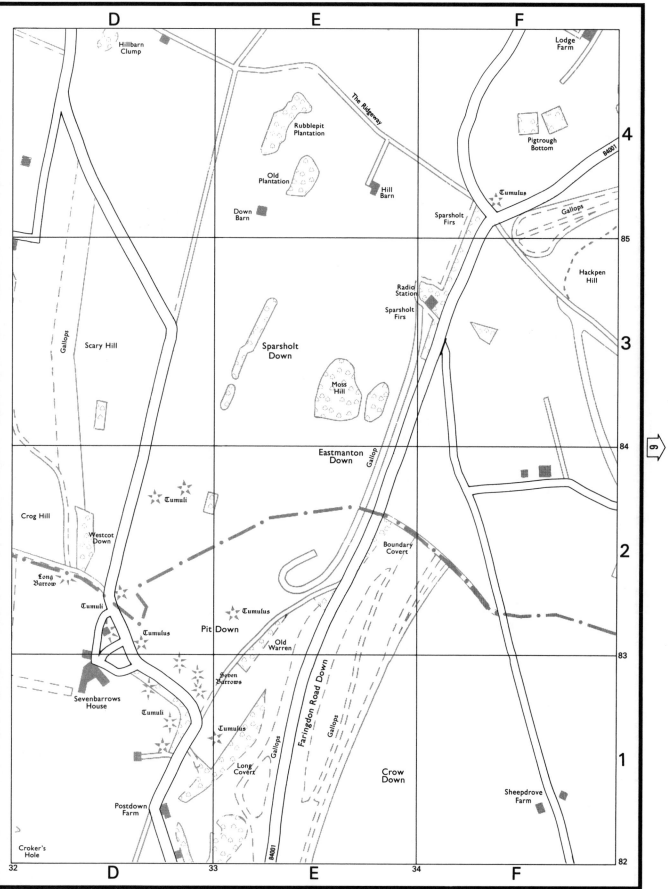

D

E

F

Hillbarn
Clump

The Ridgeway

Rubblepit
Plantation

Old
Plantation

Down
Barn

Hill
Barn

Lodge
Farm

Pigtrough
Bottom

B4001

Tumulus

Gallops

Sparsholt
Firs

85

Hackpen
Hill

Gallops

Scary Hill

Sparsholt
Down

Radio
Station

Sparsholt
Firs

3

Moss
Hill

84

6

Eastmanton
Down

Gallop

Crog Hill

Tumuli

Westcot
Down

Boundary
Covert

2

Long
Barrow

Tumuli

Tumulus

Pit Down

Tumulus

Old
Warren

83

Sevenbarrows
House

Tumuli

Seven
Barrows

Tumulus

Faringdon Road Down

Gallops

Gallops

Long
Covert

Crow
Down

Sheepdrove
Farm

1

Postdown
Farm

Croker's
Hole

B4001

82

32

D

33

E

34

F

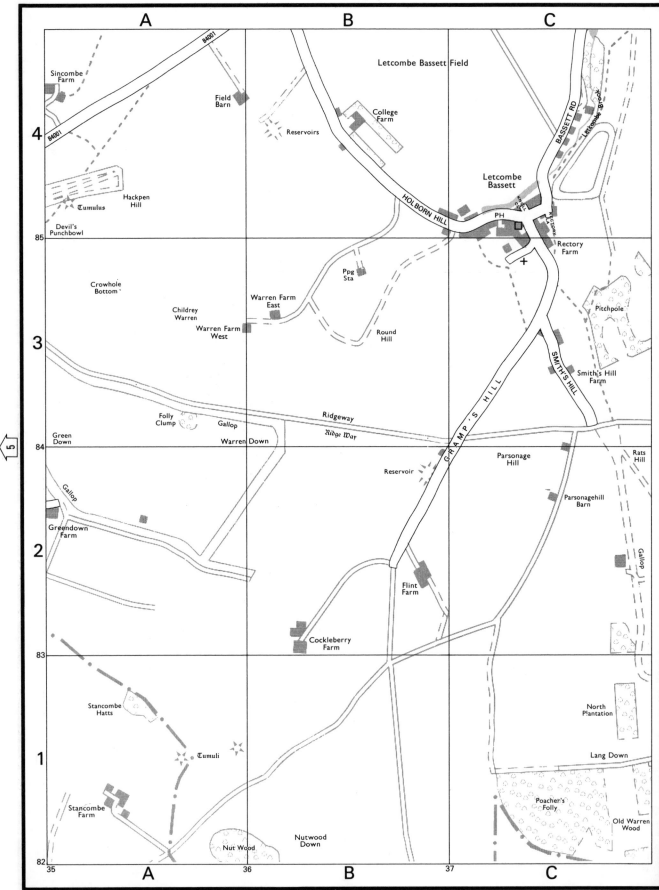

A   **B**   **C**

B4001

Sincombe
Farm

Field
Barn

Letcombe Bassett Field

College
Farm

Reservoirs

BASSETT RD

Letcombe Brook

4

B4001

Letcombe
Bassett

Tumulus

Hackpen
Hill

HOLBORN HILL

PH

SCHOOL

RECTORY

85

Devil's
Punchbowl

Rectory
Farm

Crowhole
Bottom

Childrey
Warren

Warren Farm
East

Ppg
Sta

Pitchpole

Warren Farm
West

Round
Hill

3

Smith's Hill
Farm

SMITH'S HILL

Folly
Clump

Gallop

Ridgeway

G·R·A·M·P'S HILL

Green
Down

Warren Down

Ridge Way

84

Reservoir

Parsonage
Hill

Rats
Hill

Gallop

Parsonagehill
Barn

Greendown
Farm

Gallop

2

Flint
Farm

Cockleberry
Farm

83

Stancombe
Hatts

North
Plantation

Lang Down

1

Tumuli

Stancombe
Farm

Poacher's
Folly

Old Warren
Wood

82

Nut Wood

Nutwood
Down

35   **A**   36   **B**   37   **C**

5

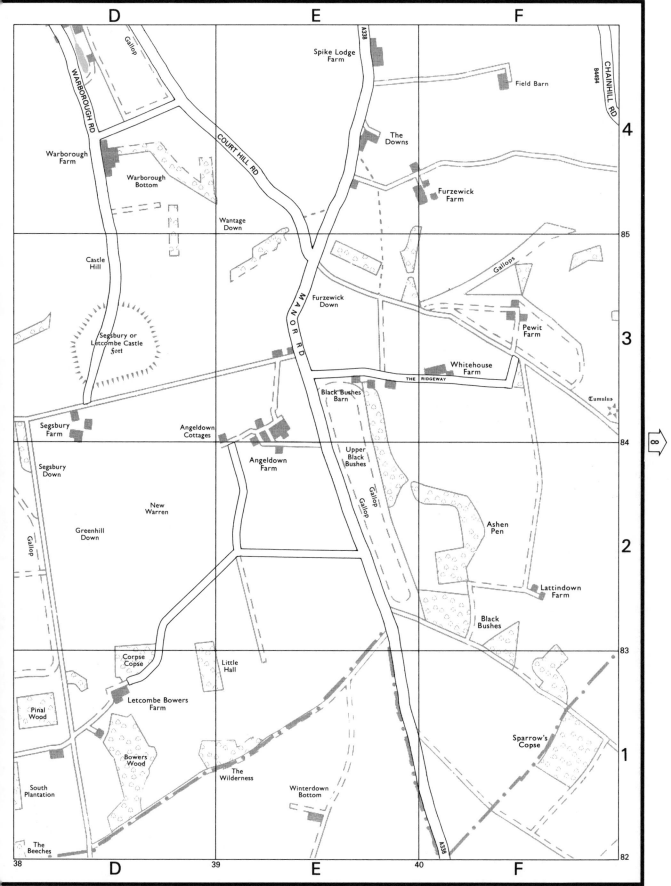

D

F

E

Gallop

Spike Lodge
Farm

A338

Field Barn

CHAINHILL RD

B4494

WARBOROUGH RD

COURT HILL RD

The
Downs

4

Warborough
Farm

Warborough
Bottom

Furzewick
Farm

Wantage
Down

85

Castle
Hill

Gallops

Furzewick
Down

Pewit
Farm

MANOR RD

Segsbury or
Letcombe Castle
Fort

3

Whitehouse
Farm

THE RIDGEWAY

Black Bushes
Barn

Tumulus

Segsbury
Farm

Angeldown
Cottages

84

8

Upper
Black
Bushes

Segsbury
Down

Angeldown
Farm

Gallop

Ashen
Pen

New
Warren

Gallop

Greenhill
Down

Gallop

2

Lattindown
Farm

Black
Bushes

83

Corpse
Copse

Little
Hall

Pinal
Wood

Letcombe Bowers
Farm

Sparrow's
Copse

Bowers
Wood

1

South
Plantation

The
Wilderness

Winterdown
Bottom

A338

The
Beeches

82

38

D

39

E

40

F

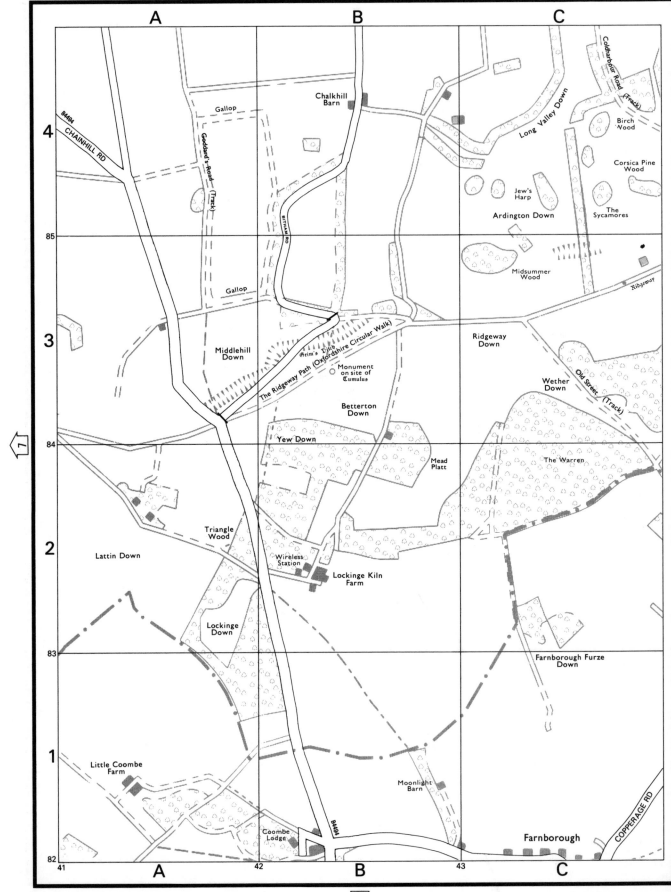

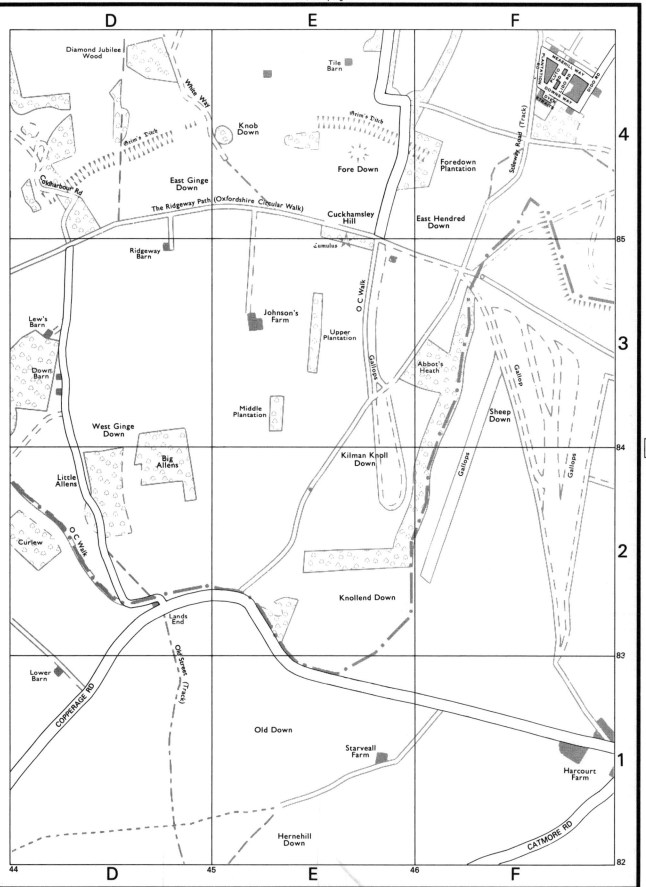

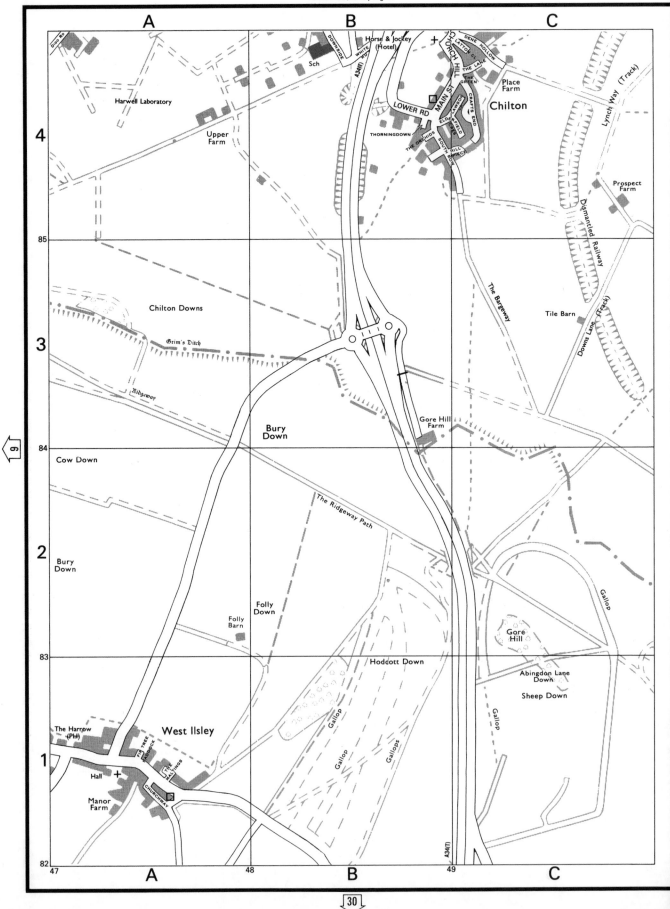

A   B   C

Diss Rd
Horse & Jockey (Hotel)
Sch
CHURCH HILL
CLATTON CLOSE
DENE HOLLOW
THE LANE
THE GREEN
Place Farm
Lynch Way (Track)
Harwell Laboratory
DOWNSIDE
A34(T)
WHITE
LOWER RD
MAIN ST
CRAFTS END
Chilton
Upper Farm
THORNINGDOWN
OAKWOOD
ELDER FIELD
SOUTH ROW
THE ORCHIDS
Prospect Farm
Dismantled Railway
Downs Lane (Track)

4

85

Chilton Downs
Grim's Ditch
The Bargeway
Tile Barn

3

Ridgeway
Bury Down
Gore Hill Farm

84

Cow Down

The Ridgeway Path

2

Bury Down

Folly Barn
Folly Down
Gallop

83

Hodcott Down
Gore Hill
Abingdon Lane Down
Sheep Down
Gallop

The Harrow (PH)
West Ilsley
FIR TREE PADDOCK
THE MALTINGS
Gallop
Gallops
Gallop

1

Hall
CHURCHWAY
Manor Farm

82
47   48   A34(T) 49

A   B   C

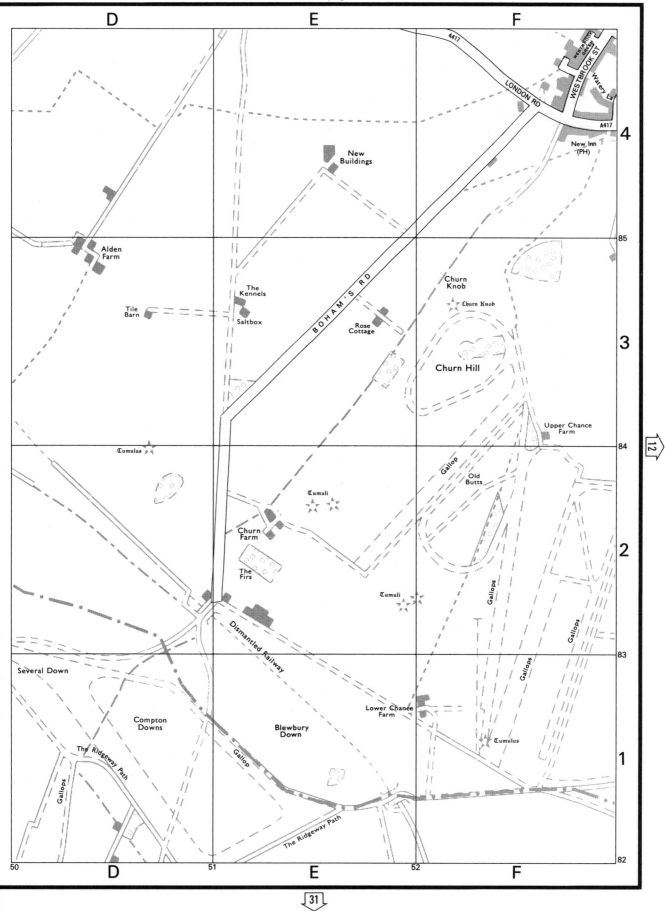

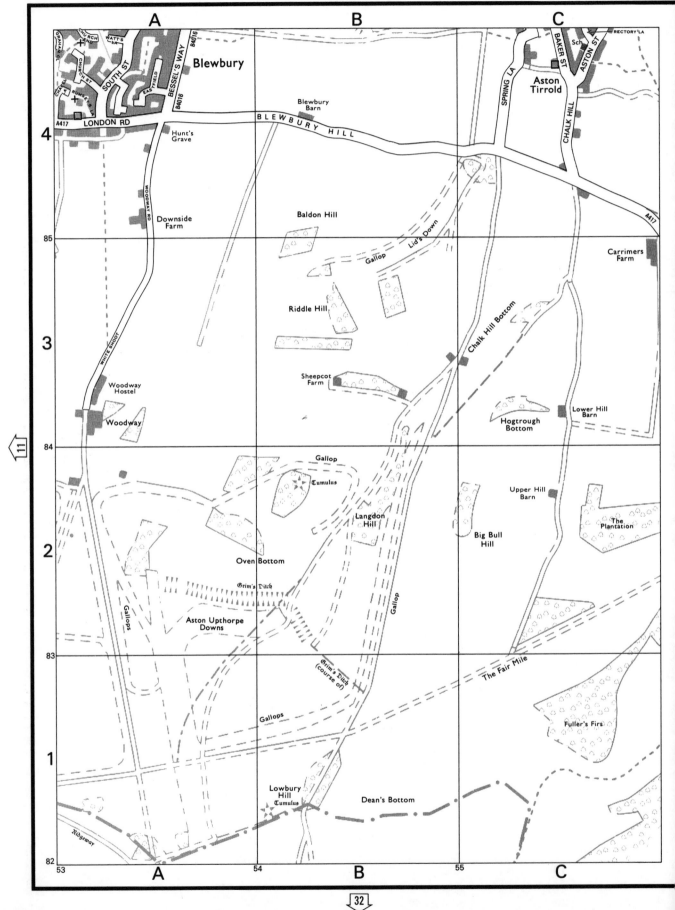

A B C

Blewbury

CHURCH LANE · WATT'S LA · GRAMMAR RD · CHAPEL · SOUTH ST · CHURCH ST · EASTFIELD · RUMSE'S LA · BESSEL'S WAY · B4016 · B4016

Blewbury Barn

BLEWBURY HILL

A417 LONDON RD

4

Hunt's Grave

WOODWAY RD

Baldon Hill

Lid's Down

Gallop

85

Downside Farm

WHITE SHOOT

Riddle Hill

3

Chalk Hill Bottom

Carrimers Farm

SPRING LA · Aston Tirrold · BAKER ST · Sch · RECTORY LA · ASTON ST · CHALK HILL

A417

Sheepcot Farm

Woodway Hostel

Lower Hill Barn

Hogtrough Bottom

Woodway

84

Gallop

Tumulus

Upper Hill Barn

The Plantation

Langdon Hill

Big Bull Hill

2

Oven Bottom

Grim's Ditch

Gallop

Aston Upthorpe Downs

83

Grim's Ditch (course of)

The Fair Mile

Gallops

Gallops

Fuller's Firs

1

Lowbury Hill Tumulus

Dean's Bottom

Ridgeway

82

53 A 54 B 55 C

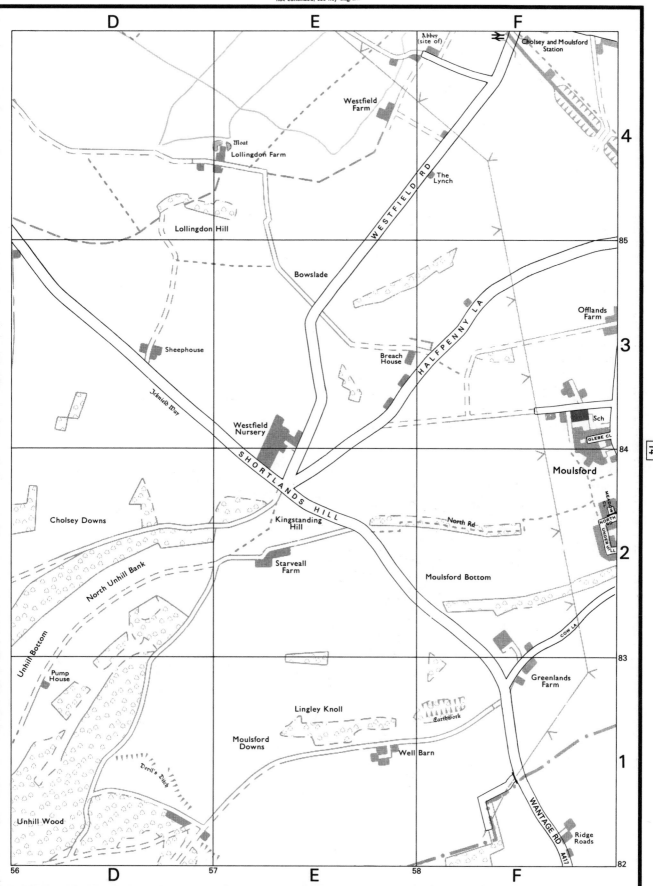

D   E   F

Abbey (site of)

Cholsey and Moulsford Station

Westfield Farm

4

Moat
Lollingdon Farm

WESTFIELD RD

The Lynch

Lollingdon Hill

85

Bowslade

HALFPENNY LA

Offlands Farm

3

Sheephouse

Breach House

Icknield Way

Sch

Westfield Nursery

GLEBE CL

84

Moulsford

SHORTLANDS HILL

MEADOW CL

NORTH RD

UNDERHILL

Cholsey Downs

Kingstanding Hill

North Rd

2

North Unhill Bank

Starveall Farm

Moulsford Bottom

COW LA

Unhill Bottom

83

Pump House

Greenlands Farm

Lingley Knoll

Earthwork

Moulsford Downs

Well Barn

1

Devil's Ditch

WANTAGE RD

Unhill Wood

Ridge Roads

A417

82

56   D   57   E   58   F

14

not continued, see key diagram

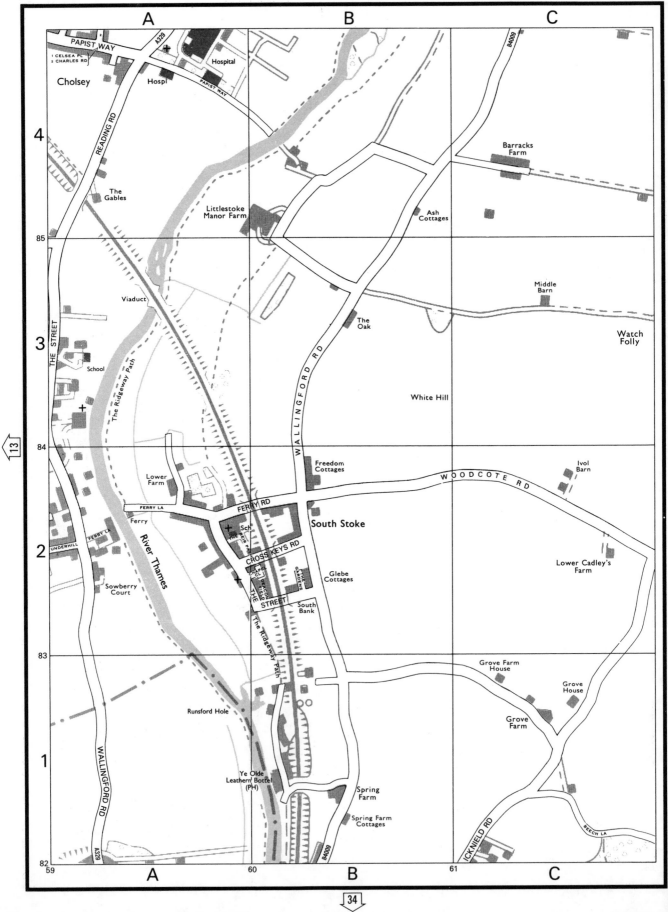

34

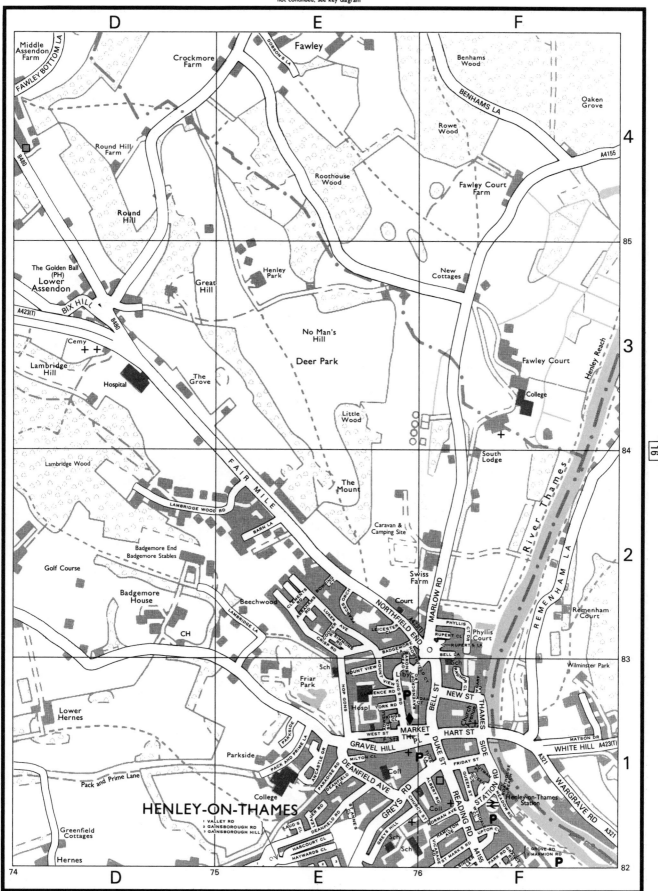

HENLEY-ON-THAMES

1 VALLEY RD
2 GAINSBOROUGH RD
3 GAINSBOROUGH HILL

16

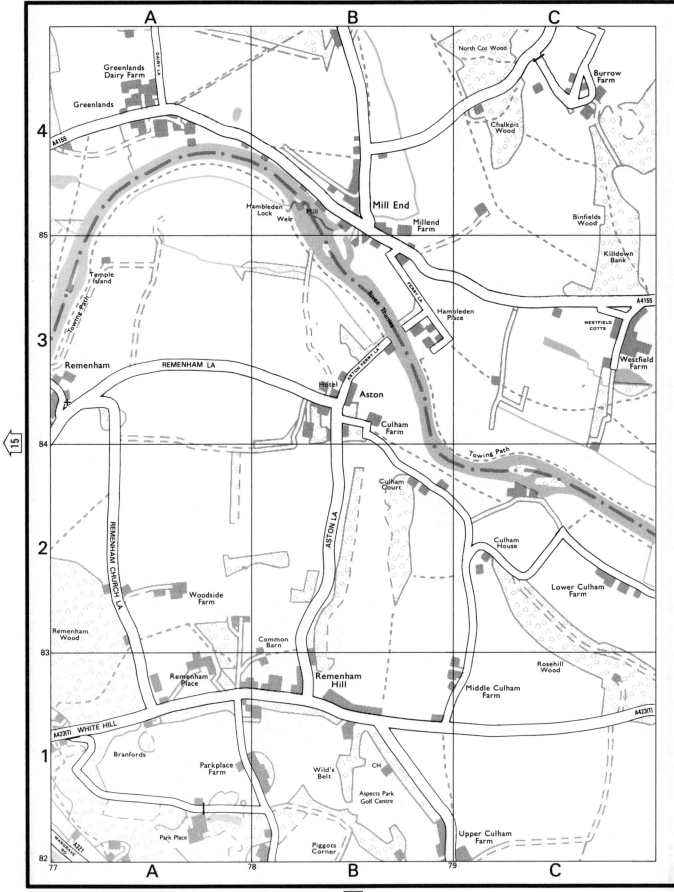

A423(T)
WHITE HILL
A321
WARGRAVE RD

Greenlands Dairy Farm
Greenlands
DAIRY LA
A4155
Towing Path
Temple Island
Remenham
REMENHAM LA
Hotel
REMENHAM CHURCH LA
Woodside Farm
Remenham Wood
Remenham Place
Branfords
Parkplace Farm
Park Place

Hambleden Lock
Weir
Mill
Mill End
Millend Farm
River Thames
FERRY LA
Hambleden Place
ASTON FERRY LA
Aston
Culham Farm
ASTON LA
Culham Court
Common Barn
Remenham Hill
Wild's Belt
CH
Aspects Park Golf Centre
Piggots Corner

North Cot Wood
Burrow Farm
Chalkpit Wood
Binfields Wood
Killdown Bank
A4155
WESTFIELD COTTS
Westfield Farm
Towing Path
Culham House
Lower Culham Farm
Rosehill Wood
Middle Culham Farm
A423(T)
Upper Culham Farm

15

36

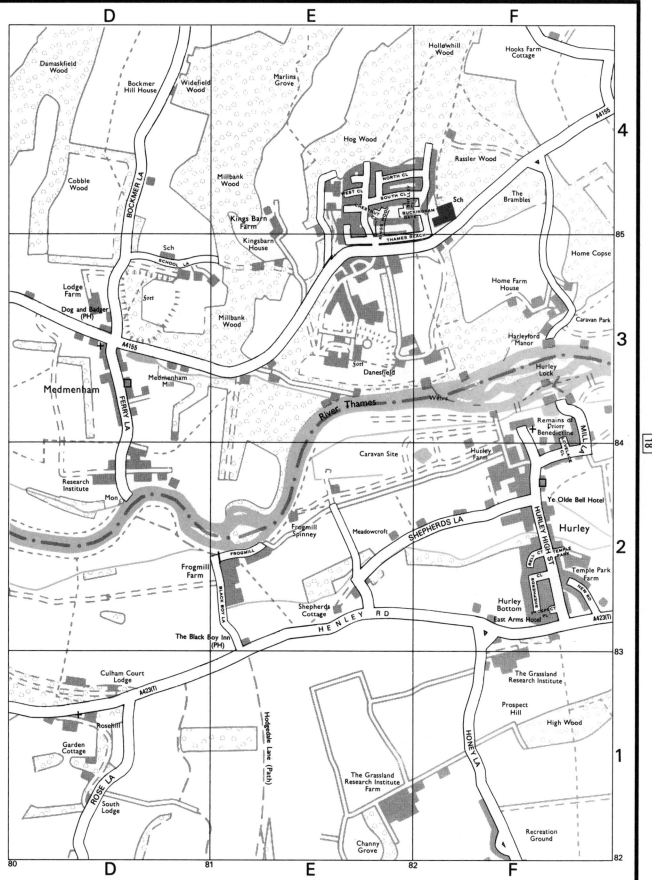

D   E   F

4

Damaskfield Wood

Bockmer Hill House

Widefield Wood

Marlins Grove

Hollowhill Wood

Hooks Farm Cottage

A4155

Cobble Wood

BOCKMER LA

Millbank Wood

Hog Wood

Rassler Wood

NORTH CL

WEST CL   SOUTH CL

CHESTNUT   KINGS WOOD

Sch

The Brambles

85

Kings Barn Farm

Kingsbarn House

BUCKINGHAM GATE

THAMES REACH

Home Copse

Sch

SCHOOL LA

Sort

Millbank Wood

Home Farm House

Caravan Park

3

Lodge Farm

Dog and Badger (PH)

A4155

Sort

Danesfield

Harleyford Manor

Hurley Lock

Medmenham Mill

Medmenham

FERRY LA

River Thames

Weirs

Remains of Priory Benedictine

MILL LA

84

Research Institute

Mon

Caravan Site

Hurley Farm

LOVELACE CL

Frogmill Spinney

Meadowcroft

SHEPHERDS LA

Ye Olde Bell Hotel

Hurley

HURLEY HIGH ST

2

FROGMILL

Frogmill Farm

BLACK BOY LA

Shepherds Cottage

HENLEY RD

BELL CT

TEMPLE PARK

Temple Park Farm

SHERIDANS CL

Hurley Bottom

PROSPECT PL

NEW RD

The Black Boy Inn (PH)

East Arms Hotel

A423(T)

83

Culham Court Lodge

A423(T)

The Grassland Research Institute

Rosehill

Hodgedale Lane (Path)

Prospect Hill

High Wood

Garden Cottage

HONEY LA

1

ROSE LA

South Lodge

The Grassland Research Institute Farm

Channy Grove

Recreation Ground

80   D   81   E   82   F   82

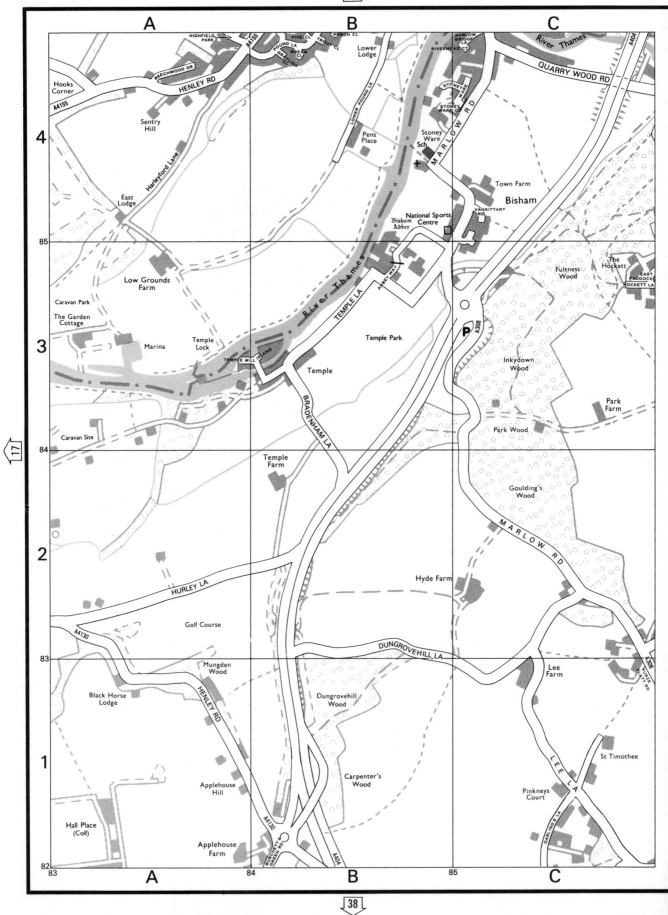

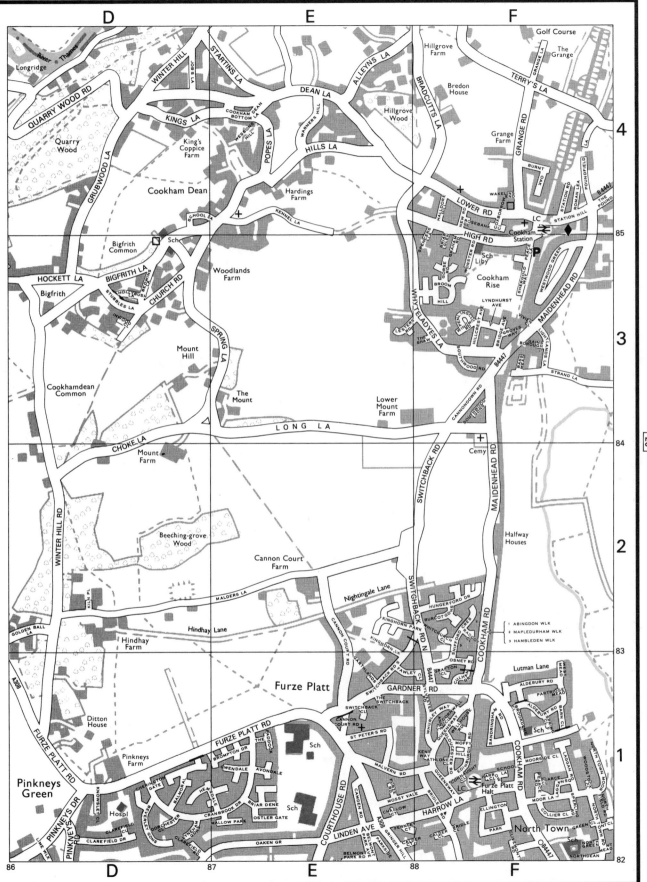

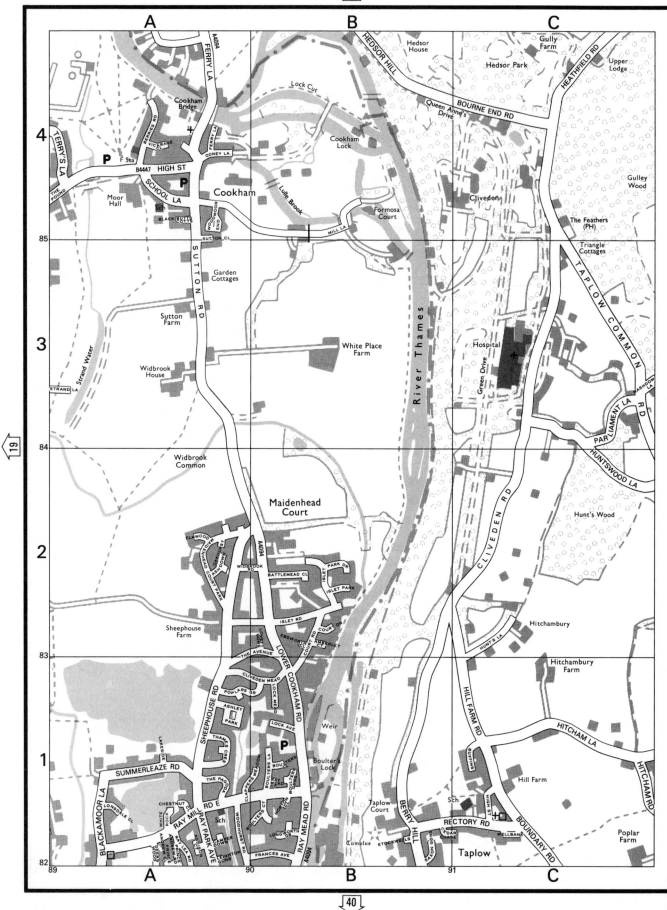

A B C

4

85

3

84

2

83

1

82

89 90 91

A B C

FERRY LA
A4094
HEDSOR HILL
Hedsor House
Gully Farm
HEATHFIELD RD
Hedsor Park
Upper Lodge
Lock Cut
BERRIES RD
Cookham Bridge
VICARAGE
Cookham Lock
Queen Anne's Drive
BOURNE END RD
Gulley Wood
TERRY'S LA
P
F Sta
ODNEY LA
HIGH ST
B4447
Cliveden
THE POUND
P
SCHOOL LA
Cookham
Lulle Brook
The Feathers (PH)
Moor Hall
WOODMOOR END MOOR
Sch
BLACKBUTTS COTTS
SUTTON CL
Formosa Court
MILL LA
Triangle Cottages
TAPLOW COMMON
SUTTON RD
Garden Cottages
Sutton Farm
River Thames
Hospital
Green Drive
ASHDOWN RD
Strand Water
Widbrook House
White Place Farm
PARLIAMENT LA
STRAND LA
HUNTSWOOD LA
Widbrook Common
Maidenhead Court
CLIVEDEN RD
Hunt's Wood
Hitchambury
ELMWOOD RD
MAIDENHEAD COURT PARK
OAKHURST
WIDBROOK
A4094
BATTLEMEAD CL
ISLET PARK DR
ISLET PARK
Hitchambury Farm
Sheephouse Farm
ISLET RD
EBSWORTH RD
COURT DR
AMBERLEY
HUNT'S LA
THE AVENUE
LODGE
HILL FARM RD
HITCHAM LA
HITCHAM RD
SHEEPHOUSE RD
CLIVEDEN MEAD
POPLARS GR
LOCK MEAD
LOWER COOKHAM RD
Weir
ASHLEY PARK
LOCK AVE
Boulter's Lock
Ruffins
Hill Farm
SUMMERLEAZE RD
THAMES CRES
P
BERRY HILL
Sch
BOUNDARY RD
BLACKMOOR LA
LONGSDALE CL
LAKESIDE
THE PAGODA
CLAPPERS MEADOW
BOULTERS
Taplow Court
RECTORY RD
WELLBANK
Poplar Farm
CHESTNUT
RAY MILL RD E
Sch
WOODHURST RD
LONGWORTH DR
Cumulus
Stockwells
CEDAR CHASE
SATON
Taplow
WHITE
RAY PARK AVE
ANDREW
PRINCE
RAY LEA RD
AMBER
LEIGHTON GDNS
FRANCES AVE
A4094

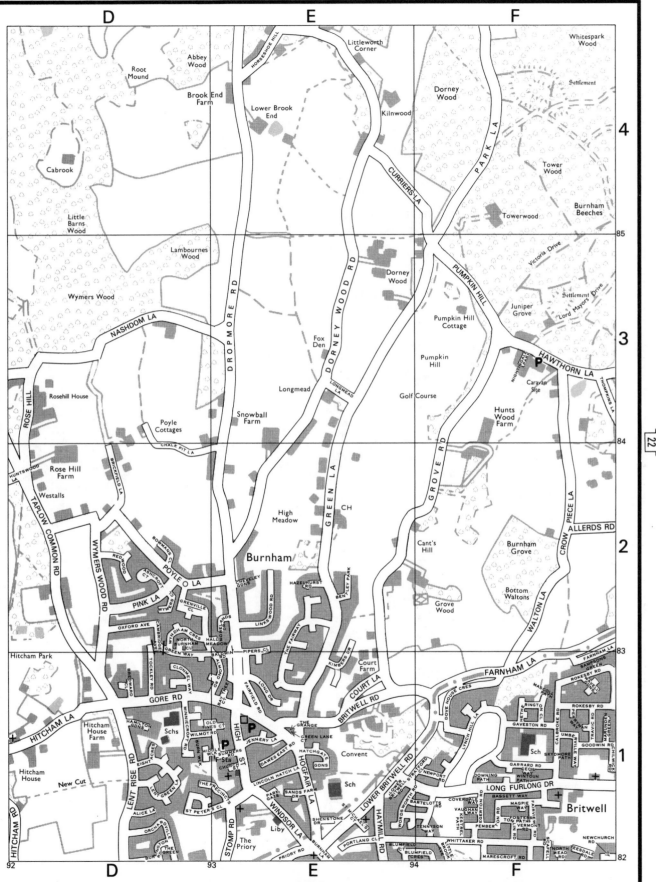

22

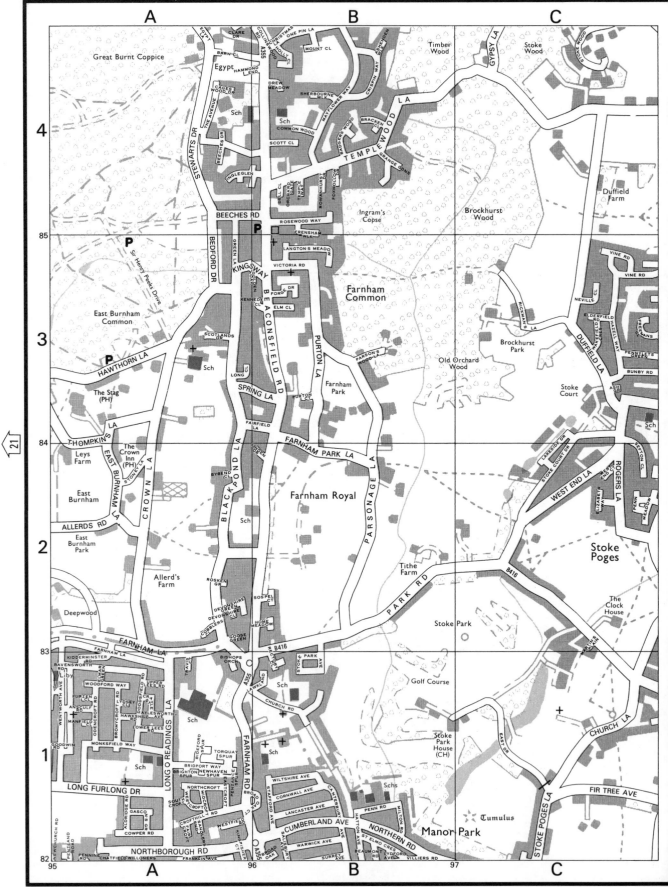

21

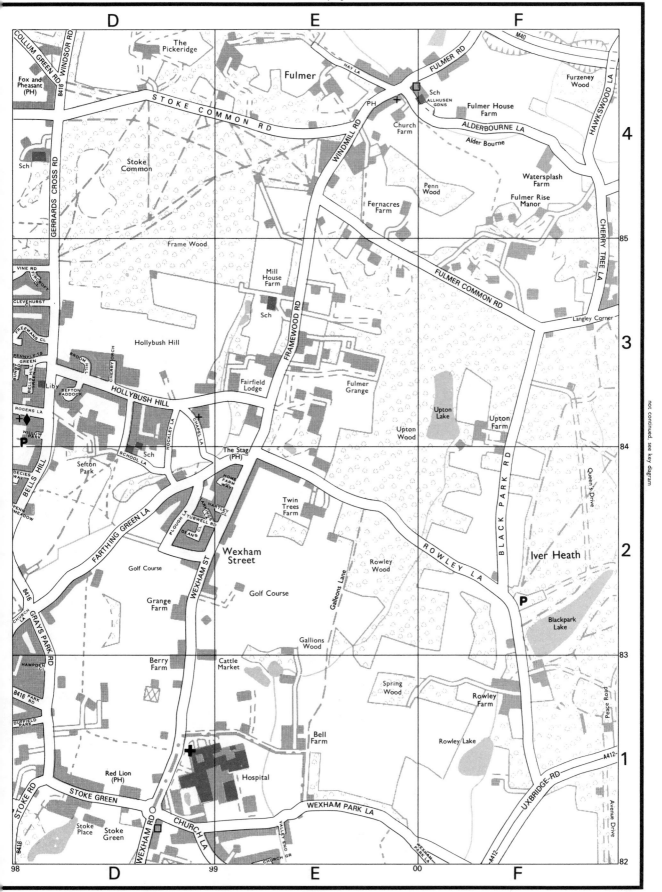

not continued, see key diagram

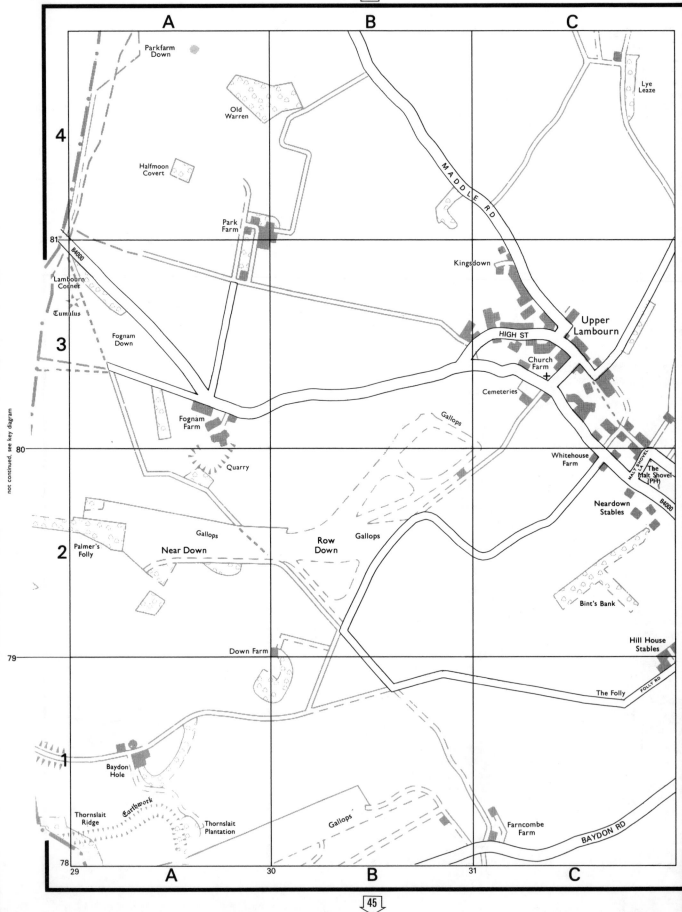

A
B
C

Parkfarm
Down

Old
Warren

4

Halfmoon
Covert

Park
Farm

MADDLE RD

Lye
Leaze

81

B4000

Kingsdown

Lambourn
Corner

HIGH ST

Upper
Lambourn

Tumulus

3

Fognam
Down

Church
Farm

Cemeteries

Fognam
Farm

Gallops

Whitehouse
Farm

MALT SHOVEL LA

The
Malt Shovel
(PH)

80

Quarry

B4000

Palmer's
Folly

Gallops

Near Down

Row
Down

Gallops

Gallops

Neardown
Stables

Bint's Bank

2

Hill House
Stables

79

Down Farm

The Folly

FOLLY RD

1

Baydon
Hole

Thornslait
Ridge

Earthwork

Thornslait
Plantation

Gallops

Farncombe
Farm

BAYDON RD

78

29

A

30

B

31

C

not continued, see key diagram

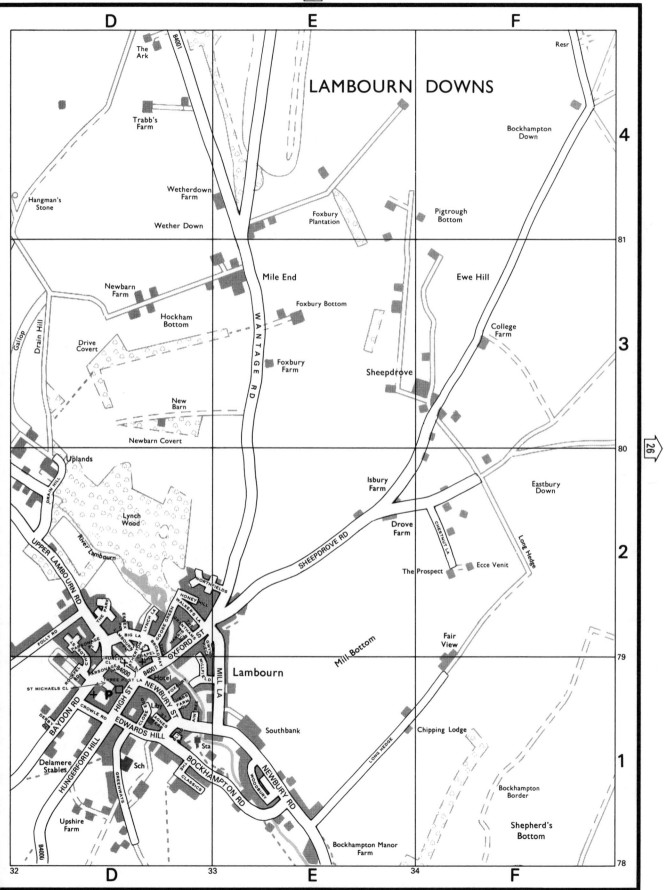

LAMBOURN DOWNS

The Ark

B4001

Trabb's
Farm

Resr

Bockhampton
Down

4

Hangman's
Stone

Wetherdown
Farm

Wether Down

Foxbury
Plantation

Pigtrough
Bottom

81

Newbarn
Farm

Mile End

Ewe Hill

Hockham
Bottom

Foxbury Bottom

Drive
Covert

WANTAGE RD

Foxbury
Farm

College
Farm

3

Gallop

Drain Hill

New
Barn

Sheepdrove

Newbarn Covert

80

26

Uplands

Isbury
Farm

Eastbury
Down

DRAIN HILL

Lynch
Wood

Drove
Farm

CHESTNUT LA

River Lambourn

SHEEPDROVE RD

The Prospect

Ecce Venit

Long Hedge

2

UPPER LAMBOURN RD

NORTHFIELDS

HONEYHILL

WALKER'S LA

Mill Bottom

Fair
View

THE PARK

LYNCH LA

GOOSE GREEN

ESSEX CL

FOLLY RD

BIG LA

BROADWAY

OXFORD ST

HAYES RD

GWYN CLOSE

79

PARSONAGE

CHAPEL LA

Lambourn

CHURCH CL

B4000

B4001

Hotel

MILL LA

ST MICHAELS CL

THREE POST LA

NEWBURY ST

FOX HILL

MILL FIELD

FOXHILL FARM

Southbank

BAYDON RD

CROWLE RD

HIGH ST

OLD CLOSE

AGNES RD

Chipping Lodge

DERBY

Liby

Long Hedge

HUNGERFORD HILL

EDWARDS HILL

GREENWAYS

Delamere
Stables

Sch

BOCKHAMPTON RD

WOODBURN

NEWBURY RD

Bockhampton
Border

F Sta

CLASSICS

Shepherd's
Bottom

Upshire
Farm

B4000

Bockhampton Manor
Farm

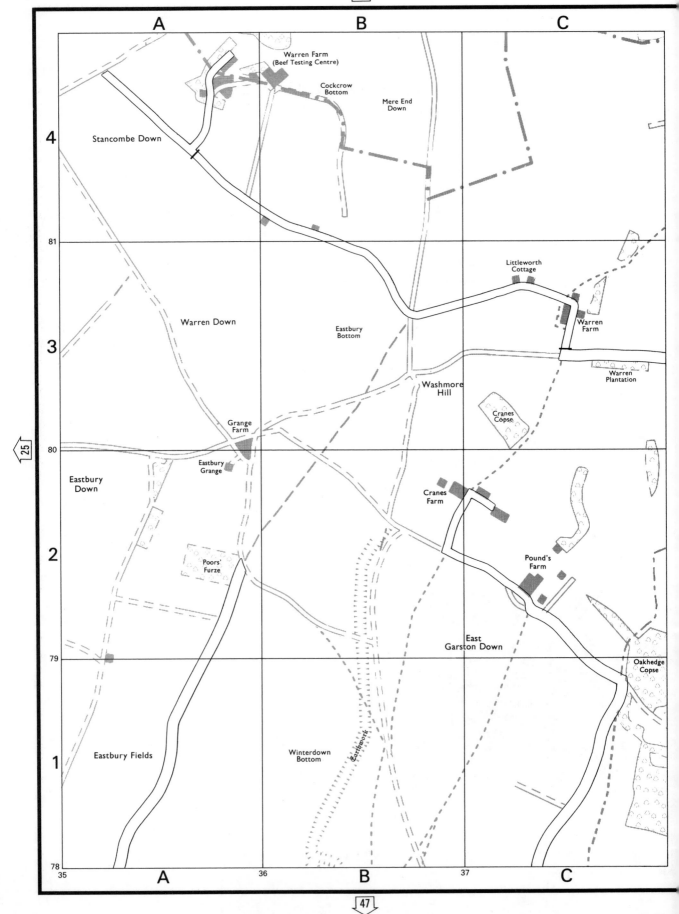

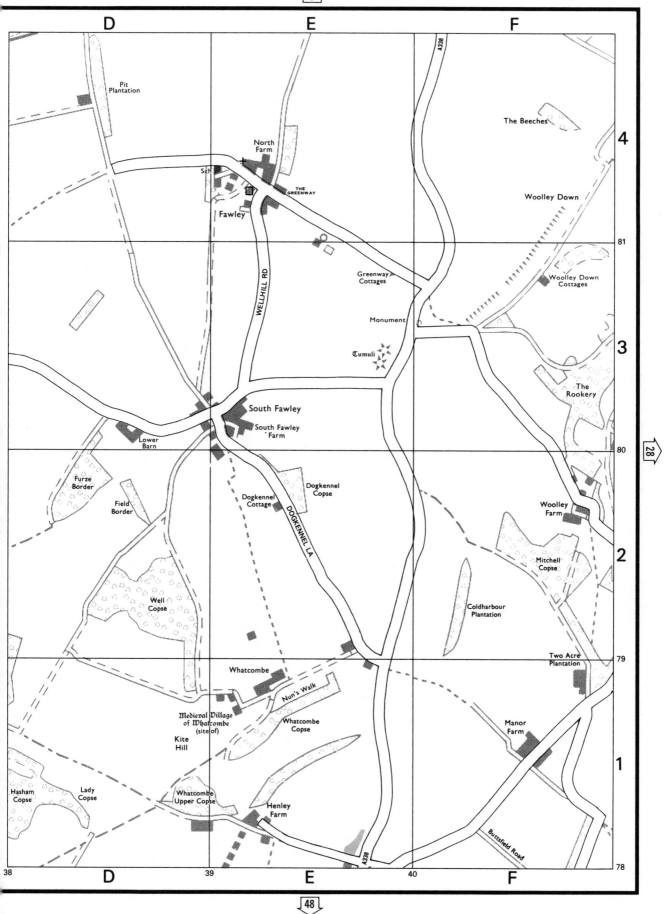

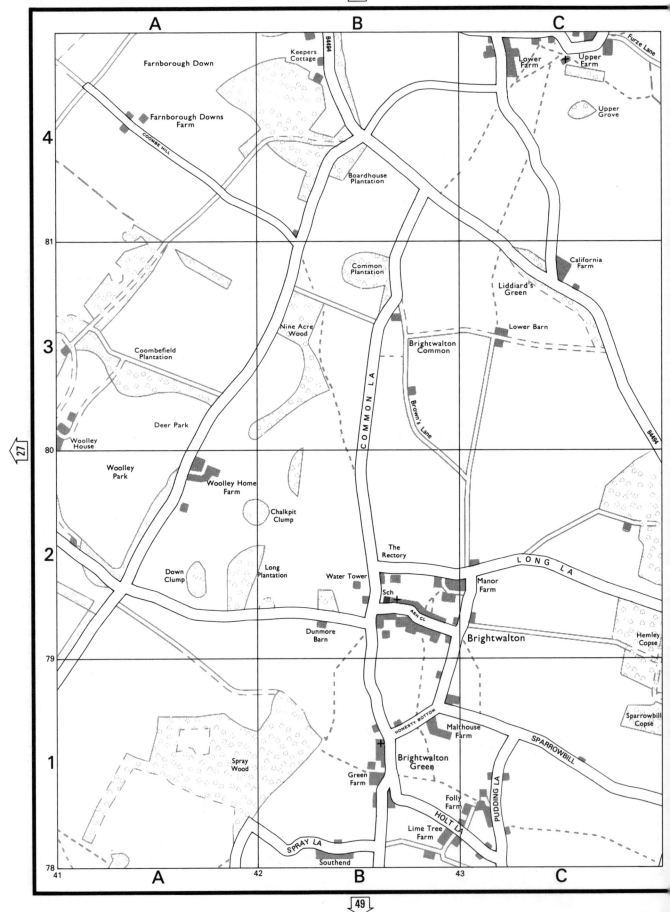

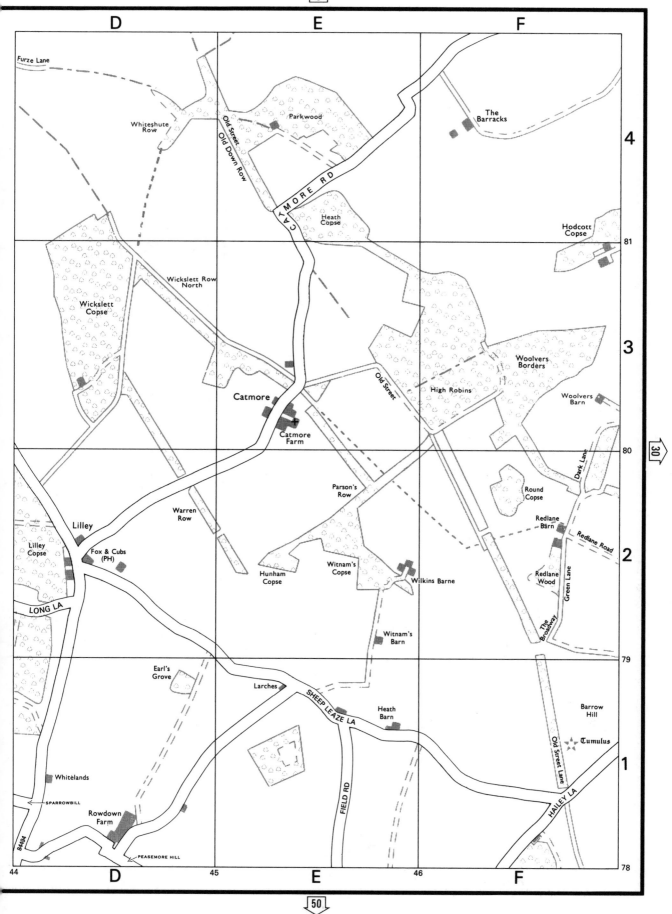

D   E   F

Furze Lane

Whiteshute Row

Old Street

Old Down Row

Parkwood

CATMORE RD

The Barracks

4

Heath Copse

Hodcott Copse

81

Wickslett Row North

Wickslett Copse

Woolvers Borders

3

Old Street

High Robins

Catmore

Woolvers Barn

Catmore Farm

80

30

Parson's Row

Round Copse

Dark Lane

Warren Row

Lilley

Redlane Barn

Lilley Copse

Fox & Cubs (PH)

Hunham Copse

Witnam's Copse

Wilkins Barne

Redlane Wood

Redlane Road

Green Lane

2

The Broadway

LONG LA

Witnam's Barn

79

Earl's Grove

Larches

SHEEP LEAZE LA

Heath Barn

Barrow Hill

Whitelands

← SPARROWBILL

Old Street Lane

Tumulus

1

B4494

Rowdown Farm

FIELD RD

HAILEY LA

PEASEMORE HILL →

44   D   45   E   46   F   78

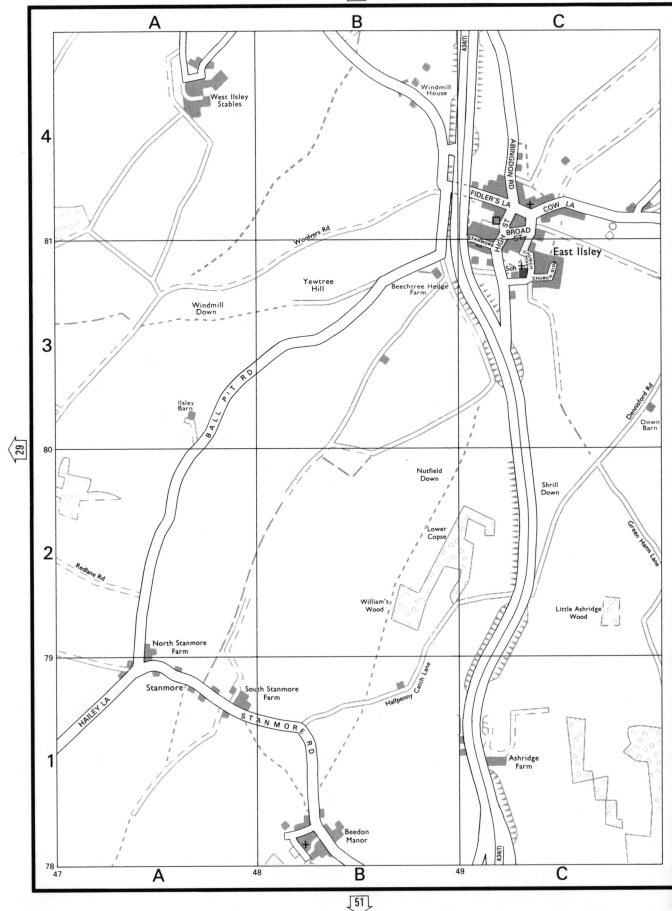

A B C

4

81

3

80

2

79

78

29

West Ilsley Stables

Windmill House

A34(T)

ABINGDON RD

FIDLER'S LA

COW LA

HIGH ST

BROAD ST

STANMORE RD

CHURCH ST

CHURCH

Sch

CHURCH SIDE

East Ilsley

Woolvers Rd

Yewtree Hill

Beechtree Hedge Farm

Windmill Down

BALL PIT RD

Ilsley Barn

Dennisford Rd

Down Barn

Nutfield Down

Shrill Down

Green Hams Lane

Lower Copse

Little Ashridge Wood

Redlane Rd

William's Wood

North Stanmore Farm

HAILEY LA

Stanmore

South Stanmore Farm

STANMORE RD

Halfpenny Catch Lane

Ashridge Farm

Beedon Manor

A34(T)

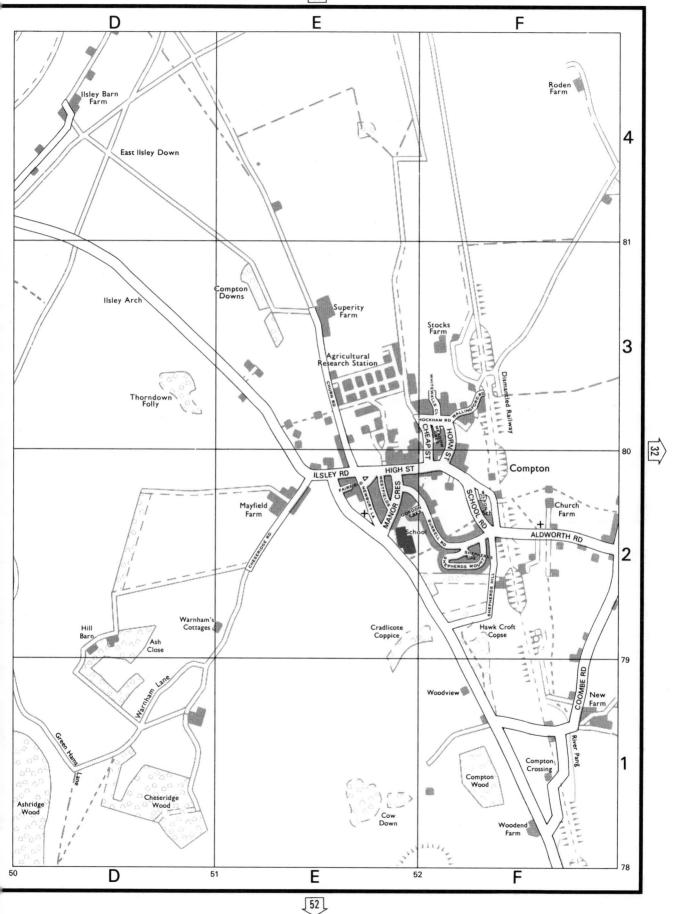

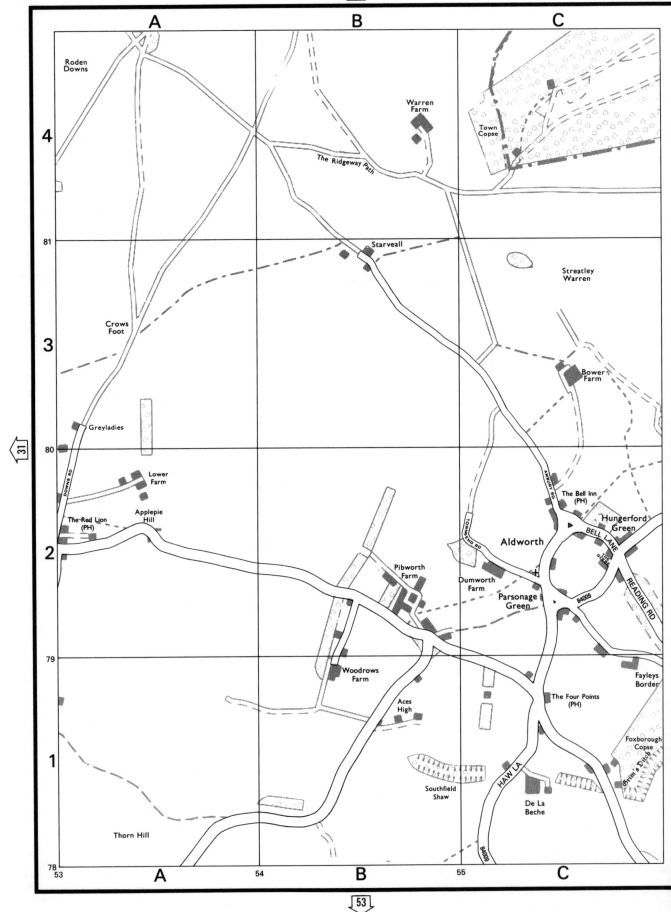

Roden
Downs

A

B

C

Warren
Farm

Town
Copse

4

The Ridgeway Path

81

Starveall

Streatley
Warren

Crows
Foot

3

Bower
Farm

Greyladies

80

DOWNS RD

Lower
Farm

The Bell Inn
(PH)

AMBURY RD

Hungerford
Green

The Red Lion
(PH)

Applepie
Hill

Aldworth

BELL LANE

2

TOWNS END RD

Pibworth
Farm

Dumworth
Farm

Parsonage
Green

B4009

READING RD

79

Woodrows
Farm

Aces
High

Fayleys
Border

The Four Points
(PH)

Foxborough
Copse

1

HAW LA

Grim's Ditch

Southfield
Shaw

De La
Beche

B4009

Thorn Hill

78
A
54
B
55
C

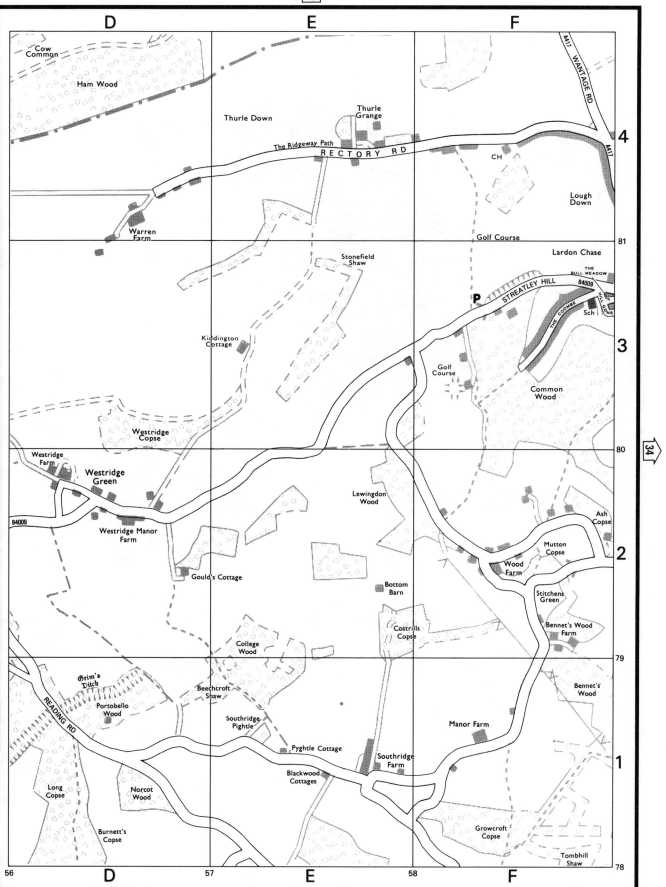

D   E   F

Cow Common

Ham Wood

Thurle Down

Thurle Grange

A417 WANTAGE RD

The Ridgeway Path

RECTORY RD

CH

4

A417

Lough Down

Warren Farm

Golf Course

81

Stonefield Shaw

Lardon Chase

THE BULL MEADOW

B4009

P

STREATLEY HILL

THE COOMBE

HILL GDNS

Sch

Kiddington Cottage

Golf Course

3

Common Wood

Westridge Copse

80

34

Westridge Farm

Westridge Green

Lewingdon Wood

Ash Copse

B4009

Westridge Manor Farm

Mutton Copse

Wood Farm

2

Gould's Cottage

Bottom Barn

Stitchens Green

Bennet's Wood Farm

College Wood

Costrills Copse

79

Grim's Ditch

Beechcroft Shaw

Bennet's Wood

READING RD

Portobello Wood

Southridge Pightle

Manor Farm

Pyghtle Cottage

Southridge Farm

1

Long Copse

Blackwood Cottages

Norcot Wood

Growcroft Copse

Burnett's Copse

Tombhill Shaw

78

56   D   57   E   58   F

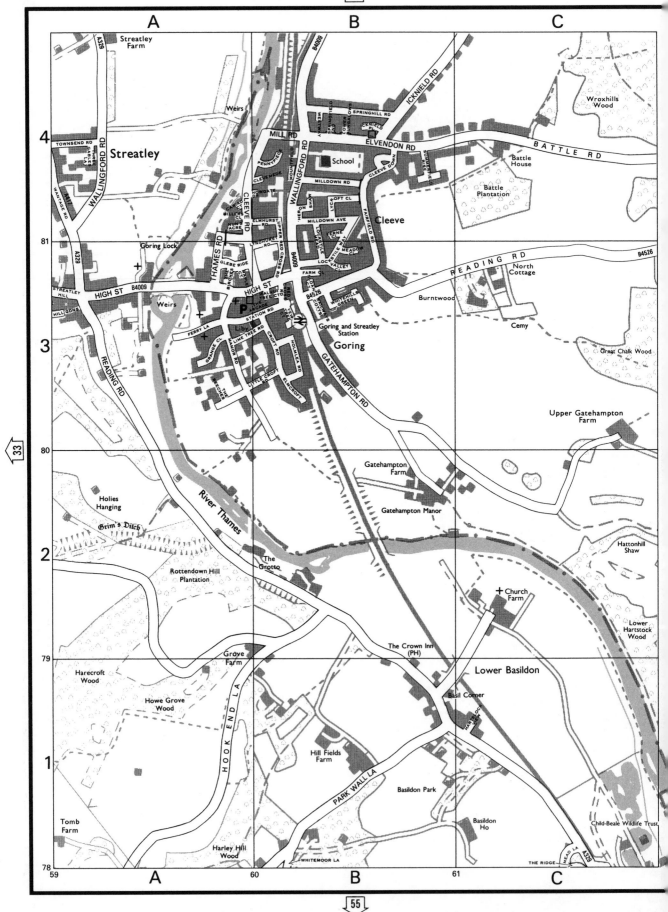

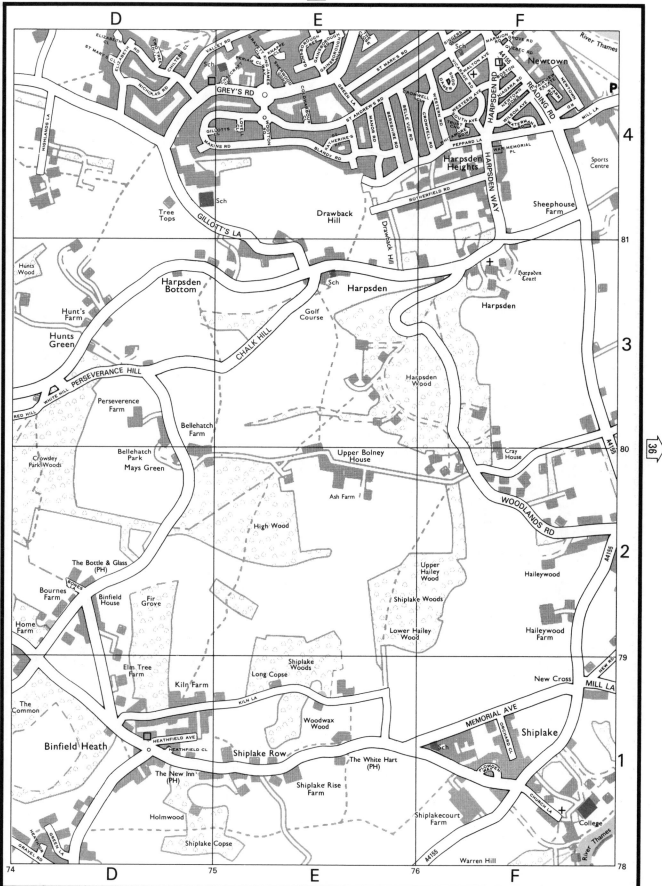

D

E

F

River Thames

Elizabeth CL
St Mary's Elizabeth Rd WHITTREE
CHILTERN CL Valley Rd GRAVEL HILL KINGS JAMES CL KNAPPE CL GAINSBOROUGH CRES GAINSBOROUGH RD
Highlands La NICHOLAS RD PERIAM CL KINGSWOOD CLOSE
Sch St MARK'S RD Sch SINGERS LA MARMION RD GROVE RD
QUEBEC RD Newtown
GREY'S RD VICTORIA RD WALTON AVE A4155 NEWTOWN
COLDHARBOUR GREEN LA St ANDREWS RD CROMWELL DAMER BOSTON NEWTOWN GDNS P
GILLOTTS CL WOOTTON St CROMWELL WESTERN RD NIAGARA RD NEWTOWN RD HARPSDEN RD
LOVELL BELLE VUE RD CL SOUTH AVE WILSON AVE FARVIEW ESTCT FRY
MAKINS RD St KATHERINE'S MANOR RD BERKSHIRE RD TRUST CHOS WATERMANS MILL LA
4
BLANDY RD PEPPARD LA WAR MEMORIAL PL Sports Centre
Tree Tops Harpsden Heights
Sch Drawback Hill HARPSDEN WAY Sheephouse Farm
GILLOTT'S LA ROTHERFIELD RD
Drawback Hill
81
Hunts Wood Harpsden Bottom Sch Harpsden + Harpsden Court
Hunt's Farm Golf Course Harpsden
Hunts Green CHALK HILL
3
PERSEVERANCE HILL Harpsden Wood
WHITE HILL Perseverence Farm
RED HILL Bellehatch Farm
Bellehatch Park Upper Bolney House Cray House A4155
Crowsley Park Woods Mays Green 80 36
Ash Farm WOODLANDS RD
The Bottle & Glass (PH) High Wood Upper Hailey Wood Haileywood
BONES Shiplake Woods A4155
Bournes Farm Binfield House Fir Grove Lower Hailey Wood Haileywood Farm
Home Farm 2
Elm Tree Farm Shiplake Woods NEW RD 79
Kiln Farm Long Copse New Cross MILL LA
The Common KILN LA MEMORIAL AVE ORCHARD CL Shiplake
Binfield Heath HEATHFIELD AVE Woodwax Wood Sch PLOWDEN WAY
HEATHFIELD CL Shiplake Row The White Hart (PH) 1
The New Inn (PH) CHURCH LA College
Shiplake Rise Farm Shiplakecourt Farm +
Holmwood HEATHFIELD GREEN LA A4155 River Thames
GRAVEL RD Shiplake Copse Warren Hill 78

74 D 75 E 76 F 78

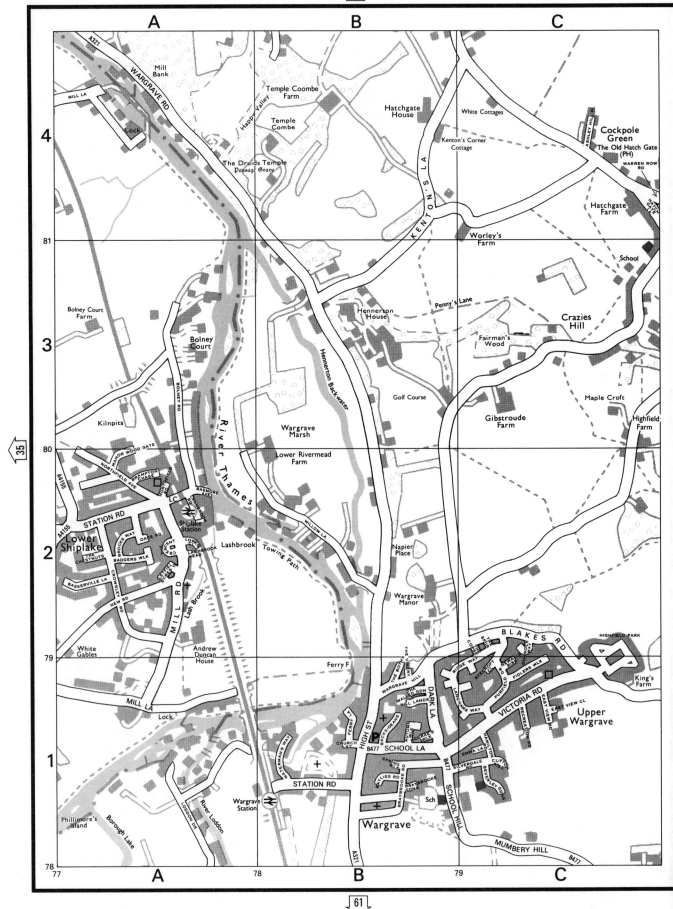

17

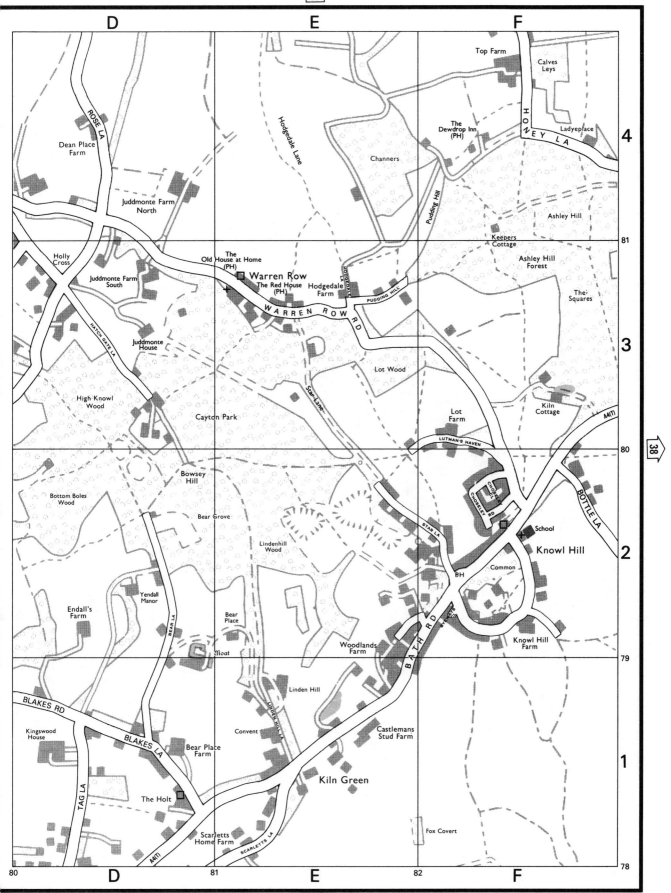

62

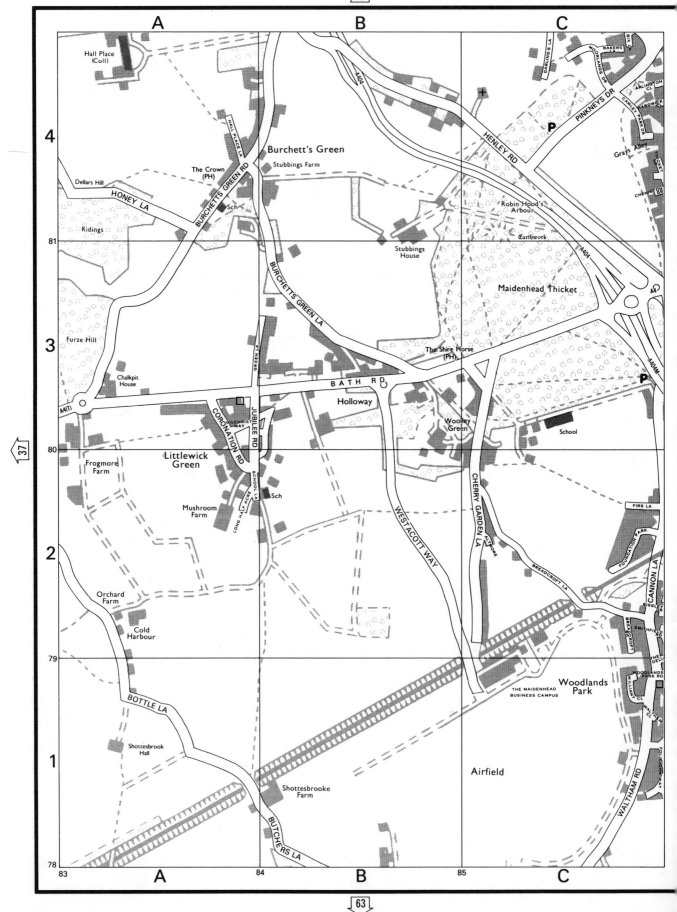

Hall Place
(Coll)

4

Burchett's Green

The Crown
(PH)

Stubbings Farm

Dellars Hill

HONEY LA

BURCHETTS GREEN RD

HALL PLACE LA

Sch

Ridings

81

Stubbings
House

Robin Hood's
Arbour

Earthwork

Maidenhead Thicket

A404

HENLEY RD

T A404

PINKNEYS DR

DARLING'S LA

WOODLANDS DR

BAKERS

CAMLEY PARK DR

HARDWICK

AALINGTON CL

Grays Alley

CHENS

BURCHETTS' GREEN LA

GREEN LA

3

Furze Hill

Chalkpit
House

A4(T)

The Shire Horse
(PH)

BATH RD

Holloway

Woolley
Green

School

A4(T)

A404(T)

P

P

GILCHRIST WAY

JUBILEE RD

CORONATION RD

80

Littlewick
Green

Frogmore
Farm

Mushroom
Farm

Sch

SCHOOL LA

LONG HALF ACRE

WESTACOTT WAY

CHERRY GARDEN LA

ALTMORE

FIRS LA

FOUNDATION PARK

2

Orchard
Farm

Cold
Harbour

BREADCROFT LA

BREADCROFT

CANNON LA

BISSLEY DR

SMITHFIELD RD

79

THE MAIDENHEAD
BUSINESS CAMPUS

Woodlands
Park

THE
DELL

WOODLANDS PARK RD

WILLANT CL

BOTTLE LA

1

Shottesbrook
Hall

Shottesbrooke
Farm

Airfield

WALTHAM RD

WALSING

FOUNTAIN

78

BUTCHERS LA

83

A

84

B

85

C

19

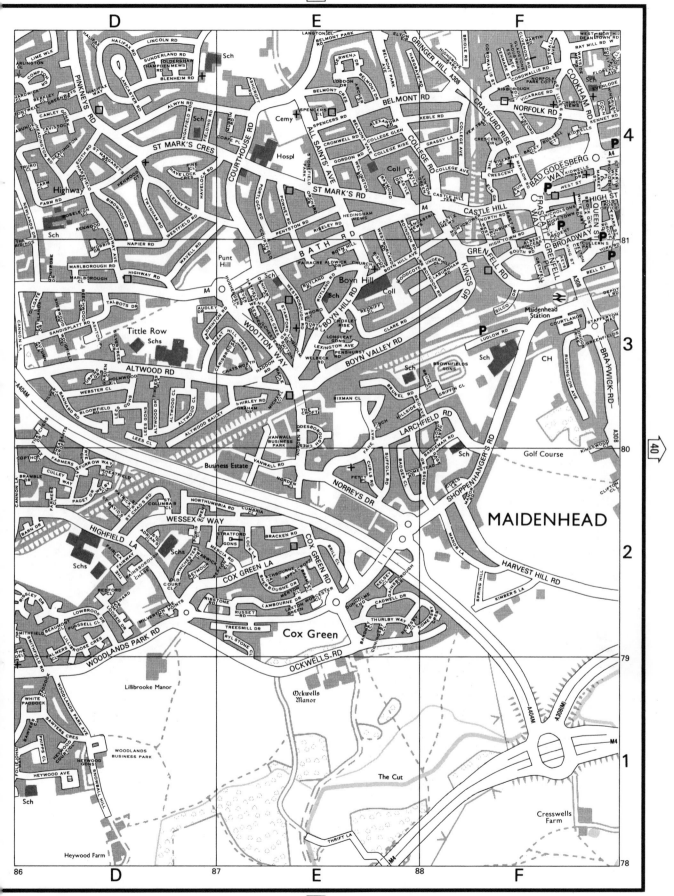

MAIDENHEAD

64
40

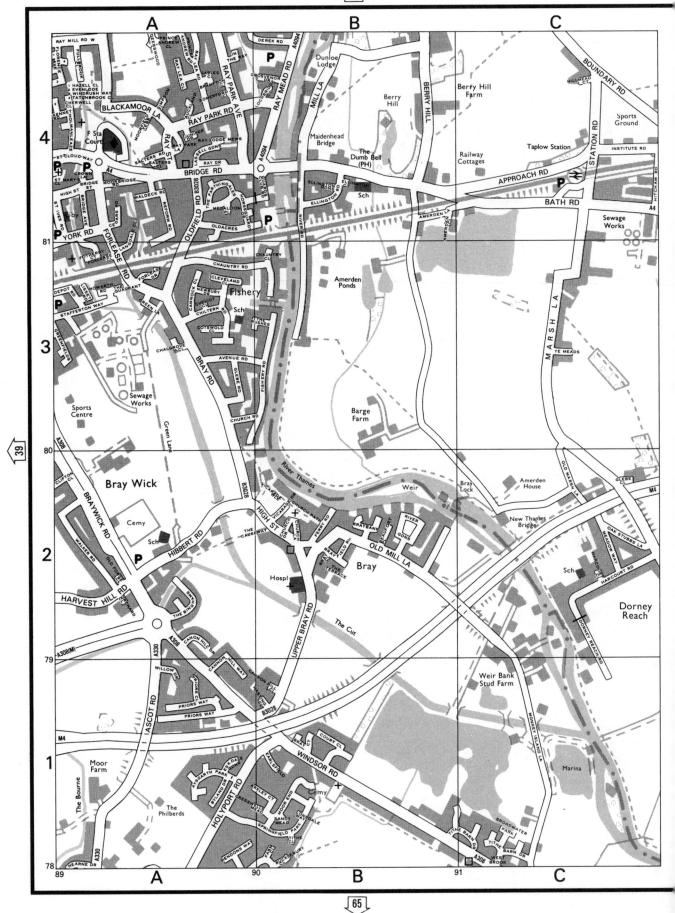

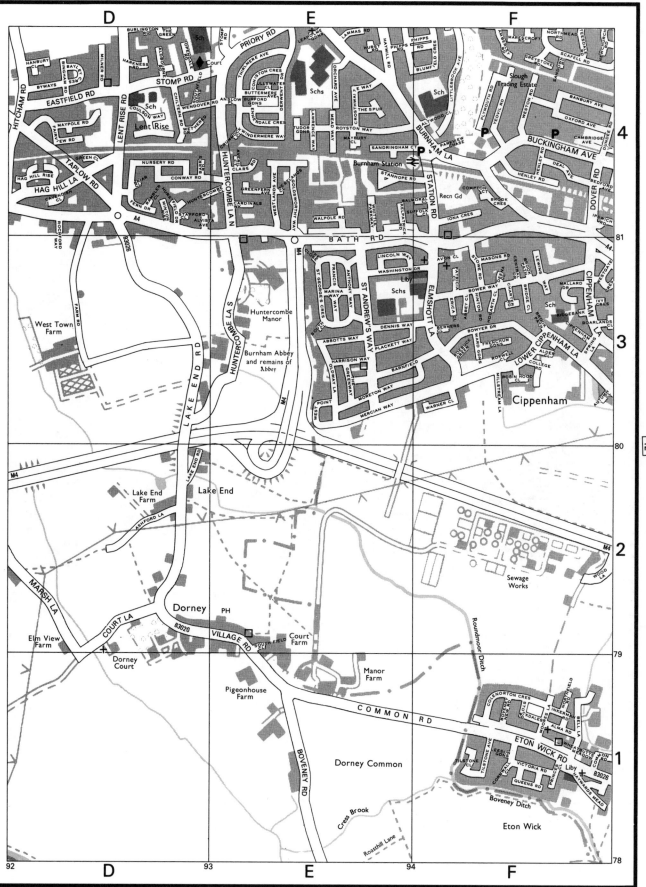

D   E   F

HITCHAM RD
EASTFIELD RD
BURLINGTON RD
THE GREEN
STOMP RD
PRIORY RD
LAMMAS RD
HURST RD
HAYMILL RD
PHIPPS RD
NORTHMEAD
TEESDALE
NEWCHURCH
MARESCROFT RD
SCAFELL RD
GREYSTOKE RD
Slough Trading Estate
BANBURY AVE
OXFORD AVE
CAMBRIDGE AVE
BUCKINGHAM AVE
BEDFORD RD
DOVER RD
IPSWICH RD

HANBURY CL
BINGHAM RD
BAY
BYWAYS
CRES
MILNER RD
HARKNESS RD
ALDERBOURNE
Court
Sch
THIRLMERE AVE
COULSTON CRES
BUTTERMERE AVE
BURFORD GDNS
ULLSWATER CL
Schs
AE WAY
THE SPUR
ALTWOOD CL
LITTLEBROOK AVE
Sch
YEOVIL RD
WESTON RD
HENLEY RD

MAYPOLE RD
FAIRLIE
YEW RD
GREEN CL
LENT RISE RD
COULSON WAY
CHILTERN RD
WENDOVER RD
ANSLOW
WINDERMERE AVE
ENNERDALE CRES
DERWENT DR
LAWRENCE WAY
TUDOR GDNS
MEAD WAY
MAYBURY RD
ROYSTON WAY
CROFTHAN
CLOSE
BURNHAM LA
PARKWAY
PARKWAY CHASE
COMPTON CT
DEAL AVE
P
P
P
Recn Gd
BROOK CRES

Sch
Lent Rise
NURSERY RD
BARR
CONWAY RD
HUNTERCOMBE LA N
CARDINALS
GREENFERN AVE
WESTLANDS AVE
GOLDSWORTHY WAY
WHITLEY
PARKWAY
SANDRINGHAM CT
Burnham Station
STANHOPE RD
BALMORAL
SUFFOLK RD
XELFA TRICK
IONA CRES
STATION RD
LINCOLN WAY
WASHINGTON DR
AVON CL
STOVE RD
MASONS RD
CIPPENHAM

HAG HILL RISE
HAG HILL LA
CAVENDISH CL
BALMORAL
TAPLOW RD
CEDAR
RAMBLER
HUNTERFIELD CL
MINTON
STAFFORD DR
ALVISTA AVE
NEIL CLARE
CHINBROOK
WINDERMERE WAY
FERN DR
A4
B3026
WALPOLE RD
BATH RD
BATH RD
81

West Town Farm
HUNTERCOMBE LA S
LAKE END RD
M4
Huntercombe Manor
Burnham Abbey and remains of Abbey
ST GEORGES CRES
MARINA WAY
FRANCIS WAY
ANTHONY WAY
ST ANDREW'S WAY
DENNIS WAY
ABBOTTS WAY
PLACKETT WAY
HARRISON WAY
OLDWAY LA
THE GREENWAY
POINT
WEST
MORETON WAY
BARNFIELD
MERCIAN WAY
WARNER CL
Liby
Schs
ELMSHOTT LA
PATRICIA
ABBEY CL
HINTON
BOWER WAY
ERICA CL
BERNERS
GORTH
CHART RD
CHART RD
CENTRAL RD
BRIDGE RD
BROOK
LEWINS WAY
MALLARD
IVY CL
Sch
RIDGEBANK
BOARLANDS CL
SPRING LA
CIPPENHAM
ALDER
ROBIN HOOD CL
BOWYER DR
FRENCHUM GDNS
ROXWELL
COLLEGE
LOWER CIPPENHAM LA
MILLSTREAM LA
Cippenham
80

M4
Lake End Farm
Lake End
ASHFORD LA
Sewage Works
M4
WOOD CL
79

MARSH LA
COURT LA
Elm View Farm
Dorney
PH
B3020
VILLAGE RD
SOUTH FIELD
Court Farm
Dorney Court
Pigeonhouse Farm
Manor Farm
BOVENEY RD
COMMON RD
Roundmoor Ditch
COLENORTON CRES
LINKERMAN
ALMA RD
ETON WICK RD
TILSTONE CL
TILSTONE AVE
LEESON GDNS
VICTORIA RD
QUEENS RD
PRINCES
Liby
B3026
HAYWARDS MEAD
1

Dorney Common
Cress Brook
Roasthill Lane
Boveney Ditch
Eton Wick
78

92   D   93   E   94   F

42

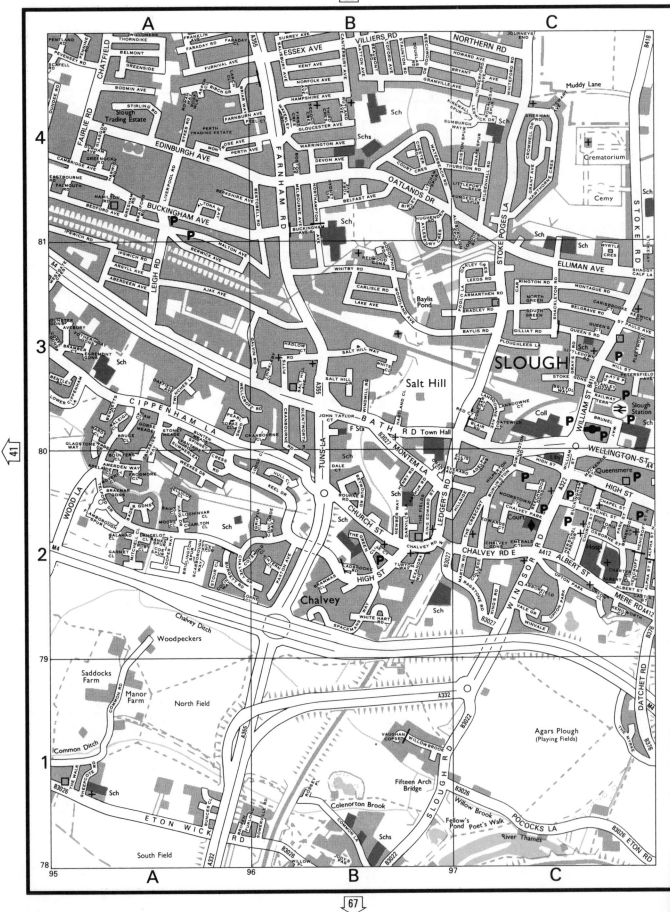

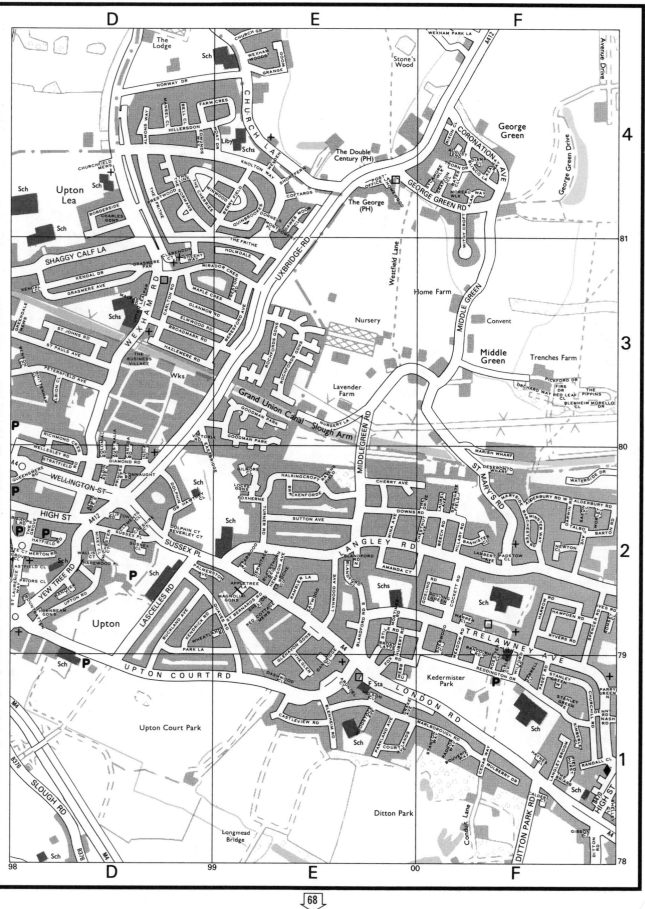

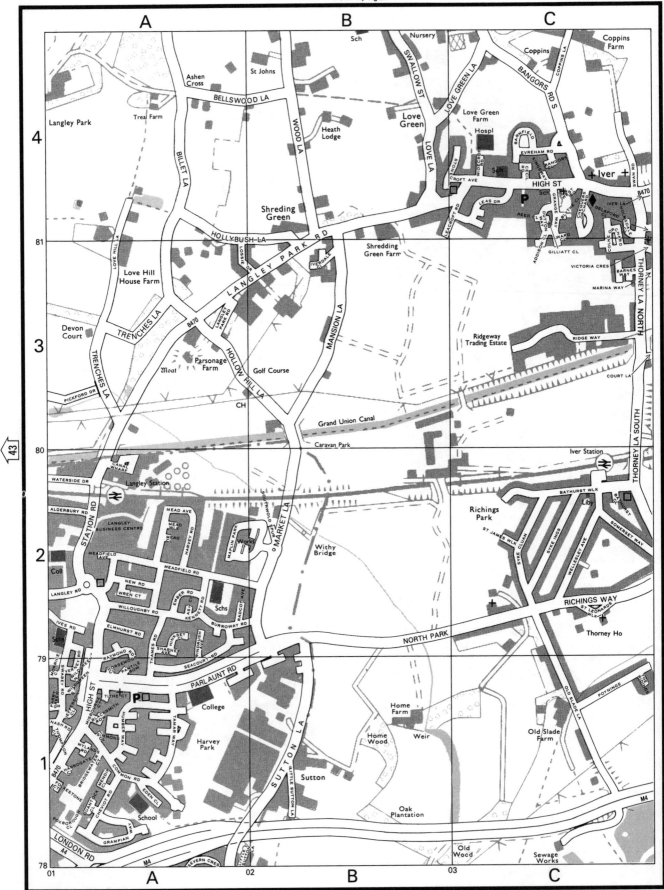

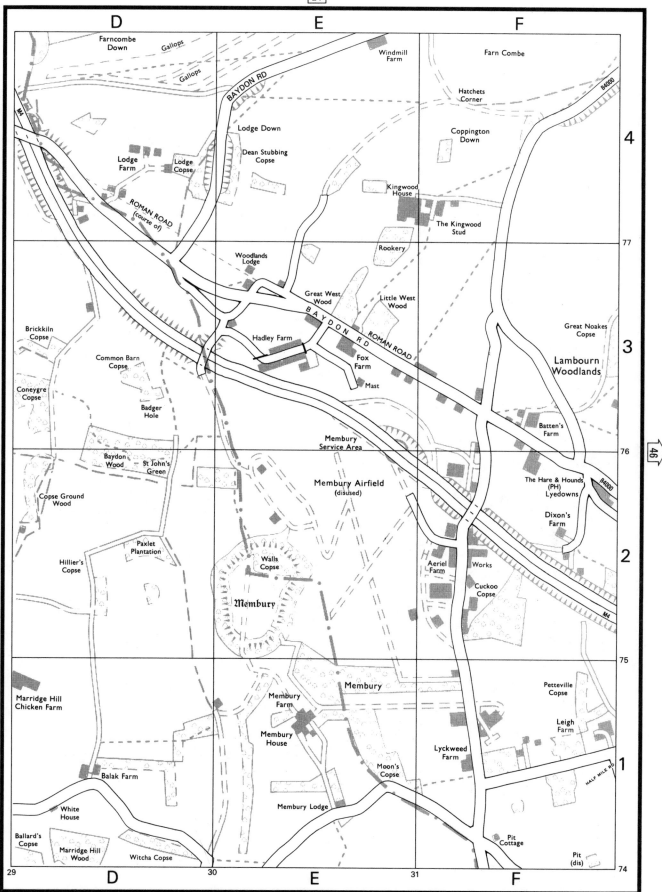

24

D

E

F

Farncombe Down

Gallops

Gallops

Gallops

Windmill Farm

Farn Combe

B4000

BAYDON RD

Hatchets Corner

Lodge Down

Coppington Down

4

Dean Stubbing Copse

Lodge Farm

Lodge Copse

M4

Kingwood House

The Kingwood Stud

ROMAN ROAD (course of)

77

Woodlands Lodge

Rookery

Great West Wood

Little West Wood

Great Noakes Copse

Brickkiln Copse

BAYDON RD

ROMAN ROAD

3

Common Barn Copse

Hadley Farm

Fox Farm

Lambourn Woodlands

Coneygre Copse

Mast

Batten's Farm

Badger Hole

76

46

Baydon Wood

St John's Green

Membury Service Area

The Hare & Hounds (PH) Lyedowns

B4000

Copse Ground Wood

Membury Airfield (disused)

Dixon's Farm

Hillier's Copse

Paxlet Plantation

Walls Copse

Aeriel Farm

Works

2

Cuckoo Copse

Membury

M4

75

Petteville Copse

Membury

Marridge Hill Chicken Farm

Membury Farm

Leigh Farm

Membury House

Lyckweed Farm

1

Moon's Copse

Balak Farm

HALF MILE RD

White House

Membury Lodge

Ballard's Copse

Pit Cottage

Marridge Hill Wood

Witcha Copse

Pit (dis)

74

29

D

30

E

31

F

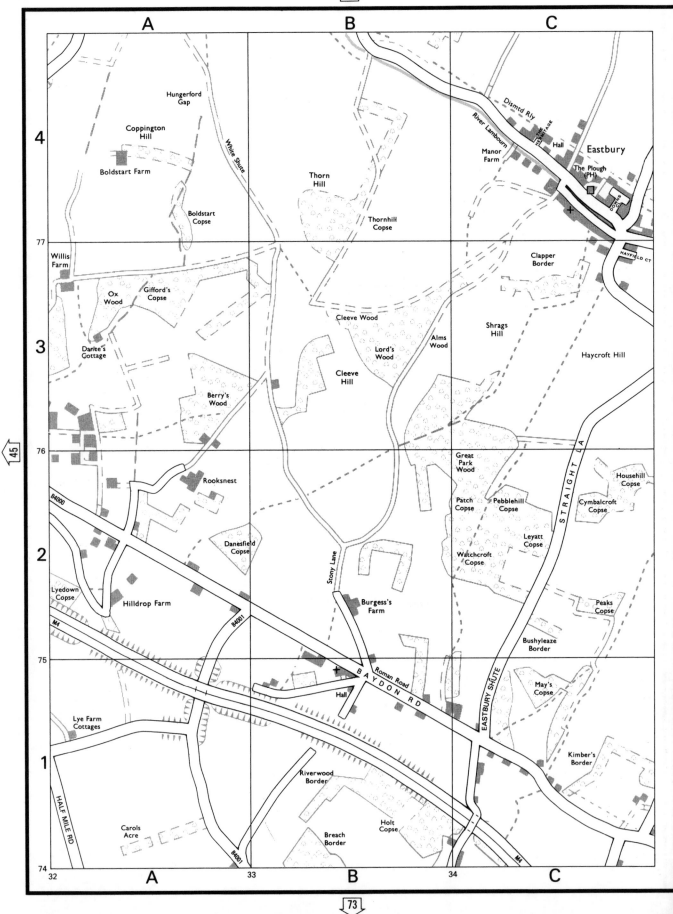

A   B   C

4

Hungerford Gap

Coppington Hill

Boldstart Farm

Boldstart Copse

White Shute

Thorn Hill

Thornhill Copse

River Lambourn

Dismtd Rly

Manor Farm

HERITAGE

Hall

Eastbury

The Plough (PH)

DOWNS

HAYFIELD CT

77

Willis Farm

Ox Wood

Gifford's Copse

Dante's Cottage

Cleeve Wood

Lord's Wood

Alms Wood

Clapper Border

Shrags Hill

Haycroft Hill

3

Berry's Wood

Cleeve Hill

76

Rooksnest

Great Park Wood

Patch Copse

Pebblehill Copse

Leyatt Copse

Watchcroft Copse

Household Copse

Cymbalcroft Copse

STRAIGHT LA

B4000

Danesfield Copse

Stony Lane

Peaks Copse

2

Lyedown Copse

Hilldrop Farm

Burgess's Farm

Bushyleaze Border

M4

B4001

75

Roman Road

BAYDON RD

Hall

EASTBURY SHUTE

May's Copse

Lye Farm Cottages

1

Riverwood Border

Holt Copse

Kimber's Border

HALF MILE RD

Carols Acre

Breach Border

B4001

M4

74

32   A   33   B   34   C

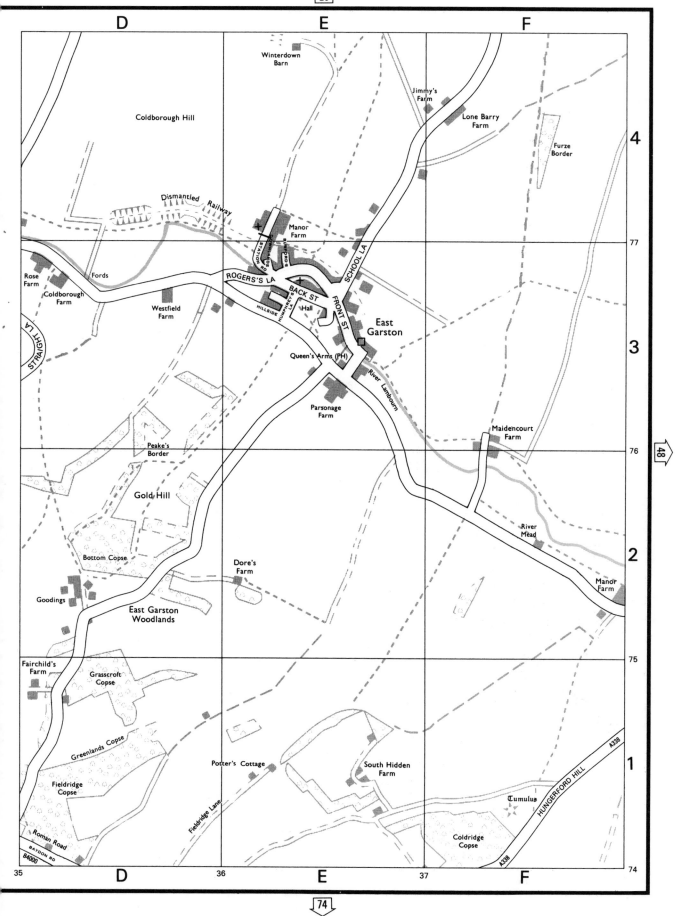

D   E   F

Winterdown
Barn

Coldborough Hill

Jimmy's
Farm

Lone Barry
Farm

4

Furze
Border

Dismantled Railway

Manor
Farm

77

Rose
Farm

Fords

ROGERS'S LA

BACK ST

SCHOOL LA

FRONT ST

Coldborough
Farm

Westfield
Farm

HILLSIDE

Hall

East
Garston

3

Queen's Arms (PH)

River Lambourn

Parsonage
Farm

Peake's
Border

Maidencourt
Farm

76

48

Gold Hill

River
Mead

Bottom Copse

2

Goodings

Dore's
Farm

East Garston
Woodlands

Manor
Farm

Fairchild's
Farm

Grasscroft
Copse

75

Greenlands Copse

Potter's Cottage

South Hidden
Farm

Fieldridge
Copse

1

Tumulus

HUNGERFORD HILL

A338

Fieldridge Lane

Roman Road

Coldridge
Copse

B4000

BAYDON RD

A338

35   D   36   E   37   F   74

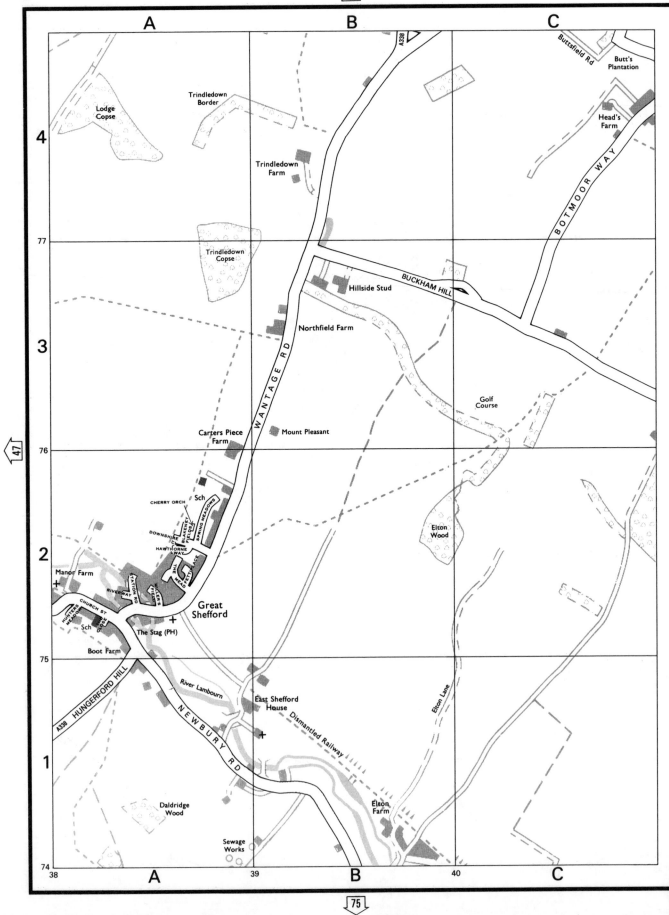

47

A   B   C

Lodge Copse

Trindledown Border

Trindledown Farm

4

Buttsfield Rd

Butt's Plantation

Head's Farm

BOTMOOR WAY

77

Trindledown Copse

BUCKHAM HILL

Hillside Stud

Northfield Farm

A338

3

Golf Course

WANTAGE RD

Carters Piece Farm

Mount Pleasant

76

Sch

CHERRY ORCH

Elton Wood

SPRING MEADOWS

DOWNSHIRE

BLAKENEY CL
FIELDS

HAWTHORNE WAY

2

Manor Farm

STATION RD

MILLER'S

THE MEAD

FESTY PLACE

Great Shefford

RIVERWAY

CHURCH ST

HUNTERS MEADOW

DOWNSHIRE CLOSE

Sch

The Stag (PH)

Boot Farm

75

HUNGERFORD HILL

A338

River Lambourn

East Shefford House

Elton Lane

NEWBURY RD

Dismantled Railway

1

Daldridge Wood

Elton Farm

Sewage Works

74

38   A   39   B   40   C

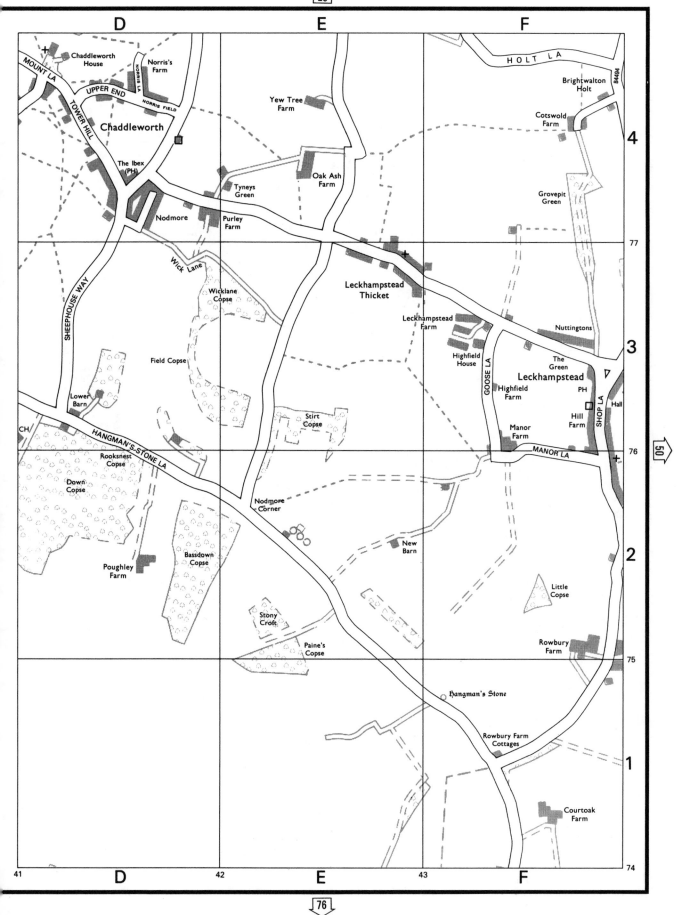

D   E   F

HOLT LA

MOUNT LA

Chaddleworth House

Norris's Farm

UPPER END

NORRIS LA

NORRIS FIELD

Brightwalton Holt

B4494

TOWER HILL

Yew Tree Farm

Cotswold Farm

4

Chaddleworth

The Ibex (PH)

Oak Ash Farm

Grovepit Green

Tyneys Green

Nodmore

Purley Farm

77

Wick Lane

Leckhampstead Thicket

SHEEPHOUSE WAY

Wicklane Copse

Leckhampstead Farm

Nuttingtons

Field Copse

Highfield House

GOOSE LA

The Green

Leckhampstead

3

Lower Barn

Highfield Farm

PH

Hall

SHOP LA

CH

HANGMAN'S-STONE LA

Stirt Copse

Hill Farm

Rooksnest Copse

Manor Farm

MANOR LA

76

50

Down Copse

Nodmore Corner

Bassdown Copse

New Barn

Little Copse

Poughley Farm

2

Stony Croft

Rowbury Farm

Paine's Copse

75

Hangman's Stone

Rowbury Farm Cottages

1

Courtoak Farm

41   D   42   E   43   F   74

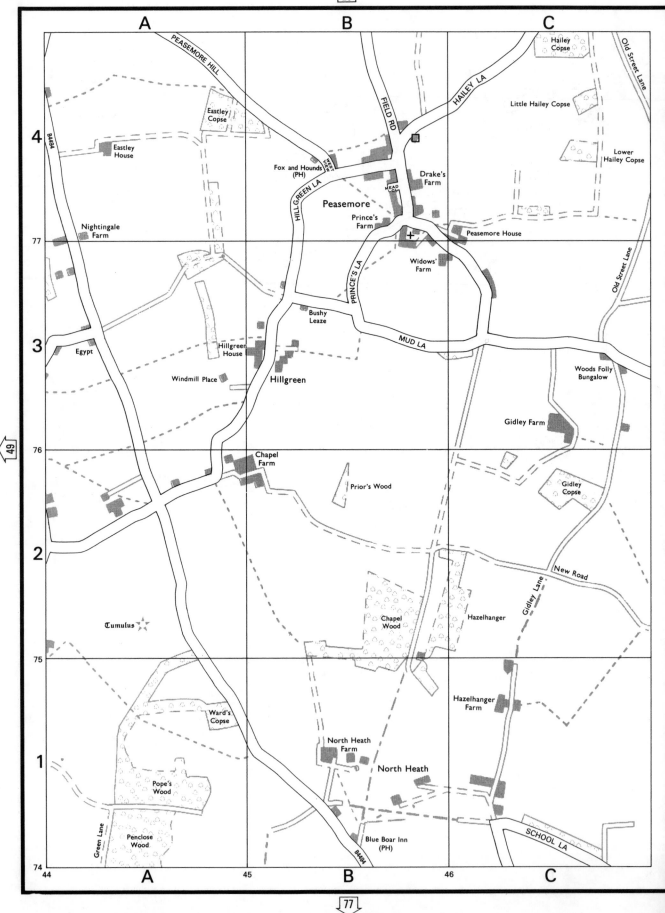

D   E   F

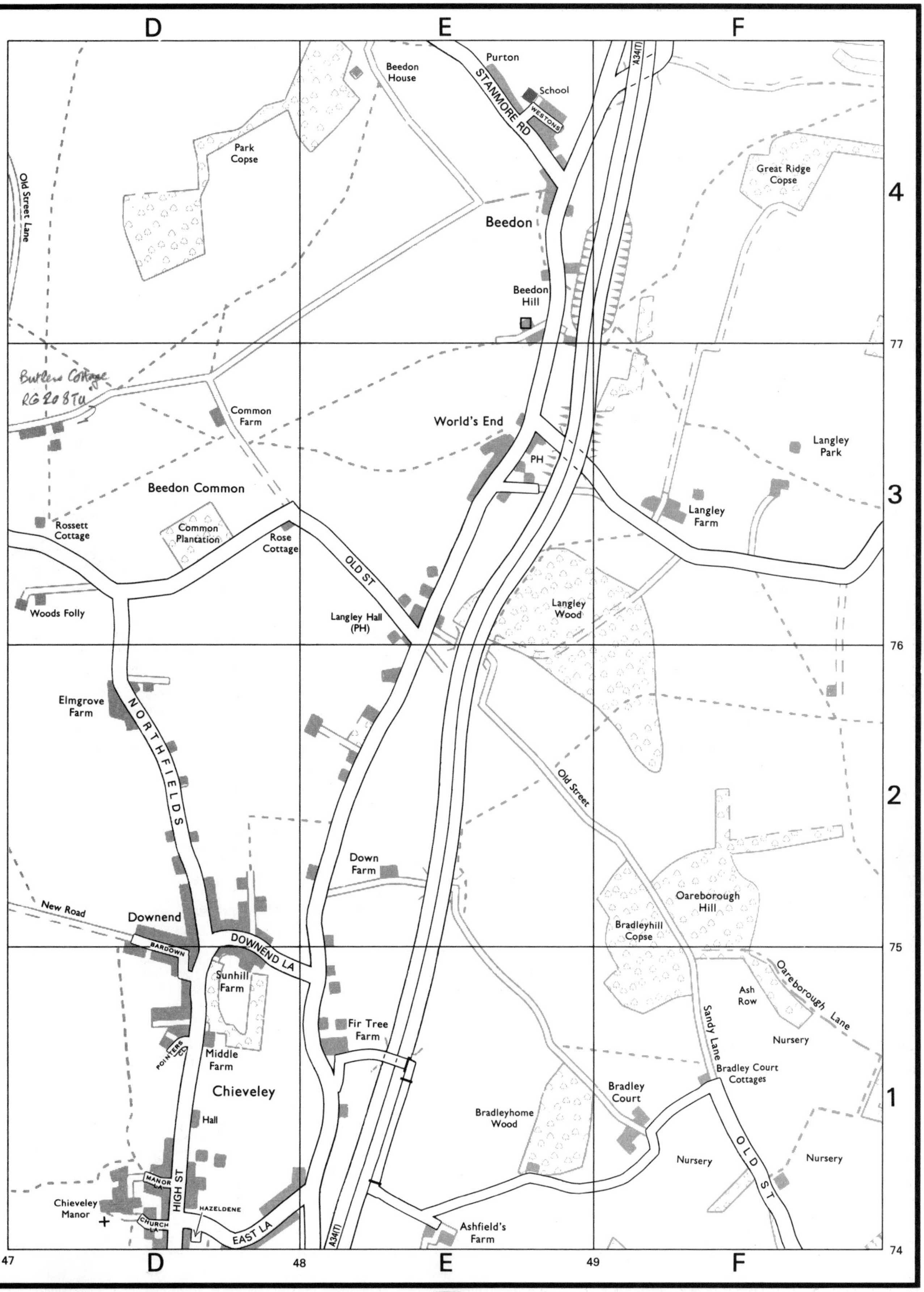

Old Street Lane

Park Copse

Beedon House

Purton

School

STANMORE RD

WESTONS

A34(T)

Great Ridge Copse

4

Beedon

Beedon Hill

77

Butlers Cottage
RG 20 8 TU

Common Farm

World's End

PH

Langley Park

Langley Farm

3

Beedon Common

Rossett Cottage

Common Plantation

Rose Cottage

OLD ST

Langley Wood

Langley Hall (PH)

Woods Folly

⬆ 52

76

Elmgrove Farm

NORTHFIELDS

Old Street

2

New Road

Downend

BARDOWN

DOWNEND LA

Down Farm

Oareborough Hill

Bradleyhill Copse

75

Sunhill Farm

POINTERS

Fir Tree Farm

Ash Row

Oareborough Lane

Nursery

Middle Farm

Sandy Lane

Bradley Court Cottages

1

Chieveley

Hall

Bradley Court

Bradleyhome Wood

OLD ST

MANOR

Chieveley Manor

HIGH ST

HAZELDENE

CHURCH LA

EAST LA

A34(T)

Ashfield's Farm

Nursery

Nursery

74

47   D   48   E   49   F

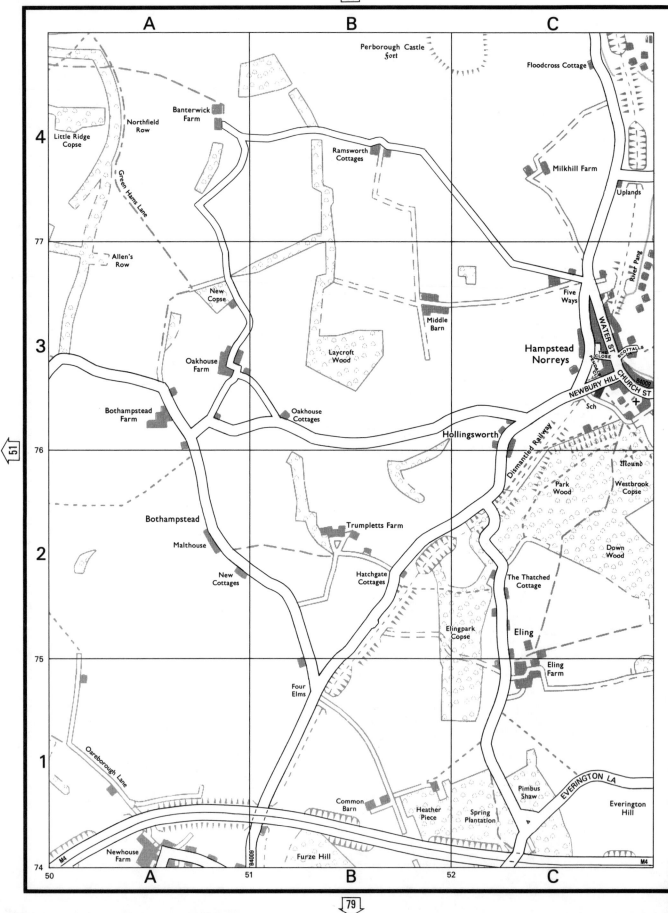

51

A · B · C

Perborough Castle Fort

Floodcross Cottage

Little Ridge Copse

Northfield Row

Banterwick Farm

Ramsworth Cottages

Milkhill Farm

Uplands

4

Green Harns Lane

Allen's Row

77

New Copse

Middle Barn

Five Ways

River Pang

WATER ST

3

Laycroft Wood

Hampstead Norreys

SCOTTALLS

THE CLOSE

PEROKES

Oakhouse Farm

NEWBURY HILL

CHURCH ST

B4009

Bothampstead Farm

Oakhouse Cottages

Hollingsworth

Sch

76

Dismantled Railway

Mound

Park Wood

Westbrook Copse

Bothampstead

Down Wood

Malthouse

Trumpletts Farm

2

New Cottages

Hatchgate Cottages

The Thatched Cottage

Elingpark Copse

Eling

75

Eling Farm

Four Elms

1

Oareborough Lane

EVERINGTON LA

Pimbus Shaw

Everington Hill

Common Barn

Heather Piece

Spring Plantation

M4

B4009

Newhouse Farm

Furze Hill

M4

74

50 · 51 · 52

A · B · C

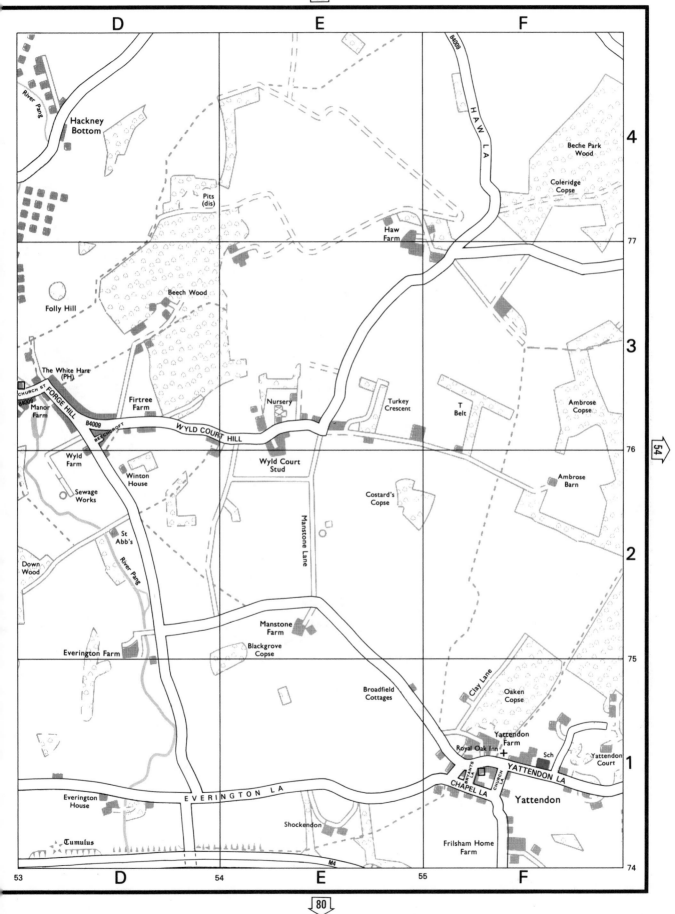

D   E   F

River Pang

Hackney
Bottom

Pits
(dis)

Beche Park
Wood

Coleridge
Copse

HAW LA

B4009

4

77

Beech Wood

Folly Hill

Haw
Farm

3

The White Hart
(PH)

CHURCH ST

B4009

Manor
Farm

FORGE HILL

Firtree
Farm

Nursery

Turkey
Crescent

T
Belt

Ambrose
Copse

B4009

BEECHCROFT

WYLD COURT HILL

76

Wyld
Farm

Winton
House

Wyld Court
Stud

Ambrose
Barn

Sewage
Works

Costard's
Copse

Manstone Lane

St
Abb's

River Pang

Down
Wood

2

Everington Farm

Manstone
Farm

Blackgrove
Copse

75

Broadfield
Cottages

Clay Lane

Oaken
Copse

Yattendon
Farm

Royal Oak Inn

Sch

Yattendon
Court

YATTENDON LA

BRYANTS LA

CHURCH LA

1

Everington
House

EVERINGTON LA

CHAPEL LA

Yattendon

Shockendon

Frilsham Home
Farm

Tumulus

M4

74

53   D   54   E   55   F

54

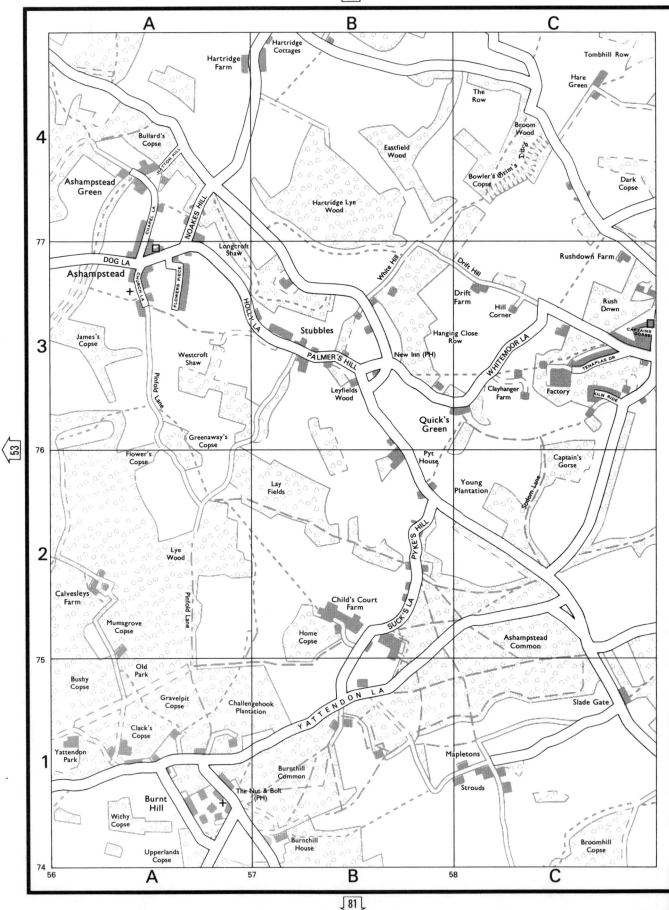

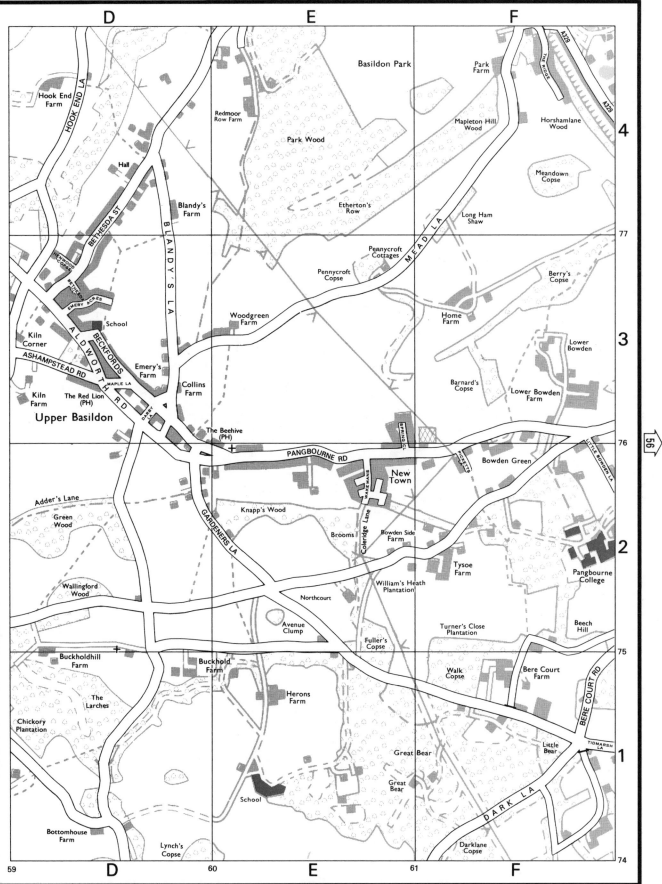

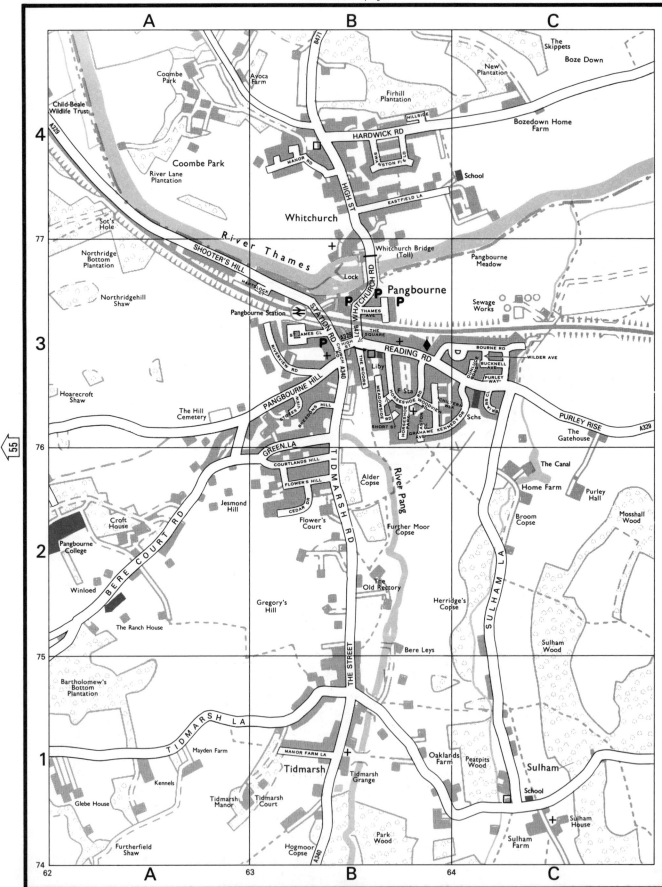

Child-Beale Wildlife Trust

Coombe Park

Avoca Farm

Firhill Plantation

HARDWICK RD

HILLSIDE

The Skippets

Boze Down

New Plantation

Bozedown Home Farm

School

Coombe Park

River Lane Plantation

MANOR RD

SWANSTON FIELD

HIGH ST

EASTFIELD LA

Whitchurch

Sot's Hole

River Thames

SHOOTER'S HILL

Northridge Bottom Plantation

Lock

Whitchurch Bridge (Toll)

Pangbourne Meadow

Northridgehill Shaw

HART-LOCK

WHITCHURCH RD

Pangbourne

THAMES AVE

Sewage Works

Pangbourne Station

STATION RD

ST JAMES CL

THE SQUARE

READING RD

BOURNE RD

WILDER AVE

BUCKNELL AVE

PURLEY WAY

Hoarecroft Shaw

PANGBOURNE HILL

CHURCH RD

A340

RIVERVIEW RD

B471

A329

HIGH ST

THE MOORS

Liby

MEADOWSIDE

HORSESHOE RD

F Sta

WOODVIEW

DUNLUCE GARDENS

CHILTERN WLK

PURLEY WAY

The Hill Cemetery

STOKES VIEW

BREEDONS HILL

SHORT ST

GRAHAME AVE

KENNEDY DR

Schs

PURLEY RISE

A329

The Gatehouse

GREEN LA

COURTLANDS HILL

FLOWER'S HILL

Alder Copse

River Pang

The Canal

Home Farm

Purley Hall

Jesmond Hill

CEDAR DR

Flower's Court

Further Moor Copse

Broom Copse

Mosshall Wood

Croft House

BERE COURT RD

TIDMARSH RD

Pangbourne College

Herridge's Copse

SULHAM LA

Sulham Wood

Winloed

The Old Rectory

Gregory's Hill

The Ranch House

Bere Leys

THE STREET

Bartholomew's Bottom Plantation

TIDMARSH LA

Mayden Farm

MANOR FARM LA

Tidmarsh

Tidmarsh Grange

Oaklands Farm

Peatpits Wood

Sulham

School

Kennels

Glebe House

Tidmarsh Manor

Tidmarsh Court

A340

Sulham House

Furtherfield Shaw

Hogmoor Copse

Park Wood

Sulham Farm

83

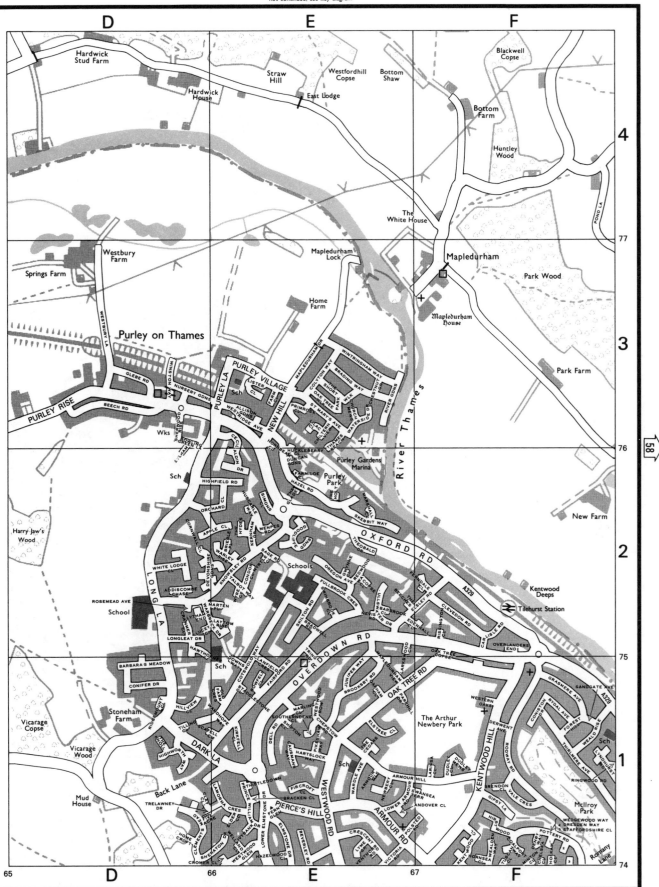

D   E   F

Hardwick Stud Farm

Hardwick House

Straw Hill

Westfordhill Copse

East Lodge

Bottom Shaw

Blackwell Copse

Bottom Farm

Huntley Wood

4

The White House

77

Westbury Farm

Springs Farm

Mapledurham Lock

Mapledurham

Park Wood

Home Farm

Mapledurham House

+

Park Farm

3

Purley on Thames

WESTBURY LA

WINSTON WAY

GLEBE RD

NURSERY GDNS

PURLEY RISE

BEECH RD

PURLEY LA

PURLEY VILLAGE

NEW HILL

MAPLEDURHAM DR

WINTRINGHAM WAY

BRACING WAY

COLTON WAY

SHORT ST

OAK TREE WLK

CHESTNUT

RIVER GDNS

WATERSIDE

Sch

LISTER CL

PARK CL

ALLISON

WESTRIDGE AVE

PRIMROSE LA

ST. MARY'S AVE

GLACIER

CLACKEN

HOLMES

58

Wks

SHERWOOD

BROWNS

CE CL

ALDIN DR

HIGHFIELD RD

HORSEACRE

HUCKLEBERRY CL

DUNCAN GDNS

FARMILOE

HAZEL RD

Purley Park

GOOSE

MARSHALL

SKERRIT WAY

+

Purley Gardens Marina

River Thames

76

Sch

Harry Jaw's Wood

ORCHARD

CL

CORNWALL CL

WARLEY

BRIERLEY

HAYDES

NUTCASTLE

SIMONS

MENPES

PYE GDNS

THEOBALD DR

NEWCOMBE

FERNDALE

OXFORD RD

New Farm

2

WHITE LODGE CL

DEVONSHIRE

KNOWSLEY RD

TALBOT WAY

SAGE RD

LONDON RD

Schools

OREGON AVE

REDWOOD

CHURNE

SKELTON RD

WINNBROOK

FULLBROOK CRES

NEVIS

BROWEL

ISBARBROOK

DR

BEESLEY RD

CLEVEDON RD

A329

EDENHALL

Kentwood Deeps

ROSEMEAD AVE

School

ADDISCOMBE CHASE

MARTEN

CLAYTON

CRAYTHAN

LONGLEAT DR

HAWTHORN

LONG LA

BARBARA'S MEADOW

CONIFER DR

HILLVIEW

FARM

RIDGMOUNT

TILLING

SCAFELL

OVERDOWN RD

COTSWOLD

LOWELL

CLANFIELD RD

SADDLE STONE

FAIRFORD RD

TRING

OAK TREE RD

PARKWOOD

OAK TREE COPSE

Tilehurst Station

CARLISLE RD

OVERLANDERS END

75

Stoneham Farm

HIGHWORTH WAY

DARK LA

Back Lane

Mud House

Vicarage Copse

Vicarage Wood

TRELAWNEY DR

AKORNIA CRES

PRINCE WILLIAM DR

THISTLEDOWN

FIRCROFT

BRACKEN CL

PIERCE'S HILL

WESTWOOD RD

DELL RD

SOUTHERNDENE

MARLING

AUSTRALS

HARTSLOCK WAY

CHEPSTOW

ELSTREE CL

JUNIPER WAY

BROOKSBY RD

MAPLEDURHAM

Sch

WARDLE AVE

LARISSA

PARPHILL

The Arthur Newbery Park

WESTERN OAKS

+

DUDLEY AVE

DERWENT

CONISTON

RYDAL AVE

GRASMERE AVE

SANDGATE AVE

A329

FOREST

WEALD RISE

THIRLMERE AVE

LYNHURST AVE

Sch

RINGWOOD RD

KENTWOOD HILL

ARMOUR HILL

SWANSEA

ANDOVER CL

BRENDON CL

PALE CRES

GIPSY LA

ROWLAND WAY

ROWAN WAY

McIlroy Park

WEDGEWOOD WAY

DRESDEN WAY

STAFFORDSHIRE CL

POTTERY RD

ARMOUR RD

1

CROMER CL

HAZELWOOD DR

BEVERLEY RD

CRESCENT RD

VICTORIA RD

HORNSEA

Romany Lane

74

65   D   66   E   67   F

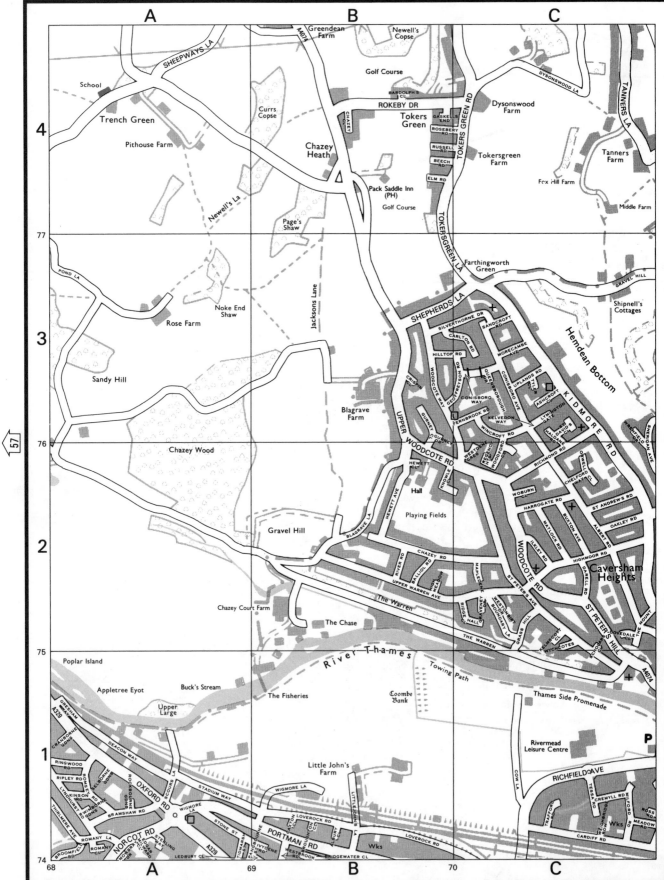

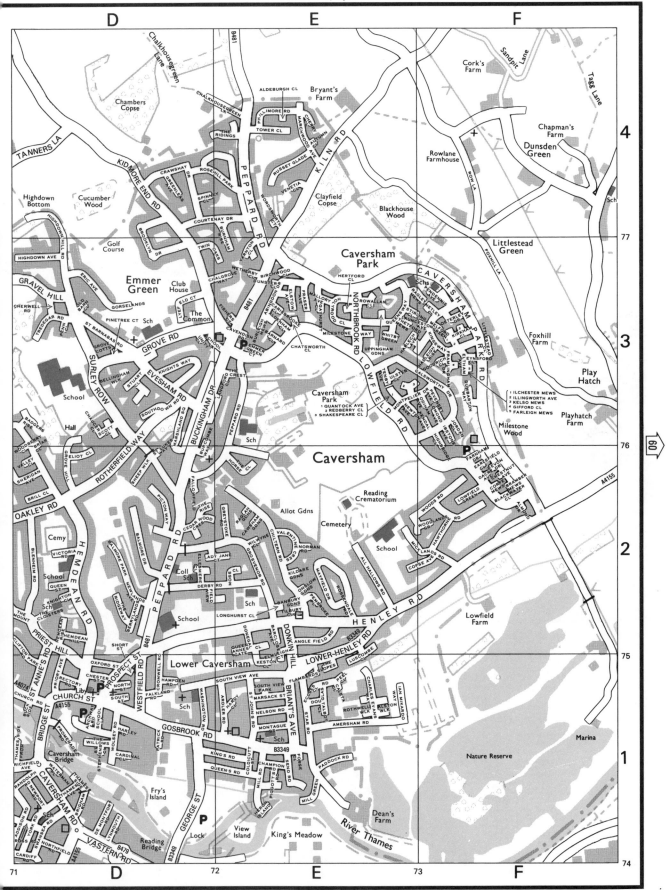

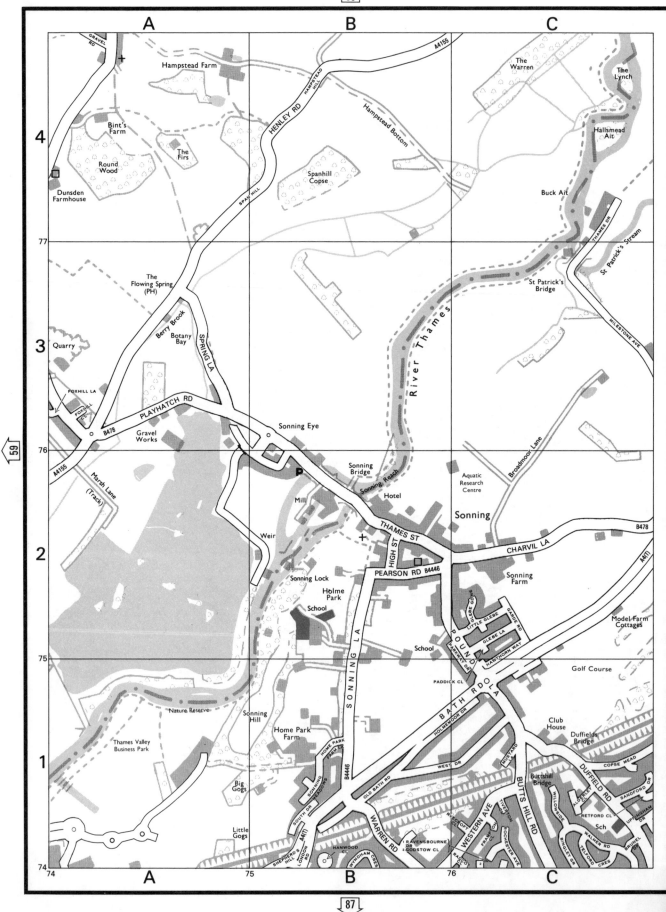

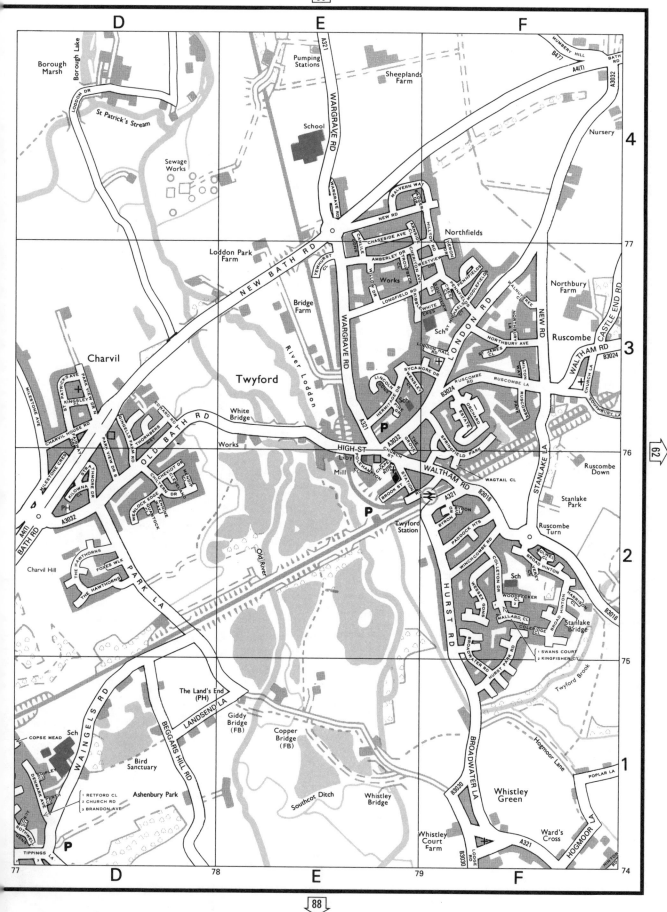

D E F

4

Borough
Marsh

Borough Lake

LODDON DR

St Patrick's Stream

Sewage
Works

Pumping
Stations

Sheeplands
Farm

School

A321

WARGRAVE RD

WARGRAVE RD

B477

MUNBERY HILL

A4(1)

BATH RD

A3032

Nursery

77

Loddon Park
Farm

NEW BATH RD

Bridge
Farm

YEWHURST CL

River Loddon

MALVERN WAY

NEW RD

CHASESIDE AVE

AMBERLEY DR

Works

LONGFIELD RD

CARLISLE CL

WILLOW DR

HILLTON RD

HERON RD

Northfields

Northbury
Farm

CASTLE END RD

77

Charvil

ST PATRICK'S AVE

MILESTONE AVE

KINGSLEY DR

PARK VIEW DR N

EDWARD RD

THORNBERS

GINGELLS FARM RD

OLD BATH RD

Twyford

White
Bridge

Sch

WHITE

KIBBLE

LONGFIELD RD

SYCAMORE DR

LINCOLN
COURT

HERMITAGE DR

ST MICHAELS RD

LODDON HALL RD

LONDON RD

NORTHBURY AVE

RUSCOMBE RD

RUSCOMBE LA

NEW RD

ST JAMES CL

WILTON RD

WALTHAM RD

Ruscombe

B3024

CHURCH LA

SOUTHBURY LA

3

MILESTONE CRES

PH

A3032

WARBERS

PARK VIEW DR S

STROMDORE DR

CHILTERN RD

CHEVIOT DR

PENNINE WAY

MENDIP DR

HIGHLAND

WELLOCK EDGE

MATTOCK WAY

PADDOCK

KILOWNA CL

Charvil Hill

BATH RD

A4110

THE HAWTHORNS

FOXES WLK

THE HAWTHORNS

PARK LA

Works

WARGRAVE RD

A321

P

A3032

HIGH ST

Mill

Liby

CHAPEL RD

POLEHAMPTON CL

BROOK ST

STATION RD

WALTHAM RD

CHURCH

THE GROVE

SPRINGFIELD PARK

ORCHARD ESTATE

B3024

RUSCOMBE RD

STANLAKE LA

RUSCOMBE PARK

Ruscombe
Down

76

P

Twyford
Station

BYRON CL

BYRON RD

A321

PADDOCK HTS

WINCHCOMBE RD

COLLEYTON DR

WESSEX GDNS

B3018

WAGTAIL CL

Stanlake
Park

Ruscombe
Turn

BROAD HINTON

FOLWELL

BROAD VERRY

HARRISON CL

B3018

2

Charvil Hill

HURST RD

WOODPECKER

MALLARD CL

COLERIDGE

BROADWATER RD

BROAD HINTON

HURST PARK RD

Stanlake
Bridge

1 SWANS COURT
2 KINGFISHER CL

75

WAINGELS RD

Sch

COPSE MEAD

STIPLEY

DENMARK AVE

ROTHWELL

TIPPINGS

P

1 RETFORD CL
2 CHURCH RD
3 BRANDON AVE

BEGGARS HILL RD

LANDSEND LA

The Land's End
(PH)

Giddy
Bridge
(FB)

Copper
Bridge
(FB)

Bird
Sanctuary

Ashenbury Park

Old River

Southcot Ditch

Whistley
Bridge

BROADWATER LA

B3030

A321

Hogmoor Lane

Whistley
Green

POPLAR LA

1

Whistley
Court
Farm

B3030

A321

Ward's
Cross

HOGMOOR LA

HINTON

74

D 78 E 79 F

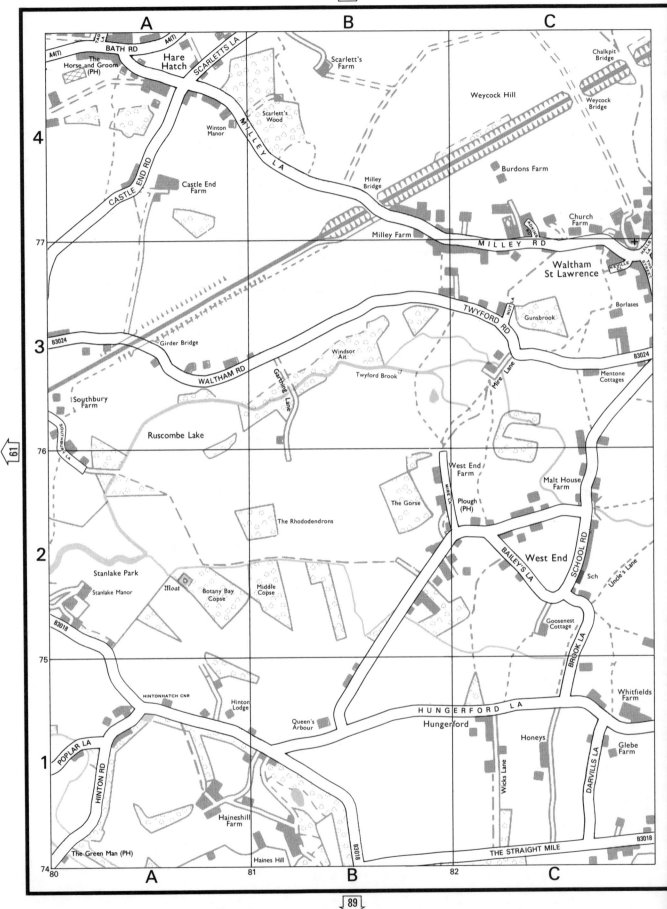

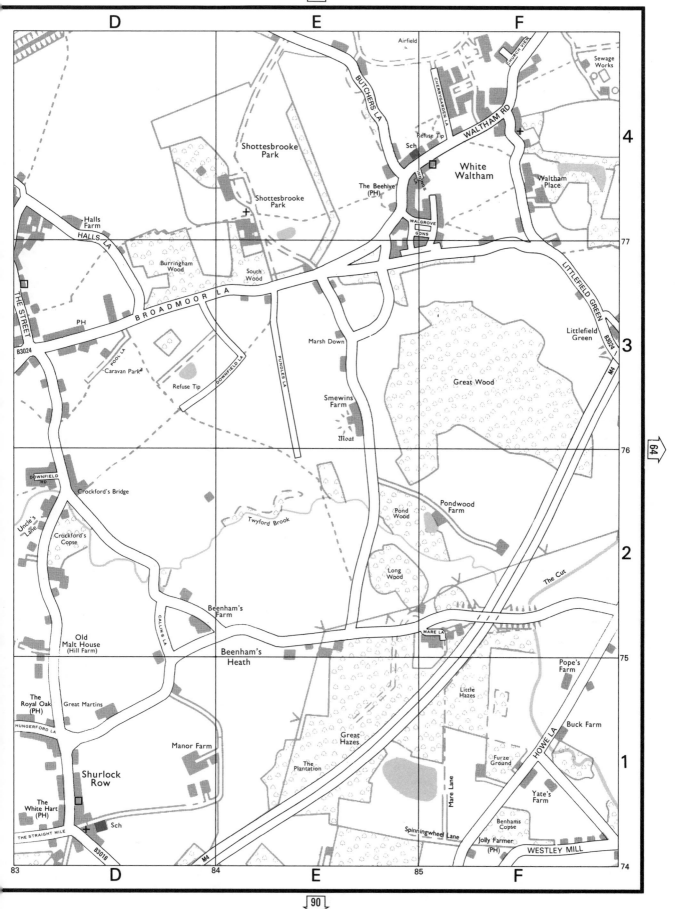

D
E
F

4

Airfield

CHURCH VIEW

Sewage Works

Shottesbrooke Park

BUTCHERS LA

CHERRYGARDEN LA

WALTHAM RD

Refuse Tip

Sch

Shottesbrooke Park

The Beehive (PH)

White Waltham

Waltham Place

THNINGS LA

Halls Farm

HALLS LA

WALGROVE GDNS

77

THE STREET

PH

BROADMOOR LA

Burringham Wood

South Wood

Marsh Down

LITTLEFIELD GREEN

Littlefield Green

B3024

3

B3024

Caravan Park

DOWNFIELD LA

PUNDLES LA

Refuse Tip

POOL LA

Great Wood

64

Smewins Farm

Moat

76

DOWNFIELD RD

Crockford's Bridge

Twyford Brook

Pond Wood

Pondwood Farm

Uncle's Lane

Crockford's Copse

Long Wood

2

The Cut

Beenham's Farm

CALLIN'S LA

MARE LA

Old Malt House (Hill Farm)

Beenham's Heath

75

Pope's Farm

The Royal Oak (PH)

Great Martins

Little Hazes

HOWE LA

Buck Farm

HUNGERFORD LA

Manor Farm

Great Hazes

Furze Ground

1

Shurlock Row

The Plantation

Mare Lane

Yate's Farm

The White Hart (PH)

Sch

Benhams Copse

THE STRAIGHT MILE

B3018

Spinningwheel Lane

Jolly Farmer (PH)

WESTLEY MILL

83

D

84

M4

E

85

F

74

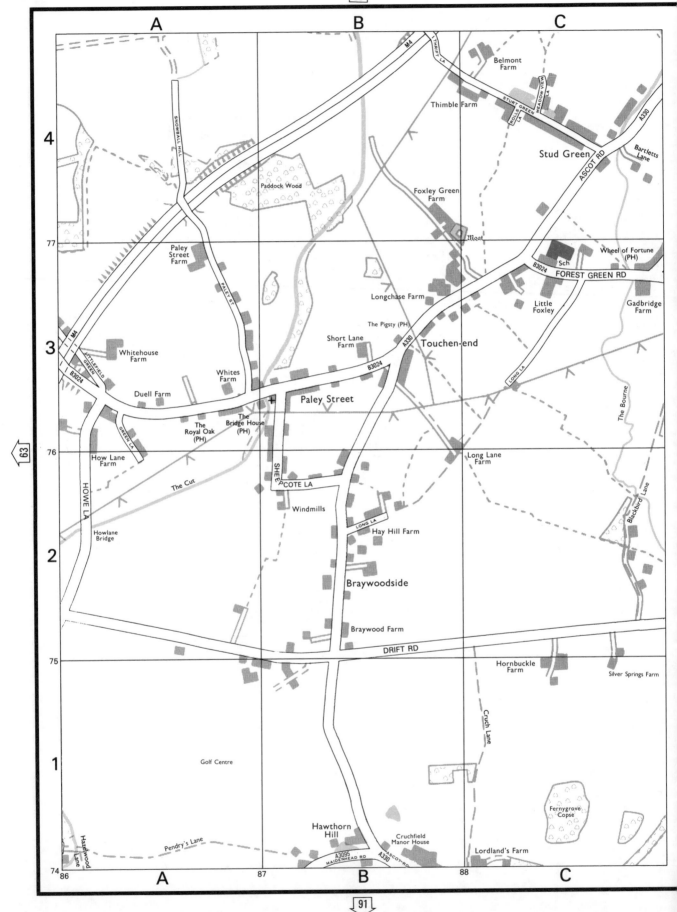

63

A   B   C

4

77

3

76

2

75

1

74

86   A   87   B   88   C

Belmont Farm
Thimble Farm
Stud Green
Bartletts Lane
Wheel of Fortune (PH)
Gadbridge Farm
FOREST GREEN RD
Little Foxley
Sch
Foxley Green Farm
Meat
Longchase Farm
The Pigsty (PH)
Touchen-end
Short Lane Farm
Paddock Wood
Paley Street Farm
Whitehouse Farm
Whites Farm
Duell Farm
Paley Street
The Royal Oak (PH)
The Bridge House (PH)
How Lane Farm
The Cut
Howlane Bridge
SHEEPCOTE LA
Windmills
Long Lane Farm
Hay Hill Farm
Braywoodside
Braywood Farm
DRIFT RD
Hornbuckle Farm
Silver Springs Farm
The Bourne
Blackbird Lane
Golf Centre
Cruch Lane
Fernygrove Copse
Hawthorn Hill
Cruchfield Manor House
Lordland's Farm
Hazelwood Lane
Pendry's Lane
A3095 MAIDENHEAD RD
A330 ASCOT RD
SNOWBALL HILL
PALEY ST
M4
THRIFT LA
STURT GREEN
ROLLS LA
MEADOW VIEW
ASCOT RD
A330
B3024
LONG LA
HOWE LA
GREEN LA
LITTLEFIELD GREEN
B3024

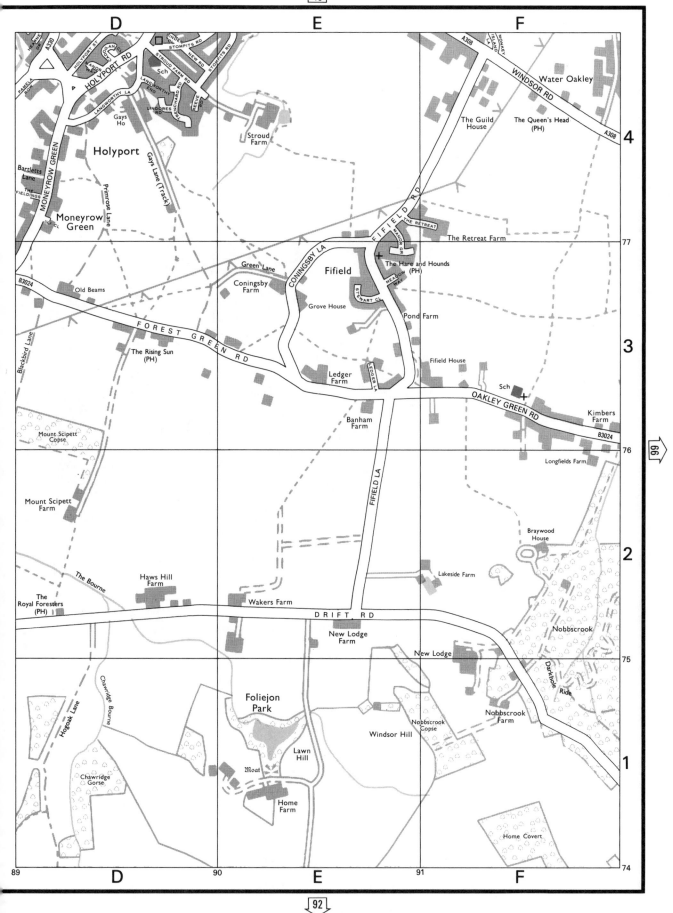

41

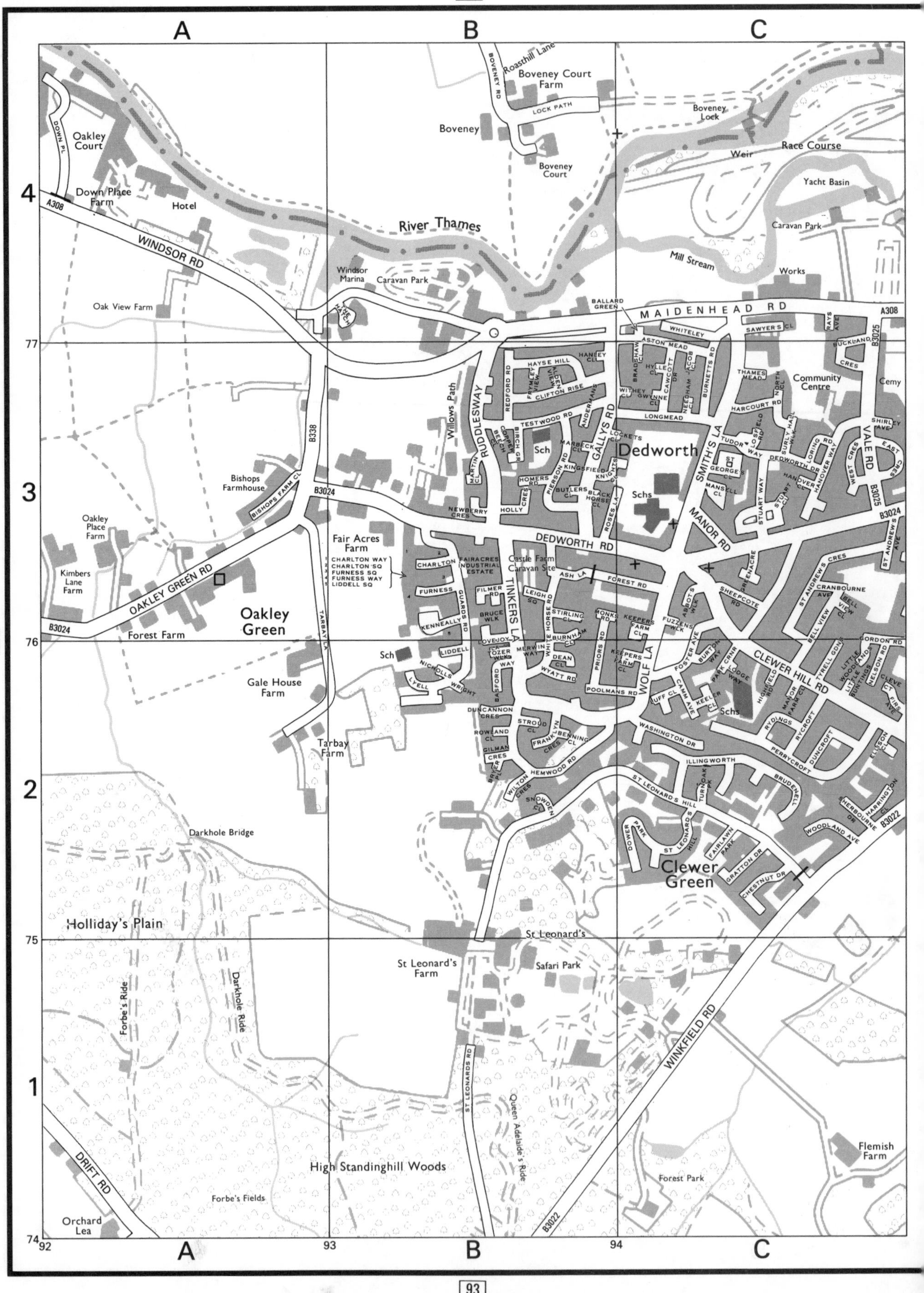

A
B
C
4
3
2
1
77
76
75
74
92
93
94
River Thames
Boveney Court Farm
Roasthill Lane
BOVENEY RD
LOCK PATH
Boveney
Boveney Court
Boveney Lock
Weir
Race Course
Yacht Basin
Caravan Park
Mill Stream
Works
Oakley Court
DOWN PL
Down Place Farm
Hotel
A308
WINDSOR RD
Windsor Marina
Caravan Park
Oak View Farm
BALLARD GREEN
MAIDENHEAD RD
WHITELEY
SAWYERS CL
RAYS AVE
BUCKLAND CRES
B3025
Cemy
Community Centre
THAMES MEAD
HARCOURT RD
ASTON MEAD
HAYSE HILL
HANLEY CL
CLIFTON RISE
REDFORD RD
BRADSHAW CL
HYLLE CL
CAWCOTT DR
JACOB CL
BURNETTS RD
WITHEY CL
GWYNNE CL
NEEDHAM CL
LONGMEAD
Willows Path
RUDDLESWAY
TESTWOOD RD
GALLYS RD
LOCKETS
Dedworth
SMITH'S LA
TUDOR WAY
SHIRLEY AVE
VALE RD
EAST CRES
WEST CRES
Sch
MARBECK CL
KINGSFIELD
KNIGHTS CL
GEORGES CL
MANSELL CL
STUART WAY
STUART CL
HANOVER WAY
DEDWORTH DR
B338
Bishops Farmhouse
BISHOPS FARM CL
B3024
HOMERS RD
BUTLERS CL
BLACK HORSE CL
Schs
MANOR RD
NEWBERRY CRES
HOLLY CRES
ROSES LA
Oakley Place Farm
Fair Acres Farm
DEDWORTH RD
CHARLTON WAY
CHARLTON SQ
FURNESS SQ
FURNESS WAY
LIDDELL SQ
CHARLTON
FAIRACRES INDUSTRIAL ESTATE
Castle Farm Caravan Site
ASH LA
FOREST RD
GREENACRE
ST ANDREWS CRES
ST ANDREW'S AVE
CRANBOURNE AVE
Kimbers Lane Farm
OAKLEY GREEN RD
FURNESS
FILMER RD
TINKERS LA
LEIGH SQ
SHEEPCOTE RD
BELL VIEW CL
BELL VIEW
KENNEALLY
GUARDS RD
BRUCE WLK
STIRLING CL
MONKS RD
KEEPERS FARM CL
FUZZENS WLK
ABBOTS WLK
Oakley Green
Forest Farm
TARBAY LA
LOVEJOY LA
WHITE HORSE RD
BURNHAM CL
PRIORS RD
WOLF LA
FOSTER AVE
BURTON WAY
PARK CNR
LODGE WAY
CLEWER HILL RD
TYRELL GDNS
GORDON RD
LITTLE WOODLANDS
BUNTINGS
NELSON RD
CLEVE CT
FIRS AVE
Sch
LIDDELL
OZER WLK
MERWIN WAY
DEAN CL
KEEPERS FARM CL
NICHOLLS
LYELL
WRIGHT
BASFORD WAY
WYATT RD
POOLMANS RD
DUFF CL
CAMM AVE
KEELER CL
HIGHFIELD RD
MANOR FARM CL
RYDINGS
RYCROFT
DUNCROFT
ELLISON CL
Gale House Farm
DUNCANNON CRES
ROWLAND CL
STROUD CL
FRANKLYN CRES
BENNING CL
WASHINGTON DR
Schs
PERRYCROFT
GILMAN CRES
Tarbay Farm
HEMWOOD RD
ILLINGWORTH
BRUDENELL
HARRINGTON CL
SHERBOURNE DR
WILTON CRES
SNOWDEN CL
ST LEONARD'S HILL
TURNOAK PARK
WOODLAND AVE
B3022
Darkhole Bridge
DOWER PARK
ST LEONARDS HILL
FAIRLAWN PARK
GRATTON DR
CHESTNUT DR
Clewer Green
Holliday's Plain
St Leonard's
St Leonard's Farm
Safari Park
Forbe's Ride
Darkhole Ride
WINKFIELD RD
ST LEONARDS RD
Queen Adelaide's Ride
DRIFT RD
High Standinghill Woods
Forbe's Fields
Orchard Lea
Forest Park
Flemish Farm

65

93

42

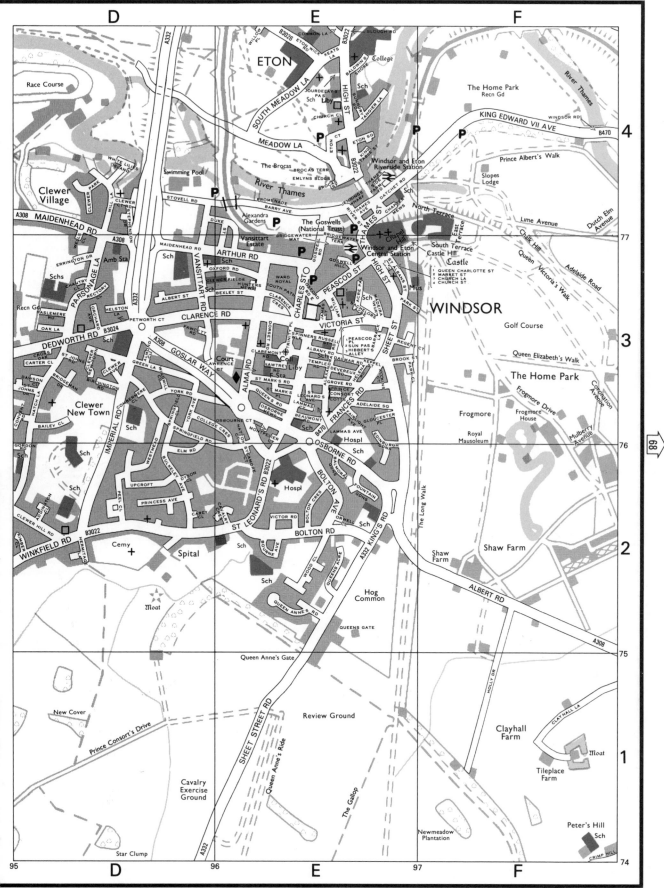

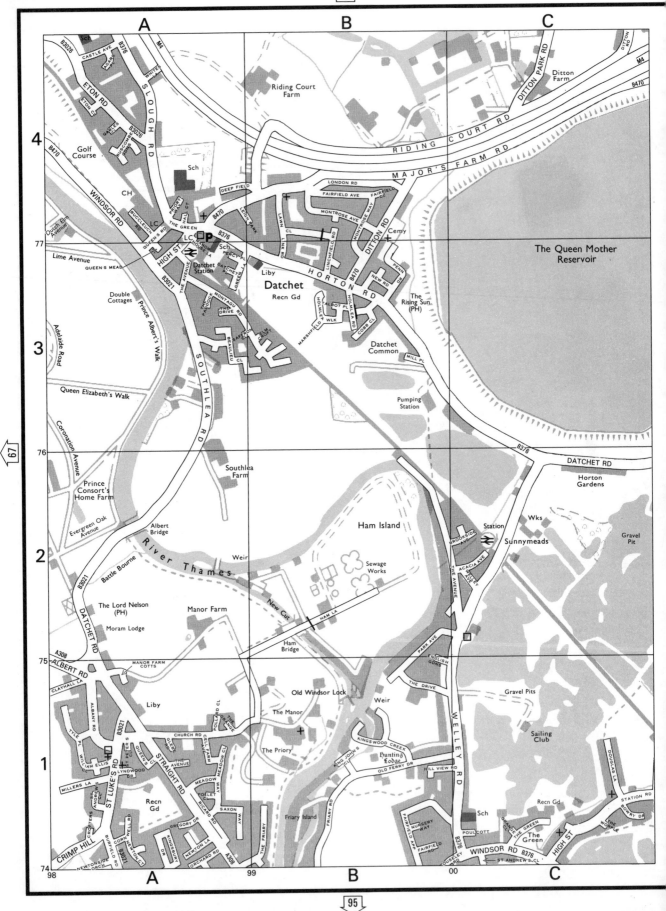

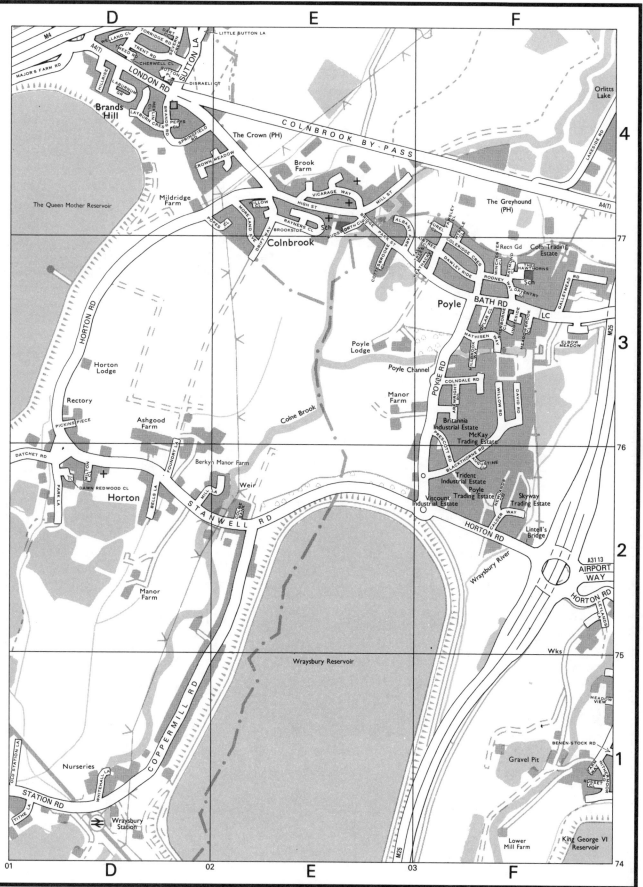

D   E   F

M4
A4(T)
MAJOR'S FARM RD
WELAND CL
TORRIDGE RD
TRENT RD
SEVERN
TWEED RD
CHERWELL CL
SUTTON LA
LITTLE SUTTON LA
LONDON RD
DISRAELI CT
HILLRISE
LABURNUM GR
MERLIN CL
BRANDS RD
LAYBURN CRES
SPRINGFIELD
PEPYS CL

Brands
Hill

Orlitts
Lake

COLNBROOK BY-PASS

The Crown (PH)

Mildridge
Farm

The Queen Mother Reservoir

Brook
Farm

VICARAGE WAY
HIGH ST
MILL ST
WILLOW CL
MORELAND AVE
DRIFT WAY
POPES CL
RAYNERS CL
BROOKSIDE
Sch
RUDSWORTH COTTAGE
PARK ST
COTTSBROOKE CL
ALBANY
CRABTREE
LAUREL
FAWLEY
CORNWALL
COLERIDGE CRES
WINCHESTER
DAWLEY RIDE
RAYMOND WAY
RODNEY
DAVENTRY
A4(T)

The Greyhound
(PH)

Colnbrook

Recn Gd
Coln Trading
Estate

THE HAWTHORNS

Sch

Poyle

BATH RD

GALLEYMEAD RD

LC

M25

HORTON RD

Poyle
Lodge

Poyle Channel

Manor
Farm

POYLE RD
MATHISEN
POPLAR CL
OSBORNE WAY
ILLSWORTH
ARKWRIGHT RD
COLNDALE RD
WILLOW RD
DAVID RD
INNESIDE
MEADOWBROOK

ELBOW
MEADOW

Horton
Lodge

Rectory

PICKINS PIECE

Ashgood
Farm

Colne Brook

Britannia
Industrial Estate

McKay
Trading Estate

PRESCOTT CL
BLACKTHORNE CL
AUGUSTINE CL

Trident
Industrial Estate

Poyle
Trading Estate

NEWLANDS

Skyway
Trading Estate

HORTON RD

DATCHET RD
PARK LA
MILTON RD
DAWN REDWOOD CL
BELLS LA
FOUNDRY LA
MILL LA
COLNE BANK
STANWELL RD

Berkyn Manor Farm

Weir

Horton

Viscount
Industrial Estate

CALDER WAY

Lintell's
Bridge

Wraysbury River

A3113
AIRPORT
WAY

HORTON RD

LEYLANDS

Manor
Farm

COPPERMILL RD

Wks

MEADOW
VIEW

Wraysbury Reservoir

BENEN-STOCK RD

OLD STATION LA
WHITEHALL LA
STATION RD
TITHE

Nurseries

Gravel Pit

WINTERBROOK
RUSSET CL

Lower
Mill Farm

King George VI
Reservoir

Wraysbury
Station

77
3
76
2
75
1
74

70

01   D   02   E   03   F   74

not continued, see key diagram

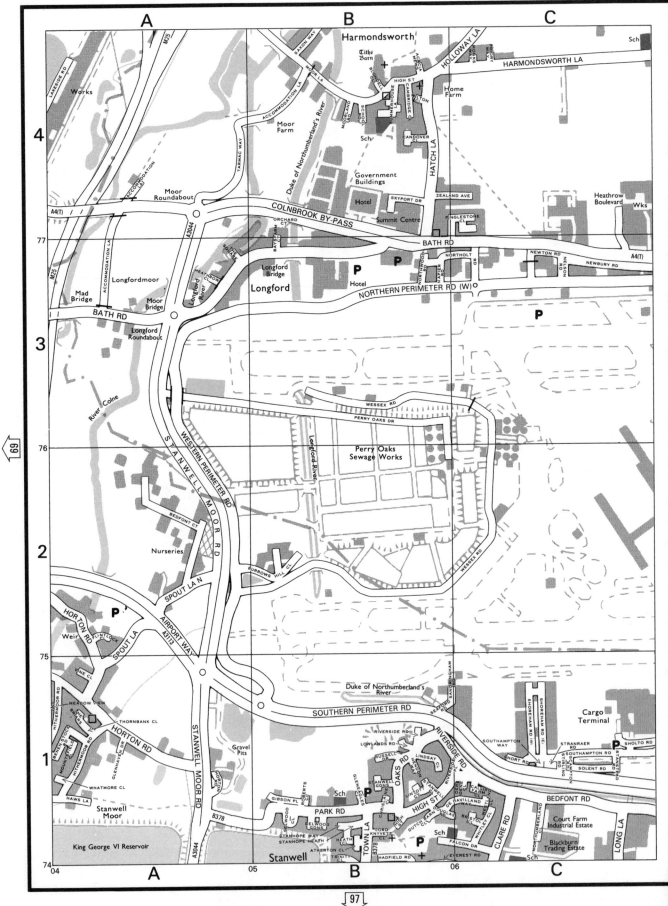

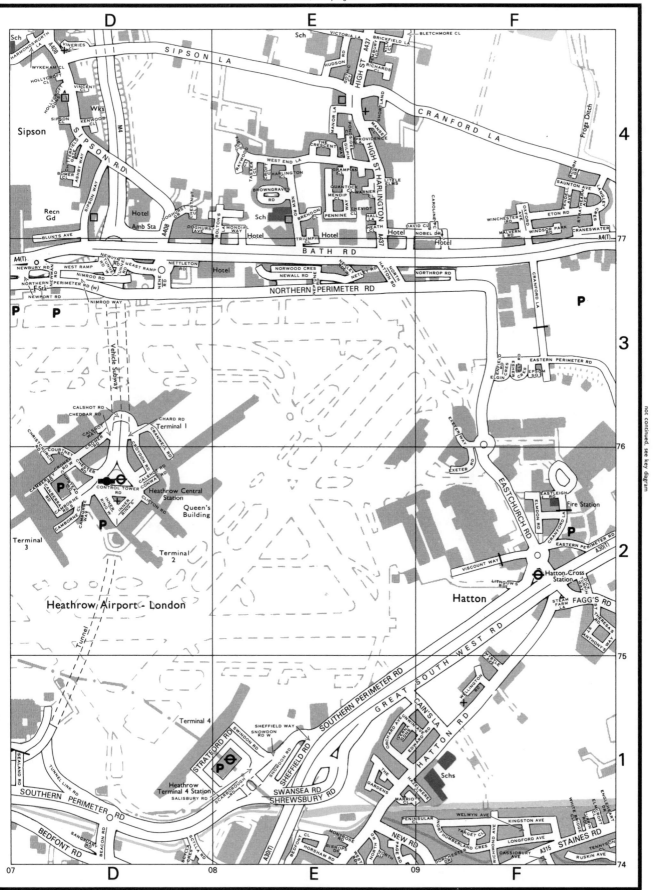

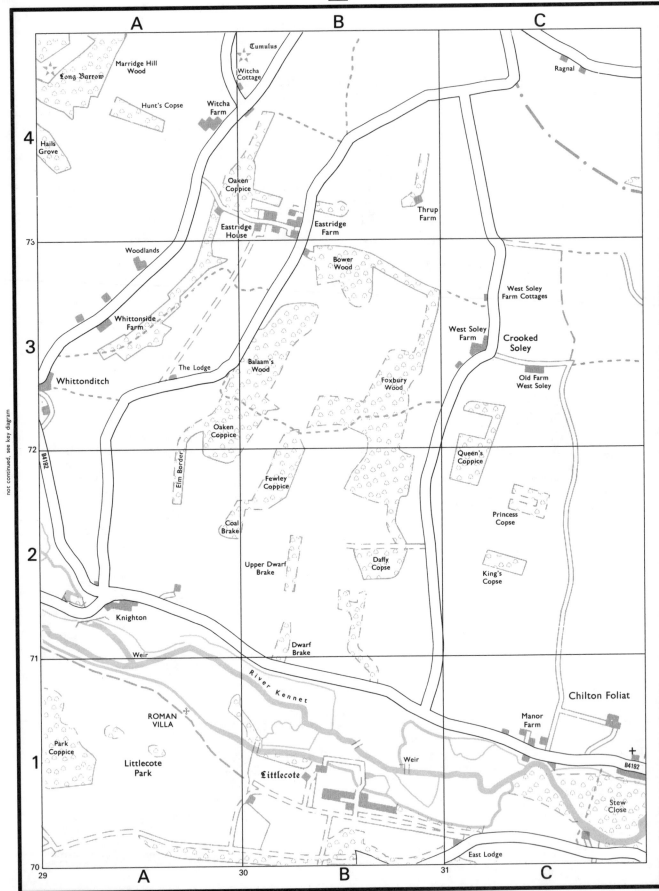

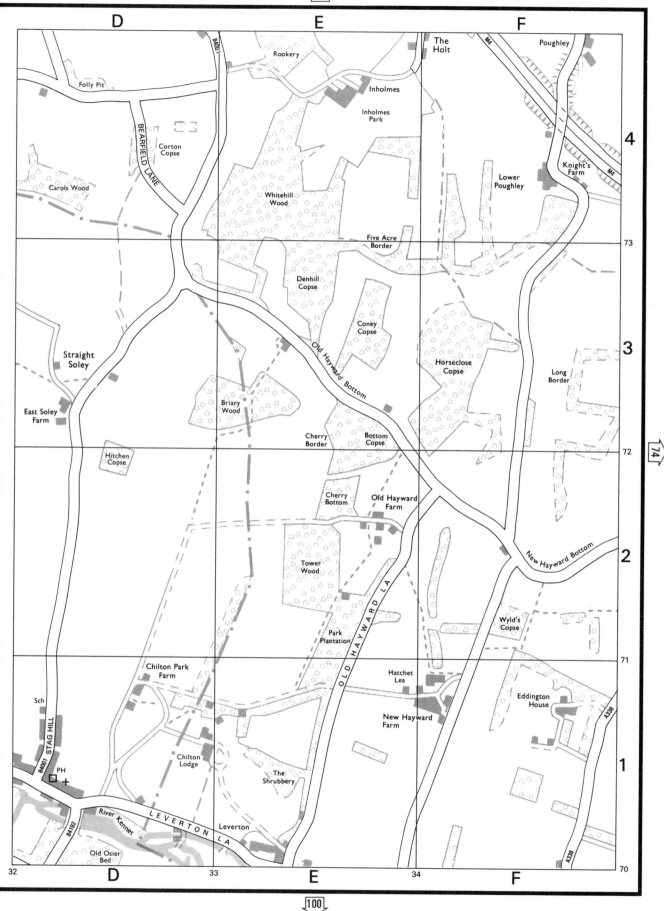

The Holt

Poughley

Inholmes

Folly Pit

Rookery

Inholmes Park

Corton Copse

Carols Wood

Whitehill Wood

Lower Poughley

Knight's Farm

BEARFIELD LANE

B4001

M4

Five Acre Border

Denhill Copse

Coney Copse

Horseclose Copse

Long Border

Straight Soley

Old Hayward Bottom

Briary Wood

East Soley Farm

Hitchen Copse

Cherry Border

Bottom Copse

Cherry Bottom

Old Hayward Farm

New Hayward Bottom

Tower Wood

Wyld's Copse

OLD HAYWARD LA

Park Plantation

Chilton Park Farm

Hatchet Lea

Eddington House

Sch

STAG HILL

PH

Chilton Lodge

The Shrubbery

New Hayward Farm

A338

B4001

River Kennet

LEVERTON LA

Leverton

B4192

Old Osier Bed

4

73

3

72

2

71

1

70

74

32

33

34

D

E

F

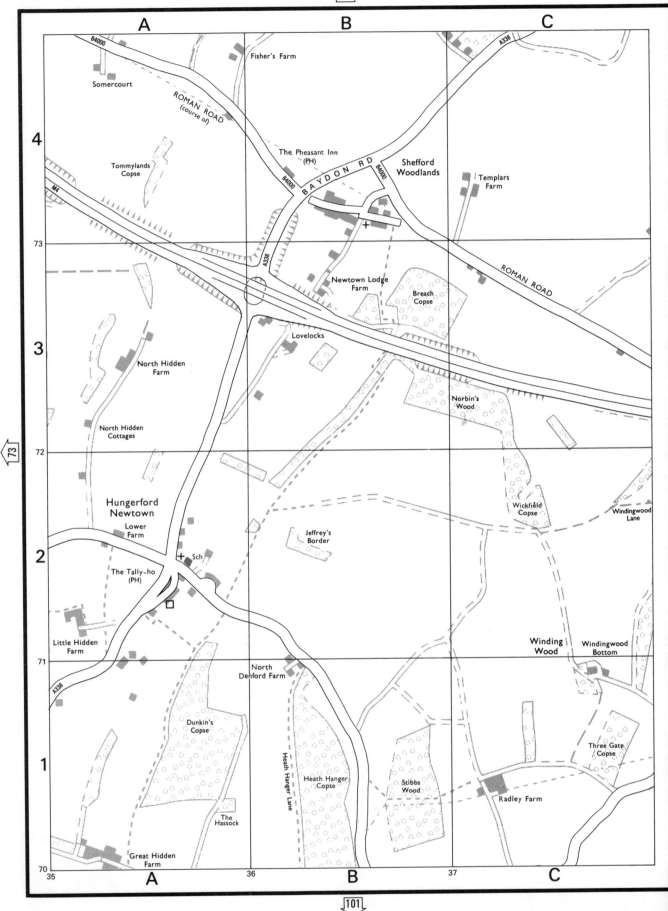

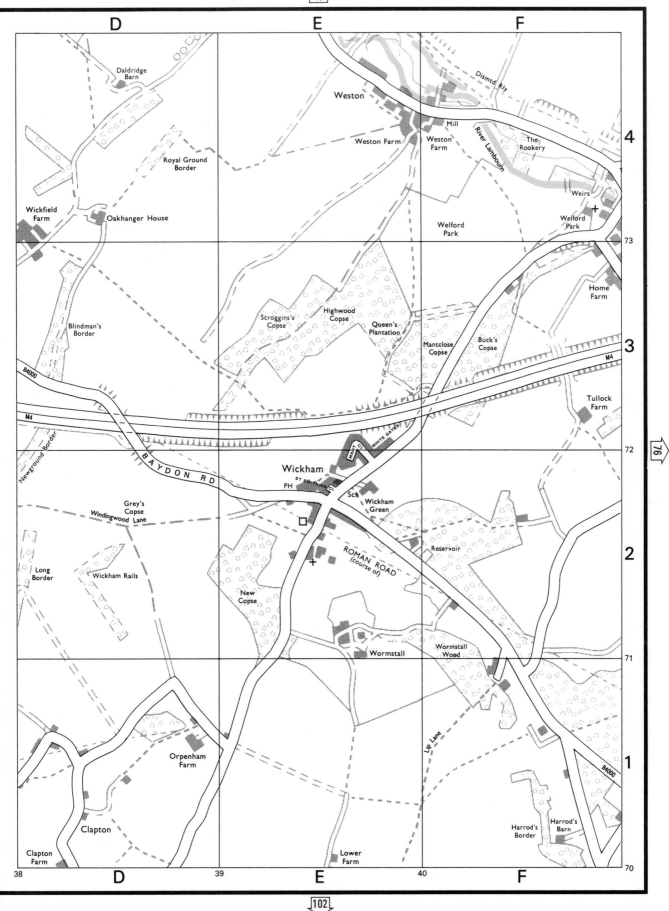

D   E   F

Daldridge Barn

Weston

Weston Farm

Weston Farm

Mill

The Rookery

River Lambourn

Dismtd Rly

4

Royal Ground Border

Wickfield Farm

Oakhanger House

Welford Park

Weirs

Welford Park

73

Home Farm

Blindman's Border

Scroggins's Copse

Highwood Copse

Queen's Plantation

Mantclose Copse

Buck's Copse

3

B4000

M4

M4

Tullock Farm

72

76

BAYDON RD

MANT CL

WHITE GATES

Newground Border

Wickham

PH

ST SWITHINS CL

Sch

Wickham Green

Grey's Copse

Windingwood Lane

ROMAN ROAD (course of)

Reservoir

2

Long Border

Wickham Rails

New Copse

Wormstall

Wormstall Wood

71

Orpenham Farm

Lip Lane

B4000

1

Clapton

Clapton Farm

Lower Farm

Harrod's Border

Harrod's Barn

70

38   D   39   E   40   F

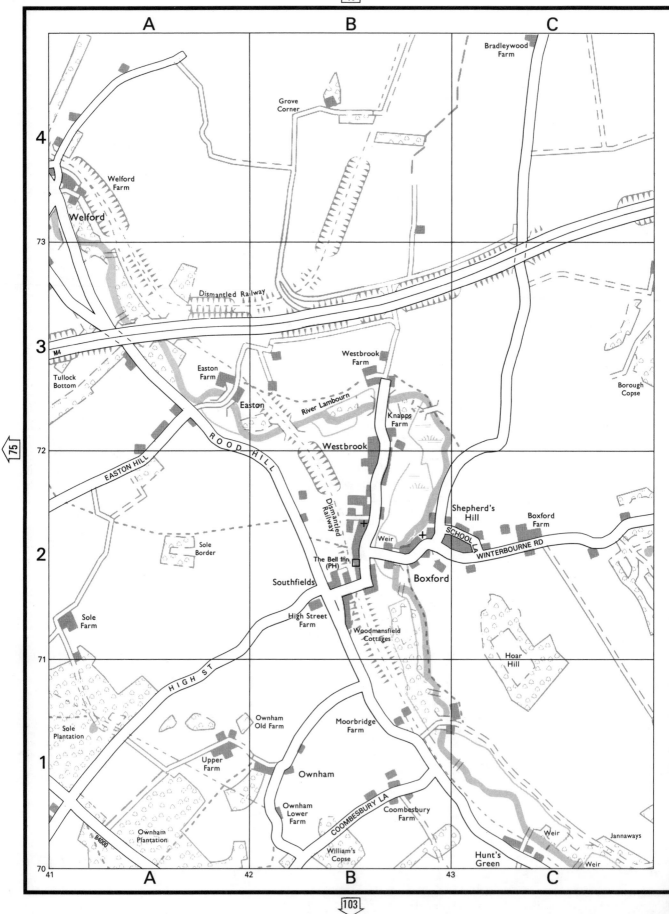

49

75

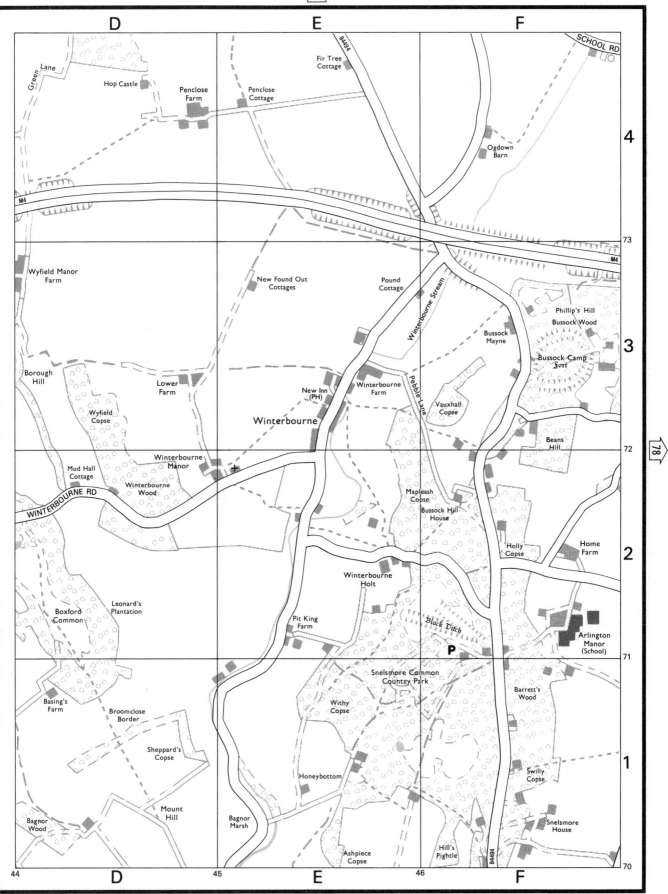

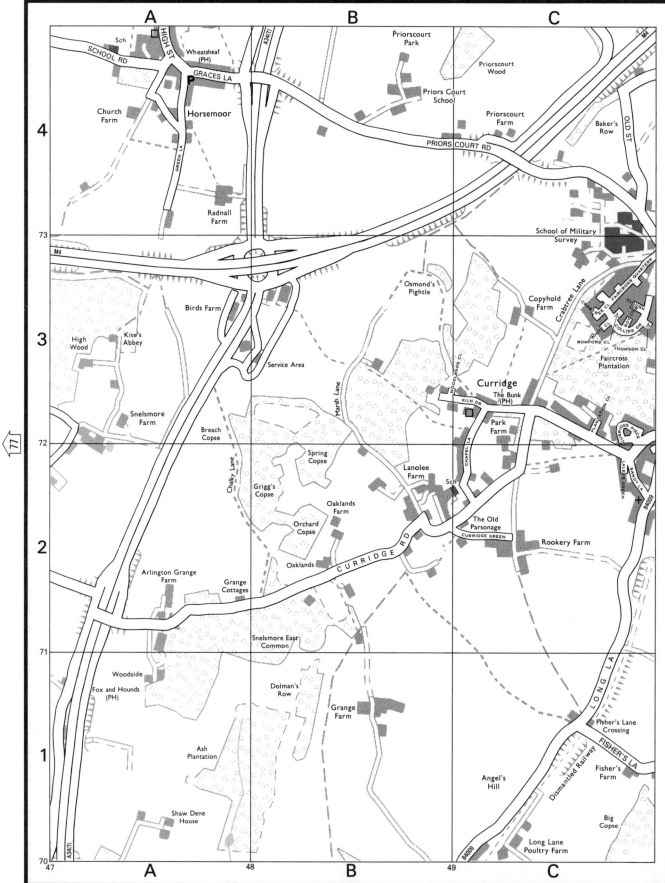

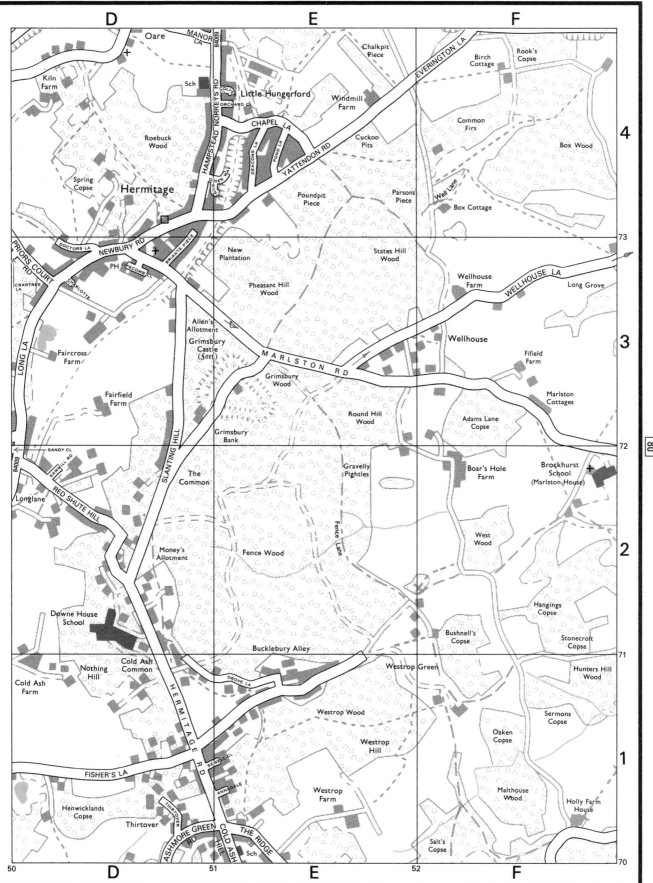

D

E

F

Oare

MANOR LA

B4009

EVERINGTON LA

Kiln
Farm

Sch

Little Hungerford

Windmill
Farm

Chalkpit
Piece

Birch
Cottage

Rook's
Copse

4

Roebuck
Wood

HAMPSTEAD NORREYS RD

ORCHARD CL

COLLIS

CHAPEL LA

YATTENDON RD

Cuckoo
Pits

Common
Firs

Box Wood

Spring
Copse

Hermitage

DEACONS LA

PILL'S WAY

POND LA

Poundpit
Piece

Parsons
Piece

Well Lane

Box Cottage

73

DOCTORS LA

NEWBURY RD

BRIANTS PIECE

New
Plantation

States Hill
Wood

WELLHOUSE LA

PRIORS COURT RD

PH

LISCOMBE CL

Pheasant Hill
Wood

Wellhouse
Farm

Long Grove

CRABTREE LA

CHARLOTTE

Allen's
Allotment

Grimsbury
Castle
(fort)

MARLSTON RD

Grimsbury
Wood

Wellhouse

Fifield
Farm

3

LONG LA

Faircross
Farm

Round Hill
Wood

Adams Lane
Copse

Marlston
Cottages

Fairfield
Farm

SLANTING HILL

Grimsbury
Bank

SANDY CL

72

B4009

The
Common

Gravelly
Pightles

Boar's Hole
Farm

Brockhurst
School
(Marlston House)

Longlane

SAWMILL RD

RED SHUTE HILL

Money's
Allotment

Fence Wood

Fence Lane

West
Wood

Hangings
Copse

2

Downe House
School

Bucklebury Alley

Bushnell's
Copse

Stonecroft
Copse

71

Cold Ash
Farm

Nothing
Hill

Cold Ash
Common

HERMITAGE RD

DROVE LA

Westrop Green

Hunters Hill
Wood

Westrop Wood

Oaken
Copse

Sermons
Copse

1

FISHER'S LA

SEWELL CL

Westrop
Hill

Henwicklands
Copse

ANNADALE

Westrop
Farm

Malthouse
Wood

Holly Farm
House

Thirtover

THIRTOVER

ASHMORE GREEN RD

COLD ASH HILL

THE RIDGE

Sch

Salt's
Copse

70

50

D

51

E

52

F

80

53

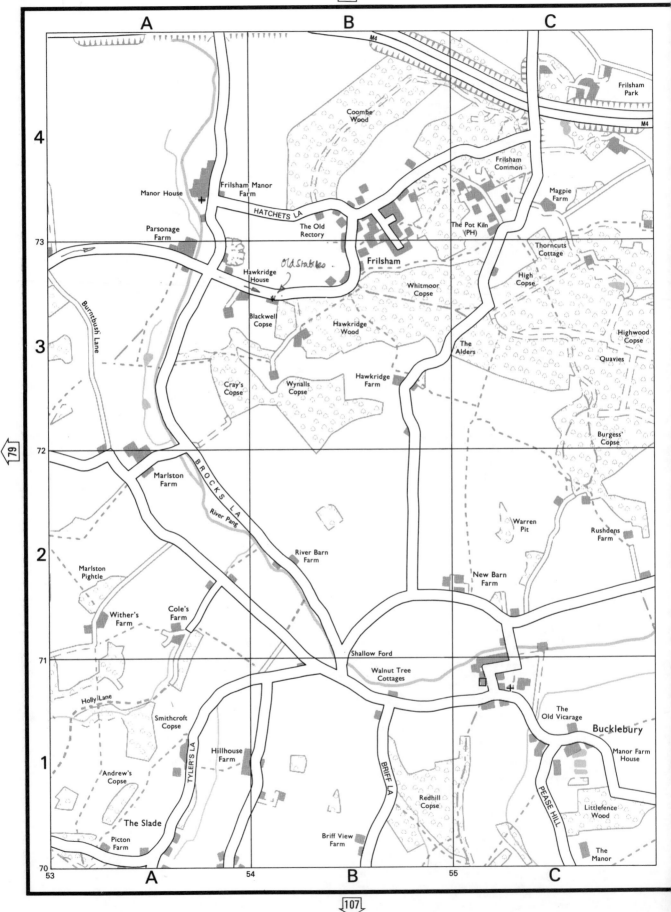

79

107

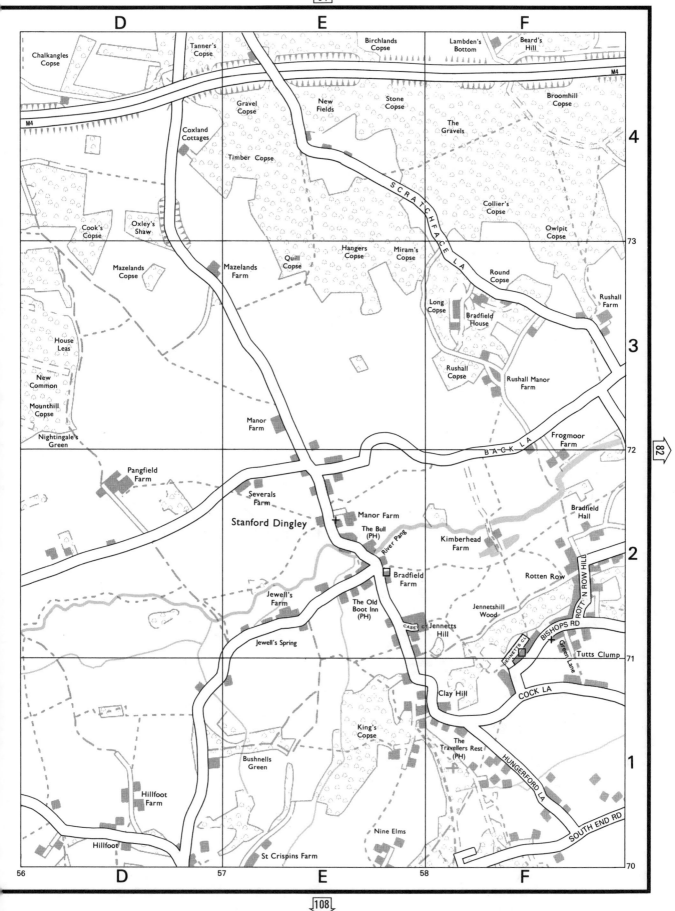

D   E   F

Chalkangles Copse

Tanner's Copse

Birchlands Copse

Lambden's Bottom

Beard's Hill

M4

M4

Gravel Copse

New Fields

Stone Copse

Broomhill Copse

Coxland Cottages

The Gravels

4

Timber Copse

Collier's Copse

Cook's Copse

Oxley's Shaw

Owlpit Copse

73

Mazelands Copse

Mazelands Farm

Quill Copse

Hangers Copse

Miram's Copse

Round Copse

Rushall Farm

House Leas

Long Copse

Bradfield House

Rushall Copse

Rushall Manor Farm

3

New Common

Mounthill Copse

SCRATCHFACE LA

Nightingale's Green

Manor Farm

Frogmoor Farm

BACK LA

72

Pangfield Farm

Severals Farm

Bradfield Hall

Stanford Dingley

Manor Farm

The Bull (PH)

Kimberhead Farm

Rotten Row

2

River Pang

Bradfield Farm

Jewell's Farm

The Old Boot Inn (PH)

Jennetshill Wood

BISHOPS RD

ROTT'N ROW HILL

Jewell's Spring

CASE

Jennetts Hill

JENNETTS CL

Green Lane

Tutts Clump

71

Clay Hill

COCK LA

King's Copse

Bushnells Green

The Travellers Rest (PH)

1

HUNGERFORD LA

Hillfoot Farm

SOUTH END RD

Nine Elms

Hillfoot

St Crispins Farm

56   D   57   E   58   F   **70**

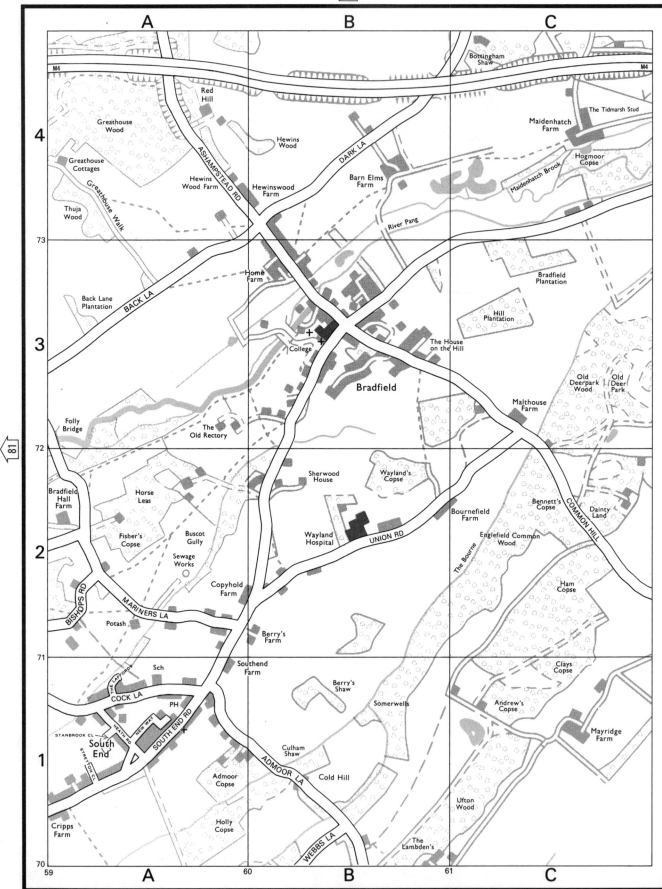

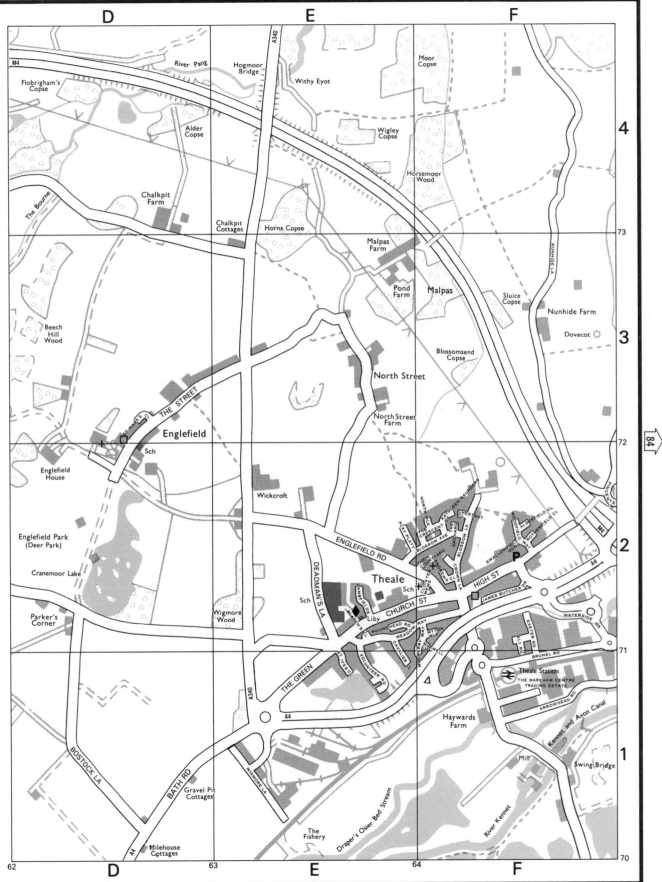

84

57
83

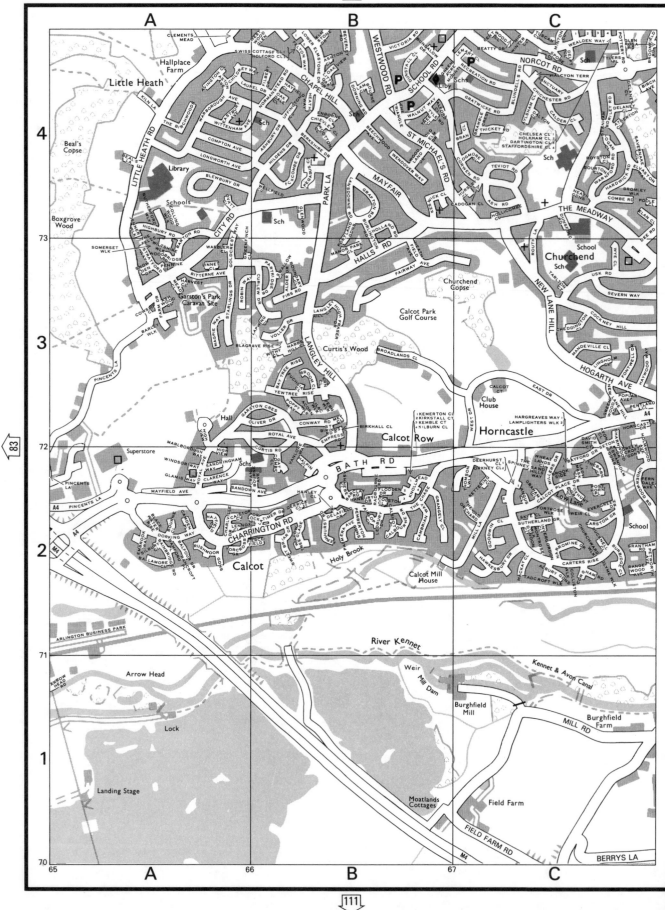

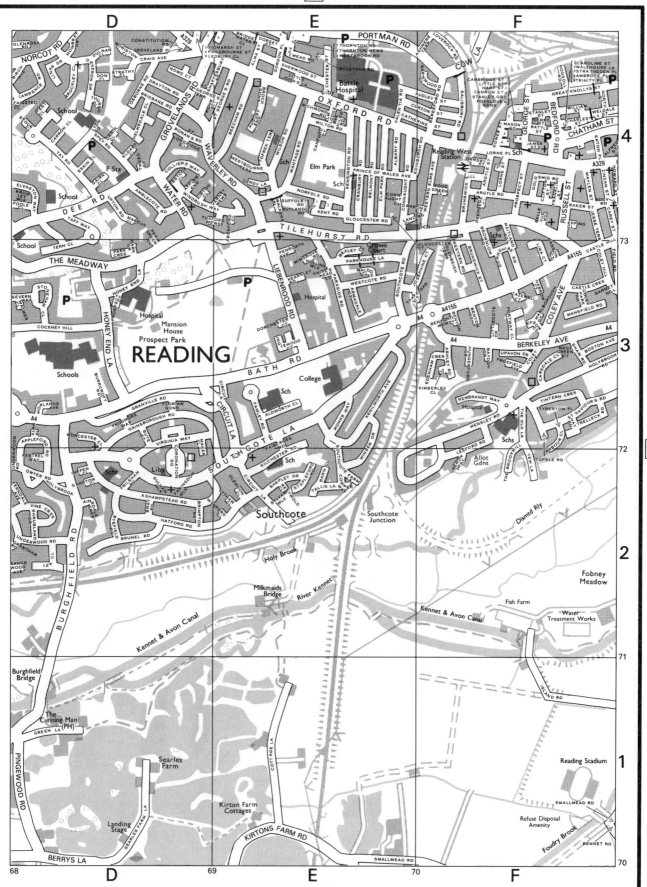

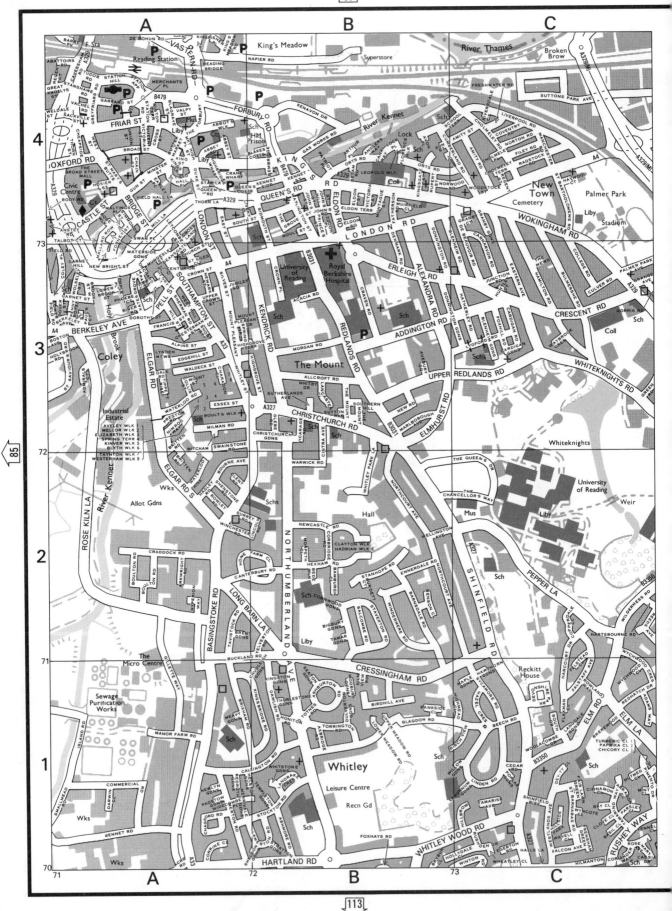

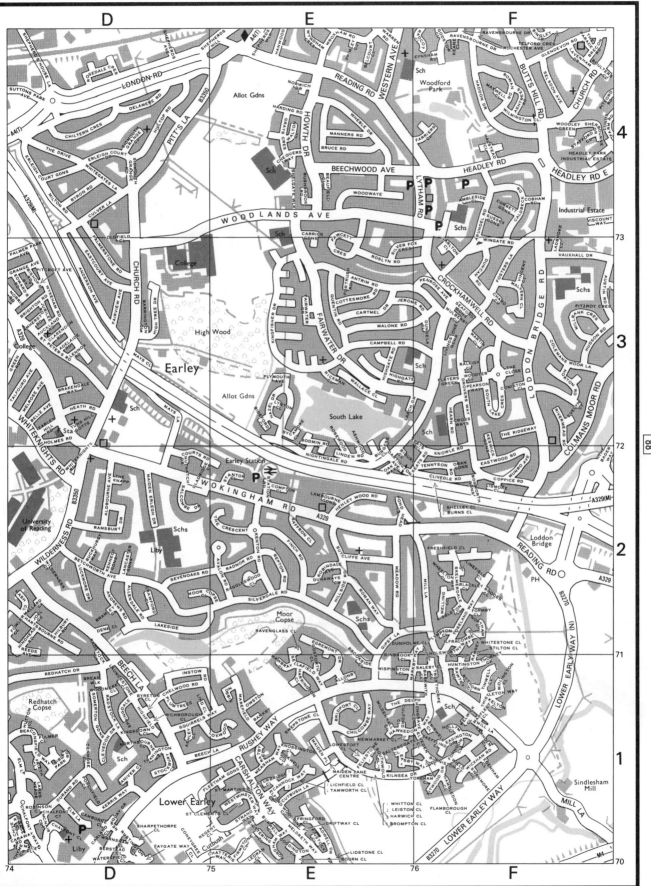

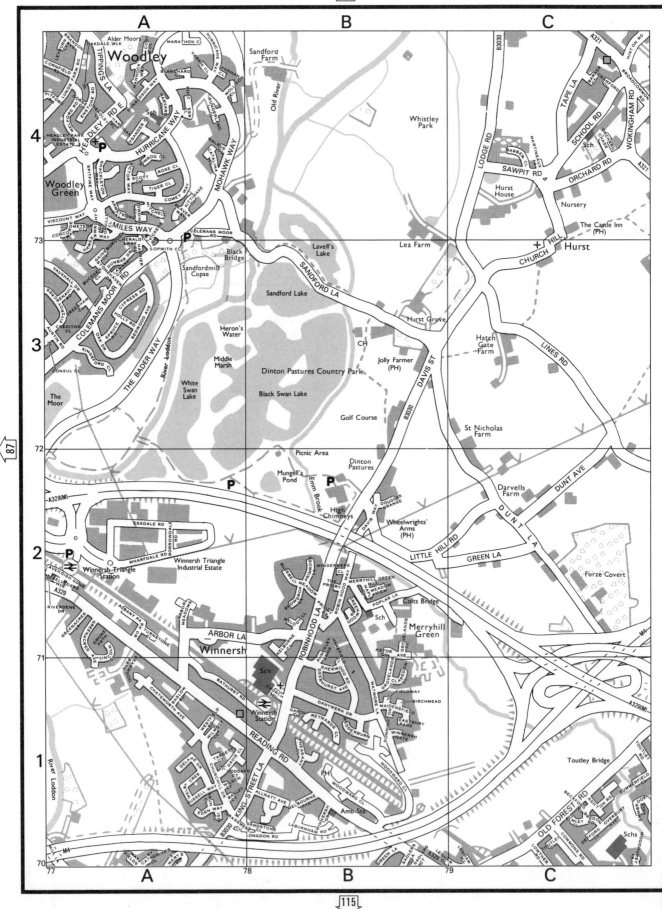

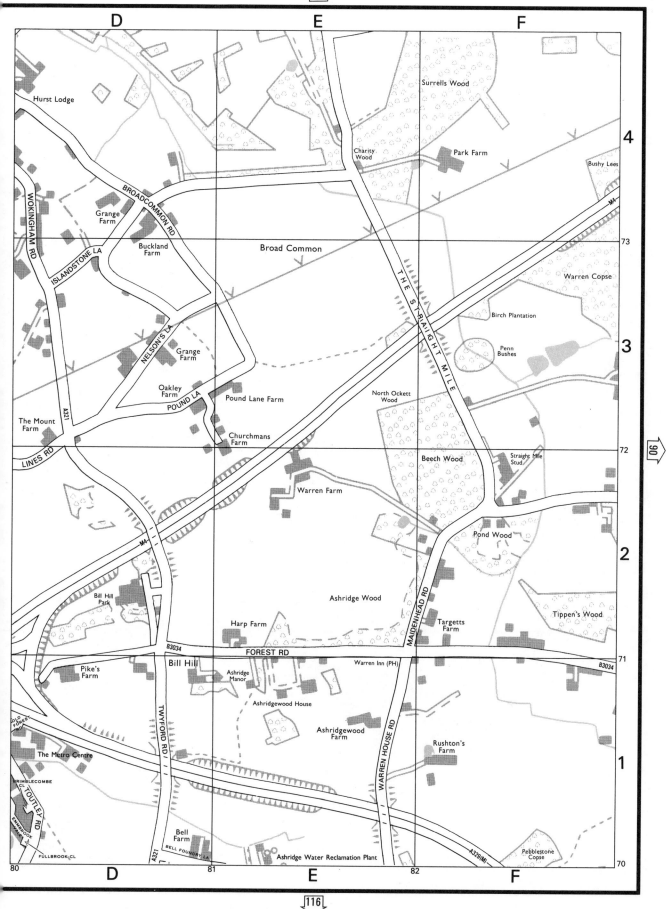

62

D   E   F

4

Hurst Lodge

Surrells Wood

Charity Wood

Park Farm

Bushy Lees

M4

BROADCOMMON RD

Grange Farm

WOKINGHAM RD

73

ISLANDSTONE LA

Buckland Farm

Broad Common

Warren Copse

Birch Plantation

NELSON'S LA

Grange Farm

THE STRAIGHT MILE

Penn Bushes

3

Oakley Farm

POUND LA

Pound Lane Farm

North Ockett Wood

A321

The Mount Farm

Churchmans Farm

72

90

LINES RD

Beech Wood

Straight Mile Stud

Warren Farm

M4

Pond Wood

2

Bill Hill Park

Ashridge Wood

MAIDENHEAD RD

Tippen's Wood

Harp Farm

Targetts Farm

B3034

FOREST RD

71

Pike's Farm

Bill Hill

Ashridge Manor

Warren Inn (PH)

B3034

OLD FOREST RD

TWYFORD RD

Ashridgewood House

WARREN HOUSE RD

Ashridgewood Farm

Rushton's Farm

1

The Metro Centre

BRIMBLECOMBE CL

TOUTLEY RD

EMMBROOK

A321

Bell Farm

BELL FOUNDRY LA

Ashridge Water Reclamation Plant

A329(M)

Pebblestone Copse

FULLBROOK CL

80   D   81   E   82   F   70

116

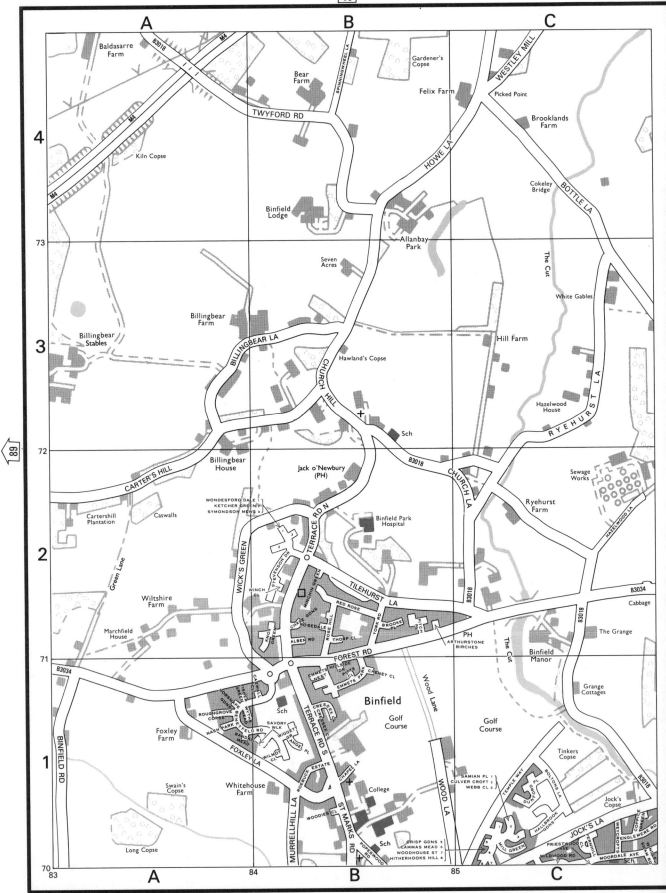

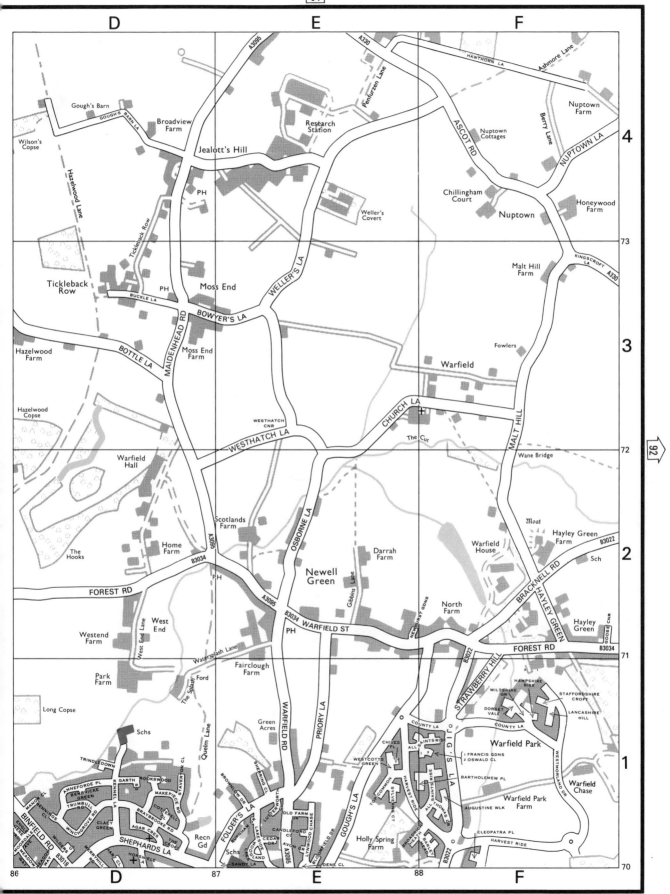

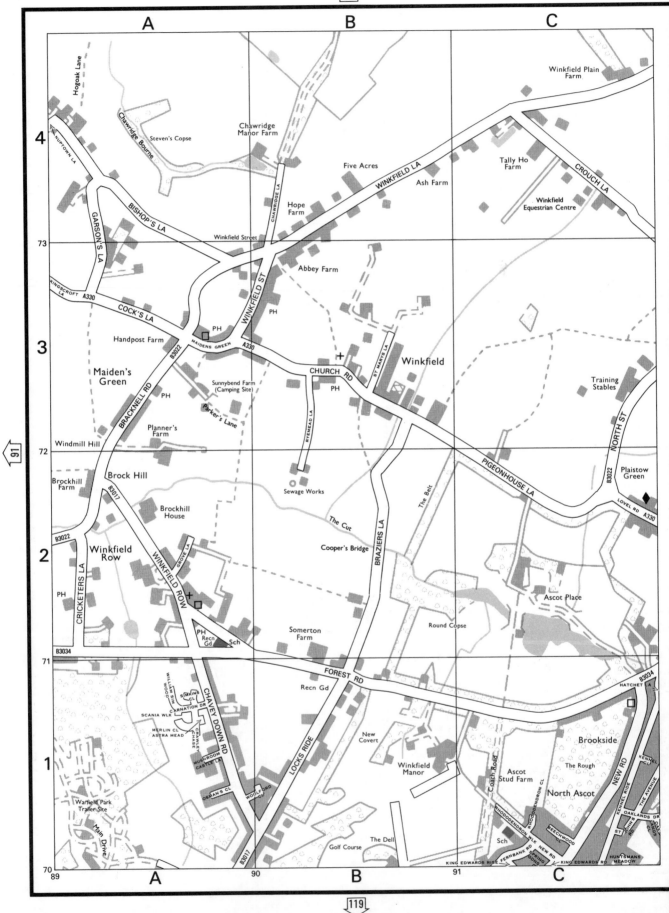

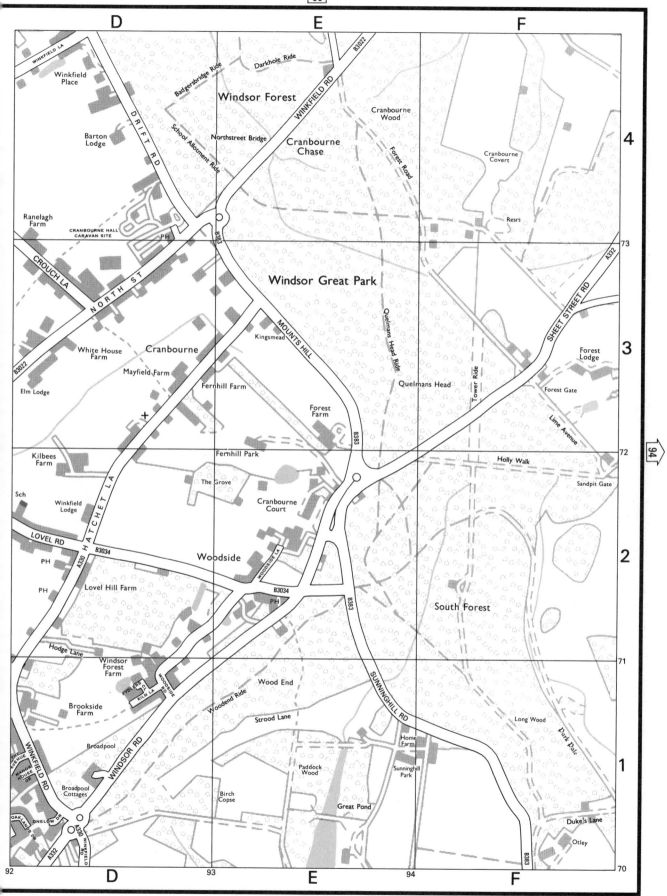

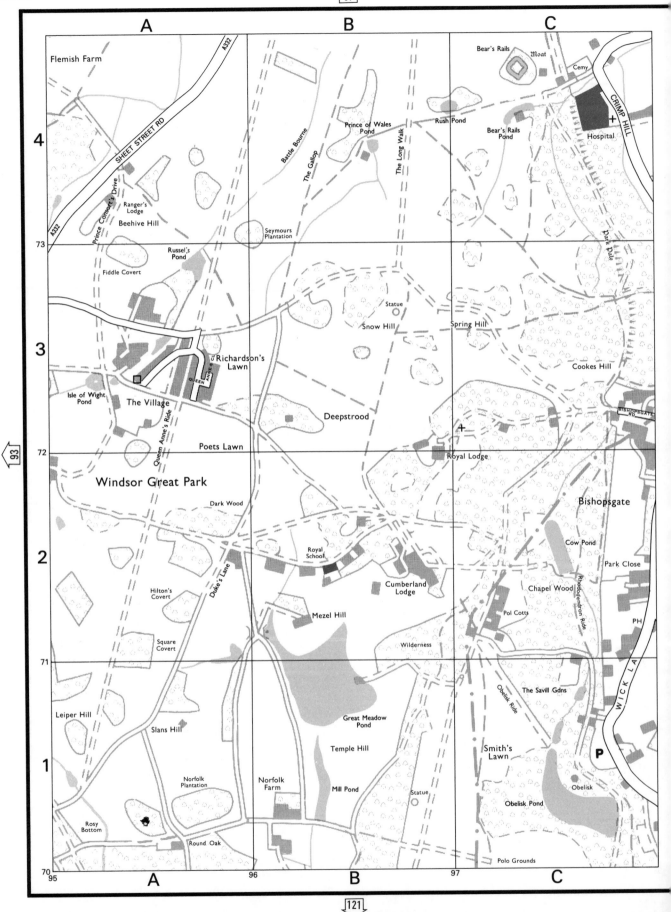

A   B   C

Flemish Farm

SHEET STREET RD

A332

4

Prince Consort's Drive

Ranger's
Lodge

Beehive Hill

Battle Bourne

The Gallop

Prince of Wales
Pond

The Long Walk

Rush Pond

Bear's Rails

Moat

Cemy

Hospital

CRIMP HILL

Bear's Rails
Pond

Park Pale

73

Russel's
Pond

Fiddle Covert

Seymours
Plantation

Statue

3

Richardson's
Lawn

QUEEN ANNE'S

Snow Hill

Spring Hill

Cookes Hill

Isle of Wight
Pond

The Village

Queen Anne's Ride

Deepstrood

Royal Lodge

BISHOPSGATE
RD

Poets Lawn

72

Windsor Great Park

Dark Wood

Bishopsgate

Cow Pond

Park Close

2

Duke's Lane

Hilton's
Covert

Royal
School

Cumberland
Lodge

Chapel Wood

Pol Cotts

Rhododendron Ride

PH

Square
Covert

Mezel Hill

Wilderness

Obelisk Ride

The Savill Gdns

WICK LA

71

Leiper Hill

Great Meadow
Pond

Smith's
Lawn

P

Slans Hill

Temple Hill

1

Norfolk
Plantation

Norfolk
Farm

Mill Pond

Statue

Obelisk Pond

Obelisk

Rosy
Bottom

Round Oak

Polo Grounds

70
95   96   97

A   B   C

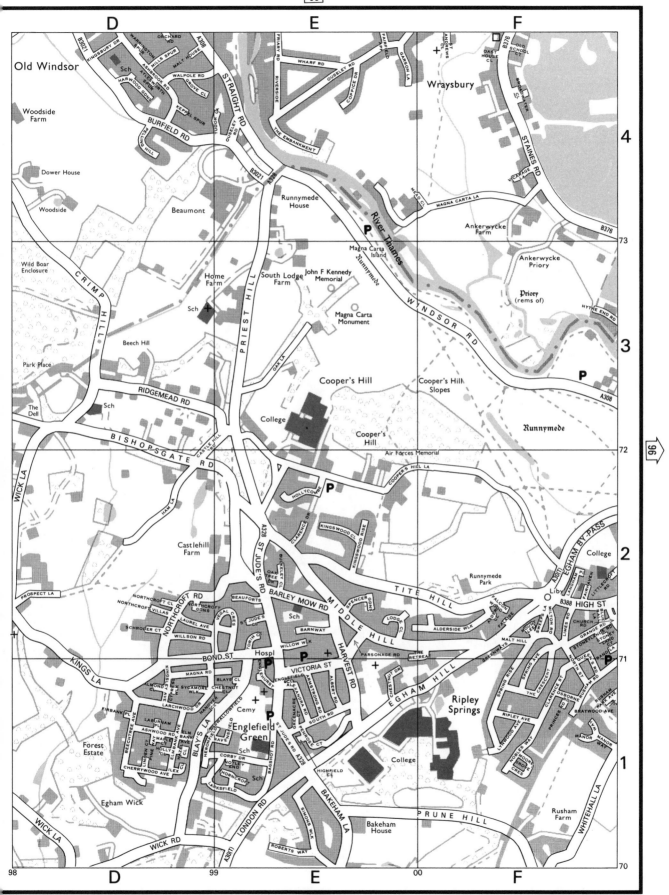

Old Windsor

Woodside Farm

Dower House

Woodside

Beaumont

Wild Boar Enclosure

Park Place

The Dell

Wick La

Forest Estate

Egham Wick

Wick La

Wick Rd

D 98

B3021 Kingsbury Dr Orchard Rd A308 Warrington Spur Mills Spur Malt House Walpole Rd Grove Cl Sch Harwood Gdns Ashworth Keppel Spur Aylesworth Bellina Hill Ouseley Rd Burfield Rd Tudor La Straight Rd B3021 A328

Home Farm Sch Priest Hill South Lodge Farm John F Kennedy Memorial Magna Carta Island Runnymede House Runnymede P

Crimp Hill Beech Hill Oak La Magna Carta Monument Cooper's Hill

Ridgemead Rd Sch Castle Hill Rd College Cooper's Hill

Bishopsgate Rd Ham La A328 Hollycombe P Clarence Dr Kingswood Cl Kingswood Rise Cooper's Hill La Air Forces Memorial

Prospect La Castlehill Farm St Jude's Rd Buckley Cl Oak Tree Dr Barley Mow Rd Middle Hill Spencer Gdns Lodge Cl Tite Hill Runnymede Park Egham By-Pass College

Northcroft Rd Northcroft Cl Northcroft Gdns Beauforts St Jude's Sch Barnway Willow Wlk Alderside Wlk Liby B388 High St

Northcroft Villas Laurel Ave Regal Cres Schroder Ct Willson Rd Bond St Hospl P Victoria St Parsonage Rd The Retreat Church Rd Grange Rd

Kings La Magna Rd Blays Cl Englefield Ale Alexandra Rd Albert Rd Egham Hill Ripley Springs Spring Rise Spring Ave Clarence St Osborne Rusham Park Ave

Almond Av Sycamore Wlk Chestnut La South Rd Penrose Ct Ripley Ave Lynwood Ave Princes Bratwood Ave

Firbank Pl Laburnam Larchwood Dr Cemy P St Jude's Rd A328 College Noble's Way Grove Cres Manor Way

Beechtree Ave Ashwood Rd Elm Bank Holly Martens Heron Wallowfield Highfield Cl Manor

Cherrywood Ave Ilex Corby Dr Sch Prune Hill Rusham Farm

Larksfield Basshot Rd Sch Thorncroft Notley End

London Rd Simons Wlk Bakeham La Bakeham House Whitehall La

A30(T) Roberts Way

Wraysbury

St Andrews Oast House Cl B376 Old School Ct Sch

Vicarage La Staines Rd

Mead Cl Magna Carta La Ankerwycke Farm B376

Ankerwycke Priory

Windsor Rd Priory (rems of) Hythe End Rd

Cooper's Hill Slopes Runnymede P A308

River Thames

The Embankment Friary Rd Wharf Rd Ouseley Rd Coppice Rd Fairfield Garron La Riverside

4 73

3 72

2 71

1 70

96

D E F

98 99 00

122

69

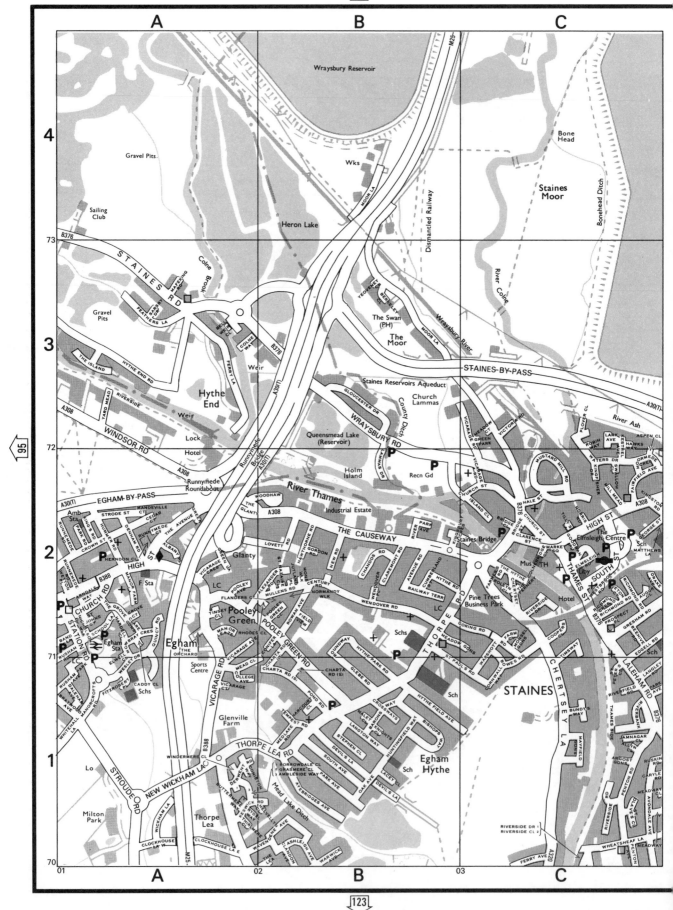

95

123

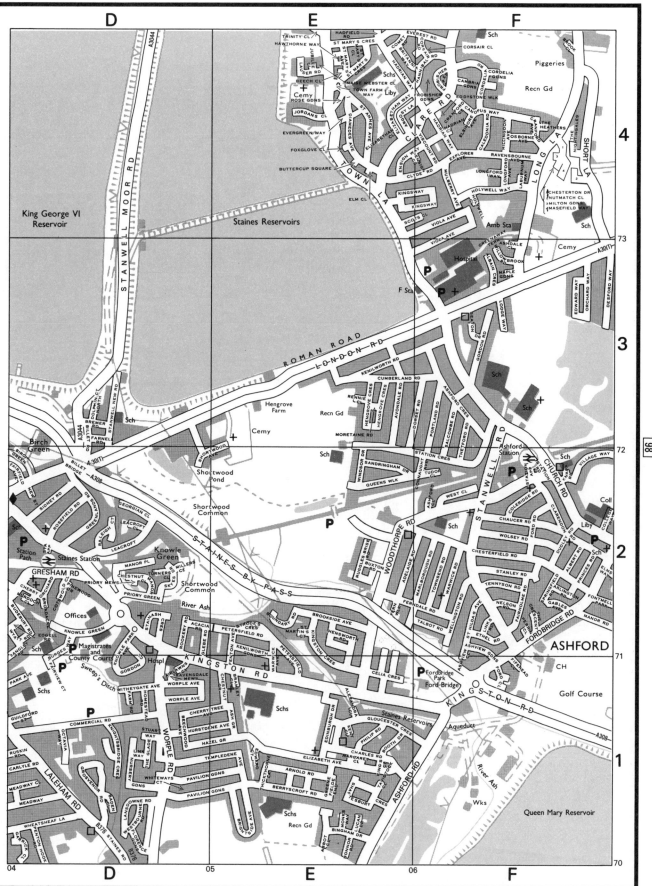

98

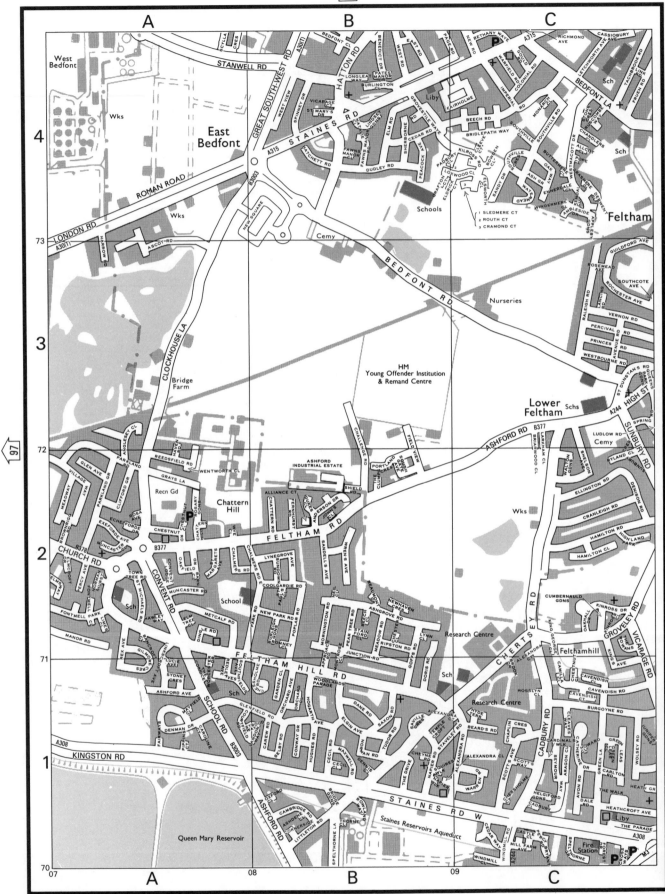

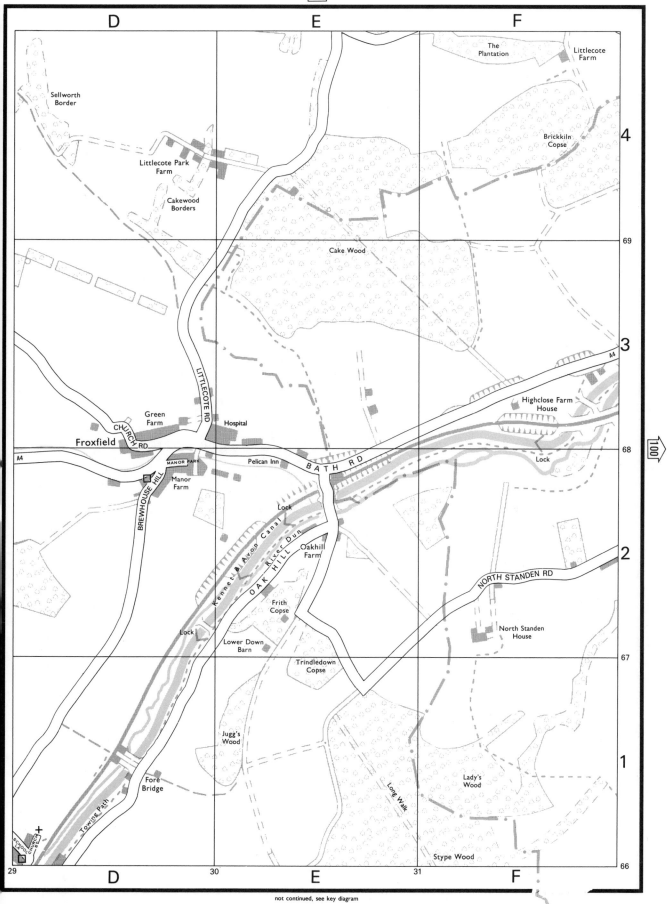

73

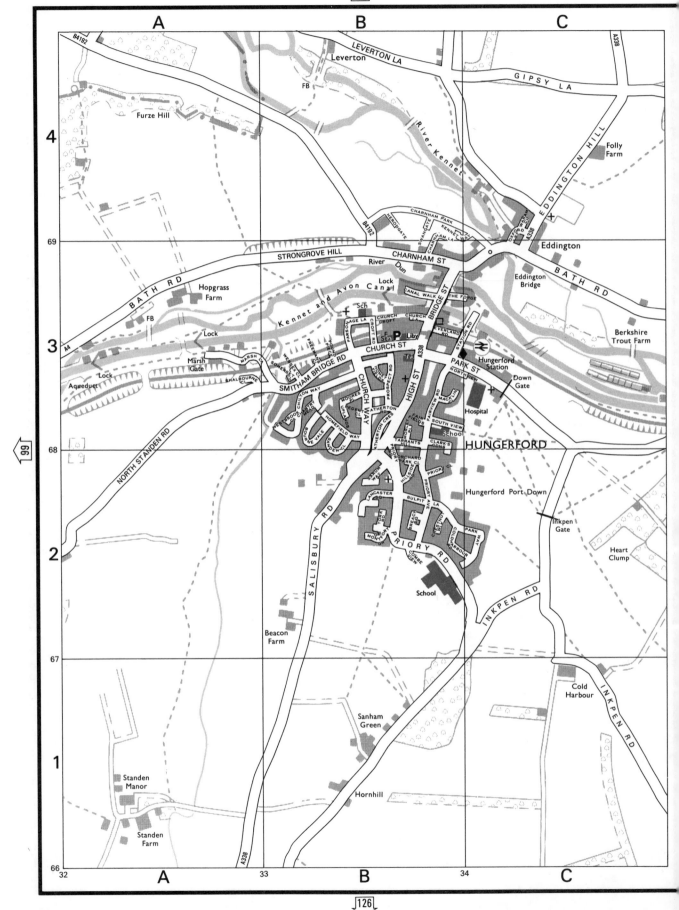

99

126

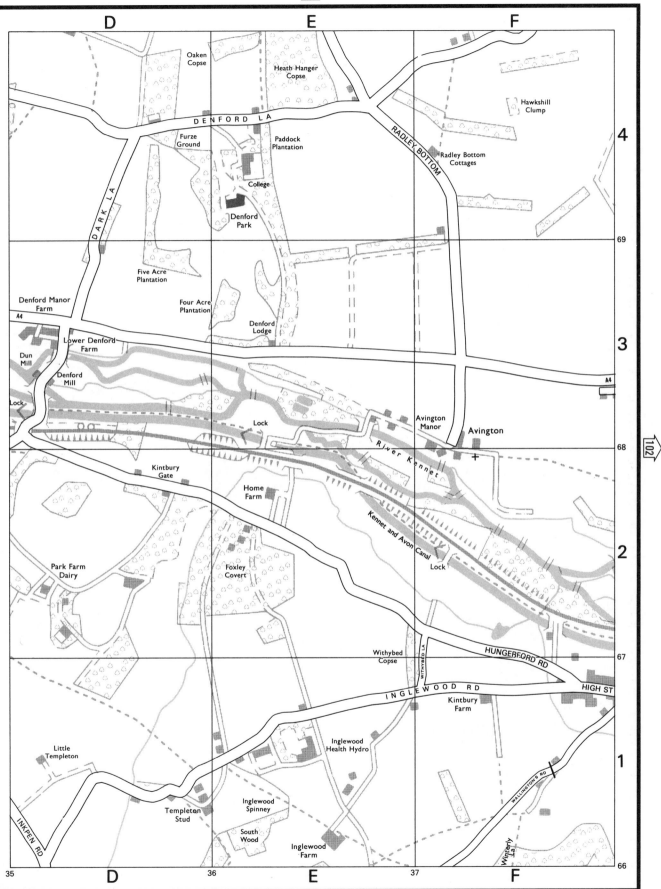

D

E

F

Oaken Copse

Heath Hanger Copse

Hawkshill Clump

DENFORD LA

4

Furze Ground

Paddock Plantation

RADLEY BOTTOM

Radley Bottom Cottages

DARK LA

College

Denford Park

69

Five Acre Plantation

Four Acre Plantation

Denford Manor Farm

A4

Denford Lodge

3

Lower Denford Farm

Dun Mill

A4

Denford Mill

Avington Manor

Lock

Avington

Lock

Lock

River Kennet

68

Kintbury Gate

Home Farm

Kennet and Avon Canal

2

Park Farm Dairy

Foxley Covert

Lock

Withybed Copse

HUNGERFORD RD

67

WITHYBED LA

INGLEWOOD RD

HIGH ST

Kintbury Farm

Little Templeton

Inglewood Health Hydro

1

WALLINGTON'S RD

Templeton Stud

Inglewood Spinney

INKPEN RD

South Wood

Inglewood Farm

Winterly La

66

35

D

36

E

37

F

75
101

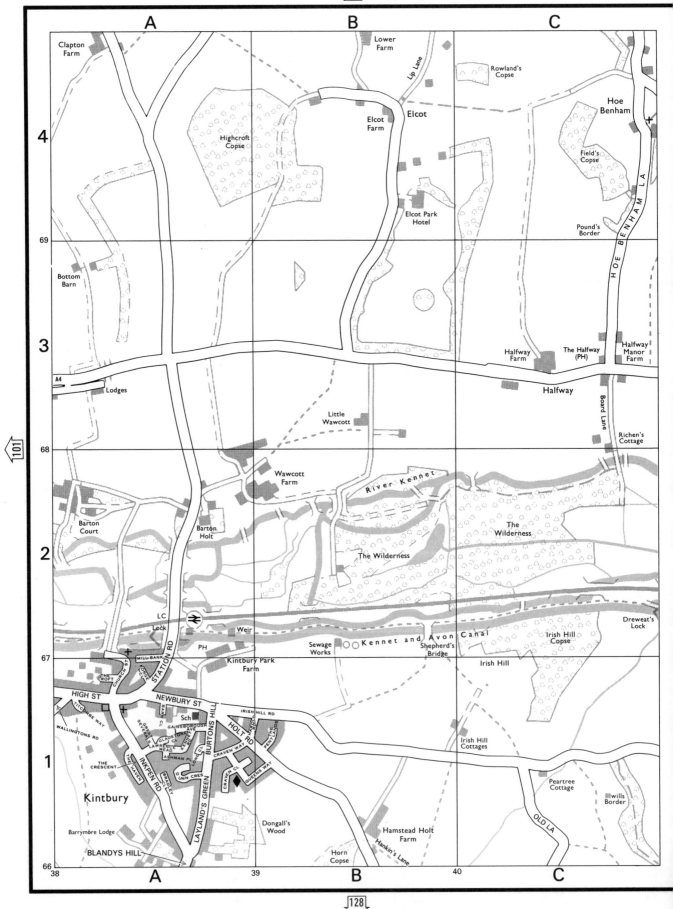

A   B   C

Clapton Farm

Lower Farm

Lip Lane

Rowland's Copse

Hoe Benham

Elcot

Elcot Farm

Highcroft Copse

4

Field's Copse

HOE BENHAM LA

Elcot Park Hotel

Pound's Border

69

Bottom Barn

3

Halfway Farm

The Halfway (PH)

Halfway Manor Farm

A4

Lodges

Halfway

Board Lane

Little Wawcott

Richen's Cottage

68

Wawcott Farm

River Kennet

Barton Court

Barton Holt

The Wilderness

The Wilderness

2

The Wilderness

Irish Hill Copse

Dreweat's Lock

LC

Lock

Weir

Kennet and Avon Canal

Shepherd's Bridge

Sewage Works

Irish Hill Copse

67

THE CROFT

MILL BANK

COTTAGE COTTAGE

STATION RD

PH

Kintbury Park Farm

Irish Hill

HIGH ST

NEWBURY ST

IRISH HILL RD

Sch

TITCOMBE WAY

CHURCH ST

GAINSBOROUGH AVE

BARR CL

Irish Hill Cottages

WALLINGTONS RD

GREAT SEVERALS

LAWRENCE MEAD

GLADSTONE CL

KENNET CL

HOLT RD

BURTONS HILL

CRAVEN WAY

PENTLANDS

1

THE CRESCENT

THE HAVEN

INKPEN RD

ASHMAN PL

BRADLEY

DUNN CRES

CRAVEN CL

QUEENS WAY

LAYLAND'S GREEN

Peartree Cottage

Illwills Border

Kintbury

Barrymore Lodge

Dongall's Wood

Hamstead Holt Farm

OLD LA

BLANDYS HILL

Horn Copse

Hankin's Lane

66

38   A   39   B   40   C

128

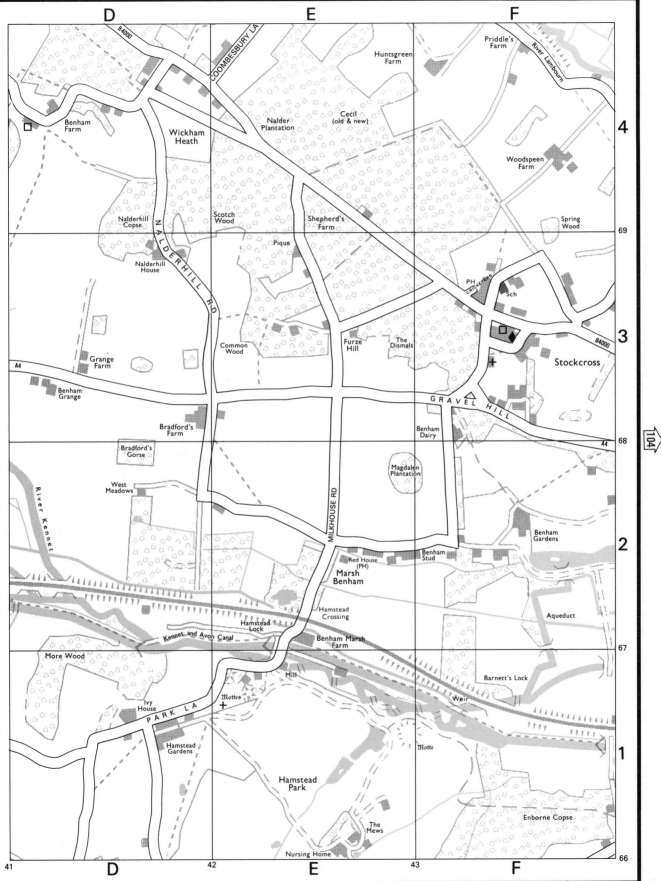

104

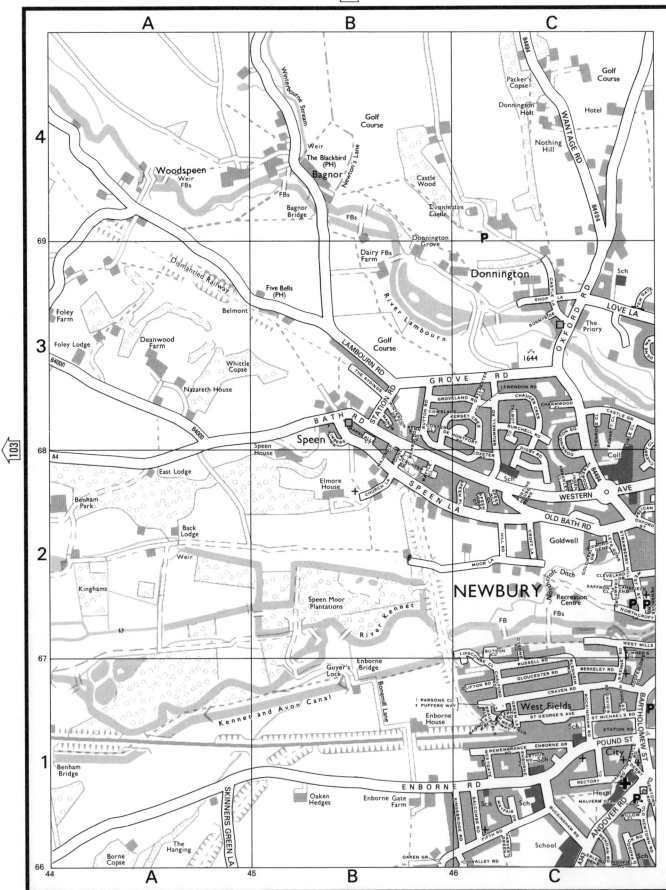

103

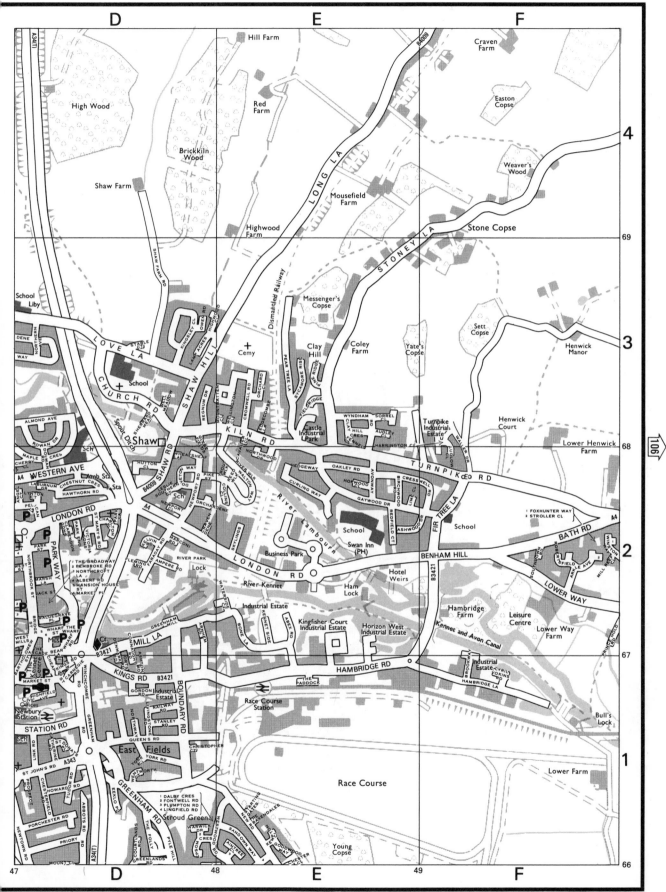

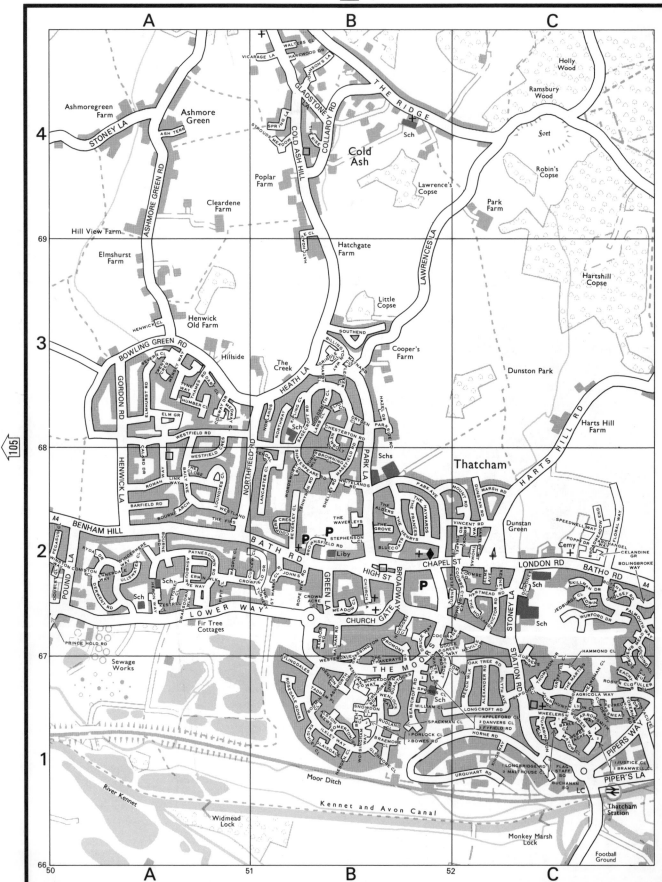

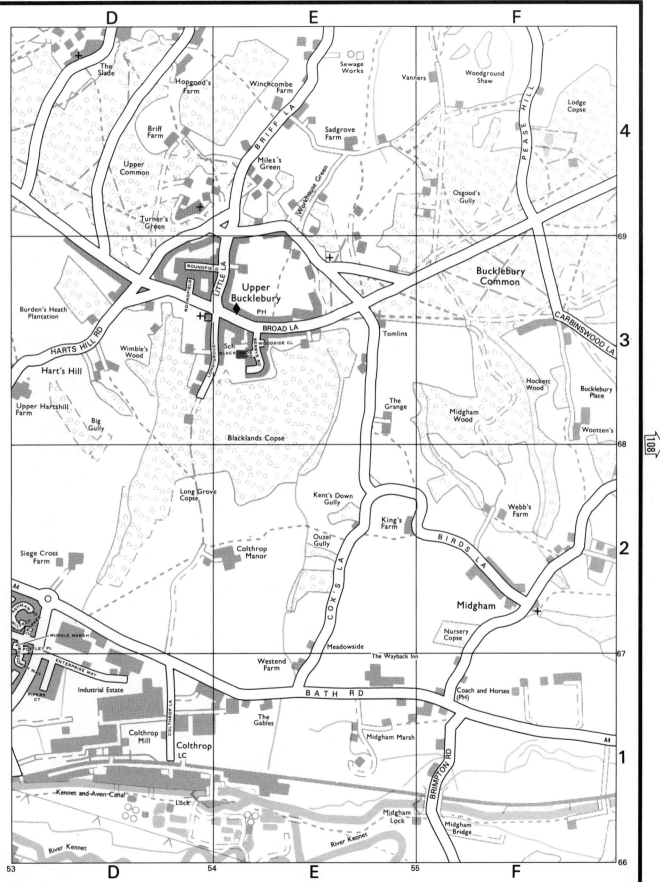

D

The Slade

Hopgood's Farm

Winchcombe Farm

Sewage Works

Vanners

Woodground Shaw

Lodge Copse

4

Briff Farm

BRIFF LA

Miles's Green

Sadgrove Farm

PEASE HILL

Upper Common

Workhouse Green

Osgood's Gully

Turner's Green

69

Bucklebury Common

Upper Bucklebury

PH

CARBINSWOOD LA

3

Burden's Heath Plantation

ROUNDFIELD

LITTLE LA

Tomlins

HARTS HILL RD

ROUNDFIELD

BROAD LA

Wimble's Wood

LONG GROVE

Sch
BLACKLANDS

HENRY'S RD

WOODSIDE CL

Hart's Hill

The Grange

Hockett Wood

Bucklebury Place

Upper Hartshill Farm

Big Gully

Midgham Wood

Wootten's

Blacklands Copse

68

Long Grove Copse

Kent's Down Gully

Webb's Farm

2

Siege Cross Farm

Colthrop Manor

King's Farm

COX'S LA

BIRDS LA

A4

Ouzel Gully

ASHMAN...
WILD...
CL...

MUNKLE MARSH

Midgham

POPLEY PL

Nursery Copse

BROAD... WAY

+

PIPERS CT

Industrial Estate

ENTERPRISE WAY

Meadowside

The Wayback Inn

67

Westend Farm

COLTHROP LA

BATH RD

Coach and Horses (PH)

The Gables

Colthrop Mill

Colthrop LC

Midgham Marsh

BRIMPTON RD

A4

1

Kennet and Avon Canal

Lock

Midgham Lock

Midgham Bridge

River Kennet

River Kennet

66

53

D

54

E

55

F

81

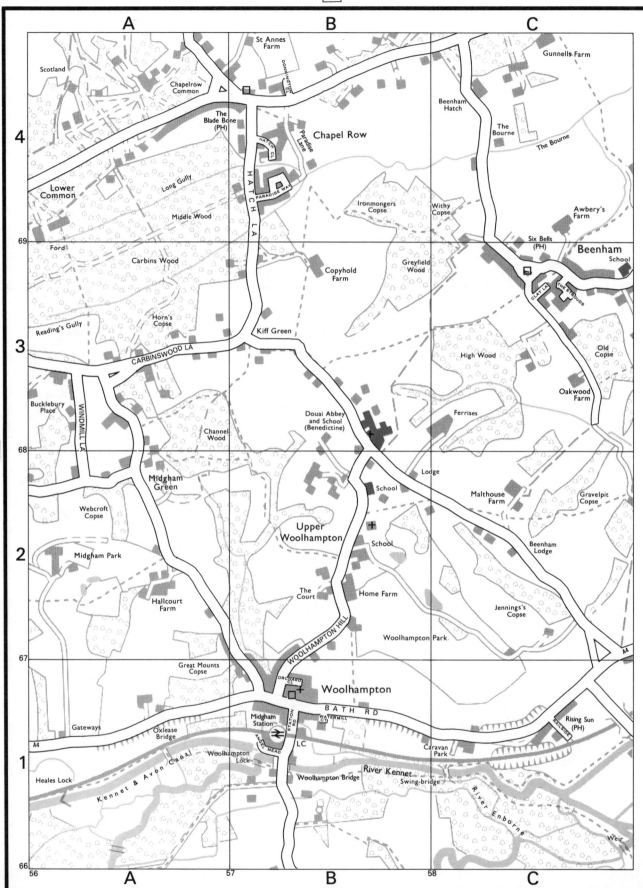

107

134

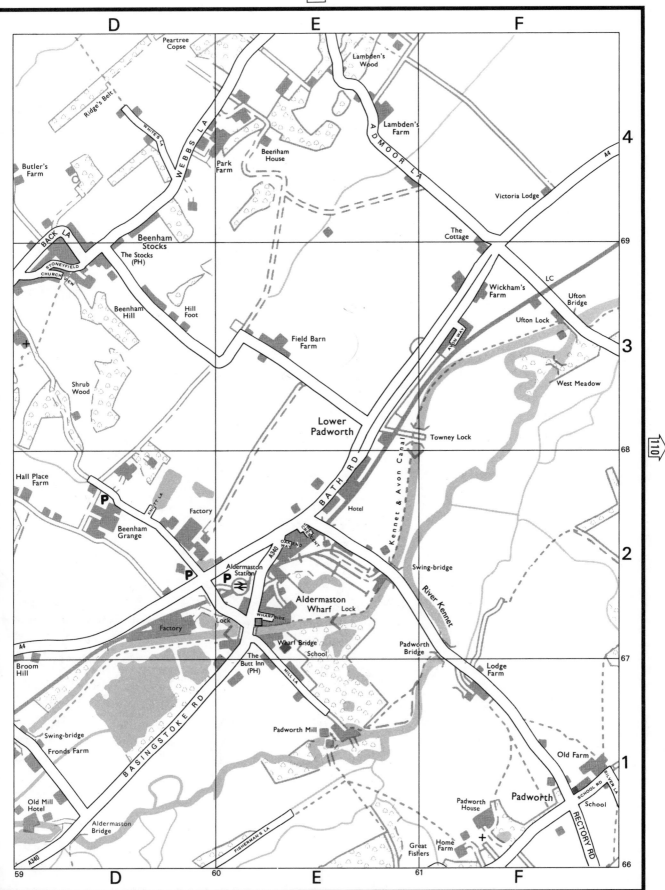

D E F

4

A4

Peartree Copse

Lambden's Wood

Lambden's Farm

ADMOOR LA

Ridge's Belt

WHITE'S LA

WEBBS LA

Butler's Farm

Park Farm

Beenham House

Victoria Lodge

The Cottage

69

BACK LA

Beenham Stocks

STONEYFIELD

CHURCH VIEW

The Stocks (PH)

Wickham's Farm

LC

Ufton Bridge

Beenham Hill

Hill Foot

Field Barn Farm

AVON WAY

Ufton Lock

3

Shrub Wood

West Meadow

Lower Padworth

Kennet & Avon Canal

Towney Lock

68

Hall Place Farm

P

KNOTT LA

Factory

Beenham Grange

P

P

Aldermaston Station

A340

OAK END WAY

CRESCENT

BATH RD

Hotel

Swing-bridge

River Kennet

2

Aldermaston Wharf

Lock

Lock

WHARFSIDE

Wharf Bridge

School

Padworth Bridge

Lodge Farm

67

A4

Factory

Broom Hill

The Butt Inn (PH)

MILL LA

Old Farm

Swing-bridge

Fronds Farm

BASINGSTOKE RD

Padworth Mill

SCHOOL RD

SILVER LA

Padworth

1

Old Mill Hotel

Aldermaston Bridge

FISHERMAN'S LA

Padworth House

Home Farm

Great Fishers

School

RECTORY RD

A340

Padworth

66

59 D 60 E 61 F

83

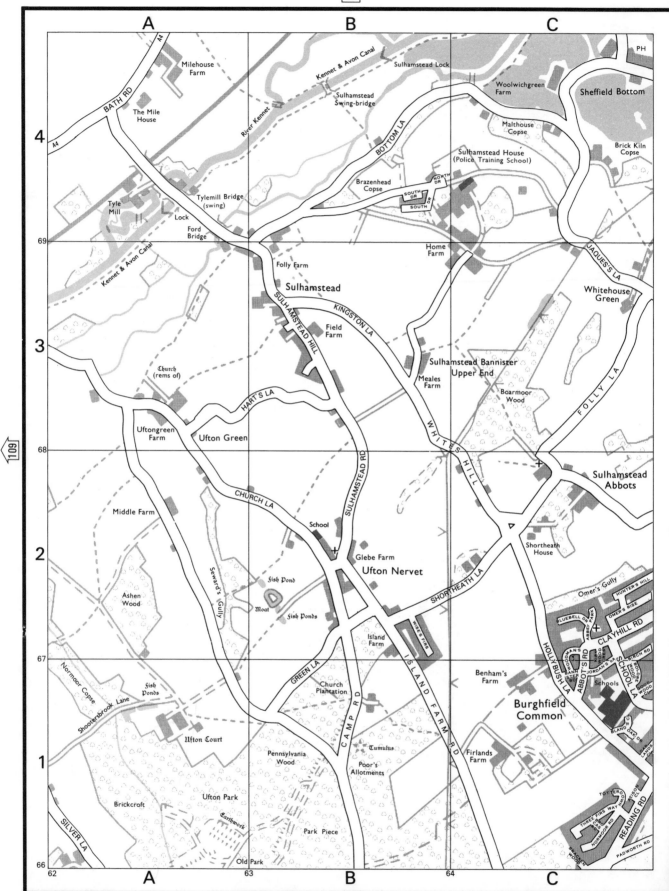

109

84

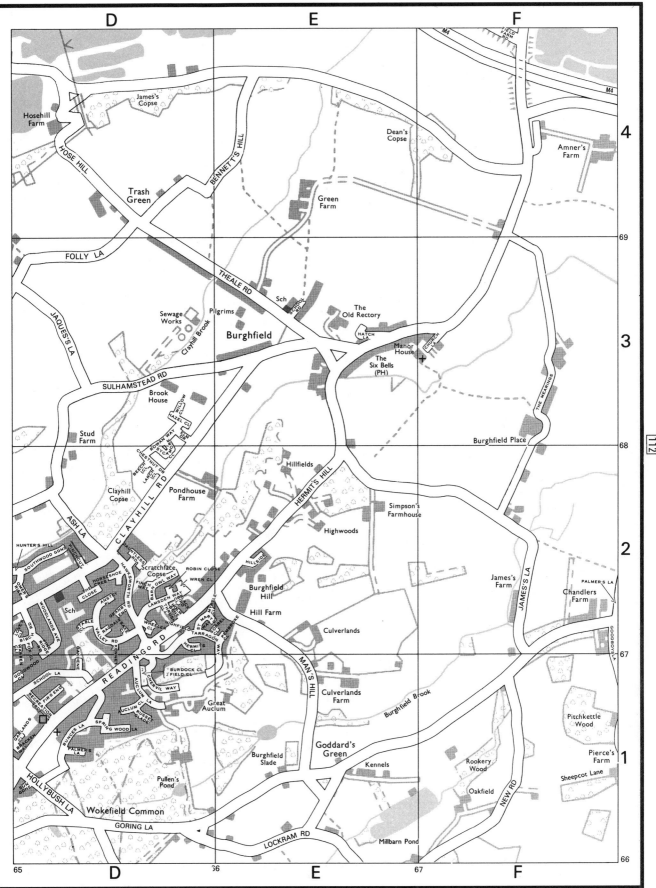

1112

85

111

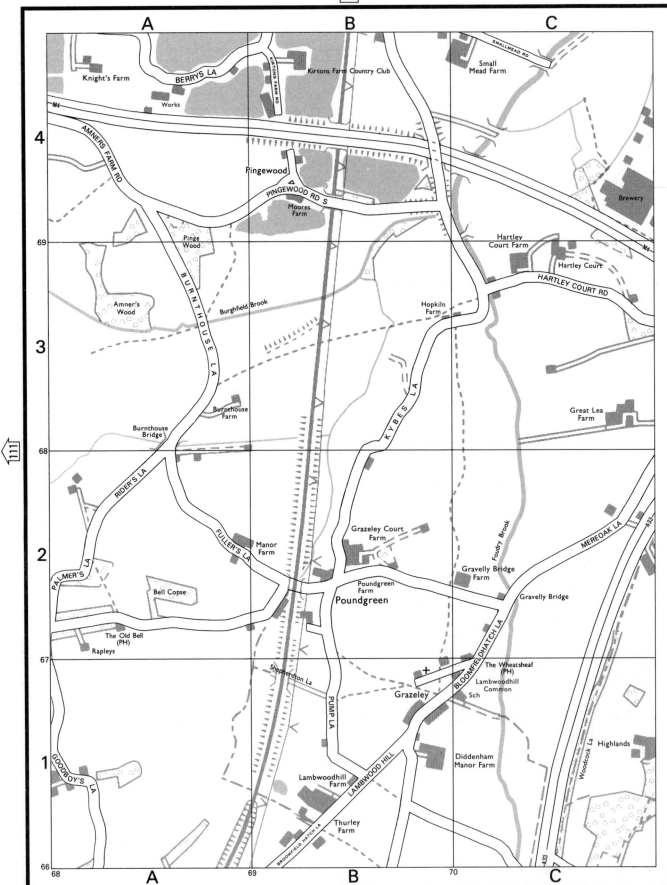

138

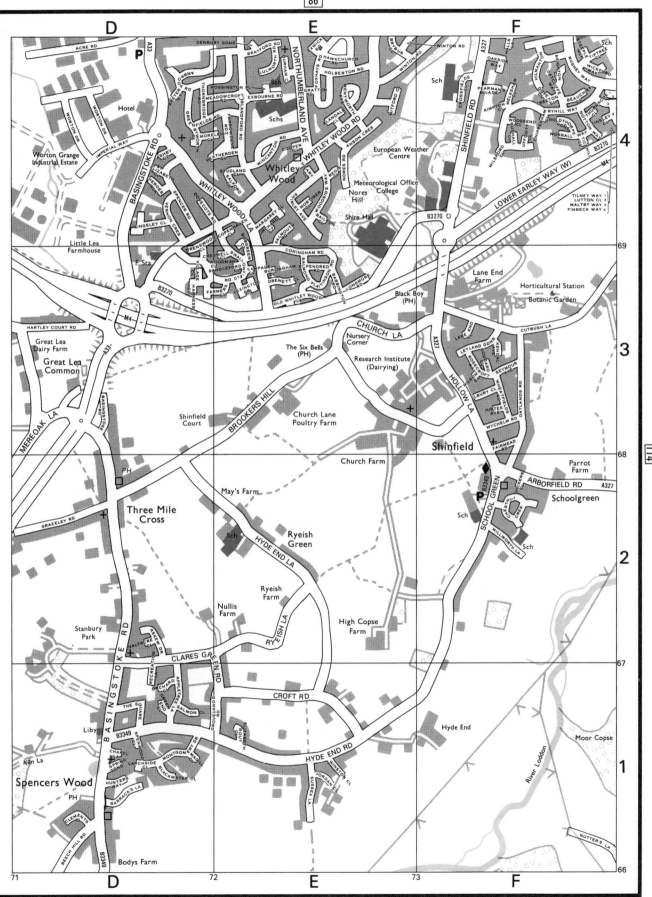

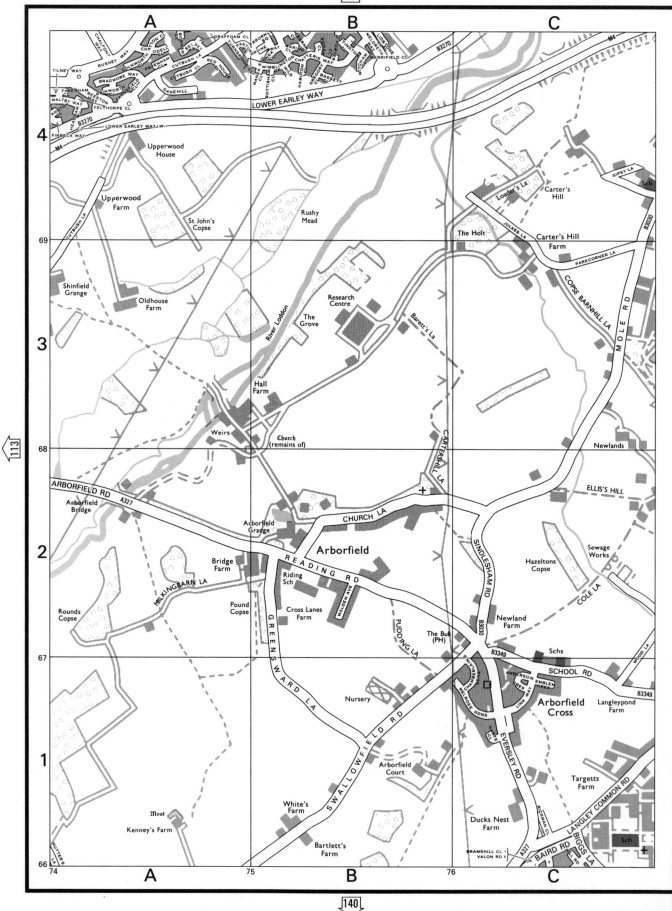

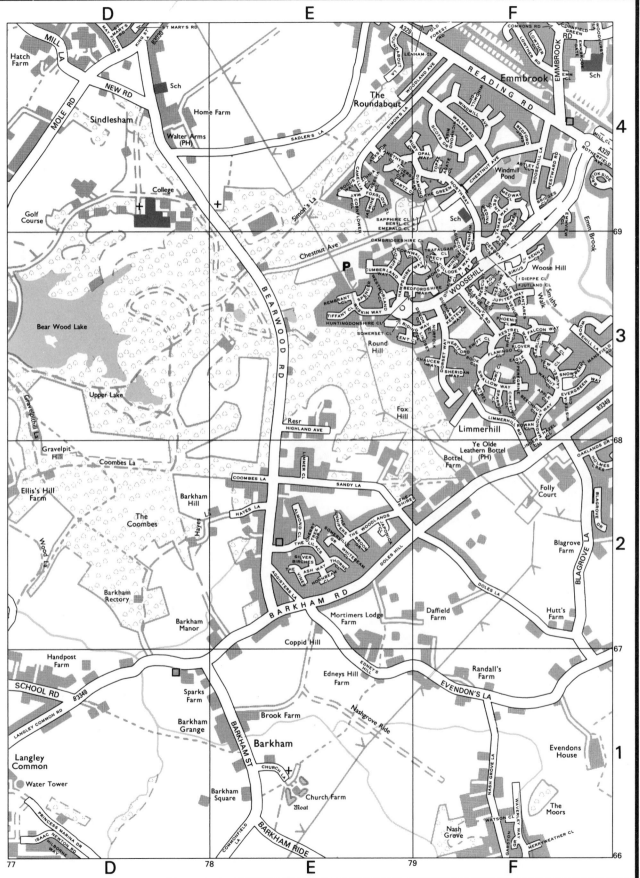

88
116

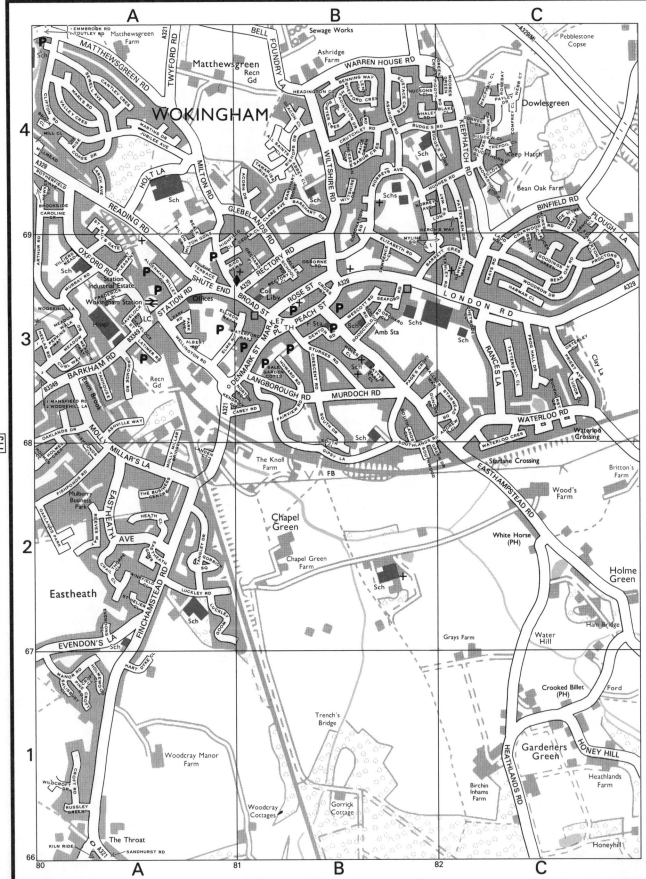

115

WOKINGHAM

D E F

Binfield Rd
Stokes Farm
Top Copse
Murrellhill Farm
Pockets Copse
Murrellhill La
Murrell Hill
St Mark's Rd
Popes Manor
Popeswood Rd
Wood La
Temple Way
Hither Copse Gr
Jock's La
Buckthorns
Sch
Queensway
Windlesham Dr
Lawrence Gr
Nettle Cl
Sampson Park
London Rd
B3408
Wilwood Rd
Longmoor Dale
Kingsmere Rd
Priestwood Ave
Priestwood Court Rd
Lindenhill Rd
Farley Copse
Farleywood
Wokingham Rd
Fanes Cl
B3408

4

St Mark's Rd
Beehive La
Milward Gdns
Springfield Oaks
Mutton Oaks
Fletcher Gdns
Golden Dale
Blonfield Dale
Arkwright Dr
Tippits Mead
Popeswood
Simmonds
Radclive Rd
Turnpike Rd
Catkin Pl
Amen Corner Business Park
Milbanke Ct
Milbanke
Western Rd
The Western Centre
Downmill Rd
Tandem

Hotel
John Nike Way
Cain Rd
Leisure-Sport Complex
Waterside Park
Cookham Rd
Longshot La
Longshot Industrial Estate
A329

69

Wr Twr Rose Farm
Amen Corner
Doncastle Rd
Doncastle
Oldbury
Willoughby Rd
A3095

B E R K S H I R E W A Y

Peacock La
Wykery Copse
Peacock Farm
Longshot La
Southern Industrial Area
Ellesfield Ave
M-I-L-L L-A

3

Plough Farm
A329
Hotel
A329(M)
B3408

Big Wood
Peacock Cottages
Burnthouse Ride
Mill Pond
Nature Reserve
Northerams
Wildridings Rd

Big Wood House
West Garden Copse
Jennett's Hill
P
Wokham
P
A3095

68

Waterloo Rd
Lock's House
Easthampstead Park
Waverley
Welbeck
Wheatley
Winscombe
Viking
Woodsworth
Yardley
Ambassador
Ringmead
Ringmead
Abbotsbury
Appledore
Schs
Liby
P
Great Hollands
Vandyke
Ashbourne
Great Hollands Rd
P
Aygarth

2

Educational Centre
Wickham Vale
Rambury
Beedon Dr
Andrews
Underwood
Highfield
Holbeck
Penwood
Burnaby
Cadogan
Holmwood Gdns
Turnberry
Flexford Green
Ullswater
Holland Pines

67

Six Oaks
Easthampstead Rd
Golf Course
Sch
Sch
Tumulus
Bywood
Crowthorne Rd
Prescott
Pembroke
A3095

Sutton Court Farm
Office
Crem
Sch
Silwood
Spinis
Sylvanus
Sarum
Southwold
Qualitas
Quintilis

1

Honey Hill
Old Wokingham Rd
Newlands
Yew Tree Corner
Playing Field
Staplehurst
Stratfield
Nine Mile Ride
Bracknell Rd
B3430
A3095
B3430

66

83 D 84 E 85 F

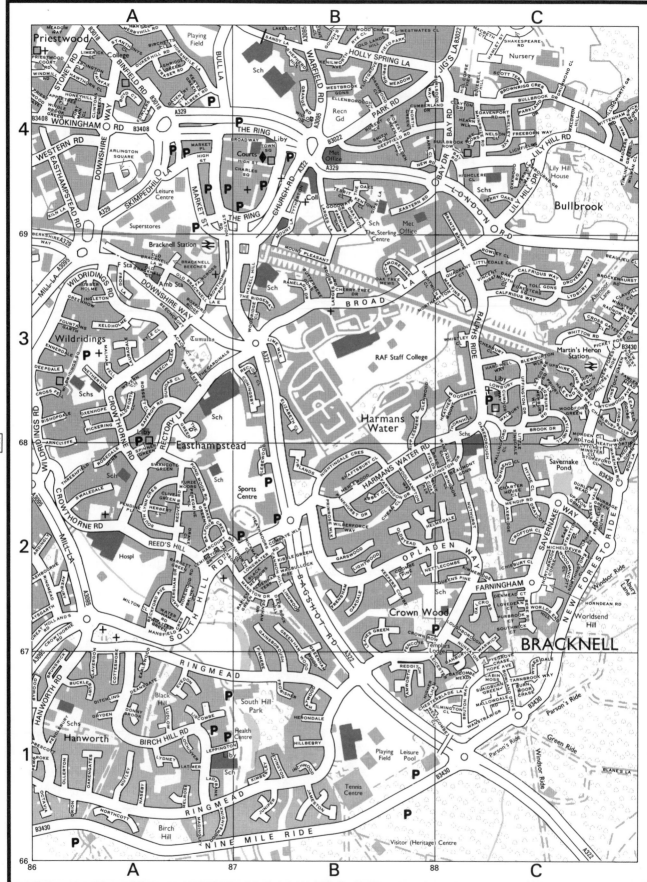

117

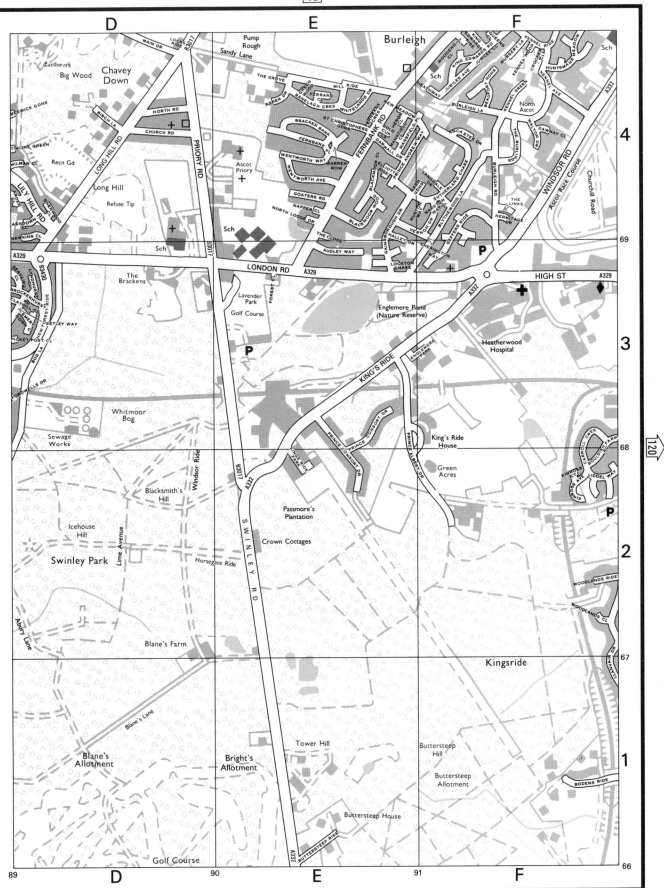

D E F

Burleigh

Earthwork

Big Wood

Chavey Down

Pump Rough

Sandy Lane

North Ascot

Sch

4

MAIN DR

LOCKS RIDE

B3017

THE GROVE

MILL RIDE

ASHER DR

GREEN WOOD

FERRARD CL

RANELAGH CRES

WHITELANDS DR

ST CHRISTOPHERS CRES

NEW MEADOW

FERNBANK RD

KING EDWARDS RD

WOODEND

HEATHWAY

KING EDWARDS
JUBILEE AVE

JUBILEE CL

QUEENS RD

HARPERT LA

KENNEL AVE

KENNEL GDNS

BEAUFORT GDNS

CROCKERS RIDE

HUNTSMANS MEADOW

Sch

WINDSOR RD

A332

BESWICK GDNS

BIRCH LA

NORTH RD

CHURCH RD

TIMLINE GREEN

Recn Gd

LONG HILL RD

PRIORY RD

Ascot Priory

BRACKEN BANK

FERNBANK PL

WENTWORTH WAY

WENTWORTH AVE

WARREN ROW

BLACKMOOR CL

ELLIOTT RISE

DARWALL DR

PRINCE ANDREW WAY

MANSFIELD PL

CUP

LANDALE

ANCASTER DR

KENNEL GREEN

WALDON DR

DAWNAY CL

BURLEIGH LA

Ascot Race Course

Churchill Road

MILMAN CL

Long Hill

Refuse Tip

GOATERS RD

NAPPER CL

NORTH LODGE DR

BLACKMOOR

VERNON DR

RUNNYMEDE WAY

MASS WAY

SUTHERLAND LA

BLYTHEWOOD WAY

OFFERS RIDE

BURLEIGH RD

THE LINKS

THE BURLINGS

HERMITAGE DR

4

LILY HILL RD

ASHDOWN CL

HAWKINS CL

Sch

Sch

THE CLOSE

HALLEY DR

CHERINGTON WAY

P

69

A329

B3430

LYNDHURST

BROCKENHURST

CLAY HILL

FOREST RIDE

OSETLEY WAY

PICKET POST CL

The Brackens

LONDON RD

A329

FOREST CL

Lavender Park Golf Course

AUDLEY WAY

LOCKTON CHASE

Englemere Pond (Nature Reserve)

A332

HIGH ST

A329

Heatherwood Hospital

3

BOG LA

PONDWELLS DR

P

KING'S RIDE

ENGLEMERE PARK

3

Whitmoor Bog

Sewage Works

Windsor Ride

B3017

King's Ride House

KINGSRIDE PARK DR

PRINCE CONSORT DR

PRINCE CONSORT DR

PRINCE ALBERT DR

Green Acres

CARROLL CRES

KINROSS CT

KINROSS AVE

LIDDEL WAY

POULTERS FARM

68

2

ABURY LANE

Blacksmith's Hill

Icehouse Hill

LIME AVENUE

Swinley Park

HORSEGATE RIDE

SWINLEY RD

Passmore's Plantation

Crown Cottages

P

WOODLANDS RIDE

WOODLANDS CL

2

Blane's Farm

Kingsride

LAVANA CL

LANAIR DR

67

BLANE'S LANE

Tower Hill

Buttersteep Hill

Buttersteep Allotment

1

Blane's Allotment

Bright's Allotment

Buttersteep House

BODENS RIDE

1

Golf Course

A332

BUTTERSTEEP RIDE

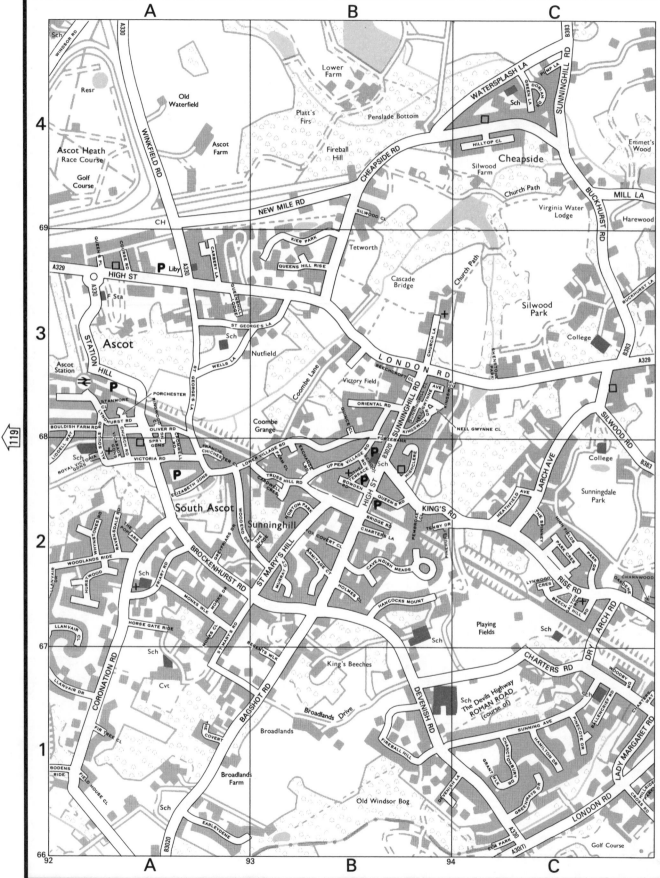

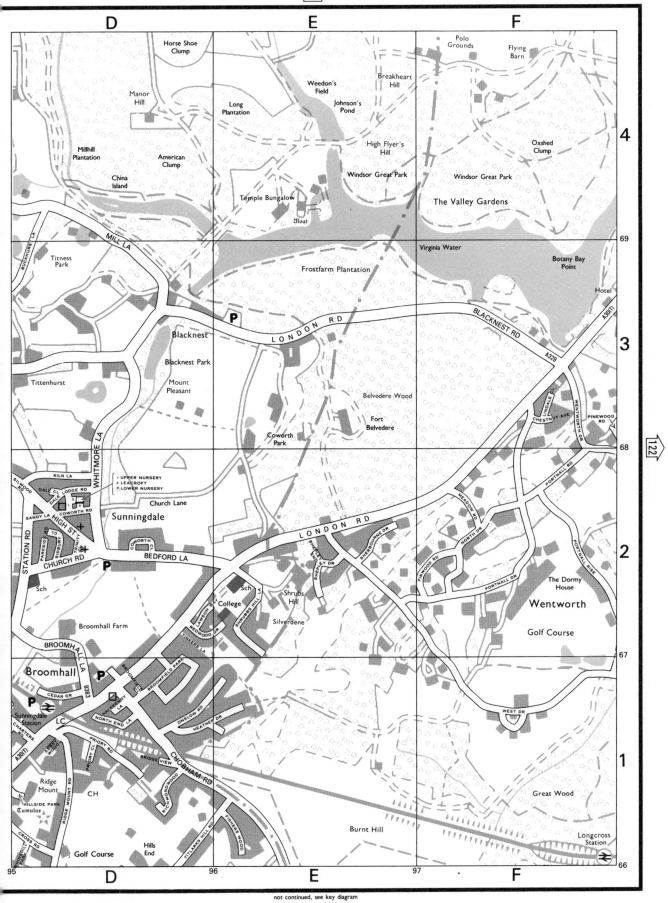

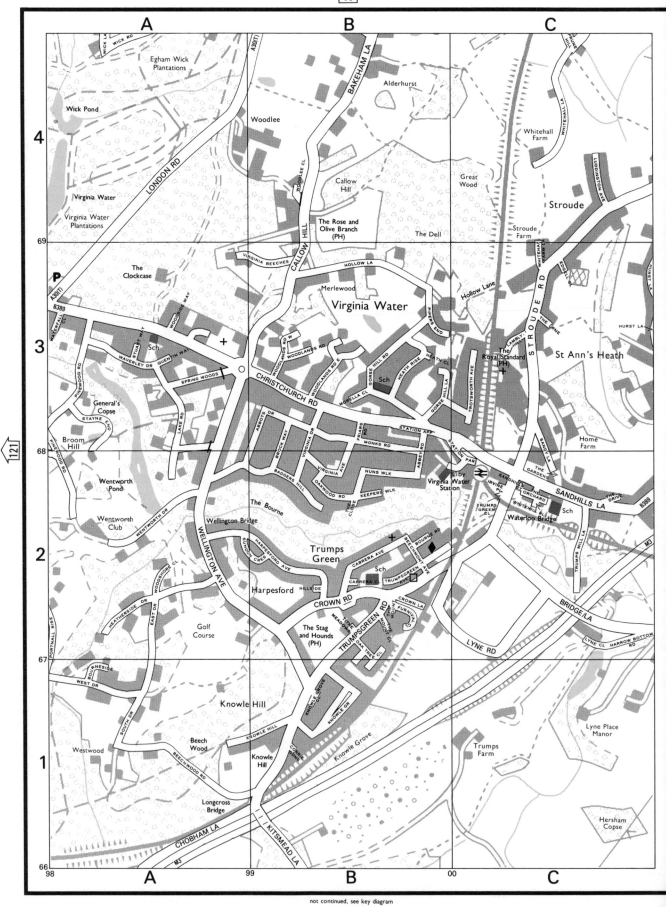

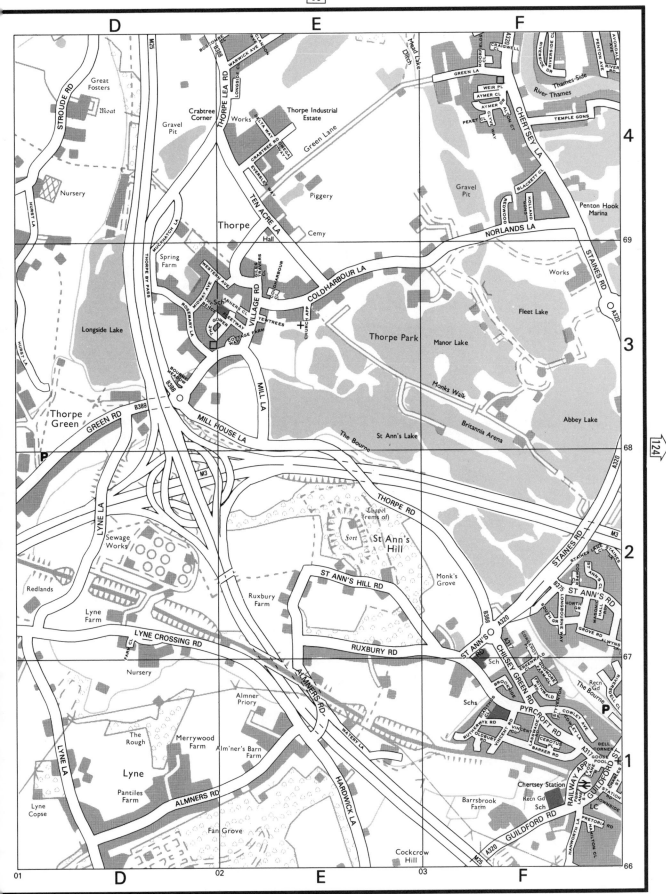

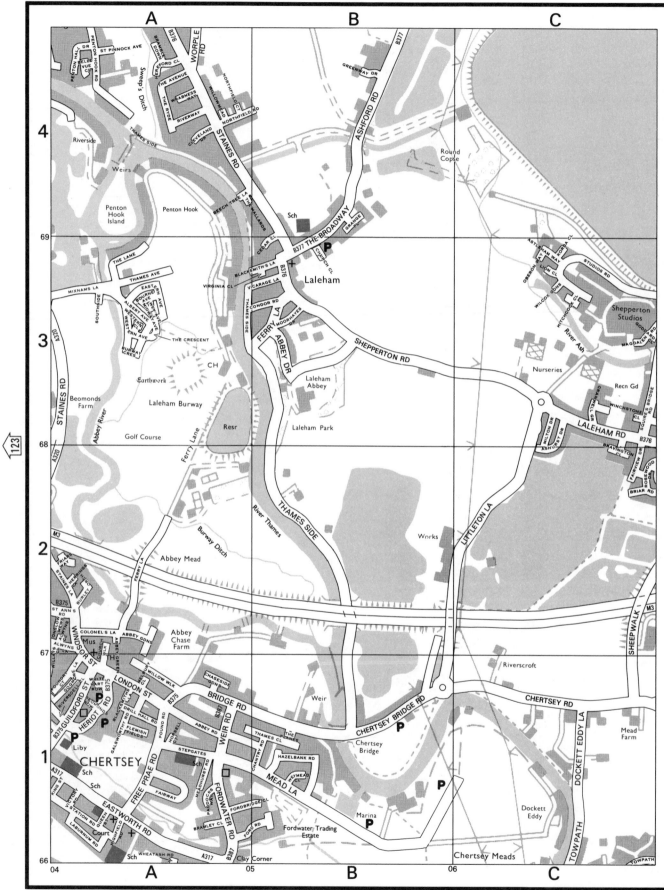

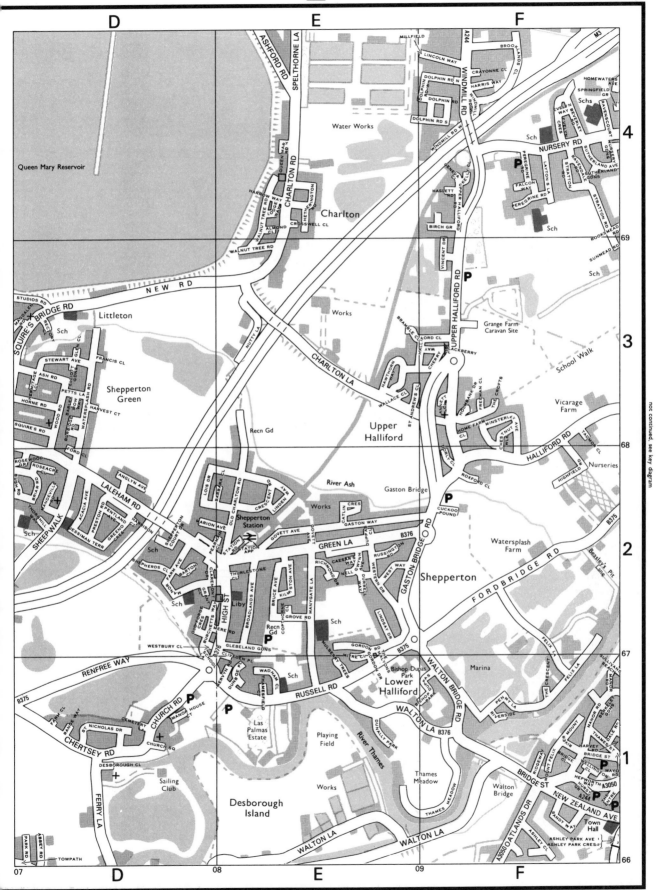

not continued, see key diagram

100

A   B   C

4

Upper Slope End Farm

A338

Elm Copse

Hightree Copse

Anvilles

Moat

Totterdown House

Prosperous Home Farm

The Heath

The Gully

Middle Copse

65

Lower Slope End Farm

Kiln Copse

Anville's Copse

Great Sadler's Copse

3

SIX ACRE LA

A338

Daniel's La

Mount Prosperous

Bitham La

BITHAM LA

POLERS RD

64

CUTTING HILL

CUTTING HILL

Happy Valley Nursery

2

Lower Spray Farm

Cowley's Copse

Lower Spray Copse

SPRAY RD

HAM RD

Dove's Farm

Ham Spray Farm

Field La

Crown & Anchor (PH)

Sch

63

CHURCH RD

Ham

Ham Spray House

Manor House

The Lynch

Eastcourt Farm

Inwood Copse

1

Manor Farm

62

Ham Hill

32   A   33   B   34   C

not continued, see key diagram

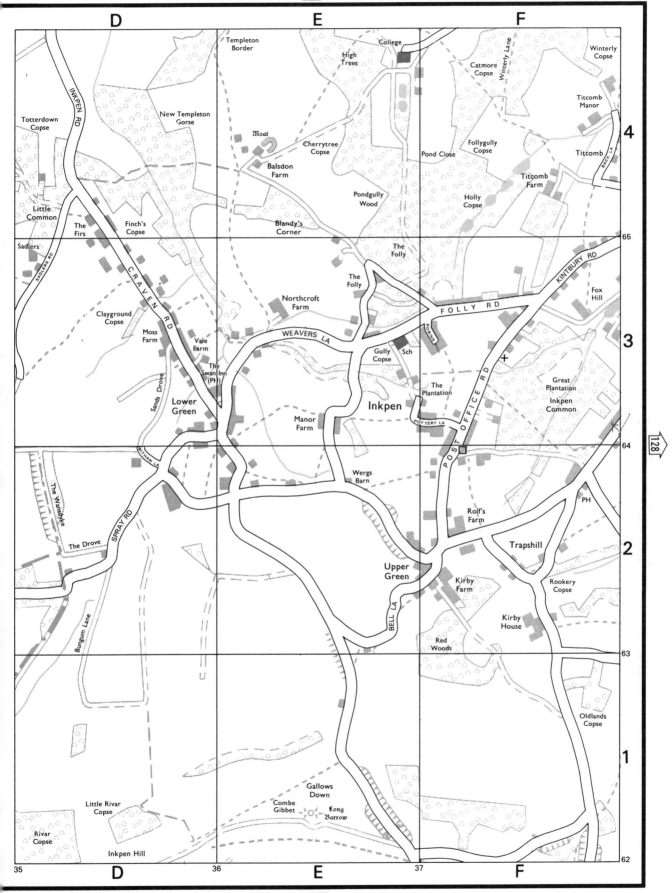

D   E   F

Templeton Border

College

High Trees

Winterly Copse

Catmore Copse

Winterly Lane

Totterdown Copse

New Templeton Gorse

Titcomb Manor

INKPEN RD

Moat

Cherrytree Copse

Pond Close

Follygully Copse

Titcomb

4

BACK LA

Balsdon Farm

Pondgully Wood

Holly Copse

Titcomb Farm

Little Common

The Firs

Finch's Copse

Blandy's Corner

65

Sadlers

SADLERS RD

CRAVEN RD

The Folly

The Folly

KINTBURY RD

Fox Hill

Clayground Copse

Northcroft Farm

FOLLY RD

Moss Farm

Vale Farm

WEAVERS LA

Gully Copse

Sch

ROBINS HILL

POST OFFICE RD

+

Great Plantation

Inkpen Common

3

Sands Drove

The Swan Inn (PH)

Inkpen

The Plantation

Lower Green

Manor Farm

POTTERY LA

64

BITHAM LA

Wergs Barn

PH

The Wansdyke

SPRAY RD

Rolf's Farm

Trapshill

2

The Drove

Bungum Lane

Upper Green

BELL LA

Kirby Farm

Rookery Copse

Kirby House

Red Woods

63

Oldlands Copse

1

Little Rivar Copse

Gallows Down

Rivar Copse

Combe Gibbet

Long Barrow

Inkpen Hill

62

35   D   36   E   37   F

102

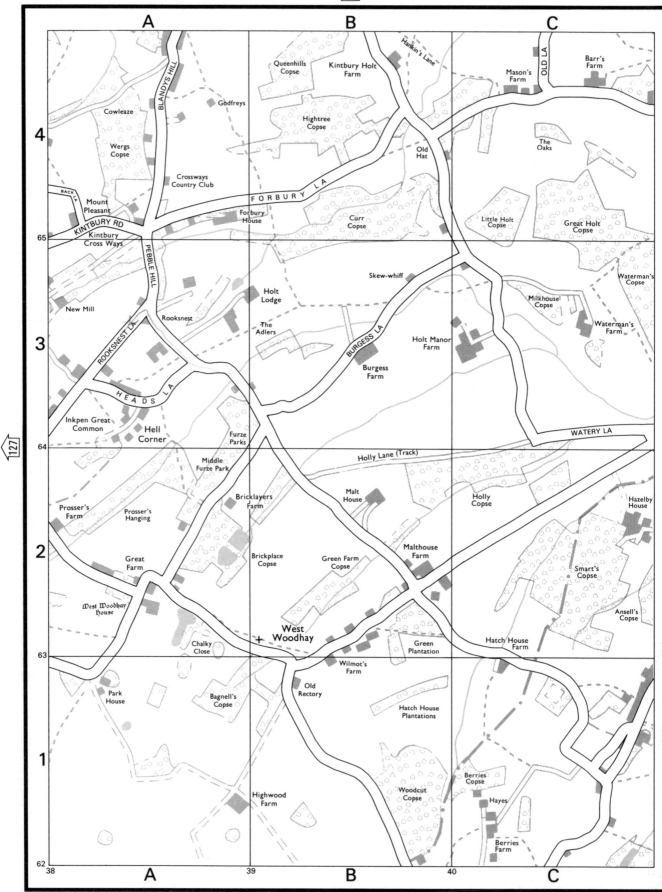

127

148

A   **B**   **C**

4

Queenhills Copse

Kintbury Holt Farm

Hankin's Lane

Mason's Farm

OLD LA

Barr's Farm

Cowleaze

Godfreys

BLANDYS HILL

Hightree Copse

Old Hat

The Oaks

Wergs Copse

Crossways Country Club

FORBURY LA

Little Holt Copse

Great Holt Copse

BACK LA

Mount Pleasant

KINTBURY RD

Forbury House

Curr Copse

65

Kintbury Cross Ways

PEBBLE HILL

Skew-whiff

Waterman's Copse

New Mill

Holt Lodge

Milkhouse Copse

Waterman's Farm

Rooksnest

ROOKSNEST LA

The Adlers

BURGESS LA

Holt Manor Farm

3

Burgess Farm

H E A D S   L A

Inkpen Great Common

Hell Corner

Furze Parks

WATERY LA

64

Middle Furze Park

Holly Lane (Track)

Prosser's Farm

Bricklayers Farm

Malt House

Holly Copse

Hazelby House

Prosser's Hanging

2

Brickplace Copse

Green Farm Copse

Malthouse Farm

Smart's Copse

Great Farm

West Woodhay House

Ansell's Copse

Chalky Close

West Woodhay

Green Plantation

Hatch House Farm

63

Park House

Wilmot's Farm

Bagnell's Copse

Old Rectory

Hatch House Plantations

1

Berries Copse

Highwood Farm

Woodcut Copse

Hayes

62

A   **B**   **C**

Berries Farm

38   39   40

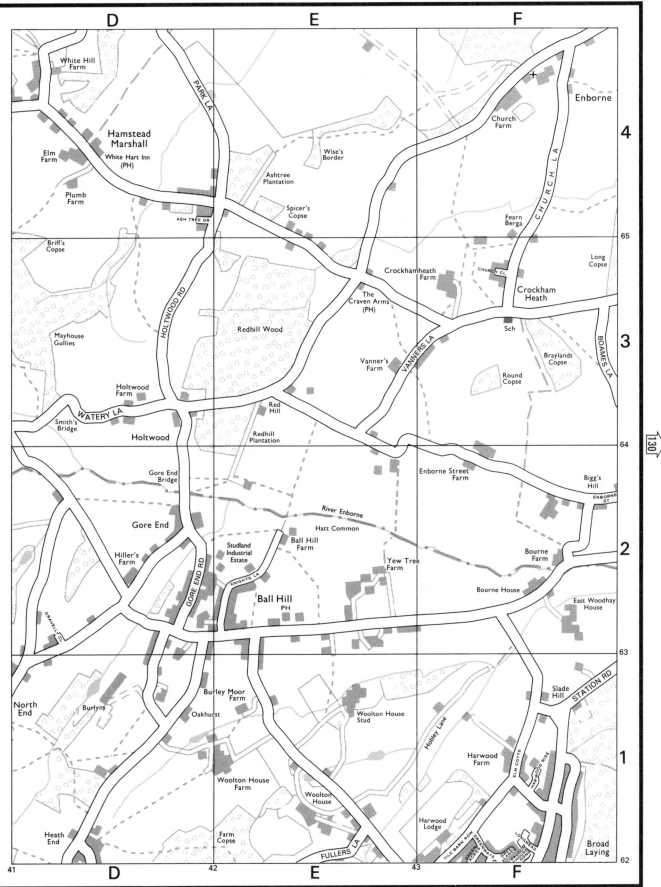

D

E

F

White Hill Farm

PARK LA

Hamstead Marshall

White Hart Inn (PH)

Elm Farm

Plumb Farm

ASH TREE GR

Ashtree Plantation

Wise's Border

Spicer's Copse

Enborne

Church Farm

CHURCH LA

Fearn Berga

4

Briff's Copse

HOLTWOOD RD

65

Crockhamheath Farm

CHURCH CL

Long Copse

Crockham Heath

Mayhouse Gullies

Redhill Wood

The Craven Arms (PH)

VANNERS LA

Sch

Braylands Copse

BOAMES LA

3

Holtwood Farm

Vanner's Farm

Round Copse

WATERY LA

Smith's Bridge

Red Hill

Holtwood

Redhill Plantation

64

Gore End Bridge

Enborne Street Farm

Bigg's Hill

ENBORNE ST

130

Gore End

River Enborne

Hatt Common

Bourne Farm

2

Hiller's Farm

GORE END RD

Studland Industrial Estate

KNIGHTS LA

Ball Hill Farm

Yew Tree Farm

Bourne House

East Woodhay House

GRAVELL CL

Ball Hill
PH

63

North End

Burlyns

Burley Moor Farm

Oakhurst

Woolton House Stud

Hobley Lane

Slade Hill

STATION RD

Harwood Farm

ELM COTTS

HARWOOD RISE

1

Woolton House Farm

Woolton House

Harwood Lodge

TILE BARN ROW

GREENWAYS C

GREEN RANGE

LONGMEAD

Broad Laying

Heath End

Farm Copse

FULLERS LA

62

41

D

42

E

43

F

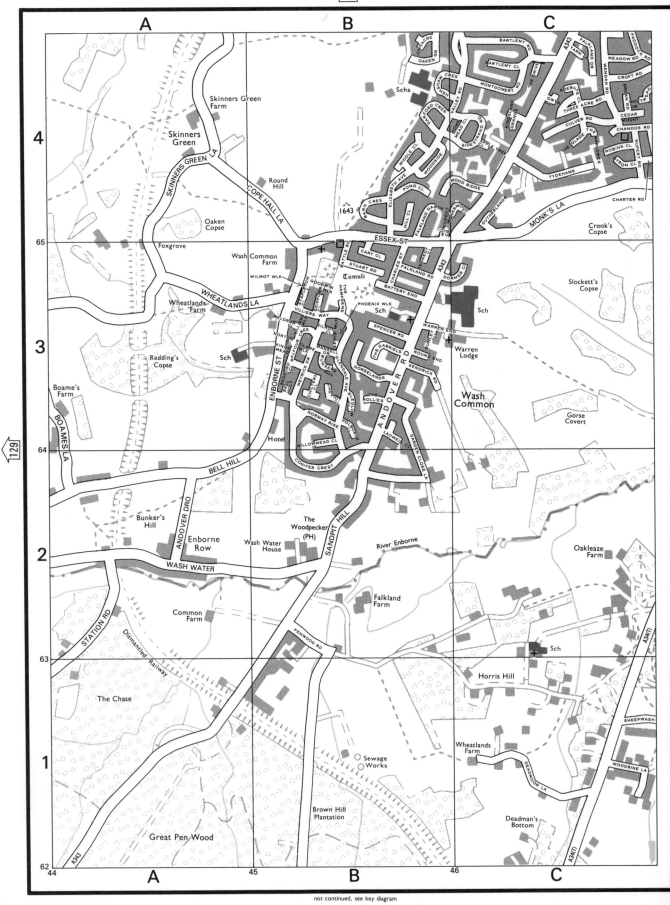

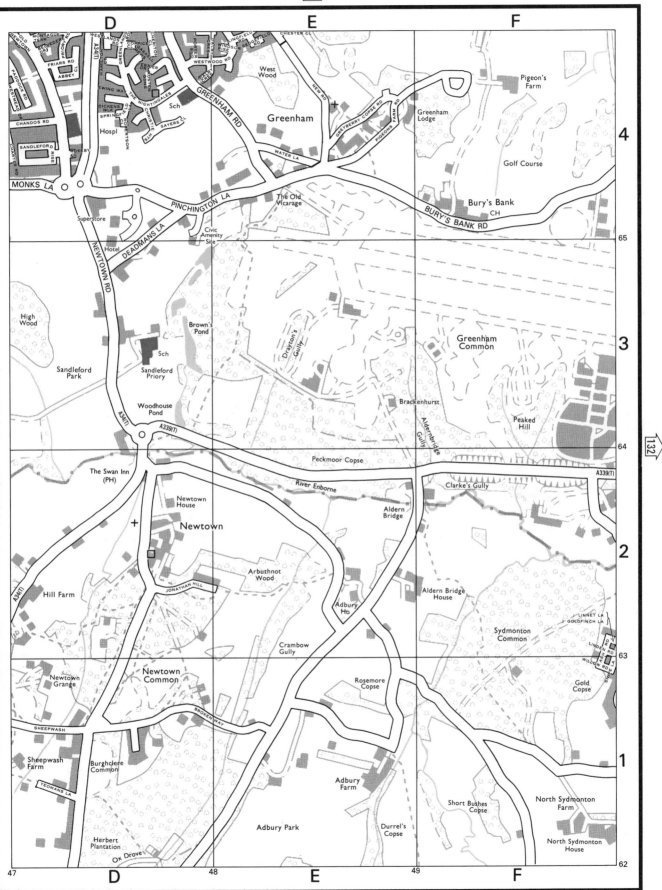

132

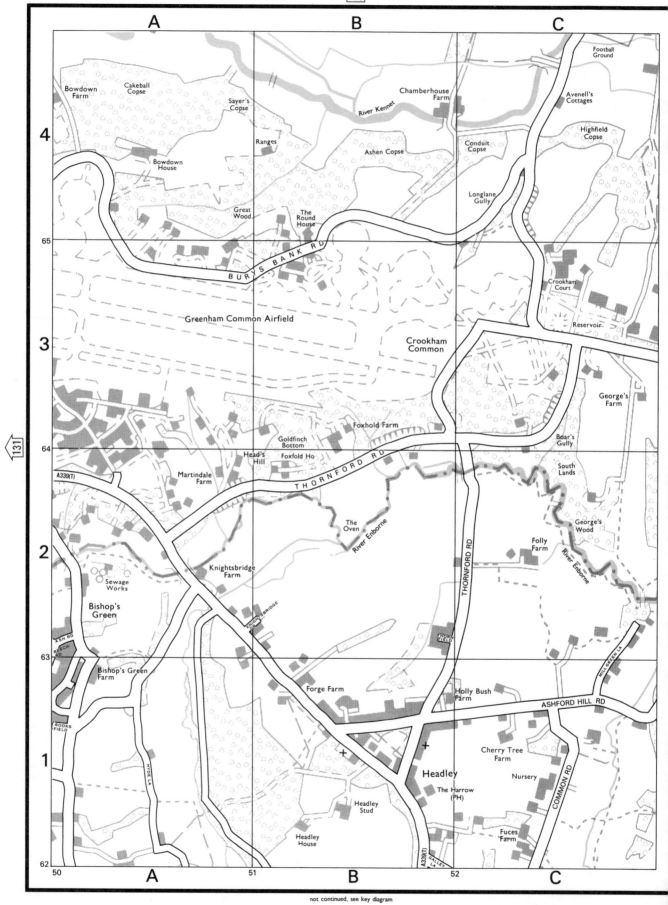

106
131

not continued, see key diagram

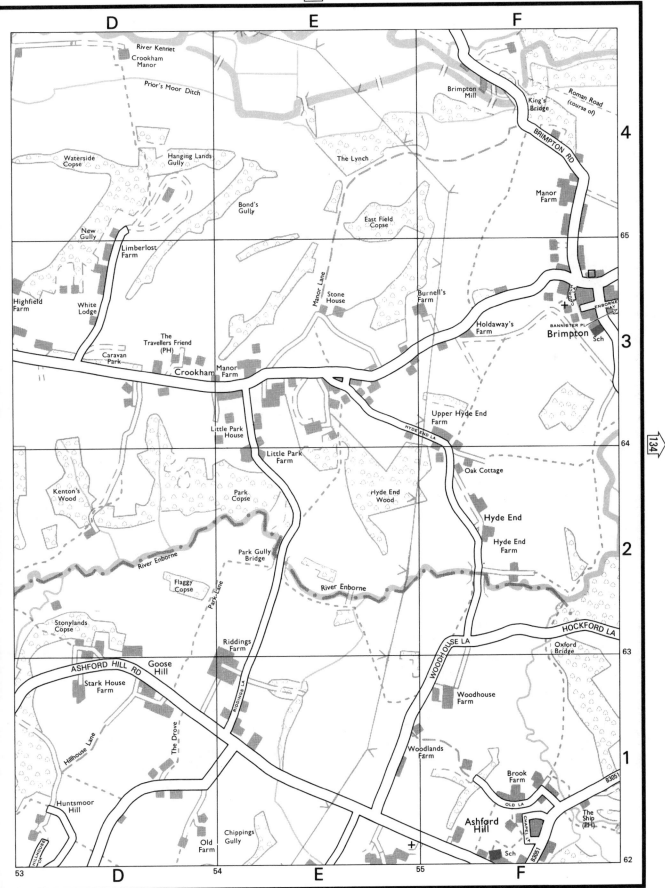

D   E   F

River Kennet
Crookham Manor
Prior's Moor Ditch

Brimpton Mill
King's Bridge
Roman Road (course of)

BRIMPTON RD

4

Waterside Copse
Hanging Lands Gully
The Lynch

Manor Farm

Bond's Gully
East Field Copse

65

New Gully
Limberlost Farm
Manor Lane
Stone House
Burnell's Farm

Highfield Farm
White Lodge
Holdaway's Farm
+ CHURCH
ENBORNE WAY
BANNISTER PL

The Travellers Friend (PH)
Brimpton
Sch

3

Caravan Park
Crookham
Manor Farm

Little Park House
Upper Hyde End Farm

HYDE END LA

64

134

Kenton's Wood
Little Park Farm
Park Copse
Hyde End Wood
Oak Cottage

Hyde End

River Enborne
Park Gully Bridge
Park Lane
Flaggy Copse
River Enborne
Hyde End Farm

2

Stonylands Copse
HOCKFORD LA
Oxford Bridge

63

ASHFORD HILL RD
Goose Hill
Stark House Farm
Riddings Farm
RIDDINGS LA
WOODHOUSE LA
Woodhouse Farm

Hillhouse Lane
The Drove

Huntsmoor Hill
Woodlands Farm

1

Brook Farm
B3051

Chippings Gully
Old Farm
OLD LA
CHAPEL LA
The Ship (PH)

Ashford Hill
+
Sch
B3051

62

53   D   54   E   55   F

not continued, see key diagram

108

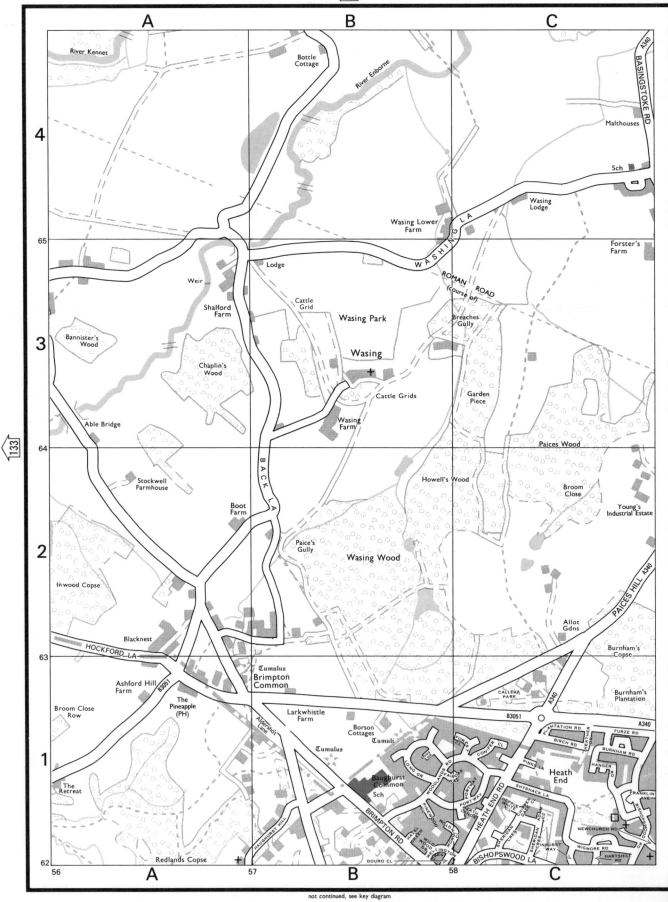

133

A   B   C

4

River Kennet

Bottle
Cottage

River Enborne

BASINGSTOKE RD

A340

Malthouses

Sch

Wasing
Lodge

65

Wasing Lower
Farm

WASHING LA

Forster's
Farm

Lodge

Weir

ROMAN   ROAD
(course of)

Shalford
Farm

Cattle
Grid

Wasing Park

Breaches
Gully

3

Bannister's
Wood

Wasing

Chaplin's
Wood

Cattle Grids

Garden
Piece

Able Bridge

Wasing
Farm

Paices Wood

64

BACK LA

Stockwell
Farmhouse

Howell's
Wood

Broom
Close

Young's
Industrial Estate

Boot
Farm

Paice's
Gully

Wasing Wood

2

Inwood Copse

Allot
Gdns

Burnham's
Copse

PAICES HILL A340

Blacknest

HOCKFORD LA

63

Burnham's
Plantation

Ashford Hill
Farm

B3051

Tumulus
Brimpton
Common

CALLEVA
PARK

A340

A340

Broom Close
Row

The Pineapple
(PH)

Larkwhistle
Farm

Aldershot Lane

B3051

PLANTATION RD

BIRCH RD

HEATHER

FURZE RD

Borson
Cottages

Tumuli

CONIFER CL

PINKS LA

Burnham RD

HANGER

1

Tumulus

HEATH END RD

Heath
End

The
Retreat

Baughurst
Common
Sch

SHYSHACK LA

Newchurch RD

FRANKLIN
AVE

BRIMPTON RD

WIGMORE RD

HARTSHILL
RD

62

Redlands Copse

BISHOPSWOOD LA

DOURO CL

56   A   57   B   58   C

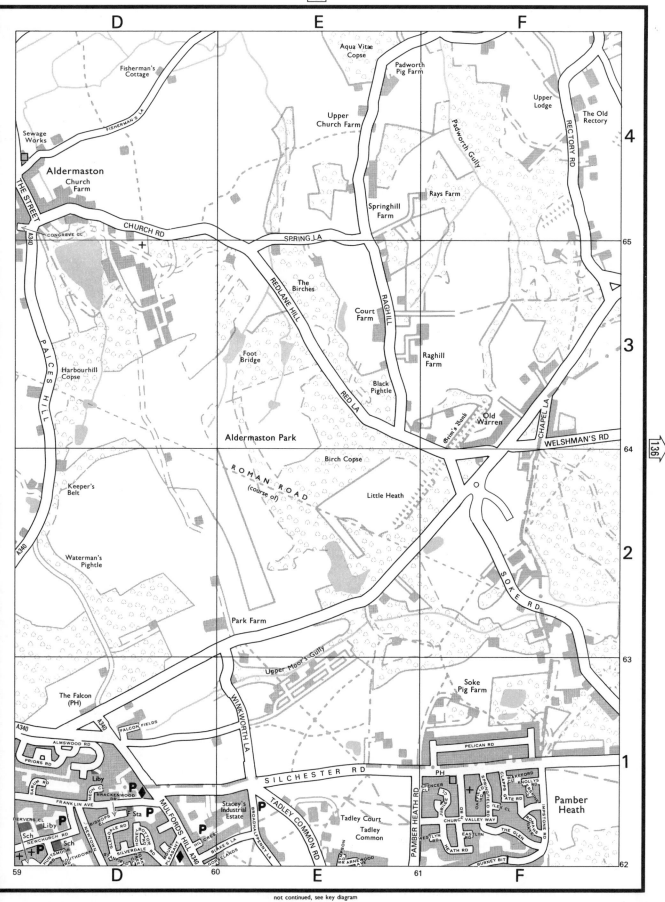

109

136

D   E   F

Fisherman's Cottage

Aqua Vitæ Copse

Padworth Pig Farm

Upper Lodge

The Old Rectory

FISHERMAN'S LA

Sewage Works

Upper Church Farm

Padworth Gully

RECTORY RD

4

Aldermaston
Church Farm

Rays Farm

THE STREET

Springhill Farm

A340

CONGREVE CL

CHURCH RD

SPRING LA

65

RAGHILL

The Birches

Court Farm

PAICES HILL

REDLANE HILL

Raghill Farm

3

Harbourhill Copse

Foot Bridge

RED LA

Black Pightle

Grim's Bank

Old Warren

CHAPEL LA

WELSHMAN'S RD

64

Aldermaston Park

Birch Copse

R O M A N   R O A D

Keeper's Belt

(course of)

Little Heath

A340

SOKE RD

2

Waterman's Pightle

Park Farm

63

Upper Moor's Gully

The Falcon (PH)

Soke Pig Farm

A340

WINKWORTH LA

Falcon Fields

ALMSWOOD RD

PELICAN RD

PH

1

PRIORS RD

Liby

P

Pamber Heath

SARUM RD

BRACKENWOOD DR

SILCHESTER RD

PAMBER HEATH RD

SPENCER CL

WAKEFORD KNOLLYS

FRANKLIN AVE

Stacey's Industrial Estate

P

TADLEY COMMON RD

CHURCH RD

CLAPPS GATE RD

Beavers CL

Liby

Sch

F Sta

P

BROADLA

PENNY LA

Tadley Court

JUBILEE RD

VALLEY WAY

THE GLEN

ROMANS FLD

Newchurch Rd

Sch

MULFORDS HILL A340

P

HILCREST

BLAKES LA

Tadley Common

WESTLYN

EASTLYN

HEATH RD

62

SILVERDALE RD

GORSELANDS

ARNEWOOD AVE

BURNEY BIT

59   D   60   E   61   F

not continued, see key diagram

A   **B**   **C**

Grim's Bank

Brent's Gully

Oval Pond

Four Houses Corner

Water Tower

ISLAND FARM RD

Cowpond Piece

Five Oaken

SILVER LA

Roundoak Piece

Gibbet Piece

CAMP RD

LONGMOOR LA

MAY'S LA

The Croft

PADWORTH RD

Holden's Firs

Tumuli

COLLEGE PIECE

The Round Oak (PH)

Fifty Acre Piece

Hundred Acre Piece

GROVES LEA

BRIARLEA RD

HIL CRES

RECTORY RD

Padworth Common

RAMPTONS LA

ROMAN ROAD (course of)

Pickling Yard Plantation

ST CATHERINE'S HILL

STEPHENS FIRS

VICTORIA RD

STEPHENS FIRS

LEIGH FIELD

CLENAPP GRANGE

LOVES WOOD

Stockwell's Piece

Pond Bar

Chaplin's Copse

SWEETTER'S PIECE

BIRCHLAND

RAVENSWORTH RD

BIRCH LA

STEPHEN'S RD

Burnt Common

Budd's Firs

Turners' Arms (PH)

WEST END RD

STANMORE GDNS

DRURY LA

Welshman's Pond

WELSHMAN'S RD

LANSWOOD

Summerlug

West End Farm

TURK'S LA

THE BRIDGES

Fox Hill

Mortimer West End

Simms's Copse

SIMMS FARM LA

Simms Stud Farm

Lovegrove's Farm

Benyon's Inclosure

Red Lion (PH)

West End Brook

ROMAN ROAD (course of)

Hungry Hill

Kiln Pond

Pond Farm

Nine Acre Copse

Simms's Plantation

Stone Hill

ROMAN ROAD (course of)

Catthaw Lands Copse

WALL LA

Kiln Yard Copse

SOKE RD

Earthwork

Earthwork

AMPHITHEATRE

Catthawlands Farm

The Drove

Manor Farm

The Devil's Highway

ROMAN ROAD (course of)

SILCHESTER RD

KINGS RD

School

Museum

CALLEVA ATREBATVM ROMAN TOWN (remains of)

CHURCH LA

Silchester Common

P

BRAMLEY RD

Calleva Arms (PH)

Silchester

Park Pale

DUKES RIDE

ROMAN FIELDS

THE LANE

ROMAN ROAD (course of)

Silchester Hall

Earthwork

A   **B**   **C**

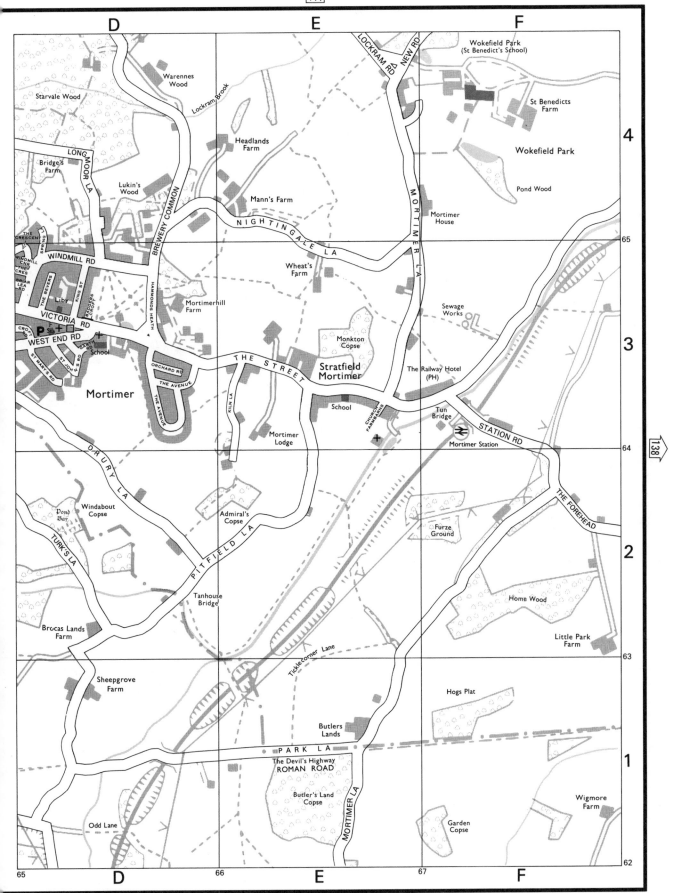

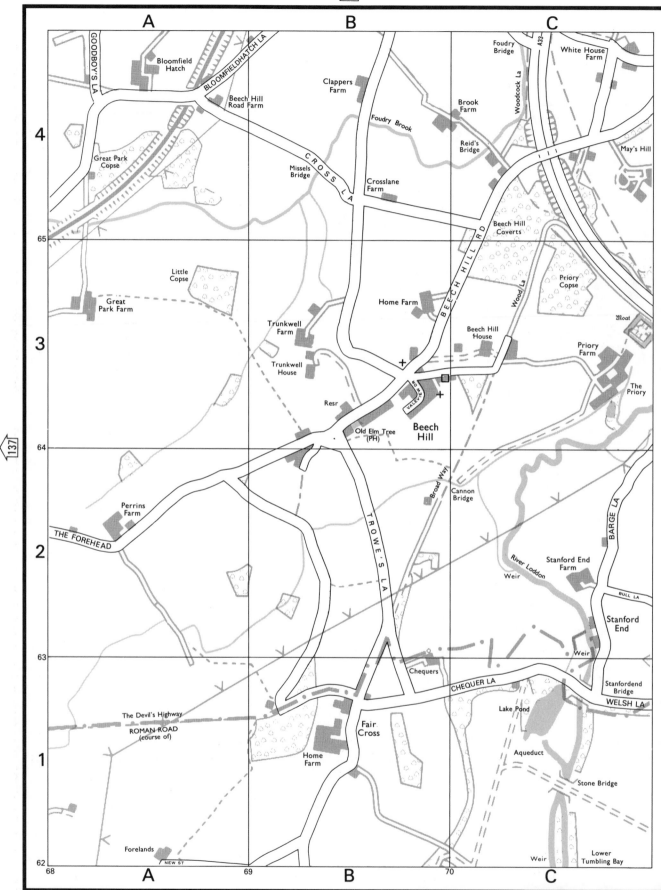

A   B   C

GOODBOY'S LA

Bloomfield
Hatch

BLOOMFIELDHATCH LA

Beech Hill
Road Farm

Clappers
Farm

Foudry
Bridge

A33

White House
Farm

Woodcock La

4

Great Park
Copse

CROSS LA

Foudry Brook

Missels
Bridge

Brook
Farm

Reid's
Bridge

May's Hill

Crosslane
Farm

Beech Hill
Coverts

65

Little
Copse

Great
Park Farm

Trunkwell
Farm

Home Farm

BEECH HILL RD

Wood La

Priory
Copse

Moat

3

Trunkwell
House

Beech Hill
House

Priory
Farm

The
Priory

Resr

Old Elm Tree
(PH)

Beech
Hill

VALLEY RD

64

Perrins
Farm

THE FOREHEAD

Broad Way

Cannon
Bridge

TROWE'S LA

BARGE LA

2

River Loddon

Stanford End
Farm

Weir

Stanford
End

BULL LA

63

Weir

Chequers

Stanfordend
Bridge

CHEQUER LA

WELSH LA

The Devil's Highway

ROMAN ROAD
(course of)

Fair
Cross

Lake Pond

1

Home
Farm

Aqueduct

Stone Bridge

Forelands

NEW ST

Weir

Lower
Tumbling Bay

62

68   A   69   B   70   C

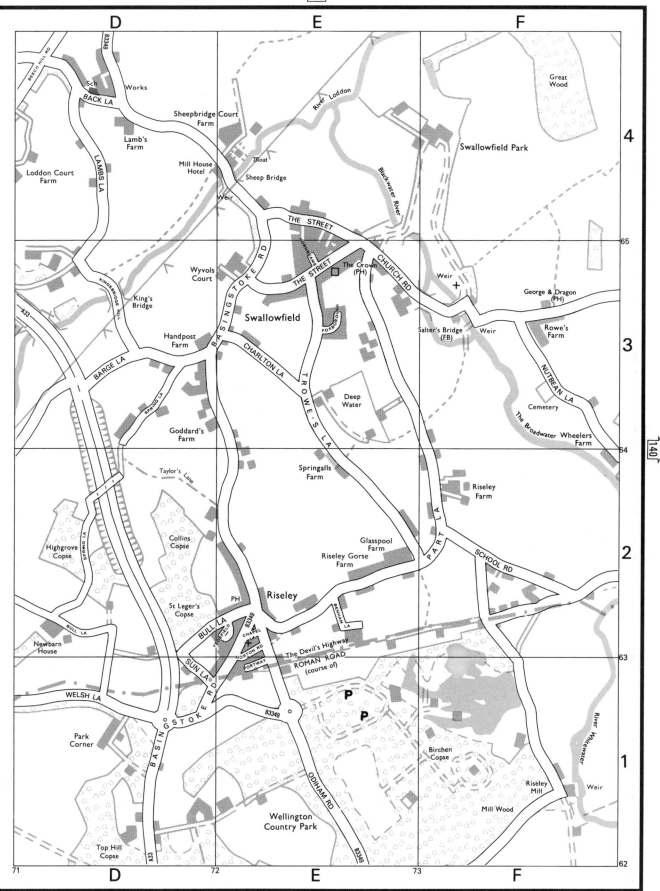

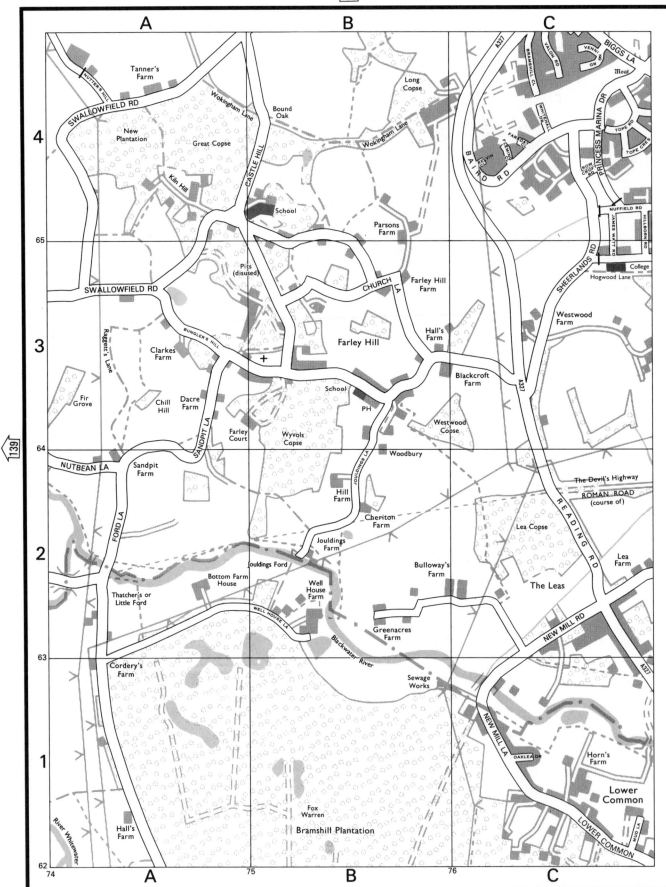

A   **B**   **C**

4

NUTTER'S HILL
Tanner's Farm
SWALLOWFIELD RD
New Plantation
Wokingham Lane
Great Copse
Kiln Hill
Castle Hill
School
Bound Oak
Long Copse
Wokingham Lane
Parsons Farm

A327
BRAMSHILL CL.
VALON RD
VENNI NG RD
BIGGS LA
Moat
WHITERALL
PRINCESS MARINA DR
TOPE RD
TOPE CRES
BAIRD RD
KELVIN RD
FARADAY
SERVICE RD
BOW CROFT RD
NUFFIELD RD
JAMES WATT RD
HILLBORN RD

65

SWALLOWFIELD RD
Pits (disused)
CHURCH LA
Farley Hill Farm
SHEERLANDS RD
College
Hogwood Lane

3

Raggett's Lane
BUNGLER'S HILL
Clarkes Farm
Farley Hill
Hall's Farm
Blackcroft Farm
Westwood Farm
A327
Fir Grove
Chill Hill
Dacre Farm
School
PH
Westwood Copse

64

NUTBEAN LA
Sandpit Farm
SANDPIT LA
Farley Court
Wyvols Copse
Woodbury
JOULDINGS LA
The Devil's Highway
ROMAN ROAD (course of)

2

FORD LA
Hill Farm
Cheriton Farm
Jouldings Farm
Bulloway's Farm
Lea Copse
READING RD
Lea Farm
The Leas
Jouldings Ford
Bottom Farm House
Well House Farm
Thatcher's or Little Ford
WELL HOUSE LA
Greenacres Farm
Blackwater River
NEW MILL RD
A327

63

Cordery's Farm
Sewage Works
NEW MILL LA
OAKLEA DR
Horn's Farm

1

River Whitewater
Hall's Farm
Fox Warren
Bramshill Plantation
Lower Common
LOWER COMMON
MUD LA

62

74   75   76

A   **B**   **C**

not continued, see key diagram

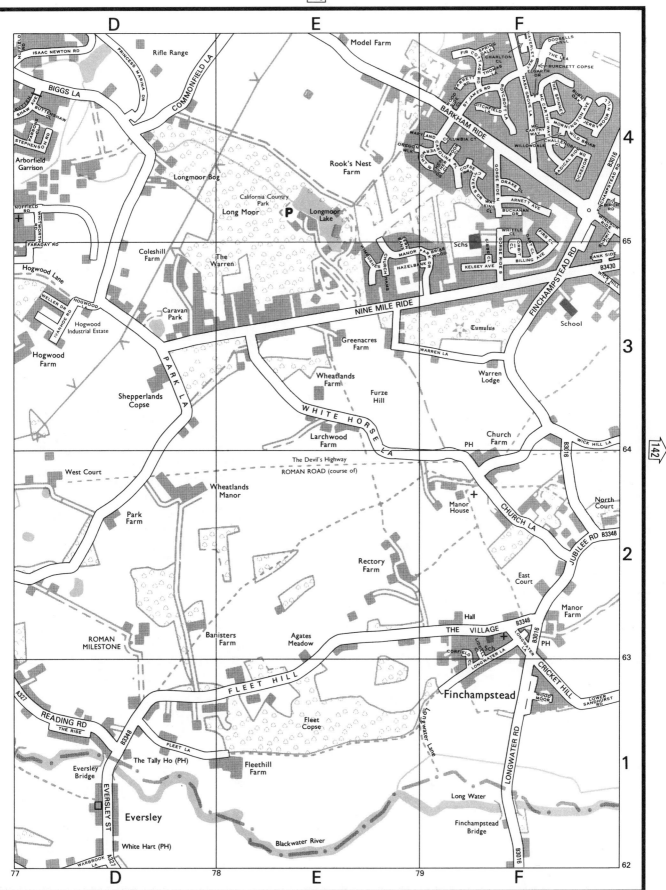

142

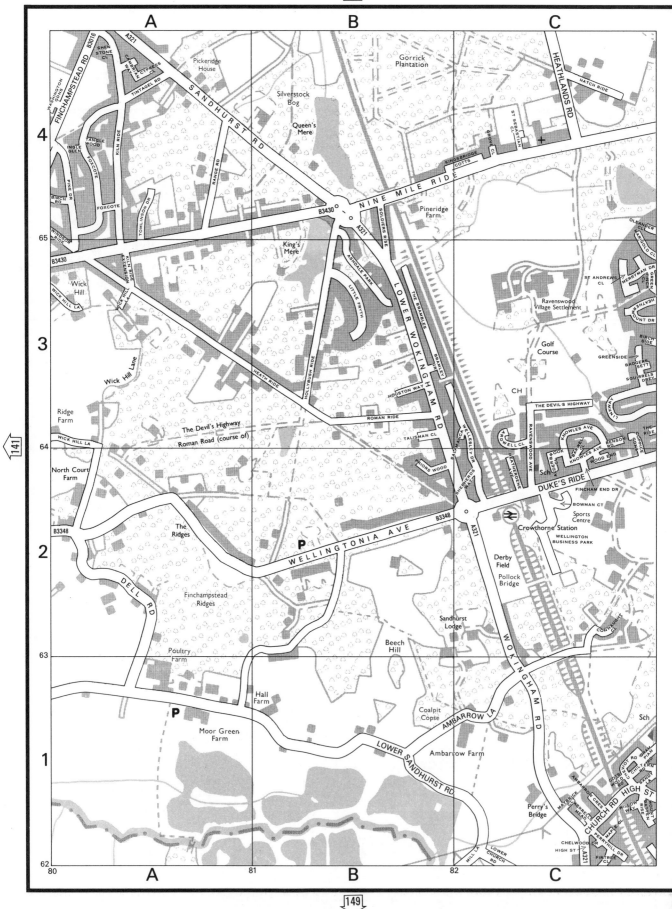

117
144
150

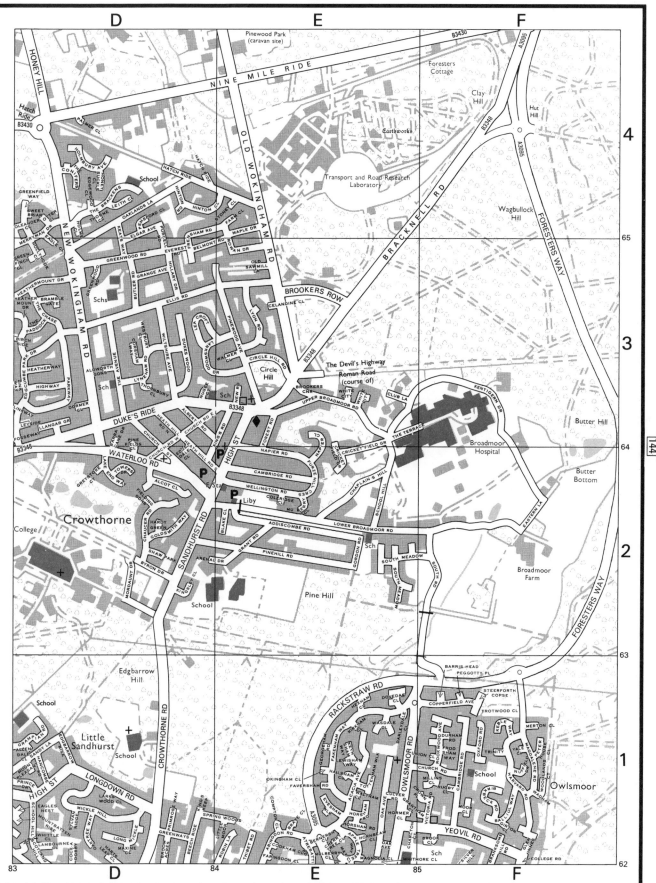

118

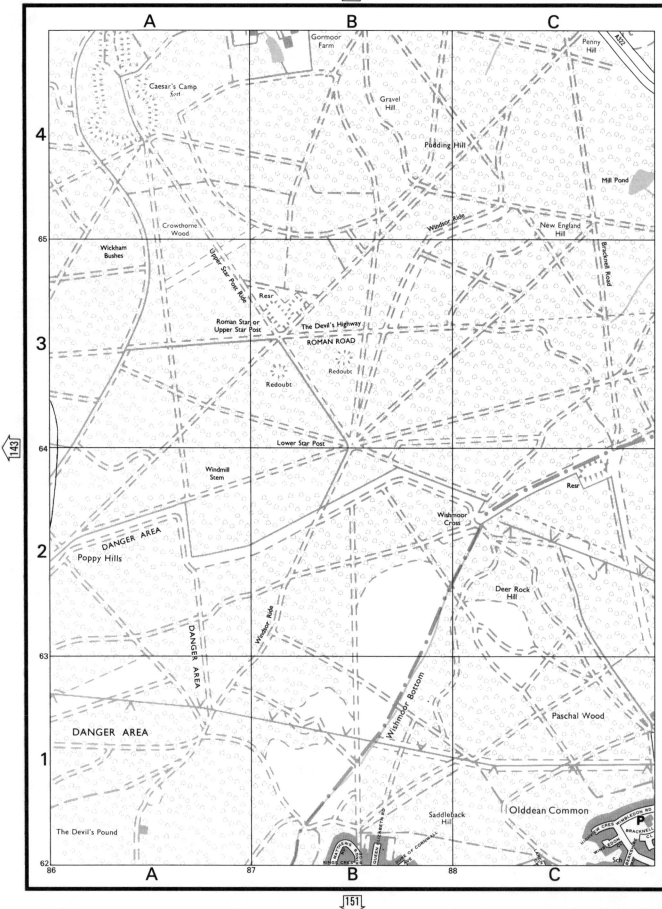

143

A   B   C

Gormoor Farm

Caesar's Camp fort

Gravel Hill

Penny Hill

Pudding Hill

Mill Pond

4

Crowthorne Wood

Windsor Ride

New England Hill

65

Wickham Bushes

Upper Star Post Ride

Bracknell Road

Resr

Roman Star or Upper Star Post

The Devil's Highway

ROMAN ROAD

3

Redoubt

Redoubt

Lower Star Post

64

Windmill Stem

Resr

Wishmoor Cross

DANGER AREA

Poppy Hills

2

Deer Rock Hill

DANGER AREA

Windsor Ride

63

Wishmoor Bottom

Paschal Wood

DANGER AREA

1

Olddean Common

P

The Devil's Pound

Saddleback Hill

Sch

62

86   A   87   B   88   C

151

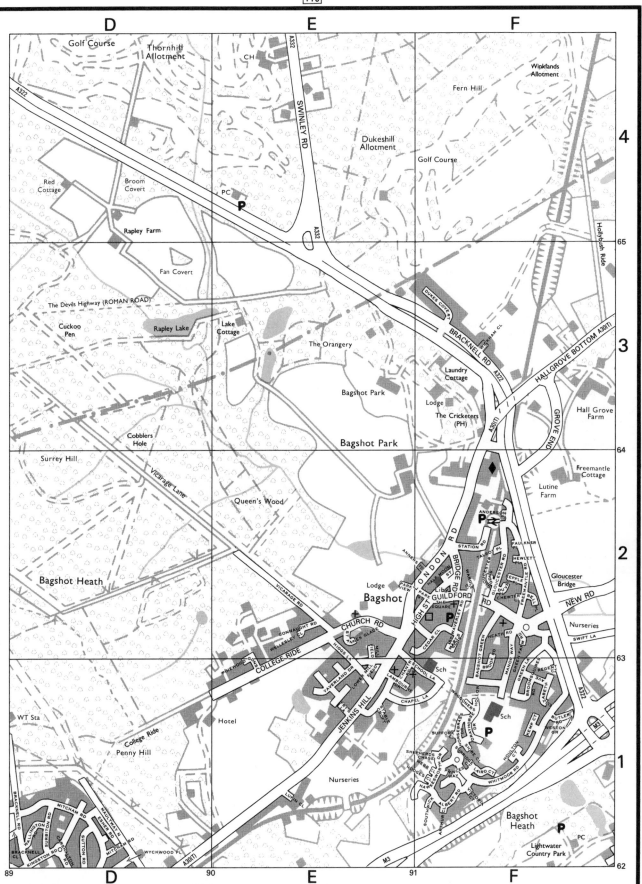

119

146

152

D

E

F

4

3

2

1

65

64

63

62

Golf Course

Thornhill Allotment

CH

A322

SWINLEY RD

Winkfands Allotment

Fern Hill

Dukeshill Allotment

Golf Course

Red Cottage

Broom Covert

PC

P

A322

Hollybush Ride

Rapley Farm

Fan Covert

A322

The Devils Highway (ROMAN ROAD)

DUKES COVERT

PETHAM CL

BRACKNELL RD

A322

HALLGROVE BOTTOM A30(T)

Cuckoo Pen

Rapley Lake

Lake Cottage

The Orangery

Laundry Cottage

A30(T)

GROVE END

Hall Grove Farm

Bagshot Park

Lodge

The Cricketers (PH)

Cobblers Hole

Bagshot Park

64

Surrey Hill

Vicarage Lane

Queen's Wood

Freemantle Cottage

Lutine Farm

ANDERSON

P

Bagshot Heath

VICARAGE RD

STATION RD

ANNE'S

LONDON RD

BRIDGE RD

TALBOT

PL

Gloucester Bridge

HEWLETT

Lodge

PARK VIEW

Libry

GUILDFORD

RD

Bagshot

HIGH ST

CEDAR CL

BEECH

GLOUCESTER RD

CHEWTER

FREEMANTLE RD

BELL

NEW RD

Nurseries

P

HEATH RD

SWIFT LA

Connaught Rd

Wellesley Cl

CHURCH RD

ST ANNE'S GLADE

HIGGS LA

MANOR

CL

BAGSHOT GREEN

BROOK

GREEN FARM CT

LA

REGENT

A322

COLLEGE RIDE

PINEWOOD

TAVERLAND DR

JENKINS HILL

LOWER MILL

LAMBOURNE

CHAPEL LA

SCHOOL LA

Sch

WAGTAIL

MANOR WAY

BROOMHURST

BUTLER

M3

KEMP CT

WESTON GR

WT Sta

College Ride

Penny Hill

Hotel

Sch

P

Nurseries

SUFFORK

SHEPHERDS CHASE

HODGES CL

HAWK

ALBERT RD

ARTHUR RD

HOULTON CT

LAIRD CT

WHITMOOR RD

Bagshot Heath

P

PC

BRACKNELL CL

WELLINGTON RD

KINGSTON RD

MITCHAM RD

SURBITON RD

MAULWAY N

ESHER RD

SUTTON RD

MITCH AV

WYCHWOOD PL

A30(T)

Lightwater Country Park

LUPIN CL

M3

89

90

91

D

E

F

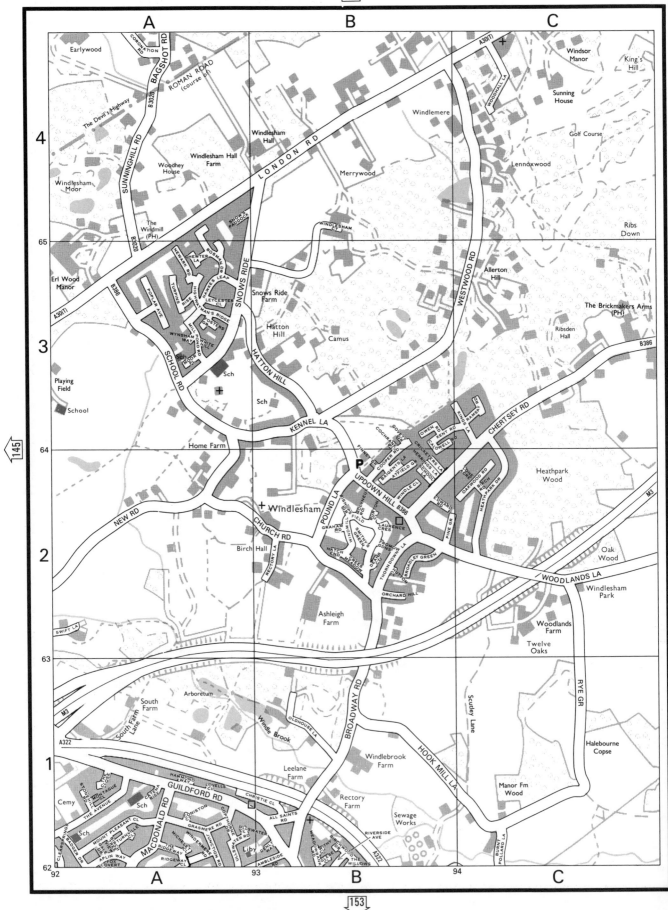

145

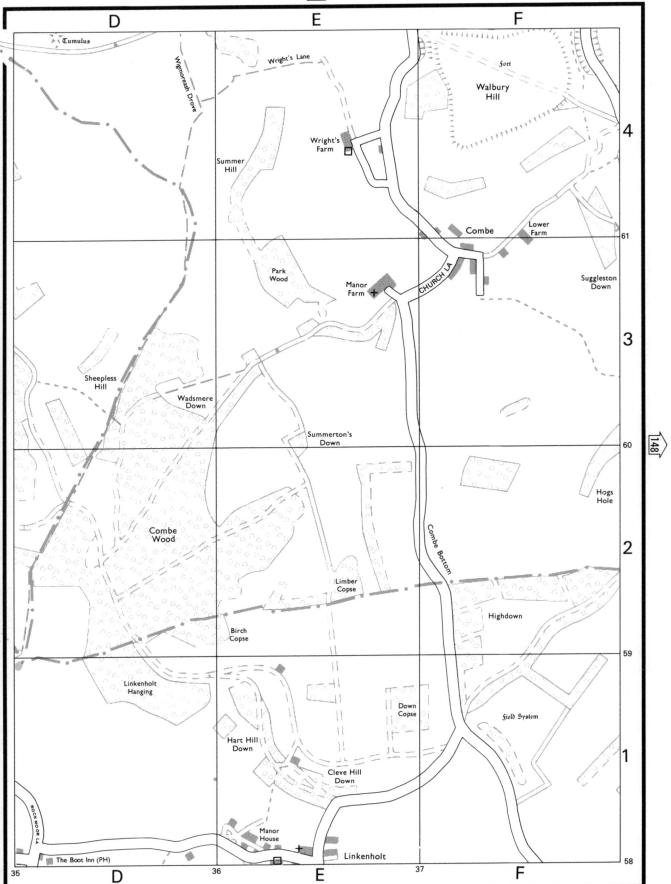

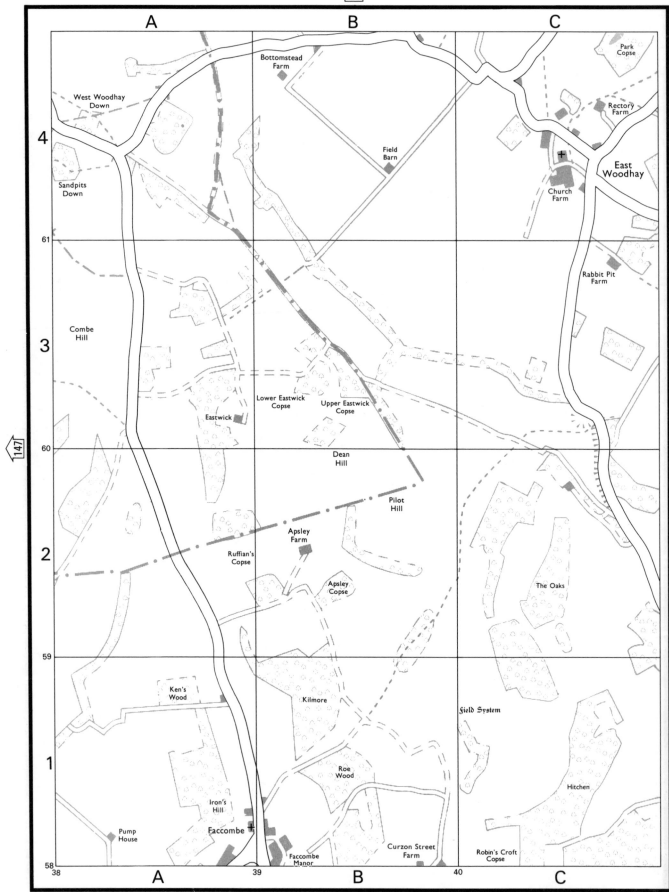

A B C

Park
Copse

Bottomstead
Farm

West Woodhay
Down

Rectory
Farm

Field
Barn

East
Woodhay

4

Sandpits
Down

Church
Farm

61

Rabbit Pit
Farm

Combe
Hill

3

Lower Eastwick
Copse

Upper Eastwick
Copse

Eastwick

60

Dean
Hill

Pilot
Hill

Apsley
Farm

Ruffian's
Copse

2

The Oaks

Apsley
Copse

59

Ken's
Wood

Kilmore

Field System

1

Roe
Wood

Hitchen

Iron's
Hill

Faccombe

Pump
House

Curzon Street
Farm

Robin's Croft
Copse

Faccombe
Manor

58

38 A 39 B 40 C

not continued, see key diagram

142

D E F

Watmore Farm
Moulsham Green
Copse Lane
Mill Farm
Pavilion
Blackwater River
Church Farm
The Yateley Lakes
FIRTREE CL
Sch
ST MICHAEL'S RD
MASON'S LA
SUN RAY
CEDARS CL
A321
LOWER CHURCH RD
HIGH ST
YATELEY RD
A321

FOX LA
B3272
CANBERRA
EXETER
MANTON
TOWER DR
CROSBY GDNS
VES CL
MOULSHAM LA
COOMBE RD
MILBRIDGE RD
RIVER RD
COSSE LA
MOULSHAM LA

4

Love Lane
CELANDINE CT
Green Lane
WEST GREEN
FALLOWFIELD
CLOVER LA
BORDER LA
HONEYSUCKLE CL
FIRGROVE RD
THE LINK
VICARAGE RD
VICARAGE LA
CHANDLERS LA
CRONDALL END
GREENLEYS
WHITES WAY
BROOME CL
SPINNEY
THE GALLOP
STABLE VIEW
PROPERT DR
WEST FRYERNE
HEATHWOOD
MILL LA

Yateley Green
Old School
FLORENCE CL
MACRAE RD
WILLOW
OAKLANDS
READING RD
Yateley
Schs
SANDHURST RD
WEYBRIDGE MEAD
KEVINS DR
PLOUGH RD
CORONATION RD
FRY'S LA
61

FIRGROVE RD
WREN CL
FALCON WAY
BRAMLING AVE
OWER
CAVES
PARTRIDGE AVE
SELWYN DR
CONNAUGHT
MONTEAGLE
KELVIN
SCHOOL LA
Liby Schools
WISTARIA LA
HOME PARK
LAWFORD CRES
CRANFORD PARK DR
WOODBOURNE
SOMERVILLE CRES
MANOR PARK DR
F Sta
P
3

ROKES PL
HOLBECHE CL
OLDCORNE HOLLOW
HUDDINGTON GLADE
GARNET FIELD
CATESBY GDNS
THROGMORTON RD
RYVES AVE
TESHMOND
TRESHAM
MALLARD
MORLEY CL
MONTEAGLE LA
HILLTOP VIEW
BYWAYS
THE DELL
LYMINGTON AVE
MINSTEAD
MERRON CL
FARM VIEW
JOHN CRES
WESTWORTH
HALL LA
HALL FARM CRES
MANOR PARK RD
CHURCH
MAPLE GDNS
BEAVER LA
DENHAM
HENLEY OR
Cricket Hill
POTLEY HILL RD
STEVENS HILL
ROUND CL
ASHFIELD GREEN
HARDWOOD
JESSE CL
Sch
B3272

Silver Fox Farm
GREENHAVEN
MONTEAGLE LA
VIGO LA
DICKENS CL
DOYLE GDNS
HARDY AVE
CHRISTIE WLK
KINGSLEY
HERIOT
WILDING CL
STOCKBRIDGE
MICHAELMAS CL
WALNUT
Sch
HANDFORD LA
LUCAS CL
NOTLEY
BROCKENHURST
MISTLETOE RD
DUNGELLS FARM CL
BARTONS LA
Hill Farm
60

P
Blackbush Market
Little Vigo
BROCKLANDS
GIBBS WAY
KEATS
CORNWALL
WORDSWORTH AVE
BYRON CL
COLEMAN
HARVEST
The Anchor (PH)
GORSELANDS
SILVER LADE
BIRCHVIEW
DUNGELLS LA
WHITLEY RD
FRESHWOOD DR
STONEY
TUDOR DR
WOODLANDS
Cemetery
Cottage Farm
2

VIGO LA
Works
Yateley Common
A30
59

Blackbushe Airport
A30
Hartford Bridge Flats
B3013
B3013
A327
B3013
Blackwater Tumulus Lodge
Barracks
MINLEY RD
Hornley Common
1

Forest Lodge
Yateley Drive
West Minley Farm
Minley Manor
Minley
A327
58

Clapperoak Cottage

80 D 81 E 82 F

150

not continued, see key diagram

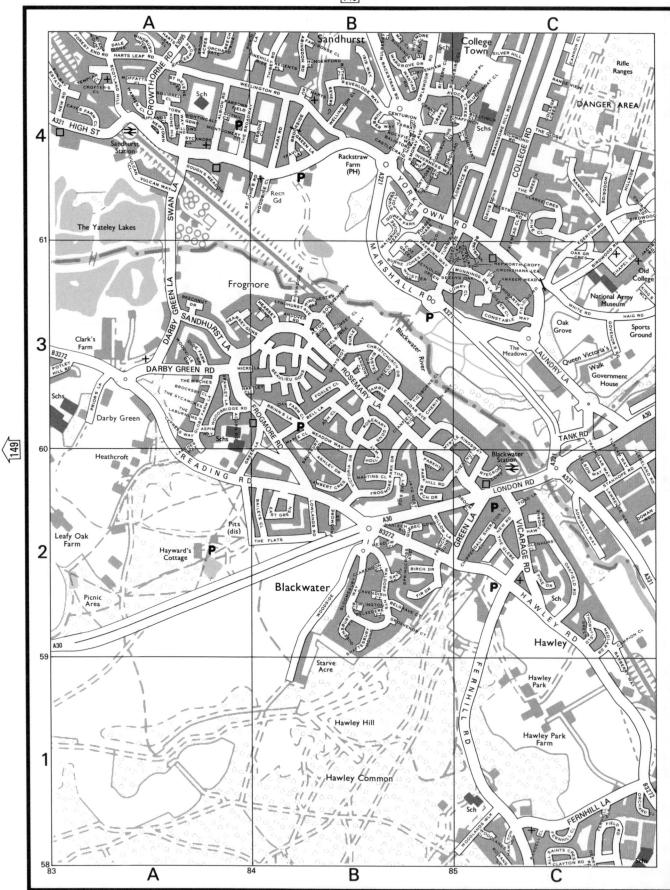

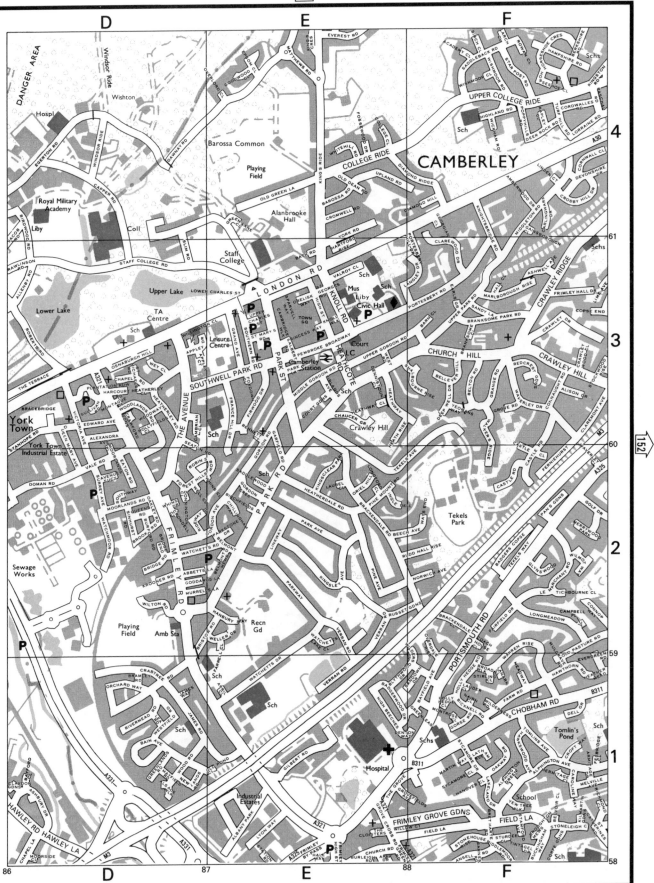

CAMBERLEY

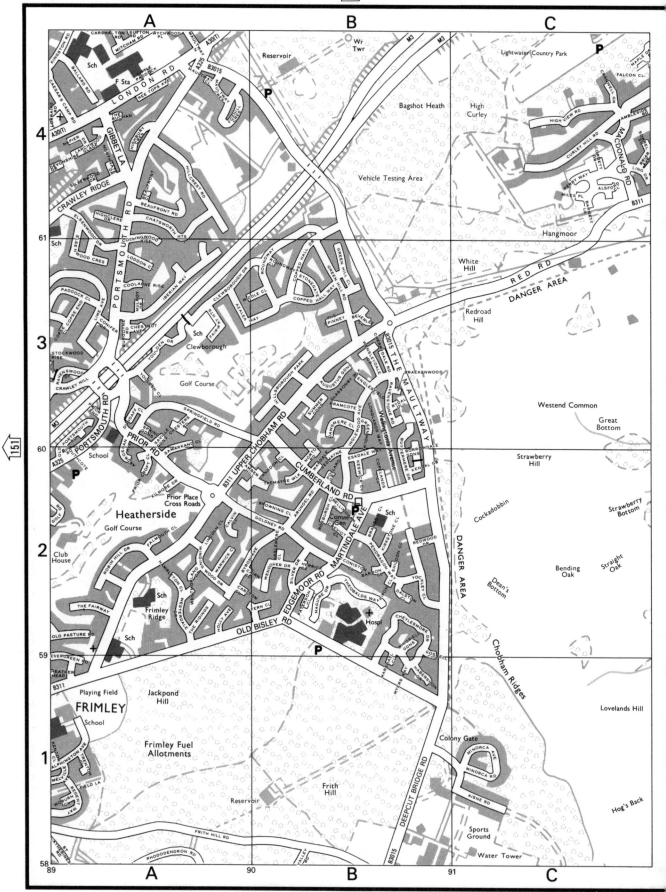

146

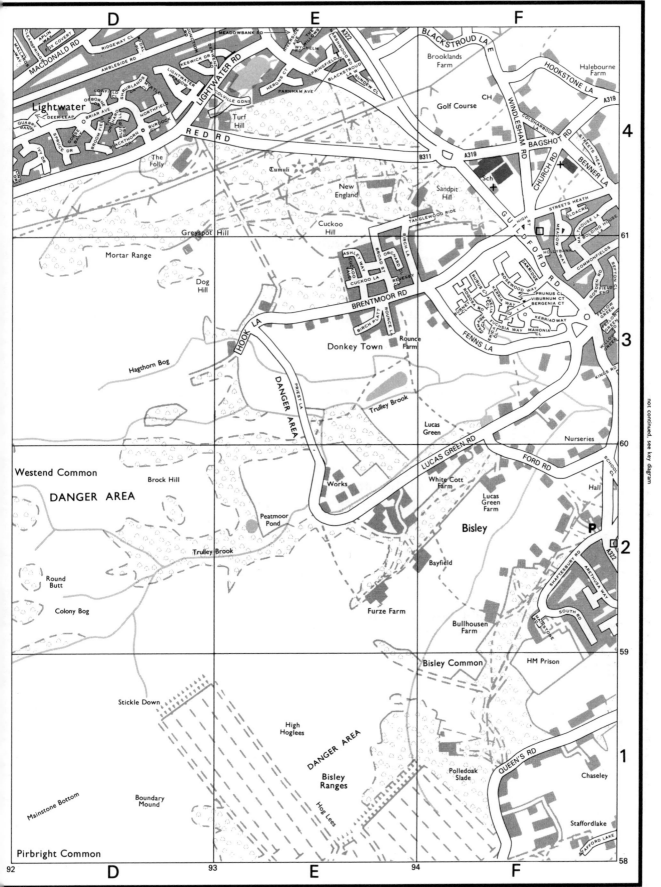

INDEX

EXPLANATION OF THE STREET INDEX REFERENCE SYSTEM

Street names are listed alphabetically and show the locality, the page number and a reference to the square in which the name falls on the map page.

Example:	Rushey Way. Read...87 E1

Rushey Way	This is the full street name, which may have been abbreviated on the map.
Read	This is the abbreviation for the town, village or locality in which the street falls.
87	This is the page number of the map on which the street name appears.
E1	The letter and figure indicate the square on the map in which the centre of the street falls. The square can be found at the junction of the vertical column carrying the appropriate letter and the horizontal row carrying the appropriate figure.

ABBREVIATIONS USED IN THE INDEX
Road Names

Approach	App	Lane	La
Avenue	Ave	North	N
Boulevard	Bvd	Orchard	Orch
Broadway	Bwy	Parade	Par
By-Pass	By-Ps	Passage	Pas
Causeway	Cswy	Place	Pl
Common	Comm	Pleasant	Plea
Corner	Cnr	Precinct	Prec
Cottages	Cotts	Promenade	Prom
Court	Ct	Road	Rd
Crescent	Cres	South	S
Drive	Dr	Square	Sq
Drove	Dro	Street,Saint	St
East	E	Terrace	Terr
Gardens	Gdns	Walk	Wlk
Grove	Gr	West	W
Heights	Hts	Yard	Yd

Aldermaston	Alde	135	D4
Aldworth	Aldw	32	C2
Arborfield	Arbo	114	B2
Ascot	Ascot	120	A3
Ashampstead	Asham	54	A4
Ashford	Ashf	97	F2
Aston Tirrold	Ast T	12	C4
Bagshot	Bags	145	E2
Ball Hill	Ball H	129	E2
Barkham	Bark	115	E1
Beech Hill	Bee H	138	B3
Beedon	Beed	51	E4
Beenham	Been	108	C3
Binfield	Binf	90	B1
Bisham	Bish	18	C4
Bisley	Bis	153	F2
Blackwater	Black	150	B2
Blewbury	Blew	12	A4
Bourne End	Bou E	3	D1
Boxford	Box	76	B2
Bracknell	Brac	118	C2
Bradfield	Brad	82	B3
Brightwalton	Brig	28	C2
Brimpton	Brim	133	F3
Bucklebury	Buck	80	C1
Burchett's Green	Bur G	38	B4
Burghfield Common	Bur C	110	C1
Burleigh	Burl	119	E4
Burnham	Burn	21	E2
Camberley	Camb	151	F4
Caversham	Caver	59	E2
Chaddleworth	Chadd	49	D4
Charvil	Char	61	D3
Chertsey	Chert	124	A1
Chieveley	Chiev	51	D1
Chilton	Chil	10	C4
Chilton Foliat	Chil F	72	C1
Cholsey	Chol	14	A4

Cold Ash	Cold A	106	B4
Combe	Combe	147	F4
Compton	Comp	31	F2
Cookham	Cook	20	A4
Crowthorne	Crow	143	D2
Datchet	Datch	68	B3
Dorney	Dorn	41	D2
East Garston	East G	47	E3
East Isley	East I	30	C3
Englefield	Eng G	95	E1
Eton	Eton	67	E4
Farnborough	Farn	8	C1
Farnham Common	Far C	22	B3
Fawley	Fawl	27	E4
Fawley (Bucks)	Faw (Bu)	15	E4
Feltham	Felt	98	C4
Finchampstead	Finch	141	F1
Flackwell Heath	Fla H	3	D4
Froxfield	Frox	99	D3
Fulmer	Fulm	23	E4
Goring	Gori	34	B3
Great Shefford	Gr She	48	A2
Greenham	Gree	131	E4
Ham	Ham	126	B1
Hambledon	Hamb	16	B4
Hampstead Norreys	Hamp N	52	C3
Hamstead Marshall	Ham M	129	D4
Harlington	Harl	71	E4
Harmonsworth	Harm	70	B4
Headley	Head	132	B1
Henley-on-Thames	Hen-O-T	15	E1
Hermitage	Herm	79	D4
Holyport	Holy	65	D4
Horton	Hort	69	D2
Hungerford	Hung	100	C3
Hurley	Hurl	17	F2
Hurst	Hurst	88	C3
Inkpen	Ink	127	E3

Iver	Iver	44	C4
Iver Heath	Iver H	23	F2
Kintbury	Kint	102	A1
Knowle Hill	Know H	37	F2
Lambourn	Lamb	25	E1
Leckhampstead	Leckh	50	A3
Letcombe Bassett	Let B	6	C4
Lightwater	Light	153	D4
Linkenholt	Link	147	E1
Little Marlow	Lit M	2	B3
Maidenhead	Maid	39	F2
Mapledurham	Maple	57	F3
Marlow	Mar	1	A1
Marlow Bottom	Mar B	1	B3
Medmenham	Medm	17	D3
Mortimer	Mort	137	D3
Moulsford	Moul	13	F2
Newbury	Newb	104	C2
Newell Green	New G	91	E2
Newtown	Newt	131	D2
Oakley Green	Oak G	66	A3
Old Windsor	Old W	95	D4
Padworth	Padw	109	F1
Pangbourne	Pang	56	A3
Peasemore	Pease	50	C4
Purley on Thames	Pur O T	57	D3
Reading	Read	85	D3
Remenham Hill	Rem H	16	B1
Sandhurst	Sand	150	B4
Shepperton	Shepp	125	F2
Shinfield	Shin	113	F3
Shiplake	Shipl	35	F1
Silchester	Silc	136	B1
Slough	Slough	42	C3
Sonning	Sonn	60	C2
South Stoke	Sou S	14	B2
Staines	Stai	96	C1
Stanford Dingley	Stan D	81	E2

Stanwell	Stan	70	B1
Stoke Poges	Sto P	22	C2
Streatley	Stre	34	A4
Sulham	Sulh	56	C1
Sulhamstead	Sulhd	110	B3
Swallowfield	Swal	139	E3
Tadley	Tad	134	C1
Taplow	Tapl	20	C1
Thatcham	That	106	C2
Theale	Thea	83	E2
Tidmarsh	Tidm	56	B1
Twyford	Twyf	61	E3
Upper Basildon	Upp B	55	D3
Virginia Water	Vir W	122	B3
Waltham St Lawrence	W St L	62	C3
Wargrave	Warg	36	B1
Wentworth	Went	121	F2
West End	West E	153	F3
West Isley	West I	10	A1
West Woodhay	West W	128	B2
Whitchurch-on-Thames	Whi-O-T	56	B4
White Waltham	Whi Wa	63	F4
Wickham	Wick	75	E2
Windlesham	Windl	146	B2
Windsor	Wind	67	F3
Winkfield	Wink	92	B3
Winnersh	Winn	88	A2
Winterbourne	Wint	77	E3
Wokingham	Woki	116	A4
Woodburn Green	Woo G	3	F4
Woodley	Wood	88	A4
Woolhampton	Wool	108	B1
Wraysbury	Wray	95	F4
Yateley	Yate	149	E3
Yattendon	Yatt	53	F1

Abattoirs Rd. Read   Avondale. Maid

Abattoirs Rd. Read ... 86 A4
Abbetts La. Camb ... 151 D2
Abbey Cl. Brac ... 118 B2
Abbey Cl. Newb ... 131 D4
Abbey Cl. Slough ... 41 F3
Abbey Cl. Woki ... 116 B4
Abbey Gdns. Chert ... 124 A2
Abbey Green. Chert ... 124 A2
Abbey Park. Bou C ... 110 C2
Abbey Rd. Bou E ... 2 C3
Abbey Rd. Chert ... 124 A1
Abbey Rd. Shepp ... 125 D1
Abbey Rd. Went ... 121 D1
Abbey Rd. Vir W ... 122 B3
Abbey Sq. Read ... 86 A4
Abbey St. Read ... 86 A4
Abbey Way. Bish ... 18 B3
Abbot Cl. Stai ... 97 E1
Abbot's Rd. Bur C ... 110 C1
Abbot's Wlk. Read ... 86 A4
Abbot's Wlk. Wind ... 66 C3
Abbots Dr. Vir W ... 122 B3
Abbots Rd. Newb ... 105 D1
Abbotsbury. Brac ... 117 F2
Abbotts Way. Slough ... 41 E3
Abelia Cl. Camb ... 153 E3
Aberford Cl. Read ... 85 E4
Abex Rd. Newb ... 105 E2
Abingdon Cl. Brac ... 118 C2
Abingdon Dr. Caver ... 59 E3
Abingdon Rd. East I ... 30 C4
Abingdon Rd. Sand ... 143 E1
Abingdon Wlk. Maid ... 19 F2
Abney Ct Dr. Bou E ... 3 D1
Aborfield Cl. Slough ... 42 C2
Abrahams Rd. Hen-O-T ... 15 E2
Acacia Ave. Crow ... 143 E1
Acacia Ave. Stai ... 125 D1
Acacia Ave. Wray ... 68 C2
Acacia Ct. Brac ... 118 A3
Acacia Mews. Harm ... 70 B4
Acacia Rd. Read ... 86 B3
Acacia Rd. Stai ... 97 D2
Academy Cl. Camb ... 151 F4
Accommodation La. Harm ... 70 A4
Ackrells Mead. Sand ... 142 C1
Acorn Dr. Woki ... 116 B4
Acorn Gr. Harl ... 71 F4
Acorn Rd. Black ... 150 A3
Acorn Pas. Wind ... 67 E3
Acre Rd. Read ... 113 D4
Acre The. Mar ... 1 C1
Adam Cl. Slough ... 42 A3
Adam Cl. Tad ... 134 C1
Adam Ct. Hen-O-T ... 15 F1
Adams Way. Read ... 86 C1
Addington Cl. Wind ... 67 D2
Addington Rd. Read ... 86 B3
Addiscombe Chase. Sulh ... 57 D2
Addiscombe Rd. Crow ... 143 E2
Addison Cl. Iver ... 44 C4
Addison Ct. Maid ... 20 A1
Addison Rd. Read ... 59 D1
Adelaide Cl. Slough ... 42 A2
Adelaide Rd. Ashf ... 97 E2
Adelaide Rd. Read ... 87 D3
Adelaide Sq. Wind ... 67 E3
Adelphi Gdns. Slough ... 42 C2
Adkins Rd. W St L ... 62 C4
Admirals Ct. Read ... 86 A3
Admiralty Way. Sand ... 150 C2
Admoor La. Been ... 109 E4
Adwell Dr. Winn ... 87 E1
Adwell Sq. Hen-O-T ... 15 E1
Adwood Ct. That ... 106 C2
Agar Cres. Brac ... 91 D1
Agars Pl. Datch ... 68 A4
Agate Cl. Woki ... 115 F4
Aggisters La. Woki ... 115 E2
Agincourt Cl. Woki ... 115 F3
Agricola Way. That ... 106 C1
Ainsdale Cres. Read ... 85 D2
Aintree Cl. Newb ... 105 E1
Aintree Cl. Stan ... 69 F3
Aintree. Lamb ... 25 D1
Airport Way. Stan ... 70 A2
Aisne Rd. Camb ... 152 C1
Ajax Ave. Slough ... 42 A3
Alan Pl. Read ... 85 D3
Alan Way. Slough ... 43 F4
Alandale Cl. Read ... 113 E4
Albain Cres. Stan ... 97 F3
Albany Park Dr. Winn ... 88 A2
Albany Park. Camb ... 151 E1
Albany Park. Stan ... 69 E4
Albany Pl. Eng G ... 96 A2
Albany Rd. Old W ... 68 A1
Albany Rd. Read ... 85 E4
Albany Rd. Wind ... 67 E3
Alben Rd. Binf ... 90 B2
Albert Ave. Chert ... 124 A3
Albert Cl. Slough ... 42 C2
Albert Rd. Ashf ... 97 F2
Albert Rd. Bags ... 145 F1
Albert Rd. Brac ... 118 A4
Albert Rd. Camb ... 151 E2
Albert Rd. Caver ... 59 D1
Albert Rd. Crow ... 143 D3
Albert Rd. Eng G ... 95 E1

Albert Rd. Hen-O-T ... 15 F1
Albert Rd. Newb ... 105 D2
Albert Rd. Old W ... 68 A1
Albert Rd. Wind ... 67 F2
Albert Rd. Woki ... 116 A3
Albert St. Maid ... 39 F4
Albert St. Slough ... 42 C2
Albert St. Wind ... 67 D3
Albion Cl. Slough ... 43 D3
Albion Rd. Sand ... 150 A4
Albion Terr. Read ... 86 B4
Albury Cl. Read ... 58 B1
Albury Gdns. Read ... 84 C2
Alcot Cl. Crow ... 143 D2
Aldborough Spur. Slough ... 42 C4
Aldbourne Ave. Read ... 87 D2
Aldbourne Rd. Burn ... 41 D4
Aldeburgh Cl. Caver ... 59 E4
Aldebury Rd. Maid ... 19 F1
Alden View. Wind ... 66 B3
Aldenham Cl. Caver ... 59 E3
Aldenham Terr. Brac ... 118 B2
Alder Cl. Eng G ... 95 F2
Alder Cl. Slough ... 41 F3
Alder Dr. Read ... 84 B3
Alder Gr. Yate ... 149 E3
Alderbourne La. Fulm ... 23 F4
Alderbrook Cl. Finch ... 142 C3
Alderbury Rd W. Slough ... 43 F2
Alderbury Rd. Slough ... 43 F2
Alderfield Cl. Thea ... 83 F2
Alderley Cl. Wood ... 60 C1
Alderman Willey Cl. Woki ... 116 A3
Alders The. That ... 106 B2
Alderside Wlk. Eng G ... 95 F2
Aldin Ave S. Slough ... 43 D2
Aldridge Rd. Slough ... 22 A1
Aldwick Dr. Maid ... 39 E3
Aldworth Cl. Brac ... 118 A3
Aldworth Cl. Read ... 85 E3
Aldworth Gdns. Crow ... 143 D3
Aldworth Rd. Comp ... 31 F2
Aldworth Rd. Upp B ... 55 D3
Alexander Rd. Stai ... 96 B2
Alexander Rd. That ... 106 C1
Alexandra Ave. Camb ... 151 D3
Alexandra Cl. Ashf ... 98 B1
Alexandra Cl. Stai ... 97 E1
Alexandra Cl. Ashf ... 98 B1
Alexandra Cl. Ashf ... 98 C2
Alexandra Rd. Ashf ... 98 C1
Alexandra Rd. Eng G ... 95 E1
Alexandra Rd. Maid ... 39 E4
Alexandra Rd. Read ... 86 B3
Alexandra Rd. Slough ... 42 B2
Alexandra Rd. Wind ... 67 E3
Alford Cl. Read ... 84 B4
Alfred St. Read ... 85 F4
Alice La. Burn ... 21 D1
Alison Cl. Bur C ... 110 C1
Alison Dr. Camb ... 151 F3
All Hallows Rd. Caver ... 59 E2
All Saints Cl. Woki ... 116 B4
All Saints Cres. Black ... 150 C1
All Saints Rise. New G ... 91 F1
All Saints' Ave. Maid ... 39 E4
All Saints' Rd. Light ... 146 B1
All Souls' Rd. Ascot ... 120 A3
Allanson Rd. Mar ... 1 C2
Allcot Cl. Felt ... 98 C4
Allcroft Rd. Read ... 86 B3
Allenby Rd. Camb ... 151 D3
Allenby Rd. Maid ... 39 D4
Allendale Cl. Sand ... 143 D1
Allendale Rd. Read ... 87 D2
Allerds Rd. Burn ... 22 A2
Alleyns La. Cook ... 19 E4
Allhusen Gdns. Fulm ... 23 F4
Alliance Ct. Ashf ... 98 B2
Allison Gdns. Pur O T ... 57 E3
Allkins Ct. Wind ... 67 E3
Allnatt Ave. Winn ... 88 B1
Allonby Cl. Read ... 87 E1
Allsmoor La. Brac ... 118 C3
Allyn Cl. Stai ... 96 C1
Alma Rd. Eton ... 41 F1
Alma Rd. Wind ... 67 E3
Alma St. Read ... 85 E4
Almners Rd. Chert ... 123 D1
Almond Ave. Newb ... 105 D3
Almond Cl. Eng G ... 95 D1
Almond Cl. Stai ... 125 E4
Almond Cl. Wind ... 67 D3
Almond Cl. Woki ... 115 E2
Almond Dr. Caver ... 59 F2
Almond Rd. Burn ... 21 E1
Almons Way. Slough ... 43 D4
Almswood Rd. Tad ... 135 D1
Alpha St N. Slough ... 42 C2
Alpha St S. Slough ... 42 C2
Alphington Ave. Camb ... 151 F1
Alphington Green. Camb ... 151 F1
Alpine St. Read ... 86 A3
Alsace Wlk. Camb ... 151 D1
Alsford Cl. Camb ... 152 C4
Alston Mews. That ... 106 B1
Alston Wlk. Caver ... 59 E1
Altmore. Bur G ... 38 C2
Alton Ct. Stai ... 123 F4

Alton Ride. Black ... 150 B3
Altona Way. Slough ... 42 A4
Altwood Bailey. Maid ... 39 D3
Altwood Cl. Burn ... 41 F4
Altwood Cl. Maid ... 39 D3
Altwood Dr. Maid ... 39 D3
Altwood Rd. Maid ... 39 D3
Alvista Ave. Burn ... 41 D4
Alwyn Rd. Maid ... 39 D4
Alwyns Cl. Chert ... 124 A2
Alwyns La. Chert ... 123 F2
Amanda Ct. Slough ... 43 E2
Ambarrow Cres. Sand ... 142 C1
Ambarrow La. Sand ... 142 C1
Ambassador. Brac ... 117 F2
Amber Hill. Camb ... 152 A2
Amberley Cl. Newb ... 104 C2
Amberley Ct. Maid ... 20 B2
Amberley Dr. Twyf ... 61 E3
Amberley Rd. Burn ... 41 F4
Amberwood Dr. Camb ... 151 F4
Amblecote Rd. Read ... 85 D4
Ambleside Cl. Wood ... 87 F4
Ambleside Dr. Felt ... 98 C4
Ambleside Dr. Felt ... 98 C4
Ambleside Rd. Light ... 153 D4
Ambleside Way. Stai ... 96 A1
Ambrook Road. Read ... 113 D4
Ambrose Pl. Read ... 85 F4
Ambury Rd. Comp ... 32 C2
Amen Corner Bsns Park. Brac ... 117 F4
Amerden Cl. Tapl ... 40 B4
Amerden La. Tapl ... 40 B4
Amerden La. Tapl ... 40 C2
Amerden Way. Slough ... 42 A2
Amersham Rd. Caver ... 59 E1
Amethyst Cl. Woki ... 115 E4
Amherst Rd. Read ... 87 D3
Amity Rd. Read ... 86 C4
Amity St. Read ... 86 C4
Amners Farm Rd. Bur C ... 112 A4
Ampere Rd. Newb ... 105 D2
Ancaster Dr. Ascot ... 119 F4
Ancastle Gr. Hen-O-T ... 15 E1
Andermans. Wind ... 66 B3
Anderson Ave. Read ... 87 D3
Anderson Cres. Arbo ... 114 C1
Anderson Dr. Ashf ... 98 B2
Anderson Pl. Bags ... 145 F2
Andover Cl. Read ... 57 E1
Andover Dro. Ham M ... 130 A2
Andover Rd. Ball H ... 130 B3
Andover Rd. Black ... 150 B3
Andover Rd. Newb ... 130 B3
Andrew Cl. Woki ... 116 C3
Andrews Cl. Thea ... 83 F2
Andrews Rd. Read ... 87 D2
Andrews Way. Mar B ... 1 B4
Angel Ct. Newb ... 105 D2
Angel Mead. Wool ... 108 B1
Angel Pl. Binf ... 90 B1
Angle Field Rd. Caver ... 59 E2
Anglers Way. Read ... 86 B4
Anglesey Cl. Ashf ... 98 A3
Angus Cl. Read ... 84 C2
Annadale. Cold A ... 79 E1
Anne Cl. Maid ... 19 F1
Anneforde Pl. Brac ... 91 D1
Anners Cl. Stai ... 123 E3
Annesley Gdns. Winn ... 88 B2
Annett Cl. Shepp ... 125 F3
Anscuff Rd. Slough ... 22 A1
Ansell Rd. Camb ... 151 F1
Anslow Pl. Slough ... 41 E4
Anson Cres. Read ... 113 E4
Anstey Pl. Bur C ... 111 D2
Anstey Rd. Read ... 86 A4
Anston Cl. Read ... 114 A4
Antares Cl. Woki ... 115 F3
Anthony Way. Slough ... 41 E3
Antrim Rd. Wood ... 87 E3
Apex Dr. Camb ... 151 E1
Aplin Way. Light ... 146 A1
Apple Cl. Pur O T ... 57 D2
Apple Cl. Woki ... 115 F3
Apple Tree Cl. Newb ... 130 C4
Apple Tree Way. Sand ... 143 E1
Appleby End. Read ... 85 D4
Appleby Gdns. Felt ... 98 C4
Applecroft. Maid ... 39 E2
Appledore. Brac ... 117 F2
Appleford Rd. That ... 106 B1
Appleford Rd. Read ... 85 D3
Appletree La. Shin ... 113 D1
Appletree La. Slough ... 43 E2
Appletree Pl. Brac ... 118 A4
Appley Ct. Camb ... 151 D3
Appley Dr. Camb ... 151 D3
Approach Rd. Ashf ... 98 B1
Approach Rd. Tapl ... 40 C4
April Cl. Camb ... 151 E1
Aquila Cl. Woki ... 115 F3
Aragon Cl. Ashf ... 98 C1
Arbor La. Winn ... 88 A2
Arbor Meadows. Winn ... 88 A2
Arborfield Rd. Shin ... 113 F2
Arbour Cl. Read ... 85 F3
Arcade The. Gori ... 34 B3
Arcade The. Newb ... 105 D2

Archangel Way. That ... 106 C2
Archer Cl. Maid ... 39 E4
Archway Rd. Caver ... 59 D1
Arden Cl. Brac ... 119 D4
Ardingly. Brac ... 118 A2
Ardler Rd. Caver ... 59 E1
Ardrossan Ave. Camb ... 152 A3
Ardwell Cl. Finch ... 142 C3
Arenal Dr. Crow ... 143 E2
Arethusa Way. Bis ... 153 F2
Argosy Gdns. Stai ... 96 C1
Argosy La. Stan ... 97 E4
Argyle Cl. Newb ... 104 C3
Argyle Rd. Read ... 85 F4
Argyle St. Read ... 85 F4
Arkle Ave. That ... 105 F2
Arkley Ct. Holy ... 40 B1
Arkwright Dr. Brac ... 117 E4
Arkwright Rd. Read ... 86 A2
Arkwright Rd. Stan ... 69 F3
Arlington Bsns Park. Read ... 84 A2
Arlington Cl. Brac ... 118 A4
Arlington Cl. Maid ... 38 C4
Arlington Rd. Ashf ... 97 F2
Arlington Square. Brac ... 118 A4
Armadale Ct. Read ... 85 E3
Armitage Ct. Ascot ... 120 B2
Armitage Dr. Camb ... 151 F1
Armour Hill. Read ... 57 E1
Armour Rd. Read ... 57 E1
Armour Wlk. Pur O T ... 57 E1
Armstrong Rd. Eng G ... 95 E1
Armstrong Way. Wood ... 88 A4
Arncliffe. Brac ... 118 A2
Arndale Way. Eng G ... 96 A2
Arnett Ave. Woki ... 141 F4
Arnewood Ave. Tad ... 135 E1
Arnhem Rd. Newb ... 105 D2
Arnold Rd. Stai ... 97 E1
Arnside Cl. Twyf ... 61 E4
Arrowhead Rd. Thea ... 83 F1
Arrowsmith Way. That ... 106 C1
Arthur Cl. Bags ... 145 F1
Arthur Pl. Read ... 86 B4
Arthur Rd. Newb ... 104 C1
Arthur Rd. Slough ... 42 B2
Arthur Rd. Wind ... 67 D3
Arthur Rd. Woki ... 116 A3
Arthurstone Birches. Binf ... 90 B2
Arun Cl. Winn ... 88 A1
Arundel Cl. Maid ... 39 D4
Arundel Ct. Slough ... 43 E1
Arundel Rd. Camb ... 152 B2
Arundel Rd. Wood ... 87 F4
Ascot Rd. Felt ... 98 A3
Ascot Rd. Holy ... 40 A1
Ascot Rd. Holy ... 64 C4
Ascot Rd. New G ... 91 F4
Ash Cl. Brig ... 28 B2
Ash Cl. Sand ... 150 B3
Ash Cl. Slough ... 44 A2
Ash Gr. Felt ... 98 C4
Ash Gr. Stai ... 97 E1
Ash Gr. Sto P ... 22 C3
Ash La. Bur C ... 111 D2
Ash La. Wind ... 66 B3
Ash Rd. Newt ... 131 F2
Ash Rd. Newt ... 132 A2
Ash Rd. Read ... 84 C4
Ash Rd. Stai ... 125 D3
Ash Terr. Cold A ... 106 A4
Ash Tree Gr. Ham M ... 129 D4
Ash Way. Woki ... 115 E2
Ashampstead Rd. Brad ... 82 A4
Ashampstead Rd. Read ... 85 D2
Ashampstead Rd. Upp B ... 55 D3
Ashbourne Gr. Maid ... 39 E2
Ashbourne Way. That ... 106 A2
Ashbourne. Brac ... 117 F2
Ashbrook Rd. Old W ... 95 D4
Ashburton Rd. Read ... 86 B1
Ashbury Dr. Camb ... 151 D1
Ashbury Dr. Read ... 84 B4
Ashby Ct. Read ... 113 D4
Ashby Way. Harm ... 71 D4
Ashcroft Cl. Caver ... 58 C3
Ashcroft Ct. Burn ... 21 D2
Ashcroft Rd. Maid ... 39 E4
Ashdale Cl. Stan ... 97 F3
Ashdale Park. Brac ... 142 B3
Ashdene Cl. Stai ... 98 B1
Ashdown Cl. Brac ... 119 D4
Ashdown. Maid ... 20 A2
Ashen Cross. Slough ... 44 A4
Ashenden Wlk. Far C ... 22 B4
Asher Dr. Burl ... 119 E4
Ashfield Green. Yate ... 149 F3
Ashford Ave. Ashf ... 98 A1
Ashford Cl. Ashf ... 97 F2
Ashford Cres. Ashf ... 97 F3
Ashford Hill Rd. Head ... 132 C1
Ashford Ind Est. Felt ... 98 B2
Ashford La. Dorn ... 41 D2
Ashford Rd. Felt ... 98 C3
Ashford Rd. Stai ... 97 E1
Ashford Rd. Stai ... 98 B1
Ashgrove Rd. Ashf ... 98 B2
Ashleigh Ave. Stai ... 96 B1
Ashley Cl. Read ... 87 D1

Ashley Cl. Shepp ... 125 F1
Ashley Dr. Black ... 150 B2
Ashley Hill Pl. Know H ... 36 C4
Ashley Park Ave. Shepp ... 125 F1
Ashley Park Cres. Shepp ... 125 F1
Ashley Park. Maid ... 20 A1
Ashley Rd. Read ... 85 F3
Ashley Way. West E ... 153 E3
Ashman Pl. Kint ... 102 A1
Ashman Rd. That ... 107 D2
Ashmere Cl. Bur C ... 84 B2
Ashmere Terr. Read ... 85 F4
Ashmore Green Rd. Cold A ... 106 A4
Ashmore Rd. Read ... 86 B1
Ashridge Green. Brac ... 118 A4
Ashridge Rd. Woki ... 116 B4
Ashton Cl. Read ... 84 B4
Ashton Pl. Maid ... 39 D3
Ashton Rd. Newb ... 105 D1
Ashton Rd. Woki ... 88 C1
Ashtrees Rd. Wood ... 87 F4
Ashurst Dr. Stai ... 124 C3
Ashview Cl. Ashf ... 97 F2
Ashview Gdns. Ashf ... 97 F2
Ashville Way. Woki ... 116 A3
Ashwell Ave. Camb ... 151 F3
Ashwood Cl. Read ... 84 A3
Ashwood Dr. Newb ... 105 E2
Ashwood Pl. Eng G ... 95 D1
Ashwood. Wood ... 87 E2
Ashworth Dr. That ... 106 B1
Askew Dr. Shin ... 113 D2
Aspen Cl. Slough ... 42 A4
Aspen Cl. Stai ... 96 C3
Aspin Way. Black ... 150 A3
Astleham Way. Stai ... 124 C3
Astley Cl. Woki ... 115 F4
Aston Ave. Read ... 57 D3
Aston Cl. Pangb ... 56 B3
Aston Ferry La. Rem H ... 16 B3
Aston La. Rem H ... 16 B2
Aston Mead. Wind ... 66 C3
Aston St. Ast T ... 12 C4
Astor Cl. Winn ... 88 B2
Astra Mead. Burl ... 92 A1
Atfield Gr. Windl ... 146 B2
Atherton Cl. Read ... 84 C4
Atherton Cl. Stan ... 70 B1
Atherton Cres. Hung ... 100 B3
Atherton Pl. Lamb ... 25 D2
Atherton Rd. Hung ... 100 B3
Athlone Cl. Maid ... 19 F1
Atrebatti Rd. Sand ... 143 E1
Auckland Cl. Maid ... 40 A4
Auckland Rd. Read ... 87 D3
Auclum Cl. Bur C ... 111 D1
Auclum La. Bur C ... 111 D1
Audley Cl. Newb ... 105 E3
Audley Dr. Maid ... 39 D2
Audley St. Read ... 85 F4
Audley Way. Burl ... 119 E3
Augur Cl. Stai ... 96 C2
August End. Read ... 85 E4
August End. Slough ... 43 F4
Augustine Cl. Stan ... 69 F2
Augustus Gdns. Camb ... 152 B3
Austen Gdns. Newb ... 131 D4
Austin Rd. Wood ... 87 F3
Australia Ave. Maid ... 39 F4
Australia Rd. Slough ... 43 D2
Autumn Cl. Caver ... 59 E4
Autumn Cl. Slough ... 41 F3
Autumn Wlk. Maid ... 39 D3
Autumn Wlk. Warg ... 36 B1
Avalon Rd. Bou E ... 3 D3
Avalon Rd. Read ... 87 E2
Avebury Sq. Read ... 86 B3
Avebury. Brac ... 118 A2
Avebury. Slough ... 42 A3
Avenue Rd. Felt ... 98 C3
Avenue Rd. Maid ... 40 A3
Avenue Rd. Stai ... 96 B2
Avenue Sucy. Camb ... 151 D2
Avenue The. Ascot ... 92 C1
Avenue The. Bou E ... 3 D2
Avenue The. Camb ... 151 D3
Avenue The. Crow ... 143 D3
Avenue The. Eng G ... 96 A2
Avenue The. Far C ... 22 A4
Avenue The. Light ... 146 A1
Avenue The. Maid ... 20 B2
Avenue The. Mort ... 137 D3
Avenue The. Old W ... 68 A1
Avenue The. Slough ... 68 A3
Avenue The. Stai ... 124 A4
Avenue The. Wray ... 68 C2
Averil Cl. Slough ... 41 E4
Avington Cl. Read ... 57 D3
Avocet Cres. Sand ... 150 C4
Avon Cl. Read ... 84 C3
Avon Cl. Slough ... 41 F3
Avon Gr. Brac ... 91 E1
Avon Pl. Read ... 86 B4
Avon Rd. Ashf ... 98 C1
Avon Way. Padw ... 109 F3
Avondale Ave. Stai ... 96 C1
Avondale Rd. Ashf ... 97 E3
Avondale. Maid ... 19 E1

157
Avonway. Newb
Birdhill Ave. Read

Avonway. Newb 105 E2
Axbridge Rd. Read 86 B1
Axbridge. Brac 118 C2
Ayebridges Ave. Stai 96 B1
Aylesbury Cres. Slough 42 B3
Aylesham Way. Yate 149 D3
Aylesworth Ave. Slough 22 A1
Aylesworth Spur. Old W 95 D4
Aylsham Cl. Read 84 C4
Aymer Cl. Stai 123 F4
Aymer Dr. Stai 123 F4
Aysgarth Park. Holy 40 A1
Aysgarth. Brac 118 A2
Azalea Way. Camb 152 A3
Azalea Way. Slough 43 F4

Babbington Rd. Read 113 E3
Bachelors Acre. Wind 67 E3
Back La. Been 109 D4
Back La. Brad 81 F2
Back La. Brim 134 B2
Back La. Kint 127 F4
Back La. Shin 139 D4
Back La. Stan D 81 F2
Back St. East G 47 E3
Backsideans. Warg 36 B1
Bacon Cl. Sand 150 B3
Bad Godesberg Way. Maid 39 F4
Baden Cl. Stai 97 D1
Bader Gdns. Slough 42 A2
Bader Way The. Wood 88 A3
Badgebury Rise. Mar B 1 B4
Badgemore La. Hen-O-T 15 E2
Badger Cl. Maid 39 E2
Badger Dr. Light 146 A1
Badger Dr. Twyf 61 E4
Badgers Copse. Camb 151 F2
Badgers Croft. Mort 137 D3
Badgers Hill. Vir W 122 B2
Badgers Holt. Yate 149 D3
Badgers Rise. Caver 59 D3
Badgers Sett. Crow 142 C3
Badgers Way. Brac 118 C4
Badgers Way. Mar B 1 B4
Badgers Wlk. Shipl 36 A2
Badgers Wood. Far C 22 B4
Badgerwood Dr. Camb 151 E1
Badminton Rd. Maid 39 D3
Bagnols Way. Newb 104 C1
Bagshot Green. Bags 145 F2
Bagshot Rd. Ascot 120 A1
Bagshot Rd. Brac 118 B2
Bagshot Rd. Eng G 95 E1
Bagshot Rd. Sunn 120 A1
Bagshot Rd. West E 153 F4
Baigents La. Windl 146 B2
Bailey Cl. Maid 39 F4
Bailey Cl. Wind 67 D3
Bailey's La. Hurst 62 C2
Baileys Cl. Black 150 B2
Baily Ave. That 106 A2
Bain Ave. Camb 151 D1
Bainbridge Rd. Bur C 84 A2
Baird Cl. Slough 42 A2
Baird Rd. Arbo 140 C4
Baird Rd. Bark 140 C4
Bakeham La. Eng G 95 E1
Baker St. Ast T 12 C4
Baker St. Read 85 F4
Bakers La. Maid 38 C4
Baldwin Rd. Burn 21 E1
Baldwin's Shore. Eton 67 E4
Balfour Cres. Brac 118 A2
Balfour Cres. Newb 130 B3
Balfour Dr. Bur C 84 A2
Balfour Rd. Mar 1 B2
Balintore Ct. Sand 150 B4
Ball Pit Rd. Beed 30 A3
Ball Pit Rd. East I 30 A3
Ballamore Cl. Bur C 84 A2
Ballard Green. Wind 66 C4
Ballard Rd. Camb 152 A4
Ballencrief Rd. Sunn 120 C1
Balliol Rd. Caver 58 B2
Balliol Way. Crow 143 F1
Balmoral Cl. Slough 41 F4
Balmoral Gdns. Wind 67 E2
Balmoral. Maid 19 D1
Balmore Dr. Caver 59 D2
Bamburgh Cl. Read 86 B2
Bamford Pl. Bur C 84 A2
Banbury Ave. Slough 41 F4
Banbury Gdns. Caver 59 E2
Banbury. Brac 118 C1
Bancroft Cl. Ashf 98 A2
Bancroft Pl. Bur C 84 A2
Band La. Eng G 96 A2
Bangors Cl. Iver 44 C4
Bangors Rd S. Iver 44 C4
Bank Side. Woki 141 F3
Banks Spur. Slough 42 A2
Bankside Cl. Read 86 B1
Bannard Rd. Maid 39 D3
Bannister Cl. Slough 43 F2
Bannister Gdns. Yate 149 F3
Bannister Pl. Brim 133 F3
Bannister Rd. Bur C 110 C1
Barbara Cl. Shepp 125 D2
Barbara's Meadow. Sulh 57 D1
Barber Cl. Hurst 88 C4
Barberry Way. Black 150 C1
Barbon Cl. Camb 152 B2
Barbrook Cl. Read 57 E2
Barchester Rd. Slough 43 F2
Barclay Rd. Bur C 84 B2
Barclose Ave. Caver 59 E2
Bardney Cl. Maid 39 E2
Bardolph's Cl. Maple 58 B4
Bardown. Chiev 51 D1
Barfield Rd. That 106 A2
Barge La. Swal 139 D3
Bargeman Rd. Maid 39 F2
Bargeman Rd. Maid 39 F3
Barholm Cl. Winn 87 F1
Barkby. Read 87 E1
Barker Ct. Hurst 88 C4
Barker Green. Brac 118 A2
Barker Rd. Chert 123 F1
Barkham Rd. Bark 115 E2
Barkham Rd. Woki 115 E2
Barkham Ride. Bark 141 F4
Barkham Ride. Woki 141 F4
Barkham St. Bark 115 E1
Barkhart Dr. Woki 116 B4
Barkhart Gdns. Woki 116 B4
Barkwith Cl. Winn 87 F1
Barley Cl. That 106 C1
Barley Fields. Woo G 3 F4
Barley Mead. New G 91 F1
Barley Mow Rd. Eng G 95 E2
Barley Mow Way. Stai 125 D3
Barley Wlk. Read 84 A3
Barn Cl. Ashf 98 A2
Barn Cl. Brac 118 B4
Barn Cl. Camb 151 F3
Barn Cl. Far C 22 A4
Barn Cl. Kint 102 A1
Barn Cl. Maid 19 F1
Barn Cl. Read 85 E2
Barn Cres. Newb 130 B4
Barn Dr. Maid 39 D2
Barn La. Hen-O-T 15 E2
Barn Owl Way. Bur C 111 D2
Barnard Cl. Caver 59 E3
Barnards Hill. Mar 1 B1
Barnes Rd. Camb 151 F1
Barnes Way. Iver 44 C3
Barnett Green. Brac 118 A2
Barnett La. Camb 152 C4
Barnfield. Iver 44 C4
Barnfield. Slough 41 E3
Barnhill Cl. Mar 1 B2
Barnhill Gdns. Mar 1 B2
Barnhill Rd. Mar 1 B2
Barnsdale Rd. Read 86 B2
Barnway. Eng G 95 E2
Barnwood Cl. Read 85 F4
Baron Ct. Read 85 F4
Barons Mead. Hen-O-T 15 E1
Barons Way. Stai 96 B1
Barossa Rd. Camb 151 E4
Barr's Rd. Burn 41 D4
Barracane Dr. Crow 143 D3
Barrack La. Wind 67 E3
Barracks La. Shin 113 D1
Barrett Cres. Woki 116 C3
Barrington Cl. Read 87 D3
Barris Head. Crow 143 F1
Barry Ave. Wind 67 E4
Barry Pl. Read 86 A4
Bartelotts Rd. Slough 21 F1
Bartholemew Pl. New G 91 F1
Bartholomew St. Newb 104 C1
Bartlemy Cl. Newb 130 C4
Bartlemy Rd. Newb 130 C4
Barton Cl. Shepp 125 D2
Barton Rd. Read 84 A4
Barton Rd. Slough 43 F2
Bartons Dr. Yate 149 E2
Barwell Cl. Crow 142 C2
Basemoors. Brac 118 C4
Basford Way. Wind 66 B2
Basil Cl. Read 86 C1
Basingstoke Rd. Alde 109 D1
Basingstoke Rd. Read 86 A2
Basingstoke Rd. Shin 139 E3
Basingstoke Rd. Swal 139 E3
Baskerville La. Shipl 36 A2
Baslow Rd. Winn 88 A1
Basmore Ave. Shipl 36 A2
Bass Mead. Cook 19 F3
Bassett Cl. Winn 114 B4
Bassett Rd. Let B 6 C4
Bassett Way. Slough 21 F1
Batcombe Mead. Brac 118 C1
Bates Cl. Slough 43 F4
Bath Rd. Been 108 B1
Bath Rd. Brad 108 B1
Bath Rd. Bur G 38 B3
Bath Rd. Burn 41 E4
Bath Rd. Camb 151 E3
Bath Rd. Frox 99 D2
Bath Rd. Harl 71 E3
Bath Rd. Harm 70 B3
Bath Rd. Hung 100 C4
Bath Rd. Know H 38 B3
Bath Rd. Maid 38 B3
Bath Rd. Newb 104 B3
Bath Rd. Padw 108 B1
Bath Rd. Read 85 E3
Bath Rd. Slough 41 E4
Bath Rd. Sonn 60 C1
Bath Rd. That 108 B1
Bath Rd. Thea 108 B1
Bath Rd. Warg 62 A4
Bath Rd. Wool 108 B1
Bathurst Cl. Iver 44 C2
Bathurst Rd. Winn 88 A1
Bathurst Wlk. Iver 44 C2
Battery End. Newb 130 B3
Battle Cl. Newb 104 B2
Battle Rd. Gori 34 C4
Battle Rd. Newb 130 B3
Battle St. Read 85 F4
Battlemead Cl. Maid 20 B2
Batty's Barn Cl. Woki 116 B3
Baxendales The. Newb 105 E1
Bay Cl. Read 86 C1
Bay Dr. Brac 118 C4
Bay Rd. Brac 118 C4
Bay Tree Ct. Burn 21 E1
Bay Tree Rise. Read 84 B3
Baydon Dr. Read 85 F3
Baydon Rd. East G 46 B2
Baydon Rd. Gr She 46 B2
Baydon Rd. Lamb 46 B2
Bayfield Ave. Camb 151 F1
Bayford Cl. Camb 151 D1
Bayford Dr. Read 84 C2
Bayley Cres. Burn 41 D4
Bayley Ct. Winn 88 A1
Baylis Rd. Slough 42 C3
Bayliss Rd. Warg 36 B1
Baysfarm Ct. Harm 70 B3
Beacon Rd. Felt 71 D1
Beaconsfield Rd. Far C 22 B3
Beaconsfield Way. Read 87 D1
Beal's La. Sulh 84 A4
Beale Cl. Woki 116 A4
Bean Oak Rd. Woki 116 C3
Beancroft Rd. That 106 B1
Bear La. Newb 105 D2
Bear La. Warg 37 D2
Beard's Rd. Ashf 98 C1
Bearwood Path. Winn 88 A1
Bearwood Rd. Woki 115 E3
Beatty Dr. Read 84 C4
Beauchief Cl. Read 113 F4
Beaufield Cl. Wood 87 E4
Beaufort Cl. Mar 1 C1
Beaufort Gdns. Ascot 119 F4
Beaufort Gdns. Mar 1 C1
Beaufort Pl. Maid 40 B2
Beauforts. Eng G 95 E2
Beaufront Cl. Camb 152 A4
Beaufront Rd. Camb 152 A4
Beaulieu Cl. Brac 119 D3
Beaulieu Cl. Datch 68 A3
Beaulieu Gdns. Sand 150 B3
Beaumont Cl. Maid 39 D2
Beaumont Dr. Ashf 98 B2
Beaumont Gdns. Brac 118 C2
Beaumont Rd. Slough 42 B4
Beaumont Rd. Wind 67 E3
Beaumont Rise. Mar 1 C1
Beaver La. Yate 149 F3
Beaver Way. Wood 88 A4
Beavers Cl. Tad 135 D1
Becket Cl. Woki 116 C3
Beckford Ave. Brac 118 A2
Beckford Cl. Woki 88 C1
Beckfords. Upp B 55 D3
Beckings Way. Fla H 3 E4
Bede Wlk. Read 86 B2
Bedfont Cl. Felt 71 E1
Bedfont Ct. Stan 70 A2
Bedfont La. Felt 98 C4
Bedfont Rd. Felt 98 B3
Bedfont Rd. Stan 70 C1
Bedford Ave. Slough 42 A4
Bedford Cl. Maid 39 D2
Bedford Cl. Newb 130 B3
Bedford Dr. Far C 22 A3
Bedford Gdns. Woki 115 F4
Bedford La. Sunn 121 D2
Bedford Rd. Read 85 F4
Bedfordshire Way. Woki 115 F3
Bedwins La. Cook 19 D3
Beech Ave. Camb 151 E2
Beech Cl. Ashf 98 B2
Beech Cl. Bur C 111 D2
Beech Cl. Stan 97 E4
Beech Dr. Black 150 B2
Beech Glen. Brac 118 A3
Beech Hill Rd. Bee H 138 C3
Beech Hill Rd. Sunn 120 C2
Beech La. Gori 14 C1
Beech La. Read 87 D1
Beech Rd. Felt 98 C4
Beech Rd. Maple 58 B4
Beech Rd. Newt 132 A2
Beech Rd. Pur O T 57 D3
Beech Rd. Read 86 C1
Beech Rd. Slough 43 F2
Beech Ride. Sand 143 D1
Beech Tree La. Stai 124 A4
Beech Wlk. That 106 C1
Beecham Rd. Read 85 E4
Beechbrook Ave. Yate 149 F3
Beechcroft Cl. Ascot 120 B3
Beechcroft. Brac 118 A3
Beechcroft. Hamp N 53 D3
Beeches Dr. Far C 22 A4
Beeches Rd. Far C 22 A4
Beeches The. Gori 34 A3
Beeches The. Read 57 E2
Beechingstoke. Mar 1 C2
Beechmont Ave. Went 122 B2
Beechnut Cl. Woki 115 F3
Beechnut Dr. Black 150 A3
Beechtree Ave. Eng G 95 D1
Beechtree Ave. Mar B 1 B3
Beechwood Ave. Read 84 B4
Beechwood Ave. Stai 97 D1
Beechwood Ave. Wood 87 E4
Beechwood Cl. Burl 92 C1
Beechwood Dr. Maid 39 D3
Beechwood Dr. Mar 18 A4
Beechwood Gdns. Slough 42 C2
Beechwood Rd. Slough 42 B4
Beechwood Rd. Went 122 A1
Beedon Dr. Brac 117 F2
Beehive La. Brac 117 E4
Beehive Rd. Brac 117 E4
Beehive Rd. Stai 96 C2
Beeston Way. Read 114 A4
Beggars Hill Rd. Char 61 D1
Beighton Cl. Read 113 F4
Beir Path The. Sou S 14 A2
Belfast Ave. Slough 42 B4
Belgrave Ct. Black 150 B2
Belgrave Rd. Slough 42 C3
Bell Cl. Slough 43 D4
Bell Corner. Chert 123 F1
Bell Ct. Hurl 17 F2
Bell Foundary La. Woki 116 B4
Bell Foundry La. Woki 116 B4
Bell Hill. Ham M 130 A2
Bell Hill. Newb 130 A2
Bell Holt. Newb 130 B3
Bell La. Comp 32 C2
Bell La. Eton 41 F1
Bell La. Hen-O-T 15 F2
Bell La. Ink 127 E2
Bell La. Sand 150 B3
Bell Pl. Bags 145 F2
Bell St. Hen-O-T 15 F1
Bell St. Maid 39 F3
Bell View Cl. Wind 66 C3
Bell View. Wind 66 C3
Bell Weir Cl. Wray 96 A3
Belle Ave. Read 87 D3
Belle Vue Cl. Stai 124 A4
Belle Vue Rd. Hen-O-T 35 E4
Belle Vue Rd. Read 85 F4
Bellever Hill. Camb 151 F3
Bellingham Cl. Camb 152 B2
Bellingham Wlk. Caver 59 D3
Bells Hill Green. Sto P 23 D3
Bells Hill. Sto P 23 D2
Bells La. Hort 69 D2
Bellswood La. Iver 44 A4
Belmont Cres. Maid 39 E4
Belmont Dr. Maid 39 E4
Belmont Mews. Camb 151 E2
Belmont Park Ave. Maid 39 E4
Belmont Park Rd. Maid 39 E4
Belmont Rd. Camb 151 E2
Belmont Rd. Crow 143 D3
Belmont Rd. Maid 39 E4
Belmont Rd. Read 85 E4
Belmont Vale. Maid 39 E4
Belmont. Slough 42 A4
Belton Rd. Camb 151 F3
Belvedere Ct. Black 150 B2
Belvedere Dr. Newb 131 D4
Belvedere Wlk. Winn 88 A2
Belvoir Cl. Camb 151 F1
Bembridge Ct. Slough 42 C2
Bembridge Pl. Read 86 B4
Benbricke Green. Brac 91 D1
Bence The. Stai 123 D3
Bencombe Rd. Mar B 1 C3
Benedict Dr. Felt 98 B4
Benedict Green. New G 91 F1
Benen-stock Rd. Stan 70 A1
Benetfeld Rd. Binf 90 A1
Benham Hill. Newb 105 F2
Benham Hill. That 105 F2
Benham La. Swal 139 E2
Benhams La. Faw (Bu) 15 F4
Benner La. West E 153 F4
Bennet Rd. Read 86 A1
Bennett Cl. Newb 104 C3
Bennett Ct. Camb 151 E3
Bennett's Hill. Bur C 111 E4
Bennetts Cl. Slough 42 A3
Benning Cl. Wind 66 B2
Benning Way. Woki 116 B4
Bennings Cl. Brac 91 D1
Benson Cl. Read 86 B2
Benson Cl. Slough 43 D3
Benson Rd. Crow 142 C3
Bentley Park. Burn 21 E2
Bentley Rd. Slough 42 A3
Benyon Ct. Read 85 F3
Benyon Mews. Read 85 F3
Beomonds Row. Chert 124 A1
Bere Court Rd. Pangb 56 A2
Bere Rd. Brac 118 C2
Beresford Ave. Slough 43 E3
Beresford Rd. Read 85 F4
Bergenia Ct. Camb 153 F3
Berkeley Ave. Read 85 F3
Berkeley Cl. Stan 96 B3
Berkeley Gdns. Shepp 125 F1
Berkeley Mews. Mar 1 C1
Berkeley Rd. Newb 104 C1
Berkley Cl. Maid 39 D4
Berkshire Ave. Slough 42 A4
Berkshire Dr. Read 84 B4
Berkshire Rd. Camb 151 F4
Berkshire Rd. Hen-O-T 35 E4
Berkshire Way. Brac 117 E3
Berners Cl. Slough 41 F3
Bernersh Cl. Sand 143 E1
Berries Rd. Cook 20 A4
Berry Field. Slough 43 E4
Berry Hill. Tapl 40 B4
Berrybank. Sand 150 C3
Berrylands Rd. Caver 59 D2
Berrys La. Bur C 85 D1
Berrys Rd. Buck 107 E3
Berryscroft Rd. Stai 97 E1
Berstead Cl. Read 87 D1
Berwick Ave. Slough 42 A3
Berwick Cl. Mar 1 B2
Berwick La. Mar 1 B2
Berwick Rd. Mar 1 B2
Beryl Cl. Woki 115 F4
Bessel's Way. Blew 12 A4
Bestobell Rd. Slough 42 B4
Betam Rd. Read 86 B4
Betchworth Ave. Read 87 D2
Bethany Waye. Felt 98 C4
Bethesda Cl. Upp B 55 D3
Bethesda St. Upp B 55 D4
Betjeman Wlk. Yate 149 D2
Betteridge Rd. That 106 C1
Beverley Cl. Camb 152 B3
Beverley Cl. Mar 1 B1
Beverley Cl. That 106 B2
Beverley Ct. Slough 43 D2
Beverley Gdns. Maid 19 D1
Beverley Gdns. Warg 36 C1
Beverley Rd. Read 57 E1
Beverley Rd. Shepp 125 F4
Bevers The. Mort 137 D3
Bexley Ct. Read 85 E3
Bexley St. Wind 67 E3
Bibury Cl. Wood 87 E2
Bicknell Rd. Camb 151 F1
Bideford Cl. Wood 87 E3
Bideford Spur. Slough 22 A1
Big La. Lamb 25 D2
Bigbury Gdns. Read 86 B2
Bigfrith La. Cook 19 D3
Biggs La. Bark 141 D4
Billet Bridge. Stai 97 D2
Billet La. Slough 44 A4
Billet Rd. Stan 97 D3
Billing Ave. Woki 141 F3
Billingbear La. Binf 90 A3
Billington Way. Cold A 106 B3
Binbrook Cl. Winn 87 E1
Binfield Rd. Binf 116 C4
Binfield Rd. Brac 118 A4
Binfield Rd. Woki 116 C4
Bingham Dr. Stai 97 E1
Bingham Rd. Burn 41 D4
Binghams The. Maid 40 A2
Bingley Gr. Wood 60 C1
Binsted Dr. Black 150 B3
Birch Ave. Read 85 D4
Birch Cl. Camb 151 F4
Birch Dr. Black 150 B2
Birch Gr. Shepp 125 F4
Birch Gr. Slough 42 A4
Birch Gr. Wind 66 B3
Birch Hill Rd. Brac 118 A1
Birch La. Burl 119 D4
Birch La. Silc 136 C3
Birch La. West E 153 E3
Birch Platt. West E 153 E3
Birch Rd. Bur C 111 D2
Birch Rd. Tad 134 C1
Birch Rd. Windl 146 C2
Birch Rd. Woki 142 A4
Birch Side. Crow 142 C3
Birch Tree View. Light 146 A1
Birch View. Read 86 C1
Birches The. Black 150 A3
Birches The. Gori 34 A3
Birchetts Cl. Brac 118 A4
Birchfields. Camb 151 E2
Birchington Rd. Wind 67 D3
Birchland Cl. Silc 136 C3
Birchmead. Winn 88 B1
Birchview Cl. Yate 149 E2
Birchwood Cl. Caver 59 E3
Birchwood Dr. Light 146 B1
Birchwood Rd. Newb 105 E2
Birchwood The. Read 57 D3
Bird Mews. Woki 116 A3
Birdhill Ave. Read 86 B1

Birds La. Wool

Browning Cl. That

Birds La. Wool 107 F2
Birdwood Rd. Maid 39 D4
Birdwood Rd. Sand 151 D4
Birkbeck Rd. Crow 143 F1
Birkdale. Brac 117 F1
Birkhall Cl. Read 84 B3
Birley Rd. Slough 42 B4
Bishop Ct. Maid 39 E3
Bishop Duppas La. Shepp . 125 F1
Bishop's La. New G 92 A4
Bishop's La. Wink 92 A4
Bishop's Rd. Read 87 D3
Bishopdale. Brac 118 A3
Bishops Cl. Tad 135 D1
Bishops Dr. Felt 71 E1
Bishops Dr. Woki 116 B4
Bishops Farm Cl. Oak G 66 A3
Bishops Gr. Windl 146 B2
Bishops Orch. Far C 22 A1
Bishops Rd. Brad 81 F2
Bishops Rd. Slough 43 D2
Bishops Way. Stai 96 B1
Bishops Wlk. Bou E 3 F3
Bishopsgate Rd. Eng G 95 D2
Bishopswood La. Tad 134 C1
Bishopswood Rd. Tad 134 C1
Bissley Dr. Maid 39 D2
Bitham La. Ham 126 B3
Bitham La. Ink 127 D2
Bitham Rd. Farn 8 B4
Bittern Cl. Sand 150 B4
Bitterne Ave. Read 84 A3
Bix Hill. Faw (Bu) 15 D3
Bix La. Maid 38 C4
Black Boy La. Hurl 17 E2
Black Butts Cotts. Cook 20 A4
Black Horse Cl. Wind 66 B3
Black Park Rd. Fulm 23 F2
Black Park Rd. Iver H 23 F2
Blackamoor La. Maid 40 A4
Blackberry Cl. Shepp 125 F3
Blackbird Cl. Bur C 111 D2
Blackbird Cl. Sand 150 B4
Blackcap Pl. Sand 150 C4
Blackdown Way. That 106 B1
Blackett Cl. Stai 123 F4
Blacklands Rd. Buck 107 E3
Blackley Cl. Winn 87 F2
Blackmeadows. Brac 118 B2
Blackmoor Cl. Burl 119 E4
Blackmoor Wood. Burl 119 E4
Blacknest Rd. Went 121 F3
Blackpond La. Far C 22 A2
Blacksmith Row. Slough 44 A1
Blacksmith's La. Stai 124 B3
Blacksmiths La. Chert 124 A1
Blackstroud La E. Light 146 B1
Blackstroud La W. Light 153 E4
Blackthorn Dell. Slough 43 E2
Blackthorn Dr. Light 153 D4
Blackthorne Rd. Stan 69 F2
Blackwater Cl. Caver 59 F2
Blackwater Cl. Shin 113 D1
Blackwater Rise. Bur C 84 A2
Blagdon Rd. Read 86 B1
Blagrave La. Caver 58 B2
Blagrave St. Read 86 A4
Blagrove Rise. Read 84 B3
Blagrove Dr. Woki 115 F2
Blagrove La. Woki 115 F2
Blair Rd. Slough 42 C3
Blaire Park. Yate 149 D4
Blake Cl. Crow 143 E2
Blake Cl. Woki 116 C4
Blake's La. Tad 135 E1
Blakeney Fields. Gr She 48 A2
Blakes Cotts. Read 86 B4
Blakes La. Warg 37 D1
Blakes Rd. Warg 36 C2
Blakes Ride. Yate 149 D3
Blanchard Cl. Wood 88 A4
Bland's Cl. Bur C 110 C1
Blandford Cl. Slough 43 E2
Blandford Rd N. Slough 43 E2
Blandford Rd S. Slough 43 E2
Blandford Rd. Read 113 E4
Blandy Rd. Hen-O-T 35 E4
Blandy's La. Upp B 55 D3
Blandys Hill. Kint 128 A4
Blatch's Cl. Thea 83 E2
Blay's La. Eng G 95 D1
Blays La. Eng G 95 E1
Bledlow Cl. Newb 130 B3
Blenheim Cl. Slough 43 F3
Blenheim Cl. Woki 115 F3
Blenheim Gdns. Read 86 C3
Blenheim Rd. Caver 59 D2
Blenheim Rd. Maid 39 D4
Blenheim Rd. Newb 104 C1
Blenheim Rd. Read 86 C3
Blenheim Rd. Slough 43 E1
Bletchmore Cl. Harl 71 E4
Blewburton Wlk. Brac 118 C3
Blewbury Dr. Read 84 A4
Blewbury Hill. Blew 12 B4
Blinco La. Slough 43 F4
Blind La. Bou E 3 D3
Blind La. Fla H 3 D3
Blind La. Lamb 25 D1

Blomfield Dale. Brac 117 E4
Blomfield Dr. Brac 91 E1
Blondell Cl. Harm 70 B4
Bloomfield Rd. Maid 39 D3
Bloomfieldhatch La. Bee H ...138 A4
Bloomfieldhatch La. Shin 112 C2
Bloomsbury Way. Black 150 B2
Blossom Ave. Thea 83 F2
Blossom La. Thea 83 F2
Bloxworth Cl. Brac 118 C3
Blue Ball La. Eng G 95 F2
Blue Coat Wlk. Brac 118 B2
Bluebell Dr. Bur C 110 C2
Bluebell Hill. Brac 118 C4
Bluebell Meadow. Winn 88 B2
Bluebell Rise. Light 153 D4
Bluecoats. That 106 B2
Bluethroat Cl. Sand 150 C4
Blumfield Cres. Burn 41 F4
Blumfield Ct. Slough 21 E1
Blundell's Rd. Read 84 C4
Blunts Ave. Harm 71 D4
Blyth Ave. That 106 C1
Blythe Cl. Iver 44 C4
Blythewood La. Ascot 119 F4
Blythwood Dr. Camb 151 E1
Boames La. Ham M 129 F3
Boarlands Cl. Slough 42 A2
Boathouse Reach. Hen-O-T ... 15 F1
Bobgreen Ct. Read 113 E4
Bobmore La. Mar 1 C2
Bockhampton Rd. Lamb 25 E1
Bockmer La. Medm 17 D4
Bodens Ride. Brac 119 F1
Bodmin Ave. Slough 42 A4
Bodmin Cl. That 106 B1
Bodmin Rd. Wood 87 E3
Body Rd. Read 85 F4
Bog La. Brac 119 D3
Boham's Rd. Blew 11 E3
Bolding House La. West E 153 F4
Boldrewood. Bur C 110 C1
Boleyn Cl. Stai 96 C2
Bolingbroke Way. That 106 C2
Bolney Rd. Shipl 36 A3
Bolton Ave. Wind 67 E2
Bolton Cres. Wind 67 E2
Bolton Rd. Wind 67 E2
Bolton's La. Harl 71 E4
Bolwell Cl. Twyf 61 F2
Bomer Cl. Harm 71 D4
Bomford Cl. Herm 78 C3
Bond St. Eng G 95 E2
Bone La. Newb 105 E2
Bones La. Shipl 35 D2
Booth Dr. Stai 97 E1
Borderside. Slough 43 D4
Borderside. Yate 149 D3
Borrowdale Cl. Stai 96 A1
Borrowdale Gdns. Camb 152 B2
Borrowdale Rd. Winn 88 A2
Boscombe Cl. Stai 123 E4
Boscowen Way. That 107 D1
Bosham Cl. Road 114 A4
Bosman Dr. Windl 146 A3
Bostock La. Thea 83 D1
Boston Ave. Read 85 F3
Boston Gr. Slough 42 B4
Boston Rd. Hen-O-T 35 F4
Bosworth Gdns. Wood 87 F2
Botany Cl. That 106 C2
Bothy The. Warg 36 B1
Botmoor Way. Chadd 48 C4
Bottisham Cl. Winn 114 B4
Bottle La. Binf 91 D3
Bottle La. Know H 38 A2
Bottle La. New G 91 D3
Bottom La. Sulhd 110 B4
Bouldish Farm Rd. Ascot 119 F3
Boult St. Read 86 B4
Boult's Wlk. Read 86 A3
Boulters Cl. Maid 20 B1
Boulters Cl. Slough 42 A2
Boulters Cl. Wood 87 F4
Boulters Ct. Maid 20 B1
Boulters Gdns. Maid 20 B1
Boulters La. Maid 20 B1
Boulton Rd. Read 86 A2
Boultons La. Binf 90 C1
Boundary Cl. Read 84 B3
Boundary La. Caver 58 C2
Boundary Pl. Woo G 3 E4
Boundary Rd. Newb 105 D1
Boundary Rd. Stai 97 E2
Boundary Rd. Tapl 40 C4
Boundary Rd. Woo G 3 E4
Bourn Cl. Winn 87 E1
Bourne Arch. That 106 A2
Bourne Ave. Chert 124 A3
Bourne Ave. Read 86 A2
Bourne Ave. Wind 67 E2
Bourne Cl. Bou E 3 D3
Bourne Cl. Bur C 84 A2
Bourne End Rd. Bou E 20 C4
Bourne End Rd. Tapl 20 C4
Bourne Meadow. Stai 123 D3
Bourne Rd. Pangb 56 C3
Bourne Rd. Slough 42 B2
Bourne Rd. That 106 A2

Bourne Rd. Went 122 B2
Bourne Vale. Hung 100 B3
Bourneside. Went 122 A1
Bourton Cl. Read 84 C4
Bouverie Way. Slough 43 F1
Boveney Cl. Slough 42 A2
Boveney New Rd. Eton 41 F1
Boveney Rd. Dorn 41 E1
Bovingdon Hts. Mar 1 C1
Bowden Cl. Felt 98 C4
Bowden Rd. Ascot 120 B2
Bower Way. Slough 41 F3
Bowes Rd. Stai 96 C1
Bowes Rd. That 106 B1
Bowfell Cl. Read 57 E1
Bowland Drive. Brac 118 C1
Bowling Ct. Hen-O-T 15 E2
Bowling Green La. Pur O T 57 D3
Bowling Green Rd. That 106 A3
Bowman Ct. Woki 142 C2
Bowmans Cl. Burn 21 D2
Bowry Dr. Wray 68 C1
Bowyer Cres. Woki 116 B4
Bowyer Dr. Slough 41 F3
Bowyer's La. New G 91 E3
Boxford Ridge. Brac 118 A3
Boyd Cl. Brac 118 A4
Boyn Hill Ave. Maid 39 E3
Boyn Hill Cl. Maid 39 E3
Boyn Hill Rd. Maid 39 E3
Boyn Valley Rd. Maid 39 E3
Boynden Rd. Maid 39 E4
Bracebridge. Camb 151 D3
Bracken Bank. Burl 119 E4
Bracken Cl. Far C 22 B4
Bracken Cl. Read 57 E1
Bracken La. Yate 149 D3
Bracken Rd. Maid 39 E2
Bracken Way. Bur C 111 D1
Bracken Way. Fla H 3 D4
Brackendale Cl. Camb 151 F2
Brackendale Rd. Camb 151 E2
Brackenforde. Slough 43 E2
Brackens The. Brac 143 D4
Brackenwood Dr. Tad 135 D1
Brackenwood. Bur C 110 C1
Brackenwood. Camb 152 B3
Bracknell Beeches. Brac 118 A3
Bracknell Cl. Camb 144 C1
Bracknell Rd. Bags 145 F3
Bracknell Rd. Brac 143 F4
Bracknell Rd. Camb 145 D1
Bracknell Rd. New G 91 F2
Bracknell Rd. New G 92 A3
Bracknell Rd. Wink 92 A3
Bradcutts La. Cook 19 F4
Bradenham La. Bish 18 B3
Bradfields. Brac 118 B2
Bradford Rd. Slough 42 A4
Brading Way. Pur O T 57 E3
Bradley Cl. Kint 102 A1
Bradley Rd. Slough 42 C3
Bradmore Way. Read 114 A4
Bradshaw Cl. Wind 66 C3
Bradwell Rd. Read 57 E2
Braemar Gdns. Slough 42 A2
Braemore Cl. That 106 B1
Brakendale Way. Read 87 D3
Bramber Cl. Slough 42 A3
Bramber Mews. Caver 59 F2
Bramble Cl. Shepp 125 E3
Bramble Cres. Read 84 C4
Bramble Dr. Maid 39 E1
Brambledown. Stai 124 A4
Bramblegate. Crow 143 D3
Brambles The. Brac 142 B3
Bramcote. Camb 152 B3
Bramley Cl. Chert 124 A1
Bramley Cl. Maid 39 E2
Bramley Cl. Read 87 D2
Bramley Cl. Stai 97 E1
Bramley Gr. Brac 142 B3
Bramley La. Black 150 A3
Bramley Rd. Camb 151 D1
Bramley Rd. Silc 136 A1
Bramling Ave. Yate 149 D3
Brammas Cl. Slough 42 B2
Brampton Chase. Shipl 36 A2
Bramshaw Rd. Read 58 A1
Bramshill Cl. Arbo 140 C4
Bramwell Cl. That 106 C1
Bran Cl. Read 84 C4
Brandon Ave. Wood 88 A4
Brandon Cl. Camb 152 B2
Brands Cl. Slough 69 D4
Branksome Cl. Camb 151 F3
Branksome Hill Rd. Sand 150 C4
Branksome Park Rd. Camb . 151 F3
Brants Bridge. Brac 118 C3
Braunfels Wlk. Newb 104 C1
Bravington Cl. Stai 124 C2
Bray Cl. Maid 40 B2
Bray Cl. Holy 40 B1
Bray Rd. Maid 40 A3
Bray Rd. Read 85 D2
Braybank. Maid 40 B2
Braybrooke Gdns. Warg 36 B1
Braybrooke Rd. Brac 91 D1
Braybrooke Rd. Warg 36 B1

Braye Cl. Sand 143 E1
Brayfield Rd. Maid 40 B2
Brayford Rd. Read 113 E4
Braywick Rd. Maid 40 A3
Braywood Ave. Eng G 96 A1
Braziers La. Wink 92 B2
Breach Sq. Hung 100 B3
Breadcroft La. Bur G 38 C2
Breadcroft Rd. Whi Wa 38 C2
Bream Cl. Mar 18 B4
Brecon Rd. Wood 87 F4
Bredon Rd. Woki 88 C1
Bredward Cl. Burn 21 D1
Breech The. Sand 150 B4
Breedons Hill. Pangb 56 B3
Bremer Rd. Stan 97 D3
Brendon Cl. Harl 71 E4
Brendon Cl. Read 57 F1
Brent Cl. That 106 B1
Brent Gdns. Read 86 A2
Brent Rd. Bou E 3 D2
Brentmoor Rd. West E 153 E3
Brereton Cl. Read 86 C1
Bret Harte Rd. Camb 151 F1
Brewery Comm. Mort 137 D4
Brewhouse Hill. Frox 99 D2
Briant's Ave. Caver 59 E1
Briants Piece. Herm 79 D3
Briar Ave. Light 153 D4
Briar Cl. Burn 41 D4
Briar Cl. Caver 59 D3
Briar Dene. Maid 19 E1
Briar Glen. Cook 19 F3
Briar Rd. Stai 125 D2
Briar Way. Slough 42 A4
Briarlea Rd. Mort 136 C3
Briars Cl. Pangb 56 C3
Briars The. Slough 43 F1
Briars The. Stan 70 A1
Briarwood Cl. Felt 98 C3
Briarwood. Woki 141 F3
Brickfield La. Burn 21 D2
Brickfield La. Harl 71 E4
Bridge Ave. Cook 19 F3
Bridge Cl. Shepp 125 D1
Bridge Cl. Slough 41 F3
Bridge Cl. Stai 96 C2
Bridge End. Camb 151 D2
Bridge Gdns. Stai 98 B1
Bridge La. Went 122 C2
Bridge Rd. Ascot 120 B2
Bridge Rd. Bags 145 F2
Bridge Rd. Camb 151 D2
Bridge Rd. Chert 124 A1
Bridge Rd. Maid 40 A4
Bridge St. Caver 59 D1
Bridge St. Hung 100 B3
Bridge St. Iver 69 E4
Bridge St. Maid 40 A4
Bridge St. Newb 105 D2
Bridge St. Read 86 A4
Bridge St. Shepp 125 F1
Bridge St. Stai 96 C2
Bridge View. Went 121 D1
Bridge Walk. Yate 149 E4
Bridgeman Dr. Wind 67 D3
Bridges Cl. Woki 115 F4
Bridges The. Silc 136 B3
Bridgestone Dr. Bou E 3 E2
Bridgewater Cl. Read 58 B1
Bridgewater Ct. Slough 44 A1
Bridgewater Terr. Wind 67 E3
Bridgewater Way. Wind 67 E3
Bridle Cl. Maid 19 F1
Bridle Rd. Maid 19 F1
Bridlepath Way. Felt 98 C4
Bridlington Spur. Slough 42 A2
Bridport Cl. Read 87 E1
Bridport Way. Slough 22 A1
Brierley Pl. Pur O T 57 E2
Briff La. Buck 107 E4
Brigham Rd. Read 59 D1
Brighton Rd. Read 87 D3
Brighton Spur. Slough 22 A1
Brightside Ave. Stai 97 E1
Brill Cl. Caver 59 D1
Brill Cl. Maid 39 E2
Brill Cl. Mar 1 B1
Brimblecombe Cl. Woki 89 D1
Brimpton Rd. Brim 133 F4
Brimpton Rd. Read 85 D2
Brimpton Rd. Tad 134 B1
Brimpton Rd. Wool 133 F4
Brinn's La. Sand 150 B3
Brisbane Rd. Read 85 D4
Bristol Cl. Stan 70 C1
Bristol Way. Slough 42 C3
Bristow Cres. Camb 151 D2
Bristow Ct. Mar 2 A2
Bristow Rd. Camb 151 D2
Britannia Way. Stan 97 E4
Britten Rd. Read 86 A3
Britwell Rd. Burn 21 E1
Brixham Rd. Read 86 A1
Broad Hinton. Twyf 61 F2
Broad La. Bou E 3 F3
Broad La. Brac 118 B3
Broad La. Buck 107 E3
Broad Oak Ct. Slough 22 B1

Broad Oak. Slough 22 B1
Broad Platts. Slough 43 E2
Broad St. East I 30 C4
Broad St. Read 86 A4
Broad St. West E 153 E3
Broad St. Woki 116 B3
Broad Street Mall The. Read .. 86 A4
Broad Wlk. Camb 151 F1
Broadacre. Stai 97 D2
Broadcommon Rd. Hurst 89 D4
Broadhalfpenny La. Tad 135 E1
Broadlands Ave. Shepp 125 E2
Broadlands Cl. Read 84 B3
Broadlands Dr. Sunn 120 B1
Broadley Green. Windl 146 B2
Broadmark Rd. Slough 43 D3
Broadmeadow End. That 106 C2
Broadmoor La. W St L 63 D3
Broadmoor La. Whi Wa 63 D3
Broadrich Heath. New G 91 F1
Broadwater Cl. Wray 95 F4
Broadwater La. Hurst 61 F1
Broadwater Park. Holy 40 C1
Broadwater Rd. Twyf 61 F2
Broadway Rd. Light 146 B1
Broadway The. Lamb 25 D2
Broadway The. Newb 105 D2
Broadway The. Sand 150 A4
Broadway The. Stai 124 B4
Broadway. Brac 118 B4
Broadway. Maid 39 F4
Broadway. That 106 B2
Brocas Rd. Bur C 110 C1
Brocas St. Eton 67 E4
Brocas Terr. Eton 67 E4
Brock Gdns. Read 85 E4
Brock La. Maid 39 F4
Brock Way. Vir W 122 B3
Brockenhurst Dr. Yate 149 E3
Brockenhurst Rd. Ascot 120 A2
Brockenhurst Rd. Brac 119 D3
Brocklands. Yate 149 D2
Brockley Cl. Read 85 D4
Brocks La. Buck 80 A2
Brocks Way. Shipl 36 A2
Brocksby Rd. Read 57 E1
Broken Furlong. Eton 42 A1
Broken Way. Newt 131 E1
Bromley Wlk. Read 84 C4
Brompton Cl. Winn 87 E1
Brompton Dr. Maid 19 E1
Bromycroft Rd. Slough 22 A1
Brook Cl. Sand 143 F1
Brook Cl. Stan 97 F4
Brook Cl. Woki 116 A4
Brook Cres. Slough 41 F4
Brook Dr. Ashf 98 C1
Brook Dr. Brac 118 C3
Brook La. Hurst 62 C2
Brook Path. Slough 41 F3
Brook Path. Slough 41 F3
Brook Rd. Bags 145 F1
Brook Rd. Camb 151 D2
Brook St W. Read 86 A3
Brook St. Twyf 61 E2
Brook St. Wind 67 E3
Brookbank. Bou E 3 E2
Brookdene Cl. Maid 19 F1
Brooke Pl. Binf 90 B2
Brookers Cnr. Crow 143 E3
Brookers Hill. Read 113 E3
Brookers Row. Brac 143 D3
Brookfield Cl. Bou E 3 E2
Brookhouse Dr. Bou E 3 E2
Brooklands Cl. Stai 125 F4
Brooklyn Dr. Caver 59 D3
Brookmill The. Read 85 F3
Brooksby Rd. Read 57 E1
Brookside Ave. Stai 97 E2
Brookside Ave. Wray 68 C2
Brookside Cl. Read 87 E1
Brookside. Chert 123 F1
Brookside. Iver 69 E4
Brookside. Read 84 C2
Brookside. Sand 150 B4
Brookside. Woki 115 F4
Brookway. Newb 105 E1
Broom Acres. Sand 143 D1
Broom Cl. Black 150 C2
Broom Cl. Read 84 B3
Broom Field. Light 153 D4
Broom Gr. Woki 115 E2
Broom Hill. Cook 19 F3
Broom Hill. Sto P 23 D3
Broome Cl. Yate 149 E4
Broomfield. Went 121 D1
Broomfield Park. Went 121 D1
Broomfield Rd. Read 58 A1
Broomfield Rd. Read 84 C4
Broomhall La. Sunn 121 D2
Broomsquire Rd. Bags 145 F1
Broughton Cl. Read 58 B1
Broughton Mews. Camb 151 F1
Brownfields Gdns. Maid 39 F3
Browngraves Rd. Harl 71 E4
Browning Cl. Camb 152 B2
Browning Cl. That 106 B2

Brownlow Dr. Brac 91 E1
Brownlow Rd. Read 85 F4
Brownrigg Cres. Brac 118 C4
Brownrigg Rd. Ashf 98 A2
Brownsfield Rd. That 106 B2
Bruan Rd. Newb 130 C4
Bruce Ave. Shepp 125 E2
Bruce Cl. Slough 42 A3
Bruce Rd. Wood 87 E4
Bruce Wlk. Wind 66 B3
Brudenell. Wind 66 C2
Brummell Rd. Newb 104 C4
Brunel Cl. Maid 39 F3
Brunel Dr. Wood 60 C1
Brunel Rd. Maid 39 E3
Brunel Rd. Read 85 D2
Brunel Rd. Thea 83 F1
Brunel Way. Slough 42 C3
Brunswick Hill. Read 85 F4
Brunswick St. Read 85 F3
Brunswick. Brac 118 A1
Bruton Way. Brac 118 C1
Bryant Ave. Slough 42 C4
Bryants La. Yatt 53 F1
Brybur Cl. Read 113 E4
Bryer Pl. Wind 66 B2
Buccaneer Cl. Wood 88 A4
Buccleuch Rd. Datch 68 A4
Buchan The. Camb 152 A4
Buchanan Dr. Woki 141 F4
Buchanan Sq. That 106 C1
Buck Side. Caver 59 D1
Buckden Cl. Wood 88 A3
Buckham Hill. Chadd 48 B3
Buckhurst Gr. Woki 116 C3
Buckhurst Hill. Brac 118 C3
Buckhurst La. Ascot 121 D3
Buckhurst Rd. Ascot 120 C4
Buckhurst Way. Read 87 D2
Buckingham Ave E. Slough ... 42 B4
Buckingham Ave. Slough 42 A4
Buckingham Dr. Caver 59 D3
Buckingham Gate. Medm 17 E4
Buckingham Gdns. Slough ... 42 C2
Buckingham Rd. Newb 104 C1
Buckingham Way. Camb 151 F1
Buckland Ave. Slough 43 D2
Buckland Cres. Wind 66 C3
Buckland Rd. Read 86 A2
Buckle La. New G 91 D3
Bucklebury Cl. Holy 40 B1
Bucklebury. Brac 118 A1
Bucknell Ave. Pangb 56 C3
Bucknell Cl. Read 84 C2
Buckthorn Cl. Woki 116 C4
Budebury Rd. Stai 97 D2
Budge's Gdns. Woki 116 C4
Budge's Rd. Woki 116 B4
Buffins. Tapl 20 B1
Bulkeley Ave. Wind 67 D2
Bulkeley Cl. Eng G 95 E2
Bull La. Brac 118 A4
Bull La. Swal 139 D2
Bull Meadow The. Stre 33 F3
Bullbrook Dr. Brac 118 C4
Bullbrook Row. Brac 118 C4
Bullfinch Cl. Sand 150 C4
Bulmershe Rd. Read 86 C3
Bulpit La. Hung 100 B2
Bunby Rd. Sto P 22 C3
Bunces Cl. Eton 42 A1
Bunces La. Bur C 111 D1
Bundy's Way. Stai 96 C1
Bungalow Dr. Read 84 B4
Bungler's Hill. Swal 140 A3
Bunkers Hill. Newb 130 B3
Bunten Meade. Slough 42 A3
Burbage Green. Brac 118 C2
Burbidge Cl. Read 84 C2
Burbidge Rd. Stai 125 D3
Burchell Rd. Newb 104 C3
Burchett Copse. Woki 141 F4
Burchetts Green La. Bur G 38 B3
Burchetts Green Rd. Bur G 38 A4
Burchetts Way. Shepp 125 D2
Burcombe Way. Caver 59 D2
Burcot Gdns. Maid 19 F2
Burdett Ct. Read 86 B2
Burdock Cl. Bur C 111 D1
Burdock Cl. Light 153 D4
Burfield Rd. Old W 95 D4
Burford Cl. Mar B 1 B3
Burford Gdns. Slough 41 E4
Burford Rd. Camb 151 D2
Burford's. East G 47 E3
Burges Way. Stan 97 D1
Burgess Cl. Wood 87 E2
Burgess La. Kint 128 B3
Burgett Rd. Slough 42 A2
Burghead Cl. Sand 150 B4
Burghfield Rd. Read 85 D2
Burgoyne Rd. Ashf 98 C1
Burgoyne Rd. Camb 152 A2
Burleigh Gdns. Ashf 98 B2
Burleigh La. Ascot 119 F4
Burleigh Mews. Caver 59 E3
Burleigh Rd. Ascot 119 F4
Burleigh Rd. Camb 151 E1
Burley Orch. Chert 124 A2

Burley Way. Black 150 B3
Burlingham Cl. Read 113 E3
Burlings The. Ascot 119 F4
Burlington Ave. Slough 42 C2
Burlington Cl. Felt 98 B4
Burlington Cl. Black 150 B2
Burlington Rd. Burn 41 D4
Burlington Rd. Read 84 B4
Burlington Rd. Slough 42 C2
Burlsdon Way. Brac 118 C4
Burn Moor Chase. Brac 118 C1
Burn Wlk. Burn 21 D1
Burne-Jones Dr. Sand 150 B3
Burnet Cl. Camb 153 F3
Burnetts Rd. Wind 66 C3
Burney Bit. Silc 135 F1
Burnham Cl. Bou E 3 D2
Burnham Cl. Wind 66 B3
Burnham Gr. Brac 91 E1
Burnham La. Slough 41 F4
Burnham Rd. Tad 134 C1
Burnham Rise. Caver 59 E3
Burniston Cl. Winn 87 F1
Burns Cl. Wood 87 F2
Burns Wlk. That 106 B2
Burnt Oak. Cook 19 F4
Burnt Oak. Woki 141 F4
Burnt Pollard La. West E 146 C1
Burnthouse La. Bur C 112 A3
Burrcroft Rd. Read 85 D3
Burrell Rd. Comp 31 F2
Burroughs Cres. Bou E 3 D2
Burroway Rd. Slough 44 A2
Burrows Hill Cl. Stan 70 B2
Burton Cl. Windl 146 B2
Burton Way. Wind 66 C2
Burtons Hill. Kint 102 A1
Burway Cres. Chert 124 A3
Burwell Cl. Winn 87 E1
Burys Bank Rd. Gree 132 A3
Burys Bank Rd. That 132 A3
Bush Rd. Stai 96 A2
Business Centre The. Woki .. 116 A2
Business Village The. Slough .. 43 D3
Butchers La. Whi Wa 63 E4
Bute St. Read 85 D3
Butler Ct. Mar 2 A2
Butler Rd. Bags 145 F1
Butler Rd. Crow 143 D3
Butlers Cl. Wind 66 B3
Butson Cl. Newb 104 C2
Buttenshaw Ave. Bark 141 D4
Buttenshaw Cl. Bark 141 D4
Butter Market. Read 86 A4
Buttercup Square. Stan 97 E4
Butterfield. Bou E 3 E2
Buttermere Ave. Slough 41 E4
Buttermere Cl. Felt 98 C4
Buttermere Dr. Camb 152 B3
Buttermere Gdns. Brac 118 B3
Buttermere Way. Stai 96 A1
Buttersteep Rise. Brac 119 E1
Butts Hill Rd. Wood 87 F4
Buxton Ave. Caver 58 C2
Buxton Rd. Ashf 97 E2
Byebend Cl. Far C 22 A2
Byfield Rd. Read 85 D2
Byeways Cl. Warg 37 F2
Byland Dr. Holy 40 A1
Byreton Cl. Read 87 D1
Byron Ave. Camb 152 A2
Byron Cl. Mar 1 C2
Byron Cl. Newb 130 C4
Byron Cl. Twyf 61 F2
Byron Cl. Yate 149 D2
Byron Dr. Crow 143 D2
Byron Rd. Read 87 D4
Byron Rd. Twyf 61 F2
Bythorn Cl. Winn 87 F1
Byways. Burn 41 D4
Byways. Yate 149 D3
Bywood. Brac 118 A1
Byworth Cl. Read 113 D4

Cabin Moss. Brac 118 C1
Cabrera Ave. Went 122 B2
Cabrera Cl. Went 122 B2
Cadbury Cl. Ashf 98 C1
Cadbury Rd. Ashf 98 C1
Caddy Cl. Eng G 96 A2
Cadogan Cl. Holy 65 D4
Cadogan Cl. Read 84 C4
Cadwell Dr. Maid 39 E2
Caesar's Camp Rd. Camb ... 152 A4
Caesar's Way. Shepp 125 E2
Cages Wood Dr. Far C 22 A4
Cain Rd. Binf 117 E4
Cain Rd. Brac 117 F4
Cain's La. Harm 71 F1
Cairn Cl. Camb 152 A4
Cairngorm Rd. That 106 B1
Caistor Cl. Bur C 84 A2
Calard Dr. That 106 A3
Calbourne Dr. Bur C 84 B2
Calbroke Rd. Slough 21 F1
Calcot Cl. Read 84 C3
Calcot Place Dr. Read 84 C2
Caldbeck Dr. Wood 87 F4
Calder Cl. Maid 19 F1

Calder Cl. Read 84 C4
Calder Ct. Maid 19 E1
Calder Cl. Slough 43 F1
Calder Way. Stan 69 F2
Caldwell Rd. Windl 146 B3
Caledonia Rd. Stan 97 F4
Caleta Ct. Caver 59 E1
Calfridus Way. Brac 118 C3
Calleva Park. Alde 134 C1
Callin's La. W St L 63 D2
Callington Rd. Read 86 B1
Callis Farm Cl. Stan 70 C1
Callow Hill. Vir W 122 B4
Calshot Pl. Bur C 84 B2
Calshot Rd. Harm 71 D3
Calshot Way. Harm 71 D3
Calvin Cl. Camb 152 A2
Camberley Rd. Harm 71 D2
Camborne Cl. Crow 143 D1
Camborne Cl. Harm 71 D2
Camborne Rd. Harm 87 D1
Camborne Rd S. Harm 71 D1
Camborne Way. Harm 71 D2
Cambria Gdns. Stan 97 F4
Cambrian Cl. Camb 151 D3
Cambrian Way. Brac 142 A4
Cambrian Way. Bur C 84 B2
Cambridge Ave. Burn 21 D2
Cambridge Ave. Slough 42 A4
Cambridge Cl. Harm 70 B4
Cambridge Rd. Crow 143 E2
Cambridge Rd. Mar 1 B1
Cambridge Rd. Sand 143 F1
Cambridge Rd. Stai 98 B1
Cambridge St. Read 85 F4
Cambridge Wlk. Camb 151 E3
Cambridgeshire Cl. Woki 115 F3
Camden Pl. Bou E 3 D2
Camden Pl. Bur C 84 A2
Camden Rd. Maid 19 E1
Camellia Way. Woki 115 E4
Camilla Cl. Ashf 98 C1
Camley Gdns. Maid 39 D4
Camley Park Dr. Maid 38 C4
Camm Ave. Wind 66 C2
Camp Rd. Padw 110 B1
Campbell Cl. Yate 149 F3
Campbell Pl. Camb 151 F2
Campbell Rd. Wood 87 E3
Camperdown. Maid 20 A1
Campion Cl. Black 150 C2
Campion Way. Woki 116 C4
Canada Rd. Slough 43 D2
Canal Walk. Hung 100 B3
Canal Way. Read 86 B4
Canal Wharf. Slough 44 A2
Canberra Cl. Yate 149 D4
Canberra Rd. Harm 71 D2
Candleford Cl. Brac 91 E1
Candover Cl. Harm 70 B4
Canford Ct. Read 85 E4
Cannock Cl. Maid 40 A3
Cannock Way. Wood 87 E1
Cannon Cl. Sand 150 C4
Cannon Court Rd. Cook 19 E2
Cannon Court Rd. Maid 19 E2
Cannon Hill Cl. Maid 40 B1
Cannon Hill. Brac 118 B2
Cannon La. Maid 38 C2
Cannon La. Whi Wa 38 C2
Cannon St. Read 85 F4
Cannondown Rd. Cook 19 F3
Canon Hill Dr. Maid 40 A2
Canopus Way. Stan 97 F4
Cansfield End. Newb 104 C2
Canterbury Ave. Slough 22 B1
Canterbury Rd. Read 86 B2
Cantley Cres. Woki 116 A4
Capper Rd. Camb 151 D4
Captains Gorse. Upp B 54 C3
Caraway Rd. Read 87 D1
Carbery La. Ascot 120 A3
Carbinswood La. Buck 108 A3
Cardiff Rd. Read 58 C1
Cardigan Gdns. Read 86 C3
Cardigan Rd. Read 86 C3
Cardinal Cl. Caver 59 D1
Cardinal's Wlk. Ashf 98 C1
Cardinals The. Brac 118 A3
Cardinals Wlk. Slough 41 E4
Cardwell Cres. Ascot 120 B2
Carew Rd. Ashf 98 B1
Carey Cl. Wind 67 D2
Carey Rd. Woki 116 B3
Carey St. Read 85 F4
Cariad Ct. Gori 34 A4
Carisbrooke Cl. Caver 59 E3
Carisbrooke Cl. Maid 39 E3
Carisbrooke Ct. Slough 42 C3
Carland Cl. Read 87 D1
Carlile Gdns. Twyf 61 E1
Carlinwark Dr. Camb 151 F4
Carlisle Rd. Camb 151 E1
Carlisle Rd. Read 57 F2
Carlisle Rd. Slough 42 B3
Carlton Cl. Camb 152 A2
Carlton Cl. Wood 87 F3
Carlton Rd. Ashf 98 C1
Carlton Rd. Caver 58 C3
Carlton Rd. Slough 43 D3

Carlyle Rd. Stai 97 D1
Carmarthen Rd. Slough 42 C3
Carnarvon Rd. Read 86 C3
Carnation Dr. Burl 92 A1
Carnegie Rd. Newb 105 D1
Carolina Pl. Woki 141 F4
Caroline Ct. Ashf 98 A1
Caroline Cl. Mar 1 C2
Caroline Dr. Woki 116 A4
Caroline Pl. Stan 71 F4
Caroline St. Read 85 F4
Caroline Way. Camb 151 F1
Carrick Gdns. Wood 87 E4
Carrington Ave. Fla H 3 C1
Carrington Rd. Slough 42 C3
Carroll Cres. Ascot 119 F3
Carron Cl. Read 85 D4
Carsdale Cl. Read 85 F3
Carshalton Rd. Camb 145 D1
Carshalton Way. Wood 87 E1
Carston Gr. Read 84 C2
Carter Cl. Wind 67 D3
Carter's Hill. Binf 90 A2
Carters Rise. Read 84 C2
Cartmel Dr. Wood 87 E3
Cary Cl. Newb 130 B3
Casey Ct. Stan D 81 E2
Cassia Dr. Read 86 C1
Cassiobury Ave. Felt 98 C4
Castle Ave. Datch 68 A4
Castle Cl. Camb 151 F2
Castle Cl. Stai 98 C1
Castle Cres. Read 85 F3
Castle Cl. Maid 39 E4
Castle Dr. Maid 39 E4
Castle End Rd. W St L 62 A4
Castle Gr. Newb 104 C3
Castle Hill Rd. Eng G 95 D3
Castle Hill Rd. Eng G 95 E3
Castle Hill Terr. Maid 39 F4
Castle Hill. Maid 39 F4
Castle Hill. Read 85 F3
Castle Hill. Swal 140 B4
Castle La. Wint 104 C3
Castle Mews. Maid 39 F4
Castle Rd. Camb 151 F2
Castle St. Read 86 A4
Castle St. Slough 42 C2
Castlecraig Ct. Sand 150 B4
Castleton Ct. Mar 1 C1
Castleview Rd. Slough 43 E1
Castor Ct. Yate 149 E3
Caswall Cl. Binf 90 B1
Caswall Ride. Yate 149 F3
Catalina Cl. Wood 88 A4
Catcliffe Way. Read 113 F4
Catena Rise. Light 146 A1
Catesby Gdns. Yate 149 D3
Catherine Dr. Ashf 98 C1
Catherine Rd. Newb 105 D2
Catherine St. Read 85 F4
Catlin Cres. Shepp 125 E2
Catmore Rd. Farn 29 E4
Catmore Rd. West I 29 E4
Caunter Rd. Newb 104 B2
Causeway The. Maid 40 B2
Causeway The. Mar 1 C1
Causeway The. Stai 96 B2
Causmans Way. Read 57 E1
Cavalier Cl. Newb 105 E3
Cavalier Cl. Thea 83 E1
Cavalry Cres. Wind 67 E2
Cavendish Cl. Ashf 98 C1
Cavendish Cl. Burn 41 D4
Cavendish Cl. Ashf 98 C1
Cavendish Ct. Black 150 B2
Cavendish Gdns. Winn 88 A2
Cavendish Meads. Ascot 120 B2
Cavendish Rd. Ashf 98 C1
Cavendish Rd. Caver 59 E3
Cavendish Rd. Read 86 A3
Caversham Park Rd. Caver ... 59 F3
Caversham Rd. Caver 59 D1
Caves Farm Cl. Sand 150 A4
Cawcott Dr. Wind 66 C3
Cawsham Gdns. Caver 59 E2
Caxton Cl. Read 58 B1
Cecil Aldin Dr. Pur O T 57 E2
Cecil Cl. Ashf 98 B1
Cecil Rd. Ashf 98 B1
Cecil Rd. Iver 44 C4
Cecil Way. Slough 21 F1
Cedar Ave. Black 150 B3
Cedar Chase. Tapl 20 B1
Cedar Cl. Bags 145 F2
Cedar Cl. Stai 124 B3
Cedar Cl. Woki 116 B3
Cedar Ct. Eng G 96 A2
Cedar Ct. Mar 1 C1
Cedar Dr. Brac 91 E1
Cedar Dr. Mar B 1 B4
Cedar Dr. Pangb 57 D3
Cedar Dr. Windl 121 D1
Cedar Mount. Newb 130 C4
Cedar Rd. Felt 98 B4
Cedar Rd. Read 86 C1
Cedar Way. Slough 43 F1
Cedar Way. Stai 98 C1

Cedar Wood Cres. Caver 59 D2
Cedars Cl. Sand 149 F4
Cedars Rd. Maid 40 A4
Cedars The. Read 57 E1
Celandine Cl. Crow 143 E3
Celandine Ct. Yate 149 D4
Celandine Gr. That 106 C2
Celia Cres. Stai 97 E1
Cell Farm Ave. Old W 68 A1
Celsea Pl. Chol 14 A4
Cemetery La. Shepp 125 D1
Central Dr. Slough 41 F3
Centre The. Shepp 125 F1
Centurion Cl. Read 86 A3
Centurion Cl. Sand 150 B4
Century Rd. Stai 96 B2
Cerotus Pl. Chert 123 F1
Ceviot Rd. Sand 142 C1
Chaffinch Cl. Sand 150 B4
Chaffinch Cl. Woki 115 F3
Chagford Rd. Read 86 A1
Chain St. Read 86 A4
Chainhill Rd. Farn 8 A4
Chalcraft Cl. Hen-O-T 35 E4
Chalfont Cl. Read 87 D1
Chalfont Ct. Read 87 D1
Chalfont Way. Read 87 D1
Chalford Rd. Newb 104 C1
Chalford. Woo G 3 F3
Chalgrove Cl. Maid 40 A3
Chalgrove Way. Caver 59 E3
Chalk Hill. Ast T 12 C4
Chalk Hill. Shipl 35 E3
Chalk Pit La. Burn 21 D2
Chalkhousegreen La. Maples . 59 D4
Chalklands. Bou E 3 D2
Chalkpit La. Mar 1 A2
Challenge Rd. Felt 98 B2
Challenor Cl. Woki 141 F4
Challis Pl. Brac 117 E4
Challow Ct. Maid 19 E1
Chalmers Rd E. Ashf 98 B2
Chalmers Rd. Ashf 98 A2
Chalvey Gdns. Slough 42 C2
Chalvey Gr. Slough 42 A2
Chalvey Park. Slough 42 C2
Chalvey Rd E. Slough 42 C2
Chalvey Rd W. Slough 42 B2
Chamberlain's Gdns. Arbo ... 114 C1
Champion Rd. Caver 59 E1
Chancellor's Way The. Read ... 86 C2
Chanctonbury Dr. Sunn 120 C1
Chandlers Cl. Felt 98 C4
Chandlers La. Yate 149 E4
Chandos Rd. Newb 131 D4
Chandos Rd. Stai 96 B2
Chantry Cl. Wind 67 D3
Chantry Mead. Hung 100 B3
Chantry Rd. Bags 145 E1
Chantry Rd. Chert 124 B1
Chapel Cl. Sou S 14 B2
Chapel Ct. That 106 C2
Chapel Hill. Read 84 B4
Chapel La. Asham 54 A4
Chapel La. Bags 145 E1
Chapel La. Binf 90 B1
Chapel La. Blew 12 A4
Chapel La. Camb 151 D1
Chapel La. Head 133 F1
Chapel La. Herm 78 C2
Chapel La. Herm 79 E4
Chapel La. Lamb 25 D2
Chapel La. Shin 113 D1
Chapel La. Silc 135 D1
Chapel La. Sto P 23 D3
Chapel La. Swal 139 E2
Chapel La. Yatt 53 F1
Chapel Rd. Camb 151 D3
Chapel Rd. Fla H 3 D4
Chapel Row. Twyf 61 E2
Chapel Sq. Sand 150 C3
Chapel St. Mar 1 C1
Chapel St. Slough 42 C2
Chapel St. That 106 B2
Chaplain's Hill. Crow 143 E2
Chaplin Cres. Ashf 98 C1
Chapman La. Bou E 3 D3
Chapman La. Fla H 3 D3
Chapter Mews. Wind 67 E4
Charadon Cl. Read 86 A3
Chard Cl. Wood 87 F3
Chard Rd. Harm 71 D3
Charlbury Cl. Brac 118 C3
Charles Evans Way. Caver 59 E1
Charles Gdns. Slough 43 D4
Charles Rd. Chol 14 A4
Charles Rd. Stai 97 E1
Charles Sq. Brac 118 B4
Charles St. Chert 123 F1
Charles St. Newb 130 B3
Charles St. Read 85 F4
Charles St. Wind 67 D3
Charlotte Cl. Herm 79 D3
Charlotte Way. Mar 1 C1
Charlton Cl. Slough 42 A2
Charlton Cl. Woki 141 F4
Charlton Cl. Sand 143 E1
Charlton La. Shepp 125 E3
Charlton La. Swal 139 E3

Charlton Pl. Newb 105 D2
Charlton Rd. Stai 125 E4
Charlton Sq. Oak G 66 B3
Charlton Way. Oak G 66 B3
Charlton. Oak G 66 B3
Charlville Dr. Bur C 84 A2
Charmwood Cl. Newb 104 C3
Charnham La. Hung 100 B4
Charnham Park. Hello 100 B4
Charnham St. Hung 100 B3
Charnwood. Ascot 120 C2
Charrington Rd. Bur C 84 B2
Charta Rd (E). Stai 96 B1
Charta Rd (S). Stai 96 B1
Charta Rd (W). Stai 96 B2
Charter Cl. Slough 42 C2
Charter Rd. Newb 131 D4
Charter Rd. Slough 41 F3
Charterhouse Cl. Brac 118 C2
Charters La. Ascot 120 B2
Charters Rd. Sun 120 C1
Charters Rd. Windl 120 C1
Charters Way. Windl 120 C1
Charvil House Rd. Char 61 D3
Charvil La. Sonn 60 C2
Charwood Rd. Woki 116 C4
Chase Gdns. Binf 90 B2
Chase The. Bur C 84 B2
Chase The. Crow 143 D3
Chase The. Mar 2 A2
Chaseside Ave. Twyf 61 E4
Chaseside Gdns. Chert 124 A1
Chatfield. Slough 42 A4
Chatham St. Read 85 F4
Chatsworth Ave. Winn 88 A1
Chatsworth Cl. Caver 59 E3
Chatsworth Cl. Maid 39 E3
Chatsworth Hts. Camb 152 A4
Chatteris Way. Winn 114 B4
Chattern Hill. Ashf 98 A2
Chattern Rd. Ashf 98 B2
Chatton Cl. Read 114 A4
Chaucer Cl. Caver 59 D3
Chaucer Cl. Woki 116 C3
Chaucer Cres. Newb 104 C3
Chaucer Rd. Ashf 97 F2
Chaucer Rd. Crow 143 D2
Chaucer Way. Woki 115 F3
Chauntry Cl. Maid 40 B3
Chauntry Rd. Maid 40 A3
Chavey Down Rd. Burl 92 A1
Chawridge La. Wink 92 B4
Chazey Cl. Maple 58 B4
Chazey Rd. Caver 58 B2
Cheam Rd. Brac 118 B2
Cheap St. Comp 31 F3
Cheap St. Newb 105 D1
Cheapside Rd. Ascot 120 B4
Cheapside. Read 86 A4
Cheddar Rd. Harm 71 D3
Cheddington Cl. Read 84 C3
Cheeseman Cl. Woki 116 B4
Chelford Way. Caver 58 C2
Chelsea Cl. Read 57 F1
Chelwood Dr. Sand 142 C1
Chelwood Rd. Read 87 D1
Cheney Cl. Binf 90 B1
Cheniston Gr. Maid 38 C4
Chepstow Rd. Read 57 E1
Chequer La. Bee H 138 C1
Chequers Orch. Iver 44 C4
Chequers Way. Wood 87 E4
Cherbury Cl. Brac 118 C3
Cherington Gate. Maid 19 D1
Cherington Way. Ascot 119 F4
Cheriton Ave. Twyf 61 E3
Cheriton Cl. Newb 131 D4
Cheriton Way. Black 150 B3
Cherries The. Slough 43 D4
Cherry Ave. Slough 43 E2
Cherry Cl. Caver 59 E4
Cherry Cl. Fla H 3 D4
Cherry Cl. Newb 104 C2
Cherry Garden La. Bur G 38 C2
Cherry Orch. Gr She 48 A2
Cherry Orch. Stai 97 D2
Cherry Orch. Sto P 23 D3
Cherry Rise. Fla H 3 D4
Cherry Tree Ave. Stai 97 D1
Cherry Tree Cl. Sand 143 E1
Cherry Tree Dr. Brac 118 B3
Cherry Tree Gr. Woki 115 E2
Cherry Tree La. Fulm 23 F3
Cherry Tree Rd. Far C 22 B3
Cherry Way. Shepp 125 F3
Cherrydale Rd. Camb 152 B3
Cherrygarden La. Whi Wa 63 F4
Cherrywood Ave. Eng G 95 D1
Cherrywood Gdns. Fla H 3 D4
Chertsey Bridge Rd. Shepp ... 124 B1
Chertsey La. Stai 96 C1
Chertsey Rd. Felt 98 C2
Chertsey Rd. Shepp 124 B1
Chertsey Rd. Windl 146 C3
Chervil Way. Bur C 111 D1
Cherwell Cl. Maid 40 A4
Cherwell Rd. Slough 69 D4
Cherwell Rd. Bou E 3 D2

Cherwell Rd. Caver 59 D3
Cheseridge Rd. Comp 31 E2
Cheshire Ct. Slough 43 D2
Chessholme Ct. Ashf 98 C1
Chessholme Rd. Ashf 98 B1
Chester Cl. Ashf 98 B2
Chester Cl. Newb 105 E1
Chester Rd. Harm 71 D2
Chester Rd. Slough 42 B4
Chester St. Caver 59 D1
Chester St. Read 85 E4
Chesterblade La. Brac 118 C1
Chesterfield Rd. Ashf 97 F2
Chesterfield Rd. Newb 105 D1
Chesterman St. Read 86 A3
Chesters Rd. Camb 152 A3
Chesterton Dr. Stan 97 D1
Chesterton Rd. That 106 B3
Chestnut Ave. Camb 152 A3
Chestnut Ave. Caver 59 F2
Chestnut Ave. Slough 43 F2
Chestnut Ave. Went 121 F3
Chestnut Cl. Ashf 98 A2
Chestnut Cl. Ashf 98 C1
Chestnut Cl. Black 150 C3
Chestnut Cl. Eng G 95 E1
Chestnut Cl. Harl 71 D4
Chestnut Cl. Maid 20 A1
Chestnut Cl. Medm 17 E4
Chestnut Cl. Thea 83 F2
Chestnut Cres. Newb 105 D2
Chestnut Cres. Shin 113 F2
Chestnut Dr. Bur C 111 D2
Chestnut Dr. Eng G 95 E1
Chestnut Dr. Wind 66 C2
Chestnut Gr. Pur O T 57 E2
Chestnut Gr. Stai 97 E1
Chestnut La. Lamb 25 F2
Chestnut Manor Cl. Stai 97 D2
Chestnut Rd. Ashf 98 A2
Chestnut Wlk. Hung 100 B2
Chestnut Wlk. Shepp 125 F3
Chestnuts The. Shipl 36 A2
Chetwode Cl. Woki 116 C3
Cheveley Gdns. Burn 21 E2
Cheviot Cl. Camb 152 B2
Cheviot Cl. Hart 71 E4
Cheviot Cl. Maid 40 A3
Cheviot Cl. Newb 130 B3
Cheviot Dr. Char 61 D2
Cheviot Rd. Slough 44 A1
Chewter Cl. Bags 145 F2
Chewter La. Windl 146 A3
Cheylesmore Dr. Camb 152 B2
Cheyne Rd. Ashf 98 B1
Chichester Ct. Slough 43 D2
Chichester Rd. Read 84 C4
Chicory Cl. Read 86 C1
Chievley Cl. Read 84 B4
Chilcombe Way. Read 87 E1
Child St. Lamb 25 D1
Childrey Way. Read 84 B4
Chillingham Way. Camb 151 E2
Chilsey Green Rd. Chert 123 F1
Chiltern Cl. Hen-O-T 35 D4
Chiltern Cl. Newb 130 B3
Chiltern Cres. Read 87 D4
Chiltern Dr. Char 61 D2
Chiltern Green. Fla H 3 D4
Chiltern Rd. Burn 41 D4
Chiltern Rd. Caver 59 E2
Chiltern Rd. Maid 40 A3
Chiltern Rd. Mar 1 B1
Chiltern Rd. Sand 142 C1
Chiltern View. Pur O T 57 E3
Chiltern Wlk. Pangb 56 C3
Chilterns Cl. Fla H 3 D4
Chilterns Park. Bou E 3 D3
Chilton Way. Hung 100 B3
Chilwick Rd. Slough 21 F1
Chippendale Cl. Black 150 C2
Chippendale Cl. Tad 134 C1
Chippenham Cl. Read 113 F4
Chipstead Rd. Harm 71 D2
Chisbury Cl. Brac 118 C2
Chitterfield Gate. Harm 71 D4
Chittering Cl. Winn 87 E1
Chive Rd. Read 87 D1
Chivers Dr. Woki 141 F4
Chives Pl. New G 91 F1
Chobham La. Went 122 A1
Chobham Rd. Camb 151 F1
Chobham Rd. Went 121 D1
Choke La. Cook 19 D2
Cholmeley Pl. Read 86 C4
Cholmeley Rd. Read 86 C4
Cholmeley Terr. Read 86 C4
Cholsey Rd. That 106 C2
Choseley Cl. Know H 37 F2
Choseley Rd. Know H 37 F2
Chrislaine Cl. Stan 70 B1
Christchurch Dr. Black 150 B3
Christchurch Gdns. Read 86 B3
Christchurch Rd. Harm 71 D2
Christchurch Rd. Read 86 B3
Christchurch Rd. Vir W 122 B3
Christie Cl. Light 146 B1
Christie Hts. Newb 131 D4
Christie Wlk. Yate 149 E2

Christmas La. Far C 22 B4
Christopher Ct. Newb 105 D1
Chudleigh Gdns. Read 86 B1
Church App. Stai 123 E3
Church Cl. Eton 67 E4
Church Cl. Ham M 129 F3
Church Cl. Lamb 25 D2
Church Cl. Maid 39 E3
Church Cl. Stai 124 B3
Church Cl. Winn 88 B1
Church Croft. Hung 100 B3
Church Dr. Maid 40 B2
Church End La. Read 84 C4
Church Farmbarns. Mort 137 E3
Church Gate. That 106 B2
Church Gr. Slough 43 E4
Church Hams. Woki 141 E3
Church Hill. Binf 90 B3
Church Hill. Camb 151 F3
Church Hill. Chil 10 B4
Church Hill. East I 30 C3
Church Hill. Hurst 88 C3
Church La. Arbo 114 B2
Church La. Ascot 120 B3
Church La. Asham 54 A3
Church La. Bark 115 E1
Church La. Binf 90 B2
Church La. Bur C 111 F3
Church La. Chiev 51 D1
Church La. Combe 147 F3
Church La. Finch 141 F2
Church La. Ham M 129 F4
Church La. Hung 100 B3
Church La. Maid 40 B2
Church La. New G 91 E3
Church La. Newb 104 B2
Church La. Padw 110 B2
Church La. Read 113 E3
Church La. Shipl 35 F1
Church La. Silc 136 C1
Church La. Slough 43 E4
Church La. Sto P 22 C1
Church La. Swal 140 B3
Church La. That 106 B2
Church La. Twyf 61 F3
Church La. Wind 67 E3
Church La. Yatt 53 F1
Church Mews. Pur O T 57 E3
Church Path. Maid 40 B2
Church Rd E. Crow 143 D3
Church Rd W. Crow 143 D2
Church Rd. Alde 135 D4
Church Rd. Ascot 120 A3
Church Rd. Ashf 97 F2
Church Rd. Bags 145 E2
Church Rd. Brac 118 B4
Church Rd. Burl 119 D4
Church Rd. Caver 59 D1
Church Rd. Cook 19 D3
Church Rd. Eng G 96 A2
Church Rd. Far C 22 B1
Church Rd. Frox 99 D3
Church Rd. Ham 126 A1
Church Rd. Lit M 2 B1
Church Rd. Maid 40 A3
Church Rd. Newb 105 D3
Church Rd. Pangb 56 B3
Church Rd. Read 87 D3
Church Rd. Sand 143 F1
Church Rd. Sand 150 C4
Church Rd. Shepp 125 D1
Church Rd. Silc 135 F1
Church Rd. Sunn 121 D2
Church Rd. Swal 139 E3
Church Rd. West E 153 F4
Church Rd. Windl 146 B2
Church Rd. Wink 92 B3
Church Rd. Wood 87 F4
Church Side. East I 30 C3
Church Sq. Shepp 125 D1
Church St. Blew 12 A4
Church St. Burn 21 E1
Church St. Caver 59 D1
Church St. Crow 143 D3
Church St. Frox 99 D1
Church St. Gr She 48 A2
Church St. Hamp N 52 C3
Church St. Hen-O-T 15 E1
Church St. Hung 100 B3
Church St. Kint 102 A1
Church St. Read 86 A3
Church St. Slough 42 B2
Church St. Slough 42 C2
Church St. Stai 96 C2
Church St. Thea 83 F2
Church St. Twyf 61 E2
Church St. Warg 36 B1
Church St. Wind 67 E3
Church View. Been 109 D3
Church View. Whi Wa 63 F4
Church View. Yate 149 E3
Church Views. Maid 39 F4
Church Way. Hung 100 B3
Church Wlk. Chert 124 A2
Churchfield Mews. Slough 43 D4
Churchill Cl. Fla H 3 D4
Churchill Cl. Fla H 3 E4

Churchill Cres. Yate 149 E3
Churchill Dr. Mar 1 C2
Churchill Dr. Winn 88 A1
Churchill Rd. Slough 43 F1
Churchward Wlk. Read 84 C2
Churchway. West I 10 A1
Churn Rd. Comp 31 E3
Cinnamon Cl. Read 86 C1
Cintra Ave. Read 86 B3
Cippenham Cl. Slough 41 F3
Cippenham La. Slough 42 A3
Circle Hill Rd. Crow 143 E3
Circuit La. Read 85 E3
City Rd. Read 84 A4
Clacy Green. Brac 91 D1
Clandon Ave. Stai 96 B1
Clanfield Cres. Read 57 E1
Clanfield Ride. Black 150 B3
Clappers Meadow. Maid 20 B1
Clapps Gate Rd. Silc 135 F1
Clapton App. Woo G 3 E4
Clare Ave. Woki 116 B4
Clare Dr. Far C 22 A4
Clare Gdns. Eng G 96 A2
Clare Rd. Maid 39 E3
Clare Rd. Slough 41 E4
Clare Rd. Stan 70 C1
Clare Rd. Stan 97 F4
Clare Wlk. Newb 130 B3
Claredon Cl. Winn 88 B1
Clarefield Cl. Maid 19 D1
Clarefield Dr. Maid 19 D1
Clarefield Rd. Maid 19 D1
Claremont Ave. Camb 151 F3
Claremont Dr. Shepp 125 D2
Claremont Gdns. Mar 1 C1
Claremont Rd. Mar 1 C1
Claremont Rd. Stai 96 B2
Claremont Rd. Wind 67 E3
Clarence Cres. Wind 67 E3
Clarence Dr. Eng G 95 E2
Clarence Rd. Hen-O-T 15 E1
Clarence Rd. Wind 67 D3
Clarence St. Eng G 95 F1
Clarence St. Stai 96 C2
Clarence Way. Read 84 A2
Clarendon Ct. Black 150 B2
Clarendon Cl. Slough 43 D3
Clarendon Gdns. Newb 105 D2
Clarendon Rd. Ashf 97 F2
Clarendon Rd. Read 87 D3
Clares Green Rd. Shin 113 D2
Clarewood Dr. Camb 151 F3
Clark's Gdns. Hung 100 B3
Clarke Cres. Sand 150 C4
Classics The. Lamb 25 D1
Claverdon. Brac 118 A1
Clay Cl. Fla H 3 D4
Clay Cl. Pur O T 57 D1
Clay Hill Cres. Newb 105 E3
Clay La. Been 108 C3
Claydon Gdns. Camb 151 D1
Clayhall La. Old Wind 67 F1
Clayhill Cl. Brac 119 D3
Clayton Gr. Brac 118 C4
Clayton Rd. Black 150 C1
Clayton Wlk. Read 86 B2
Claytons Meadow. Bou E 3 D2
Clearsprings. Camb 153 D4
Clearsprings. Light 146 A1
Cleaves Way. Ashf 98 C1
Cleeve Ct. Felt 98 C4
Cleeve Down. Gori 34 B4
Cleeve Rd. Gori 34 A4
Clements Cl. Shin 113 D1
Clements Cl. Slough 43 D2
Clements Mead. Sulh 57 D1
Clements Rd. Hen-O-T 15 E2
Clent Rd. Read 86 A2
Cleopatra Pl. New G 91 F1
Cleve Ct. Wind 66 C2
Clevedon Dr. Read 87 D1
Clevedon Rd. Read 57 F2
Clevehurst Cl. Sto P 23 D3
Cleveland Cl. Maid 40 A3
Cleveland Cl. Woo G 3 F4
Cleveland Dr. Stai 124 A4
Cleveland Gr. Newb 104 C2
Cleveland. Char 61 D2
Clevemede. Gori 34 B4
Clewborough Dr. Camb 152 A3
Clewer Ave. Wind 67 D3
Clewer Ct Rd. Wind 67 D3
Clewer Fields. Wind 67 D3
Clewer Hill Rd. Wind 66 C2
Clewer New Town. Wind 67 D3
Clewer Park. Wind 67 D4
Clifford Gr. Ashf 98 A2
Clifford Way. Bou E 3 D3
Clifton Cl. Maid 40 A2
Clifton Rd. Harm 71 D2
Clifton Rd. Newb 104 C1
Clifton Rd. Slough 43 D2
Clifton Rd. Woki 116 A4
Clifton Rise. Warg 36 C1
Clifton Rise. Wind 66 B3
Clifton St. Read 85 F4
Clintons Green. Brac 118 A4
Clive Ct. Slough 42 B2

Clive Green. Brac 118 A4
Clivedale Rd. Wood 87 F4
Cliveden Mead. Maid 20 B1
Cliveden Pl. Shepp 125 E4
Cliveden Rd. Tapl 20 C2
Clivemont Rd. Maid 39 F4
Clockhouse La E. Stai 96 A1
Clockhouse La W. Eng G 96 A1
Clockhouse La. Ashf 98 A3
Clockhouse La. Felt 98 A3
Cloister Mews. Thea 83 F2
Cloisters The. Camb 151 E1
Cloisters The. Caver 59 D1
Clonmel Way. Burn 21 D1
Close End. Lamb 25 D1
Close The. Bou E 3 D3
Close The. Bur C 111 D2
Close The. Burl 119 E4
Close The. Gr She 48 A2
Close The. Hamp N 52 C3
Close The. Hen-O-T 35 E4
Close The. Light 146 A1
Close The. Sand 150 C4
Close The. Slough 41 E4
Close The. That 106 A2
Close The. Vir W 122 B2
Close The. Wood 87 F3
Clough Dr. Herm 78 C3
Clove Cl. Read 86 C1
Clover Cl. Woki 116 C4
Clover La. Yate 149 D3
Club La. Crow 143 E3
Clumps The. Felt 98 B2
Clyde Rd. Stan 97 F4
Clyve Way. Stai 123 F4
Coach House Cl. Camb 151 E4
Coach Ride. Mar 1 B2
Coalport Way. Read 57 F1
Cobb Cl. Datch 68 B3
Cobbett's La. Yate 149 F3
Cobblers Cl. Far C 22 A2
Cobham Rd. Wood 87 F4
Cochrane Cl. That 106 C2
Cochrane Pl. Windl 146 B3
Cock La. Brad 82 A1
Cock's La. New G 92 A3
Cock's La. Wink 92 A3
Cock-a-Dobby. Sand 143 D1
Cockett Rd. Slough 43 F2
Cockney Hill. Read 84 C3
Cody Cl. Read 88 A4
Coe Spur. Slough 42 A2
Coftards. Slough 43 E4
Cold Ash Hill. Cold A 79 F2
Cold Harbour. Hen-O-T 35 E4
Coldharbour Cl. Stai 123 E3
Coldharbour La. Stai 123 E3
Coldharbour La. West E 153 F4
Coldharbour Rd. Hung 100 B2
Coldicutt St. Caver 59 E1
Coldmoorholme La. Bou E 2 C2
Colemans Moor La. Wood 87 F3
Colemans Moor Rd. Wood 88 A3
Colenorton Cres. Eton 41 F1
Coleridge Ave. Yate 149 F3
Coleridge Cl. Crow 143 E2
Coleridge Cl. Twyf 61 F2
Coleridge Cres. Stan 69 F3
Coleridge Rd. Ashf 97 F2
Coley Ave. Read 85 F3
Coley Hill. Read 85 F3
Coley Park Rd. Read 85 F3
Coley Pl. Read 86 A3
Colin Way. Slough 42 A2
Collaroy Rd. Cold A 106 B4
College Ave. Maid 39 F4
College Ave. Slough 42 C2
College Ave. Stai 96 A1
College Cl. Camb 151 E4
College Cres. Sand 150 C4
College Cres. Wind 67 E3
College Glen. Maid 39 E4
College Piece. Mort 136 C3
College Rd. Maid 40 B2
College Rd. Read 86 C3
College Rd. Slough 41 F3
College Ride. Bags 145 E4
College Ride. Camb 151 E4
College Rise. Maid 39 E4
College Way. Ashf 97 F2
Colleton Dr. Twyf 61 F3
Collier Cl. Maid 19 F1
Colliers Way. Read 85 D4
Collingwood Rise. Camb 152 A4
Collingwood Wlk. Read 84 A4
Collins Cl. Newb 105 E2
Collins Dr. Herm 78 C3
Collinswood Rd. Far C 22 B4
Collis St. Read 86 A3
Colliston Wlk. Read 84 C2
Collum Green Rd. Sto P 22 C4
Coln Cl. Maid 39 F4
Colnbrook By-Pass. Iver 69 E4
Colnbrook By-Pass. Slough ... 69 E4
Colndale Rd. Stan 69 E4
Colne Bank. Hort 69 E2
Colne Orchard. Iver 44 C4
Colne Way. Wray 96 A3
Colnebridge Cl. Stai 96 C2

Colnworth Cl. Read 114 A4
Colonel's La. Chert 124 A2
Colonial Rd. Felt 98 C4
Colonial Rd. Slough 43 D2
Colston Cl. Bur C 84 B2
Colthrop La. That 107 D1
Columbia Ct. Woki 141 F4
Colville Gdns. Light 153 E4
Colwyn Cl. Yate 149 E3
Colyer Cl. Herm 79 E4
Colyton Way. Pur O T 57 E3
Combe Rd. Read 84 C4
Combe View. Hung 100 B2
Combermere Cl. Wind 67 D3
Comet Rd. Stan 97 E4
Comet Way. Wood 88 A4
Comfrey Cl. Woki 116 C4
Commercial Rd. Read 86 A1
Commercial Rd. Stai 97 D1
Common Hill. Brad 82 C2
Common La. Brig 28 B3
Common La. Eton 42 B1
Common Rd. Dorn 41 E1
Common Rd. Eton 42 A1
Common Rd. Fla H 3 D4
Common Rd. Head 132 C1
Common Rd. Slough 44 A1
Common The. Fla H 3 D4
Common Wood. Far C 22 B4
Commonfield La. Bark 141 D4
Commonfields. West E 153 E4
Commons Rd. Woki 88 C1
Compton Ave. Read 57 D3
Compton Cl. Brac 117 F2
Compton Cl. Read 87 E4
Compton Cl. Sand 143 E1
Compton Ct. Slough 41 F4
Compton Dr. Maid 39 D4
Comsaye Wlk. Brac 118 B2
Concorde Way. Slough 42 B2
Concorde Way. Wood 88 A4
Condor Cl. Sulh 57 E2
Condor Rd. Stai 124 B3
Conegar Ct. Slough 42 C3
Coneygree Cl. Read 87 D1
Congreve Cl. Alde 135 D4
Conifer Cl. Tad 134 C1
Conifer Crest. Newb 130 B2
Conifer Dr. Camb 152 A3
Conifer Dr. Sulh 57 D1
Conifer La. Stai 96 B2
Conifers The. Brac 143 D4
Coningham Rd. Read 113 E3
Coningsby Cl. Maid 39 E2
Coningsby La. Holy 65 E3
Coningsby. Brac 118 B3
Conisboro Ave. Caver 58 C3
Conisboro Way. Caver 58 C3
Coniston Cl. Camb 152 B2
Coniston Cl. That 106 A2
Coniston Cl. Wood 87 F3
Coniston Cres. Slough 41 E4
Coniston Ct. Light 146 B1
Coniston Dr. Read 57 F1
Coniston Way. Stai 96 A1
Connaught Ave. Ashf 97 F2
Connaught Cl. Crow 142 C2
Connaught Cl. Maid 19 F1
Connaught Cl. Read 85 E4
Connaught Cl. Yate 149 D3
Connaught Rd. Bags 145 E2
Connaught Rd. Camb 151 F3
Connaught Rd. Newb 105 D2
Connaught Rd. Read 85 E4
Connaught Rd. Slough 43 D2
Conniston Cl. Mar 1 A1
Connop Way. Camb 151 F2
Constable Way. Sand 150 C3
Constitution Rd. Read 85 D4
Consul Cl. Wood 88 A3
Control Tower Rd. Harm 71 D2
Convent Lodge. Ashf 98 A2
Convent Rd. Ashf 98 A2
Convent Rd. Wind 67 D3
Conway Dr. Ashf 98 B1
Conway Dr. That 106 A3
Conway Rd. Burn 41 D4
Conway Rd. Harm 71 D2
Conway Rd. Read 84 B3
Conway Rd. Slough 41 D4
Cookham Cl. Sand 143 E1
Cookham Dean Bottom La. Cook 19 E4
Cookham Rd. Brac 117 F4
Cookham Rd. Maid 19 F1
Cookham Rd. Maid 19 F2
Coolarne Rise. Camb 152 A3
Coolgardie Rd. Ashf 98 B2
Coombe Ct. That 106 C2
Coombe Hill. Farn 28 A4
Coombe Pine. Brac 118 B2
Coombe Rd. Comp 31 F2
Coombe Sq. That 106 C2
Coombe Rd. Yate 149 D4
Coombes La. Woki 115 E2
Coombe The. Stre 33 F3
Coombesbury La. Box 76 B1
Cooper Cl. Read 113 E4
Cooper Rd. Hen-O-T 15 E2

Cooper Rd. Windl 146 B2
Cooper Way. Slough 42 A2
Cooper's Hill La. Eng G 95 E2
Coopers Cl. Stai 96 C2
Coopers Cres. That 106 B2
Cope Hall La. Ham M 130 B4
Copelands Cl. Camb 152 B2
Copenhagen Cl. Read 113 E4
Copped Hall Dr. Camb 152 B3
Copped Hall Way. Camb 152 B3
Copper Beech Cl. Wind 66 B3
Copperage Rd. Farn 9 D1
Copperdale Cl. Read 86 C2
Coppermill Rd. Hort 69 D1
Coppermill Rd. Wray 69 D1
Coppice Cl. Newb 131 D4
Coppice Dr. Wray 95 E4
Coppice Gdns. Crow 142 C3
Coppice Gdns. Yate 149 E3
Coppice Green. Brac 90 C1
Coppice Rd. Wood 87 F2
Coppice The. Ashf 98 A1
Coppins La. Iver 44 C4
Copse Ave. Caver 59 F2
Copse Cl. Camb 152 A3
Copse Cl. Mar 1 B1
Copse Cl. Read 57 E2
Copse Dr. Woki 116 A4
Copse End. Camb 152 A3
Copse Mead. Wood 60 C1
Copse The. Warg 36 C2
Copse Way. Woki 141 F4
Copthorn Cl. Maid 39 D2
Copthorne Cl. Shepp 125 E2
Copthorne Dr. Light 146 A1
Corbett Dr. Camb 152 C4
Corbett Gdns. Wood 87 F4
Corbridge Rd. Read 86 B2
Corby Cl. Wood 61 D1
Corby Dr. Eng G 95 E1
Cordelia Gdns. Stan 97 F3
Cordelia Rd. Stan 97 F4
Corderoy Cl. That 106 C1
Corderoy Pl. Chert 123 F2
Cordwalles Rd. Camb 151 F4
Cordwallis Rd. Maid 39 F4
Cordwallis St. Maid 39 F4
Cores End Rd. Bou E 3 D2
Corfe Gdns. Camb 151 F1
Corfe Gdns. Slough 42 A3
Corfe Mews. Caver 59 F2
Corfe Pl. Maid 39 E4
Corfield Cl. Finch 141 F2
Coriander Way. Read 86 C1
Cormorant Pl. Sand 150 C4
Cornbunting Cl. Sand 150 B4
Cornerside. Ashf 98 B1
Cornfield Green. Woki 115 E4
Cornfield Rd. Wood 88 A4
Cornfields. Yate 149 D2
Cornflower Cl. Woki 115 E4
Cornwall Ave. Slough 22 B1
Cornwall Cl. Camb 151 F4
Cornwall Cl. Eton 41 F1
Cornwall Cl. Maid 19 F1
Cornwall Cl. Pur O T 57 D2
Cornwall Cl. Woki 115 E3
Cornwall Way. Stai 96 C1
Cornwell Rd. Old W 68 A1
Cornwood Gdns. Read 86 B2
Coronation Ave. Slough 43 F4
Coronation Rd. Ascot 120 A1
Coronation Rd. Bish 38 A4
Coronation Rd. Brac 120 A1
Coronation Rd. Yate 149 F4
Coronation Sq. Read 85 D2
Coronation Sq. Woki 116 B4
Corrie Gdns. Went 122 B1
Corrine Cl. Read 86 A1
Corsair Cl. Stan 97 F4
Corsair Rd. Stan 97 F4
Corsham Rd. Read 84 C2
Corsham Way. Crow 143 D3
Corwen Rd. Read 84 C1
Coster Cl. Newb 104 B3
Cotswold Cl. Maid 40 A3
Cotswold Cl. Slough 42 B2
Cotswold Cl. Stai 97 D2
Cotswold Rd. Sand 142 C1
Cotswold Way. Read 57 E1
Cottage Farm Way. Stai 123 E3
Cottage La. Bur C 85 E1
Cotterell Cl. Brac 91 D1
Cottesbrooke Cl. Stan 69 E3
Cottesmore Rd. Wood 87 E3
Cottesmore. Brac 118 A1
Coulson Way. Burn 41 D4
County La. New G 91 F1
Course Rd. Ascot 120 A3
Court Cl. Holy 40 B1
Court Cres. Slough 42 B4
Court Dr. Maid 20 B2
Court Gdns. Camb 151 E3
Court Hill Rd. Farn 7 D4
Court Hill Rd. Let B 7 D4
Court La. Burn 21 E1
Court La. Iver 44 C3
Court La. Slough 41 D2
Court Rd. Maid 20 B2

Courtenay Dr. Caver 59 D4
Courtfield Rd. Ashf 98 A1
Courtfields Dr. Maid 39 E3
Courthouse Rd. Maid 39 E4
Courtlands Ave. Slough 43 E1
Courtlands Hill. Pangb 56 B2
Courtlands Rd. Newb 105 D1
Courtlands. Maid 39 F3
Courtney Rd. Harm 71 D2
Courts Rd. Read 87 D2
Courtyard The. Thea 83 F2
Coventry Rd. Read 86 C4
Coverdale Way. Slough 21 F1
Covert The. Sunn 120 A1
Cow La. East I 30 C4
Cow La. Moul 13 F2
Cow La. Read 58 C1
Cowley Ave. Chert 123 F1
Cowley La. Chert 123 F1
Coworth Cl. Sunn 121 D2
Coworth Rd. Sunn 121 D2
Cowper Cl. Chert 123 F1
Cowper Rd. Slough 22 A1
Cowper Way. Read 85 E2
Cowslade. Newb 104 B3
Cowslip Cl. Read 84 A3
Cox Green La. Maid 39 E2
Cox Green Rd. Maid 39 E2
Cox Green. Sand 150 B4
Cox's La. Wool 107 E2
Coxborrow Cl. Cook 19 F4
Coxeter Rd. Newb 104 C2
Crabtree Cl. Herm 78 C3
Crabtree Rd. Camb 151 D1
Crabtree Rd. Stai 123 E4
Craddock Rd. Read 86 A2
Crafts End. Chil 10 C4
Craig Ave. Read 85 D4
Craigwell Cl. Stai 123 F4
Crail Cl. Woki 116 A2
Crake Pl. Sand 150 B4
Cramond Ct. Felt 98 C4
Cranborne Gdns. Read 58 A1
Cranbourne Ave. Bur C 84 B2
Cranbourne Ave. Wind 66 C3
Cranbourne Cl. Slough 42 B3
Cranbourne Hall Caravan Site. Wink 93 D4
Cranbourne Rd. Slough 42 B3
Cranbrook Dr. Maid 19 E1
Cranbury Rd. Read 85 E4
Crane Cl. Sand 150 B4
Crane Wharf. Read 86 A4
Craneswater. Harl 71 F4
Cranford Ave. Stan 97 F4
Cranford Cl. Hurst 88 C4
Cranford Cl. Stan 97 F4
Cranford La. Harl 71 F4
Cranford La. Harm 71 F4
Cranford La. Harm 71 F3
Cranford Park Dr. Yate 149 E3
Cranleigh Rd. Felt 98 C2
Cranmer Cl. Sulh 57 D2
Cranwell Gr. Light 152 C4
Cranwell Gr. Stai 124 C3
Cranwell Rd. Harm 71 D2
Craufurd Rise. Maid 39 F4
Craven Cl. Kint 102 A1
Craven Dene. Newb 105 D2
Craven Rd. Ink 127 D3
Craven Rd. Newb 104 C1
Craven Rd. Read 86 B3
Craven Way. Kint 102 A1
Crawford Cl. Read 87 D2
Crawford Gdns. Camb 151 D3
Crawford Pl. Newb 104 C2
Crawley Chase. Burl 92 A1
Crawley Dr. Camb 151 F3
Crawley Hill. Camb 151 F3
Crawley Ridge. Camb 151 F3
Crawley Wood Cl. Camb 151 F3
Crawshay Dr. Caver 59 D4
Crayle St. Slough 22 A1
Crayonne Cl. Stai 125 F4
Crecy Cl. Woki 115 F3
Creden Cl. Maid 39 E4
Crediton Cl. Wood 88 A3
Crees Meadow. Windl 146 B2
Cremyll Rd. Read 58 C1
Crescent Ave. Read 86 C4
Crescent Dr. Maid 39 F4
Crescent Rd. Read 57 F1
Crescent Rd. Shepp 125 E2
Crescent The. Ashf 97 F2
Crescent The. Chert 124 A3
Crescent The. Eng G 95 F1
Crescent The. Eng G 95 F1
Crescent The. Harl 71 E4
Crescent The. Kint 102 A1
Crescent The. Maid 39 F4
Crescent The. Mort 137 D3
Crescent The. Padw 109 E2
Crescent The. Read 87 E2
Crescent The. Shepp 125 F1
Crescent The. Shipl 36 A2
Crescent The. Slough 42 C2
Crescent The. Thea 83 F2
Cress Rd. Slough 42 A2

Cressex Cl. Binf 90 B1
Cressingham Rd. Read 86 B3
Cressington Pl. Bou E 3 D2
Cresswell Rd. Newb 105 E2
Cresswells Mead. Holy 40 B1
Crest Cl. Twyf 61 F3
Crest The. Caver 59 E3
Creswell Cl. Read 113 E3
Cricket Field Gr. Crow 143 E2
Cricket Hill La. Yate 149 F2
Cricket Hill. Finch 141 F1
Cricketers La. Burl 92 A2
Cricketers La. Windl 146 B2
Cricketers. Box 103 F3
Crimp Hill. Eng G 95 D3
Crimp Hill. Old W 95 D3
Crisp Gdns. Binf 90 C1
Crisp Rd. Hen-O-T 15 E2
Crispin Cl. Caver 58 B3
Crispin Way. Far C 22 B4
Crocker Cl. Ascot 119 F4
Crockhamwell Rd. Wood 87 F3
Crocus Way. Woki 115 E4
Croft Cl. Harl 71 E4
Croft Cl. Woki 116 A1
Croft La. Newb 104 C2
Croft La. Yate 149 E4
Croft Rd. Gori 34 B3
Croft Rd. Hung 100 B3
Croft Rd. Mort 136 C3
Croft Rd. Newb 130 C4
Croft Rd. Woki 116 A1
Croft Road. Shin 113 E1
Croft The. Brac 91 D1
Croft The. Kint 102 A1
Croft The. Maid 39 E3
Croft The. Mar 2 A2
Croft Way. Camb 151 F1
Crofter's Cl. Sand 150 A4
Crofters. Old W 68 A1
Crofthill Rd. Slough 22 A1
Crofton Cl. Brac 118 C2
Crofts The. Shepp 125 F3
Cromer Cl. Read 57 E1
Cromer Rd W. Harn 71 D2
Cromer Rd. Harm 71 D3
Cromwell Cl. Hen-O-T 35 F4
Cromwell Dr. Slough 42 C4
Cromwell Gdns. Mar 1 C1
Cromwell Rd. Ascot 120 A3
Cromwell Rd. Camb 151 E4
Cromwell Rd. Caver 59 D1
Cromwell Rd. Hen-O-T 35 F4
Cromwell Rd. Maid 39 E4
Cromwell Rd. Mar 1 C1
Cromwell Rd. Newb 105 E3
Crondall End. Yate 149 E4
Crondell Ct. Camb 151 D2
Cropper Cl. That 107 D2
Crosby Gdns. Yate 149 D4
Crosby Hill Dr. Camb 151 F4
Cross Fell. Brac 118 A3
Cross Gates Cl. Brac 118 C3
Cross Keys Rd. Sou S 14 B2
Cross La. Bee H 138 B4
Cross Oak. Wind 67 D3
Cross Rd. Windl 121 D1
Cross St. Read 86 A4
Cross St. Woki 116 B3
Crossfields Cl. Read 113 F4
Crossland Rd. Read 86 A4
Crossways. Stai 96 B1
Crossways. Stai 98 C1
Crossways. Wood 87 F3
Crosswell Cl. Stai 125 E4
Crosthwaite Way. Slough 41 E4
Crouch La. Wink 92 C4
Crow Piece La. Burn 21 F2
Crowfield Dr. That 106 A2
Crowle Rd. Lamb 25 D1
Crown Acre Cl. That 106 B2
Crown La. Burn 22 A2
Crown La. Maid 40 A4
Crown La. Mar 1 B1
Crown La. Thea 83 F2
Crown La. Went 122 B2
Crown Meadow. Iver 69 D4
Crown Pl. Read 86 B3
Crown Pl. Sand 143 F1
Crown Rd. Mar 1 B1
Crown Rd. Went 122 B2
Crown Row. Brac 118 B2
Crown St. Eng G 96 A2
Crown St. Read 86 A3
Crowsley Rd. Shipl 36 A2
Crowthorne Rd N. Brac 118 A3
Crowthorne Rd. Brac 117 F1
Crowthorne Rd. Brac 118 A2
Crowthorne Rd. Sand 143 D1
Croxley Rise. Maid 39 E3
Croydon Rd. Harm 71 D2
Cruikshank Lea. Sand 150 C3
Crummock Cl. Slough 41 E4
Crutchley Rd. Woki 116 B4
Cuckoo La. West E 153 E3
Cuckoo Pound. Shepp 125 F2
Cuckoo Vale. West E 153 E3
Culford Cl. Winn 87 E1
Culham Dr. Maid 19 F1

Cullen Cl. Yate 149 E3
Cullern's Pas. Maid 39 F3
Culley Way. Maid 39 D2
Culloden Way. Woki 115 F3
Culver Croft. Binf 90 C1
Culver La. Read 87 D4
Culver Rd. Newb 130 C4
Culver Rd. Read 86 C3
Culver Rd. Sand 143 E1
Cumberland Ave. Slough 22 B1
Cumberland Dr. Brac 118 B4
Cumberland Rd. Ashf 97 D3
Cumberland Rd. Camb 152 B2
Cumberland Rd. Read 86 C4
Cumberland St. Stai 96 B2
Cumberland Way. Woki 115 E3
Cumbernauld Gdns. Ashf 98 C2
Cumbria Cl. Maid 39 E2
Cumnor Way. Brac 118 C3
Curl Way. Woki 116 A3
Curlew Cl. That 106 B2
Curlew Dr. Read 84 B3
Curley Hill Rd. Light 152 C2
Curling Way. Newb 105 E2
Curls Rd. Maid 39 E2
Curridge Green. Herm 78 C2
Curridge Piece. Herm 78 C3
Curridge Rd. Herm 78 B2
Curriers La. Burn 21 F4
Curtis Rd. Read 84 B2
Curzon St. Read 85 F4
Cutbush Cl. Read 114 A4
Cutbush La. Read 114 A4
Cutting Hill. Ham 126 A2
Cygnet Cl. That 106 A2
Cypress Cl. Brac 142 A4
Cypress Rd. Stai 125 F4
Cypress Rd. Wood 88 A3
Cypress Way. Black 150 A3
Cypress Wlk. Eng G 95 D1
Cyril Vokins Rd. Gree 105 F4

Dacre Ave. Caver 59 F2
Dagmar Rd. Wind 67 E3
Dairy La. Hamb 16 A4
Dalby Cres. Newb 131 D4
Dalby Cres. Newb 131 E4
Dalcross. Brac 118 C2
Dale Cl. Sunn 121 D2
Dale Ct. Slough 42 B2
Dale Gdns. Sand 150 A4
Dale Lodge Rd. Sunn 121 D2
Dale Rd. Ashf 98 C1
Dale Rd. Read 86 A3
Dale Rd. Shepp 125 F1
Daleham Ave. Eng G 96 A1
Dalston Cl. Camb 152 B2
Dalton Cl. Read 84 C4
Damar Gdns. Hen-O-T 35 F4
Damask Cl. Camb 153 F3
Dandridge Cl. Slough 43 E1
Dandridge Dr. Bou E 3 E2
Dane Rd. Ashf 98 B1
Danehill. Read 114 A4
Danvers Cl. That 106 B1
Danywern Dr. Winn 88 B1
Darby Green La. Black 150 A3
Darby Green Rd. Black 150 A3
Darby La. Upp B 55 D3
Darell Rd. Caver 58 C2
Dark La. Brad 82 B4
Dark La. Read 57 D1
Dark La. Warg 36 B1
Dark La. Wick 101 D4
Darleydale Cl. Crow 143 E1
Darling's La. Bish 18 C1
Darrell Cl. Slough 43 F1
Dart Cl. Slough 69 D4
Dart Cl. That 106 A3
Dart Cl. Woki 141 F3
Dartington Ave. Wood 87 E2
Dartmouth Cl. Brac 118 C3
Darvill's La. Slough 42 B2
Darvills La. St L 62 C1
Darwall Dr. Burl 119 E4
Darwin Cl. Read 86 A1
Darwin Rd. Slough 43 F2
Dashwood Cl. Brac 118 B4
Dashwood Cl. Slough 43 E1
Datchet Pl. Slough 68 A3
Datchet Rd. Datch 42 C1
Datchet Rd. Hort 68 C2
Datchet Rd. Old W 68 A2
Datchet Rd. Slough 42 C1
Datchet Rd. Wind 67 E4
Dauntless Rd. Bur C 111 D2
Davenport Rd. Brac 118 C4
Daventry Cl. Stan 69 F3
Daventry Ct. Brac 118 A4
David Cl. Harl 71 E4
David Rd. Stan 69 F3
David Smith Ct. Read 84 C3
Davis Cl. Mar 1 C1
Davis Cl. Winn 88 A1
Davis Gdns. Sand 150 C4
Davis St. Hurst 88 B3
Davis Way. Hurst 88 A2
Dawes East Rd. Burn 21 E1
Dawes Moor Cl. Slough 43 E4

Dawley Ride. Stan 69 F3
Dawlish Rd. Read 86 B1
Dawn Redwood Cl. Hort 69 D2
Dawnay Cl. Ascot 119 F4
Dawnay Rd. Sand 151 D4
Dawsmere Rd. Camb 152 B3
Dawson Cl. Wind 67 D3
De Beauvoir Rd. Read 86 C3
De Bohun Rd. Read 86 A4
De Havilland Way. Stan 70 C1
De Montfort Gr. Hung 100 B2
De Montfort Rd. Newb 104 C3
De Montfort Rd. Read 59 D1
De Vitre Green. Woki 116 C4
Deacon Cl. Woki 116 B4
Deacon Way. Read 58 A1
Deaconfield. Sou S 14 B2
Deacons La. Herm 79 E4
Deadman's La. Thea 83 E2
Deadmans La. Gree 131 D4
Deadmoor La. Ball H 130 C1
Deadmoor La. Newt 130 C1
Deal Ave. Slough 41 F4
Dean Cl. Wind 66 B2
Dean La. Cook 19 E4
Dean St. Mar 1 B1
Deanfield Ave. Hen-O-T 15 E1
Deanfield Cl. Mar 1 B2
Deanfield Rd. Hen-O-T 15 E1
Deans Cl. Sto P 23 D2
Deans Ct. Windl 146 B2
Deansgate Rd. Read 86 A3
Deansgate. Brac 118 A1
Decies Way. Sto P 23 D2
Dedmere Ct. Mar 1 C1
Dedmere Rd. Mar 1 C1
Dedmere Rise. Mar 1 C1
Dedworth Dr. Wind 66 C3
Dedworth Rd. Wind 66 B3
Dee Rd. Read 85 D4
Deena Cl. Slough 41 F3
Deep Field. Datch 68 A4
Deep Well Dr. Camb 151 F3
Deepcut Bridge Rd. Camb 152 B1
Deepdene Cl. Read 85 F4
Deepfield Rd. Brac 118 B4
Deer Leap. Camb 153 D4
Deer Rock Hill. Brac 118 B2
Deer Rock Rd. Camb 151 F4
Deerhurst Ave. Winn 88 B1
Deerhurst Cl. Read 84 C2
Deerswood. Maid 20 A1
Defford Cl. Woki 88 C1
Delafield Dr. Bur C 84 B2
Delaford Cl. Iver 44 C4
Delamere Rd. Read 87 D4
Delane Dr. Winn 88 A1
Delaney Cl. Read 84 C4
Delft Cl. Read 84 C4
Dell Cl. Far C 22 B4
Dell Gr. Camb 151 F1
Dell Rd. Finch 142 A2
Dell Rd. Read 57 E1
Dell The. Whi Wa 38 C2
Dell The. Yate 149 E3
Dellars Hill. Hurl 38 A4
Delph The. Winn 87 E1
Delta Way. Stai 123 E4
Denbury Gdns. Read 113 E4
Denby Way. Read 57 F1
Dene Cl. Brac 118 B4
Dene Cl. Read 87 D2
Dene Hollow. Chil 10 C4
Dene Way. Newb 105 D3
Denford La. Hung 101 D4
Denford La. Wick 101 D4
Denham Cl. Maid 39 E3
Denham Dr. Yate 149 F3
Denham Gr. Brac 118 B2
Denham Rd. Eng G 96 A2
Denhose Cl. Read 87 D1
Denison Rd. Felt 98 C2
Denly Way. Light 146 B1
Denman Dr. Ashf 98 A1
Denmark Ave. Wood 61 D1
Denmark Rd. Newb 105 D2
Denmark Rd. Read 86 B3
Denmark St. Maid 39 F4
Denmark St. Woki 116 B3
Denmead Ct. Brac 118 C2
Dennis Cl. Ashf 98 B1
Dennis Way. Slough 41 E3
Dennisford Rd. East I 31 D3
Dennistoun Cl. Camb 151 E3
Denny Rd. Slough 43 F1
Denton Cl. That 106 B1
Denton Rd. Woki 116 B3
Denton Way. Camb 151 E1
Depot Rd. Maid 40 A3
Deppdale. Brac 118 A3
Derby Cl. Lamb 25 D1
Derby Rd. Caver 59 D2
Derby Rd. Newb 104 C1
Derby St. Read 85 F4
Derek Rd. Maid 40 B4
Deri Dene Cl. Stan 70 C1
Derrick Cl. Bur C 84 B2
Derry Rd. Black 150 C1
Derwent Ave. Read 57 F1

Derwent Cl. Felt 98 C4
Derwent Cl. Woki 115 F3
Derwent Dr. Maid 39 E4
Derwent Dr. Slough 41 E4
Derwent Rd. Light 153 D4
Derwent Rd. Stai 96 A1
Derwent Rd. That 106 A2
Desborough Cl. Shepp 125 D1
Desborough Cres. Maid 39 E3
Deseronto Wharf. Slough 43 F2
Desford Way. Ashf 97 F3
Devenish La. Sunn 120 B1
Devenish Rd. Ascot 120 B1
Devenish Rd. Sunn 120 B1
Devereux Rd. Wind 67 E3
Deveron Dr. Read 85 D4
Devil's Highway The. Brac 142 C3
Devil's Highway The. Finch 142 C3
Devil's La. Stai 96 B1
Devitt Cl. Read 86 C1
Devon Ave. Slough 42 B4
Devon Cl. Sand 150 B4
Devon Cl. Woki 115 F3
Devon Dr. Caver 59 F2
Devonshire Cl. Slough 22 A2
Devonshire Dr. Camb 151 F4
Devonshire Gdns. Sulh 57 D2
Devonshire Green. Far C 22 A2
Devonshire Park. Read 86 C1
Dhoon Rise. Maid 39 F3
Diamedes Ave. Stan 97 E4
Diamond Hill. Camb 151 F4
Diamond Rd. Slough 43 D2
Diamond Ridge. Camb 151 F4
Diamond Way. Woki 115 F4
Diana Cl. Slough 43 F4
Dianthus Cl. Chert 123 F1
Dick Turpin Way. Harm 71 F2
Dickens Way. Yate 149 E3
Dickens Wlk. Newb 131 D4
Dido Rd. Chil 9 F4
Dieppe Cl. Woki 115 F3
Digby Rd. Newb 104 C2
Dines Way. Herm 79 E4
Dingle Rd. Ashf 98 A2
Disraeli Ct. Slough 69 D4
Ditchfield La. Woki 141 F4
Ditchling. Brac 118 A1
Ditton Park Rd. Datch 68 C4
Ditton Rd. Datch 68 B4
Ditton Rd. Slough 68 C4
Dobson's La. Faw (Bu) 15 E4
Dockett Eddy La. Shepp 124 C1
Doctors La. Herm 79 D3
Doddington Cl. Winn 87 E1
Doddsfield Rd. Slough 22 A1
Dodsells Well. Woki 141 F4
Dog La. Asham 54 A3
Doghurst Ave. Harl 71 D4
Doghurst Dr. Harl 71 D4
Dogkennel La. Fawl 27 E2
Doles Hill. Woki 115 E2
Doles La. Woki 115 F2
Dolman Rd. Newb 105 D2
Dolphin Ct N. Stai 97 D3
Dolphin Ct. Slough 43 D2
Dolphin Ct. Stan 97 D3
Dolphin Rd N. Stai 125 F4
Dolphin Rd S. Stai 125 F4
Dolphin Rd W. Stai 125 F4
Dolphin Rd. Slough 43 D2
Dolphin Rd. Stai 125 F4
Doman Rd. Camb 151 D2
Domoney Cl. That 106 C2
Don Cl. Read 85 D4
Donaldson Way. Read 88 A4
Doncastle Rd. Brac 117 F3
Donegal Cl. Caver 59 E2
Donkin Hill. Caver 59 E2
Donnington Cl. Buck 108 B4
Donnington Cl. Camb 151 D2
Donnington Gdns. Read 86 C3
Donnington Pl. Winn 88 B1
Donnington Rd. Read 86 B3
Donnington Sq. Newb 104 C3
Donnybrook. Brac 118 A1
Dorchester Cl. Maid 19 D1
Dorchester Ct. Read 85 E3
Dorchester Dr. Felt 71 F1
Dorian Dr. Ascot 120 C4
Doris Rd. Ashf 98 B1
Dorking Way. Bur C 84 A2
Dorly Cl. Shepp 125 F2
Dormer Cl. Crow 143 D3
Dormer Cl. Newb 130 C3
Dornels. Slough 23 D4
Dorney Reach Rd. Dorn 40 C2
Dorney Wood Rd. Burn 21 E3
Dorothy St. Read 86 A3
Dorset Cl. Ashf 97 E3
Dorset Rd. Wind 67 E3
Dorset St. Read 85 E4
Dorset Vale. New G 91 F1
Dorset Way. Woki 115 F3
Doublet Cl. That 106 A2
Douglas Ct. Mar 2 A2
Douglas Grange. Hurst 88 C4
Douglas La. Wray 68 C2
Douglas Rd. Caver 59 E1

Douglas Rd. Slough 42 B4
Douglas Rd. Stan 70 B1
Doultons The. Stan 97 D1
Douro Cl. Tad 134 B1
Dove Cl. Read 113 F4
Dove House Cres. Slough 21 F1
Dovecote Rd. Read 113 D4
Dovedale Cl. Caver 58 C2
Dovedale Cl. Crow 143 E1
Dover Rd. Slough 41 F4
Dover St. Read 86 A3
Doveton Way. Newb 105 D2
Dowding Cl. Wood 88 A4
Dower Park. Wind 66 C2
Down Pl. Oak G 66 A4
Downend La. Chiev 51 D1
Downfield La. W St L 63 D3
Downfield Rd. W St L 63 D2
Downing Path. Slough 21 F1
Downing Rd. Read 84 B4
Downlands. East G 47 E3
Downmill Rd. Brac 117 F4
Downs Cl. Lamb 46 C4
Downs Rd. Comp 32 A2
Downs Rd. Slough 43 E2
Downs Way. Chil 9 F4
Downs Way. Read 57 E1
Downshire Cl. Gr She 48 A2
Downshire Sq. Read 85 F3
Downshire Way. Brac 118 A3
Downside. Chert 123 F1
Downside. Chil 10 B4
Doyle Gdns. Yate 149 E2
Drake Ave. Slough 43 E1
Drake Ave. Stai 96 C2
Drake Cl. Brac 118 A2
Drake Cl. Woki 141 F4
Draper Cl. That 106 B1
Drawback Hill. Shipl 35 E3
Draycott. Brac 118 C2
Drayhorse Dr. Bags 145 F1
Drayton Cl. Brac 118 B4
Drayton Rd. Read 85 D4
Dresden Way. Read 57 F1
Drew Meadow. Far C 22 B4
Drewett Cl. Read 113 E3
Drift Rd. Holy 65 E2
Drift Rd. Wink 93 D4
Drift Way. Iver 69 E4
Driftway Cl. Winn 87 E1
Drill Hall Rd. Chert 124 A1
Drive The. Ashf 98 B1
Drive The. Bou E 2 C2
Drive The. Newb 130 C4
Drive The. Read 87 D4
Drive The. Slough 43 F2
Drive The. Slough 68 A3
Drive The. Vir W 122 C2
Drive The. Wray 68 B1
Droitwich Cl. Brac 118 C3
Dromepath. Winn 88 A2
Dropmore Rd. Burn 21 E3
Drove La. Herm 79 E1
Drovers Way. Brac 118 C3
Drovers Way. Wood 87 F3
Druce Way. That 106 B2
Drummond Cl. Brac 118 C4
Drury La. Mort 137 D2
Dry Arch Rd. Sunn 120 C2
Dryden Cl. That 106 B3
Dryden. Brac 118 A1
Du Pre Wlk. Bou E 3 E2
Dudley Cl. Read 57 F1
Dudley Mews. Read 57 F1
Dudley Rd. Ashf 97 F2
Dudley Rd. Felt 98 B4
Duffield La. Sto P 22 C3
Duffield Park. Sto P 23 D1
Duffield Rd. Wood 60 C1
Duke Of Cornwall Ave. Camb 144 B1
Duke St. Hen-O-T 15 F1
Duke St. Read 86 A4
Duke St. Wind 67 E4
Duke's Ride. Crow 143 D3
Duke's Ride. Finch 143 D3
Dukes Cl. Ashf 98 B2
Dukes Covert. Bags 145 F3
Dukes Pl. Mar 1 B1
Dukes Ride. Silc 136 A1
Dukes Wood. Crow 143 D3
Dukeshill Rd. Brac 118 A4
Dulnan Cl. Read 85 D4
Dulverton Gdns. Read 86 B1
Dumas Cl. Yate 149 E3
Dumbarton Way. Caver 59 F3
Dunally Park. Shepp 125 E1
Dunaways Cl. Read 87 E2
Dunbar Dr. Wood 88 A3
Dunboe Pl. Shepp 125 E1
Duncan Dr. Woki 116 C3
Duncan Gdns. Pur O T 57 E2
Duncan Rd. Wood 87 F3
Duncannon Cres. Wind 66 B2
Duncroft. Wind 66 C2
Dundaff Cl. Camb 152 A3
Dundas Cl. Brac 118 A3
Dundee Rd. Slough 42 A4
Dundela Cl. Wood 87 F3
Dunford Pl. Binf 90 C1

Dungells Farm Cl. Yate 149 E2
Dungells La. Yate 149 E2
Dungrovehill La. Bish 18 B2
Dunholme Cl. Winn 87 F1
Dunholme End. Maid 39 E2
Dunkirk Cl. Woki 115 F3
Dunluce Gdns. Pangb 56 C3
Dunn Cres. Kint 102 A1
Dunnock Way. Warg 36 C2
Dunoon Cl. Read 84 C2
Dunsfold Rd. Read 84 C4
Dunsmore Gdns. Yate 149 D3
Dunstall Cl. Read 84 B4
Dunstan Rd. That 106 C2
Dunster Cl. Caver 59 E3
Dunster Gdns. Slough 42 A3
Dunt Ave. Hurst 88 C2
Dunt La. Hurst 88 C2
Duppas Cl. Shepp 125 E2
Durand Rd. Read 87 D1
Durham Ave. Slough 42 A4
Durham Cl. Read 113 E4
Durham Cl. Woki 115 F3
Durham Rd. Sand 143 F1
Durley Mead. Brac 118 C2
Durrell Way. Shepp 125 E2
Dutch Barn Cl. Stan 70 B1
Dutton Way. Iver 44 C4
Duval Pl. Bags 145 F2
Dwyer Rd. Read 85 D2
Dyer Straits. Chil 9 F4
Dyson Cl. Wind 67 D2
Dysonswood La. Maple 58 C4
Eagle Cl. Brac 143 D4
Eagle Cl. Woki 115 F3
Eagles Nest. Crow 143 D1
Earley Hill Rd. Read 87 D3
Earley Pl. Read 86 A4
Earleydene. Sunn 120 A1
Earls Gr. Camb 151 F3
Earlsfield Cl. Caver 59 F2
Earlsfield. Holy 40 B1
Earlswood. Brac 118 A1
Easby La. Winn 87 E1
Easington Dr. Winn 87 F1
East Burnham La. Burn 22 A2
East Cres. Wind 66 C3
East Dr. Read 84 C3
East Dr. Sto P 22 C1
East Dr. Vir W 122 A2
East Green. Black 150 B2
East La. Chiev 51 D1
East Paddock. Bish 18 C3
East Ramp. Harm 71 D3
East Rd. Felt 98 B4
East Rd. Maid 39 F3
East Rd. Maid 39 F4
East Ridge. Bou E 3 D2
East St. Read 86 A4
East Stratton Cl. Brac 118 C2
East View. Warg 36 C1
East View Rd. Warg 36 C1
Eastbourne Rd. Slough 42 A4
Eastbridge. Slough 43 D3
Eastbury Ave. Read 57 D3
Eastbury Park. Winn 88 B1
Eastbury Shute. Lamb 46 C1
Eastchurch Rd. Harm 71 F2
Eastcourt Ave. Read 87 D3
Eastcroft. Slough 22 A1
Easterfield La. Whi-O-T 56 B4
Eastern Ave. Chert 124 A3
Eastern Ave. Read 86 C3
Eastern Dr. Bou E 3 E2
Eastern La. Crow 143 F2
Eastern Perimeter Rd. Harm 71 F3
Eastern Rd. Brac 118 B4
Eastfield Cl. Slough 43 D2
Eastfield La. White 56 B4
Eastfield Rd. Burn 41 D4
Eastfield. Blew 12 A4
Easthampstead Rd. Brac 116 C2
Easthampstead Rd. Brac 118 A4
Eastheath Ave. Woki 116 A2
Eastheath Gdns. Woki 116 A2
Eastleigh Rd. Harm 71 F2
Eastlyn Rd. Silc 135 F1
Easton Hill. Wick 76 A3
Eastwood Rd. Wood 87 F2
Eastworth Rd. Chert 124 A1
Eaton Pl. Read 85 F4
Eaton Rd. Camb 151 D2
Ebborn Sq. Winn 114 B4
Ebsworth Cl. Maid 20 B2
Eccles Cl. Caver 59 E1
Echelforde Dr. Ashf 98 A2
Eddington Hill. Hung 100 C4
Eddington Rd. Brac 117 F2
Eddystone Wlk. Stan 97 F4
Eden Cl. Slough 44 A1
Eden Way. Winn 88 A1
Edenhall Cl. Read 57 E2
Edenham Cl. Winn 87 F1
Edenham Cres. Read 85 F3
Edgar Milward Cl. Read 58 A1
Edgbarrow Rise. Sand 143 D1
Edgcumbe Park Dr. Crow 143 D3
Edgecombe La. Newb 105 E3

Edgedale Cl. Crow 143 D3
Edgehill St. Read 86 A3
Edgell Cl. Vir W 122 C3
Edgell Rd. Stai 96 C2
Edgemoor Rd. Camb 152 B2
Edgewood Cl. Brac 143 D4
Edinburgh Ave. Slough 42 A4
Edinburgh Dr. Stai 97 E1
Edinburgh Gdns. Wind 67 E3
Edinburgh Rd. Maid 19 F1
Edinburgh Rd. Mar 1 C2
Edinburgh Rd. Read 85 F4
Edith Rd. Maid 39 E4
Edmunds Way. Slough 43 D4
Edney's Hill. Woki 115 E1
Edward Ave. Camb 151 D3
Edward Ct. Stai 97 E1
Edward Rd. Harm 71 F1
Edward Rd. Twyf 61 D3
Edward Rd. Windl 146 B2
Edward Way. Ashf 97 F3
Edwards Ct. Slough 42 C2
Edwards Hill. Lamb 25 D1
Edwin Cl. That 106 C2
Eeklo Pl. Newb 105 D1
Egerton Rd. Read 86 C1
Egerton Rd. Sand 150 C4
Egerton Rd. Slough 21 F1
Egham By-Pass. Eng G 96 A2
Egham Hill. Eng G 95 E1
Egremont Dr. Read 87 E2
Egremont Gdns. Slough 42 A3
Egypt La. Far C 22 A4
Eight Acres. Burn 21 D4
Elan Cl. Read 84 C4
Elbow Meadow. Stan 69 F3
Eldart Cl. Read 85 D4
Elder Cl. Read 57 E1
Elderfield Cres. Chil 10 B4
Elderfield Rd. Sto P 22 C3
Eldon Pl. Read 86 B4
Eldon Rd. Read 86 B4
Eldon Sq. Read 86 B4
Eldon St. Read 86 B4
Eldon Terr. Read 86 B4
Eldrick Ct. Felt 98 B4
Elford Cl. Wood 87 E1
Elgar Ave. Crow 143 D4
Elgar Rd. Read 86 A3
Elgarth Dr. Woki 141 F4
Elgin Ave. Ashf 98 B1
Elgin Cres. Harm 71 F3
Eliot Cl. Caver 59 E2
Eliot Cl. That 106 B3
Eliot Dr. Mar 1 C2
Elizabeth Ave. Bags 145 F1
Elizabeth Ave. Newb 130 B4
Elizabeth Ave. Stai 97 E1
Elizabeth Cl. Brac 118 B3
Elizabeth Cl. Hen-O-T 35 D4
Elizabeth Ct. Read 85 F4
Elizabeth Gdns. Ascot 120 A2
Elizabeth Rd. Hen-O-T 35 D4
Elizabeth Rd. Mar 1 C2
Elizabeth Rd. Woki 116 B3
Elizabeth Rout Cl. Shin 113 E1
Elizabeth Way. Sto P 22 C2
Elizabethan Cl. Stan 97 E4
Elizabethan Way. Stan 97 E4
Ellesfield Ave. Brac 117 F3
Ellesmere Cl. Caver 59 D2
Elliman Ave. Slough 42 C3
Ellington Ct. Tapl 40 B4
Ellington Gdns. Tapl 40 B4
Ellington Park. Maid 19 F1
Ellington Rd. Felt 98 C2
Ellington Rd. Tapl 40 B4
Elliott Gdns. Stai 125 D3
Elliott Rise. Burl 119 E4
Ellis Ave. Slough 42 C2
Ellis Rd. Crow 143 D3
Ellison Cl. Wind 66 C2
Ellison Way. Woki 116 A3
Elm Bank. Yate 149 E4
Elm Cl. Far C 22 B3
Elm Cl. Stan 97 E4
Elm Cotts. Ball H 129 F1
Elm Croft. Datch 68 B3
Elm Dr. Bur C 111 D3
Elm Gr. Maid 39 F4
Elm Gr. That 106 A3
Elm La. Bou E 2 C3
Elm La. Read 86 C1
Elm Lodge Ave. Read 85 E4
Elm Park Rd. Read 85 E4
Elm Park. Windl 120 C1
Elm Rd. Felt 98 B4
Elm Rd. Maple 58 B4
Elm Rd. Read 86 C1
Elm Rd. Wind 67 D2
Elm Tree Cl. Ashf 98 A2
Elmar Green. Slough 22 A1
Elmbank Ave. Eng G 95 D1
Elmcroft Cl. Felt 71 F1
Elmcroft Dr. Ashf 98 A2
Elmcroft. Gori 34 B3
Elmdon Rd. Harm 71 F2
Elmhurst Rd. Gori 34 B4
Elmhurst Rd. Read 86 B3

Elmhurst Rd. Slough 44 A2
Elmhurst Rd. That 106 A3
Elmleigh Ct. Caver 59 E2
Elmley Cl. Woki 88 C1
Elms Ave. That 106 C2
Elms Dr. Bou E 3 E2
Elmshott La. Slough 41 F3
Elmsleigh Stai 96 C2
Elmstone Dr. Read 57 E1
Elmsway. Ashf 98 A2
Elmwood Rd. Slough 43 D3
Elmwood. Maid 20 A2
Elsenwood Cres. Camb 152 A3
Elsenwood Dr. Camb 152 A4
Elsinore Ave. Stan 97 F4
Elsley Rd. Read 57 F2
Elstow Ave. Caver 59 E3
Elstree Cl. Read 57 E1
Elsworth Cl. Felt 98 C4
Eltham Ave. Caver 59 F3
Elton Dr. Maid 39 E4
Elvaston Way. Read 85 D4
Elvedon Cl. Winn 87 F1
Elvendon Rd. Gori 34 B4
Elwell Cl. Eng G 96 A1
Ely Ave. Slough 42 B4
Ely Rd. Harm 71 F3
Ely Rd. Thea 83 F2
Embankment The. Wray 95 E4
Ember Rd. Slough 44 A2
Emblem Cres. Arbo 114 C1
Embrook Way. Read 84 A2
Emerald Cl. Woki 115 F4
Emerald Ct. Slough 42 C2
Emery Acres. Upp B 55 D3
Emery Down Cl. Brac 119 D3
Emlyns Bldgs. Eton 67 E4
Emm Cl. Woki 115 F4
Emma The. Warg 36 C1
Emmbrook Gate. Woki 115 F4
Emmbrook Rd. Woki 115 F4
Emmbrook Vale. Woki 89 D1
Emmer Green Ct. Caver 59 E3
Emmets Nest. Binf 90 B1
Emmets Park. Binf 90 B1
Emmview Cl. Woki 115 F4
Empress Rd. Read 84 B3
Enborne Cl. Read 84 B4
Enborne Gr. Newb 104 C1
Enborne Pl. Newb 104 C1
Enborne Rd. Ham M 104 C1
Enborne Rd. Newb 104 C1
Enborne St. Ham M 130 B3
Enborne St. Newb 130 B3
Enborne Way. Brim 133 F3
Enfield Rd. Harm 71 F3
Englefield Cl. Eng G 95 E1
Englefield Rd. Thea 83 E2
Engleheart Dr. Felt 71 F1
Englehurst. Eng G 95 E1
Englemere Park. Burl 119 F3
Englemere Rd. Brac 90 C1
Englesfield. Camb 152 B3
English Gdns. Wray 68 B1
Ennerdale Cl. Felt 98 C4
Ennerdale Cres. Slough 41 E4
Ennerdale Rd. Read 86 B2
Ennerdale Way. That 106 A2
Ennerdale. Brac 118 A3
Ensign Cl. Stan 97 E4
Ensign Way. Stan 97 E4
Enstone Rd. Wood 88 A4
Enterprise Way. That 107 D1
Epping Cl. Read 85 F4
Epping Way. Brac 118 C3
Epsom Cl. Camb 151 E4
Epsom Cres. Newb 105 D1
Epsom Ct. Read 85 F3
Epson Sq. Harm 71 F3
Eric Ave. Caver 59 D3
Erica Cl. Camb 153 F3
Erica Cl. Slough 41 F3
Eriswell Cl. Winn 87 F1
Erkenwald Cl. Chert 123 F1
Erleigh Court Dr. Read 87 D4
Erleigh Court Gdns. Read 87 D4
Erleigh Dene. Newb 104 C1
Erleigh Rd. Read 86 B3
Ermin Wlk. That 106 A2
Errington Dr. Wind 67 D3
Erskine Cl. Silc 135 F1
Esher Cres. Harm 71 F3
Esher Rd. Camb 145 D1
Eskdale Gdns. Holy 40 A1
Eskdale Rd. Winn 88 A2
Eskdale Way. Camb 152 B2
Eskin Cl. Read 85 D4
Essex Ave. Slough 42 A4
Essex Pl. Lamb 25 D2
Essex St. Newb 130 B4
Essex St. Read 86 A3
Ethel Rd. Ashf 97 F2
Eton Cl. Datch 68 A4
Eton Ct. Eton 67 E4
Eton Pl. Mar 1 B1
Eton Rd. Datch 68 A4
Eton Rd. Harl 71 F4
Eton Sq. Eton 67 E4

Eton Wick Rd. Eton 42 A1
Eustace Cres. Woki 116 B4
Evedon. Brac 118 A1
Evelyn Cres. Shepp 125 F4
Evelyn Ct. Wood 87 F3
Evelyn Way. Shepp 125 F4
Evendon's La. Bark 115 F1
Evendons Cl. Woki 116 A2
Evenlode Rd. Bou E 3 D2
Evenlode Way. Sand 150 B4
Evenlode. Maid 39 F4
Everard Ave. Slough 42 C2
Everest Rd. Camb 151 E4
Everest Rd. Crow 143 D3
Everest Rd. Stan 97 F4
Evergreen Dr. Read 84 C2
Evergreen Rd. Camb 152 A1
Evergreen Way. Stan 97 E4
Evergreen Way. Woki 115 F3
Everington La. Yatt 53 D1
Everland Rd. Hung 100 B3
Eversley Rd. Arbo 114 C1
Eversley St. Finch 141 D1
Eversley Way. Stai 123 E4
Evesham Rd. Caver 59 D3
Evesham Wlk. Crow 143 E1
Evreham Rd. Iver 44 C4
Evreux Cl. That 106 C1
Ewing Way. Newb 131 D4
Exbourne Rd. Read 113 E4
Exchange Rd. Ascot 120 B2
Exeforde Ave. Ashf 98 A2
Exeter Cl. Read 113 D4
Exeter Gdns. Yate 149 D4
Exeter Rd. Stan 71 F2
Exeter Rd. Thea 83 F2
Exeter Way. Stan 71 F3
Exmoor Rd. That 106 B2
Explorer Ave. Stan 97 F4
Exwick Sq. Read 113 E4
Eylham. Pur O T 57 D3
Eynsford Cl. Caver 59 F3
Eynsham Rd. Wood 87 F4

Fagg's Rd. Harm 71 F2
Fair Lawn Green. Read 86 C1
Fair Mile. Hen-O-T 15 E2
Fairacre. Maid 39 E3
Fairacres Ind Est. Wind 66 B3
Faircroft. Slough 22 A1
Faircross Quarters. Herm 78 C3
Faircross Rd. Read 85 E3
Faircross. Brac 118 A3
Fairfax. Brac 118 A4
Fairfield App. Wray 68 B1
Fairfield Ave. Datch 68 B4
Fairfield Ave. Stai 68 B4
Fairfield Dr. Camb 151 F2
Fairfield La. Far C 22 A2
Fairfield Rd. Burn 21 E1
Fairfield Rd. Gori 34 B4
Fairfield Rd. Wray 68 B1
Fairfield. Comp 31 E2
Fairfields. Hung 100 B3
Fairford Rd. Maid 39 F4
Fairford Rd. Read 57 E1
Fairhaven. Eng G 95 F2
Fairholme Rd. Ashf 97 F2
Fairholme. Felt 98 C4
Fairlawn Park. Wind 66 C2
Fairlawns Cl. Stai 97 D1
Fairlea. Maid 39 D2
Fairlie Rd. Slough 42 A4
Fairlight Ave. Wind 67 E3
Fairlop Cl. Bur C 84 B2
Fairmead Cl. Sand 150 C4
Fairmead Rd. Shin 113 F3
Fairoak Way. Tad 134 B1
Fairsted Cl. Read 85 D4
Fairview Ave. Read 87 D4
Fairview Ct. Stai 97 D1
Fairview Dr. Stai 124 C2
Fairview Rd. Burn 41 D4
Fairview Rd. Hung 100 B3
Fairview Rd. Slough 21 F1
Fairview Rd. Woki 116 B3
Fairwater Dr. Wood 87 E3
Fairway Ave. Read 84 B3
Fairway Dr. Char 61 D3
Fairway Hts. Camb 152 A3
Fairway The. Burn 21 E2
Fairway The. Camb 152 A2
Fairway The. Fla H 3 E4
Fairway The. Maid 39 D2
Fairway. Chert 124 A1
Fairways. Ashf 98 A1
Fakenham Cl. Read 114 A4
Fakenham Way. Crow 143 E1
Falaise. Eng G 95 F2
Falcon Ave. Read 86 C1
Falcon Cl. Camb 152 C4
Falcon Dr. Stan 70 C2
Falcon Fields. Tad 135 D1
Falcon House Gdns. Ball H ... 129 F1
Falcon Way. Shepp 125 F4
Falcon Way. Woki 115 F3
Falcon Way. Yate 149 D3

Falcons Croft. Woo G 3 F4
Falconwood. Eng G 95 F2
Falkland Dr. Newb 130 C4
Falkland Garth. Newb 130 B4
Falkland Rd. Caver 59 D1
Falkland Rd. Newb 130 B3
Fallowfield Cl. Caver 59 D2
Fallowfield. Yate 149 D4
Falmouth Cl. Camb 152 A2
Falmouth Rd. Read 113 D4
Falmouth Rd. Slough 42 A4
Falmouth Way. That 106 C2
Falstaff Ave. Read 86 C1
Fane Way. Maid 39 E3
Fanes Cl. Brac 117 F4
Faraday Cl. Arbo 140 C4
Faraday Cl. Slough 42 A4
Faraday Rd. Bark 141 D4
Faraday Rd. Newb 105 D2
Faraday Rd. Slough 42 A4
Farcrosse St. Sand 150 B4
Fareham Dr. Yate 149 D4
Faringdon Cl. Sand 143 E1
Faringdon Dr. Brac 118 B2
Faringdon Wlk. Read 85 D2
Farleigh Mews. Caver 59 F3
Farley Copse. Brac 117 F4
Farm Cl. Ascot 120 B2
Farm Cl. Brac 117 F4
Farm Cl. Brac 143 E4
Farm Cl. Chert 123 D2
Farm Cl. Gori 34 B3
Farm Cl. Holy 40 B1
Farm Cl. Maid 39 D4
Farm Cl. Pur O T 57 E3
Farm Cl. Shepp 125 D1
Farm Cl. Stai 96 C2
Farm Cl. Yate 149 E3
Farm Cres. Slough 43 E4
Farm Dr. Read 84 A3
Farm Lea. Woo G 3 F4
Farm Rd. Bou E 2 C2
Farm Rd. Burn 41 D3
Farm Rd. Camb 151 F1
Farm Rd. Hen-O-T 35 F4
Farm Rd. Maid 39 D4
Farm Rd. Stai 97 D1
Farm View. Yate 149 E3
Farm Way. Stan 69 F1
Farm Yd. Wind 67 E4
Farman Cl. Wood 88 A4
Farmer's Rd. Stai 96 C2
Farmers Cl. Maid 39 D2
Farmers Cl. Read 113 E3
Farmers Way. Maid 39 D2
Farmiloe Cl. Pur O T 57 E2
Farnburn Ave. Slough 42 A4
Farnell Rd. Stan 97 D3
Farnham Cl. Brac 118 B4
Farnham Dr. Caver 59 F2
Farnham La. Slough 22 A2
Farnham Park La. Far C 22 B2
Farnham Rd. Slough 42 B4
Farningham. Brac 118 C2
Farnsfield Cl. Read 114 A4
Farrell Cl. Camb 151 E2
Farriers Cl. Wood 87 F4
Farrowdene Rd. Read 113 E4
Farthing Green La. Sto P 23 D2
Farthingales The. Maid 40 A4
Fatherson Rd. Read 86 B4
Faulkner Pl. Bags 145 F2
Faversham Rd. Crow 143 E1
Fawcett Cres. Wood 87 E3
Fawcett Rd. Wind 67 D3
Fawler Mead. Brac 118 C3
Fawley Bottom La. Faw (Bu) ... 15 E4
Fawley Cl. Maid 19 E1
Fawley Rd. Read 85 E3
Fawns Manor Cl. Felt 98 B4
Fawns Manor Rd. Felt 98 B4
Fawsley Cl. Stan 69 F4
Faygate Way. Read 87 D1
Feathers La. Wray 96 A3
Felbridge Cl. Camb 151 F1
Felix La. Shepp 125 F2
Felixstowe Cl. Winn 87 E1
Fellow Green Rd. West E 153 F3
Fellow Green. West E 153 F3
Fells The. Read 84 A3
Felstead Cl. Read 86 C2
Feltham Hill Rd. Ashf 98 A2
Feltham Rd. Ashf 98 A2
Felthorpe Cl. Read 114 A4
Felton Way. Read 84 B4
Fencote. Brac 118 B2
Fennel Cl. Newb 105 E3
Fennel Cl. Read 86 C1
Fenns La. West E 153 F3
Fenton Ave. Stai 97 E2
Fern Cl. Camb 152 B2
Fern Cl. Read 84 B3
Fern Dr. Burn 41 D4
Fern Glen. Read 57 E1
Fern La. Lit M 2 C3
Fern Wlk. Ashf 97 E2
Fernbank Cres. Burl 119 E4
Fernbank Pl. Burl 119 E4
Fernbank Rd. Burl 119 E4

Fernbank. Woki 141 E4
Fernbrook Rd. Caver 58 C3
Ferndale Ave. Read 85 D2
Ferndale Cl. Read 57 E2
Ferndale Rd. Ashf 97 F2
Ferne Cl. Gori 34 B4
Fernery The. Stai 96 C2
Fernhill Cl. Black 150 C1
Fernhill Cl. Brac 90 C1
Fernhill La. Black 150 C1
Fernhill Rd. Black 150 C1
Fernhill Wlk. Black 150 C1
Fernhurst Rd. Ashf 98 B2
Fernhurst Rd. Bur C 84 B2
Ferniehurst. Camb 151 F2
Fernley Ct. Maid 19 E1
Ferrard Cl. Burl 119 E4
Ferrier Gr. Newb 131 D4
Ferry Ave. Stai 96 C1
Ferry La. Bou E 3 D1
Ferry La. Gori 34 A2
Ferry La. Hamb 16 B3
Ferry La. Medm 17 D3
Ferry La. Shepp 125 D1
Ferry La. Sou S 14 A2
Ferry La. Stai 124 B3
Ferry La. Warg 36 B1
Ferry La. Wray 96 A3
Ferry Rd. Maid 40 B2
Ferry Rd. Sou S 14 B2
Fettiplace. Gr She 48 A2
Fetty Pl. Maid 39 E2
Fidler's La. East I 30 C4
Fidlers Wlk. Warg 36 C1
Field Cl. Bur C 111 D1
Field Cl. Harl 71 E4
Field End. Warg 36 C1
Field End. West E 153 F3
Field Farm Rd. Bur C 84 C1
Field House Cl. Brac 120 A1
Field La. Camb 151 F1
Field Park. Brac 118 B4
Field Rd. Black 150 C1
Field Rd. Pease 29 E1
Field Rd. Read 86 A3
Field View. Caver 59 D2
Field View. Felt 98 B2
Field View. Stai 96 B2
Fielden Pl. Brac 118 B4
Fieldfare Ave. Yate 149 D3
Fieldhead Gdns. Bou E 3 D2
Fielding Gdns. Crow 143 D2
Fielding Rd. Maid 39 D4
Fielding Rd. Sand 150 C3
Fieldings The. Holy 65 D4
Fieldridge. Newb 105 E3
Fields The. Slough 42 B2
Fieldway. Winn 88 B1
Fifehead Cl. Ashf 97 F1
Fifield La. Holy 65 E2
Fifield Rd. Holy 65 E4
Fifth Rd. Newb 104 C1
Filbert Dr. Read 84 B4
Filey Rd. Read 86 C4
Filey Spur. Slough 42 A2
Filmer Rd. Wind 66 B3
Finbeck Way. Read 113 F4
Finch Cl. Maid 39 E3
Finch Rd. Read 87 E2
Finch Way. Bur C 111 D2
Fincham End Dr. Crow 142 C2
Finchampstead Rd. Finch 142 A4
Finchampstead Rd. Woki 142 A4
Findhorn Cl. Sand 150 B4
Finmere. Brac 118 B1
Finney Dr. Windl 146 B2
Finstock Cl. Winn 87 E1
Finstock Green. Brac 118 C3
Fir Cottage Rd. Bark 141 F4
Fir Cottage Rd. Woki 141 F4
Fir Dr. Black 150 B2
Fir Tree Ave. Sto P 22 C1
Fir Tree Cl. Ascot 120 A1
Fir Tree La. Newb 105 F2
Fir Tree Paddock. West I 10 A1
Fir's End. Bur C 111 D1
Firbank Pl. Eng G 95 D1
Fircroft Cl. Read 57 E1
Fircroft Cl. Sto P 23 D3
Fireball Hill. Sunn 120 B1
Firglen Dr. Yate 149 E4
Firgrove Rd. Yate 149 D3
Firlands Ave. Camb 151 E3
Firlands. Brac 118 B2
Firmstone Cl. Winn 87 E1
Firs Ave. Wind 66 C2
Firs Cl. Woki 141 F4
Firs Dr. Slough 43 F3
Firs La. Maid 38 C2
Firs Rd. Read 84 B3
Firs The. That 106 A2
First Ave. Mar 2 A1
First Cres. Slough 42 B4
Firtree Cl. Sand 142 C1
Firview Cl. Mar 1 C1

Firwood Dr. Camb 151 E3
Firwood Rd. Went 121 F2
Fisher Green. Binf 90 A1
Fisherman's La. Alde 135 D4
Fisherman's Way. Bou E 3 D2
Fishermans Retreat. Mar 1 C1
Fishers Ct. Caver 59 E3
Fishers Wood. Went 121 E1
Fishery Rd. Maid 40 B3
Fishponds Cl. Woki 116 A2
Fishponds Rd. Woki 116 A2
Fitzrobert Pl. Eng G 96 A1
Fitzroy Cres. Wood 88 A3
Five Acre. Read 57 E1
Five Acres. Woo G 3 F4
Flag Staff Sq. That 106 C1
Flambards. Caver 59 E1
Flamborough Cl. Winn 87 F1
Flamborough Spur. Slough 42 A2
Flamingo Cl. Woki 115 F3
Flanders Ct. Stai 96 B2
Flats The. Black 150 B2
Flaxman Cl. Read 86 C1
Flecker Cl. That 106 B3
Fleet Cl. Woki 115 F3
Fleet Hill. Finch 141 E1
Fleet St. Finch 141 D1
Fleetham Gdns. Wood 87 E1
Fleetway. Stai 123 E3
Fleetwood Rd. Slough 42 C3
Fleming Cl. Arbo 140 C4
Fleming Rd. Newb 105 D2
Flemish Fields. Chert 124 A1
Fletcher Gdns. Brac 117 E4
Flexford Green. Brac 117 F2
Flintgrove. Brac 118 B4
Flintlock Cl. Stan 70 A2
Flodden Dr. Bur C 84 B2
Floral Way. That 106 C2
Florence Ave. Maid 39 F4
Florence Ave. Maid 40 A4
Florence Cl. Yate 149 E3
Florence Gdns. Stai 97 D1
Florence Rd. Sand 150 C4
Florence Wlk. Read 86 B4
Florian Gdns. Read 85 D3
Flower's Hill. Pangb 56 B2
Flowers Piece. Asham 54 A3
Fobney St. Read 86 A4
Fokerham Rd. That 106 C1
Folder's La. Brac 91 E1
Foliejohn Way. Whi Wa 38 C1
Folkestone Cl. Slough 44 A1
Follet Cl. Old W 68 A1
Folly La. Bur 110 C3
Folly La. Sulhd 110 C3
Folly Rd. Ink 127 F3
Folly Rd. Lamb 25 D2
Folly The. Newb 105 D1
Fontmell Cl. Ashf 98 A2
Fontmell Park. Ashf 98 A2
Fontwell Cl. Maid 39 D4
Fontwell Dr. Read 84 C3
Fontwell Rd. Newb 105 D2
Forbes Chase. Sand 150 B4
Forbury La. Kint 128 B4
Forbury Rd. Read 86 B4
Forbury The. Read 86 A4
Ford Cl. Ashf 97 F1
Ford Cl. Stai 125 D2
Ford La. Swal 140 A2
Ford Rd. Ashf 97 F2
Ford Rd. Bis 153 F2
Ford Rd. Chert 124 A1
Ford Rd. West E 153 F2
Fordbridge Cl. Chert 124 A1
Fordbridge Rd. Ashf 97 F2
Fordbridge Rd. Shepp 125 F2
Fordham Way. Winn 87 E1
Fordwater Rd. Chert 124 A1
Fordwells Dr. Brac 118 C3
Forehead The. Bee H 137 F2
Forest Cl. Brac 119 E3
Forest Cl. Tad 134 C1
Forest Dr. Stai 98 C1
Forest End Rd. Sand 150 A4
Forest Green Rd. Holy 65 D3
Forest Green. Brac 118 B4
Forest Hill. Read 57 F1
Forest Hills. Camb 151 D2
Forest Rd. Ascot 92 C1
Forest Rd. Binf 90 B2
Forest Rd. Burl 92 C1
Forest Rd. Crow 143 E3
Forest Rd. New G 92 C1
Forest Rd. Wind 66 C3
Foresters Sq. Brac 118 C3
Foresters Way. Crow 143 F2
Forge Cl. Caver 59 E1
Forge Cl. Kint 102 A1
Forge Dr. Far C 22 B3
Forge Hill. Hamp N 53 D3
Forge The. Hung 100 B3
Forlease Cl. Maid 40 A3
Forlease Dr. Maid 40 A3
Forlease Rd. Maid 40 A3
Formby Cl. Winn 87 F2
Forndon Cl. Winn 87 F1

Fortrose Cl. Sand 150 B4
Fortrose Wlk. Read 84 C2
Forty Green Dr. Mar 1 A1
Fosseway. Crow 143 D3
Fossewood Dr. Camb 151 E4
Foster Ave. Wind 66 C2
Fosters Gr. Windl 146 A3
Fosters La. Wood 87 F3
Fosters Path. Slough 21 F1
Fotherby Ct. Maid 40 A3
Fotheringay Gdns. Slough 42 A3
Foundary Ct. Chert 124 A1
Foundation Park. Maid 38 C2
Foundry La. Hort 69 D2
Fountain Gdns. Wind 67 E2
Fountains Garth. Brac 118 A3
Fourth Ave. Mar 2 A1
Fowler Cl. Read 87 D2
Fowlers La. Read 118 A4
Fox Cl. Bur C 111 D2
Fox Covert Cl. Ascot 120 B2
Fox Covert. Light 153 D4
Fox Dr. Yate 149 E4
Fox La. Yate 149 D4
Fox Lane N. Chert 123 F1
Fox Lane S. Chert 123 F1
Fox Rd. Slough 43 E1
Foxborough Cl. Slough 44 A1
Foxborough. Swal 139 E3
Foxbury. Lamb 25 D1
Foxcombe Dr. Read 84 B4
Foxcote. Woki 142 A4
Foxdown Cl. Camb 151 E4
Foxes Piece. Mar 1 C2
Foxes Wlk. Char 61 D2
Foxglove Cl. Stan 97 E4
Foxglove Cl. Woki 115 D4
Foxglove Gdns. Read 85 F4
Foxhays Rd. Read 113 E4
Foxherne. Slough 43 E2
Foxhill Cl. Caver 60 A3
Foxhill Cres. Camb 152 A4
Foxhill La. Caver 59 F3
Foxhill Rd. Read 86 C3
Foxhollow Dr. Far C 22 B4
Foxhunt Gr. Read 84 C2
Foxhunter Way. That 105 F2
Foxley Cl. Sand 150 B3
Foxley La. Binf 90 B1
Framewood Rd. Sto P 23 E3
Framlingham Dr. Caver 59 F3
Frampton Cl. Wood 60 C1
France Hill Dr. Camb 151 E3
Frances Ave. Maid 20 B1
Frances Rd. Wind 67 E3
Frances The. That 106 B2
Francis Chichester Cl. Ascot .. 120 A2
Francis Cl. Stai 125 D3
Francis Gdns. New G 91 F1
Francis St. Read 86 A3
Francis Way. Slough 41 E3
Frank London Cl. Bou E 3 E2
Franklin Ave. Slough 42 A4
Franklin Ave. Tad 135 D1
Franklin St. Read 85 F4
Franklyn Cres. Wind 66 B2
Frascati Way. Maid 39 F4
Fraser Ave. Caver 59 E3
Fraser Mead. Sand 150 C3
Fraser Rd. Brac 118 A4
Frederick Pl. Wind 116 A3
Free Prae Rd. Chert 124 A1
Freeborn Way. Brac 118 C4
Freeman Cl. Shepp 125 F3
Freemans Cl. Hung 100 B3
Freemans Cl. Sto P 23 D3
Freemantle Rd. Bags 145 F2
Freesia Cl. Woki 115 E4
French Gdns. Black 150 B2
Frenchum Gdns. Slough 44 F3
Frensham Cl. Yate 149 D3
Frensham Green. Read 86 C1
Frensham Rd. Crow 143 D4
Frensham Wlk. Far C 22 B3
Frensham. Brac 118 B2
Freshfield Cl. Winn 87 F2
Freshwater Rd. Read 86 C4
Freshwood Dr. Yate 149 E2
Friar St. Read 86 A4
Friars Keep. Brac 118 A3
Friars Rd. Newb 131 D4
Friars Rd. Vir W 122 B3
Friars Way. Chert 124 A2
Friary Rd. Ascot 120 A2
Friary Rd. Wray 68 B1
Friary Rd. Wray 95 E4
Friary The. Old W 68 B1
Friday St. Hen-O-T 15 F1
Frieth Cl. Read 87 D1
Frilsham Rd. Read 85 D2
Frimley By-Pass. Camb 151 E1
Frimley Cl. Wood 87 E4
Frimley Green Rd. Camb 151 E1
Frimley Grove Gdns. Camb ... 151 F1
Frimley Hall Dr. Camb 151 F3
Frimley High St. Camb 151 E1
Frimley Rd. Camb 151 D2
Fringford Cl. Winn 87 E1
Frith Hill Rd. Camb 152 A1

Frithe The. Slough 43 D4
Frithwald Rd. Chert 123 F1
Frobisher Cres. Stan 97 F4
Frobisher Gdns. Stan 97 F4
Frobisher. Brac 118 B1
Frodsham Way. Sand 143 F1
Frog Hall Dr. Woki 116 C3
Frog La. Brac 118 A3
Frogmill. Hurl 17 E2
Frogmore Cl. Slough 42 A2
Frogmore Gr. Black 150 B2
Frogmore Park Dr. Black 150 B2
Frogmore Rd. Sand 150 B3
Frogmore Way. Read 85 D3
Fromer Rd. Bou E 3 E2
Fromont Dr. That 106 B2
Fromow Gdns. Windl 146 B2
Front St. East G 47 E3
Froxfield Ave. Read 85 F3
Froxfield Down. Brac 118 C2
Fruen Rd. Felt 98 C4
Fry Rd. Ashf 97 E2
Fry's La. Bags 145 E1
Fry's La. Yate 149 F4
Frymley View. Wind 66 B3
Fuchia Cl. Camb 153 F3
Fuchsia Cl. Read 84 B3
Fullbrook Cl. Maid 40 A4
Fullbrook Cl. Woki 89 D1
Fullbrook Cres. Read 57 E2
Fuller Cl. That 106 C1
Fuller's La. Bur C 112 A2
Fullers La. Ball H 129 E1
Fulmead Rd. Read 85 E4
Fulmer Cl. Read 87 D1
Fulmer Common Rd. Fulm 23 E1
Fulmer Rd. Fulm 23 F4
Furlong Cl. Bou E 3 D2
Furlong Rd. Bou E 3 D2
Furness Sq. Oak G 66 B3
Furness Way. Oak G 66 B3
Furness. Oak G 66 B3
Furnival Ave. Slough 42 A4
Furnival Cl. Went 122 B2
Furrow Way. Maid 39 D2
Furze Hill Cres. Crow 143 E2
Furze Platt Rd. Maid 19 D1
Furze Platt Rd. Maid 19 E1
Furze Rd. Maid 19 E1
Furze Rd. Tad 134 C1
Furzebank. Ascot 120 B3
Furzemoors. Brac 118 A2
Furzen Cl. Slough 22 A1
Fuzzens Wlk. Wind 66 C3
Fydlers Cl. Ascot 93 D1
Fyfield Cl. Black 150 B3
Fyfield Rd. That 106 B1
Fylingdales. That 106 B2

Gables Ave. Ashf 97 F2
Gables Cl. Datch 68 A4
Gables Cl. Maid 40 A4
Gage Cl. Maid 39 F2
Gainsborough Ave. Kint 102 A1
Gainsborough Cl. Camb 151 F4
Gainsborough Cl. Wood 88 A3
Gainsborough Cres. Hen-O-T .. 35 E4
Gainsborough Dr. Ascot 119 E4
Gainsborough Dr. Maid 39 E2
Gainsborough Hill. Hen-O-T ... 35 E4
Gainsborough Rd. Hen-O-T 35 E4
Gainsborough Rd. Read 85 D3
Gainsborough. Brac 118 B2
Gainsborough. Cook 19 F3
Gairn Cl. Read 85 D4
Galahad Cl. Slough 42 A2
Gale Dr. Light 146 A1
Galley La. Head 132 B1
Galleymead Rd. Stan 69 F3
Gallop The. Yate 149 E4
Gallys Rd. Wind 66 B3
Galsworthy Dr. Caver 59 F3
Galsworthy Rd. Chert 124 A1
Galton Rd. Sunn 120 C2
Galvin Rd. Slough 42 B3
Garde Rd. Sonn 60 C2
Garden Cl. Ashf 98 B1
Garden Cl. Maid 39 D3
Garden Close La. Newb 130 B2
Gardeners La. Brad 55 E2
Gardens The. Ham 71 E1
Gardens The. Sou S 14 B2
Gardens The. Vir W 122 C2
Gardner Rd. Maid 19 F1
Garfield Rd. Camb 151 E3
Garford Cres. Newb 130 B4
Garlands Cl. Bur C 111 D1
Garnet Cl. Slough 42 A2
Garnet Ct. Mar 1 B1
Garnet Field. Yate 149 D3
Garnet Hill. Read 86 A3
Garnet St. Read 86 A3
Garrard Rd. Slough 21 F1
Garrard St. Read 86 A4
Garrett Rd. Woki 141 F4
Garrick Cl. Stai 97 D1
Garson La. Wray 95 E4
Garson's La. New G 92 A4

Garston Cl. Read 85 D2
Garston Cres. Read 84 A3
Garston Gr. Woki 115 F1
Garswood. Brac 118 B2
Garth Cl. Winn 88 B1
Garth Rd. Mort 137 D3
Garth Sq. Brac 91 D1
Garthlands. Maid 19 E1
Gas Works Rd. Read 86 B4
Gascon's Gr. Slough 22 A1
Gaskell Mews. Newb 131 D4
Gaskells End. Maple 58 B4
Gaston Bridge Rd. Shepp 125 E2
Gaston Way. Shepp 125 E2
Gatcombe Cl. Read 84 B2
Gatehampton Rd. Gori 34 B3
Gatewick Cl. Slough 42 C3
Gatward Ave. Maid 39 D2
Gaveston Rd. Slough 21 F1
Gayhurst Cl. Caver 59 E3
Geffers Ride. Ascot 119 F4
Geneva Cl. Shepp 125 F4
Geoffreyson Rd. Caver 58 C3
George Cl. Mar 1 C2
George Green Rd. Slough 43 F4
George St. Caver 59 D1
George St. Read 85 F4
George St. Stai 96 C2
Georgeham Rd. Crow 143 E1
Georgian Cl. Camb 151 F4
Georgian Cl. Stai 97 D2
Georges Dr. Fla H 3 E4
Gerrards Cross Rd. Sto P 23 D4
Gibbet La. Camb 152 A4
Gibbons Cl. Sand 150 B4
Gibbs Cl. Woki 141 F3
Gibbs Way. Yate 149 D2
Gibraltar La. Cook 2 B1
Gibson Ct. Slough 43 F1
Gibson Pl. Stan 70 B1
Gifford Cl. Caver 59 F3
Gilbert Rd. Camb 151 E1
Gilbey Wlk. Bou E 3 E2
Gilchrist Way. Bish 38 A3
Giles Travers Cl. Stai 123 E3
Gillette Way. Read 86 A1
Gilliat Rd. Slough 42 C3
Gilliatt Cl. Iver 44 C4
Gillott's La. Shipl 35 E4
Gillotts Cl. Hen-O-T 35 D4
Gilman Cres. Wind 66 B2
Gilmore Cl. Slough 43 E2
Gilmore Cres. Ashf 98 A2
Gilpin Way. Harl 71 E4
Gilroy Cl. Newb 130 B3
Gingells Farm Rd. Char 61 D3
Gipsy La. Brac 118 B4
Gipsy La. Hung 100 C4
Gipsy La. Read 57 F1
Gipsy La. Read 87 E2
Gipsy La. Woki 114 B4
Gipsy La. Woki 116 B2
Girton Cl. Crow 143 F1
Glade Rd. Mar 1 C1
Glade The. Ascot 120 B2
Glade The. Newb 130 C4
Glade The. Pur O T 57 E2
Glade The. Stai 97 D1
Gladridge Cl. Read 87 E2
Gladstone Cl. Kint 102 A1
Gladstone Ind Est. Maid 39 F4
Gladstone La. Cold A 106 B4
Gladstone Way. Slough 42 A3
Glaisdale. That 106 B1
Glamis Way. Read 84 A2
Glanmor Rd. Slough 43 D3
Glanty The. Stai 96 A2
Glasgow Rd. Slough 42 A4
Glassonby Wlk. Camb 152 B3
Glebe Cl. Dorn 40 C2
Glebe Cl. Light 146 B1
Glebe Cl. Moul 13 F3
Glebe Gdns. Sonn 60 C2
Glebe La. Sonn 60 C2
Glebe Rd. Maid 40 A3
Glebe Rd. Old W 68 A1
Glebe Rd. Pur O T 57 D3
Glebe Rd. Read 86 B3
Glebe Rd. Stai 96 B1
Glebe Rd. Stai 97 D2
Glebe Ride. Gori 34 A3
Glebe The. Aldw 32 C2
Glebe The. Black 150 C2
Glebefields. Newb 105 D3
Glebeland Gdns. Shepp 125 E2
Glebeland Rd. Camb 150 C2
Glebelands Rd. Woki 116 B4
Glebewood. Brac 118 B2
Glen Ave. Ashf 98 A2
Glen Cl. Stai 125 D3
Glen Innes. Sand 143 F1
Glen The. Silc 135 F1
Glen The. Slough 43 E1
Glenapp Grange. Mort 136 C3
Glenavon Gdns. Slough 43 E2
Glenavon Gdns. Yate 149 E2
Glenbeigh Terr. Read 85 F3
Glendale Ave. Newb 130 B3
Glendale Rd. Tad 135 D1

Glendevon Rd. Wood 87 F4
Gleneagles Cl. Stan 70 B1
Glenfield Rd. Ashf 98 B1
Glenhaven Dr. Stan 70 B1
Glenhurst Cl. Black 150 C2
Glenmore Cl. That 106 B1
Glenrosa Rd. Read 85 D4
Glentworth Pl. Slough 42 B3
Glenwood Dr. Read 84 B4
Glenwood. Brac 118 B3
Globe Farm La. Black 150 A3
Glory Cl. Woo G 3 F4
Glory Mill La. Woo G 3 F4
Gloucester Ave. Slough 42 B4
Gloucester Cres. Stai 97 E1
Gloucester Ct. Read 85 E4
Gloucester Dr. Stai 96 B3
Gloucester Gdns. Bags 145 F2
Gloucester Pl. Wind 67 E3
Gloucester Rd. Bags 145 F2
Gloucester Rd. Maid 19 F1
Gloucester Rd. Newb 104 C1
Gloucester Rd. Read 85 E4
Glyme Wlk. Read 84 C2
Glynswood. Camb 151 F2
Goaters Rd. Burl 119 E4
Goddard Cl. Shin 113 F3
Goddard Cl. Stai 124 C3
Goddard Ct. Winn 88 A1
Goddards La. Camb 151 D2
Goddington Rd. Bou E 3 D3
Godolphin Rd. Slough 42 B3
Godstow Cl. Wood 87 F4
Goffs Rd. Ashf 98 B2
Gogmore Farm Cl. Chert 123 F1
Gogmore La. Chert 124 A1
Gold Cup La. Burl 119 E4
Goldcrest Cl. Yate 149 D3
Goldcrest Way. Read 84 A3
Golden Ball La. Cook 19 D2
Golden Oak. Far C 22 B3
Golden Orb Wood. Brac 117 E4
Goldfinch La. Newt 131 F2
Golding Cl. That 106 C2
Goldney Rd. Camb 152 B2
Goldsmid Rd. Read 85 F4
Goldsmith Cl. That 106 B3
Goldsmith Way. Crow 143 D2
Goldsworthy Way. Slough 41 E4
Goldthorpe Gdns. Read 113 F4
Goldwell Dr. Newb 104 C2
Golf Dr. Camb 152 A2
Goodboy's La. Bur C 112 A1
Goodboy's La. Mort 112 A1
Goodchild Rd. Woki 116 B3
Goodings Green. Woki 116 C3
Goodliffe Gdns. Pur O T 57 E2
Goodman Park. Slough 43 E3
Goodman Pl. Stai 96 C2
Goodrich Cl. Caver 59 F3
Goodways Dr. Brac 118 B4
Goodwin Cl. Bur C 84 C2
Goodwin Meadows. Woo G 3 F3
Goodwin Rd. Slough 21 F1
Goodwin Wlk. Newb 130 B3
Goodwood Cl. Bur C 111 D1
Goodwood Cl. Camb 151 E4
Goodwood Rise. Mar B 1 B4
Goodwood Way. Newb 105 E1
Goose Cnr. New G 91 F2
Goose Green Way. That 106 C2
Goose Green. Far C 22 A4
Goose Green. Lamb 25 D2
Goose La. Leckh 49 F3
Goose Pool. Chert 123 F1
Gordon Ave. Camb 151 E2
Gordon Cl. Stai 97 D1
Gordon Cres. Camb 151 E2
Gordon Cres. Comp 31 F2
Gordon Dr. Shepp 125 E1
Gordon Pl. Read 85 E4
Gordon Rd. Ashf 97 F3
Gordon Rd. Camb 151 E3
Gordon Rd. Crow 143 E2
Gordon Rd. Maid 39 E4
Gordon Rd. Newb 105 D1
Gordon Rd. Shepp 125 E2
Gordon Rd. Stai 96 B2
Gordon Rd. That 106 A3
Gordon Rd. Wind 66 C3
Gordon Wlk. Yate 149 F3
Gore End Rd. Ball H 129 D2
Gore Rd. Burn 21 D1
Goring La. Bur C 111 F2
Goring Rd. Stai 96 C2
Gorrick Sq. Brac 116 A2
Gorse Bank. Light 153 D4
Gorse Dr. Wood 88 A4
Gorse Hill La. Vir W 122 B3
Gorse Hill Rd. Vir W 122 B3
Gorse Meade. Slough 42 A3
Gorse Rd. Camb 151 F1
Gorse Rd. Cook 19 F3
Gorse Ride N. Woki 141 F4
Gorse Ride S. Woki 141 F3
Gorselands. Caver 59 D3
Gorselands. Newb 130 B3
Gorselands. Tad 135 E1

Gorselands. Yate 149 E2
Gosbrook Rd. Caver 59 D1
Gosden Rd. West E 153 F3
Gosforth Cl. Read 87 E1
Goslar Way. Wind 67 D3
Gosling Green. Slough 43 F2
Gosling Rd. Slough 43 F2
Gosnell Cl. Camb 152 B2
Gossmore Cl. Mar 1 C1
Gossmore La. Mar 1 C1
Goswell Hill. Wind 67 E3
Goswells Rd. Wind 67 E4
Gothic Cl. Harl 71 E4
Gothic Ct. Sand 150 A4
Gough's Barn La. New G 91 D4
Gough's La. New G 91 E1
Gough's Meadow. Sand 150 A4
Gould Rd. Felt 98 C4
Govenor's Rd. Sand 150 C3
Govett Ave. Shepp 125 E2
Govett Gr. Windl 146 B3
Gower Park. Sand 150 C4
Gower St. Read 85 F4
Gower The. Stai 123 E3
Graces La. Chiev 78 A4
Graffham Cl. Read 114 A4
Grafton Cl. Maid 19 F1
Grafton Cl. Slough 43 F4
Grafton Ct. Felt 98 B4
Grafton Rd. Read 84 B4
Graham Cl. Blew 12 A4
Graham Cl. Maid 39 E3
Graham Cl. Read 84 C2
Graham Rd. Cook 19 F3
Graham Rd. Windl 146 B2
Grahame Ave. Pangb 56 B3
Gramp's Hill. Let B 6 C3
Grampian Cl. Harl 71 E4
Grampian Rd. Sand 143 D1
Grampian Way. Slough 44 A1
Granby Cl. Read 86 C4
Granby End. Bur C 111 D2
Granby Gdns. Read 86 C4
Grand Ave. Camb 151 E3
Grange Ave. Crow 143 D3
Grange Ave. Read 87 D3
Grange Cl. Gori 34 A3
Grange Cl. Wray 68 C3
Grange Dr. Bou E 3 E2
Grange Gdns. Far C 22 B4
Grange La. Cook 19 F4
Grange Pl. Stai 124 B4
Grange Rd. Brac 118 B4
Grange Rd. Camb 151 F3
Grange Rd. Cook 19 F4
Grange Rd. Eng G 95 F2
Grange Rd. Hen-O-T 15 F1
Grange The. Burn 21 E1
Grange The. Old W 68 A1
Grange Way. Iver 44 C4
Grangely Cl. Bur C 84 B2
Grangewood. Slough 43 E4
Grant Ave. Slough 42 C4
Grant Cl. Shepp 125 D2
Grant Rd. Crow 143 E2
Grant Wlk. Sunn 120 C1
Grantham Cl. Sand 143 F1
Grantham Rd. Read 84 C2
Granthams The. Lamb 25 D2
Granville Ave. Slough 42 B4
Granville Rd. Read 85 D3
Grasmere Ave. Read 57 F1
Grasmere Ave. Slough 43 D3
Grasmere Cl. Felt 98 C4
Grasmere Cl. Stai 96 A1
Grasmere Par. Slough 43 D3
Grasmere Rd. Light 146 A1
Grass Hill. Caver 58 C2
Grassington Pl. That 106 B2
Grassmead. That 106 C1
Grassmere Cl. Winn 88 A1
Grassy La. Maid 39 F4
Grattan Ct. Mar 2 A2
Gratton Dr. Wind 66 C2
Gratton Rd. Read 113 E4
Gratwicke Rd. Read 84 C4
Gravel Hill. Box 103 F3
Gravel Hill. Caver 59 D3
Gravel Hill. Hen-O-T 15 E1
Gravel Rd. Caver 35 D1
Gravelly Cl. Ball H 129 D2
Graveney Dr. Caver 59 D2
Gravett Cl. Hen-O-T 35 E4
Gray's Pl. Slough 42 C3
Gray's Rd. Slough 42 C3
Grayling Cl. Mar 18 B4
Grays Cres. Wood 87 E4
Grays La. Ashf 98 A2
Grays Park Rd. Sto P 23 D2
Grayshot Dr. Sand 150 B3
Grazeley Rd. Shin 113 D2
Great Hill Cres. Maid 39 E3
Great Hollands Rd. Brac 117 F2
Great Hollands Sq. Brac 117 F2
Great Knollys St. Read 85 F4
Great Severals. Kint 102 A1
Great South West Rd. Felt 71 F1
Great South West Rd. Harm ... 71 F1
Green Acre Mount. Read 84 B4

Green Cl. Burn

Green Cl. Burn 41 D4
Green Cl. Maid 19 F1
Green Cres. Fla H 3 E4
Green Croft. Woki 116 C4
Green Dr. Woki 116 B4
Green Dragon La. Fla H 3 D4
Green End Cl. Shin 113 D1
Green End. Yate 149 E4
Green Farm Rd. Bags 145 F2
Green Finch Cl. Brac 142 C3
Green Hill Cl. Camb 152 B3
Green Hill Rd. Camb 152 B3
Green La. Ascot 120 C4
Green La. Ashf 98 C1
Green La. Bags 145 F1
Green La. Black 150 C2
Green La. Bur C 85 D1
Green La. Bur G 38 A3
Green La. Burn 21 E2
Green La. Caver 35 D1
Green La. Far C 22 A3
Green La. Hen-O-T 35 E4
Green La. Holy 64 A3
Green La. Hurst 88 C2
Green La. Maid 40 A3
Green La. Maid 40 A4
Green La. Newb 104 C1
Green La. Padw 110 B1
Green La. Pangb 56 B2
Green La. Sand 150 B3
Green La. Sand 150 B4
Green La. Shepp 125 E2
Green La. Slough 68 A3
Green La. Stai 96 A2
Green La. Stai 123 F4
Green La. That 106 B2
Green La. Wind 67 D3
Green La. Woki 88 B1
Green La. Yate 149 D4
Green Lane Cl. Camb 151 D4
Green Lane Ct. Burn 21 E1
Green Leas Cl. Ashf 98 C1
Green Leas. Ashf 98 C1
Green Park. Stai 96 C3
Green Rd. Read 87 D3
Green Rd. Vir W 123 F4
Green The. Brac 118 A3
Green The. Burn 21 D1
Green The. Chil 10 C4
Green The. Datch 68 A4
Green The. Slough 42 B2
Green The. Thea 83 E1
Green The. Woki 115 F4
Green The. Woo G 3 F3
Green The. Wray 68 C1
Green Verges. Mar 1 C2
Green Way. Burn 21 D2
Green Wood. Burl 119 E4
Greenacre Ct. Eng G 95 E1
Greenacre. Wind 66 C3
Greenacres Ave. Winn 88 A2
Greenacres La. Winn 88 A2
Greenacres. Ball H 129 F1
Greencroft Gdns. Read 84 C3
Greendale Mews. Slough 43 D3
Greene Fielde End. Stai 97 E1
Greenfell Ave. Maid 39 F3
Greenfern Av. Slough 41 E4
Greenfield Way. Brac 143 D4
Greenfields Rd. Read 113 D4
Greenfields. Maid 40 A3
Greenfinch Cl. Read 84 A3
Greenham Cl. Wood 88 A3
Greenham Mill. Newb 105 D2
Greenham Rd. Newb 105 D1
Greenham Wood. Brac 118 C3
Greenhaven. Yate 149 D3
Greenholme. Camb 152 B3
Greenlands Rd. Camb 151 D1
Greenlands Rd. Newb 105 D1
Greenlands Rd. Stai 97 D2
Greenlands. Ball H 129 F1
Greenlands. Fla H 3 D3
Greenleas Ave. Caver 59 D4
Greenleas Cl. Yate 149 E4
Greenleas. Camb 151 F1
Greeno Cres. Stai 125 D2
Greenock Rd. Slough 42 A4
Greenside. Bou E 3 D3
Greenside. Crow 142 C3
Greenside. Slough 42 A4
Greensward La. Arbo 114 B1
Greenway Dr. Stai 124 A4
Greenway The. Fawl 27 E4
Greenway The. Slough 41 E3
Greenways Dr. Maid 39 D4
Greenways Dr. Sunn 120 C1
Greenways. Ball H 129 F1
Greenways. Eng G 95 F2
Greenways. Lamb 25 D1
Greenways. Sand 143 D1
Greenwood Gr. Winn 114 B4
Greenwood Rd. Crow 143 D3
Greenwood Rd. Read 84 C3
Gregory Cl. Winn 114 B4
Gregory Dr. Old W 68 A1
Grenfell Pl. Maid 39 F3
Grenfell Rd. Maid 39 F3

Grenville Cl. Burn 21 D2
Gresham Rd. Slough 42 A4
Gresham Rd. Stai 96 C2
Gresham Rd. Stai 97 D2
Gresham Way. Read 58 A1
Grey's Rd. Hen-O-T 35 E4
Greyberry Copse Rd. Gree .. 131 E4
Greyfriars Dr. Ascot 120 A2
Greyfriars Rd. Read 86 A4
Greys Ct. Read 86 B4
Greys Hill. Hen-O-T 15 E1
Greystoke Ct. Crow 143 D2
Greystoke Rd. Caver 59 E2
Greystoke Rd. Slough 41 F4
Griffin Cl. Maid 39 F3
Griffin Cl. Slough 42 B2
Griffiths Cl. That 106 C1
Grindle Cl. Cold A 106 B3
Gringer Hill. Maid 39 F4
Grosvenor Cl. Black 150 B2
Grosvenor Dr. Maid 40 B4
Grosvenor Rd. Caver 59 E2
Grosvenor Rd. Stai 97 D1
Grove Cl. Brac 142 C4
Grove Cl. Old W 95 D4
Grove Cl. Slough 43 D2
Grove Cotts. Caver 59 D3
Grove Cross Rd. Camb 151 E1
Grove Ct. Eng G 96 A2
Grove End. Windl 145 F3
Grove Hill. Caver 59 D2
Grove La. Wink 92 A2
Grove Rd. Burn 21 F2
Grove Rd. Camb 151 F3
Grove Rd. Caver 59 D3
Grove Rd. Chert 123 F2
Grove Rd. Hen-O-T 15 F1
Grove Rd. Maid 39 F4
Grove Rd. Newb 104 C3
Grove Rd. Shepp 125 E2
Grove Rd. Wind 67 E3
Grove The. Burl 119 E4
Grove The. Camb 151 E1
Grove The. Eng G 96 A2
Grove The. Read 86 B4
Grove The. Slough 43 D2
Grove The. That 106 B2
Grove The. Twyf 61 E3
Grovefields Ave. Camb 151 E1
Groveland Pl. Read 85 D4
Groveland Rd. Newb 104 C3
Grovelands Ave. Winn 88 B1
Grovelands Cl. Winn 88 B2
Grovelands Rd. Read 85 D4
Grovelands Rd. Shin 113 E1
Groveley Rd. Ashf 98 C2
Groves Lea. Mort 136 C3
Groves Way. Cook 19 F3
Grovestile Waye. Felt 98 B4
Grubwood La. Cook 19 D4
Guards Club Rd. Maid 40 B4
Guards Rd. Oak G 66 B3
Guildford Ave. Felt 98 C3
Guildford Rd. Bags 145 F2
Guildford Rd. Bis 153 F4
Guildford Rd. Light 153 F4
Guildford Rd. West E 153 F4
Guildford St. Chert 124 A1
Guildford St. Stai 97 D1
Gun St. Read 86 A4
Gunthorpe Rd. Mar 2 A2
Gurney Cl. Caver 58 B3
Gurney Dr. Caver 58 B3
Gwendale. Maid 19 E1
Gweneth Cl. Mar 1 B2
Gwent Cl. Maid 39 D2
Gwyn Cl. Newb 130 C4
Gwynne Cl. Read 57 E2
Gwynne Cl. Wind 66 C3
Gwyns Piece. Lamb 25 D2
Gypsy La. Mar 1 C2
Gypsy La. Sto P 22 C4

Habershon Dr. Camb 152 B1
Haddon Dr. Wood 87 F4
Haddon Rd. Maid 39 E3
Hadfield Rd. Stan 70 B1
Hadfield Rise. Caver 59 F3
Hadleigh Rise. Caver 59 F3
Hadlow Cl. Slough 42 B3
Hadrian Cl. Stan 97 F4
Hadrian Way. Stan 97 F4
Hadrian Wlk E. Read 86 B2
Hag Hill La. Burn 41 D4
Hag Hill Rise. Burn 41 D4
Hagley Rd. Read 86 A2
Haig Dr. Slough 42 A2
Haig Rd. Sand 150 C3
Hailey La. Beed 29 F1
Hailsham Cl. Crow 143 E1
Halcyon Terr. Read 84 C4
Haldane Rd. Caver 58 C3
Hale End. Brac 118 C3
Hale St. Stai 96 C2
Hale Way. Camb 151 E1
Halewood. Brac 117 F2
Half Mile Rd. Lamb 46 A1
Half Moon St. Bags 145 F2
Halfacre Cl. Shin 113 D2

Halfpenny La. Chol 13 F3
Halfpenny La. Went 121 D1
Halifax Cl. Maid 39 D4
Halifax Rd. Maid 39 D4
Halifax Way. Maid 39 D4
Halkingcroft. Slough 43 E2
Hall Cl. Camb 151 F3
Hall Ct. Datch 68 A4
Hall Farm Cres. Yate 149 E3
Hall La. Harl 71 E4
Hall La. Yate 149 E3
Hall Meadow. Burn 21 E2
Hall Place La. Bur G 38 A4
Hallbrook Gdns. Binf 90 C1
Halldore Hill. Cook 19 F4
Halley Dr. Ascot 119 E4
Hallgrove Bottom. Windl 145 F3
Halliford Rd. Shepp 125 F3
Halliford Rd. Shepp 125 F3
Halls La. Read 86 C1
Halls La. W St L 63 D3
Halls Rd. Read 84 B3
Halpin Cl. Read 84 B2
Halstead Cl. Wood 87 F4
Ham La. Eng G 95 D2
Ham La. Old W 68 B2
Ham Rd. Ham 126 A2
Hamble Ave. Black 150 B3
Hambleden Wlk. Maid 19 F2
Hambledon Cl. Winn 87 F1
Hambleton Cl. Camb 152 A2
Hambridge La. Gree 105 F1
Hambridge Rd. Newb 105 E1
Hamilton Ave. Hen-O-T 15 F1
Hamilton Cl. Chert 123 F1
Hamilton Cl. Felt 98 C2
Hamilton Ct. Black 150 C1
Hamilton Ct. Newb 131 D4
Hamilton Dr. Sunn 120 C1
Hamilton Gdns. Burn 21 D1
Hamilton Rd. Felt 98 C2
Hamilton Rd. Read 86 C3
Hamilton Rd. Slough 42 A4
Hamilton Rd. Warg 36 C1
Hamlet St. Brac 118 C4
Hammond Cl. That 106 C1
Hammond End. Far C 22 B4
Hammond Way. Light 146 A1
Hammonds Heath. Mort 137 D3
Hampden Cl. Sto P 23 D1
Hampden Rd. Caver 59 D1
Hampden Rd. Maid 39 D4
Hampden Rd. Slough 43 F2
Hampdens The. Newb 130 B3
Hampshire Ave. Slough 42 B4
Hampshire Rd. Camb 151 F4
Hampshire Rise. New G 91 F1
Hampshire Way. Woki 115 E3
Hampstead Hill. Caver 60 B4
Hampstead Norreys Rd. Herm 79 D4
Hampton Rd. Newb 104 C1
Hanbury Cl. Burn 41 D4
Hanbury Dr. Bur C 84 B2
Hanbury Way. Camb 151 E2
Hancocks Mount. Ascot 120 B2
Hancombe Rd. Sand 143 D1
Handford La. Yate 149 E3
Hanger Rd. Tad 134 C1
Hangerfield Cl. Yate 149 E3
Hangman's Stone La. Chadd .. 49 D3
Hanley Cl. Wind 66 B3
Hannibal Rd. Stan 97 F4
Hanover Cl. Camb 151 F1
Hanover Cl. Eng G 95 D1
Hanover Cl. Slough 43 D2
Hanover Cl. Wind 66 C3
Hanover Gdns. Brac 117 F1
Hanover Way. Wind 66 C3
Hanwood Cl. Wood 87 E4
Hanworth Cl. Brac 118 B2
Hanworth Rd. Chert 123 F1
Hanworth Rd. Brac 118 A1
Harcourt Cl. Dorn 40 C2
Harcourt Cl. Hen-O-T 15 E1
Harcourt Cl. Stai 96 B1
Harcourt Dr. Read 86 C2
Harcourt Rd. Brac 118 A2
Harcourt Rd. Camb 151 D3
Harcourt Rd. Dorn 40 C2
Harcourt Rd. Wind 66 C3
Hardell Cl. Eng G 96 A2
Harding Rd. Wood 87 E4
Hardwell Way. Brac 118 C3
Hardwick Cl. Maid 39 D4
Hardwick La. Chert 123 E1
Hardwick Rd. Read 84 C4
Hardwick Rd. Whi-O-T 56 B4
Hardy Ave. Yate 149 E2
Hardy Cl. Caver 59 E1
Hardy Cl. Slough 42 A3
Hardy Cl. That 106 B3
Hardy Green. Crow 143 D2
Hare Shoots. Maid 39 F3
Harefield Cl. Winn 88 B1
Harefield Rd. Maid 39 D4
Harewood Dr. Cold A 106 B4
Harewood Pl. Slough 43 D2
Hargrave Rd. Maid 39 E4
Hargreaves Way. Read 84 C2

Harkness Rd. Burn 41 D4
Harlech Ave. Caver 59 E3
Harlech Rd. Black 150 B2
Harley Rd. Caver 59 D1
Harlington Cl. Harl 71 E4
Harlton Cl. Winn 114 B4
Harmans Water Rd. Brac 118 B2
Harmar Cl. Woki 116 C3
Harmondsworth La. Harm 70 C4
Harness Cl. Read 113 D3
Harold Rd. Kint 102 A1
Harpesford Ave. Went 122 B2
Harpton Cl. Yate 149 E4
Harrier Cl. Wood 88 A3
Harrington Cl. Newb 105 F3
Harrington Cl. Read 87 E1
Harrington Cl. Wind 66 C2
Harris Cl. Lamb 25 D2
Harris Cl. Read 88 A4
Harris Way. Stai 125 F4
Harrison Cl. Twyf 61 F2
Harrison Cl. Stai 125 D2
Harrison Way. Slough 41 E3
Harrogate Ct. Slough 44 A1
Harrogate Rd. Caver 58 C2
Harrow Bottom Rd. Went 122 C2
Harrow Cl. Maid 19 F1
Harrow Ct. Read 85 F3
Harrow La. Maid 19 F1
Harrow Rd. Ashf 98 A3
Harrow Rd. Slough 43 F2
Harrow Way. Stai 125 E4
Hart Cl. Brac 91 D1
Hart Dyke Cl. Brac 116 A1
Hart St. Hen-O-T 15 F1
Hart St. Read 85 F4
Hart's La. Sulhd 110 B3
Hartford Rise. Camb 151 E3
Hartigan Pl. Read 88 A4
Hartland Cl. Slough 42 B3
Hartland Rd. Read 86 B1
Hartley Cl. Black 150 A3
Hartley Cl. Sto P 23 E2
Hartley Court Rd. Shin 112 C3
Hartley Way. That 106 C2
Hartmead Rd. That 106 C2
Harts Cl. Arbo 114 C1
Harts Hill Rd. That 106 B2
Harts Leap Cl. Sand 150 A4
Harts Leap Rd. Sand 150 A4
Hartsbourne Rd. Read 87 D2
Hartshill Rd. Tad 134 C1
Hartslock Ct. Pangb 56 A3
Hartslock Way. Read 57 E1
Hartstock View. Upp B 34 C1
Harvard Cl. Wood 88 A4
Harvard Rd. Crow 143 F1
Harvest Cl. Read 84 A3
Harvest Cl. Yate 149 D2
Harvest Ct. Stai 125 D3
Harvest Green. Newb 104 C1
Harvest Hill Rd. Maid 39 F2
Harvest Hill. Bou E 3 E1
Harvest Rd. Eng G 95 E1
Harvest Ride. New G 91 F1
Harvey Rd. Shepp 125 F1
Harvey Rd. Slough 44 A2
Harwich Cl. Winn 87 E1
Harwich Rd. Slough 42 A4
Harwood Gdns. Old W 95 D4
Harwood Rise. Mar 1 B1
Harwood Rise. Ball H 129 F1
Haslemere Cl. Camb 152 B2
Haslemere Rd. Wind 67 D3
Haslett Rd. Shepp 125 F4
Hasting Cl. Maid 40 B1
Hatch Cl. Buck 108 B4
Hatch End. Windl 146 B2
Hatch Gate La. Know H 37 D3
Hatch La. Buck 108 B4
Hatch La. Bur C 111 E3
Hatch La. Harm 70 B4
Hatch La. Wind 67 D3
Hatch Ride. Brac 142 C4
Hatch Ride. Brac 143 D4
Hatch The. Oak G 66 C4
Hatchet La. Ascot 93 D2
Hatchet La. Old W 93 D2
Hatchet La. Wink 93 D2
Hatchets La. Buck 80 B4
Hatchett Rd. Felt 98 B4
Hatchgate Cl. Cold A 106 B4
Hatchgate Copse. Brac 117 F2
Hatchgate Gdns. Burn 21 E1
Hatfield Cl. Maid 39 E3
Hatfield Ct. Bur C 84 A2
Hatfield Rd. Slough 43 D2
Hatford Rd. Read 85 D2
Hatherley Rd. Read 86 C3
Hatherwood. Yate 149 F3
Hatton Ave. Far C 22 B1
Hatton Ct. Wind 67 E3
Hatton Hill. Asham 54 A4
Hatton Hill. Windl 146 B3
Hatton Rd. Felt 98 B4
Hatton Rd. Harm 71 F1
Haughurst Hill. Tad 134 B1
Havelock Cres. Maid 39 D4
Havelock Rd. Maid 39 D4

Havelock Rd. Woki 116 A3
Havelock St. Woki 116 A3
Haven Rd. Ashf 98 A3
Haven The. Kint 102 A1
Haversham Dr. Brac 118 A2
Haw La. Asham 53 F4
Hawkchurch Rd. Read 113 E4
Hawkedon Way. Winn 87 F1
Hawker Way. Wood 88 A4
Hawkes Cl. Woki 116 A4
Hawkes Leap. Windl 146 A3
Hawkesbury Dr. Bur C 84 C2
Hawkesworth Dr. Bags 145 F1
Hawkins Cl. Brac 119 D4
Hawkins Way. Woki 116 C3
Hawks Hill. Bou E 3 E1
Hawkshill Rd. Slough 22 A1
Hawksway. Stai 96 C3
Hawkswood Ave. Camb 151 F1
Hawkswood La. Fulm 23 F4
Hawksworth Rd. Bur C 111 D2
Hawley Cl. Bur C 84 B2
Hawley La. Camb 151 D2
Hawley Rd. Black 150 C2
Hawley Way. Ashf 98 A2
Haws La. Stan 70 A1
Hawthorn Cl. Brac 118 A4
Hawthorn Cl. Mar 1 C2
Hawthorn Gdns. Read 86 C1
Hawthorn La. Burn 22 A3
Hawthorn La. New G 91 F4
Hawthorn Rd. Camb 151 F1
Hawthorn Rd. Newb 105 D2
Hawthorn Way. Shepp 125 E3
Hawthorn Way. Sonn 60 C1
Hawthorne Cres. Black 150 C2
Hawthorne Cres. Slough 42 C4
Hawthorne Rd. Caver 59 F2
Hawthorne Rd. Stai 96 B2
Hawthorne Way. Gr She 48 A3
Hawthorne Way. Stan 97 E4
Hawthornes. Sulh 57 D2
Hawthorns The. Char 61 D2
Hawthorns The. Stan 69 F3
Hawtrey Cl. Slough 43 D2
Hawtrey Rd. Wind 67 E3
Hay La. Fulm 23 E4
Hay Rd. Read 85 F3
Hayes La. Bark 115 E2
Hayes Pl. Mar 1 B1
Hayfield Cl. Read 84 B4
Hayley Green. New G 91 F2
Haymill Rd. Slough 21 E1
Haynes Cl. Slough 43 F1
Hayse Hill. Wind 66 B3
Haywards Cl. Hen-O-T 15 E1
Haywards Mead. Eton 41 F1
Haywards The. That 106 B2
Haywood Ct. Read 86 C4
Haywood Way. Read 84 C3
Haywood. Brac 118 B3
Hazel Cl. Bur C 111 D3
Hazel Cl. Eng G 95 D1
Hazel Cl. Mar B 1 B3
Hazel Cl. Woki 115 F3
Hazel Cres. Read 86 C1
Hazel Dr. Wood 87 E3
Hazel Gr. Stai 97 E1
Hazel Green. Tad 134 B1
Hazel Gr. That 106 B3
Hazel Rd. Pur O T 57 E2
Hazelbank Rd. Chert 124 B1
Hazelbank. Woki 141 F3
Hazeldene. Chiev 51 D1
Hazelhurst Rd. Burn 21 E2
Hazell Cl. Maid 39 F4
Hazell Hill. Brac 118 B3
Hazell Way. Sto P 22 C3
Hazelmere Cl. Harm 71 F1
Hazelwood Cl. Read 57 E1
Hazelwood La. Binf 90 C2
Hazlemere Rd. Slough 43 D3
Heacham Cl. Read 114 A4
Headington Cl. Maid 39 D4
Headington Dr. Woki 116 B4
Headington Rd. Woki 116 B4
Headington Rd. Maid 39 D4
Headley Cl. Wood 88 A4
Headley Park Ind Est. Wood ... 87 F4
Headley Rd E. Wood 88 A4
Headley Rd. Wood 87 F4
Heads La. Ink 128 A3
Heads La. West W 128 A3
Heardman Cl. That 106 C1
Hearmon Cl. Yate 149 F3
Hearn Rd. Wood 87 F3
Hearn Wlk. Brac 118 C4
Hearne Dr. Holy 40 A1
Hearsey Gdns. Black 150 A3
Heath Cl. Harl 71 E4
Heath Cl. Stan 70 B1
Heath Cl. Vir W 122 B3
Heath Cl. Woki 116 A2
Heath Dr. Caver 35 D1
Heath End Rd. Tad 134 C1
Heath Gr. Ashf 98 C1
Heath Hill Rd N. Crow 143 D3
Heath Hill Rd S. Crow 143 D3
Heath La. That 106 B3

Heath La. That

Heath Rd. Bags 145 F2
Heath Rd. Beac 3 F4
Heath Rd. Brad 82 A1
Heath Rd. Read 87 D3
Heath Rd. Silc 135 F1
Heath Ride. Finch 142 B3
Heath Ride. Woki 142 B3
Heath Rise. Camb 151 E3
Heath Rise. Vir W 122 B3
Heathacre. Stan 69 F3
Heathcote Rd. Camb 151 E3
Heathcroft Ave. Ashf 98 C1
Heather Cl. Woki 141 F4
Heather Dr. Tad 134 C1
Heather Dr. Went 121 D1
Heather Mead. Camb 151 F1
Heatherdale Rd. Camb 151 E2
Heatherden Cl. Read 113 E4
Heatherdene Ave. Finch 142 C2
Heatherley Cl. Camb 151 D3
Heatherley Rd. Camb 151 D3
Heathermount Dr. Crow 143 D3
Heathermount. Brac 118 C3
Heathers The. Stan 97 F4
Heatherside Dr. Vir W 122 A2
Heatherway. Crow 143 D3
Heathfield Ave. Ascot 120 C2
Heathfield Ave. Read 84 B3
Heathfield Ave. Shipl 35 D1
Heathfield Ave. Shipl 35 D1
Heathfield Rd. Bou E 20 C4
Heathfield Rd. Tapl 20 C4
Heathlands Dr. Maid 39 D3
Heathlands Rd. Woki 116 C1
Heathlands. Tad 134 C1
Heathmoors. Brac 118 B2
Heathpark Dr. Windl 146 C2
Heathrow Cl. Harm 70 A3
Heathway Cl. Camb 151 E3
Heathway. Burl 119 F4
Heathway. Camb 151 E3
Heathway. Read 84 B4
Heathwood Cl. Yate 149 E4
Heavens Lea. Bou E 3 E1
Hebden Cl. That 106 B1
Hedge Lea. Woo G 3 E4
Hedgeway. Newb 105 E2
Hedingham Mews. Maid 39 E4
Hedley Rd. Fla H 3 D4
Hedsor Hill. Bou E 3 E1
Hedsor La. Bou E 3 F1
Hedsor Rd. Bou E 3 D1
Heelas Rd. Woki 116 A3
Helena Rd. Wind 67 E3
Helgiford Gdns. Ashf 98 C1
Hellyer Way. Bou E 3 E2
Helmsdale Cl. Read 85 D4
Helmsdale. Brac 118 C2
Helston Gdns. Read 86 A1
Helston La. Wind 67 D3
Helvellyn Cl. Stai 96 B1
Hemdean Hill. Caver 59 D2
Hemdean Rd. Caver 59 D2
Hemdean Rise. Caver 59 D2
Hempson Ave. Slough 43 E2
Hemsdale. Maid 19 D1
Hemwood Rd. Wind 66 B2
Hencroft St N. Slough 42 C2
Hencroft St S. Slough 42 C2
Hendon Way. Stan 70 B1
Hendons Way. Holy 40 A1
Hengrave Cl. Winn 87 F1
Hengrove Cres. Ashf 97 E3
Henley Gdns. Yate 149 E3
Henley Rd. Bur G 18 A1
Henley Rd. Caver 60 B4
Henley Rd. Hurl 18 A1
Henley Rd. Maid 18 A1
Henley Rd. Mar 18 A4
Henley Rd. Shipl 60 B4
Henley Rd. Slough 41 F4
Henley Wood Rd. Read 87 E2
Henry Rd. Slough 42 B2
Henry St. Read 86 A3
Henrys The. That 106 B2
Henshaw Cres. Newb 130 B4
Hensworth Rd. Stai 97 E2
Henwick Cl. That 106 A3
Henwick La. That 106 A2
Henwood Copse. Upp B 55 D3
Hepplewhite Cl. Tad 134 C1
Hepworth Croft. Sand 150 B3
Hepworth Way. Shepp 125 F1
Herald Way. Wood 88 A3
Herbert Cl. Brac 118 A2
Hereford Cl. Stai 124 A4
Herewood Cl. Newb 104 C2
Heriot Rd. Chert 124 A1
Hermit's Hill. Bur C 111 E2
Hermitage Cl. Camb 151 F1
Hermitage Cl. Slough 43 E2
Hermitage Cl. Stai 125 D3
Hermitage Dr. Ascot 119 F4
Hermitage Dr. Twyf 61 E3
Hermitage La. Wind 67 D2
Hermitage Rd. Cold A 79 D1
Hermitage Rd. Herm 79 D1
Hermitage The. Lamb 46 C4
Hermits Cl. Bur C 111 D2

Herndon Cl. Eng G 96 A2
Heroes Wlk. Read 113 D4
Heron Cl. Burl 119 E4
Heron Dr. Twyf 61 F3
Heron Island. Caver 59 E1
Heron Rd. Woki 115 F3
Heron Shaw. Gori 34 B4
Heron Way. Bur C 85 F2
Heron Way. That 106 A2
Heron's Way. Woki 116 C4
Herondale. Brac 118 B1
Heronfield. Eng G 95 D1
Herongate. Hung 100 B4
Herons Ct. Light 153 E4
Herons Pl. Mar 1 C2
Herrick Cl. Camb 152 B2
Herrings La. Chert 124 A2
Herrings La. Windl 146 B2
Herriot Cl. Yate 149 E2
Herschel Park Dr. Slough 42 C2
Herschel St. Slough 42 C2
Hertford Cl. Caver 59 E3
Hertford Cl. Woki 115 F3
Hetherington Cl. Slough 21 F1
Hetherington Rd. Stai 125 E4
Hever Cl. Maid 39 E3
Hewett Ave. Caver 58 B2
Hewett Cl. Caver 58 B2
Hewlett Pl. Bags 145 F2
Hexham Cl. Crow 143 E1
Hexham Rd. Read 86 B2
Heywood Ave. Whi Wa 39 D1
Heywood Court Cl. Whi Wa 39 D1
Heywood Gdns. Whi Wa 39 D1
Hibbert Rd. Maid 40 A2
Hibbert's Alley. Wind 67 E3
Hicks La. Black 150 A3
Higgs La. Bags 145 E2
High Beech. Brac 118 C3
High Beeches. Camb 151 E1
High Fields. Sunn 120 C2
High Heavens Wood. Mar B 1 B4
High Meadow. Caver 58 B2
High Rd. Cook 19 F3
High St Harlington. Harl 71 E4
High St. Ascot 120 A3
High St. Ascot 120 B2
High St. Bags 145 F2
High St. Box 76 A2
High St. Brac 118 A4
High St. Brac 118 B4
High St. Burn 21 E1
High St. Camb 151 E3
High St. Chiev 51 D1
High St. Comp 31 E2
High St. Cook 20 A4
High St. Crow 143 E2
High St. Datch 68 A3
High St. East I 30 C4
High St. Eng G 96 A2
High St. Eton 67 E4
High St. Felt 98 C3
High St. Gori 34 B3
High St. Harl 71 E4
High St. Harm 70 B4
High St. Hung 100 B3
High St. Iver 44 C4
High St. Iver 69 E4
High St. Kint 102 A1
High St. Lamb 24 C3
High St. Lamb 25 D1
High St. Maid 39 F4
High St. Maid 40 A2
High St. Maid 40 B3
High St. Mar 1 C1
High St. Pangb 56 B3
High St. Read 86 A4
High St. Sand 143 D1
High St. Sand 149 F4
High St. Shepp 125 E2
High St. Slough 42 B2
High St. Slough 42 C2
High St. Slough 44 A1
High St. Sonn 60 B2
High St. Stai 96 C2
High St. Stan 70 B1
High St. Stre 34 A3
High St. Sunn 121 D2
High St. Tapl 20 C1
High St. That 106 B2
High St. Thea 83 F2
High St. Twyf 61 E2
High St. Warg 36 B1
High St. West E 153 F4
High St. Whi-O-T 56 B4
High St. Wick 76 A2
High St. Wind 67 E3
High St. Wray 68 C1
High Town Rd. Maid 39 F3
High Tree Dr. Read 87 D3
High View Cl. Mar B 1 B4
High View Rd. Light 152 C4
Highbeeches Cl. Mar B 1 B3
Highbridge Cl. Caver 59 F2
Highbridge Wharf. Read 86 A4
Highbury Cres. Camb 152 A4
Highbury Rd. Read 84 A3
Highclere Cl. Brac 118 C4
Highclere Dr. Camb 152 A4

Highclere. Ascot 120 B2
Highdown Ave. Caver 59 F4
Highdown Hill Rd. Caver 59 D4
Highdown Hill Rd. Maple 59 D4
Higher Alham. Brac 118 C1
Highfield Cl. Eng G 95 E1
Highfield Ave. Newb 105 D1
Highfield Cl. Woki 116 A3
Highfield Ct. Bur C 111 D2
Highfield La. Maid 39 D2
Highfield Park. Mar 18 A4
Highfield Park. Warg 36 C1
Highfield Rd. Bou E 3 D2
Highfield Rd. Chert 124 A1
Highfield Rd. Fla H 3 D4
Highfield Rd. Maid 39 D4
Highfield Rd. Newb 104 C1
Highfield Rd. Pur O T 57 E2
Highfield Rd. Shepp 125 F2
Highfield Rd. Wind 66 C2
Highfield. Brac 117 F2
Highfield. Read 87 D1
Highgate Rd. Wood 87 E3
Highgrove Park. Maid 39 F4
Highgrove St. Read 86 B3
Highgrove Terr. Read 86 A3
Highland Ave. Woki 115 F4
Highland Park. Felt 98 C2
Highland Rd. Camb 151 F4
Highlands La. Shipl 35 D4
Highlands. Fla H 3 D4
Highlea Ave. Fla H 3 D4
Highmead Cl. Read 86 C1
Highmoor Rd. Caver 58 C2
Highview Cres. Camb 144 C1
Highview. Read 84 A3
Highway Ave. Maid 39 D3
Highway Rd. Maid 39 D3
Highway. Crow 143 D3
Highwayman's Ridge. Windl . 146 A3
Highwood Cl. Newb 105 E3
Highwood Cl. Yate 149 E2
Highwoods Cl. Mar B 1 B4
Highwoods Dr. Mar B 1 B4
Highworth Way. Sulh 57 D1
Hilary Cl. Read 113 E4
Hilborne Way. Bark 115 D1
Hilbury Rd. Read 87 D2
Hilcot Rd. Read 85 E4
Hildens Dr. Read 84 B4
Hilfield. Yate 149 F3
Hill Cl. Newb 130 B4
Hill Copse View. Brac 118 C4
Hill Farm App. Woo G 3 F4
Hill Farm Rd. Mar B 1 C3
Hill Farm Rd. Tapl 20 C1
Hill Gdns. Stre 34 A3
Hill Lands. Warg 36 B1
Hill Piece. Chil 10 C4
Hill Rd. Bark 114 C1
Hill Rd. Newb 104 C2
Hill St. Read 86 A3
Hill Top Dr. Mar 1 A1
Hill View Rd. Wray 68 B1
Hillary Dr. Crow 143 D3
Hillary Rd. Slough 43 F2
Hillberry. Brac 118 B1
Hillborn Rd. Bark 140 C4
Hillbrow. Read 86 C1
Hillcrest Ave. Cook 19 E3
Hillcrest Rd. Camb 152 A4
Hillcrest. Tad 135 D1
Hillersdon. Slough 43 D4
Hillgreen La. Pease 50 B4
Hillhouse La. Head 133 E1
Hillingdon Ave. Stan 97 F4
Hillmead Ct. Tapl 40 C4
Hillrise. Slough 69 D4
Hills La. Cook 19 E4
Hillsborough Park. Camb 152 B3
Hillside Dr. Binf 90 B1
Hillside Park. Read 86 C1
Hillside Park. Windl 120 C1
Hillside Rd. Hung 100 B2
Hillside Rd. Mar 1 C2
Hillside Rd. Read 87 E2
Hillside. Bur C 111 E2
Hillside. East G 47 E3
Hillside. Maid 39 E3
Hillside. Sand 150 C4
Hillside. Slough 42 C2
Hillside. Went 122 B2
Hillside. Whi-O-T 56 B4
Hilltop Cl. Ascot 120 C4
Hilltop Rd. Caver 58 B3
Hilltop Rd. Read 87 D4
Hilltop Rd. Twyf 61 F4
Hilltop View. Yate 149 D3
Hillview Cl. Read 57 D1
Hilmanton. Read 113 F4
Hilperton Rd. Slough 42 C2
Hindhead Rd. Read 87 D2
Hinksey Cl. Slough 44 A2
Hinton Cl. Crow 143 D4
Hinton Dr. Crow 143 D4
Hinton Rd. Hurst 62 A1
Hinton Rd. Hurst 88 C4
Hinton Rd. Slough 41 F3

Hintonhatch Cnr. Hurst 62 A1
Hirstwood. Pur O T 57 F1
Hirtes Ave. Shin 113 F3
Hitcham La. Tapl 20 C1
Hitcham Rd. Burn 41 D4
Hitchcock Cl. Stai 124 C3
Hitherhooks Hill. Binf 90 C1
Hitherhooks Hill. Brac 117 F4
Hithermoor Rd. Stan 70 A1
Hobart Dr. Mar 2 A2
Hobbis Dr. Maid 39 D3
Hockett La. Bish 19 D3
Hockett La. Cook 19 D3
Hockford La. Head 134 A2
Hockham Rd. Comp 31 F3
Hockley La. Sto P 23 D3
Hodgedale La. Warg 37 E3
Hodges Cl. Bags 145 F1
Hodsoll Rd. Read 85 F4
Hoe Benham La. Wick 102 C3
Hogarth Ave. Ashf 98 B1
Hogarth Ave. Read 84 C3
Hogarth Cl. Sand 150 C3
Hogarth Cl. Slough 41 F3
Hogfair La. Burn 21 E1
Hogmoor La. Hurst 61 F1
Hogwood La. Bark 141 D3
Holbeche Cl. Yate 149 D3
Holbeck. Brac 117 F2
Holberton Rd. Read 113 E4
Holborn Hill. Let B 6 B4
Holborne Cl. Newb 130 B3
Holford Cl. Read 84 B4
Holkam Cl. Read 57 F1
Holland Gdns. Stai 123 F4
Holland Pines. Brac 117 F1
Holland Rd. Mar 1 C2
Holland Rd. Read 84 B4
Hollands The. That 106 C2
Hollicombe Cl. Read 84 C4
Hollies The. Newb 130 B3
Hollins Wlk. Read 85 E3
Hollow Hill La. Iver 44 B3
Hollow La. Shin 113 F3
Hollow La. Vir W 122 B3
Holloway La. Harm 70 C4
Holly Ave. Camb 152 A2
Holly Cl. Eng G 95 D1
Holly Cl. Far C 22 B4
Holly Cres. Wind 66 B3
Holly Dr. Maid 39 F4
Holly Dr. Old Wind 67 F1
Holly Hedge Cl. Camb 151 F1
Holly Hedge Rd. Camb 151 F1
Holly La. Asham 54 B3
Holly Rd. Wood 88 A3
Holly Spring La. Brac 118 B4
Holly Way. Black 150 B2
Hollybank. West E 153 F3
Hollybush Hill. Sto P 23 D3
Hollybush La. Cook 19 D3
Hollybush La. Iver 44 A3
Hollybush La. Sulh 110 C2
Hollybush Ride. Brac 142 B3
Hollybush Ride. Finch 142 B3
Hollycombe. Eng G 95 E2
Hollycroft Cl. Harm 71 D4
Hollycroft Gdns. Harm 71 D4
Hollydale Cl. Read 86 C1
Hollyhock Cl. Brac 143 D3
Hollym Cl. Winn 87 F1
Holmanleaze. Maid 40 A4
Holmbank Dr. Shepp 125 F3
Holmbury Ave. Brac 143 D4
Holmdale. Slough 43 E3
Holmdene. Bur C 111 D2
Holme Cl. Brac 143 D4
Holmemoor Dr. Sonn 60 C1
Holmes Cl. Ascot 120 B2
Holmes Cl. Woki 116 A2
Holmes Cres. Woki 116 A2
Holmes Rd. Read 87 D3
Holmewood Cl. Woki 116 A1
Holmlea Rd. Datch 68 B3
Holmlea Rd. Gori 34 B3
Holmlea Wlk. Datch 68 B3
Holmsdale Cl. Iver 44 C4
Holmwood Ave. Read 84 C2
Holmwood Cl. Maid 39 D3
Holsworthy Cl. Winn 87 F2
Holt La. Brig 49 F4
Holt La. Woki 116 A4
Holt Rd. Kint 102 A1
Holt The. Pur O T 57 E2
Holton Heath. Brac 118 C3
Holtspur Ave. Woo G 3 F4
Holtspur La. Woo G 3 F3
Holtwood Rd. Ham M 129 D3
Holybrook Cres. Read 85 D2
Holybrook Rd. Read 85 F3
Holyport St. Holy 65 D4
Holyrood Cl. Caver 59 E3
Holywell Cl. Stan 97 F4
Holywell Way. Stan 97 F4
Hombrook Dr. Brac 117 F4
Home Croft. Sulh 57 D1
Home Farm Cl. Read 86 B2
Home Farm Cl. Shepp 125 F3

Home Farm Way. Sto P 23 E4
Home Mead Cl. Newb 130 C4
Home Meadow Dr. Fla H 3 D4
Home Meadow. Far C 22 B2
Home Park Farm La. Sonn 60 B1
Home Park Rd. Yate 149 E3
Homefield Way. Hung 100 B3
Homers Rd. Wind 66 B3
Homestead Rd. Maid 39 E2
Homestead Rd. Stai 97 D1
Homewaters Ave. Shepp 125 F4
Homewood. Slough 43 E4
Hone Hill. Sand 150 A4
Honesty Bottom. Brig 28 B1
Honey End La. Read 85 D3
Honey Hill. Brac 117 D1
Honey Hill. Lamb 25 D2
Honey La. Hurl 17 F1
Honeybottom Rd. Tad 135 D1
Honeyfields. Hung 100 B3
Honeyhill Rd. Brac 118 A4
Honeysuckle Cl. Brac 143 D4
Honeysuckle Cl. Yate 149 D3
Honiton Rd. Read 86 B1
Honnor Rd. Stai 97 D1
Hook End La. Upp B 34 A1
Hook La. West E 153 E3
Hook Mill La. Light 146 B1
Hookstone La. West E 153 F4
Hop Gdns. Hen-O-T 15 E1
Hope Ave. Brac 118 C1
Hopeman Cl. Sand 150 B4
Hopwood Cl. Newb 105 E2
Horewood Rd. Brac 118 A2
Hormer Cl. Sand 143 D1
Horn St. Comp 31 F3
Hornbeam Cl. Pur O T 57 E3
Hornbeam Cl. Sand 143 E1
Hornbeam Cl. Woki 115 E2
Hornbeam Gdns. Slough 43 D2
Hornbeams. Swal 139 E3
Horncastle Dr. Read 84 C3
Horndean Rd. Brac 118 C1
Horne Rd. Stai 125 D3
Horne Rd. That 106 C1
Hornsea Cl. Read 57 F2
Horse Cl The. Caver 59 E2
Horse Gate Ride. Ascot 120 A2
Horsebrass Dr. Bags 145 F1
Horseguards Dr. Maid 40 A4
Horsell Ct. Chert 124 A1
Horsemoor Cl. Slough 44 A1
Horseshoe Cl. Camb 151 F4
Horseshoe Cres. Bur C 111 D2
Horseshoe Cres. Camb 151 F4
Horseshoe Hill. Burn 21 E4
Horseshoe Park. Pangb 56 B3
Horseshoe Rd. Pangb 56 B3
Horsham Rd. Crow 143 E1
Horsham Rd. Felt 71 E1
Horsnape Gdns. Binf 90 A1
Horsneile La. Brac 118 A4
Horton Cl. Maid 20 B1
Horton Rd. Datch 68 B3
Horton Rd. Hort 69 D3
Horton Rd. Stan 69 F2
Horton Rd. Poyle 69 E2
Hose Hill. Bur C 111 D4
Hosier St. Read 86 A4
Houlton Ct. Bags 145 F1
Houston Way. Finch 142 B3
Howard Ave. Slough 42 C4
Howard Cl. Ashf 98 C1
Howard Rd. Ashf 97 E2
Howard Rd. Newb 105 D1
Howard Rd. Woki 116 B3
Howard St. Read 85 F4
Howarth Rd. Maid 40 A3
Howe La. Holy 63 F1
Howgate Dr. Gori 34 B4
Howth Dr. Wood 87 E4
Hubberholme. Brac 118 A3
Hubert Rd. Slough 43 E2
Huckleberry Cl. Pur O T 57 E2
Huddington Glade. Yate 149 D3
Hudson Rd. Harl 71 E4
Hudson Rd. Wood 87 F3
Hugh Fraser Dr. Read 84 B3
Hughenden Cl. Maid 39 E3
Hughenden Rd. Slough 42 B4
Hughes Rd. Ashf 98 B1
Hughes Rd. Woki 116 C4
Hull Cl. Slough 42 B2
Humber Cl. That 106 A3
Humber Cl. Woki 115 F3
Humber Way. Sand 150 B4
Humber Way. Slough 43 F3
Hummer Rd. Eng G 96 A2
Humphrey's La. East G 47 E3
Hungerford Ave. Slough 42 C4
Hungerford Cl. Sand 150 B4
Hungerford Dr. Maid 19 F2
Hungerford Dr. Read 85 F3
Hungerford Hill. East G 47 F1
Hungerford La. Lamb 25 D1
Hungerford La. Hurst 62 C1
Hungerford La. W St L 62 C1
Hungerford Rd. Kint 101 F2
Hunt's La. Tapl 20 C2

Hunter's Hill. Bur C 110 C2
Huntercombe Cl. Burn 41 E4
Huntercombe Cl. Slough 41 E4
Huntercombe La N. Slough 41 E4
Huntercombe La S. Burn 41 E3
Huntercombe La S. Slough 41 E3
Hunters Meadow. Gr She 48 A2
Hunters Mews. Wind 67 E3
Hunters Way. Shin 113 D1
Huntingdonshire Cl. Woki 115 E3
Huntingfield Way. Stai 96 B1
Huntington Cl. Winn 87 F1
Huntley Ct. Read 86 C3
Huntsmans Meadow. Ascot .. 119 F4
Huntsmoor Rd. Tad 135 D1
Huntswood La. Burn 20 C2
Huntswood La. Tapl 20 C2
Hurley High St. Hurl 17 F2
Hurley La. Bish 18 A2
Hurley La. Hurl 18 A2
Hurricane Way. Read 88 A4
Hurricane Way. Wood 88 A4
Hursley Cl. Read 84 C4
Hurst Gr. Shepp 125 F1
Hurst La. Vir W 123 D4
Hurst Park Rd. Twyf 61 F1
Hurst Rd. Slough 41 E4
Hurst Rd. Twyf 61 F2
Hurstdene Ave. Stai 97 D1
Hurstfield Dr. Burn 41 D4
Hurstwood. Ascot 120 A2
Huscarle Way. Pur O T 57 E2
Hutsons Cl. Woki 116 B4
Hutton Cl. Newb 105 D2
Hutton Cl. Read 87 D1
Hutton Cl. Windl 146 B2
Hyde End La. Brim 133 E3
Hyde End La. Shin 113 E2
Hyde End Rd. Shin 113 E1
Hyde Green. Mar 1 C1
Hyde La. Newt 132 A1
Hyde Terr. Ashf 98 C1
Hydes The. Pur O T 57 E2
Hylle Cl. Wind 66 C3
Hyperion Way. Read 86 A2
Hythe Cl. Brac 118 C2
Hythe End Rd. Wray 96 A3
Hythe Field Ave. Stai 96 B1
Hythe Park Rd. Stai 96 B2
Hythe Rd. Stai 96 B2
Hythe The. Stai 96 C2

Ian Mikardo Way. Caver 59 E1
Iberian Way. Camb 152 A3
Ibstock Cl. Read 85 D4
Ibstone Ave. Caver 59 F3
Icknield Pl. Gori 34 B4
Icknield Rd. Gori 34 B4
Ilbury Cl. Shin 113 F3
Ilchester Cl. Maid 39 E3
Ilchester Mews. Caver 59 F3
Ilex Cl. Eng G 95 D1
Ilex Cl. Silc 135 F1
Ilex Cl. Yate 149 D3
Ilfracombe Way. Winn 87 F2
Ilkley Rd. Caver 58 C2
Ilkley Way. That 106 B1
Illingworth Ave. Caver 59 F3
Illingworth Gr. Brac 118 C4
Illingworth. Wind 66 C2
Ilsley Rd. Comp 31 E2
Imperial Rd. Felt 98 C4
Imperial Rd. Wind 67 D3
Imperial Way. Read 113 D4
Impstone Rd. Silc 135 F1
In The Ray. Maid 40 A2
Inchwood. Brac 118 B1
India Rd. Slough 43 D2
Ingle Dell. Camb 151 E2
Ingle Glen. Woki 142 N4
Ingleglen. Far C 22 A4
Ingleside. Stan 69 F3
Ingleton. Brac 118 A3
Inglewood Ave. Camb 152 B3
Inglewood Ct. Read 85 C3
Inglewood Rd. Kint 101 F1
Inhurst Way. Tad 134 C1
Inkerman Rd. Eton 41 F1
Inkpen Cl. Read 85 D2
Inkpen Rd. Hung 100 C2
Inkpen Rd. Kint 102 A1
Inkpen Rd. Kint 127 D4
Inner Ring E. Harm 71 D2
Inner Ring W. Harm 71 D2
Innings La. Whi Wa 63 E4
Institute Rd. Burn 40 C4
Institute Rd. Mar 1 C1
Institute Rd. Tapl 40 C4
Instow Rd. Read 87 D1
Invergordon Cl. Read 84 C2
Inverness Way. Sand 150 B4
Inwood Cl. Cook 19 D3
Iona Cres. Slough 41 F4
Ipswich Rd. Slough 42 A4
Irish Hill Rd. Kint 102 A1
Irvine Pl. Vir W 122 C4
Irvine Way. Winn 114 B4
Isaac Newton Rd. Bark 115 D1
Isis Cl. Winn 88 A1

Isis Way. Bou E 3 D2
Isis Way. Sand 150 B4
Island Cl. Stai 96 C2
Island Farm Rd. Bur C 110 B1
Island Farm Rd. Bur C 136 C4
Island Farm Rd. Sulhd 110 B1
Island Rd. Bur C 85 F1
Island Rd. Read 85 F1
Island The. Eng G 96 A3
Islandstone La. Hurst 89 D3
Islet Park Dr. Maid 20 B2
Islet Park. Maid 20 B2
Islet Rd. Maid 20 B2
Ivanhoe Rd. Bark 141 D3
Iver La. Iver 44 C4
Iverdale Cl. Iver 44 B3
Iverna Gdns. Harm 71 E1
Ives Cl. Yate 149 D4
Ives Rd. Slough 44 A2
Ivy Cl. Holy 65 D4
Ivy Cres. Slough 41 F3
Ivy Dr. Light 153 D4
Ivybank. Read 57 E1
Ivydene Rd. Read 58 B1

Jack St. Newb 105 D2
Jackson Cl. Brac 118 A2
Jacob Cl. Brac 117 E4
Jacob Cl. Wind 66 C3
Jacob Rd. Sand 151 D4
James Butcher Dr. Thea 83 F2
James Cl. Mar 1 C2
James Rd. Camb 151 D1
James St. Read 85 F4
James St. Wind 67 E3
James Watt Rd. Bark 140 C4
James Way. Camb 151 D1
James's La. Bur C 111 F2
Jameston. Brac 118 B1
Jamnagar Cl. Stai 96 C1
Janson Ct. Read 85 F3
Japonica Cl. Woki 115 E2
Jaques's La. Sulhd 110 C3
Jarry Ct. Mar 1 C2
Jasmine Cl. Woki 115 E4
Jays Nest Cl. Black 150 B2
Jedburgh Cl. That 106 C2
Jefferson Cl. Slough 44 A1
Jeffries Ct. Bou E 3 D1
Jellicoe Cl. Slough 42 A2
Jenkins Hill. Bags 145 E1
Jennery La. Burn 21 E1
Jennetts Cl. Brad 81 F2
Jennings Field. Fla H 3 E4
Jennings Wharf. Wind 67 E4
Jenny's Wlk. Yate 149 F3
Jerome Cl. Mar 1 C2
Jerome Rd. Wood 87 F3
Jerrymoor Hill. Woki 141 F4
Jesmond Dene. Newb 104 C2
Jesse Cl. Yate 149 F3
Jesse Terr. Read 85 F4
Jessiman Terr. Stai 125 D2
Jevington. Brac 118 B1
Jig's La. New G 91 E1
Job's La. Cook 19 D4
Jock's La. Binf 90 C1
Joel Ct. Read 87 D2
John Childs Cl. Newb 105 D1
John Hunt Cl. That 106 C1
John Nike Way. Binf 117 E4
John Taylor Ct. Slough 42 B3
John's Cl. Ashf 98 B2
Johnson's La. Cold A 106 B4
Jonathan Hill. Newt 131 D2
Jordan Cl. Caver 59 F3
Jordan Cl. Shin 113 E1
Jordan's La. Bur C 110 C1
Jordans Cl. Stan 97 E4
Joseph Ct. New G 91 F1
Josephine Ct. Read 85 F3
Jouldings La. Swal 140 B2
Jourdelay's Pas. Eton 67 E4
Journeys End. Slough 42 C4
Jubilee Ave. Burl 119 F4
Jubilee Ave. Woki 116 A4
Jubilee Cl. Burl 119 F4
Jubilee Cl. Silc 135 F1
Jubilee Cl. Stan 97 E4
Jubilee Rd. Bish 38 A3
Jubilee Rd. Finch 141 F2
Jubilee Rd. Read 87 D3
Jubilee Sq. Read 86 A3
Judy's Pas. Eton 42 B1
Julkes La. Arbo 114 B4
Junction Rd. Ashf 98 B2
Junction Rd. Light 146 A1
Junction Rd. Read 86 C3
Juniper Dr. Maid 40 A4
Juniper Gdns. Ashf 98 C1
Juniper La. Fla H 3 E4
Juniper Rd. Mar B 1 B1
Juniper Way. Read 57 E1
Juniper. Brac 118 B1
Junnipers The. Woki 115 E2
Jupiter Way. Woki 115 E3
Justice Cl. That 106 C1
Jutland Cl. Woki 115 F3

Jutland Pl. Stai 96 B2

Katesgrove La. Read 86 A3
Kathleen Saunders Ct. Thea .. 83 F2
Kaywood Cl. Slough 43 E2
Keane Cl. Wood 87 F4
Kearsley Rd. Read 85 E3
Keates Green. Brac 118 A4
Keats Cl. Wood 87 F2
Keats La. Eton 67 E4
Keats Rd. Wood 87 F2
Keats Way. Crow 143 D3
Keats Way. Yate 149 D2
Keble Rd. Maid 39 F4
Keble Way. Crow 143 F1
Ketcher Green. Binf 90 B2
Keel Dr. Slough 42 B2
Keeler Cl. Wind 66 C2
Keepers Combe. Brac 118 B2
Keepers Farm Cl. Wind 66 C2
Keepers Farm Cl. Wind 66 C3
Keepers Wlk. Vir W 122 B2
Keephatch Rd. Woki 116 C4
Keighley Cl. That 106 B1
Kelburne Cl. Winn 88 B2
Kelly La. That 125 F4
Kelmscott Cl. Caver 58 C2
Kelpatrick Rd. Slough 41 E4
Kelsey Ave. Woki 141 F3
Kelsey Cl. Maid 39 E2
Kelsey Gr. Yate 149 F3
Kelso Mews. Caver 59 F3
Kelton Cl. Winn 87 F1
Kelvedon Way. Caver 58 C3
Kelvin Cl. Arbo 140 C4
Kelvin Rd. Newb 105 D2
Kemble Ct. Bur C 84 B2
Kemerton Cl. Bur C 84 B2
Kemp Ct. Bags 145 F1
Kempton Cl. Newb 105 E1
Kenavon Dr. Read 86 B4
Kendal Ave. Caver 59 F3
Kendal Ave. Shin 113 F3
Kendal Cl. Felt 98 C4
Kendal Cl. Slough 43 D3
Kendal Cl. That 106 B2
Kendal Dr. Slough 43 D3
Kendal Gr. Camb 152 B2
Kendrick Cl. Woki 116 B3
Kendrick Rd. Newb 130 B3
Kendrick Rd. Read 86 B3
Kendrick Rd. Slough 43 D2
Kenilworth Ave. Brac 118 B4
Kenilworth Ave. Read 85 E3
Kenilworth Ct. Slough 42 C2
Kenilworth Gdns. Stai 97 E2
Kenilworth Rd. Ashf 97 D3
Kenneally. Oak G 66 B3
Kennedy Cl. Far C 22 B3
Kennedy Cl. Maid 39 E3
Kennedy Cl. Mar 1 C2
Kennedy Cl. Newb 130 B3
Kennedy Dr. Pangb 56 C3
Kennedy Gdns. Read 87 D2
Kennel Ave. Ascot 119 F4
Kennel Cl. Ascot 92 C1
Kennel Green. Ascot 119 F4
Kennel La. Brac 91 D1
Kennel La. Cook 19 E4
Kennel La. Windl 146 B3
Kennel Ride. Ascot 92 C1
Kennel Wood. Ascot 119 F4
Kennet Cl. That 106 C2
Kennet Cl. Woki 115 F3
Kennet Pl. Bur C 111 D2
Kennet Rd. Kint 102 A1
Kennet Rd. Maid 39 F4
Kennet Rd. Newb 104 C2
Kennet Side. Newb 105 E2
Kennet Side. Read 86 B4
Kennet St. Read 86 B4
Kennet Way. Hung 100 C4
Kennett Rd. Bou E 3 D2
Kennett Rd. Slough 44 A2
Kensington Rd. Read 85 E4
Kent Ave. Slough 42 B4
Kent Cl. Stai 97 E1
Kent Cl. Woki 115 E3
Kent Rd. Read 85 E4
Kent Rd. Windl 146 B3
Kent Way. Maid 19 F1
Kentigern Dr. Brac 143 F3
Kenton Cl. Brac 118 B4
Kenton Cl. Camb 152 A1
Kenton Cl. Mar 1 C1
Kenton Rd. Read 87 E2
Kenton's La. Warg 36 B4
Kenton's La. Windl 66 C3
Kentwood Cl. Read 57 F1
Kentwood Hill. Read 57 F1
Kenwood Cl. Harm 71 D4
Kenwood Cl. Maid 39 D4
Keppel Spur. Old W 95 D4
Keppel St. Wind 67 E3
Kepple Pl. Bags 145 F2
Kernham Dr. Pur O T 57 E2
Kerria Way. Camb 153 F3
Kerris Way. Read 87 D1
Kersey Cres. Newb 104 C3

Kesteven Way. Woki 115 F3
Keston Cl. Caver 59 E1
Kestrel Ave. Stai 96 C3
Kestrel Cl. That 106 A2
Kestrel Path. Slough 21 F1
Kestrel Way. Read 85 D2
Kestrel Way. Woki 115 F3
Keswick Cl. Camb 152 B2
Keswick Cl. Read 84 B4
Keswick Cl. Slough 42 C3
Keswick Dr. Light 153 D4
Keswick Gdns. Wood 87 F3
Keswick Rd. Stai 96 A1
Ketcher Green. Binf 90 B2
Kettering Cl. Bur C 84 C2
Kevins Dr. Yate 149 F4
Keynsham Way. Crow 143 E1
Keys La. Maid 39 F3
Keys La. Maid 39 F3
Kibble Green. Brac 118 B2
Kibblewhite Cres. Twyf 61 E3
Kidderminster Rd. Slough 22 A1
Kidmore End Rd. Caver 59 D4
Kidmore End Rd. Maple 59 D4
Kidmore Rd. Caver 58 C3
Kidwells Cl. Maid 39 F4
Kidwells Park Dr. Maid 39 F4
Kier Park. Ascot 120 B3
Kilburn Cl. Bur C 84 B2
Kildare Gdns. Caver 59 E1
Killarney Dr. Maid 39 F4
Kilmartin Gdns. Camb 151 F1
Kilmington Cl. Brac 118 C1
Kilmiston Ave. Shepp 125 E2
Kilmore Dr. Camb 152 A2
Kilmuir Cl. Sand 150 B4
Kiln Cl. Harl 71 E4
Kiln Cl. Herm 79 E4
Kiln Dr. Herm 78 C3
Kiln La. Ascot 93 D1
Kiln La. Bou E 3 E2
Kiln La. Brac 118 A4
Kiln La. Mort 137 E3
Kiln La. Shipl 35 E1
Kiln La. Sulh 84 A4
Kiln La. Sunn 121 D2
Kiln Pl. Maid 19 D2
Kiln Rd. Caver 59 E4
Kiln Rd. Newb 105 E3
Kiln Ride Extension. Woki 142 A3
Kiln Ride. Upp B 54 C3
Kiln Ride. Woki 142 A4
Kiln View Rd. Read 86 B1
Kilnsea Dr. Read 87 E1
Kilnsea Dr. Winn 87 E1
Kilowna Cl. Char 61 D2
Kilross Rd. Felt 98 C4
Kimber Cl. Wind 67 D2
Kimber's Cl. Newb 104 C2
Kimber's La. Maid 39 F2
Kimberley Cl. Read 85 F3
Kimberley Cl. Slough 43 F1
Kimberley. Brac 118 B1
Kimbers Dr. Burn 21 E1
Kimbers Dr. Newb 104 B3
Kimmeridge. Brac 118 C2
Kimpton Cl. Read 113 F4
King Edward St. Slough 42 B2
King Edward VII Ave. Wind 67 F4
King Edwards Rd. Burl 119 F4
King Edwards Rise. Burl 92 C1
King Edwards Rise. Burl 119 F4
King George Cl. Ashf 98 C2
King James Way. Hen-O-T 35 E4
King John's Cl. Wray 68 B1
King St. Chert 124 A1
King St. Maid 39 F3
King St. Mort 137 D3
King St. Read 86 A4
King Stable St. Eton 67 E4
King Street La. Winn 88 B1
King's Ave. Ashf 98 C1
King's Cl. Stai 97 E1
King's Cres. Camb 151 E4
King's Gr. Maid 39 F3
King's Keep. Sand 143 D1
King's Meadow Rd. Read 86 A4
King's Rd. Ascot 120 B2
King's Rd. Caver 59 E1
King's Rd. Crow 143 D3
King's Rd. Eng G 96 A2
King's Rd. Hen-O-T 15 E1
King's Rd. Read 86 B4
King's Rd. Slough 42 C2
King's Rd. Wind 67 E2
King's Ride. Ascot 119 E3
King's Ride. Brac 119 E3
King's Ride. Camb 151 E4
King's Ride Park. Brac 119 E2
King's Wlk. Sand 150 C3
Kingfisher Cl. Slough 22 A1
Kingfisher Ct. Twyf 61 F2
Kingfisher Dr. Stai 96 C2
Kingfisher Dr. Wood 87 E3
Kingfisher Dr. Yate 149 D3
Kingfisher Pl. Read 86 A4
Kinghorn La. Maid 19 E2
Kinghorn Park. Maid 19 E2
Kings Cl. Hen-O-T 15 E1
Kings La. Cook 19 D4

Kings La. Eng G 95 D1
Kings La. Windl 146 C3
Kings Mead. Newb 130 B3
Kings Rd W. Newb 105 D1
Kings Rd. Newb 105 D1
Kings Rd. Silc 136 A1
Kings Rd. West E 153 F3
Kings Wlk. Read 86 A4
Kings Wood. Medm 17 E4
Kingsbridge Cotts. Brac 142 C4
Kingsbridge Hill. Swal 139 D3
Kingsbridge Rd. Newb 104 C1
Kingsbridge Rd. Read 86 B1
Kingsbury Cres. Stai 96 B2
Kingsbury Dr. Old W 68 A1
Kingsclear Park. Camb 151 E2
Kingsdown Cl. Read 87 D1
Kingsfield. Wind 66 B3
Kingsford Cl. Wood 88 A3
Kingsgate St. Read 86 B4
Kingsland Grange. Newb 130 C4
Kingsley Ave. Camb 151 E2
Kingsley Ave. Eng G 95 D1
Kingsley Cl. Char 61 D3
Kingsley Cl. Crow 143 D2
Kingsley Cl. Newb 105 D3
Kingsley Cl. Read 113 D4
Kingsley Dr. Mar B 1 B3
Kingsmere Rd. Brac 117 F4
Kingston Ave. Felt 71 F1
Kingston Cres. Stai 97 E2
Kingston Gdns. Read 86 B1
Kingston La. Sulhd 110 B3
Kingston Rd. Camb 152 A4
Kingston Rd. Stai 97 E1
Kingsway. Black 150 C3
Kingsway. Caver 59 F3
Kingsway. Far C 22 B3
Kingsway. Iver 44 C4
Kingsway. Stan 97 E4
Kingsway. That 106 C1
Kingswick Cl. Ascot 120 B3
Kingswick Dr. Ascot 120 B3
Kingswood Cl. Eng G 95 E2
Kingswood Creek. Wray 68 B1
Kingswood Ct. Maid 39 F3
Kingswood Rise. Eng G 95 E2
Kinross Ave. Ascot 119 F2
Kinross Cl. Ashf 98 C2
Kinross Ct. Ascot 119 F2
Kinross Dr. Ashf 98 C2
Kinson Rd. Read 58 A1
Kintbury Rd. Kint 127 E3
Kipling Cl. That 106 B3
Kipling Cl. Yate 149 E2
Kirkfell Cl. Read 57 E1
Kirkham Cl. Caver 59 F3
Kirkham Cl. Crow 143 E1
Kirkstall Ct. Bur C 84 B2
Kirkstone Cl. Camb 152 B2
Kirkwall Spur. Slough 42 C4
Kirkwood Cres. Bur C 110 C2
Kirton Cl. Read 85 D4
Kirtons Farm Rd. Bur C 85 E1
Kitsmead La. Went 122 B1
Kittiwake Cl. Wood 88 A4
Kitwood Dr. Winn 87 F1
Klondyke. Mar 1 B1
Knapp Rd. Ashf 97 F2
Knapp The. Read 87 D2
Knappe Cl. Hen-O-T 35 E4
Knighton Cl. Caver 59 D2
Knights Cl. Stai 96 B1
Knights Cl. Wind 66 B3
Knights La. Ball H 129 E2
Knights Way. Caver 59 D3
Knightsbridge Cres. Stai 97 D1
Knightsbridge Dr. Head 132 A2
Knightsbridge Rd. Camb 151 F4
Knightswood. Brac 118 A1
Knoll Cl. Let B 6 C4
Knoll Rd. Camb 151 E3
Knoll The. Pur O T 57 D1
Knoll Wlk. Camb 151 E3
Knollmead. Bur C 84 B2
Knollys Rd. Silc 135 F1
Knolton Way. Slough 43 E4
Knossington Cl. Read 87 E1
Knott La. Been 109 D2
Knowle Cl. Caver 58 B2
Knowle Gr. Went 122 B1
Knowle Green. Stai 97 D2
Knowle Grove Cl. Went 122 B1
Knowle Hill. Went 122 B1
Knowle Park Ave. Stai 97 D2
Knowle Rd. Wood 87 F2
Knowles Ave. Finch 142 C3
Knowles Ave. Finch 142 C3
Knowsley Cl. Maid 19 D1
Knowsley Rd. Sulh 57 E2
Knox Green. Binf 90 B2
Korda Cl. Stan 124 C3
Krooner Rd. Camb 151 D2
Kybes La. Shin 112 B3
Kyle Cl. Brac 118 A3

La Roche Cl. Slough 43 E2
Laburnam Pl. Eng G 95 D1
Laburnham Rd. Maid 39 F3

Laburnham Rd. Read	87	D1
Laburnum Cl. Mar	1	C2
Laburnum Gdns. Read	86	C1
Laburnum Gr. Newb	105	D2
Laburnum Gr. Slough	69	D4
Laburnum Rd. Chert	124	A1
Laburnum Way. Stan	97	F4
Laburnums The. Black	150	A3
Lacey Cl. Stai	96	B1
Ladbroke Cl. Wood	87	F3
Ladbrooke Rd. Slough	42	B2
Ladwell Cl. Newb	130	B3
Lady Jane Ct. Caver	59	E2
Lady Margaret Rd. Sunn	120	C1
Ladybank. Brac	118	A1
Ladymask Cl. Read	84	C2
Laffords The. Brad	82	A1
Laggan Rd. Maid	19	F1
Laggan Sq. Maid	19	F1
Laird Ct. Bags	145	F1
Lake Ave. Slough	42	B3
Lake End Rd. Burn	41	D3
Lake End Rd. Dorn	41	D2
Lake End Way. Crow	143	D2
Lake Rd. Vir W	122	A3
Lake Side The. Black	150	B2
Lakeland Dr. Camb	151	F1
Lakeside Dr. Sto P	22	C2
Lakeside Rd. Iver	69	F4
Lakeside. Brac	91	E1
Lakeside. Maid	20	A1
Lakeside. Read	87	D2
Lalande Cl. Woki	115	F3
Laleham Rd. Shepp	125	D2
Laleham Rd. Stai	96	C1
Laleham Rd. Stai	125	D2
Laleys Green. Herm	78	C2
Lamb Cl. That	106	B3
Lambert Ave. Slough	43	F2
Lambert Cres. Black	150	B2
Lambfields. Thea	83	E2
Lambly Hill. Vir W	122	B2
Lambourn Pl. Lamb	25	D2
Lambourn Rd. Newb	104	B3
Lambourne Cl. Read	84	B4
Lambourne Dr. Bags	145	E1
Lambourne Dr. Maid	39	E2
Lambourne Gdns. Read	87	E2
Lambourne Gr. Brac	118	C4
Lambridge La. Hen-O-T	15	E2
Lambridge La. Shipl	15	E2
Lambridge Wood Rd. Hen-O-T	15	D2
Lambs La. Shin	139	D4
Lambwood Hill. Shin	112	B1
Lamerton Rd. Read	86	B1
Lammas Ave. Wind	67	E3
Lammas Ct. Wind	67	E3
Lammas Dr. Wray	96	B2
Lammas Mead. Binf	90	C1
Lammas Rd. Slough	41	E4
Lamorna Cres. Read	57	E1
Lamp Acres. Newb	105	D3
Lamplighters Wlk. Read	84	C2
Lamsden Way. Bur C	111	D2
Lanark Cl. Camb	151	F1
Lanark Cl. Wood	88	A3
Lancashire Hill. New G	91	F1
Lancaster Ave. Slough	22	B1
Lancaster Cl. Hung	100	B2
Lancaster Cl. Read	86	B3
Lancaster Cl. That	106	B2
Lancaster Gdns. Read	87	D2
Lancaster Rd. Maid	39	D4
Lancaster Sq. Hung	100	B2
Lancastria Mews. Maid	39	E4
Lancelot Cl. Slough	42	A2
Lancing Cl. Read	85	E4
Lancing Rd. Felt	98	C3
Landen Ct. Woki	116	A2
Landon Way. Ashf	98	A1
Landrake Cres. Read	86	B1
Landseer Cl. Sand	150	C3
Landsend La. Char	61	D1
Lane End Cl. Shin	113	F3
Lane The. Chert	124	A3
Lane The. Chil	10	C4
Lane The. Silc	136	A1
Lane The. Vir W	122	C3
Lanes Wood. Mort	136	C3
Langborough Rd. Woki	116	B3
Langdale Cl. Maid	40	A3
Langdale Dr. Ascot	119	F4
Langdale Gdns. Read	86	C1
Langdon Cl. Camb	152	B2
Langford Cl. Caver	59	F2
Langham Pl. Eng G	95	F2
Langhams Way. Warg	36	C1
Langley Broom. Slough	43	F1
Langley Common Rd. Arbo	114	C1
Langley Common Rd. Bark	114	C1
Langley Cres. Harl	71	F4
Langley Dr. Camb	151	E3
Langley Hill Cl. Read	84	B3
Langley Hill. Read	84	B3
Langley Park Rd. Iver	44	B3
Langley Park Rd. Slough	44	B3
Langley Rd. Slough	43	E2
Langley Rd. Stai	96	C1
Langley Way. Mar	1	B1
Langton Cl. Maid	39	E4
Langton Way. Stai	96	B1
Langton's Meadow. Far C	22	B3
Langworthy End. Holy	65	D4
Langworthy La. Holy	65	D4
Laniver Cl. Read	87	D1
Lansdowne Ave. Slough	42	C3
Lansdowne Ct. Slough	42	C3
Lansdowne Rd. Read	84	B4
Lansdowne Rd. Stai	97	D1
Lapwing Cl. Read	84	B3
Larch Ave. Ascot	120	C2
Larch Ave. Sunn	120	C2
Larch Ave. Woki	116	A4
Larch Cl. Bur C	111	D2
Larch Cl. Camb	151	F4
Larch Cl. Slough	42	A4
Larch Dr. Wood	87	F3
Larches Way. Black	150	A3
Larchfield Rd. Maid	39	F3
Larchside Cl. Shin	113	D1
Larchwood Dr. Eng G	95	D1
Larchwood Glade. Camb	152	A4
Larges Bridge Dr. Brac	118	B3
Larges La. Brac	118	B4
Larissa Cl. Read	57	F1
Lark Ave. Stai	96	C3
Larkham Cl. Felt	98	C3
Larkings La. Sto P	23	D2
Larks-Meade. Read	87	D1
Larksfield. Eng G	95	E1
Larkspur Cl. Woki	115	E4
Larkswood Cl. Read	57	E2
Larkswood Cl. Sand	143	D1
Larkswood Dr. Crow	143	D3
Lascelles Rd. Slough	43	D2
Lashbrook Mead. Shipl	36	A2
Lashbrook Rd. Shipl	36	A2
Lassell Gdns. Maid	40	A4
Lasswade Rd. Chert	123	F1
Latham Ave. Camb	151	F1
Latimer Dr. Bur C	84	B2
Latimer Rd. Woki	116	A3
Latimer. Brac	118	A1
Latton Cl. Chil	10	C4
Laud Way. Woki	116	C3
Laud's Cl. Hen-O-T	15	E1
Launceston Ave. Caver	59	F3
Launcestone Cl. Read	87	D1
Launder Cl. Camb	151	F1
Laundry La. Sand	150	C3
Lauradale. Brac	118	A3
Laurel Ave. Eng G	95	D2
Laurel Ave. Slough	43	F2
Laurel Cl. Camb	151	E2
Laurel Cl. Stan	69	F4
Laurel Cl. Woki	115	F3
Laurel Dr. Read	57	D3
Laurence Cres. Windl	146	B2
Lauser Rd. Stan	97	E4
Lavenham Dr. Wood	87	F4
Lawford Cres. Yate	149	E3
Lawkland. Far C	22	A1
Lawn Cl. Datch	68	B4
Lawrence Cl. Woki	116	B3
Lawrence Ct. Wind	67	E3
Lawrence Gr. Binf	117	E4
Lawrence Mead. Kint	102	A1
Lawrence Rd. Read	85	D4
Lawrence Way. Sand	150	C2
Lawrence Way. Slough	41	E4
Lawrences La. Cold A	106	B3
Lawson La. Chil	10	B4
Lawson Way. Windl	121	D2
Laxton Green. Maid	39	E2
Layburn Cres. Slough	69	D4
Layland's Green. Kint	102	A1
Laytm Rise. Sulh	57	E2
Layton's La. Shepp	125	F4
Le Marchant Rd. Camb	151	F2
Lea Cl. Mar B	1	B3
Lea Cl. Read	85	D2
Lea Croft. Crow	143	D3
Lea Rd. Camb	151	D1
Lea The. Stai	96	B1
Lea The. Woki	141	F4
Leacroft Cl. Stai	97	D2
Leacroft Cl. Iver	44	C4
Leacroft. Stai	97	D2
Leacroft. Sunn	121	D2
Leafield Copse. Brac	118	C3
Leaholme Gdns. Slough	41	E4
Leas Dr. Iver	44	C4
Leaver Rd. Hen-O-T	15	E1
Leaves Green. Brac	118	B2
Ledbury Cl. Read	58	A1
Ledbury Dr. Bur C	84	B2
Ledger La. Holy	65	E3
Ledger's Rd. Slough	42	B2
Ledran Cl. Winn	87	E1
Lee La. Bish	18	C1
Lee La. Maid	18	C1
Leeds Rd. Slough	42	C4
Lees Gdns. Maid	39	D3
Lees Cl. Maid	39	D3
Lees Wlk. Mar	1	B1
Leeson Gdns. Eton	41	F1
Leicester Cl. Hen-O-T	15	E2
Leicester. Brac	118	C1
Leigh Field. Mort	136	C3
Leigh Park. Datch	68	B4
Leigh Rd. Slough	42	A3
Leigh Sq. Wind	66	B3
Leighton Gdns. Maid	20	A1
Leiston Cl. Winn	87	E1
Leiston Spur. Slough	42	C4
Leith Cl. Slough	42	A4
Lemart Cl. Read	84	C4
Lemington Gr. Brac	118	A2
Leney Cl. Woki	116	B4
Lenham Cl. Woki	88	C1
Lennox Cl. Bur C	84	A2
Lennox Rd. Read	87	D3
Lent Green La. Burn	21	D1
Lent Rise Rd. Burn	41	D4
Leopold Wlk. Read	86	B4
Leppington. Brac	118	A1
Lerwick Dr. Slough	42	C4
Lesford Rd. Read	85	F3
Leslie Southern Ct. Newb	105	D2
Lesters Rd. Cook	19	D3
Letchworth Ave. Felt	98	C4
Letcombe Sq. Brac	118	C3
Letcombe St. Read	86	A4
Leverton La. Hung	73	D1
Lewendon Rd. Newb	104	C3
Lewins Way. Slough	41	F3
Lewis Wlk. Newb	130	B3
Lewisham Way. Crow	143	E1
Lexington Ave. Maid	39	E3
Lexington Gr. Read	113	E3
Leyburn Cl. Wood	88	A4
Leycester Cl. Windl	146	A3
Leyland Gdns. Shin	113	F3
Leylands La. Stan	69	F2
Leys Gdns. Newb	104	C2
Leyside. Crow	143	D3
Lichfield Cl. Wood	87	E1
Lichfields. Brac	118	C4
Liddel Way. Ascot	119	F2
Liddell Cl. Finch	141	F2
Liddell Sq. Oak G	66	B3
Liddell. Oak G	66	B2
Lido Rd. Chil	9	F4
Lidstone Cl. Winn	114	B4
Liebenrood Rd. Read	85	E3
Lightlands La. Cook	19	F3
Lightwater Meadow. Light	153	D4
Lightwater Rd. Light	153	E4
Lightwood. Brac	118	B2
Lilac Cl. Pur O T	57	E3
Lilacs The. Woki	115	E2
Lillibrooke Cres. Maid	39	D2
Lily Hill Dr. Brac	118	C4
Lily Hill Rd. Brac	118	C4
Lima Ct. Read	85	F3
Lime Ave. Camb	152	A3
Lime Cl. Newb	105	E2
Lime Cl. Woki	115	F3
Lime Tree Rd. Gori	34	A3
Lime Wlk. Brac	118	B3
Lime Wlk. Maid	39	D4
Limecroft. Yate	149	E3
Limefield Cl. Winn	87	F2
Limerick Cl. Brac	118	A4
Limes Cl. Ashf	98	A2
Limes Rd. Eng G	95	F2
Limmer Cl. Woki	115	E2
Limmerhill Rd. Woki	115	F3
Linchfield Rd. Datch	68	B3
Lincoln Cl. Camb	152	A2
Lincoln Cl. Winn	88	A2
Lincoln Gdns. Twyf	61	E3
Lincoln Hatch La. Burn	21	E1
Lincoln Rd. Maid	39	D4
Lincoln Rd. Read	86	B2
Lincoln Way. Slough	41	E3
Lincoln Way. Stai	125	F4
Lind Cl. Read	87	D1
Lindale Cl. Went	121	F3
Lindale Rd. Crow	143	E1
Linden Ave. Maid	19	E1
Linden Cl. Holy	65	D4
Linden Cl. Newb	104	C2
Linden Cl. Woki	115	F2
Linden Ct. Camb	151	F4
Linden Ct. Eng G	95	D1
Linden Dr. Far C	22	B2
Linden Hill La. Warg	37	E1
Linden Rd. Newt	131	F2
Linden Rd. Read	86	C1
Linden Rd. Wood	87	E2
Linden Way. Shepp	125	E2
Lindenhill Rd. Brac	117	F4
Lindores Rd. Holy	65	D4
Lindsay Cl. Stan	70	B1
Lindsay Dr. Shepp	125	E2
Lindsey Cl. Woki	115	F3
Lindsey Gdns. Felt	98	B4
Lines Rd. Hurst	88	C3
Ling Dr. Light	152	C4
Lingfield Rd. Newb	131	E4
Lingholm Cl. Maid	39	E3
Lingholm Cl. Read	84	C3
Lingwood. Brac	118	B2
Link Rd. Datch	68	B3
Link Rd. Felt	98	C4
Link Rd. Newb	105	D1
Link The. Slough	43	D4
Link The. Yate	149	E4
Link Way. Arbo	114	C1
Link Way. Stai	97	D1
Link Way. That	106	A2
Links App. Fla H	3	D4
Links Dr. Read	85	D4
Links Rd. Ashf	97	F2
Links Rd. Fla H	3	E4
Links The. Burl	119	F4
Links Way. Fla H	3	D4
Linkscroft Ave. Ashf	98	A1
Linkswood Rd. Burn	21	E2
Linkway. Camb	151	E2
Linkway. Crow	142	C3
Linnet Ave. Newt	131	F2
Linnet Cl. Read	84	A3
Lintott Ct. Stan	70	B1
Lion Cl. Stai	124	C3
Lip La. Wick	75	F2
Lipscomb Cl. Herm	79	D3
Lipscombe Cl. Newb	104	C2
Liscombe. Brac	118	A1
Lisle Cl. Newb	104	C3
Lismore Cl. Wood	87	F2
Lisset Rd. Maid	40	A3
Lister Cl. Pur O T	57	E3
Liston Rd. Mar	1	B1
Litcham Spur. Slough	42	B4
Lithgow's Rd. Harm	71	F2
Littington Cl. Winn	114	B4
Little Bowden La. Pangb	55	F2
Little Buntings. Wind	66	C2
Little Cl. Fla H	3	D3
Little Croft Rd. Gori	34	B3
Little Croft. Yate	149	E3
Little Elms. Harl	71	E4
Little Fryth. Woki	142	B3
Little Glebe. Sonn	60	C2
Little Heath Rd. Read	84	A4
Little Hill Rd. Hurst	88	A2
Little John's La. Read	85	E4
Little La. Buck	107	E3
Little London Dr. Silc	136	A1
Little Marlow Rd. Mar	1	C2
Little Moor. Sand	143	E1
Little Oak Dr. Read	84	B4
Little Paddock. Camb	152	A4
Little Ringdale. Brac	118	C3
Little St. Read	85	F4
Little Sutton La. Iver	44	B1
Little Sutton La. Slough	69	D4
Little Vigo. Yate	149	D2
Little Woodlands. Wind	66	C2
Littlebrook Ave. Slough	21	F1
Littlebrook Ave. Slough	41	F4
Littlecote Dr. Read	85	F3
Littlecote Rd. Frox	99	D3
Littlecroft Rd. Eng G	95	F2
Littledale Cl. Brac	118	C3
Littledown Rd. Slough	42	C3
Littlefield Green. Whi Wa	63	F3
Littlejohn's La. Read	58	B1
Littleport Spur. Slough	42	C4
Littlestead Cl. Caver	59	F3
Littleton La. Stai	124	C2
Littleton Rd. Stai	98	B1
Liverpool Rd. Read	86	C4
Liverpool Rd. Slough	42	A4
Livery Cl. Read	86	B4
Livingstone Gdns. Wood	87	F3
Livingstone Rd. Newb	105	D1
Llangar Gr. Crow	143	D3
Llanvair Cl. Ascot	120	A2
Llanvair Dr. Ascot	119	F2
Lochbridge Rd. Maid	40	B4
Lochinvar Cl. Slough	42	A2
Lochinver. Brac	118	A1
Lock Ave. Maid	20	B1
Lock La. Maid	39	E2
Lock Mead. Maid	20	B1
Lock Path. Dorn	66	B4
Lock Pl. Read	86	B4
Lock Rd. Mar	1	C1
Lockbridge Rd. Bou E	3	D2
Locke Gdns. Slough	43	E2
Lockets Cl. Wind	66	B3
Lockram Rd. Bur C	111	E1
Lockram Rd. Mort	111	E1
Locks Ride. Burl	92	B1
Lockstile Mead. Gori	34	B3
Lockstile Way. Gori	34	B3
Lockton Chase. Ascot	119	E3
Loddon Bridge Rd. Winn	87	F3
Loddon Bridge Rd. Wood	87	F3
Loddon Cl. Camb	152	A3
Loddon Dr. Char	61	D4
Loddon Dr. Maid	39	E4
Loddon Hall Rd. Twyf	61	F3
Loddon Rd. Bou E	3	D2
Loddon Spur. Slough	42	C4
Lodge Cl. Eng G	95	E2
Lodge Cl. Mar	1	C1
Lodge Gr. Yate	149	F3
Lodge Rd. Hurst	88	C4
Lodge Way. Ashf	97	F3
Lodge Way. Stai	125	E4
Lodge Way. Wind	66	C2
Lois Dr. Shepp	125	D2
Lomond Ave. Caver	59	F3
London Rd. Ascot	119	F3
London Rd. Ashf	97	E3
London Rd. Bags	145	F2
London Rd. Binf	117	E4
London Rd. Black	150	B2
London Rd. Blew	11	F4
London Rd. Brac	118	C3
London Rd. Camb	151	E3
London Rd. Datch	68	B4
London Rd. Eng G	95	E1
London Rd. Newb	105	E2
London Rd. Read	86	B4
London Rd. Read	87	D4
London Rd. Slough	43	F1
London Rd. Stan	97	E3
London Rd. Sunn	121	E3
London Rd. That	105	E2
London Rd. That	106	C2
London Rd. Twyf	61	F3
London Rd. Went	121	E2
London Rd. Windl	146	B4
London St. Chert	124	A1
London St. Read	86	A4
Lone Acre. Windl	146	C2
Long Barn La. Read	86	B2
Long Cl. Far C	22	A3
Long Cl. Kint	102	A1
Long Dr. Burn	21	E1
Long Furlong Dr. Slough	21	F1
Long Gr. Tad	134	B1
Long Grove. Buck	107	E3
Long Half Acre. Bish	38	A2
Long Hedge. Lamb	25	E1
Long Hill Rd. Burl	119	D4
Long La. Brig	28	C2
Long La. Cold A	78	C1
Long La. Cook	19	E3
Long La. Herm	78	C1
Long La. Holy	64	B2
Long La. Holy	64	C3
Long La. Pur O T	57	D2
Long La. Stan	97	F4
Long La. Sulh	57	D2
Long La. Wint	78	C1
Long Mickle. Sand	143	D1
Long Readings La. Slough	22	A1
Long's Way. Woki	116	C4
Longacre. Newb	130	B4
Longbourne Way. Chert	123	F2
Longbridge Rd. That	106	C1
Longcroft Rd. That	106	C1
Longdon Rd. Winn	88	B1
Longdown Rd. Sand	143	D1
Longfield Rd. Twyf	61	E3
Longford Ave. Felt	71	F1
Longford Ave. Stan	97	F4
Longford Cl. Camb	151	E2
Longford Way. Stan	97	F4
Longhurst Cl. Caver	59	E2
Longlands Way. Camb	152	B3
Longleat Dr. Sulh	57	D2
Longleat Gdns. Maid	39	E3
Longleat Way. Felt	98	B4
Longmead La. Slough	21	E3
Longmead. Ball H	129	F1
Longmead. Wind	66	C3
Longmeadow. Camb	151	F2
Longmoor La. Mort	137	D4
Longmoors. Brac	117	F4
Longmore Rd. Read	113	E3
Longridge Cl. Read	85	D4
Longshot Ind Est. Brac	117	F4
Longshot La. Brac	117	F4
Longside Cl. Stai	123	E4
Longview. Beac	3	F4
Longwater La. Finch	141	F2
Longwater Rd. Brac	118	B2
Longwater Rd. Finch	141	F1
Longworth Ave. Read	84	A4
Longworth Dr. Maid	20	B1
Lonsdale Cl. Maid	20	A1
Lonsdale Way. Holy	40	B1
Loosen Dr. Maid	39	D2
Lord Knyvett Cl. Stan	70	B1
Loring Rd. Wind	66	C3
Lorne Cl. Slough	42	A2
Lorne Pl. Read	85	F4
Lorne St. Read	85	F4
Lorraine Rd. Camb	151	F4
lory Hill La. Beac	3	F4
Losfield Rd. Wind	66	C3
Lossie Dr. Iver	44	A3
Loughborough. Brac	118	C2
Loundyes Cl. That	106	A2
Lovatt Cl. Read	84	A4
Love Green La. Iver	44	C4
Love Hill La. Slough	44	A3
Love La. Iver	44	B4
Love La. Newb	105	D3
Love La. Yate	149	D4
Love's Cl. Bur C	111	D2
Lovedean Ct. Brac	118	C2
Lovejoy La. Wind	66	B3
Lovel La. Wink	93	D2
Lovel Rd. Wink	93	D2
Lovelace Cl. Hurl	17	F2
Lovelace Rd. Brac	117	F3

Name	Page	Grid
Lovell Cl. Hen-O-T	35	E4
Lovells Cl. Light	146	A1
Loverock Rd. Read	58	B1
Loverock Rd. Read	58	B1
Loves Wood. Mort	136	C3
Lovett Gdns. Maid	20	B2
Lovett Rd. Stai	96	B2
Lowbrook Dr. Maid	39	D2
Lowbury. Brac	118	C3
Lower Armour Rd. Read	57	E1
Lower Boyndon Rd. Maid	39	F3
Lower Britwell Rd. Slough	21	E1
Lower Broadmoor Rd. Crow	143	E2
Lower Brook St. Read	86	A3
Lower Bungalows. Gori	34	B4
Lower Canes. Yate	149	D3
Lower Charles St. Camb	151	E3
Lower Church Rd. Sand	149	F4
Lower Cippenham La. Slough	41	F3
Lower Common. Finch	140	C1
Lower Cookham Rd. Maid	20	B1
Lower Earley Way (W). Read	113	F4
Lower Earley Way. Read	114	B4
Lower Earley Way. Winn	114	B4
Lower Early Way (N). Winn	87	F1
Lower Elmstone Dr. Read	57	E1
Lower Field Rd. Read	86	A3
Lower Henley Rd. Caver	59	E2
Lower Lees Rd. Slough	22	A1
Lower Meadow Rd. Read	86	B1
Lower Mill Field. Bags	145	E1
Lower Nursery. Sunn	121	D2
Lower Pound La. Mar	18	B4
Lower Rd. Chil	10	B4
Lower Rd. Cook	19	F4
Lower Ridge. Bou E	3	D2
Lower Sandhurst Rd. Finch	142	B1
Lower Sandhurst Rd. Sand	142	B1
Lower Village Rd. Ascot	120	B2
Lower Way. That	105	F2
Lower Way. That	105	A2
Lower Wokingham Rd. Brac	142	B3
Lower Wokingham Rd. Finch	142	B3
Lowes Cl. Shipl	36	A2
Lowes Comm. Finch	140	C1
Lowestoft Cl. Winn	87	E1
Lowfield Cl. Light	153	D4
Lowfield Green. Caver	59	F2
Lowfield Rd. Caver	59	E3
Lowlands Rd. Black	150	A1
Lowlands Rd. Stan	70	B1
Lowry Cl. Sand	150	B3
Lowther Cl. Woki	115	F4
Lowther Rd. Woki	115	F4
Loxwood Cl. Felt	98	B4
Loxwood. Read	87	E1
Lucan Dr. Stai	97	E1
Lucas Cl. Yate	149	E3
Lucas Green Rd. West E	153	F2
Lucey Cl. Sulh	57	D2
Lucie Ave. Ashf	98	A1
Luckley Rd. Brac	116	A2
Luckley Wood. Brac	116	A2
Luckmore Dr. Read	87	D2
Luddington Ave. Vir W	122	C4
Ludlow Cl. Newb	105	F3
Ludlow Rd. Felt	98	C3
Ludlow Rd. Maid	39	F3
Ludlow. Brac	118	A1
Luff Cl. Wind	66	C2
Luker Ave. Hen-O-T	15	E2
Lulworth Rd. Read	113	E4
Lunds Farm Rd. Wood	88	A4
Lundy La. Read	85	E4
Lupin Cl. Bags	145	E1
Luscombe Cl. Caver	59	F2
Lutman's Haven. Know H	37	F3
Lutterworth Cl. Brac	91	E1
Lutton Cl. Read	113	F4
Lych Gate Cl. Sand	149	F4
Lycroft Cl. Gori	34	B4
Lydbury. Brac	118	C3
Lydford Ave. Slough	42	B4
Lydford Rd. Read	86	C3
Lydney. Brac	118	A1
Lydsey Cl. Slough	22	A1
Lyefield Ct. Caver	59	D3
Lyell. Oak G	66	B2
Lyme Gr. Read	57	E1
Lymington Ave. Yate	149	E3
Lymington Gate. Caver	58	C3
Lynch Hill La. Slough	21	F1
Lynch La. Lamb	25	D1
Lynden Mews. Read	86	A2
Lyndhurst Ave. Black	150	B3
Lyndhurst Ave. Cook	19	F3
Lyndhurst Rd. Brac	119	D3
Lyndhurst Rd. Ascot	120	A3
Lyndhurst Rd. Gori	34	B4
Lyndhurst Rd. Read	58	A1
Lyndwood Dr. Old W	68	A1
Lyne Cl. Went	122	C2
Lyne Crossing Rd. Chert	123	D2
Lyne La. Chert	123	D1
Lyne Rd. Went	122	C2
Lynegrove Ave. Ashf	98	B2
Lyneham Gdns. Maid	19	D1
Lyneham Rd. Crow	143	D3
Lynmouth Rd. Read	59	D1
Lynn Cl. Ashf	98	B2
Lynton Cl. Wood	87	E3
Lynton Ct. Newb	105	D2
Lynton Green. Maid	39	F4
Lynwood Ave. Eng G	95	F1
Lynwood Ave. Slough	43	E2
Lynwood Chase. Brac	91	E1
Lynwood Cres. Sunn	120	C2
Lyon Cl. That	106	C1
Lyon Rd. Crow	143	E3
Lyon Sq. Read	85	D4
Lyon Way. Camb	151	E1
Lysander Cl. Wood	88	A4
Lytham Cl. Read	85	E2
Lytham End. Sulh	57	D2
Lytham Rd. Wood	87	F4
Lytham. Brac	117	F2
Macbeth Ct. Brac	118	C4
Macdonald Rd. Light	153	D4
Mace Cl. Read	87	D1
Mackay Cl. Read	84	C2
Mackenzie St. Slough	42	C2
Macklin Cl. Hung	100	B3
Macphail Cl. Wood	116	C4
Macrae Rd. Yate	149	E3
Maddle Rd. Lamb	24	B4
Madeira Wlk. Wind	67	E3
Madingley. Brac	118	A1
Mafeking Rd. Wray	96	A3
Magdalen Rd. Stai	124	C3
Magdalene Rd. Crow	143	F1
Magill Cl. Shin	113	D1
Magna Carta La. Wray	95	F4
Magna Rd. Eng G	95	D1
Magnolia Cl. Sand	143	E1
Magnolia Gdns. Slough	43	E2
Magnolia Way. Woki	115	F3
Magpie Cl. That	106	A2
Magpie Way. Read	84	A3
Magpie Way. Slough	21	F1
Maguire Dr. Camb	152	B2
Mahonia Cl. Camb	153	F3
Maiden Erlegh Dr. Read	87	D2
Maiden Lane Centre. Read	87	E1
Maiden Pl. Read	87	E1
Maidenhead Bsns Cps. Whi Wa	38	C1
Maidenhead Court Park. Maid	20	A2
Maidenhead Rd. Binf	89	E2
Maidenhead Rd. Cook	19	F3
Maidenhead Rd. New G	91	D3
Maidenhead Rd. Oak G	66	C4
Maidenhead Rd. Wind	66	C4
Maidens Green. Burl	92	A3
Maidensfield. Winn	88	B1
Main Dr. Burl	119	D4
Main St. Chil	10	B4
Main St. Yate	149	E4
Mainprize Rd. Brac	118	C4
Mainstone Rd. Bis	153	F2
Maise Webster Cl. Stan	97	E4
Maitland Rd. Read	85	F4
Majendie Cl. Newb	104	B3
Major's Farm Rd. Datch	68	C4
Makepeace Rd. Brac	91	D1
Maker Cl. Read	85	D2
Makins Rd. Hen-O-T	35	E4
Malders La. Cook	19	E2
Malders La. Maid	19	E2
Maldon Cl. Read	85	E3
Malet Cl. Stai	96	B1
Malham Fell. Brac	118	A3
Malham Rd. That	106	B2
Mallard Cl. Read	87	D2
Mallard Cl. Twyf	61	F2
Mallard Dr. Slough	41	F3
Mallard Row. Read	86	A4
Mallards The. Stai	124	A4
Mallards Way. Light	153	D4
Mallory Ave. Caver	59	E3
Mallow Park. Maid	19	E1
Mallowdale Rd. Brac	118	C1
Malone Rd. Wood	87	E3
Malpas Rd. Slough	43	D3
Malt Hill. Eng G	95	F2
Malt Hill. New G	91	F3
Malt House. Old W	95	D4
Malt Shovel La. Lamb	24	C2
Maltby Way. Read	114	A4
Malthouse Cl. That	106	C1
Malthouse La. Read	85	F4
Malthouse La. West E	153	F4
Maltings Pl. Read	86	A4
Maltings The. West I	10	A1
Malton Ave. Slough	42	A3
Malvern Cl. Wood	87	F3
Malvern Ct. Newb	104	C1
Malvern Rd. Harl	71	D1
Malvern Rd. Maid	19	E1
Malvern Way. Twyf	61	E4
Malyons The. Shepp	125	E2
Man's Hill. Bur C	111	E1
Manchester Rd. Read	86	C4
Mandeville Cl. Read	84	C3
Mandeville Ct. Eng G	96	A2
Mandeville Rd. Stai	125	D2
Manea Cl. Winn	114	B4
Manfield Cl. Slough	22	A1
Manners Rd. Wood	87	E4
Mannock Way. Read	88	A4
Manor Cl. Brac	91	D1
Manor Cres. Comp	31	E2
Manor Cl. Mar	1	B2
Manor Farm Ave. Shepp	125	D2
Manor Farm Cl. Wind	66	C2
Manor Farm Cotts. Old W	68	A1
Manor Farm La. Eng G	96	A2
Manor Farm La. Tidm	56	B1
Manor Farm Rd. Read	86	A1
Manor Gr. Holy	65	E3
Manor House Ct. Shepp	125	D1
Manor House Dr. Ascot	93	D1
Manor House La. Slough	68	A3
Manor La. Chiev	51	D1
Manor La. Harl	71	E4
Manor La. Herm	79	D4
Manor La. Leckh	49	F3
Manor La. Maid	39	F2
Manor La. Newb	105	F3
Manor La. That	105	F3
Manor Leaze. Stai	96	A2
Manor Park Cl. Read	84	B3
Manor Park Dr. Woki	141	F3
Manor Park Dr. Yate	149	E3
Manor Park. Frox	99	D2
Manor Pl. Newb	104	B3
Manor Pl. Stai	97	D2
Manor Rd. Ashf	98	A2
Manor Rd. Farn	7	D4
Manor Rd. Gori	34	A3
Manor Rd. Hen-O-T	35	E4
Manor Rd. Maid	39	F2
Manor Rd. Shepp	125	F1
Manor Rd. Whi-O-T	56	B4
Manor Rd. Wind	66	C3
Manor Rd. Woki	116	A1
Manor Way. Bags	145	F2
Manor Way. Eng G	95	F1
Manor Way. Holy	65	D4
Manor Wood Gate. Shipl	36	A2
Manorcrofts Rd. Eng G	96	A1
Manse Cl. Harl	71	E4
Mansel Cl. Slough	43	D4
Mansell Cl. Wind	66	C3
Mansell Dr. Newb	130	B3
Mansfield Cl. Burl	119	E4
Mansfield Cres. Brac	118	A2
Mansfield Pl. Burl	119	E4
Mansfield Rd. Read	85	F3
Mansfield Rd. Woki	115	F3
Mansion House St. Newb	105	D2
Mansion La. Iver	44	B3
Manston Dr. Brac	118	B2
Mant Cl. Wick	75	E3
Manygate La. Shepp	125	D2
Maple Cl. Maid	39	E3
Maple Cl. Sand	142	C1
Maple Cl. Sand	150	B3
Maple Cl. Winn	88	B2
Maple Cres. Newb	105	D2
Maple Cres. Slough	43	D3
Maple Ct. Eng G	95	D1
Maple Ct. Gori	34	A3
Maple Dr. Brac	143	E4
Maple Dr. Camb	152	C4
Maple Gdns. Read	86	C1
Maple Gdns. Stan	97	F3
Maple Gdns. Yate	149	E3
Maple La. Upp B	55	D3
Maple Rise. Mar	1	C2
Mapledene. Caver	58	C2
Mapledurham Dr. Pur C T	57	E3
Mapledurham View. Read	57	E1
Mapledurham Wlk. Maid	19	F2
Maplin Park. Slough	44	B2
Marathon Cl. Read	88	A4
Marbeck Cl. Wind	66	B3
Marchant Ct. Mar	2	A2
Marchwood Ave. Caver	59	E4
Marconi Cl. Newb	105	D2
Marcus Cl. Read	85	D4
Mardale. Camb	152	B2
Mare La. Whi Wa	63	F2
Marefield Rd. Mar	1	B1
Marefield. Read	87	E1
Marescroft Rd. Slough	41	F4
Marfleet Cl. Winn	87	F1
Margaret Cl. Read	113	E4
Margaret Cl. Stai	97	E1
Marigold Cl. Brac	142	C3
Marina Way. Iver	44	C3
Marina Way. Slough	41	E3
Mariners La. Brad	82	A2
Marion Ave. Shepp	125	D2
Marish Wharf. Slough	43	F2
Markby Way. Winn	87	F1
Market La. Slough	44	B2
Market Pl. Brac	118	A4
Market Pl. Hen-O-T	15	E1
Market Pl. Newb	105	D2
Market Pl. Read	86	A4
Market Pl. Woki	116	B3
Market Sq. Mar	1	B1
Market Sq. Stai	96	C2
Market St. Brac	118	A4
Market St. Gree	105	F1
Market St. Maid	39	F4
Market St. Newb	105	D1
Market St. Wind	67	E3
Markham Centre The. Thea	83	F1
Marks Rd. Woki	116	A4
Marlborough Ave. Read	86	B3
Marlborough Cl. Maid	39	D3
Marlborough Rd. Ashf	97	F2
Marlborough Rd. Read	85	F3
Marlborough Rd. Slough	43	F1
Marlborough Rise. Camb	151	F3
Marlborough Way. Read	84	A2
Marlin Ct. Mar	1	B1
Marling Cl. Read	57	E1
Marlow Bottom. Mar B	18	B2
Marlow Bridge La. Bish	18	C4
Marlow Mill. Mar	1	C1
Marlow Rd. Bish	18	C2
Marlow Rd. Bou E	2	B3
Marlow Rd. Hen-O-T	15	F2
Marlow Rd. Lit M	2	B3
Marlow Rd. Maid	39	F4
Marlow Rd. Mar B	1	A3
Marlowes The. Newb	130	C4
Marlston Rd. Herm	79	E3
Marmion Rd. Hen-O-T	35	F4
Marriott Cl. Harm	71	E1
Mars Cl. Woki	115	F3
Marsack St. Caver	59	E1
Marsh La. Herm	78	B2
Marsh La. Hung	100	A3
Marsh La. Newb	105	D2
Marsh La. Tapl	40	C3
Marsh Rd. That	106	C2
Marshall Cl. Camb	152	B2
Marshall Cl. Read	57	E2
Marshall Rd. Sand	150	B3
Marshalls Ct. Newb	104	B3
Marshfield. Old W	68	B3
Marshland Sq. Caver	59	D3
Marshwood Rd. Light	153	E4
Marston Way. Ascot	119	F4
Marten Pl. Sulh	57	D2
Martin Cl. Wind	66	B3
Martin Cl. Wood	87	F3
Martin Rd. Maid	39	F4
Martin Rd. Slough	42	C2
Martin Way. Camb	151	F1
Martin's Plain. Sto P	22	C2
Martindale Ave. Camb	152	B2
Martineaux La. Hurst	88	C4
Martins Cl. Black	150	B4
Martins Dr. Woki	116	A4
Martins La. Brac	118	C3
Martins The. That	106	C1
Marunden Green. Slough	21	F1
Maryland. Woki	141	F4
Mary Mead. New G	91	F1
Maryside. Slough	43	F2
Mascoll Path. Slough	21	F1
Masefield Rd. That	106	B2
Masefield Way. Stan	97	F4
Mason Cl. Yate	149	F3
Mason Pl. Sand	149	F3
Mason St. Read	85	F4
Masonic Hall Rd. Chert	123	F2
Masons Rd. Slough	41	F3
Mathisen Way. Stan	69	F3
Matlock Rd. Caver	58	C2
Matson Dr. Rem H	15	F1
Mattewsgreen Rd. Woki	116	A4
Matthews La. Stai	96	C2
Matthews Rd. Camb	144	B1
Maultway Cl. Camb	152	A4
Maultway Cres. Camb	152	A4
Maultway N. Camb	145	D1
Maultway The. Camb	152	B3
Mawbray Cl. Read	87	E1
Maxine Cl. Sand	143	D1
Maxwell Cl. Wood	87	F4
Maxwell Rd. Ashf	98	B1
May Cl. Sand	143	E1
May Fields. Woki	115	D4
May Tree Cl. Mar B	1	B3
May's La. Padw	136	A4
Maybrick Cl. Sand	142	C1
Maybury Cl. Slough	41	E4
Mayfair Dr. Newb	104	C1
Mayfield Ave. Read	84	A4
Mayfield Cl. Ashf	98	A1
Mayfield Dr. Caver	59	E2
Mayfield Gdns. Stai	96	C1
Mayfield Rd. Camb	151	D2
Mayfield Rd. Woo G	3	F3
Mayflower Dr. Yate	149	D4
Mayflower Way. Far C	22	B4
Maynard Cl. Cold A	106	B3
Mayo Rd. Shepp	125	F1
Mayow Cl. That	106	C1
Maypole Rd. Burn	41	D4
Mays Cl. Read	87	D3
Mays La. Read	87	D3
Mays Rd. Woki	116	C3
Mc Carthy Way. Woki	141	F4
McCrae's Wlk. Warg	36	B1
Mead Ave. Slough	44	A2
Mead Cl. Eng G	95	D2
Mead Cl. Mar	1	C2
Mead Cl. Pease	50	B4
Mead Cl. Read	84	A3
Mead Cl. Slough	44	A2
Mead Cl. Stai	96	A1
Mead La. Chert	124	A1
Mead La. Upp B	55	F4
Mead The. Gr She	48	A2
Mead Way. Slough	41	E4
Mead Wlk. Slough	44	A2
Meadfield Ave. Slough	44	A2
Meadfield Rd. Slough	44	A2
Meadhurst Rd. Chert	124	A1
Meadow Cl. Black	150	B2
Meadow Cl. Gori	34	B4
Meadow Cl. Mar	1	C1
Meadow Cl. Moul	13	F2
Meadow Cl. Old W	68	A1
Meadow Cl. That	106	B2
Meadow Cres. Comp	31	F3
Meadow Ct. Stai	96	C3
Meadow Gdns. Stai	96	B2
Meadow La. Eton	67	E4
Meadow Rd. Ashf	98	B2
Meadow Rd. Hen-O-T	15	F1
Meadow Rd. Newb	130	C4
Meadow Rd. Read	58	C1
Meadow Rd. Read	87	E2
Meadow Rd. Slough	43	F2
Meadow Rd. Went	121	F2
Meadow Rd. Woki	116	A3
Meadow View La. Holy	64	C4
Meadow View. Mar B	1	C2
Meadow View. Stan	69	F1
Meadow View. Winn	88	B2
Meadow Walk. Woki	116	A3
Meadow Way. Bou E	3	D3
Meadow Way. Brac	91	D1
Meadow Way. Dorn	40	C2
Meadow Way. Holy	65	E3
Meadow Way. Old W	68	A1
Meadow Way. Sand	150	B3
Meadow Way. Thea	83	F2
Meadow Way. West E	153	F3
Meadow Way. Woki	116	A3
Meadowbank Rd. Light	146	B1
Meadowbrook Cl. Stan	69	F3
Meadowcroft Rd. Read	113	E4
Meadows The. Fla H	3	D4
Meadowside Rd. Pangb	56	B3
Meadway Cl. Stai	97	D1
Meadway The. Read	84	C4
Meadway. Ashf	98	A2
Meadway. Camb	151	F1
Meadway. Stai	97	D1
Meare Estate. Woo G	3	F4
Mearings The. Bur C	111	F3
Measham Way. Read	87	E1
Meashill Way. Chil	9	F4
Meavy Gdns. Read	86	A1
Medallion Pl. Maid	40	A4
Medina Cl. Woki	115	F4
Medlake Rd. Stai	96	B1
Medlar Dr. Black	150	C2
Medway Cl. That	106	A3
Medway Cl. Woki	115	F4
Melbourne Ave. Slough	42	B4
Melbourne Ave. Winn	88	B1
Melbury Cl. Chert	124	A1
Meldreth Way. Winn	87	E1
Meldrum Cl. Newb	130	B3
Melford Green. Caver	59	F3
Melksham Cl. Read	113	F4
Melling Cl. Winn	87	F2
Melody Cl. Winn	88	B2
Melrose Ave. Read	87	D3
Melrose Gdns. Arbo	114	C1
Melrose. Brac	118	A1
Melton Ct. Maid	39	F3
Melville Ave. Camb	151	F1
Membury Wlk. Brac	118	C3
Memorial Ave. Shipl	35	F1
Menair Cl. Read	87	D1
Mendip Cl. Char	61	D2
Mendip Cl. Harl	71	E4
Mendip Cl. Slough	44	A1
Mendip Rd. Brac	118	C2
Menpes Rd. Purl	57	E2
Meon Cl. Tad	135	D1
Merchants Pl. Read	86	A4
Mercia Rd. Maid	39	E2
Mercian Way. Slough	41	E3
Mercury Ave. Woki	115	F3
Mere Cl. Mar	1	C1
Mere Rd. Shepp	125	D2
Mere Rd. Slough	42	C2
Mereoak La. Shin	112	C2
Merlewood. Brac	118	B2
Merlin Cl. Slough	69	D4
Merlin Mead. Burl	92	A1
Merrifield Cl. Winn	114	B4
Merrivale Gdns. Read	86	A1
Merron Cl. Yate	149	E3
Merryhill Green Hill. Winn	88	B2
Merryhill Rd. Brac	118	A4
Merryman Dr. Brac	143	D3
Merryweather Cl. Woki	115	F1
Merrywood Park. Camb	151	F2
Mersey Way. That	106	A3
Merton Cl. Maid	39	E2

Merton Rd. Crow 143 F1
Merton Rd. Read 86 A1
Merton Rd. Slough 43 D2
Merton Rd. Slough 43 D2
Mervyn Rd. Shepp 125 E1
Merwin Way. Wind 66 B2
Metcalf Rd. Ashf 98 A2
Meteor Cl. Wood 88 A4
Mews The. Read 86 C3
Mey Cl. Read 84 B3
Meyrick Dr. Newb 130 B3
Michael Cl. Maid 39 E3
Michaelmas Cl. Yate 149 E2
Micheldever Way. Brac 118 C2
Michelet Cl. Light 146 A1
Micklands Rd. Caver 59 F2
Mickle Hill. Sand 143 D1
Midcroft. Slough 22 A1
Middle Cl. Camb 152 B3
Middle Cl. Newb 130 B4
Middle Gordon Rd. Camb .. 151 D2
Middle Green. Slough 43 D2
Middle Hill. Eng G 95 E2
Middle Wlk. Burn 21 E1
Middlefields. Twyf 61 F3
Middlegreen Rd. Slough 43 E3
Middlemoor Rd. Camb 151 F1
Middleton Rd. Camb 151 F4
Midway Ave. Chert 124 A3
Midway Ave. Stai 123 D3
Midwinter Cl. Read 84 C4
Milbanke Ct. Brac 117 F4
Milbanke Way. Brac 117 F4
Mildenhall Cl. Winn 87 E1
Mildenhall Rd. Slough 42 C4
Mile Elm. Mar 2 A2
Miles Pl. Camb 152 C4
Miles Way. Wood 88 A4
Milestone Ave. Char 61 D3
Milestone Cres. Char 61 D2
Milestone Way. Caver 59 E3
Milford Rd. Read 58 C1
Milkhouse Rd. Box 103 E2
Mill Bank. Kint 102 A2
Mill Cl. Woki 115 F4
Mill Farm Ave. Stai 98 C1
Mill Field. Bags 145 E2
Mill Green. Binf 90 C1
Mill Green. Caver 59 E1
Mill House La. Stai 123 D3
Mill La. Ascot 121 D4
Mill La. Brac 117 F3
Mill La. Bur C 84 C2
Mill La. Cook 20 B4
Mill La. Hen-O-T 35 F4
Mill La. Hort 69 D2
Mill La. Hurl 17 F2
Mill La. Lamb 25 E2
Mill La. Newb 105 D2
Mill La. Padw 109 E1
Mill La. Read 86 A4
Mill La. Read 87 F2
Mill La. Sand 149 E4
Mill La. Shipl 36 A1
Mill La. Stai 123 E3
Mill La. Tapl 40 B4
Mill La. Wind 67 D4
Mill La. Winn 87 F1
Mill La. Winn 87 F1
Mill La. Yate 149 E4
Mill Mead. Stai 96 C2
Mill Pl. Datch 68 B3
Mill Pond Rise. Windl 146 A3
Mill Rd. Bur C 84 C1
Mill Rd. Caver 59 E1
Mill Rd. Gori 34 B4
Mill Rd. Mar 1 C1
Mill Rd. Shipl 36 A2
Mill Reef Cl. That 105 F2
Mill Ride. Burl 119 E4
Mill St. Iver 69 E4
Mill St. Slough 42 C3
Millbank Cres. Wood 87 F3
Millbank. Mar 1 C1
Millboard Rd. Bou E 3 D2
Millbridge Rd. Yate 149 D4
Millbrook Way. Stan 69 F3
Milldown Ave. Gori 34 B4
Milldown Rd. Gori 34 B4
Miller's Field. Gr She 48 A2
Millers Cl. Gori 34 A4
Millers Cl. Stai 97 D2
Millers Gr. Read 84 C2
Millers La. Old W 68 A1
Milley La. Warg 62 A4
Milley Rd. W St L 62 C3
Millfield. Lamb 25 D1
Millfield. Stai 125 E4
Millgreen La. Head 132 C2
Millins Cl. Sand 143 F1
Millmead. Woki 116 A4
Millmere. Yate 149 E4
Mills Spur. Old W 95 D4
Millside. Bou E 3 E2
Millstream La. Slough 41 F3
Millstream Way. Woo G 3 F4
Millworth La. Shin 113 F2
Milman Cl. Brac 119 D4
Milman Rd. Read 86 A3
Milner Rd. Burn 41 D4
Milsom Cl. Shin 113 F3
Milton Cl. Brac 118 A2
Milton Cl. Hen-O-T 15 E1
Milton Cl. Hort 69 D2
Milton Dr. Stai 124 C3
Milton Dr. Woki 116 A3
Milton Gdns. Stan 97 F4
Milton Gdns. Woki 116 A3
Milton Rd. Eng G 95 F2
Milton Rd. Far C 22 B1
Milton Rd. Read 87 D4
Milton Rd. Woki 116 A4
Milton Way. Twyf 61 F3
Milverton Cl. Maid 39 D2
Milward Gdns. Brac 117 E4
Mina Ave. Slough 43 E2
Minchin Green. Binf 90 B2
Minden Cl. Woki 115 F3
Minley Rd. Yate 149 F1
Minniecroft Rd. Burn 21 D1
Minorca Ave. Camb 152 C1
Minorca Rd. Camb 152 C1
Minstead Cl. Brac 118 C3
Minstead Dr. Yate 149 E3
Minster St. Read 86 A4
Minster Way. Slough 43 F2
Minsterley Ave. Shepp 125 F3
Mint Cl. Read 86 C1
Minton Cl. Read 84 C4
Minton Rise. Burn 41 D4
Mirador Cres. Slough 43 E3
Mire La. W St L 62 B2
Misborne Ct. Slough 44 A1
Mistletoe Rd. Yate 149 E2
Mitcham Cl. Read 86 A3
Mitcham Rd. Camb 145 D1
Mitcham Rd. Camb 145 D1
Mitchell Cl. Slough 42 A2
Mitchell Way. Wood 88 A4
Mitford Cl. Read 113 E4
Mitre Cl. Shepp 125 E2
Mixnams La. Chert 124 A3
Moat Dr. Slough 43 E4
Modbury Gdns. Read 86 B1
Moffatts Cl. Sand 150 A4
Moffy Hill. Maid 19 F1
Mohawk Way. Wood 88 A4
Mole Rd. Arbo 114 C3
Moles Cl. Woki 116 B3
Mollison Cl. Wood 88 A4
Molly Millar Bridge. Woki . 116 A2
Molly Millar's La. Woki 116 A2
Molyneux Rd. Windl 146 B2
Monarch Cl. Felt 98 C4
Mondial Way. Stan 71 E4
Moneyrow Green. Holy 65 D4
Monk's La. Newb 130 C4
Monkey Island La. Holy 40 C1
Monks Cl. Ascot 120 A2
Monks Dr. Ascot 120 A2
Monks Hollow. Mar B 1 C3
Monks Rd. Vir W 122 B3
Monks Rd. Wind 66 B3
Monks Way. Harm 70 C4
Monks Way. Read 85 E3
Monks Way. Stai 97 E1
Monks Wlk. Ascot 120 A2
Monksfield Way. Slough 22 A1
Monkshood Cl. Woki 116 C4
Monkswood Cl. Newb 130 C4
Mons Cl. Woki 115 F3
Mons Wlk. Stai 96 B2
Monsell Gdns. Stai 96 C2
Montacute Dr. That 106 C1
Montagu Rd. Slough 68 A3
Montague Cl. Camb 151 D3
Montague Cl. Light 146 A1
Montague Rd. Slough 42 C3
Montague St. Caver 59 E1
Montague St. Read 86 B4
Montague Terr. Newb 131 D4
Monteagle La. Yate 149 D3
Monteagle La. Yate 149 E3
Montem La. Slough 42 B2
Montgomery Cl. Sand 150 A4
Montgomery Dr. Shin 113 D1
Montgomery Pl. Slough 43 E4
Montgomery Rd. Newb 130 C4
Montpelier Ct. Wind 67 E3
Montpelier Dr. Caver 59 E3
Montrose Ave. Datch 68 B4
Montrose Ave. Slough 42 A4
Montrose Cl. Ashf 98 B2
Montrose Cl. Camb 151 F1
Montrose Dr. Maid 39 D3
Montrose Rd. Felt 71 E1
Montrose Way. Datch 68 B4
Montrose Wlk. Read 84 C2
Monument Cl. Newb 130 B4
Monycrower Dr. Maid 39 F4
Moor Cl. Sand 143 F1
Moor Cl. Woki 141 F4
Moor Copse Cl. Read 87 D2
Moor End. Holy 40 B1
Moor La. Harm 70 B4
Moor La. Maid 19 F1
Moor La. Newb 104 C2
Moor La. Stan 96 B3
Moor Pl. Windl 146 A3
Moorbridge Rd. Maid 40 A4
Moordale Ave. Brac 90 C1
Moore Cl. Slough 42 A2
Moore Grove Cres. Eng G .. 95 F1
Moores Green. Woki 116 C4
Moores La. Eton 41 F1
Moores Pl. Hung 100 B3
Moorfield Terr. Maid 40 A4
Moorfields Cl. Stai 123 F4
Moorhayes Dr. Stai 124 B3
Moorland Rd. Harm 70 B4
Moorlands Ave. Iver 69 E4
Moorlands Dr. Maid 38 C4
Moorlands Pl. Camb 151 D2
Moorlands Rd. Camb 151 D2
Moormede Cres. Stai 96 C2
Moors The. Pangb 56 B3
Moors The. That 106 B1
Moorside. Woo G 3 F4
Moorside Cl. Camb 151 D1
Moorside Cl. Maid 19 F1
Moorside. Woo G 3 F4
Moorstown Ct. Slough 42 C2
Moray Ave. Sand 150 B4
Mordaunt Dr. Crow 143 D2
Morden Cl. Brac 118 C3
Moreau Wlk. Slough 43 F4
Morecambe Ave. Caver 58 C3
Moreland Ave. Iver 69 E4
Moreleigh Cl. Read 113 E4
Morella Cl. Vir W 122 B3
Morello Dr. Slough 43 F3
Moretaine Rd. Ashf 97 E3
Moreton Way. Slough 41 E3
Morgan Rd. Read 86 B3
Moriston Cl. Read 85 D4
Morlands Ave. Read 85 D3
Morley Cl. Slough 43 F2
Morley Cl. Yate 149 D3
Morley Pl. Hung 100 B3
Mornington Ave. Woki 141 F4
Mornington Cl. Tad 134 C1
Mornington Rd. Ashf 98 B2
Morpeth Cl. Read 86 B2
Morrice Cl. Slough 44 A1
Mortimer Cl. Read 113 E4
Mortimer La. Mort 137 E3
Mortimer Rd. Slough 43 E2
Morton Rd. Hort 69 D3
Moss Cl. Caver 59 E2
Mossy Vale. Maid 19 E1
Moulsham Copse La. Yate . 149 D4
Moulsham La. Yate 149 D4
Mount Cl The. Went 122 B2
Mount Cl. Far C 22 B4
Mount Cl. Newb 105 D1
Mount Felix. Shepp 125 F1
Mount La. Brac 118 B4
Mount La. Chadd 49 D4
Mount Lee. Eng G 95 F2
Mount Pleasant Cl. Light . 146 A1
Mount Pleasant Gr. Read .. 86 A3
Mount Pleasant. Brac 118 B3
Mount Pleasant. Read 86 A3
Mount Pleasant. Sand 143 D1
Mount Pleasant. Tad 135 D1
Mount Pleasant. Woki 116 A3
Mount Rd. That 106 C2
Mount St. Read 86 A3
Mount The. Caver 58 C2
Mount The. Caver 59 D2
Mount The. Read 86 B3
Mount The. Went 122 B2
Mount View. Hen-O-T 15 E1
Mountain Ash. Mar B 1 B3
Mountbatten Cl. Newb 105 E3
Mountbatten Cl. Slough 43 D2
Mountbatten Rise. Sand .. 142 C1
Mountfield. Gori 34 B4
Mounts Hill. Old W 93 E3
Mounts Hill. Wink 93 E3
Mountsfield Cl. Stan 70 A1
Mowbray Cres. Eng G 96 A2
Mowbray Dr. Read 85 D4
Mower Cl. Woki 116 C4
Moyleen Rise. Mar 1 B1
Muckhatch La. Stai 123 D4
Mud La. Finch 140 C1
Mud La. Pease 50 B3
Muirfield Cl. Read 86 B4
Mulberry Ave. Stan 97 F4
Mulberry Cl. Crow 143 E2
Mulberry Cl. Sand 143 E1
Mulberry Cl. Wood 87 F3
Mulberry Dr. Slough 43 F1
Mulberry Trees. Shepp 125 E1
Mulberry Way. Thea 83 F2
Mulfords Hill. Tad 135 D1
Mullins Rd. Stai 96 B2
Mulroy Dr. Camb 152 A3
Mumbery Hill. Warg 36 C1
Muncaster Cl. Ashf 98 A2
Muncaster Rd. Ashf 98 A2
Munces Rd. Mar B 1 B3
Mundaydean La. Mar 1 A2
Mundesley Spur. Slough 42 C4
Mundesley St. Read 86 A3
Munkle Marsh. That 107 D2
Munnings Dr. Sand 150 C3
Munro Ave. Wood 87 F2
Murdoch Cl. Stai 97 D2
Murdoch Rd. Woki 116 B3
Murray Ct. Ascot 120 B2
Murray Rd. Woki 116 A3
Murrellhill La. Binf 117 E4
Murrells La. Camb 151 D2
Murrin Rd. Maid 39 E4
Mushroom Castle La. Burl . 92 A1
Mustard La. Sonn 60 C1
Mustard Mill Rd. Stai 96 C2
Muswell Cl. Thea 83 F2
Mutton Oaks. Brac 117 E4
Myers Way. Camb 152 B1
Myline Sq. Woki 116 B3
Myrke The. Datch 42 C1
Myrke The. Slough 42 C1
Myrtle Ave. Harm 71 F1
Myrtle Cl. Bur C 111 D2
Myrtle Cl. Light 153 D4
Myrtle Cl. Stan 69 F3
Myrtle Cl. Sulh 57 E2
Myrtle Cres. Slough 42 C3
Myrtle Dr. Black 150 B3
Myton Wlk. Thea 83 F2

Nabbs Hill Cl. Read 84 B3
Nairn Cl. Camb 151 F1
Nalderhill Rd. Box 103 D3
Napier Cl. Crow 143 E3
Napier Dr. Camb 152 A4
Napier Rd. Ashf 98 B1
Napier Rd. Crow 143 E2
Napier Rd. Harm 70 B3
Napier Rd. Maid 39 E4
Napier Rd. Read 86 B4
Napier Wlk. Ashf 98 B1
Napper Cl. Burl 119 E4
Narromine Dr. Read 84 C2
Naseby. Brac 118 A1
Nash Cl. Read 87 D2
Nash Gdns. Ascot 119 F4
Nash Grove La. Woki 115 F1
Nash Park. Binf 90 A1
Nash Rd. Slough 44 A1
Nashdom La. Burn 21 D3
Natalie Cl. Felt 98 B4
Neath Gdns. Read 84 C4
Needham Cl. Wind 66 C3
Neil Cl. Ashf 98 B2
Nell Gwynn Ave. Shepp ... 125 E2
Nell Gwynne Ave. Ascot .. 120 B3
Nell Gwynne Cl. Ascot 120 B3
Nelson Cl. Brac 118 C4
Nelson Cl. Slough 43 E1
Nelson Rd. Ashf 97 F2
Nelson Rd. Caver 59 E1
Nelson Rd. Harm 70 B4
Nelson Rd. Wind 66 C2
Nelson Way. Sand 150 C2
Nelson's La. Hurst 89 D3
Nene Rd. Harm 71 D3
Neptune Cl. Woki 115 F3
Neptune Rd. Harm 71 E3
Netherton. Brac 118 A3
Netley Cl. Caver 59 F3
Netley Rd (N). Harm 71 E3
Netley Rd. Stan 71 E3
Nettlecombe. Brac 118 C2
Nettleton Rd. Harm 71 D3
Nevelle Cl. Brac 117 E4
Neville Cl. Sto P 22 C3
Neville Cl. W St L 62 C3
Neville Dr. That 106 C2
Nevis Rd. Read 57 E2
New Bath Rd. Char 61 E3
New Bath Rd. Twyf 61 E3
New Bath Rd. Warg 61 E3
New Bright St. Read 86 A3
New Cut. Mar 1 B1
New Forest Ride. Brac 118 C2
New Forest Ride. Burl 119 D3
New Ham Rd. Harm 71 E3
New Hill. Pur O T 57 E3
New Lane Hill. Read 84 C3
New Meadow. Burl 119 E4
New Mile Rd. Ascot 120 B4
New Mill La. Finch 140 C1
New Mill Rd. Bark 140 C2
New Park Rd. Ashf 98 B2
New Rd. Black 150 C2
New Rd. Bou E 3 D2
New Rd. Brac 118 B4
New Rd. Bur C 111 F1
New Rd. Burl 92 C1
New Rd. Cook 19 F4
New Rd. Crow 143 E3
New Rd. Datch 68 B3
New Rd. Felt 71 E1
New Rd. Harl 71 E4
New Rd. Holy 65 D4
New Rd. Hurl 17 F2
New Rd. Mar B 1 B3
New Rd. Mort 111 F1
New Rd. Newb 105 E1
New Rd. Read 86 B3
New Rd. Sand 150 A4
New Rd. Shipl 36 A2
New Rd. Slough 44 A2
New Rd. Stai 96 B2
New Rd. Stai 125 D3
New Rd. Twyf 61 E4
New Rd. Twyf 61 F3
New Rd. Windl 146 A2
New Rd. Woki 115 D4
New Square. Felt 98 B4
New St. Bee H 138 A1
New St. Hen-O-T 15 F1
New St. Stai 97 D2
New Way. Brad 82 A1
New Wickham La. Eng G 96 A1
New Wickham La. Stai 96 A1
New Wokingham Rd. Crow . 143 F4
New Zealand Ave. Shepp . 125 F1
Newall Rd. Harm 71 E3
Newalls Rise. Warg 36 C1
Newark Rd. Windl 146 A3
Newark St. Read 86 A3
Newber Way. Slough 42 B2
Newbery Cl. Read 57 E1
Newbewrry Cres. Wind 66 B3
Newbold Rd. Newb 104 B3
Newbolt Cl. That 106 B3
Newbury Dr. Maid 40 A3
Newbury Hill. Hamp N 52 C3
Newbury La. Comp 31 E2
Newbury Rd. Gr She 48 A1
Newbury Rd. Harm 70 C3
Newbury Rd. Herm 79 D3
Newbury Rd. Lamb 25 E1
Newbury Rd. Stan 71 D4
Newbury St. Kint 102 A1
Newbury St. Lamb 25 D1
Newcastle Rd. Read 86 B2
Newchurch Rd. Slough 41 F4
Newchurch Rd. Tad 135 D1
Newfield Gdns. Mar 1 C2
Newfield Rd. Mar 1 C1
Newhaven Cres. Ashf 98 B2
Newhaven Spur. Slough 22 A1
Newhurst Gdns. New G 91 E2
Newlands Ave. Caver 59 D2
Newlands Cl. Yate 149 E3
Newlands Dr. Maid 39 D4
Newlands Dr. Stan 69 F2
Newlyn Gdns. Read 86 A1
Newlyn Rd. Harm 71 D3
Newman Rd. Harm 71 D3
Newmarket Cl. Winn 87 E1
Newport Cl. Newb 105 D2
Newport Rd. Harm 71 D3
Newport Rd. Newb 105 D2
Newport Rd. Read 59 D1
Newport Rd. Slough 21 F1
Newquay Dr. Read 87 D1
Newton Ave. Caver 59 E3
Newton Cl. Slough 43 F2
Newton Ct. Old W 68 A1
Newton La. Old W 68 A1
Newton Rd. Harm 70 C3
Newton Rd. Hen-O-T 35 F4
Newton Rd. Mar 1 C2
Newtonside Orch. Old W 68 A1
Newtown Gdns. Hen-O-T 35 F4
Newtown Rd. Hen-O-T 35 F4
Newtown Rd. Newb 131 D4
Newtown Rd. Sand 150 A4
Newtown. Tad 135 D1
Niagara Rd. Hen-O-T 35 F4
Nicholas Rd. Hen-O-T 35 D4
Nicholls. Oak G 66 B2
Nicholson Wlk. Eng G 96 A2
Nicholsons La. Maid 39 F4
Nideggen Cl. That 106 B2
Nightingale Cres. Brac 118 B2
Nightingale Gdns. Sand .. 150 A4
Nightingale La. Mort 137 E3
Nightingale Park. Burn 21 F3
Nightingale Rd. Wood 87 E2
Nightingales The. Newb ... 131 D4
Nightingales The. Stan 97 F4
Nimrod Cl. Wood 88 A4
Nimrod Rd. Harm 71 D3
Nimrod Way. Harm 71 D3
Nimrod Way. Read 86 A3
Nine Mile Ride. Bark 142 B4
Nine Mile Ride. Brac 142 B4
Nine Mile Ride. Woki 142 B4
Nixey Cl. Slough 43 D2
Noakes Hill. Asham 54 A4
Nobel Dr. Stan 71 F4
Nobles Way. Eng G 95 F1
Norcot Rd. Read 84 C4
Norden Cl. Maid 39 E2
Norden Rd. Maid 39 E3
Norelands Dr. Burn 21 E2
Nores Rd. Read 113 E4
Norfolk Ave. Slough 42 B4
Norfolk Cl. Woki 115 F3
Norfolk Park Cotts. Maid ... 39 F4
Norfolk Rd. Maid 39 F4
Norlands La. Stai 123 F4
Norlands. That 106 B3
Norman Ave. Hen-O-T 15 F1
Norman Cl. Ashf 98 B1
Norman Rd. Caver 59 E2
Normandy Wlk. Stai 96 B2
Normanhurst. Ashf 98 A2

Normans The. Slough 43 D4
Normanstead Rd. Read 84 B4
Normay Rise. Newb 130 B3
Normoor Rd. Bur C 110 C1
Norreys Ave. Woki 116 B4
Norreys Dr. Maid 39 E2
Norris Field. Chadd 49 D4
Norris La. Chadd 49 D4
Norris Rd. Read 87 D3
Norris Rd. Stai 96 C2
North Burnham Cl. Burn 21 D2
North Cl. Felt 71 E1
North Cl. Medm 17 E4
North Cl. Wind 66 C3
North Croft. Woo G 3 F3
North Dr. Sulhd 110 B4
North Dr. Went 121 F2
North End La. Went 121 D1
North Fryerne. Yate 149 E4
North Gr. Chert 123 F2
North Green. Brac 118 B4
North Green. Maid 19 F1
North Green. Slough 42 C3
North Hatton Rd. Harm 71 E3
North Links Rd. Fla H 3 D4
North Lodge Dr. Burl 119 E4
North Park. Iver 44 B2
North Rd. Burl 119 D4
North Rd. Felt 71 E1
North Rd. Maid 39 F4
North Rd. Moul 13 F2
North St. Caver 59 D1
North St. Eng G 95 F1
North St. Read 85 F4
North St. Wink 93 D3
North Standen Rd. Hung 100 A2
North Star La. Maid 39 E3
North Town Cl. Maid 19 F1
North Town Mead. Maid 19 F1
North Town Moor. Maid 19 F1
North Town Rd. Maid 19 F1
North Wlk. Thea 83 F2
Northam Cl. Winn 87 F2
Northampton Ave. Slough ... 42 B4
Northampton Cl. Brac 118 C3
Northborough Rd. Slough ... 22 A1
Northbourne Cl. Read 87 D1
Northbrook Copse. Brac 118 C2
Northbrook Rd. Caver 59 E3
Northbrook St. Newb 105 D2
Northbury Ave. Twyf 61 F3
Northbury La. Twyf 61 F3
Northcott. Brac 118 A1
Northcourt Ave. Read 86 B2
Northcroft Cl. Eng G 95 D2
Northcroft Gdns. Eng G 95 D2
Northcroft Rd. Eng G 95 D2
Northcroft La. Newb 104 C2
Northcroft Rd. Eng G 95 D2
Northcroft Villas. Eng G 95 D2
Northcroft. Slough 22 A1
Northdean. Maid 19 F1
Northend Cl. Fla H 3 E4
Northern Ave. Newb 105 D3
Northern Hts. Bou E 3 D3
Northern Perimeter Rd W. Harm 70 C3
Northern Perimeter Rd. Harm . 71 E3
Northern Rd. Slough 22 B1
Northern Woods. Fla H 3 E4
Northfield Ave. Shipl 36 A2
Northfield Ct. Chert 124 A4
Northfield Ct. Hen-O-T 15 E2
Northfield End. Hen-O-T 15 E2
Northfield Rd. Eton 41 F1
Northfield Rd. Maid 19 F1
Northfield Rd. Read 59 D1
Northfield Rd. Shipl 36 A2
Northfield Rd. Stai 124 A4
Northfield Rd. That 106 A2
Northfield. Light 153 D4
Northfields. Chiev 51 D2
Northfields. Lamb 25 D2
Northgate Dr. Camb 152 A4
Northmead Rd. Slough 41 F4
Northolt Rd. Harm 70 C3
Northrop Rd. Harm 71 F3
Northumberland Ave. Read .. 86 B2
Northumberland Cl. Stan 70 C1
Northumberland Cres. Felt .. 71 F1
Northview. Hung 100 B3
Northway. Newb 105 D1
Northway. That 106 B3
Northway. Woki 115 F4
Northwood Dr. Newb 105 E2
Northwood Rd. Harm 70 B3
Norton Cl. Newb 130 B3
Norton Park. Ascot 120 B2
Norton Rd. Camb 152 B3
Norton Rd. Read 86 C4
Norton Rd. Swal 139 E2
Norton Rd. Woki 116 B3
Norton Rd. Wood 87 F3
Norway Dr. Slough 43 D4
Norwich Ave. Camb 151 F2
Norwich Dr. Wood 87 E4
Norwood Cres. Harm 71 E3
Norwood Rd. Read 86 C4
Notley End. Eng G 95 E1

Notton Way. Read 113 F4
Nuffield Dr. Crow 143 F1
Nuffield Rd. Bark 140 C4
Nugee Ct. Crow 143 D3
Nugent Ct. Mar 1 C2
Nun's Acre. Gori 34 A4
Nuneaton. Brac 118 C2
Nunhide La. Sulh 83 F3
Nuns Wlk. Vir W 122 B2
Nuptown La. Burl 91 F4
Nursery Gdns. Purl 57 D3
Nursery Gdns. Shepp 125 F4
Nursery Gdns. Stai 97 D1
Nursery La. Burl 119 F4
Nursery La. Slough 43 E3
Nursery Rd. Burn 41 D4
Nursery Rd. Shepp 125 F4
Nursery Way. Wray 68 B1
Nursery Wlk. Mar 1 A1
Nut La. W St L 62 C3
Nutbean La. Swal 139 F3
Nuthatch Dr. Read 87 D2
Nuthurst. Brac 118 C2
Nutley Cl. Yate 149 E3
Nutley. Brac 118 A1
Nutmatch Cl. Stan 97 F4
Nutmeg Cl. Read 86 C1
Nutter's Hill. Swal 140 A4
Nutty La. Stai 125 E3

Oak Ave. Sand 143 E1
Oak Ave. Stai 96 B1
Oak Dr. Bur C 110 C1
Oak Dr. Wood 88 A3
Oak End Way. Padw 109 E2
Oak Farm Cl. Sand 150 B3
Oak Grove Cres. Sand 150 C3
Oak Hill. Frox 99 E2
Oak La. Eng G 95 F4
Oak La. Wind 67 D3
Oak Stubbs La. Dorn 40 C2
Oak Tree Ave. Mar 1 C2
Oak Tree Cl. Mar 1 B2
Oak Tree Cl. Tad 135 D1
Oak Tree Cl. Went 122 B2
Oak Tree Copse. Read 57 F2
Oak Tree Dr. Eng G 95 E2
Oak Tree Mews. Brac 118 B3
Oak Tree Rd. Mar 1 B2
Oak Tree Rd. Read 57 E1
Oak Tree Rd. That 106 C1
Oak Tree Wlk. Pur O T 57 E3
Oak View. Read 84 B4
Oak Way. Felt 98 C4
Oak Way. Wood 88 A4
Oakdale Cl. Read 84 B4
Oakdale. Brac 118 B2
Oakdene. Bur C 111 D1
Oakdene. Sunn 120 C2
Oaken Gr. Maid 19 E1
Oaken Gr. Newb 130 B4
Oakengates. Brac 118 A1
Oakfield Ave. Slough 42 A3
Oakfield Rd. Ashf 98 A2
Oakfield Rd. Black 150 C2
Oakfield Rd. Bou E 3 D2
Oakfield Rd. Silc 135 F1
Oakhall Dr. Ashf 98 C2
Oakham Cl. Read 57 E1
Oakhurst. Maid 20 A2
Oaklands Cl. Ascot 92 C1
Oaklands Dr. Ascot 92 C1
Oaklands Dr. Woki 116 A3
Oaklands La. Crow 143 D3
Oaklands Park. Woki 116 A2
Oaklands. Yate 149 E3
Oaklea Dr. Finch 140 C1
Oakley Cres. Slough 42 C3
Oakley Green Rd. Holy 66 A3
Oakley Green Rd. Oak G 66 A3
Oakley Rd. Camb 151 D2
Oakley Rd. Caver 58 C2
Oakley Rd. Newb 105 E2
Oakridge. West E 153 F3
Oaks Rd. Shipl 36 A2
Oaks Rd. Stan 70 B1
Oaks The. Brac 118 B4
Oaks The. Yate 149 E3
Oakside Way. Read 113 F4
Oaktree Way. Sand 143 D1
Oakway Dr. Camb 151 F1
Oakwood Rd. Brac 118 C4
Oakwood Rd. Vir W 122 B2
Oakwood Rd. Windl 146 C2
Oareborough. Brac 118 C3
Oast House Ct. Wray 95 F4
Oatlands Dr. Shepp 125 F1
Oatlands Dr. Slough 42 B4
Oatlands Rd. Shin 113 F3
Oban Ct. Slough 42 B2
Oban Gdns. Wood 87 F2
Obelisk Way. Camb 151 E3
Oberon Way. Stai 124 C3
Ockwells Rd. Maid 39 E2
Octavia Way. Stai 97 D1
Octavia. Brac 118 A1
Oddfellows Rd. Newb 104 C1
Odell Cl. Read 114 A4

Odencroft Rd. Slough 22 A1
Odiham Ave. Caver 59 F3
Odiham Rd. Swal 139 E1
Odney La. Cook 20 A4
Ogmore Cl. Read 84 C4
Okingham Cl. Sand 143 E1
Old Barn Cl. Caver 59 D3
Old Bath Rd. Char 61 D3
Old Bath Rd. Newb 104 C2
Old Bath Rd. Sonn 60 B1
Old Bisley Rd. Camb 152 B2
Old Bracknell Cl. Brac 118 A3
Old Bracknell La E. Brac ... 118 A3
Old Bracknell La W. Brac .. 118 A3
Old Charlton Rd. Shepp 125 E2
Old Court Cl. Maid 39 D2
Old Dean Rd. Camb 151 E4
Old Elm Dr. Read 84 B4
Old Farm Cres. Read 57 E1
Old Farm Dr. Brac 91 E1
Old Ferry Dr. Wray 68 B1
Old Fives Ct. Burn 21 D1
Old Forest Rd. Read 88 C1
Old Forge Cl. Maid 40 A2
Old Forge Cres. Shepp 125 D2
Old Green La. Camb 151 E4
Old Hayward La. Hung 73 E2
Old Kiln Rd. Fla H 3 D4
Old La The. Read 85 F3
Old La. Ham M 102 C1
Old La. Head 133 F1
Old Lands Hill. Brac 118 B4
Old Marsh La. Dorn 40 C2
Old Mill La. Maid 40 B2
Old Newtown Rd. Newb 104 C1
Old Orchard The. Bur C 84 C2
Old Pasture Rd. Camb 151 F2
Old Pond Cl. Camb 151 E1
Old Portsmouth Rd. Camb . 152 A3
Old Post Office La. Maid 39 F4
Old Sawmill La. Crow 143 E3
Old School Ct. Wray 95 F4
Old School La. Yate 149 E3
Old Slade La. Iver 44 C1
Old St. Chiev 51 E3
Old St. Chiev 51 F1
Old St. Herm 78 C4
Old Station La. Wray 69 D1
Old Station Way. Bou E 3 F3
Old Vicarage Way. Bou E 3 E2
Old Watery La. Woo G 3 F4
Old Welmore. Yate 149 F3
Old Whitley Wood. Read 113 E3
Old Wokingham Rd. Brac .. 143 E3
Oldacre. West E 153 F4
Oldacres. Maid 40 A4
Oldfield Cl. Read 87 D4
Oldfield Rd. Maid 40 A4
Oldhouse La. Light 146 B1
Oldmoor La. Woo G 3 F4
Oldstead. Brac 118 B2
Oldway La. Slough 41 E3
Oleander Cl. Brac 143 D4
Oliver Dr. Read 84 B3
Oliver Rd. Ascot 120 A3
Oliver's Paddock. Mar B 1 B3
Ollerton. Brac 118 A1
Omega Way. Stai 123 E4
Omer's Rise. Bur C 110 C2
One Pin La. Far C 22 B4
Onslow Dr. Ascot 93 D1
Onslow Gdns. Caver 59 E2
Onslow Mews. Chert 124 A2
Onslow Rd. Went 121 D1
Opal Way. Woki 115 F4
Opendale Rd. Burn 41 D4
Opladen Way. Brac 118 C2
Orbit Cl. Woki 141 F3
Orchard Ave. Ashf 98 B1
Orchard Ave. Harm 71 E1
Orchard Ave. Read 41 E4
Orchard Ave. Slough 41 E4
Orchard Ave. Wind 67 D3
Orchard Chase. Hurst 88 C4
Orchard Cl. Ashf 98 B1
Orchard Cl. Black 150 C1
Orchard Cl. Hen-O-T 15 F1
Orchard Cl. Herm 79 E4
Orchard Cl. Maid 40 A2
Orchard Cl. Newb 105 E3
Orchard Cl. Pur O T 57 E2
Orchard Cl. Shin 113 D1
Orchard Cl. Shipl 35 F1
Orchard Cl. West E 153 E3
Orchard Cl. Woki 116 B3
Orchard Cl. Wool 108 B1
Orchard Ct. Harm 70 B4
Orchard Ct. Read 113 E4
Orchard Dr. Bou E 3 E2
Orchard Estate. Twyf 61 F3
Orchard Gate. Far C 22 B4
Orchard Gate. Sand 150 A4
Orchard Gr. Fla H 3 D4
Orchard Gr. Maid 39 D4
Orchard Hill. Windl 146 B2

Orchard Park Cl. Hung 100 B2
Orchard Pl. Woki 116 B3
Orchard Rd. Hurst 88 C4
Orchard Rd. Mort 137 D3
Orchard Rd. Old W 68 A1
Orchard St. Read 86 A3
Orchard The. Eng G 96 A2
Orchard The. Fla H 3 D4
Orchard The. Light 153 D4
Orchard The. Mar 1 C2
Orchard The. Thea 83 F2
Orchard The. Vir W 122 F2
Orchard Way. Ashf 97 F3
Orchard Way. Camb 151 D1
Orchard Way. Slough 43 F3
Orchardene. Newb 105 D2
Orchardville. Burn 21 D1
Orchids The. Chil 10 B4
Oregon Ave. Read 57 D2
Oregon Wlk. Woki 141 F4
Oriel Hill. Camb 151 D2
Oriental Rd. Ascot 120 B3
Orion. Brac 118 A1
Orkney Cl. Bur C 84 C2
Ormonde Rd. Woki 116 A3
Ormsby St. Read 85 F4
Orrin Cl. Read 85 D4
Orts Rd. Newb 105 D1
Orts Rd. Read 86 B4
Orville Cl. Wood 88 A4
Orwell Cl. Caver 58 C2
Orwell Cl. Wind 67 E2
Osborne Ave. Stan 97 F4
Osborne Dr. Light 153 D4
Osborne La. New G 91 E2
Osborne Mews. Wind 67 E3
Osborne Rd. Eng G 95 F1
Osborne Rd. Read 85 D4
Osborne Rd. Wind 67 E2
Osborne Rd. Woki 116 B3
Osborne St. Slough 42 C2
Osbourne Ct. Wind 67 E3
Osman's Cl. Burl 92 A1
Osnaburgh Hill. Camb 151 D3
Osney Rd. Maid 19 F1
Osterley Cl. Woki 116 C3
Osterley Dr. Caver 59 F3
Ostler Gate. Maid 19 E1
Oswald Cl. New G 91 E1
Otter Cl. Brac 143 D4
Ouseley Rd. Old W 95 E4
Overbury Ave. Woki 88 C1
Overdale Rise. Camb 151 F2
Overdown Rd. Read 57 E1
Overlanders End. Read 57 F2
Overlord Cl. Camb 151 E4
Owen Rd. Newb 105 D3
Owen Rd. Windl 146 B3
Owl Cl. Woki 115 F3
Owlsmoor Rd. Sand 143 E1
Owston. Read 87 E1
Oxenhope. Brac 118 A3
Oxford Ave. Burn 21 D2
Oxford Ave. Harl 71 F4
Oxford Ave. Slough 41 F4
Oxford Cl. Stai 98 B1
Oxford Rd E. Wind 67 E3
Oxford Rd. Mar 1 B1
Oxford Rd. Newb 104 B3
Oxford Rd. Read 58 A1
Oxford Rd. Sand 143 F1
Oxford Rd. Wind 67 D3
Oxford Rd. Woki 116 A3
Oxford St. Caver 59 D1
Oxford St. Hung 100 C1
Oxford St. Lamb 25 D2
Oxford St. Newb 104 C2

Pack and Prime La. Hen-O-T . 15 E1
Padbury Cl. Felt 98 C4
Paddick Cl. Sonn 60 C2
Paddock Cl. Camb 152 A3
Paddock Cl. Wha 39 D1
Paddock Hts. Twyf 61 F2
Paddock Rd. Caver 59 E1
Paddock Rd. Newb 130 C4
Paddock The. Crow 143 D3
Paddock The. Maid 19 E1
Paddock The. Newb 105 E1
Paddock The. Slough 68 A3
Paddocks The. Fla H 3 D4
Paddocks Way. Chert 124 A1
Padstow Cl. Slough 43 F2
Padstow Gdns. Read 86 A1
Padworth Rd. Mort 136 B4
Padworth Rd. Silc 136 B4
Page Rd. Felt 98 B4
Page's Croft. Woki 116 B3
Paget Cl. Mar 1 C2
Paget Dr. Maid 39 D2
Paget Rd. Slough 43 F1
Pagoda The. Maid 20 A1
Paice Green. Woki 116 B3
Paices Hill. Alde 135 D3
Paley St. Holy 64 A3
Palmer Cl. Brac 143 D4
Palmer Park Ave. Read 87 D3
Palmer School Rd. Woki 116 B3
Palmer's Hill. Asham 54 B3

Palmer's La. Bur C 111 D1
Palmer's La. Bur C 112 A2
Palmera Ave. Bur C 84 B2
Palmers Cl. Maid 39 D2
Palmerston Ave. Slough 43 D2
Palmerstone Rd. Read 87 D3
Pamber Heath Rd. Silc 135 F1
Pamela Row. Holy 65 D4
Pan's Gdns. Camb 151 F2
Panbourne Hill. Pangb 56 B3
Pangbourne Rd. Upp B 55 E2
Pangbourne St. Read 58 A1
Pankhurst Dr. Brac 118 B2
Pantile Row. Slough 44 A1
Papist Way. Chol 14 A4
Paprika Cl. Read 86 C1
Parade The. Ashf 98 C1
Parade The. Bou E 3 D2
Parade The. Wood 87 F4
Paradise Rd. Hen-O-T 15 E1
Paradise Way. Buck 108 B4
Park Ave. Camb 151 E2
Park Ave. Stai 96 B1
Park Ave. Stai 97 E1
Park Ave. That 106 B2
Park Ave. Woki 116 A3
Park Ave. Wray 68 B2
Park Cl. Wind 67 E3
Park Cres. Read 85 D3
Park Cres. Sunn 120 C2
Park Crnr. Wind 66 C2
Park Dr. Sunn 120 C2
Park End. Newb 105 D2
Park Gr. Read 85 D3
Park La. Bark 141 D3
Park La. Bee H 137 E1
Park La. Box 103 D1
Park La. Burn 21 F4
Park La. Camb 151 E3
Park La. Char 61 D2
Park La. Hort 69 D2
Park La. Newb 105 D2
Park La. Read 84 B4
Park La. Slough 43 D2
Park La. That 106 B2
Park Rd. Ashf 98 A2
Park Rd. Brac 118 B4
Park Rd. Camb 151 E2
Park Rd. Eng G 96 A2
Park Rd. Far C 22 B2
Park Rd. Hen-O-T 15 F1
Park Rd. Sand 150 B4
Park Rd. Shepp 125 D1
Park Rd. Stan 70 B1
Park Rd. Sto P 22 B2
Park Rd. Woki 116 A3
Park St. Bags 145 F2
Park St. Camb 151 E3
Park St. Hung 100 B3
Park St. Maid 39 F4
Park St. Newb 105 D2
Park St. Slough 42 C2
Park St. Stan 69 E3
Park St. Wind 67 E3
Park The. Lamb 25 D2
Park View Dr N. Char 61 D3
Park View Dr S. Char 61 D3
Park View. Bags 145 F2
Park Wall La. Upp B 34 B3
Park Way. Hung 100 C2
Park Way. Newb 105 D2
Park Wlk. Pur O T 57 E3
Parkcorner La. Arbo 114 C3
Parkgate. Burn 21 E1
Parkhill Cl. Black 150 B2
Parkhill Dr. Read 57 E1
Parkhill Rd. Black 150 B2
Parkhouse La. Read 85 E3
Parkland Ave. Slough 43 E1
Parkland Dr. Brac 118 C4
Parkland Gr. Ashf 98 A2
Parkland Rd. Ashf 98 A2
Parkside Rd. Read 85 E3
Parkside Rd. Sunn 121 D2
Parkside Rd. That 106 B3
Parkside. Hen-O-T 15 E1
Parkside. Maid 19 E1
Parkstone Dr. Camb 151 E2
Parkview Chase. Slough 41 F4
Parkview. Fla H 3 D4
Parkway Dr. Sonn 60 C2
Parkway. Camb 151 E2
Parkway. Crow 143 D3
Parkway. Mar 2 A2
Parlaunt Rd. Slough 44 A1
Parliament La. Burn 20 C3
Parnham Ave. Light 153 E4
Parry Green N. Slough 43 F1
Parry Green S. Slough 44 A1
Parsley Cl. Read 86 C1
Parson's Wood La. Far C 22 B3
Parsonage Gdns. Mar 1 C1
Parsonage La. Far C 22 B2
Parsonage La. Hung 100 B3
Parsonage La. Lamb 25 D1
Parsonage La. Wind 67 D2
Parsonage Pl. Lamb 25 D2
Parsonage Rd. Eng G 95 E2
Parsons Cl. Bark 141 D4

Parsons Cl. Newb 104 C1
Parsons Field. Sand 150 A4
Part La. Swal 139 F2
Parthia Cl. Read 86 A3
Partridge Ave. Yate 149 D3
Partridge Dr. Read 84 B3
Partridge Mead. Maid 19 F1
Paschal Rd. Camb 151 F4
Pasture Ct. Read 114 A4
Patches Field. Mar B 1 C3
Paterson Cl. Camb 152 B2
Paterson Rd. Ashf 97 E2
Pates Manor Dr. Felt 98 B4
Patricia Cl. Slough 41 F3
Patrick Rd. Caver 59 D1
Patriot Pl. Read 86 B4
Patten Ash Dr. Woki 116 C4
Patten Ave. Yate 149 E3
Pavenham Cl. Read 114 A4
Pavilion Gdns. Stai 97 D1
Pavy Cl. That 106 C1
Paxton Ave. Slough 42 B2
Payley Dr. Woki 116 C4
Paynesdown Rd. That 106 A2
Peace La. Cook 19 F3
Peach St. Woki 116 B3
Peachy Dr. That 106 C1
Peacock Ave. Felt 98 B4
Peacock La. Brac 117 E3
Peacock Rd. Mar 2 A2
Pear Tree La. Newb 105 E3
Pear Tree Rd. Ashf 98 B2
Pearce Cl. Maid 19 F1
Pearce Rd. Maid 19 F1
Pearces Orch. Hen-O-T 15 E2
Pearl Gdns. Slough 42 A3
Pearmain Cl. Shepp 125 D2
Pearman's Glade. Read 113 F4
Pearson Rd. Sonn 60 B2
Pearson Way. Wood 87 F3
Peascod Pl. Wind 67 E3
Peascod St. Wind 67 E3
Pease Hill. Buck 107 F4
Peasemore Hill. Pease 50 A4
Pebble Hill. Kint 128 A3
Peddlars Gr. Yate 149 F3
Peel Cl. Caver 59 E1
Peel Cl. Wind 67 D2
Peel Ct. Slough 42 A4
Peg's Green Cl. Read 85 D3
Pegasus Cl. That 106 A2
Pegasus Ct. Read 84 B4
Peggotty Pl. Crow 143 F1
Peket Cl. Stai 123 F4
Pelican La. Newb 105 D2
Pelican Rd. Alde 135 F1
Pell St. Read 86 A3
Pelling Hill. Old W 95 D4
Pemberton Gdns. Bur C 84 B2
Pemberton Rd. Slough 21 F1
Pembroke Broadway. Camb . 151 E3
Pembroke Cl. Ascot 120 B2
Pembroke Cl. Bur C 111 E2
Pembroke Pl. Caver 59 E2
Pembroke Rd. Newb 105 D2
Pembroke. Brac 118 A1
Pembury Ct. Harl 71 E4
Pendals Cl. Hamp N 52 C3
Pendell Ave. Harl 71 F4
Pendennis Ave. Caver 59 F3
Pendine Pl. Brac 118 A2
Pendlebury. Brac 118 A1
Pendragon Way. Camb 152 B2
Pendred Rd. Read 113 E3
Peninsular Cl. Felt 71 F1
Penling Cl. Cook 19 F3
Penn Cl. Caver 59 D3
Penn Meadow. Sto P 22 C2
Penn Rd. Datch 68 B3
Penn Rd. Farc 22 B1
Penn Rd. Newb 104 B3
Pennfields. Twyf 61 F3
Pennine Cl. Read 84 A3
Pennine Rd. Slough 42 A4
Pennine Way. Char 61 D2
Pennine Way. Harl 71 E4
Pennylets Green. Sto P 23 D3
Pennypiece. Gori 34 B4
Pennyroyal Ct. Read 86 A3
Penroath Ave. Read 85 E3
Penrose Ave. Wood 87 F3
Penrose Cl. Newb 104 C3
Penrose Cl. Eng G 95 E1
Penry La. Shepp 125 F1
Pensford Ct. Crow 143 D4
Penshurst Rd. Maid 39 E3
Pentland Ave. Stai 125 D2
Pentland Cl. Read 84 C3
Pentland Pl. That 106 B1
Pentland Rd. Slough 42 A4
Pentlands The. Kint 102 B1
Penton Ave. Stai 123 F4
Penton Hall Dr. Stai 124 A4
Penton Hook Rd. Stai 124 A4
Penton Rd. Stai 96 C1
Penwood Ct. Maid 39 D4
Penwood Gdns. Brac 117 D2
Penwood La. Mar 1 B1
Penwood Rd. Ball H 130 B2

Penyston Rd. Maid 39 E4
Penzance Spur. Slough 22 A1
Peppard La. Hen-O-T 35 F4
Peppard Rd. Caver 59 E3
Pepper La. Read 86 B2
Pepys Cl. Slough 69 D4
Perch Cl. Mar 18 B4
Percival Rd. Felt 98 C3
Percy Ave. Ashf 98 A2
Percy Bryant Rd. Stai 98 C1
Percy Pl. Slough 68 A3
Peregrine Cl. Brac 118 A2
Peregrine Cl. Woki 115 F3
Peregrine Rd. Shepp 125 F4
Periam Cl. Hen-O-T 35 E4
Perkins Way. Woki 116 A3
Perrin Cl. Ashf 97 F2
Perry Oaks Dr. Harm 70 B3
Perry Oaks. Brac 118 C4
Perry Way. Brac 118 C4
Perry Way. Camb 152 C4
Perrycroft. Wind 66 C2
Perryhill Dr. Sand 142 C1
Perryman Way. Slough 21 F1
Perserverance Hill. Hen-O-T ... 35 D3
Perth Ave. Slough 42 A4
Perth Cl. Wood 61 D1
Perth Trad Est. Slough 42 A4
Peterhouse Cl. Crow 143 F1
Petersfield Ave. Slough 43 D3
Petersfield Ave. Stai 97 E1
Petersfield Rd. Stai 97 E2
Petrel Cl. Woki 115 F3
Petts La. Stai 125 D3
Petworth Ave. Read 84 C2
Petworth Ct. Wind 67 D3
Pevensey Ave. Caver 59 F3
Pevensey Rd. Slough 42 A4
Pewsey Vale. Brac 118 C2
Pheasant La. Winn 88 B1
Pheasants Croft. Maid 39 D3
Philip Dr. Fla H 3 E4
Philip Rd. Stai 97 E1
Phillimore Rd. Caver 59 E4
Phipps Cl. Whi Wa 39 D1
Phipps Rd. Burn 41 F4
Phoebe Ct. Read 86 A3
Phoenix Cl. Woki 115 F3
Phoenix Wlk. Newb 130 B3
Phyllis Court Dr. Faw (Bu) 15 F2
Pickering. Brac 118 A3
Picket Post Cl. Brac 118 C3
Picketts La. Pangb 55 F2
Pickford Dr. Slough 43 F3
Pickins Piece. Hort 69 D3
Pickwell Cl. Wood 87 E1
Picton Way. Caver 59 D2
Pierce's Hill. Read 57 E1
Piercefield. Bur C 84 B2
Pierson Rd. Wind 66 B3
Pigeonhouse La. Wink 92 C2
Pigeons Farm Rd. Gree 131 E4
Piggott's Rd. Caver 59 E1
Pigott Rd. Woki 116 C4
Pike Cl. Mar 18 B4
Pike St. Newb 105 D2
Pikeshaw Way. Read 57 E1
Pimento Dr. Read 86 C1
Pincents La. Sulh 84 A3
Pinchcut. Bur C 111 D2
Pinchington La. Gree 131 D4
Pine Ave. Camb 151 E2
Pine Cl. Maid 39 D4
Pine Cl. Sand 150 C4
Pine Croft Rd. Woki 116 A1
Pine Dr. Black 150 C2
Pine Dr. Mort 136 C3
Pine Dr. Woki 142 A4
Pine Gr. Twyf 61 E3
Pine Gr. Windl 146 B2
Pine Mount Rd. Camb 151 E2
Pine Ridge Rd. Bur C 111 D2
Pine Ridge. Newb 105 E3
Pine Way. Eng G 95 D1
Pinecote Dr. Sunn 120 C1
Pinecroft. Mar 1 B2
Pinefields Cl. Crow 143 D2
Pinehill Rd. Crow 143 E2
Pinehill Rise. Sand 150 B4
Pinehurst. Ascot 120 B2
Pinetree Ct. Caver 59 D3
Pinewood Ave. Crow 143 E3
Pinewood Cl. Tad 134 B1
Pinewood Dr. Stai 97 D2
Pinewood Gdns. Bags 145 E2
Pinewood Rd. Vir W 122 A3
Pinewood Rd. Went 122 A3
Pingewood Rd S. Bur C 112 B4
Pingewood Rd S. Shin 112 B4
Pingewood Rd. Bur C 85 D1
Pinglestone Cl. Harm 70 C4
Pink La. Burn 21 D2
Pinkneys Dr. Maid 38 C4
Pinkneys Rd. Maid 39 D4
Pinks La. Tad 134 C1
Pipers Cl. Burn 21 E1
Pipers Ct. That 107 D1
Pipers End. Vir W 122 B3
Pipers Way. That 107 D1

Pipit Cl. That 106 A2
Pippins Ct. Ashf 98 A1
Pippins The. Slough 43 F3
Pipsons Cl. Yate 149 E3
Pitch Pl. Binf 90 B2
Pitcroft Ave. Read 87 D3
Pitfield La. Mort 137 E2
Pitfield La. Silc 137 E2
Pitford Rd. Wood 88 A4
Pitt's La. Read 87 D4
Pitts Cl. Binf 90 B1
Pitts Rd. Slough 42 B3
Plackett Way. Slough 41 E3
Plaitinson Rd. Read 113 E3
Planes The. Chert 124 B1
Plantation Cl. Herm 78 C3
Plantation Rd. Camb 151 D3
Plantation Rd. Chil 9 F4
Plantation Rd. Tad 134 C1
Plantation Row. Camb 151 D3
Platt La. Lamb 45 E3
Play Platt. Thea 83 F2
Players Green. Wood 87 F3
Playhatch Rd. Caver 60 A3
Plough La. Sto P 23 D2
Plough La. Woki 116 C3
Plough Rd. Yate 149 F4
Ploughlands. Brac 117 F4
Ploughlands. Brac 117 F4
Ploughlees La. Slough 42 C3
Plover Cl. Stai 96 C3
Plover Cl. Woki 115 F3
Plowden Way. Shipl 35 F1
Plumpton Rd. Newb 105 E1
Plumtrees. Read 87 D1
Pluto Rd. Chil 9 A4
Plymouth Ave. Wood 87 E3
Plymouth Rd. Slough 41 F4
Plympton Cl. Winn 87 F2
Pococks La. Eton 42 C1
Poffley Pl. Read 107 D2
Pointers Cl. Chiev 51 D1
Points The. Maid 39 D2
Polehampton Cl. Twyf 61 E2
Pollard Cl. Old W 68 A1
Pollard Gr. Camb 152 B2
Pollardrow Ave. Brac 117 F4
Polsted Rd. Read 57 E1
Pond Cl. Newb 130 B4
Pond Croft. Yate 149 F3
Pond Head La. Read 87 D2
Pond La. Herm 79 E4
Pond La. Maple 57 F4
Pond Moor Rd. Brac 118 A2
Pond Rd. Stai 96 B1
Pondside Cl. Harl 71 E4
Pool La. Slough 42 C3
Pool La. W St L 63 D3
Poole Cl. Read 85 D4
Pooley Ave. Stai 96 A2
Pooley Green Cl. Stai 96 B2
Pooley Green Rd. Stai 96 B2
Poolmans Rd. Wind 66 B2
Pope Cl. Felt 98 C4
Popes Cl. Iver 69 E4
Popes La. Cook 19 E4
Popeswood Rd. Binf 117 E4
Popham Cl. Brac 118 C2
Poplar Ave. Read 84 C3
Poplar Ave. Windl 146 A3
Poplar Cl. Stan 69 F3
Poplar Gdns. Read 86 C1
Poplar La. Hurst 62 A1
Poplar La. Winn 88 B2
Poplar Rd. Ashf 98 B2
Poplars Gr. Maid 20 A1
Poplars The. Ascot 120 A2
Poppy Dr. That 106 C2
Poppy Way. Read 84 B3
Poppyhills Rd. Camb 151 F4
Porchester Rd. Newb 105 D1
Porchester. Ascot 120 A3
Porchfield Cl. Read 87 D1
Porlock Cl. That 106 B1
Porlock Pl. Bur C 84 B2
Porter Cl. Winn 114 B4
Porter End. Newb 131 D4
Portesbery Hill Dr. Camb 151 F3
Portesbury Rd. Camb 151 F3
Portland Cl. Slough 21 E1
Portland Cres. Felt 98 B2
Portland Gdns. Read 84 B4
Portland Rd. Ashf 97 F3
Portlands. Mar 1 B1
Portlock Rd. Maid 39 E4
Portman Cl. Brac 118 A4
Portman Rd. Read 58 B1
Portnall Dr. Went 121 F2
Portnall Rd. Went 121 F2
Portnall Rise. Went 121 F2
Portrush Rd. Wood 87 E3
Portsmouth Rd. Camb 152 A4
Portway Cl. Read 85 F3
Portway. Swal 139 E1
Portway. Tad 134 C1
Post Horn Pl. Read 84 C2
Post Office La. Slough 43 E4
Post Office Rd. Ink 127 F3
Posting House Mews. Newb . 104 C2

Potley Hill Rd. Yate 149 F3
Pottery La. Ink 127 F3
Pottery Rd. Read 57 F1
Potts Pl. Mar 1 B1
Poulcott. Wray 68 C1
Pound Cres. Mar 1 B1
Pound La. Hurst 89 D3
Pound La. Lit M 2 B2
Pound La. Mar 1 B1
Pound La. Newb 104 B2
Pound La. Sonn 60 C1
Pound La. That 106 A2
Pound La. Windl 146 B2
Pound Piece. Hung 100 B3
Pound Rd. Chert 124 A1
Pound St. Newb 104 C1
Pound The. Cook 19 F4
Poundfield La. Cook 19 F4
Powis Cl. Maid 39 D2
Powney Rd. Maid 39 E4
Poyle La. Burn 21 D2
Poyle Rd. Stan 69 F3
Poynings. Iver 44 C1
Precincts The. Burn 21 E1
Prescott Rd. Stan 69 F3
Prescott. Brac 117 F1
Preston Rd. Read 86 A3
Preston Rd. Slough 43 E3
Preston Rd. Stai 125 D2
Prestwood. Slough 43 D4
Pretoria Rd. Chert 123 F1
Priest Ave. Woki 116 C3
Priest Hill. Caver 59 D2
Priest Hill. Eng G 95 E3
Priest La. West E 153 E3
Priestwood Ave. Brac 117 F4
Priestwood Court Rd. Brac ... 118 A4
Primrose Cl. Pur O T 57 D2
Primrose La. Winn 88 B2
Primrose Lea. Mar 1 B1
Primrose Way. Sand 143 D1
Primrose Wlk. Brac 118 B2
Prince Albert Dr. Brac 119 E2
Prince Andrew Cl. Maid 20 A1
Prince Andrew Rd. Maid 20 A1
Prince Andrew Way. Burl 119 E4
Prince Consort Cotts. Wind 67 E3
Prince Consort Dr. Brac 119 E3
Prince Dr. Sand 143 D1
Prince Hold Rd. That 106 A2
Prince of Wales Ave. Read 85 E4
Prince William Dr. Read 57 E1
Prince's La. Pease 50 B3
Prince's St. Read 86 B4
Princes Cl. Eton 41 F1
Princes Rd. Ashf 97 F2
Princes Rd. Bou E 3 E2
Princes Rd. Eng G 95 F1
Princes Rd. Felt 98 C3
Princes St. Slough 43 D2
Princes Way. Bags 145 F1
Princess Ave. Wind 67 D2
Princess Marina Dr. Bark 115 D1
Princess Marina Dr. Bark 140 C4
Princess St. Maid 39 F3
Princess Way. Camb 151 E3
Prior Croft Cl. Camb 152 A2
Prior End. Camb 152 A3
Prior Rd. Camb 152 A3
Prior's La. Black 150 A3
Priors Cl. Maid 40 A1
Priors Cl. Slough 43 D2
Priors Court Rd. Chiev 78 C4
Priors Rd. Tad 135 D1
Priors Rd. Wind 66 B2
Priors Way. Maid 40 A1
Priors Wood. Woki 142 B3
Priory Ave. Caver 59 D1
Priory Ave. Hung 100 B2
Priory Cl. Hung 100 B2
Priory Cl. Went 121 D1
Priory Ct. Winn 88 B2
Priory Green. Stai 97 D2
Priory La. New G 91 E1
Priory Mews. Stai 97 D2
Priory Rd. Burl 119 D4
Priory Rd. Hung 100 B2
Priory Rd. Newb 105 D1
Priory Rd. Slough 41 E4
Priory Rd. Went 121 D1
Priory The. Winn 88 B2
Priory Way. Datch 68 A4
Priory Way. Harm 70 C4
Priory Wlk. Brac 118 C3
Proctors Rd. Woki 116 C3
Promenade Rd. Caver 59 D1
Promenade. Wind 67 E4
Prospect Ct. Read 85 D3
Prospect La. Eng G 95 D2
Prospect Pl. Hurl 17 F2
Prospect Pl. Newb 105 D1
Prospect Pl. Stai 96 C2
Prospect Rd. Hung 100 B3
Prospect Rd. Mar 1 B1
Prospect St. Caver 59 D1
Prospect St. Read 85 F4
Providence La. Harl 71 E4
Providence Pl. Maid 39 F4
Prune Hill. Eng G 95 E1

Prunus Cl. Camb 153 F3
Pudding Hill. Know H 37 E3
Pudding La. Brig 28 C1
Puffers Way. Newb 104 C1
Pump La N. Lit M 1 C3
Pump La s. Lit M 2 A2
Pump La. Shin 112 B1
Pump La. Wink 120 C4
Pumpkin Hill. Burn 21 F3
Pundles La. Whi Wa 63 E3
Purbrook Ct. Brac 118 C2
Purcell Rd. Crow 143 D4
Purfield Dr. Warg 36 C1
Purley La. Pur O T 57 E3
Purley Rise. Pur O T 56 C3
Purley Village. Pur O T 57 E3
Purley Way. Pangb 56 C3
Purssell Cl. Maid 39 D2
Purton Ct. Far C 22 B3
Purton La. Far C 22 B3
Putman Pl. Hen-O-T 15 F1
Pyegrove Chase. Brac 118 C1
Pyke's Hill. Asham 54 B2
Pyle Hill. Newb 105 D1
Pyrcroft Rd. Chert 123 F1

Quadrant Ct. Brac 118 C3
Quadrant The. Maid 40 A3
Qualitas. Brac 117 F1
Quantock Ave. Caver 59 E3
Quantock Cl. Char 61 D2
Quantock Cl. Harl 71 E4
Quantock Cl. Slough 44 A1
Quantocks The. That 106 B1
Quarrington Cl. That 106 C1
Quarry Bank. Light 153 D4
Quarry La. Yate 149 F3
Quarrydale Dr. Mar 1 C1
Quartz Cl. Woki 115 E4
Quaves Rd. Slough 43 E2
Quebec Gdns. Black 150 B2
Quebec Rd. Hen-O-T 35 F4
Queen Anne's Cl. Old W 94 A3
Queen Anne's Rd. Wind 67 E2
Queen Annes Gate. Caver 59 E2
Queen Charlotte St. Wind 67 E3
Queen Cl. Hen-O-T 15 F1
Queen Elizabeth Rd. Camb .. 144 B1
Queen Mary Ave. Camb 151 D3
Queen Mary Rd. Stai 125 E4
Queen St. Caver 59 D2
Queen St. Chert 124 A1
Queen St. Hen-O-T 15 F1
Queen St. Maid 39 F4
Queen Victoria St. Read 86 A4
Queen's Cl. Old W 68 A1
Queen's Cotts. Read 86 B4
Queen's Dr. Slough 42 C3
Queen's Dr The. Read 86 B2
Queen's La. Maid 39 F4
Queen's Mead. Datch 68 A3
Queen's Pl. Ascot 120 A3
Queen's Rd. Ascot 120 B2
Queen's Rd. Bis 153 F1
Queen's Rd. Caver 59 E1
Queen's Rd. Datch 68 A4
Queen's Rd Eng G 95 F1
Queen's Rd. Mar 1 B1
Queen's Rd. Newb 105 D1
Queen's Rd. Read 86 B4
Queen's Rd. Slough 42 C3
Queen's Rd. Wind 67 E3
Queens Acre. Wind 67 E2
Queens Cl. Burl 119 F4
Queens Gate. Wind 67 E2
Queens Hill Rise. Ascot 120 B3
Queens Park Gdns. Felt 98 C3
Queens Park Gdns. Felt 98 C3
Queens Pine. Brac 118 C2
Queens Rd. Camb 151 D2
Queens Rd. Eton 41 F1
Queens Way. Kint 102 A1
Queens Wlk. Ashf 97 E2
Queensborough Dr. Caver 58 C3
Queensbury Pl. Black 150 B2
Queenshill Lodge. Ascot 120 A3
Queensmere Rd. Slough 43 D2
Queensway. Caver 59 E3
Queensway. Maid 19 F1
Quentin Rd. Wood 87 E3
Quentin Way. Vir W 122 A3
Quinbrookes. Slough 43 E4
Quince Cl. Ascot 120 B3
Quincy Rd. Eng G 96 A2
Quintilis. Brac 117 F1
Quoiting Sq. Mar 1 B1
Quoitings Dr. Mar 1 B1

Rackstraw Rd. Crow 143 E1
Radbourne Rd. Bur C 84 B2
Radcliffe Way. Brac 117 F4
Radcot Ave. Slough 44 A2
Radcot Cl. Maid 19 F2
Radcot Cl. Wood 87 F4
Radical Ride. Woki 141 F4
Radley Bottom. Wick 101 E4
Radnor Cl. Hen-O-T 15 F1
Radnor Rd. Brac 118 C3
Radnor Rd. Read 87 E2

173

Radnor Way. Slough

Rutherford Wlk. Read

Radnor Way. Slough 43 F1
Radstock La. Read 87 D1
Radstock Rd. Read 86 C4
Raeburn Way. Sand 150 B3
Raeburn Way. Sand 150 B4
Ragdale. Bur C 111 D2
Raggleswood Cl. Read 87 E2
Raghill. Alde 135 E3
Raglan Gdns. Caver 59 E2
Ragley Mews. Caver 59 E3
Ragmans Cl. Mar B 1 B4
Ragstone Rd. Slough 42 C2
Railside. Wool 108 C1
Railton Cl. Read 113 E4
Railway App. Chert 123 F1
Railway Rd. Newb 105 D1
Railway Terr. Slough 42 C3
Railway Terr. Stai 96 B2
Railways Cotts. Gori 34 B3
Rainsborough Chase. Maid 39 D2
Rainworth Cl. Read 114 A4
Raleigh Cl. Slough 42 A3
Raleigh Cl. Wood 87 F3
Raleigh Ct. Stai 97 D2
Raleigh Rd. Felt 98 C3
Ralphs Ride. Brac 118 C3
Rambler Cl. Burn 41 D4
Rambler La. Slough 43 E2
Rambury Cl. Brac 117 F2
Ramptons La. Silc 136 A3
Ramsay Rd. Windl 146 C3
Ramsbury Dr. Read 87 D2
Ramsey Cl. Winn 87 F1
Rances La. Woki 116 C3
Randall Cl. Slough 43 F1
Randall Mead. Binf 90 A1
Randell Cl. Black 150 C1
Randolph Rd. Read 59 D1
Randolph Rd. Slough 43 F2
Ranelagh Cres. Burl 119 E4
Ranelagh Dr. Brac 118 B3
Range Rd. Brac 142 A4
Range Ride. Sand 150 C4
Range View. Sand 150 C4
Range Way. Shepp 125 D1
Rangewood Ave. Read 84 C2
Rapley Cl. Camb 151 F4
Rapley Green. Brac 118 B2
Ratby Cl. Read 87 E1
Raven Cl. Yate 149 D3
Ravendale Mews. Stai 97 D1
Ravendale Rd. Shepp 125 F4
Ravenglass Cl. Read 87 E2
Ravens Field. Slough 43 E2
Ravensbourne Ave. Stan 97 F4
Ravensbourne Dr. Wood 87 F4
Ravenscourt. Shepp 125 F4
Ravenscroft Rd. Hen-O-T 15 E1
Ravensdale Rd. Ascot 120 A2
Ravensfield. Eng G 95 E1
Ravenshoe Cl. Bou E 3 D2
Ravenstone Rd. Camb 152 B3
Ravenswood Ave. Crow 142 C3
Ravenswood Ave. Finch 142 C3
Ravenswood Dr. Camb 152 A3
Ravensworth Rd. Silc 136 C3
Ravensworth Rd. Slough 22 A1
Rawlinson Rd. Camb 151 D3
Ray Dr. Maid 40 A4
Ray Lea Cl. Maid 40 A4
Ray Lea Rd. Maid 40 A4
Ray Lodge Mews. Maid 40 A4
Ray Mead Ct. Maid 20 B1
Ray Mead Rd. Maid 40 A4
Ray Mill Rd E. Maid 20 A1
Ray Mill Rd W. Maid 40 A4
Ray Park Ave. Maid 40 A4
Ray Park La. Maid 40 A4
Ray Park Rd. Maid 40 A4
Ray St. Maid 40 A4
Raymond Cl. Stan 69 F3
Raymond Rd. Maid 39 E4
Raymond Rd. Slough 44 A2
Rayners Cl. Iver 69 E4
Rays Ave. Wind 66 C4
Raywood Cl. Harl 71 E4
Reading Bridge. Read 86 A4
Reading Rd. Aldw 33 D1
Reading Rd. Arbo 114 B2
Reading Rd. Bark 140 C2
Reading Rd. Black 150 A2
Reading Rd. Bur C 111 E2
Reading Rd. Chol 14 A4
Reading Rd. Finch 140 C2
Reading Rd. Gori 34 C3
Reading Rd. Hen-O-T 15 F1
Reading Rd. Moul 14 A4
Reading Rd. Pangb 56 B3
Reading Rd. Stre 34 A3
Reading Rd. Woki 115 F4
Reading Rd. Wood 87 E4
Recreation La. Shin 113 D1
Recreation Rd. Bou E 3 D2
Recreation Rd. Bur C 111 D1
Recreation Rd. Read 84 C4
Recreation Rd. Warg 36 C1
Rectory Cl. Brac 118 B3
Rectory Cl. Far C 22 A1
Rectory Cl. Newb 104 C1
Rectory Cl. Sand 149 F4
Rectory Cl. Stai 125 D3
Rectory Cl. Wind 67 D3
Rectory Cl. Woki 116 B3
Rectory La. Blew 12 C4
Rectory La. Brac 118 A3
Rectory La. Windl 146 B2
Rectory Rd. Caver 59 D1
Rectory Rd. Padw 135 F4
Rectory Rd. Stre 33 E4
Rectory Rd. Tapl 20 C1
Rectory Rd. Woki 116 B3
Red Cottage Mews. Slough 43 E2
Red Cross Rd. Gori 34 B3
Red Ct. Slough 42 C3
Red Hill. Shipl 35 D3
Red House Cl. Read 114 A4
Red La. Alde 135 E3
Red Leaf Cl. Slough 43 F3
Red Lion Way. Woo G 3 F3
Red Rd. West E 152 C4
Red Rose. Binf 90 B2
Red Shute Hill. Herm 79 D2
Redberry Cl. Caver 59 E3
Redcrest Gdns. Camb 151 F3
Reddington Dr. Slough 43 F1
Redditch. Brac 118 B1
Redfield Ct. Newb 105 E2
Redford Rd. Wind 66 B3
Redhatch Dr. Read 87 D1
Redlands Rd. Read 86 B3
Redlane Hill. Alde 135 E3
Redleaves Ave. Ashf 98 A1
Redmayne. Camb 152 B2
Redriff Cl. Maid 39 E3
Redruth Gdns. Read 86 A1
Redshots Cl. Mar 1 C2
Redvers Rd. Brac 118 A2
Redwood Ave. Wood 88 A3
Redwood Dr. Camb 152 B2
Redwood Dr. Windl 121 D2
Redwood Gdns. Slough 42 B3
Redwood Way. Read 57 E2
Redwood. Burn 21 D2
Redwood. Stai 123 F4
Reed Cl. Iver 44 C4
Reed Wlk. Newb 105 E2
Reed's Hill. Brac 118 A2
Reeds Ave. Read 86 C2
Reedsfield Rd. Ashf 98 A2
Reeve Rd. Holy 65 D4
Reeves Way. Woki 116 A2
Reform Rd. Maid 40 A4
Regency Hts. Caver 58 C2
Regent Cl. Hung 100 B3
Regent Cl. Read 87 E1
Regent Ct. Bags 145 F1
Regent Ct. Maid 39 F4
Regent Ct. Read 86 A4
Regent Ct. Wind 67 E3
Regent St. Read 86 C4
Regent Way. Camb 152 A1
Regents Pl. Sand 150 B4
Regents Wlk. Ascot 120 B1
Regis Cl. Read 113 E4
Regnum Dr. Newb 105 D3
Reid Ave. Maid 39 F3
Rembrandt Way. Read 85 F3
Rembrant Cl. Woki 115 E3
Remembrance Rd. Newb 104 C1
Remenham Church La. Rem H 16 A2
Remenham La. RemH 15 F2
Renault Rd. Wood 88 A3
Renfree Way. Shepp 125 D1
Rennie Cl. Ashf 97 E3
Repton Cl. Maid 39 E2
Repton Rd. Read 87 E2
Restwold Cl. Read 85 E2
Retford Cl. Wood 60 C1
Retreat The. Eng G 95 F2
Retreat The. Holy 65 E4
Revel Rd. Woo G 3 E4
Revesby Cl. Maid 39 E2
Revesby Cl. West E 153 E3
Rex Ave. Ashf 98 A2
Reynards Cl. Winn 88 B1
Reynolds Green. Sand 150 B3
Rhodes Cl. Eng G 96 A2
Rhodes Cl. Winn 87 F2
Rhododendron Cl. Burl 92 C1
Rhododendron Rd. Camb 152 A1
Rhododendron Wlk. Burl 92 C1
Ribbleton Cl. Winn 87 F2
Ribstone Rd. Maid 39 D2
Ricard Rd. Old W 68 A1
Richards Cl. Harl 71 E4
Richborough Cl. Read 87 D1
Richfield Ave. Read 58 C1
Richings Way. Iver 44 C2
Richmond Ave. Felt 71 F1
Richmond Ave. Felt 98 C4
Richmond Cl. Camb 151 F1
Richmond Cres. Slough 43 D3
Richmond Cres. Stai 96 C2
Richmond Dr. Shepp 125 E2
Richmond Rd. Caver 58 C2
Richmond Rd. Read 85 E4
Richmond Rd. Sand 150 C4
Richmond Rd. Stai 96 C2
Richmond Rise. Woki 115 F4
Richmondwood. Went 121 D1
Rickman Cl. Arbo 114 C1
Rickman Cl. Brac 118 B2
Rickman Cl. Wood 87 E3
Rickman's La. Sto P 22 C3
Riddings La. Head 133 E1
Rider's La. Bur C 112 A2
Rideway Cl. Camb 151 D2
Ridge Hall Cl. Caver 58 C2
Ridge Mount Rd. Windl 121 D1
Ridge The. Cold A 106 B4
Ridge The. Upp B 55 F4
Ridge Way. Iver 44 C3
Ridge Way. Warg 36 C1
Ridgebank. Slough 41 F3
Ridgemead Rd. Eng G 95 D3
Ridgemount Cl. Sulh 57 D1
Ridgeway Cl. Light 153 D4
Ridgeway Cl. Mar 1 C2
Ridgeway The. Brac 118 B3
Ridgeway The. Caver 59 D2
Ridgeway The. Light 146 A1
Ridgeway The. Mar 1 C2
Ridgeway The. Wood 87 F3
Ridgeway. Iver 44 C3
Ridgeway. Shepp 125 F1
Riding Court Rd. Datch 68 C4
Riding Way. Woki 115 F3
Ridings The. Camb 152 A2
Ridings The. Caver 59 E4
Ridings The. Iver 44 C1
Ridings The. Maid 39 D3
Ridlington Cl. Winn 87 F1
Riley Rd. Mar 1 B1
Riley Rd. Read 84 C4
Ring The. Brac 118 B4
Ringmead. Brac 117 F2
Ringwood Cl. Ascot 120 A3
Ringwood Rd. Black 150 B3
Ringwood Rd. Read 58 A1
Ringwood. Brac 117 F1
Ripley Ave. Eng G 95 F1
Ripley Cl. Slough 43 F1
Ripley Rd. Read 58 A1
Ripon Cl. Camb 152 B2
Ripplesmere. Brac 118 B3
Ripplesmore Cl. Sand 150 A4
Ripston Rd. Ashf 98 B2
Risborough Rd. Maid 39 F4
Rise Rd. Sunn 120 C2
Rise The. Caver 59 D2
Rise The. Cold A 106 B4
Rise The. Crow 142 C3
Rise The. Crow 143 D3
Rise The. Finch 141 D1
Rise The. Woki 116 A4
Riseley Rd. Maid 39 E4
Rissington Cl. Read 57 F2
River Gdns. Maid 40 B2
River Gdns. Pur O T 57 E3
River Mount. Shepp 125 F1
River Park Ave. Stai 96 B2
River Park. Newb 105 D2
River Rd. Caver 58 B2
River Rd. Read 86 A3
River Rd. Stai 123 F4
River Rd. Tapl 40 B4
River Rd. Yate 149 D4
River St. Wind 67 E4
River View. Fla H 3 D4
River Wlk. Newb 105 E2
Riverbank. Stai 96 C1
Riverdene Dr. Winn 88 A2
Riverfield Rd. Stai 96 C1
Rivermead Ct. Bish 18 C4
Rivermead Rd. Camb 151 D1
Rivermead Rd. Wood 87 F3
Riverpark Dr. Mar 1 C1
Riversdale Ct. Read 86 C4
Riversdell Cl. Chert 123 F1
Riverside Ave. Light 153 E4
Riverside Cl. Stai 123 F4
Riverside Dr. Stai 96 C2
Riverside Dr. Stai 123 F4
Riverside Pl. Stan 70 C1
Riverside Rd. Stai 96 C1
Riverside Rd. Stan 70 B1
Riverside Rd. Stan 70 C1
Riverside. Bou E 3 E2
Riverside. Eng G 96 A3
Riverside. Shepp 125 F1
Riverside. Wray 95 E4
Riverview Rd. Pangb 56 B3
Riverway. Gr She 48 A2
Riverway. Stai 124 A4
Riverwoods Ave. Mar 2 A1
Riverwoods Dr. Mar 2 A1
Rixman Cl. Maid 39 E3
Rixon Cl. Slough 43 F4
Road Hill. Box 76 B2
Roasthill La. Dorn 41 E1
Roberts Cl. Stan 70 B1
Roberts Rd. Camb 151 D3
Roberts Rd. Sand 151 D3
Roberts Way. Eng G 95 E1
Robertsfield. That 105 F2
Robertson Cl. Newb 131 D4
Robin Cl. Bur C 111 D2
Robin Cl. Bur C 111 D2
Robin Hill Dr. Camb 152 A2
Robin Hood Cl. Slough 41 F3
Robin Hood Way. Winn 88 B2
Robin La. Sand 143 E1
Robin Way. Read 84 A3
Robin Way. Stai 96 C3
Robin's Bow. Camb 151 D2
Robindale Ave. Read 87 E2
Robinhood La. Winn 88 B2
Robins Cl. Newb 130 C4
Robins Grove Cres. Yate 149 D3
Robins Hill. Ink 127 F3
Robinson Ct. Read 87 D1
Rochester Ave. Felt 98 C3
Rochester Ave. Wood 60 C1
Rochford Way. Burn 41 D4
Rochfords Gdns. Slough 43 E3
Rockbourne Gdns. Read 58 A1
Rockfield Way. Sand 150 B4
Rockfield. Lamb 25 D1
Rockingham Rd. Newb 104 C1
Rockmoor La. Link 147 D1
Rodney Way. Stan 69 F3
Rodway Rd. Read 57 F1
Roebuck Estate. Binf 90 B1
Roebuck Green. Slough 41 F3
Roebuts Cl. Newb 130 C4
Rogers La. Sto P 22 C2
Rogers's La. East G 47 E3
Rogosa Rd. Camb 153 F3
Rokeby Cl. Brac 118 B4
Rokeby Cl. Newb 131 D4
Rokeby Dr. Maple 58 B4
Rokes Pl. Yate 149 D3
Rokesby Rd. Slough 21 F1
Rolls La. Holy 64 C4
Roman Fields. Silc 136 A1
Roman Lea. Cook 19 F4
Roman Ride. Finch 142 B3
Roman Way. Bou E 3 D2
Roman Way. Read 87 E2
Roman Way. That 106 A3
Romans Gate. Silc 135 F1
Romany Cl. Read 58 A1
Romany La. Read 58 A1
Romney Cl. Ashf 98 B2
Romney Ct. Mar 1 C2
Romsey Cl. Black 150 B3
Romsey Cl. Slough 43 F2
Romsey Rd. Read 58 A1
Rona Ct. Read 85 D4
Ronaldsay Spur. Slough 42 C4
Rood Hill. Wick 76 B2
Rook Cl. Woki 115 F3
Rook Rd. Bou E 3 E2
Rookery Ct. Mar 1 B1
Rookery Rd. Stai 97 D2
Rooksfield. Newt 132 A1
Rooksmead Rd. Shepp 125 F4
Rooksnest La. Kint 128 A3
Rookswood. Brac 91 D1
Rookwood Ave. Sand 143 F1
Rope Wlk. That 106 B2
Rosa Ave. Ashf 98 A2
Rosary Gdns. Ashf 98 A2
Rosary Gdns. Yate 149 E3
Rose Cl. Wood 88 A4
Rose Gdns. Stan 97 E4
Rose Hill. Binf 90 B2
Rose Hill. Burn 21 D3
Rose Kiln La. Bur C 86 A2
Rose Kiln La. Read 86 A2
Rose La. Know H 37 D4
Rose St. Woki 116 B3
Rose Wlk. Read 86 A4
Rose Wlk. Slough 42 A4
Roseacre Cl. Stai 125 D2
Rosebank Cl. Cook 19 F4
Rosebay. Woki 116 C4
Rosebery Rd. Maple 58 B4
Rosecroft Way. Shin 113 F3
Rosedale Cres. Read 87 D4
Rosedale Gdns. Brac 118 A2
Rosedale Gdns. That 106 B1
Rosedale. Binf 90 B2
Rosedene La. Sand 150 B3
Rosefield Rd. Stai 97 D2
Rosehill Park. Caver 59 E4
Roseleigh Cl. Maid 39 D4
Rosemary Ave. Read 86 C1
Rosemary Gdns. Black 150 B3
Rosemary La. Sand 150 B3
Rosemary La. Stai 123 D3
Rosemead Ave. Felt 98 C3
Rosemead Ave. Sulh 57 D2
Rosery The. Bou E 3 D2
Roses La. Wind 66 B3
Rosewood Dr. Stai 124 C2
Rosewood Way. Camb 153 F3
Rosewood Way. Far C 22 B4
Rosewood. Wood 87 E2
Rosier Cl. That 106 C1
Rosken Gr. Far C 22 A2
Roslyn Rd. Wood 87 E3
Ross Rd. Maid 39 F2
Ross Rd. Read 58 C1
Ross Rd. Read 59 D1
Rossendale Rd. Caver 59 E2
Rossett Cl. Brac 118 A3
Rossey Pl. Eton 42 B1
Rossington Pl. Read 113 E4
Rossiter Cl. Slough 43 F1
Rosslyn Cl. Ashf 98 C1
Rother Cl. Sand 150 B4
Rotherfield Ave. Woki 116 A4
Rotherfield Cl. Thea 83 F2
Rotherfield Rd. Hen-O-T 35 F4
Rotherfield Way. Caver 59 D2
Rothwell Gdns. Wood 61 D1
Rothwell Wlk. Caver 59 E1
Rotton Row Hill. Brad 81 F2
Roughgrove Copse. Binf 90 A1
Rounce La. West E 153 E3
Round Cl. Yate 149 F3
Round End. Newb 130 B3
Roundabout La. Woki 115 E4
Roundfield. Buck 107 D3
Roundhead Rd. Thea 83 E2
Roundway Cl. Camb 152 B3
Roundway. Camb 152 B3
Roundway. Stai 96 B2
Routh Ct. Felt 98 B4
Routh La. Read 84 C3
Row La. Caver 59 F4
Rowallan Cl. Caver 59 E3
Rowan Ave. Stai 96 B2
Rowan Cl. Camb 151 F4
Rowan Cl. Woki 115 F3
Rowan Dr. Brac 143 E4
Rowan Dr. Crow 143 E3
Rowan Dr. Newb 105 D3
Rowan Dr. Wood 87 F4
Rowan Way. Bur C 111 D3
Rowan Way. Slough 42 A4
Rowanhurst Dr. Far C 22 B4
Rowans Cl. Black 150 C1
Rowans The. Ashf 98 C2
Rowcroft Rd. Arbo 140 C4
Rowe Ct. Read 85 D4
Rowland Cl. Wind 66 B2
Rowland Way. Read 86 C1
Rowland Way. Stai 98 B1
Rowley Cl. Brac 118 C3
Rowley La. Sto P 23 E2
Rowley Rd. Read 86 A2
Roxburgh Cl. Camb 152 B2
Roxford Cl. Shepp 125 F2
Roxwell Cl. Slough 41 F3
Roy Cl. Herm 78 C3
Royal Ave. Read 84 B3
Royal Victoria Gdns. Ascot 120 A2
Roycroft La. Woki 141 F4
Royston Cl. Read 84 C4
Royston Way. Slough 41 E4
Rubus Cl. Camb 153 F3
Ruby Cl. Slough 42 A2
Ruby Cl. Woki 115 F4
Rudd Hall Rise. Camb 151 F2
Ruddlesway. Wind 66 B3
Rudland Cl. That 106 B1
Rudsworth Cl. Iver 69 E4
Rugby Cl. Sand 143 F1
Ruggles-Brise Rd. Ashf 97 E2
Rumsey's La. Blew 12 A4
Runnemede Rd. Eng G 96 A2
Runnymede Ct. Eng G 96 A2
Rupert Cl. Hen-O-T 15 F2
Rupert Rd. Newb 130 C4
Rupert St. Read 86 B4
Rupert's La. Hen-O-T 15 F2
Ruscombe Gdns. Datch 68 A4
Ruscombe La. Twyf 61 F3
Ruscombe Park. Twyf 61 F3
Ruscombe Rd. Twyf 61 F3
Ruscombe Way. Felt 98 C4
Rushall Cl. Read 113 F4
Rusham Park Ave. Eng G 95 F1
Rusham Rd. Eng G 95 F1
Rushbrook Rd. Wood 87 E4
Rushburn. Woo G 3 F3
Rushden Dr. Read 86 C1
Rushes The. Maid 40 A3
Rushes The. Mar 18 B4
Rushey Way. Read 87 E1
Rushington Ave. Maid 39 F3
Rushmoor Gdns. Bur C 84 A2
Ruskin Ave. Felt 71 F1
Ruskin Rd. Stai 96 C1
Ruskin Way. Woki 115 E3
Russell Ct. Maid 39 F4
Russell Dr. Stan 70 B1
Russell Rd. Maple 58 B4
Russell Rd. Newb 104 C1
Russell Rd. Shepp 125 E1
Russell St. Read 85 F4
Russell St. Wind 67 E3
Russell Way. Winn 88 A1
Russet Cl. Stan 69 F1
Russet Gdns. Camb 151 E2
Russet Glade. Bur C 111 D1
Russet Glade. Caver 59 E4
Russet Rd. Maid 39 E2
Russington Rd. Shepp 125 E2
Russley Green. Woki 116 A1
Rustington Cl. Read 87 D1
Ruston Way. Ascot 119 F4
Rutherford Wlk. Read 84 A4

Rutherwyk Rd. Chert ... 123 F1
Rutland Pl. Maid ... 39 E3
Rutland Rd. Maid ... 39 E3
Rutland Rd. Read ... 85 E4
Ruxbury Rd. Chert ... 123 E2
Ryan Mount. Sand ... 150 A4
Ryans Mount. Mar ... 1 B1
Rycroft. Wind ... 66 C2
Rydal Ave. Read ... 57 F1
Rydal Cl. Camb ... 152 B3
Rydal Dr. That ... 106 A2
Rydal Pl. Light ... 153 D4
Rydal Way. Stai ... 96 A1
Ryde The. Stai ... 124 A4
Rydings. Wind ... 66 C2
Rye Cl. Brac ... 118 B4
Rye Cl. Maid ... 39 D2
Rye Cl. New G ... 91 F1
Rye Ct. Slough ... 43 D2
Rye Gr. Light ... 146 C1
Ryecroft. Warg ... 36 C1
Ryecroft Cl. Wood ... 60 C1
Ryecroft Gdns. Black ... 150 C2
Ryehurst La. Binf ... 90 C3
Ryeish La. Shin ... 113 E2
Ryemead La. Wink ... 92 B3
Ryhill Way. Read ... 113 F4
Ryland Cl. Felt ... 98 C2
Rylstone Cl. Maid ... 39 E2
Rylstone Rd. Read ... 85 E4
Ryvers Rd. Slough ... 43 F2
Ryves Ave. Yate ... 149 D3

Sackville St. Read ... 86 A4
Saddleback Rd. Camb ... 151 F4
Saddlewood. Camb ... 151 E2
Sadler's La. Woki ... 115 E4
Sadlers Ct. Woki ... 88 B1
Sadlers Rd. Ink ... 127 D3
Saffron Cl. Datch ... 68 A3
Saffron Cl. Newb ... 104 C2
Saffron Ct. Read ... 87 E2
Saffron Rd. Brac ... 118 A3
Sage Cl. Read ... 87 D1
Sage Rd. Sulh ... 57 E2
Sagecroft Rd. That ... 106 B3
St Adrian's Cl. Maid ... 39 D2
St Agnes Terr. Lamb ... 25 D1
St Albans St. Wind ... 67 E3
St Andrew's Ave. Wind ... 66 C3
St Andrew's Cl. Old W ... 68 A1
St Andrew's Cl. Shepp ... 125 E3
St Andrew's Cl. Wray ... 68 C1
St Andrew's Cres. Wind ... 66 C3
St Andrew's Rd. Caver ... 58 C2
St Andrew's Rd. Hen-O-T ... 35 E4
St Andrew's Way. Slough ... 41 E3
St Andrews Cl. Woki ... 142 C3
St Andrews. Brac ... 117 F2
St Ann's Cl. Chert ... 123 F2
St Ann's Hill Rd. Chert ... 123 E2
St Ann's Rd. Chert ... 123 F2
St Anne's Cl. Hen-O-T ... 15 E1
St Anne's Rd. Caver ... 59 D1
St Annes Ave. Stan ... 97 E4
St Annes Glade. Bags ... 145 E2
St Anthony's Way. Harm ... 71 F2
St Anthonys Cl. Brac ... 118 A4
St Barnabas Cl. Caver ... 59 D3
St Barnabas Rd. Read ... 86 C1
St Bartholomews Rd. Read ... 86 C4
St Bernards Rd. Slough ... 43 E2
St Birinus Rd. Read ... 84 B3
St Catherine's Cl. Woki ... 88 A1
St Catherines Rd. Camb ... 151 F1
St Chad's Rd. Maid ... 39 D2
St Christophers Gdns. Burl ... 119 E4
St Clements Cl. Wood ... 87 E1
St Columba's Cl. Maid ... 39 D2
St David's Cl. Caver ... 58 C3
St David's Cl. Maid ... 39 D2
St David's Rd. Newb ... 104 C1
St Donats Pl. Newb ... 105 D1
St Dunstan's Rd. Felt ... 98 C2
St Edward's Rd. Read ... 87 D3
St Elizabeth Cl. Read ... 113 D4
St Elmo Cres. Far C ... 22 B1
St George's Ave. Newb ... 104 C1
St George's Cl. Wind ... 66 C3
St George's Cres. Slough ... 41 E3
St George's La. Ascot ... 120 A3
St George's Rd. Read ... 85 E4
St George's Terr. Read ... 85 D4
St Georges Rd. Camb ... 151 E3
St Giles Cl. Read ... 86 A3
St Helens Cres. Sand ... 150 A4
St Helier Cl. Woki ... 116 A2
St Hilda's Ave. Ashf ... 97 F2
St Ives Cl. Thea ... 83 E1
St Ives Rd. Maid ... 40 A4
St James Cl. Pangb ... 56 B3
St James Cl. Twyf ... 61 F3
St James Rd. Woki ... 141 F4
St James Wlk. Iver ... 44 C2
St John's Hill. Read ... 86 B4
St John's Rd. Ascot ... 92 C1
St John's Rd. Caver ... 59 E1
St John's Rd. Mort ... 137 D3

St John's Rd. Newb ... 105 D1
St John's Rd. Read ... 86 B4
St John's Rd. Sand ... 150 B4
St John's Rd. That ... 106 B2
St John's St. Read ... 86 B4
St Johns Ct. Eng G ... 96 A2
St Johns Dr. Wind ... 67 D3
St Johns Rd. Slough ... 43 D3
St Johns Rd. Wind ... 67 D3
St Jude's Cl. Eng G ... 95 E2
St Jude's Rd. Eng G ... 95 E2
St Katherine's Rd. Hen-O-T ... 35 E4
St Laurence Way. Slough ... 43 D2
St Leonard's Ave. Wind ... 67 E3
St Leonard's Hill. Wind ... 66 C2
St Leonard's Rd. Wind ... 67 E2
St Leonards Rd. Wind ... 66 B1
St Leonards Wlk. Iver ... 44 C2
St Luke's Rd. Maid ... 39 F4
St Luke's Rd. Old W ... 68 A1
St Lukes Way. Caver ... 59 D2
St Margaret's Rd. Maid ... 39 D4
St Margarets Ave. Ashf ... 98 A2
St Mark's Cl. Brad ... 83 D3
St Mark's Pl. Wind ... 67 E3
St Mark's Rd. Binf ... 117 E4
St Mark's Rd. Hen-O-T ... 35 E4
St Mark's Rd. Maid ... 39 E4
St Mark's Rd. Wind ... 67 E3
St Marks Cl. That ... 106 B2
St Marks Cres. Maid ... 39 D4
St Marks Rd. Binf ... 90 B1
St Martin's Ct. Stai ... 97 E2
St Martins Cl. Wood ... 87 E1
St Mary's Ave. Pur O T ... 57 E3
St Mary's Ave. Stan ... 97 E4
St Mary's Butts. Read ... 86 A4
St Mary's Cl. Hen-O-T ... 35 D4
St Mary's Cl. Maid ... 40 A4
St Mary's Cl. Stan ... 97 E4
St Mary's Cres. Stan ... 97 E4
St Mary's Dr. Felt ... 98 B4
St Mary's Gdns. Bags ... 145 F2
St Mary's Gdns. Bags ... 145 F2
St Mary's Hill. Ascot ... 120 B2
St Mary's Rd. Ascot ... 120 A2
St Mary's Rd. Camb ... 151 E3
St Mary's Rd. Mort ... 137 D3
St Mary's Rd. Newb ... 105 D2
St Mary's Rd. Newb ... 105 D2
St Mary's Rd. Slough ... 43 E2
St Mary's Rd. Woki ... 88 A1
St Mary's Way. Bur C ... 111 D2
St Mary's Wlk. Maid ... 39 F4
St Marys Cl. Sand ... 150 B4
St Marys La. Wink ... 92 B3
St Michael's Ct. Slough ... 21 E1
St Michael's Rd. Newb ... 104 C1
St Michael's Rd. Read ... 84 B4
St Michael's Rd. Sand ... 149 F4
St Michaels Ct. Lamb ... 25 D1
St Michaels Ct. Twyf ... 61 F3
St Michaels Rd. Camb ... 151 D3
St Micheals Rd. Ashf ... 98 A2
St Nazaire Cl. Stan ... 96 B2
St Nicholas Dr. Shepp ... 125 D1
St Nicholas' Rd. Newb ... 104 C1
St Olave's Cl. Stai ... 96 C1
St Patrick's Ave. Char ... 61 D3
St Patrick's Cl. Maid ... 39 D2
St Paul's Cl. Ashf ... 98 B2
St Paul's Ct. Read ... 86 A3
St Paul's Gate. Woki ... 116 A3
St Paul's Rd. Stai ... 96 B1
St Pauls Ave. Slough ... 43 D3
St Peter St. Mar ... 1 C1
St Peter's Ave. Caver ... 58 C2
St Peter's Cl. Burn ... 21 D1
St Peter's Cl. Old W ... 68 A1
St Peter's Cl. Stai ... 96 C1
St Peter's Gdns. Yate ... 149 E3
St Peter's Hill. Caver ... 58 C2
St Peter's Rd. Maid ... 19 E1
St Peter's Rd. Read ... 87 D3
St Pinnock Ave. Stai ... 124 A4
St Ronan's Rd. Read ... 85 D4
St Saviour's Rd. Read ... 85 F3
St Sebastians Cl. Woki ... 142 C4
St Stephens Cl. Caver ... 59 D1
St Swithins Cl. Wick ... 75 E2
St Theresa's Rd. Harm ... 71 F2
St Thomas Cl. That ... 106 C2
Saint Catherine's Hill. Silc ... 136 C3
Saint-Cloud Way. Maid ... 40 A4
Salamanca. Finch ... 142 C3
Salcombe Dr. Read ... 87 D2
Salcombe Rd. Ashf ... 97 F3
Salcombe Rd. Newb ... 104 C1
Salcombe Rd. Read ... 86 B2
Sale Garden Cotts. Woki ... 116 B3
Saleby Cl. Winn ... 87 F1
Salford Cl. Read ... 113 E4
Salisbury Ave. Slough ... 42 B4
Salisbury Cl. Woki ... 116 A1
Salisbury Rd. Harm ... 71 E1
Salisbury Rd. Hung ... 100 B2
Salisbury Rd. Read ... 85 F4
Salisbury Rd. Sand ... 150 B3
Salmon Cl. Shin ... 113 D1

Salmond Rd. Read ... 113 E3
Salt Hill Ave. Slough ... 42 B3
Salt Hill Dr. Slough ... 42 B3
Salt Hill Way. Slough ... 42 B3
Salters' Rd. Maid ... 40 A4
Saltersgate Cl. Winn ... 87 E1
Salwey Cl. Brac ... 118 A2
Samarkand Cl. Camb ... 152 A2
Samian Pl. Binf ... 90 C1
Sampage Cl. Read ... 113 E3
Sampson Park. Brac ... 117 E4
Sampsons Green. Slough ... 21 F1
Sanctuary Cl. Read ... 84 C4
Sanctuary Rd. Stan ... 71 D1
Sandcroft Rd. Caver ... 58 C3
Sandell's Ave. Ashf ... 98 B2
Sanden Cl. Hung ... 100 B3
Sandford Down. Brac ... 118 C2
Sandford Dr. Wood ... 60 C1
Sandford La. Hurst ... 88 B3
Sandgate Ave. Read ... 57 F1
Sandhills Ct. Vir W ... 122 C2
Sandhills La. Vir W ... 122 C2
Sandhills Way. Read ... 84 C2
Sandhurst La. Black ... 150 A3
Sandhurst Rd. Brac ... 142 A4
Sandhurst Rd. Crow ... 143 D2
Sandhurst Rd. Yate ... 149 F4
Sandisplatt Rd. Maid ... 39 D3
Sandleford Cl. Read ... 113 E3
Sandleford Rise. Newb ... 131 D4
Sandlers End. Slough ... 22 A1
Sandown Ave. Read ... 84 A2
Sandown Cl. Black ... 150 B3
Sandown Dr. Camb ... 151 F1
Sandown Rd. Slough ... 41 F4
Sandown Way. Newb ... 105 E1
Sandpit Hill. Newb ... 130 B2
Sandpit La. Swal ... 140 A3
Sandringham Cl. Slough ... 41 E4
Sandringham Dr. Ashf ... 97 E2
Sandringham Rd. Maid ... 19 F1
Sandringham Rd. Stan ... 70 C1
Sandringham Way. Read ... 84 A2
Sands Farm Dr. Burn ... 21 E1
Sandstone Cl. Winn ... 88 B1
Sandy Cl. Herm ... 79 D2
Sandy Dr. Felt ... 98 C4
Sandy La. Brac ... 118 B4
Sandy La. Camb ... 151 F3
Sandy La. Herm ... 78 C2
Sandy La. Sand ... 143 D1
Sandy La. Sunn ... 121 D2
Sandy La. Vir W ... 122 C3
Sandy La. Woki ... 115 E2
Sandy Mead. Holy ... 40 B1
Sandy Way. Shepp ... 125 F1
Sandygate Cl. Mar ... 1 B2
Sandygate Rd. Mar ... 1 B2
Sapgood Cl. That ... 106 C1
Sapphire Cl. Woki ... 115 F4
Sarsby Dr. Wray ... 96 A3
Sarum Cres. Woki ... 116 B4
Sarum Rd. Tad ... 135 D1
Sarum Way. Hung ... 100 B2
Sarum. Brac ... 117 F1
Saturn Cl. Woki ... 115 F3
Saunton Ave. Harl ... 71 F4
Savernake Cl. Read ... 84 C4
Savernake Way. Brac ... 118 C2
Savill Way. Mar ... 1 C1
Saville Cres. Ashf ... 98 B1
Saville Gdns. Camb ... 152 A3
Savory Wlk. Binf ... 90 B1
Savoy Gr. Black ... 150 B2
Sawmill Rd. Herm ... 79 D2
Sawpit Rd. Hurst ... 88 C4
Sawtry Cl. Winn ... 87 F1
Sawyer's Cl. Wind ... 66 C4
Sawyers Cl. Whi Wa ... 39 D1
Sawyers Cres. Whi Wa ... 39 D1
Saxe Cl. Bur C ... 111 D2
Saxon Cl. Slough ... 43 F2
Saxon Gdns. Tapl ... 20 B1
Saxon Rd. Ashf ... 98 B1
Saxon Way. Harm ... 70 B4
Saxon Way. Old W ... 68 A1
Sayers Cl. Gree ... 131 D4
Scafell Cl. Read ... 57 E1
Scafell Rd. Slough ... 41 F4
Scampton Rd. Stan ... 70 C1
Scania Wlk. Burl ... 92 A1
Scarborough Rd. Stan ... 71 E1
Scarborough Way. Slough ... 42 A3
Scarletts La. Warg ... 37 E1
Scholars Cl. Caver ... 58 C2
School Green. Shin ... 113 F2
School Hill. Crow ... 143 E2
School Hill. Sand ... 143 D1
School Hill. Warg ... 36 B1
School La. Bags ... 145 F1
School La. Bish ... 38 A2
School La. Box ... 76 C2
School La. Bur C ... 111 D1
School La. Caver ... 59 D1
School La. Caver ... 59 D3
School La. Cook ... 19 D4
School La. Cook ... 20 A4
School La. East G ... 47 E3

School La. Eng G ... 96 A2
School La. Frox ... 99 D1
School La. Lit M ... 2 B3
School La. Maid ... 19 F1
School La. Medm ... 17 D3
School La. Padw ... 109 F1
School La. Shepp ... 125 D2
School La. Sto P ... 23 D2
School La. W St L ... 62 C2
School La. Warg ... 36 B1
School La. Windl ... 146 B2
School La. Yate ... 149 D3
School Rd. Ascot ... 120 B2
School Rd. Ashf ... 98 A1
School Rd. Bark ... 114 C1
School Rd. Bis ... 153 F2
School Rd. Bur C ... 111 E3
School Rd. Chiev ... 78 A4
School Rd. Comp ... 31 F2
School Rd. Harm ... 70 B4
School Rd. Hurst ... 88 C4
School Rd. Read ... 84 B4
School Rd. Read ... 114 C1
School Rd. Swal ... 139 F2
School Rd. Windl ... 146 A3
School Rd. Woki ... 116 B3
School Rd. Woo G ... 3 F3
School Terr. Read ... 86 C4
Schroder Ct. Eng G ... 95 D2
Scotland Hill. Sand ... 143 D1
Scotlands Dr. Far C ... 22 A3
Scots Cl. Stan ... 97 E4
Scots Dr. Woki ... 115 F4
Scott Cl. Caver ... 59 D3
Scott Cl. Far C ... 22 B4
Scott Cl. Wood ... 88 A4
Scott Terr. Brac ... 118 C4
Scott's Ave. Ashf ... 98 C1
Scott's Way. Ashf ... 98 C1
Scottalls La. Hamp N ... 52 C3
Scours La. Read ... 58 A1
Scratchface La. Brad ... 81 F3
Scrivens Mead. That ... 106 C2
Scylla Cres. Felt ... 98 A4
Scylla Rd. Felt ... 71 D1
Seacourt Rd. Slough ... 44 A1
Seaford Gdns. Wood ... 87 F3
Seaford Rd. Stan ... 70 B1
Seaford Rd. Woki ... 116 B3
Sealand Rd. Stan ... 71 D1
Searles Farm La. Bur C ... 85 D1
Seaton Dr. Ashf ... 97 F3
Seaton Gdns. Read ... 86 B1
Seaton Rd. Camb ... 151 D3
Second Cres. Slough ... 42 B4
Sedgefield Rd. Newb ... 131 E4
Sedgmoor Gdns. Fla H ... 3 D4
Sedgmoor La. Fla H ... 3 D4
Sedgmoor Rd. Fla H ... 3 D4
Seebys Oak. Sand ... 150 B3
Sefton Cl. Sto P ... 22 C2
Sefton Cl. West E ... 153 F3
Sefton Paddock. Sto P ... 23 D3
Segsbury Gr. Brac ... 118 C3
Selborne Gdns. Read ... 58 A1
Selbourne Cl. Black ... 150 B3
Selby Rd. Ashf ... 98 B1
Selcourt Cl. Wood ... 87 E4
Sellafield Way. Read ... 87 E1
Selsdon Ave. Wood ... 87 F4
Selsey Way. Read ... 114 A4
Selwood Cl. Stan ... 70 B1
Selwood Gdns. Stan ... 70 B1
Selwyn Dr. Yate ... 149 D3
Send Rd. Caver ... 59 E1
Setley Way. Brac ... 119 D3
Seton Dr. Read ... 84 C3
Sett The. Yate ... 149 D3
Sevenoaks Rd. Read ... 87 D2
Severn Cl. Sand ... 150 B4
Severn Cl. That ... 106 A3
Severn Cres. Slough ... 69 D4
Severn Way. Read ... 84 C3
Sewell Ave. Woki ... 116 A4
Sewell Cl. Cold A ... 79 D1
Seymour Ave. Shin ... 113 F3
Seymour Cl. Maid ... 39 D2
Seymour Court Rd. Mar ... 1 B2
Seymour Court Rd. Mar B ... 1 B2
Seymour Ct La. Mar B ... 1 A3
Seymour Park Rd. Mar ... 1 B1
Seymour Plain. Mar ... 1 B3
Seymour Plain. Mar B ... 1 B3
Seymour Rd. Slough ... 42 B2
Seymour Way. Ashf ... 98 C1
Shackleton Rd. Slough ... 42 C3
Shackleton Way. Wood ... 88 A4
Shaftesbury Cres. Stai ... 97 E1
Shaftesbury Mount. Black ... 150 B2
Shaftesbury Rd. Bis ... 153 F2
Shaftesbury Rd. Read ... 85 D4
Shaftsbury Cl. Brac ... 118 B2
Shaggy Calf La. Slough ... 43 D3
Shakespeare Cl. Caver ... 59 E3
Shakespeare Rd. That ... 106 B2
Shakespeare Way. Brac ... 118 C4
Shalbourne Cl. Hung ... 100 A3
Shalbourne Rise. Camb ... 151 E3
Sharney Ave. Slough ... 44 A2

Sharnwood Dr. Read ... 84 C3
Sharpethorpe Cl. Read ... 87 D1
Shaw Farm Rd. Newb ... 105 D3
Shaw Hill. Newb ... 105 D3
Shaw Park. Crow ... 143 D2
Shaw Rd. Newb ... 105 D2
Shaw Rd. Read ... 85 F3
Shaw The. Cook ... 19 F3
Sheehy Way. Slough ... 43 D3
Sheep Leaze La. Pease ... 29 E1
Sheep Wlk. Caver ... 59 D2
Sheepcote La. Bou E ... 3 F1
Sheepcote La. Holy ... 64 B2
Sheepcote Rd. Eton ... 42 A1
Sheepcote Rd. Wind ... 66 C3
Sheepdrove Rd. Lamb ... 25 E2
Sheephouse Rd. Maid ... 20 A1
Sheephouse Way. Chadd ... 49 D3
Sheepridge La. Bou E ... 2 C4
Sheepridge La. Fla H ... 2 C4
Sheepwalk. Shepp ... 124 C2
Sheepwalk. Stai ... 124 C2
Sheepwash. Newt ... 131 D1
Sheepways La. Maple ... 58 A4
Sheerlands Rd. Arbo ... 140 C4
Sheerlands Rd. Bark ... 140 C3
Sheerlands Rd. Bark ... 140 C4
Sheet St. Wind ... 67 E3
Sheet Street Rd. Old W ... 94 A4
Sheet Street Rd. Wind ... 67 E1
Sheet Street Rd. Wind ... 94 A4
Sheffield Rd. Harm ... 71 E1
Sheffield Way. Harm ... 71 E1
Shefford Cres. Woki ... 116 B4
Sheldon Gdns. Read ... 86 B1
Shelgate Wlk. Wood ... 87 E4
Shelley Ave. Brac ... 118 C4
Shelley Cl. Medm ... 17 E4
Shelley Cl. Slough ... 43 F1
Shelley Cl. Wood ... 87 E2
Shelley Rd. Mar ... 1 C2
Shelley Rd. That ... 106 B2
Shelley Walk. Yate ... 149 D3
Shelson Ave. Felt ... 98 C2
Shelton Cl. Slough ... 43 E2
Shenstone Cl. Woki ... 142 A4
Shenstone Dr. Burn ... 21 E1
Shenstone Park. Ascot ... 120 C3
Shenstone Rd. Read ... 86 A2
Shephards La. Brac ... 91 D1
Shepherd's House La. Read ... 87 D4
Shepherds Ave. Read ... 87 D4
Shepherds Chase. Bags ... 145 F1
Shepherds Cl. Hurl ... 17 F2
Shepherds Cl. Shepp ... 125 D2
Shepherds Hill. Brac ... 118 B4
Shepherds Hill. Comp ... 31 F2
Shepherds Hill. Wood ... 87 E4
Shepherds La. Caver ... 58 B3
Shepherds La. Hurl ... 17 F2
Shepherds Mount. Comp ... 31 F2
Shepherds Rise. Comp ... 31 F2
Shepherds Way. Crow ... 142 C2
Shepherds Wlk. Wood ... 87 E4
Shepley Dr. Read ... 85 E2
Shepley Dr. Went ... 121 E2
Shepley End. Went ... 121 E2
Shepperton Court Dr. Shepp ... 125 D2
Shepperton Rd. Stai ... 124 B3
Sheraton Cl. Black ... 150 C2
Sheraton Dr. Read ... 57 F1
Sherborne Cl. Stan ... 69 F3
Sherborne Rd. Felt ... 98 B4
Sherbourne Dr. Went ... 121 E2
Sherbourne Dr. Wind ... 66 C2
Sherbourne Dr. Wood ... 87 F4
Sherbourne Wlk. Far C ... 22 B4
Shergold Way. Cook ... 19 F3
Sheridan Ave. Caver ... 59 D2
Sheridan Cres. Tad ... 134 C1
Sheridan Way. Woki ... 115 F3
Sherman Rd. Read ... 86 A3
Sherman Rd. Slough ... 42 C4
Sherrardmead. Newb ... 105 D3
Sherring Cl. Brac ... 91 E1
Sherwood Cl. Brac ... 119 D4
Sherwood Cl. Slough ... 43 F2
Sherwood Dr. Maid ... 39 D3
Sherwood Gdns. Hen-O-T ... 35 E4
Sherwood Rd. Winn ... 88 B1
Sherwood Rise. Purl ... 57 D3
Sherwood St. Read ... 85 E4
Shield Rd. Felt ... 98 B2
Shifford Cres. Maid ... 19 F2
Shildon Cl. Camb ... 152 B2
Shinfield Rd. Read ... 86 C2
Shinfield Rise. Read ... 86 C1
Shipley Cl. Wood ... 61 D1
Shipton Cl. Read ... 57 E1
Shire Cl. Bags ... 145 F1
Shire's Head Cl. Read ... 85 E3
Shires The. Woki ... 115 F2
Shires Way. Yate ... 149 E4
Shirley Ave. Read ... 113 E4
Shirley Ave. Wind ... 66 C3
Shirley Rd. Maid ... 39 E3
Sholto Rd. Stan ... 97 F3
Shooter's Hill. Pangb ... 56 A3
Shop La. Leckh ... 49 F3

Shop La. Newb 104 C3
Shoppenhanger's Rd. Maid 39 F2
Shoreham Rd (E). Stan 70 C1
Shoreham Rd (W). Stan 70 C1
Short La. Stan 97 F4
Short Rd. Stan 70 C1
Short St. Caver 59 D1
Short St. Pangb 56 B3
Short St. Read 86 A3
Short The. Pur O T 57 E3
Shortfern. Slough 43 E4
Shortheath La. Sulhd 110 C2
Shortland. Harl 71 E4
Shortlands Hill. Moul 13 E2
Shortwood Ave. Ashf 97 D2
Shrewsbury Rd. Harm 71 E1
Shrivenham Cl. Sand 150 B4
Shrubbs Hill La. Went 121 E2
Shrubland Dr. Read 85 D2
Shrublands Dr. Light 153 D4
Shute End. Woki 116 A3
Shyshack La. Tad 134 C1
Sibley Park Rd. Read 87 D1
Sibson. Read 87 E1
Sidbury Cl. Sunn 121 D2
Sidestrand Rd. Newb 130 C4
Sidmouth Grange Cl. Read 87 D4
Sidmouth Grange Rd. Read 87 D4
Sidmouth St. Read 86 B4
Sidney Rd. Stai 97 D2
Silbury Cl. Bur C 84 A2
Silchester Rd. Read 85 E2
Silchester Rd. Tad 135 E1
Silco Dr. Maid 39 F3
Silver Birches. Woki 115 E2
Silver Cl. Maid 39 D3
Silver Dr. Camb 152 B2
Silver Fox Cres. Wood 87 E3
Silver Hill. Sand 150 C4
Silver La. Padw 136 A4
Silver St. Read 86 A3
Silverdale Rd. Read 87 E2
Silverdale Rd. Tad 135 D1
Silverdale Rd. Warg 36 C1
Silverglades. Yate 149 E2
Silverthorne Dr. Caver 58 C3
Silvertrees Dr. Maid 39 D3
Silverwood Dr. Camb 152 A4
Silwood Cl. Ascot 120 B4
Silwood Rd. Sunn 120 C3
Silwood. Brac 117 F1
Simkins Cl. Burl 92 A1
Simmonds Cl. Brac 117 F4
Simmonds St. Read 86 A4
Simmons Cl. Slough 44 A1
Simmons Rd. Hen-O-T 15 E2
Simms Farm La. Silc 136 C3
Simon's La. Woki 115 E4
Simons Cl. Pur O T 57 E2
Simons Wlk. Eng G 95 E1
Simpson Cl. Maid 40 A4
Sindlesham Rd. Arbo 114 C2
Singer La. Hen-O-T 15 F1
Singers Cl. Hen-O-T 35 F4
Sinhurst Rd. Camb 151 D2
Sipson Cl. Harm 71 D4
Sipson Rd. Harl 71 D4
Sipson Rd. Harm 71 D4
Sipson Way. Harm 71 D4
Sirius Cl. Woki 115 F3
Six Acre La. Ham 126 A4
Skeffling Way. Winn 87 F1
Skelmersdale Way. Winn 87 F2
Skerrit Way. Read 57 E2
Skillman Dr. That 106 C2
Skilton Rd. Read 57 E2
Skimpedhill La. Brac 118 A4
Skinners Green La. Ham M .. 130 A4
Skippons Cl. Newb 130 B3
Skydmore Path. Slough 21 F1
Skye Cl. Read 84 C2
Skyes Dr. Stai 97 D2
Skylings. Newb 105 E2
Skyport Dr. Harm 70 B4
Slaidburn Green. Brac 118 C1
Slanting Hill. Herm 79 D3
Sledmere Ct. Felt 98 C4
Slim Rd. Camb 151 D3
Sloan Ct. Gori 34 B3
Slopes The. Caver 59 E1
Slough Rd. Datch 68 A4
Slough Rd. Eton 42 C1
Slough Rd. Slough 42 C1
Slumburgh Way. Slough 42 C4
Smallmead Rd. Bur C 85 E1
Smallmead Rd. Read 86 A1
Smith Sq. Brac 118 B4
Smith's Hill. Let B 6 C3
Smith's La. Wind 66 C3
Smitham Bridge Rd. Hung .. 100 B3
Smithfield Cl. Whi Wa 39 D2
Smithfield Rd. Maid 39 D2
Smithy's Green. Windl 146 B2
Snape Spur. Slough 42 C4
Snipe La. Newt 131 F1
Snow's Paddock. Windl 146 A4
Snowball Hill. Whi Wa 64 A4
Snowberry Cl. Woki 115 F3
Snowden Cl. Wind 66 B2

Snowden Dr. Read 84 A3
Snowden Cl. That 106 B1
Snowdon Rd W. Harm 71 E1
Snowdon Rd. Harm 71 E1
Snowdrop Gr. Winn 88 B2
Snows Ride. Windl 146 A3
Soham Cl. Winn 114 B4
Soho Cres. Bou E 3 E2
Soke Rd. Alde 135 F2
Soke Rd. Silc 135 F2
Soldiers Rise. Brac 142 B4
Solent Rd. Stan 70 C1
Somerford Cl. Maid 40 A4
Somersby Cres. Maid 39 F2
Somerset Cl. Hung 100 B3
Somerset Cl. Woki 115 E3
Somerset Way. Iver 44 C2
Somerset Wlk. Read 84 A3
Somerton Gdns. Read 87 D1
Somerton Gr. That 106 B1
Somerville Cres. Yate 149 F3
Somerville Cl. Woki 115 E2
Somerville Rd. Eton 42 B1
Sonning La. Sonn 60 B1
Sonning Meadows. Sonn 60 B1
Sonninge Cl. Sand 150 B4
Sopwith Cl. Wood 88 A4
Sorrel Cl. Bur C 111 D2
Sorrel Cl. Newb 105 E3
Sorrel Cl. Woki 116 C4
Sorrel Dr. Light 152 C4
Sospel Ct. Far C 22 B2
South Ave. Hen-O-T 35 F4
South Ave. Stai 96 B1
South Cl. Medm 17 E4
South Cl. Slough 41 E3
South Cl. Woki 116 B2
South Dr. Read 86 C1
South Dr. Sonn 60 B1
South Dr. Sulhd 110 B4
South Dr. Went 122 A1
South Dr. Woki 116 B3
South End Rd. Brad 82 A1
South Gate Ave. Felt 98 B2
South Gr. Chert 123 F2
South Green. Slough 42 C3
South Hill Rd. Brac 118 A2
South Lake. Wood 87 F3
South Lynn Cres. Brac 118 A2
South Meadow La. Eton 67 E4
South Meadow. Crow 143 E2
South Path. Wind 67 E3
South Pl. Mar 117 F3
South Rd. Bis 153 F2
South Rd. Crow 143 F2
South Rd. Eng G 95 E1
South Rd. Maid 39 F3
South Row. Chil 10 B4
South St. Blew 12 A4
South St. Caver 59 D1
South St. Read 86 B4
South St. Stai 96 C2
South View Ave. Caver 59 E1
South View Park. Caver 59 E1
South View. Hung 100 B3
Southampton Cl. Black 150 B3
Southampton Rd. Stan 70 C1
Southampton St. Read 86 A3
Southampton Way. Stan 70 C1
Southbourne Dr. Bou E 3 D2
Southbury La. Twyf 61 F3
Southcote Ave. Felt 98 C3
Southcote Dr. Camb 152 A3
Southcote Farm La. Read .. 85 E2
Southcote La. Read 85 E2
Southcote Rd. Read 85 E3
Southcroft. Slough 22 A1
Southdown Rd. Caver 59 D3
Southdown Rd. Tad 135 D1
Southdown Rd. That 105 F2
Southend. That 106 B3
Southern Hill. Read 86 B3
Southern Perimeter Rd. Harm 71 E1
Southern Perimeter Rd. Stan .. 70 B1
Southern Rd. Camb 151 E3
Southerndene Cl. Read 57 E1
Southfield Gdns. Burn 41 D4
Southfields Ave. Ashf 98 A1
Southlands Cl. Woki 116 B3
Southlands Rd. Woki 116 B2
Southlea Rd. Datch 68 A3
Southside. Chert 124 A3
Southview Cl. Twyf 61 F3
Southview Rd. Mar 1 C2
Southville Cl. Felt 98 C4
Southville Cres. Felt 98 C4
Southville Rd. Felt 98 C4
Southwark Cl. Yate 149 E3
Southway. Camb 151 D2
Southwell Park Rd. Camb .. 151 E3
Southwick Ct. Brac 118 C2
Southwick. Bags 145 F1
Southwold Cl. Winn 87 E1
Southwold Spur. Slough 44 B2
Southwold. Brac 117 F1
Southwood Gdns. Bur C 111 D2
Southwood Gdns. Cook 19 F3
Southwood Rd. Cook 19 F3

Southwood. Woki 116 B2
Spackman Cl. That 106 B1
Spackmans Way. Slough 42 B2
Spade Oak Meadows. Bou E 2 C2
Span Hill. Caver 60 B4
Sparrow Cl. Woki 115 F3
Sparrowbill. Brig 28 C1
Sparvell Way. Camb 151 E3
Speedwell Way. That 106 C2
Speen Hill Cl. Newb 104 C2
Speen La. Newb 104 B2
Speen Lodge Ct. Newb 104 C2
Speen Pl. Newb 104 C2
Spelthorne Gr. Stai 98 C1
Spelthorne La. Stai 125 E4
Spencer Cl. Silc 135 F1
Spencer Cl. Woki 115 E3
Spencer Gdns. Eng G 95 E2
Spencer Rd. Brac 117 F4
Spencer Rd. Newb 130 B3
Spencer Rd. Read 113 D4
Spencer Rd. Slough 43 F2
Spencers Cl. Maid 39 E4
Spencers La. Cook 19 F3
Spencers Rd. Maid 39 E4
Spenwood Cl. Shin 113 D1
Sperling Rd. Maid 19 F1
Spey Rd. Read 85 D4
Spinfield La W. Mar 1 B1
Spinfield La. Mar 1 A1
Spinfield Mount. Mar 1 A1
Spinfield Park. Mar 1 B1
Spinis. Brac 117 F1
Spinner Green. Brac 118 A2
Spinners Wlk. Mar 1 B1
Spinners Wlk. Wind 67 E3
Spinney Cl. Caver 59 D4
Spinney Dr. Felt 98 B4
Spinney The. Camb 152 B3
Spinney The. Read 84 C2
Spinney The. Sunn 120 C2
Spinney The. Woki 141 F4
Spinney The. Yate 149 E4
Spinney. Slough 42 A3
Spinningwheel La. Binf 90 B4
Spitfire Way. Wood 88 A4
Spittal St. Mar 1 B1
Spode Cl. Read 84 C4
Spout La N. Stan 70 A2
Spout La. Stan 70 A2
Spray La. Brig 28 B1
Spray Rd. Ham 126 C2
Spray Rd. Ink 127 D2
Spriggs Cl. That 106 B1
Spring Ave. Eng G 95 F1
Spring Cl. Maid 19 F1
Spring Cl. Pangb 55 E3
Spring Gdns. Ascot 120 A3
Spring Gdns. Bou E 3 D2
Spring Gdns. Burl 92 C1
Spring Gdns. Camb 152 A3
Spring Gdns. Mar 1 C2
Spring Gdns. Shin 113 D1
Spring Gdns. Woo G 3 F4
Spring Gr. Read 86 A3
Spring Hill. Maid 39 F2
Spring La. Alde 135 E4
Spring La. Ast T 12 C4
Spring La. Caver 60 A3
Spring La. Cold A 106 B4
Spring La. Cook 19 E3
Spring La. Far C 22 B3
Spring La. Mort 137 D3
Spring La. Slough 41 F3
Spring La. Swal 139 D2
Spring Meadow. Brac 118 B4
Spring Meadows. Gr She 48 A2
Spring Rise. Eng G 95 F1
Spring Wlk. Warg 36 B1
Spring Wood La. Bur C 111 D1
Spring Woods. Sand 143 E1
Spring Woods. Vir W 122 A3
Springate Field. Slough 43 F2
Springcross Ave. Black 150 B2
Springdale. Read 87 D1
Springdale. Woki 141 F4
Springfield Cl. Wind 67 D3
Springfield End. Gori 34 B4
Springfield Gr. Shepp 125 F4
Springfield La. Newb 131 D4
Springfield Park. Holy 40 B1
Springfield Park. Twyf 61 F2
Springfield Rd. Ashf 97 F2
Springfield Rd. Binf 117 E4
Springfield Rd. Camb 152 A3
Springfield Rd. Silc 135 F1
Springfield Rd. Slough 69 D4
Springfield Rd. Wind 67 D3
Springfield. Light 153 E4
Springhill Rd. Gori 34 B4
Spruce Dr. Light 153 D4
Spruce Rd. Wood 88 A3
Spur The. Slough 41 E4
Spur The. Warg 36 C2
Spurcroft Rd. That 106 C1
Square The. Bags 145 F2
Square The. Harm 70 C4
Square The. Pangb 56 B3

Square The. Shin 113 D1
Squire's Bridge Rd. Stai 124 C3
Squires Rd. Stai 125 D3
Squires Wlk. Ashf 98 B1
Squirrel Cl. Sand 150 A4
Squirrel Rise. Mar B 1 B3
Squirrels Drey. Crow 142 C3
Squirrels Way. Read 87 D1
Stable Cl. Bur C 111 D2
Stable Croft. Bags 145 E1
Stable Ct. Newb 105 D3
Stable View. Yate 149 E4
Stables Ct. Mar 1 A1
Staddlestone Cl. Read 57 E1
Stadium Way. Read 58 A1
Staff College Rd. Camb 151 D3
Staff College Rd. Sand 151 D3
Stafferton Way. Maid 40 A3
Stafford Ave. Slough 22 B1
Stafford Cl. Burn 41 D4
Stafford Cl. Wood 87 F4
Stafford Lake. Bis 153 F1
Staffordshire Cl. Read 57 F1
Staffordshire Croft. New G .. 91 F1
Stag Hill. Chil F 73 D1
Stainash Cres. Stai 97 D2
Stainash Par. Stai 97 D2
Staines By-Pass. Stai 97 E2
Staines La. Chert 124 A2
Staines Lane Cl. Chert 123 F2
Staines Rd W. Ashf 98 B1
Staines Rd. Felt 98 A4
Staines Rd. Stai 123 F2
Staines Rd. Wray 95 F4
Stainford Cl. Ashf 98 B2
Stamford Ave. Camb 151 F1
Stamford Rd. Maid 39 E3
Stanbrook Cl. Brad 82 A1
Stanfield. Tad 135 D1
Stanham Rd. Read 84 C4
Stanhope Heath. Stan 70 B1
Stanhope Rd. Read 86 B2
Stanhope Rd. Sand 150 C2
Stanhope Rd. Slough 41 E4
Stanhope Way. Stan 70 B1
Stanlake La. Twyf 61 F2
Stanley Cl. Mar 1 C2
Stanley Cotts. Slough 42 C3
Stanley Gr. Read 85 F4
Stanley Green E. Slough 43 F1
Stanley Green W. Slough 43 F1
Stanley Rd. Ashf 97 F2
Stanley Rd. Newb 105 D1
Stanley Rd. Woki 116 C3
Stanley St. Read 85 F4
Stanmore Cl. Ascot 120 A3
Stanmore Gdns. Mort 136 C3
Stanmore Rd. Beed 30 B1
Stanmore Rd. East I 30 C4
Stanshawe Rd. Read 86 A4
Stanstead Rd. Stan 70 C1
Stanton Cl. Read 87 E2
Stanton Way. Slough 43 F1
Stanwell Cl. Stan 70 B1
Stanwell Gdns. Stan 70 B1
Stanwell Moor Rd. Harm 70 A2
Stanwell Moor Rd. Stan 70 A2
Stanwell New Rd. Stai 97 D3
Stanwell Rd. Ashf 97 F2
Stanwell Rd. Felt 71 D1
Stanwell Rd. Felt 98 A4
Stanwell Rd. Hort 69 E2
Stanwell Rd. Stan 69 E2
Stapleford Rd. Read 85 E2
Staplehurst. Brac 117 F1
Stapleton Cl. Mar 1 C2
Stapleton Cl. Newb 130 B3
Star La. Know H 37 F2
Star La. Read 86 A4
Star Post Rd. Camb 151 F4
Star Rd. Caver 59 E1
Starling Cl. Woki 115 F3
Starlings Dr. Read 84 A3
Starmead Dr. Woki 116 C3
Starting Gates. Newb 105 E1
Startins La. Cook 19 E4
Starwood Ct. Slough 43 E2
Statham Ct. Brac 117 F4
Station App. Ashf 97 F2
Station App. Mar 1 C1
Station App. Read 86 A4
Station App. Shepp 125 E2
Station App. Stai 97 D2
Station App. Vir W 122 B3
Station Cres. Ashf 97 F2
Station Hill. Ascot 120 A3
Station Hill. Cook 19 F4
Station Hill. Read 86 A4
Station Par. Vir W 122 B3
Station Rd. Ashf 97 F2
Station Rd. Bags 145 F2
Station Rd. Ball H 130 A2
Station Rd. Bou E 3 D2
Station Rd. Brac 118 A4
Station Rd. Camb 151 E1
Station Rd. Chert 124 A1
Station Rd. Cook 19 F4
Station Rd. East G 47 E3
Station Rd. Eng G 96 A2
Station Rd. Gori 34 B3

Station Rd. Gr She 48 A2
Station Rd. Hen-O-T 15 F1
Station Rd. Hung 100 B3
Station Rd. Kint 102 A1
Station Rd. Lamb 25 D1
Station Rd. Mar 1 C1
Station Rd. Newb 104 B3
Station Rd. Newb 105 D1
Station Rd. Pangb 56 B3
Station Rd. Read 86 A4
Station Rd. Read 87 E2
Station Rd. Shepp 125 E2
Station Rd. Shipl 36 A2
Station Rd. Slough 41 F4
Station Rd. Slough 44 A2
Station Rd. Sunn 121 D2
Station Rd. Tapl 40 C4
Station Rd. That 106 C1
Station Rd. Twyf 61 E2
Station Rd. Warg 36 B1
Station Rd. Woki 116 A3
Station Rd. Wool 108 B1
Station Rd. Wray 69 D1
Station Rise. Mar 117 F3
Staunton Rd. Slough 42 B4
Staveley Rd. Ashf 98 B1
Staverton Cl. Brac 91 D1
Staverton Cl. Woki 116 C3
Staverton Rd. Read 86 B2
Stayne End. Went 122 A3
Steam Farm La. Harm 71 F2
Steeple Wlk. Read 113 F4
Steerforth Copse. Crow 143 F1
Stepgates. Chert 124 A1
Stephen Cl. Stai 96 B1
Stephen Rd. Mort 136 C3
Stephen's Cl. Mort 136 C3
Stephens Firs. Mort 136 C3
Stephenson Cl. That 106 B2
Stephenson Rd. Bark 141 D4
Stephenson Rd. Wind 67 D4
Sterling Way. Read 58 A1
Stevens Hill. Yate 149 F3
Stevenson Dr. Binf 90 B2
Stewart Ave. Slough 42 C4
Stewart Ave. Stai 125 D3
Stewart Cl. Holy 65 E3
Stewarts Dr. Far C 22 A4
Stewarts Way. Mar B 1 B4
Stile Rd. Slough 43 E2
Stilton Cl. Winn 87 F1
Stilwell Cl. Yate 149 F3
Stirling Cl. Camb 151 F1
Stirling Cl. Caver 59 E3
Stirling Cl. Wind 66 B3
Stirling Rd. Slough 42 A4
Stirling Rd. Stan 70 C1
Stockbridge Way. Yate 149 E2
Stockbury Cl. Read 87 D1
Stockdales Rd. Eton 41 F1
Stockton Rd. Read 86 B1
Stockwells. Tapl 20 B1
Stockwood Rise. Camb 151 F3
Stoke Common Rd. Fulm 23 D4
Stoke Common Rd. Sto P 23 D4
Stoke Court Dr. Sto P 22 C2
Stoke Gdns. Slough 42 C3
Stoke Green. Sto P 23 D1
Stoke Park Ave. Far C 22 C4
Stoke Poges La. Slough 42 C4
Stoke Rd. Slough 42 C4
Stoke Wood. Sto P 22 C4
Stokeford Cl. Brac 118 C2
Stokes View. Pangb 56 B3
Stokesay. Slough 42 C3
Stokesley Rise. Woo G 3 F4
Stomp Rd. Burn 21 E1
Stomp Rd. Burn 41 D4
Stomp Rd. Slough 41 D4
Stompits Rd. Holy 65 E4
Stone Cres. Felt 98 C4
Stone House La. Cook 2 B1
Stone St. Read 58 A1
Stonea Cl. Winn 114 B4
Stonecroft Ave. Iver 44 C4
Stonefield Park. Maid 39 E4
Stonegate. Camb 152 B3
Stoneham Cl. Read 85 D3
Stonehaven Dr. Wood 88 A3
Stonehill Rd. Light 146 A1
Stonehouse Rise. Camb 151 F1
Stoneleigh Ct. Camb 151 F1
Stoney Cl. Yate 149 E2
Stoney La. Burn 22 A2
Stoney La. Cold A 105 E3
Stoney La. Newb 105 E3
Stoney La. That 106 C2
Stoney Meade. Slough 42 A3
Stoney Rd. Brac 118 A4
Stoney Ware Cl. Bish 18 C4
Stoney Ware. Bish 18 C4
Stoneyfield. Been 109 D3
Stoneyland Ct. Eng G 95 F2
Stoneylands Rd. Eng G 95 F2
Stookes Way. Yate 149 D2
Stour Cl. Read 85 D4
Stour Cl. Slough 42 A2
Stovell Rd. Wind 67 D4
Stowe Rd. Slough 41 F3

Straight Bit. Fla H 3 D4
Straight La. Lamb 46 C3
Straight Mile The. Hurst 89 E3
Straight Mile The. W St L 62 C1
Straight Rd. Old W 68 A1
Strand La. Cook 19 F3
Strand Way. Wood 87 E1
Stranraer Rd. Stan 70 C1
Stratfield Rd. Slough 43 D2
Stratfield. Brac 117 F1
Stratford Dr. Bou E 3 E2
Stratford Gdns. Maid 39 E2
Stratford Rd. Harm 71 E1
Stratford Way. Read 84 A3
Strathcona Cl. Fla H 3 E4
Strathcona Way. Fla H 3 E4
Strathearn Ave. Harl 71 F4
Stratheden Pl. Read 85 F4
Strathmore Dr. Char 61 D2
Strathy Cl. Read 85 D4
Stratton Gdns. Read 86 B1
Stratton Rd. Shepp 125 F4
Strawberry Hill. New G 91 F1
Strawberry Hill. Newb 104 C2
Streatley & Goring Bridge. Gori 34 A3
Streatley Hill. Stre 33 F3
Street The. Alde 135 D4
Street The. Brad 83 D3
Street The. Mort 137 E3
Street The. Moul 14 A3
Street The. Sou S 14 A2
Street The. Swal 139 E4
Street The. Tidm 56 B1
Street The. W St L 63 D3
Streets Heath. West E 153 F4
Stretton Cl. Brad 82 A1
Strode Cl. Eng G 96 A2
Strode's Cres. Stai 97 E2
Stroller Cl. That 105 F2
Strongrove Hill. Hung 100 B3
Stroud Cl. Wind 66 B2
Stroud Farm Rd. Holy 65 D4
Stroud Way. Ashf 98 A1
Stroude Rd. Vir W 122 C3
Stroude Rd. Vir W 123 D4
Strouds Meadow. Cold A 106 B4
Strouds The. Been 108 C3
Stuart Cl. Caver 59 D3
Stuart Cl. Wind 66 C3
Stuart Rd. Newb 130 B3
Stuart Way. Stai 97 D1
Stuart Way. Vir W 122 A3
Stuart Way. Wind 66 C3
Stubbles La. Cook 19 D3
Stubbs Folly. Sand 150 B4
Studios Rd. Stai 124 C3
Studland Cl. Read 113 E4
Sturbridge Cl. Wood 87 E1
Sturdee Dr. Camb 151 F1
Sturges Rd. Woki 116 B3
Sturt Green. Holy 64 C4
Styventon Pl. Chert 123 F1
Suck's La. Asham 54 B2
Suffolk Cl. Slough 41 F4
Suffolk Cl. Woki 115 E3
Suffolk Rd. Maid 39 E2
Suffolk Rd. Read 85 E4
Suffork Cl. Bags 145 F1
Sulham La. Pangb 56 C2
Sulham La. Pur O T 56 C2
Sulham La. Sulh 56 C2
Sulham Wlk. Read 85 D2
Sulhamstead Hill. Sulhd 110 B3
Sulhamstead La. Sulhd 110 B2
Sulhamstead Rd. Bur 111 D3
Sulhamstead Rd. Sulhd 111 D3
Sullivan Rd. Camb 151 D3
Summer Gdns. Camb 152 B3
Summerfield Cl. Woki 88 C1
Summerfield Rise. Gori 34 B4
Summerhouse La. Harm 70 B4
Summerlea. Slough 42 A3
Summerleaze Rd. Maid 20 A1
Summers Rd. Burn 21 E1
Summit Cl. Woki 141 F4
Sun Gdns. Bur C 111 D1
Sun La. Maid 39 F4
Sun La. Swal 139 D1
Sun Pas. Wind 67 E3
Sun Ray Estate. Sand 150 A4
Sun St. Read 86 B4
Sunbury Cres. Felt 98 C3
Sunbury Rd. Eton 67 E4
Sunbury Rd. Felt 98 C3
Sunderland Cl. Wood 88 A4
Sunderland Rd. Maid 39 D4
Sundew Cl. Camb 153 E4
Sundew Cl. Woki 116 C4
Sundon Cres. Went 122 B2
Sundown Rd. Ashf 98 B2
Sunley Cl. Newb 130 B3
Sunning Ave. Sunn 120 C1
Sunninghill Cl. Ascot 120 B3
Sunninghill Rd. Ascot 120 B3
Sunninghill Rd. Windl 146 A4
Sunninghill Rd. Wink 93 E1
Sunnybank. Mar 1 B2

Sunnyside. Newb 104 C3
Surbiton Rd. Camb 145 D1
Surley Row. Caver 59 D3
Surly Hall Wlk. Wind 66 C3
Surrey Ave. Camb 151 D2
Surrey Ave. Slough 22 B1
Surrey Rd. Read 86 A2
Surridge Ct. Bags 145 F1
Sussex Cl. Slough 43 D2
Sussex Gdns. Wood 87 F4
Sussex La. Shin 113 E1
Sussex Pl. Slough 43 D2
Sutcliffe Ave. Read 87 E2
Sutherland Ave. Shepp 125 F4
Sutherland Chase. Ascot 119 F4
Sutherland Gdns. Shepp 125 F4
Sutherland Gr. Read 84 C2
Sutherlands Ave. Read 86 B3
Sutherlands. Newb 130 C4
Sutton Ave. Slough 43 E2
Sutton Cl. Cook 20 A4
Sutton Cl. Maid 39 E3
Sutton La. Slough 44 B1
Sutton Pl. Slough 69 D4
Sutton Rd. Camb 145 D1
Sutton Rd. Cook 20 A3
Sutton Rd. Newb 104 B3
Sutton Wlk. Read 86 B3
Suttons Park Ave. Read 86 C4
Swabey Rd. Slough 44 A1
Swainstone Rd. Read 86 A3
Swaledale. Brac 118 A2
Swallow Cl. Read 84 B3
Swallow Cl. Stai 96 C2
Swallow Cl. Yate 149 D3
Swallow St. Iver 44 B4
Swallow Way. Woki 115 F3
Swallowfield Dr. Read 113 E3
Swallowfield Gdns. Thea 83 F2
Swallowfield Rd. Arbo 114 B1
Swallowfield. Eng G 95 D1
Swan La. Sand 150 A4
Swan Pl. Read 86 A4
Swan Rd. Iver 44 C4
Swancote Green. Brac 118 A2
Swangate. Hung 100 B4
Swanholm Gdns. Read 84 C2
Swanmore Cl. Winn 87 F1
Swanscourt. Twyf 61 F2
Swansdown Wlk. That 106 A2
Swansea Rd. Harm 71 E1
Swansea Rd. Read 59 D1
Swansea Terr. Read 57 E1
Swanston Field. Whi-O-T 56 B4
Sweeps La. Eng G 95 F2
Sweet Briar Dr. Bur C 84 B2
Sweetbriar. Brac 143 D4
Sweetzer's Piece. Silc 136 C3
Swepstone Cl. Read 87 E1
Swift Cl. Woki 115 F3
Swift La. Windl 145 F2
Swinbrook Cl. Read 57 E2
Swindon Rd. Harm 71 E1
Swinley Rd. Brac 119 E2
Swiss Cottage Cl. Read 84 B4
Switchback Cl. Maid 19 E1
Switchback Rd N. Cook 19 E1
Switchback Rd N. Maid 19 F2
Switchback Rd S. Maid 19 E1
Switchback Rd. Cook 19 F2
Switchback The. Maid 19 E1
Sycamore Cl. Bur C 111 D2
Sycamore Cl. Camb 151 F1
Sycamore Cl. Sand 150 A4
Sycamore Cl. Wood 87 E3
Sycamore Ct. Wind 67 E2
Sycamore Dr. Camb 151 F1
Sycamore Dr. Mar B 1 B1
Sycamore Dr. Twyf 61 E3
Sycamore Rd. Read 86 C1
Sycamore Rise. Brac 118 B3
Sycamore Rise. Newb 105 E3
Sycamore Wlk. Eng G 95 D1
Sycamore Wlk. Slough 43 F4
Sycamores The. Black 150 A3
Sydings The. Newb 104 B3
Sydney Cl. Brac 143 E4
Sydney Cres. Ashf 98 A1
Sydney Gr. Slough 42 B4
Syke Cluan. Iver 44 C2
Syke Ings. Iver 44 C2
Sykes Rd. Slough 42 A4
Sylvan Ridge. Sand 143 D1
Sylvan Wlk. Read 85 E2
Sylvanus. Brac 117 F1
Sylverns Ct. New G 91 F1
Sylvester Cl. Newb 104 C3
Sylvester Rd. Maid 19 F1
Symondson Mews. Binf 90 B2
Sympson Rd. Tad 135 E1

Tachbrook Rd. Felt 98 C4
Tadcroft Wlk. Read 84 C2
Tadham Pl. That 106 B1
Tadley Common Rd. Tad 135 E1
Tadmor Cl. Shepp 125 F3
Taff Way. Read 85 D4
Tag La. Warg 37 D1
Talbot Ave. Slough 43 F2

Talbot Cl. Caver 59 E1
Talbot Cl. Newb 104 C3
Talbot Ct. Read 86 A4
Talbot Pl. Bags 145 F2
Talbot Pl. Datch 68 B3
Talbot Rd. Ashf 97 F2
Talbot Way. Sulh 57 E2
Talbots Dr. Maid 39 D3
Talfourd Ave. Read 87 D3
Talisman Cl. Woki 142 B3
Tall Trees. Stan 69 F3
Tallis La. Read 85 E2
Tamar Gdns. Read 86 B2
Tamar Way. Woki 115 F4
Tamar Way. Slough 44 A1
Tamarind Way. Read 86 C1
Tamarisk Ave. Read 86 C1
Tamarisk Rise. Woki 116 B4
Tamarisk Way. Slough 42 A2
Tamworth Cl. Wood 87 E1
Tamworth. Brac 118 B1
Tandem. Brac 117 E4
Tangier La. Eton 67 E4
Tanglewood Ride. West E 153 F4
Tanglewood. Woki 142 A4
Tangley Dr. Brac 116 A2
Tanglyn Ave. Stai 125 D2
Tanhouse La. Woki 116 A3
Tank Rd. Sand 150 C3
Tanner Ct. Newb 105 D2
Tanners La. Maple 58 C4
Tanners Yd. Bags 145 F2
Tape La. Hurst 88 C4
Taplow Common Rd. Burn 21 D2
Taplow Common Rd. Tapl 21 D2
Taplow Rd. Burn 41 D4
Tarbat Ct. Sand 150 B4
Tarbay La. Oak G 66 B2
Target Cl. Felt 71 F1
Targett Ct. Winn 88 A1
Tarleton Cl. Read 84 C3
Tarmac Way. Harm 70 A4
Tarn La. Newb 130 C4
Tarnbrook Way. Brac 118 C1
Tarragon Cl. Read 86 C1
Tarragon Way. Bur C 111 D2
Tarrants Hill. Hung 100 B3
Tasker Cl. Harl 71 E4
Tatchbrook Cl. Maid 40 A4
Tattersall Cl. Woki 116 C3
Tavistock Cl. Maid 39 D4
Tavistock Cl. Stai 97 E1
Tavistock Rd. Read 86 A2
Tawfield. Brac 117 F1
Tay Rd. Read 85 D4
Taylor's Cl. Mar 1 C1
Tazewell Cl. Read 85 F3
Tebbit Cl. Brac 118 B4
Teesdale Rd. Slough 41 F4
Tekels Ave. Camb 151 E2
Tekels Way. Camb 151 F2
Telford Cres. Wood 60 C1
Telford Dr. Slough 42 A2
Telston Cl. Bou E 3 D3
Tempest Rd. Stai 96 B1
Templar Cl. Sand 150 A4
Templars Pl. Mar 1 C1
Temple Gdns. Stai 123 F4
Temple La. Bish 18 B3
Temple Mill Island. Bish 18 B3
Temple Park. Hurl 17 F2
Temple Pl. Read 86 A3
Temple Rd. Wind 67 E3
Temple Way. Binf 90 C1
Temple Way. Brac 117 F4
Temple Way. Far C 22 B4
Templecroft. Ashf 98 B1
Templedene Ave. Stai 97 E1
Templeton Gdns. Read 86 B1
Templewood La. Far C 22 B4
Ten Acre La. Stai 123 E4
Tenaplas Dr. Upp B 54 C3
Tenby Ave. Caver 59 E3
Tenby Dr. Ascot 120 B2
Tennyson Rd. Ashf 97 F2
Tennyson Rd. That 106 B2
Tennyson Rd. Wood 87 F2
Tennyson Way. Slough 21 F1
Tern Cl. Read 85 D3
Terrace Rd N. Binf 90 B2
Terrace Rd S. Binf 90 B1
Terrace The. Ascot 120 B2
Terrace The. Crow 143 E3
Terrace The. Maid 40 B2
Terrace The. Woki 116 A3
Terrington Hill. Mar 1 B1
Terry's La. Cook 19 F4
Tesimond Dr. Yate 149 D3
Tessa Rd. Read 58 C1
Test Cl. Read 85 D4
Testwood Rd. Wind 66 B3
Teviot Rd. Read 84 C4
Thakerays The. That 106 B1
Thames Ave. Chert 124 A3
Thames Ave. Pangb 56 B3
Thames Ave. Read 59 D1
Thames Ave. Wind 67 E4
Thames Cl. Bou E 3 D2
Thames Cl. Chert 124 B1

Thames Cres. Maid 20 A1
Thames Dr. Char 60 C4
Thames Ind Est. Mar 1 C1
Thames Mead. Wind 66 C3
Thames Rd. Gori 34 A3
Thames Rd. Slough 44 A2
Thames Rd. That 106 A3
Thames Reach. Medm 17 E4
Thames Reach. Pur O T 55 E3
Thames Side Prom. Read 59 D1
Thames Side. Chert 124 B1
Thames Side. Hen-O-T 15 F1
Thames Side. Read 59 D1
Thames Side. Stai 96 C1
Thames Side. Wind 67 E4
Thames St. Shepp 125 F1
Thames St. Sonn 60 B2
Thames St. Stai 96 C2
Thames St. Wind 67 E4
Thamesfield Ct. Shepp 125 E1
Thamesfield Gdns. Mar 1 C1
Thanington Way. Read 87 D1
Thatchers Dr. Maid 39 D3
Theal Cl. Sand 150 B4
Theale Rd. Bur C 111 E3
Theobald Dr. Read 57 E2
Theobalds Way. Camb 152 B2
Thetford Mews. Caver 59 E3
Thetford Rd. Ashf 97 F3
Thibet Rd. Sand 150 B4
Thicket Gr. Maid 38 C4
Thicket Rd. Read 84 C4
Thickthorne La. Stai 97 E1
Third Ave. Mar 1 C1
Third Cres. Slough 42 B4
Thirkleby Cl. Slough 42 B3
Thirlmere Ave. Read 57 F1
Thirlmere Ave. Slough 41 E4
Thirlmere Cl. Stai 96 A1
Thirtover. Cold A 79 D1
Thistledown. Read 57 E1
Thistleton Way. Winn 87 F1
Thomas Dr. New G 91 F1
Thomas La. Woki 141 F4
Thomas Rd. Bou E 3 E2
Thompkins La. Burn 22 A3
Thompson Cl. Herm 78 C3
Thompson Cl. Slough 44 A1
Thompson Dr. That 106 C1
Thomson Wlk. Bur C 84 C2
Thone Cl. Brac 143 D4
Thorburn Chase. Sand 150 B3
Thorn Dr. Slough 43 F4
Thorn La. Read 86 A4
Thorn St. Read 86 A4
Thornaby Pl. Woo G 3 F4
Thornbank Cl. Stan 70 A1
Thornbers Way. Char 61 D3
Thornbridge Rd. Read 113 D4
Thornbury Cl. Crow 143 D3
Thorncroft. Eng G 95 E1
Thorndike. Slough 42 A4
Thorndown La. Windl 146 B2
Thorndown La. Windl 146 B2
Thorne Cl. Stai 98 B1
Thorne Cl. Woki 115 E2
Thorney Cl. Winn 87 F1
Thorney La N. Iver 44 C3
Thorney La S. Iver 44 C3
Thornfield Green. Black 150 C2
Thornfield. Head 132 B2
Thornford Rd. Gree 132 B2
Thornford Rd. Head 132 C2
Thornford Rd. That 132 B2
Thornhill Way. Stai 125 D2
Thornhill. Brac 118 C3
Thorningdown. Chil 10 B4
Thornton Mews. Read 85 E4
Thornton Rd. Read 85 E4
Thorp Cl. Binf 90 B2
Thorpe By Pass. Stai 123 D3
Thorpe Cl. Woki 116 A2
Thorpe Lea Rd. Stai 96 A1
Thorpe Rd. Chert 123 E2
Thorpe Rd. Stai 96 B2
Thorpe Rd. Stai 123 E2
Thrale Mews. Read 85 D4
Three Acre Rd. Newb 130 C4
Three Firs Way. Bur C 110 C1
Three Gables La. Stre 34 A4
Three Post La. Lamb 25 D1
Threshfield. Brac 118 A2
Thrift La. Holy 64 B4
Throgmorton Rd. Yate 149 D3
Thrush Cl. Bur C 111 D2
Thurlby Way. Maid 39 E2
Thurlestone Cl. Shepp 125 E2
Thurlestone Gdns. Read 86 B1
Thurnscoe Cl. Read 113 F4
Thurso Cl. Read 85 D4
Thurston Rd. Slough 42 C4
Thyme Cl. Read 87 D1
Tichborne Cl. Black 150 B3
Tichbourne Cl. Camb 151 F2
Tickenor Dr. Woki 141 F4
Tickhill Cl. Read 113 F4
Tidmarsh La. Pangb 56 A1
Tidmarsh La. Tidm 56 A1
Tidmarsh Rd. Pangb 56 B2

Tidmarsh Rd. Tidm 56 B2
Tidmarsh St. Read 58 A1
Tiffany Cl. Woki 115 E3
Tiger Cl. Wood 88 A4
Tigerseye Cl. Woki 115 E4
Tilbury Cl. Caver 59 E2
Tile Barn Row. Ball H 129 F1
Tilecotes Cl. Mar 1 B1
Tilehurst La. Binf 90 B2
Tilehurst Rd. Read 85 E4
Tilling Cl. Read 57 D1
Tilly's La. Stai 96 C2
Tilney Way. Read 113 F4
Tilstone Ave. Eton 41 F1
Tilstone Cl. Eton 41 F1
Timbers Wlk. Maid 39 D3
Timline Green. Brac 118 C4
Timsway. Stai 96 C2
Tindal Cl. Yate 149 E3
Tinkers Cl. Wind 66 B3
Tinkers La. Windl 121 D2
Tinsey Cl. Stai 96 A2
Tinsley Cl. Read 113 F4
Tintagel Dr. Camb 151 F1
Tintagel Rd. Brac 142 A4
Tintern Cl. Slough 42 B2
Tintern Cres. Read 85 F3
Tinwell Cl. Winn 87 F1
Tippett Rise. Read 86 A3
Tippings La. Wood 88 A4
Tippits Mead. Brac 117 E4
Tiptree Cl. Read 113 F4
Titcombe Way. Kint 102 A1
Tite Hill. Eng G 95 E2
Tithe Barn Dr. Holy 40 B1
Tithe Cl. Holy 40 B1
Tithe Ct. Slough 44 A1
Tithe La. Wray 69 D1
Tithe Meadows. Went 122 B2
Tithebarn Gr. Read 84 C2
Titlarks Hill Rd. Went 121 D1
Tiverton Cl. Wood 60 C1
Toad La. Black 150 C2
Tockley Rd. Burn 21 D1
Tofrek Terr. Read 85 E4
Tokers Green Rd. Maple 58 C4
Tokersgreen La. Caver 58 B3
Tokersgreen La. Maple 58 B3
Toll Gdns. Brac 118 C3
Tollgate. Maid 39 D3
Tolpuddle Way. Yate 149 F3
Tomlin Cl. That 106 C1
Tomlin Rd. Slough 21 F1
Tomlins Ave. Camb 151 F1
Tomlinson Dr. Brac 142 A4
Top Common. New G 91 F1
Topaz Cl. Slough 42 A3
Topaz Cl. Woki 115 F4
Tope Cres. Bark 140 C4
Tope Rd. Bark 140 C4
Torcross Gr. Bur C 84 A2
Torin Cl. Eng G 95 E2
Torquay Spur. Slough 22 A1
Torridge Rd. Slough 69 D4
Torrington Rd. Read 86 B1
Toseland Way. Winn 87 F2
Totnes Rd. Read 86 B1
Tottenham Wlk. Crow 143 E1
Totterdown. Bur C 110 C1
Toutley Cl. Woki 88 C1
Toutley Rd. Woki 89 D1
Tower Cl. Caver 59 E4
Tower Cl. Fla H 3 E4
Tower Hill. Chadd 49 D4
Towers Dr. Crow 143 D2
Town Farm Way. Stan 97 E4
Town La. Bou E 3 E2
Town La. Stan 70 B1
Town La. Stan 97 E4
Town Sq. Brac 118 B4
Town Square. Camb 151 E3
Town Tree Rd. Ashf 98 A2
Townsend Cl. Brac 118 C2
Townsend Rd. Aldw 32 C2
Townsend Rd. Ashf 97 F2
Townsend Rd. Stre 34 A4
Towpath. Shepp 124 C1
Tozer Wlk. Wind 66 B2
Trafalgar Cl. Woki 115 F3
Trafalgar Ct. Read 85 F3
Trafalgar Way. Sand 150 C2
Trafford Rd. Read 58 C1
Travic Rd. Slough 21 F1
Travis Ct. Slough 22 A1
Travis La. Sand 150 B4
Tredegar Rd. Caver 59 D3
Tree Cl. Read 84 B4
Tree Tops Ave. Camb 152 A4
Trees Rd. Bou E 3 D2
Treesmill Dr. Maid 39 E2
Treeton Cl. Read 113 F4
Trefoil Cl. Woki 116 C4
Trelawney Ave. Slough 43 F2
Trelawney Dr. Read 57 E1
Trelleck Rd. Read 85 F3
Tremayne Wlk. Camb 152 B2
Trenchard Rd. Holy 65 D4
Trenches La. Slough 44 A3
Trent Cl. Woki 115 F4

Trent Cres. That ... 106 A3
Trent Rd. Slough ... 69 D4
Trenton Cl. Camb ... 152 A1
Tresham Cres. Yate ... 149 D3
Trevelyan. Brac ... 117 F1
Triangle The. Read ... 84 B4
Trindledown. Brac ... 91 D1
Tring Rd. Read ... 57 E1
Trinity Ave. Mar ... 1 B2
Trinity Cl. Stan ... 70 B1
Trinity Cl. Sunn ... 121 D2
Trinity Pl. Read ... 85 F4
Trinity Pl. Wind ... 67 E3
Trinity Rd. Mar ... 1 B1
Trinity. Crow ... 143 F1
Triumph Cl. Harl ... 71 E3
Trotsworth Ave. Vir W ... 122 C3
Trotwood Cl. Crow ... 143 F1
Trout Cl. Mar ... 18 B4
Trout Wlk. Newb ... 105 E2
Troutbeck Cl. Twyf ... 61 E3
Trowe's La. Bee H ... 138 B2
Trowe's La. Swal ... 139 E3
Trumbull Rd. Brac ... 91 D1
Trumps Green Cl. Vir W ... 122 C2
Trumps Mill La. Went ... 122 C2
Trumpsgreen Ave. Went ... 122 B2
Trumpsgreen Rd. Went ... 122 B2
Truro Cl. Maid ... 39 D4
Truss Hill Rd. Ascot ... 120 B2
Trust Cnr. Hen-O-T ... 35 F4
Trusthorpe Cl. Winn ... 87 F1
Tubbs Farm Cl. Lamb ... 25 D1
Tubwell Rd. Sto P ... 23 D2
Tudor Cl. Ashf ... 97 F2
Tudor Cl. Woki ... 116 C3
Tudor Dr. Yate ... 149 E2
Tudor Gdns. Slough ... 41 E4
Tudor La. Old W ... 95 E4
Tudor Rd. Ashf ... 98 B1
Tudor Rd. Newb ... 105 D1
Tudor Rd. Read ... 86 A4
Tudor Way. Wind ... 66 C3
Tunnel Link Rd. Stan ... 71 D1
Tunnel Rd E. Harm ... 71 D3
Tunnel Rd W. Harm ... 71 D3
Tuns Hill Cotts. Read ... 87 D3
Tuns La. Hen-O-T ... 15 F1
Tuns La. Slough ... 42 B2
Tupsley Rd. Read ... 85 F3
Turf Hill Rd. Camb ... 151 F4
Turk's La. Silc ... 137 D2
Turnberry. Brac ... 117 F1
Turnbridge Cl. Read ... 114 A4
Turner Pl. Sand ... 150 B3
Turner Rd. Slough ... 43 E2
Turners Cl. Stai ... 97 D2
Turners Dr. That ... 106 C1
Turnery The. That ... 106 B2
Turnfields. That ... 106 B2
Turnoak Park. Wind ... 66 C2
Turnpike Rd. Brac ... 117 F4
Turnpike Rd. Newb ... 105 F2
Turnpike Rd. That ... 105 F2
Turnstone Cl. Winn ... 88 A2
Turnstone End. Yate ... 149 D3
Turnville Cl. Light ... 146 A1
Turpin Rd. Felt ... 71 F1
Turpins Gr. Maid ... 39 D4
Turpins Rise. Windl ... 146 A3
Turton Way. Slough ... 42 B2
Tuscam Way. Sand ... 150 C2
Tuscan Cl. Read ... 57 F1
Tuxford Mews. Read ... 85 D4
Tweed Ct. Read ... 85 D4
Tweed Rd. Slough ... 69 D4
Twin Oaks. Caver ... 59 D3
Twinches La. Slough ... 42 A3
Two Tree Hill. Hen-O-T ... 35 D4
Twyford Rd. Binf ... 89 D1
Twyford Rd. Maid ... 90 B4
Twyford Rd. W St L ... 62 C3
Twynham Rd. Maid ... 39 D4
Tyberton Pl. Read ... 85 F3
Tydehams. Newb ... 130 C4
Tyle Pl. Old W ... 68 A1
Tyle Rd. Read ... 84 B4
Tyler Cl. Caver ... 58 C3
Tyler's La. Buck ... 80 A1
Tylers Pl. Read ... 84 C4
Tyne Way. That ... 106 A3
Tyrell Gdns. Wind ... 66 C2
Tytherton. Brac ... 118 B4

Uffington Cl. Read ... 84 B4
Uffington Dr. Brac ... 118 C3
Uffcott Cl. Maid ... 113 F4
Ullswater Cl. Light ... 146 A1
Ullswater Cl. Slough ... 41 E4
Ullswater Cl. That ... 106 A3
Ullswater Dr. Caver ... 57 E2
Ullswater Rd. Light ... 146 A1
Ullswater. Brac ... 117 F1
Ulster Cl. Caver ... 59 E3
Umberville Way. Slough ... 21 F1
Underhill Cl. Maid ... 39 F3
Underhill. Moul ... 14 A2

Underwood Rd. Read ... 85 D2
Underwood. Brac ... 117 F2
Union Cl. Sand ... 143 F1
Union Rd. Brad ... 82 B2
Union St. Read ... 86 A4
Unity Cl. Caver ... 59 D3
Unwin Ave. Harm ... 71 E1
Upavon Dr. Read ... 85 F3
Upavon Gdns. Brac ... 118 C2
Upcroft. Wind ... 67 D2
Updown Hill. Windl ... 146 B2
Upland Rd. Camb ... 151 E4
Uplands Cl. Sand ... 150 A4
Uplands Rd. Caver ... 58 C3
Uplands. Hung ... 100 B3
Uplands. Mar B ... 1 B3
Upper Bray Rd. Maid ... 40 B2
Upper Broadmoor Rd. Crow ... 143 E3
Upper Charles St. Camb ... 151 E3
Upper Chobham Rd. Camb ... 152 A2
Upper College Ride. Camb ... 151 F4
Upper Crown St. Read ... 86 A3
Upper End. Chadd ... 49 D4
Upper Gordon Rd. Camb ... 151 E3
Upper Halliford Rd. Shepp ... 125 F3
Upper Lambourn Rd. Lamb ... 25 D2
Upper Lees Rd. Slough ... 22 A1
Upper Meadow Rd. Read ... 86 B1
Upper Nursery. Sunn ... 121 D2
Upper Park Rd. Camb ... 151 F3
Upper Red Cross Rd. Gori ... 34 B3
Upper Redlands Rd. Read ... 86 C3
Upper Village Rd. Ascot ... 120 B2
Upper Warren Ave. Caver ... 58 B2
Upper Woodcote Rd. Caver ... 58 B3
Uppingham Dr. Wood ... 60 C1
Uppingham Gdns. Caver ... 59 E3
Upshire Gdns. Brac ... 118 C3
Upton Cl. Hen-O-T ... 15 F1
Upton Cl. Slough ... 42 C2
Upton Court Rd. Slough ... 43 D1
Upton Lea Par. Slough ... 43 D3
Upton Park. Slough ... 42 C2
Upton Rd. Read ... 85 D4
Upton Rd. Slough ... 43 D2
Urquhart Rd. That ... 106 C1
Usk Rd. Read ... 84 C3
Uxbridge Rd. Slough ... 43 E3

Vachel Rd. Read ... 86 A4
Vale Cres. Read ... 57 F1
Vale Gr. Slough ... 42 C2
Vale Rd. Camb ... 151 D2
Vale Rd. Wind ... 66 C3
Valentia Rd. Read ... 85 E4
Valentine Cres. Caver ... 59 E2
Valeview Dr. Bee H ... 138 B3
Valley Cl. Caver ... 59 D2
Valley Cl. Gori ... 34 B3
Valley Cres. Woki ... 116 A4
Valley End. Iver H ... 23 E1
Valley Rd. Bur C ... 111 D2
Valley Rd. Camb ... 152 B1
Valley Rd. Hen-O-T ... 35 D4
Valley Rd. Newb ... 130 C4
Valley Way. Silc ... 135 F1
Valon St. Arbo ... 140 C4
Valpy St. Read ... 86 A4
Valroy Cl. Camb ... 151 E3
Vandyke. Brac ... 117 F2
Vanlore Way. Read ... 84 B3
Vanners La. Ham M ... 129 E3
Vansittart Rd. Bish ... 18 C4
Vansittart Rd. Wind ... 67 D3
Vantage Rd. Slough ... 42 A3
Vanwall Bsns Park. Maid ... 39 E3
Vanwall Rd. Maid ... 39 E2
Vastern Rd. Caver ... 59 D1
Vaughan Copse. Eton ... 42 B1
Vaughan Way. Slough ... 21 F1
Vauxhall Dr. Wood ... 88 A3
Vegal Cres. Eng G ... 95 E2
Venetia Cl. Caver ... 59 E4
Venning Rd. Bark ... 140 C4
Ventnor Rd. Read ... 57 E1
Venus Cl. Woki ... 115 F3
Verey Cl. Twyf ... 61 F2
Vermont Rd. Slough ... 21 F1
Vermont Woods. Woki ... 141 F4
Verney Cl. Mar ... 1 B1
Verney Mews. Read ... 85 E4
Verney Rd. Slough ... 44 A1
Vernon Cres. Read ... 113 D4
Vernon Dr. Ascot ... 119 F4
Vernon Rd. Felt ... 98 C3
Verran Rd. Camb ... 151 E2
Viburnum St. Camb ... 153 F3
Vicarage Ave. Stai ... 96 A2
Vicarage Cl. Cook ... 20 A4
Vicarage Cres. Stai ... 96 A2
Vicarage Ct. Felt ... 98 B4
Vicarage Ct. Stai ... 96 A1
Vicarage Dr. Maid ... 40 B2
Vicarage Gdns. Ascot ... 120 A2
Vicarage La. Cold A ... 106 B4
Vicarage La. Stai ... 124 B3
Vicarage La. Wray ... 95 F4
Vicarage La. Yate ... 149 E4
Vicarage Rd. Ashf ... 98 C1

Vicarage Rd. Bags ... 145 E2
Vicarage Rd. Black ... 150 C2
Vicarage Rd. Hen-O-T ... 35 F4
Vicarage Rd. Maid ... 39 F4
Vicarage Rd. Read ... 86 B3
Vicarage Rd. Stai ... 96 A1
Vicarage Rd. Stai ... 96 C3
Vicarage Rd. Yate ... 149 E4
Vicarage Way. Iver ... 69 E4
Vicarage Wlk. Maid ... 40 B2
Vickers Cl. Shin ... 113 F2
Vickers Cl. Wood ... 88 A4
Victor Rd. That ... 106 C2
Victor Rd. Wind ... 67 E2
Victor Way. Wood ... 88 A4
Victoria Ave. Camb ... 151 D3
Victoria Cres. Iver ... 44 C3
Victoria Gdns. Newb ... 105 D2
Victoria La. Harl ... 71 E4
Victoria Rd. Ascot ... 120 A2
Victoria Rd. Caver ... 59 D2
Victoria Rd. Eton ... 41 F1
Victoria Rd. Far C ... 22 B3
Victoria Rd. Mar ... 1 C1
Victoria Rd. Mort ... 136 C3
Victoria Rd. Read ... 84 B4
Victoria Rd. Sand ... 143 F1
Victoria Rd. Slough ... 43 D3
Victoria Rd. Stai ... 96 C3
Victoria Rd. Warg ... 36 C1
Victoria St. Eng G ... 95 E1
Victoria St. Read ... 86 B4
Victoria St. Slough ... 42 C2
Victoria St. Wind ... 67 E3
Victory Rd. Chert ... 124 A1
Vigo La. Yate ... 149 E2
Vigo La. Yate ... 149 E3
Viking. Brac ... 117 F2
Village Cl. Read ... 113 D3
Village Rd. Dorn ... 41 E2
Village Rd. Stai ... 123 E3
Village The. Finch ... 141 F2
Village The. Old W ... 94 A3
Village Way. Ashf ... 98 A2
Village Way. Yate ... 149 E4
Villiers Mead. Woki ... 116 A3
Villiers Rd. Slough ... 42 B4
Villiers Way. Newb ... 130 B3
Villiers Wlk. Newb ... 130 B3
Vincent Cl. Chert ... 123 F1
Vincent Cl. Harm ... 71 D4
Vincent Cl. Wood ... 87 F3
Vincent Dr. Shepp ... 125 F3
Vincent Rd. Chert ... 123 F1
Vincent Rd. That ... 106 C2
Vincent Rise. Brac ... 118 C3
Vine Cl. Stan ... 70 A1
Vine Cres. Read ... 85 D2
Vine Rd. Sto P ... 22 C3
Vineries Cl. Harm ... 71 D4
Vinery The. Warg ... 36 B1
Vines The. Woki ... 115 E2
Vineyard Dr. Bou E ... 3 D3
Viola Ave. Stan ... 97 F4
Virginia Ave. Vir W ... 122 B2
Virginia Beeches. Vir W ... 122 A1
Virginia Cl. Stai ... 124 B3
Virginia Dr. Vir W ... 122 B3
Virginia Way. Read ... 85 D3
Viscount Rd. Stan ... 97 F4
Viscount Way. Harm ... 71 F2
Viscount Way. Wood ... 88 A4
Vivien Cl. Cook ... 19 F3
Voller Dr. Read ... 84 B3
Volunteer Rd. Thea ... 83 E1
Vulcan Cl. Sand ... 150 A4
Vulcan Way. Sand ... 150 A4

Wabone Rd. Bou E ... 3 D2
Wade Dr. Slough ... 42 A3
Wadham Cl. Shepp ... 125 E1
Wadham. Crow ... 143 F1
Wagbullock Rise. Brac ... 118 B2
Waggoners Hollow. Bags ... 145 F1
Wagner Cl. Whi Wa ... 38 C2
Wagtail Cl. Twyf ... 61 F2
Waingels Rd. Char ... 61 D1
Waingels Rd. Wood ... 61 D1
Wakefield Cres. Sto P ... 22 C3
Wakeford Cl. Silc ... 135 F1
Wakelins End. Cook ... 19 F4
Wakeman Rd. Bou E ... 3 D2
Wakemans. Pangb ... 55 D2
Walbury. Brac ... 118 C3
Waldeck Rd. Maid ... 40 A4
Waldeck St. Read ... 86 A3
Waldegrave Pl. Newb ... 105 D2
Walden Ave. Arbo ... 114 B2
Waldens Cl. Bou E ... 3 D2
Waldorf Hts. Black ... 150 B2
Waldron Hill. Brac ... 118 C4
Walgrove Gdns. Whi Wa ... 63 F4
Walk The. Ashf ... 98 C1
Walk The. Eton ... 42 A1
Walker Rd. Maid ... 40 A2
Walker's La. Lamb ... 25 D2
Walker's Ridge. Camb ... 151 F3

Walkers Pl. Read ... 85 E4
Wall La. Silc ... 136 B1
Wallace Cl. Mar ... 1 C2
Wallace Cl. Shepp ... 125 E3
Wallace Cl. Wood ... 87 E3
Walled Gdn The. Warg ... 36 B1
Waller Dr. Newb ... 105 F3
Wallingford Cl. Brac ... 118 C3
Wallingford Rd. Comp ... 31 F3
Wallingford Rd. Gori ... 14 B3
Wallingford Rd. Sou S ... 14 B3
Wallingford Rd. Stre ... 34 A4
Wallington Rd. Camb ... 145 D1
Wallington's Rd. Kint ... 101 F1
Wallis Ct. Slough ... 43 D2
Wallner Way. Woki ... 116 C3
Walmer Cl. Crow ... 143 E3
Walmer Cl. Read ... 85 D3
Walmer Rd. Wood ... 60 C1
Walnut Cl. Woki ... 115 F3
Walnut Cl. Yate ... 149 E2
Walnut Tree Cl. Bou E ... 3 D1
Walnut Tree Cl. Twyf ... 61 F3
Walnut Tree Ct. Gori ... 34 B3
Walnut Tree Rd. Stai ... 125 E3
Walnut Tree Rd. Stai ... 125 E4
Walnut Way. Bou E ... 3 D1
Walnut Way. Read ... 84 B4
Walpole Rd. Old W ... 95 D4
Walpole Rd. Slough ... 41 E4
Walrus Cl. Wood ... 88 A4
Walter Rd. Woki ... 115 F4
Walters Cl. Cold A ... 106 B4
Waltham Cl. Crow ... 143 E1
Waltham Cl. Whi Wa ... 38 C1
Waltham Rd. Twyf ... 61 F2
Waltham Rd. Twyf ... 62 A3
Waltham Rd. Whi Wa ... 38 C1
Walton Ave. Hen-O-T ... 35 F4
Walton Bridge Rd. Shepp ... 125 F1
Walton Cl. Wood ... 87 E4
Walton Dr. Ascot ... 119 F4
Walton Gdns. Felt ... 98 C2
Walton La. Burn ... 21 F2
Walton La. Shepp ... 125 F1
Walton Way. Newb ... 105 E2
Wandhope Way. Read ... 57 E1
Wanstway Gr. Brac ... 118 C1
Wantage Cl. Brac ... 118 C2
Wantage Rd. Gr She ... 48 B3
Wantage Rd. Lamb ... 25 E3
Wantage Rd. Read ... 85 E4
Wantage Rd. Sand ... 150 B4
Wantage Rd. Stre ... 33 F4
Wapshott Rd. Stai ... 96 C2
War Memorial Pl. Hen-O-T ... 35 F4
Waram Cl. Hung ... 100 C4
Warbler Cl. Read ... 84 A3
Warborough Ave. Read ... 84 A4
Warborough Rd. Let B ... 7 D4
Warbreck Dr. Sulh ... 57 D2
Warbrook La. Finch ... 141 D1
Ward Cl. Iver ... 44 C3
Ward Cl. Woki ... 116 B4
Ward Gdns. Slough ... 41 F3
Ward Royal. Wind ... 67 D3
Ward Stone Park. Brac ... 118 C1
Wardle Ave. Read ... 57 E1
Wardle Cl. Bags ... 145 F2
Wareham Rd. Brac ... 118 C2
Warfield Rd. Brac ... 91 E1
Warfield Rd. Felt ... 98 C4
Warfield St. New G ... 91 E2
Wargrave Hill. Warg ... 36 B1
Wargrave Rd. Rem H ... 36 A4
Wargrave Rd. Twyf ... 61 E3
Wargrove Dr. Sand ... 150 B4
Waring Cl. Winn ... 114 B4
Warley Rise. Sulh ... 57 E2
Warner Cl. Harl ... 71 E4
Warner Cl. Slough ... 41 F3
Warners Hill. Cook ... 19 E4
Warnford Rd. Read ... 84 C4
Warnsham Cl. Read ... 87 D1
Warren Cl. Bur C ... 111 D2
Warren Cl. Sand ... 150 A4
Warren Cl. Slough ... 43 F2
Warren Down. Brac ... 117 F4
Warren End. Newb ... 130 B3
Warren House Rd. Bint ... 89 E1
Warren House Rd. Woki ... 116 B4
Warren La. Woki ... 141 F3
Warren Rd. Ashf ... 98 C1
Warren Rd. Wood ... 60 B1
Warren Rise. Camb ... 151 D2
Warren Row Rd. Know H ... 37 E3
Warren Row. Burl ... 119 E4
Warren The. Caver ... 58 C2
Warrington Ave. Slough ... 42 B4
Warrington Spur. Old W ... 95 D4
Warwick Ave. Slough ... 22 B1
Warwick Ave. Stai ... 97 E1
Warwick Ave. Stai ... 123 E4
Warwick Cl. Camb ... 152 A3
Warwick Cl. Maid ... 39 D2
Warwick Dr. Newb ... 105 D1
Warwick Rd. Ashf ... 97 F2
Warwick Rd. Read ... 86 B2
Warwick. Brac ... 118 C2

Wasdale Cl. Crow ... 143 E1
Wash Hill Lea. Bou E ... 3 E2
Wash Hill. Bou E ... 3 F2
Wash Water. Ham M ... 130 A2
Wash Water. Newb ... 130 A2
Washing La. Brim ... 134 B3
Washington Ct. Mar ... 2 A2
Washington Dr. Slough ... 41 E3
Washington Dr. Wind ... 66 C2
Washington Gdns. Woki ... 142 A4
Washington Rd. Caver ... 59 D1
Watchetts Dr. Camb ... 151 E1
Watchetts Lake Cl. Camb ... 151 E2
Watchetts Rd. Camb ... 151 D2
Watchmoor Rd. Camb ... 151 D2
Water La. Gree ... 131 E4
Water Rd. Read ... 85 D4
Water St. Hamp N ... 52 C3
Waterbeach Rd. Slough ... 42 B4
Waterfall Cl. Vir W ... 122 A3
Waterford Way. Woki ... 116 B3
Waterham Rd. Brac ... 118 A2
Waterhouse Mead. Sand ... 150 C4
Waterloo Cres. Woki ... 116 C3
Waterloo Rd. Crow ... 143 D2
Waterloo Rd. Read ... 86 A3
Waterloo Rd. Woki ... 116 C3
Waterloo Rise. Read ... 86 A2
Waterman Pl. Read ... 59 D1
Waterman's Rd. Hen-O-T ... 35 F4
Waterman's Way. Warg ... 36 B3
Watermead. Felt ... 98 C4
Watermill Ct. Wool ... 108 B1
Waters Dr. Stai ... 96 C2
Watersfield Cl. Read ... 87 D1
Waterside Ct. Newb ... 105 D2
Waterside Dr. Pur O T ... 57 E3
Waterside Dr. Slough ... 44 A2
Wareside Dr. Thea ... 83 F2
Waterside Gdns. Read ... 86 A4
Waterside Park Ind Est. Brac ... 117 F4
Waterside. Woo G ... 3 F4
Watersplash La. Ascot ... 120 C4
Watersplash La. Wink ... 120 C4
Watersplash Rd. Stai ... 125 D3
Watery La. Chert ... 123 E1
Watery La. Kint ... 128 C3
Watery La. Woo G ... 3 F4
Watkins Cl. Woki ... 141 F4
Watlington St. Read ... 86 B4
Watmore La. Winn ... 88 B1
Watson Cl. Woki ... 115 F1
Watt's La. Blew ... 12 A4
Wavell Cl. Read ... 86 C1
Wavell Gdns. Slough ... 21 F1
Wavell Rd. Maid ... 39 D3
Wavendene Ave. Stai ... 96 B1
Waverley Cl. Camb ... 151 F2
Waverley Dr. Camb ... 151 F3
Waverley Dr. Vir W ... 122 A3
Waverley Rd. Bags ... 145 F2
Waverley Rd. Read ... 85 E4
Waverley Rd. Slough ... 42 B4
Waverley Way. Woki ... 115 F1
Waverley Way. Woki ... 141 F4
Waverley. Brac ... 117 F2
Waverleys The. That ... 106 B2
Waybrook Cres. Read ... 86 C3
Wayland Cl. Brac ... 118 C3
Waylen St. Read ... 85 F4
Ways End. Camb ... 151 F2
Wayside Mews. Maid ... 39 F4
Weald Rise. Read ... 57 F1
Wealden Way. Read ... 57 F1
Wealden Way. Read ... 84 C4
Weavers La. Ink ... 127 E3
Weavers Wlk. Newb ... 105 D2
Webb Cl. Bags ... 145 F1
Webb Cl. Binf ... 90 C1
Webb Cl. Slough ... 43 E1
Webb Ct. Woki ... 116 C4
Webbs Acre. That ... 106 C1
Webbs La. Been ... 109 D4
Webster Cl. Maid ... 39 D3
Wedderburn Cl. Winn ... 88 B1
Wedgewood Way. Read ... 57 F1
Weekes Dr. Slough ... 42 A2
Weighbridge Row. Read ... 58 C1
Weir Cl. Read ... 84 C2
Weir Pl. Stai ... 123 F4
Weir Rd. Chert ... 124 A1
Welbeck Rd. Maid ... 39 E3
Welbeck. Brac ... 117 F2
Welby Cl. Maid ... 39 D2
Welby Cres. Winn ... 88 A1
Weldale St. Read ... 85 F4
Welford Rd. Wood ... 88 A4
Well Cl. Camb ... 151 D2
Well House La. Swal ... 140 B2
Well Meadow. Newb ... 105 D3
Welland Cl. Read ... 57 E1
Welland Cl. Slough ... 69 D4
Wellbank. Tapl ... 20 C1
Wellcroft Rd. Slough ... 42 A3
Weller Dr. Bark ... 141 D3
Weller Dr. Camb ... 151 E2
Weller's La. New G ... 91 E4
Wellesley Ave. Iver ... 44 C2
Wellesley Cl. Bags ... 145 E2

178

Wellesley Dr. Brac Wolsey Rd. Ashf

Wellesley Dr. Brac 142 C3
Wellesley Dr. Finch 142 C3
Wellesley Rd. Slough 43 D2
Welley Ave. Wray 68 C2
Welley Rd. Hort 68 C1
Welley Rd. Wray 68 C1
Wellfield Cl. Read 84 B4
Wellhill Rd. Fawl 27 E3
Wellhouse La. Buck 79 F3
Wellhouse La. Herm 79 F3
Wellhouse Rd. Maid 19 F1
Wellington Ave. Read 86 B2
Wellington Ave. Vir W 122 A2
Wellington Ave. Went 122 A2
Wellington Busn Park. Woki 142 C2
Wellington Cl. Newb 105 E3
Wellington Cl. Sand 150 B4
Wellington Cl. Shepp 125 F1
Wellington Cres. Tad 134 B1
Wellington Dr. Brac 118 C2
Wellington Rd. Ashf 97 F2
Wellington Rd. Crow 143 E2
Wellington Rd. Harm 71 F1
Wellington Rd. Maid 39 E4
Wellington Rd. Sand 150 B4
Wellington Rd. Woki 116 A3
Wellington St. Slough 43 D2
Wellingtonia Ave. Finch 142 B2
Wells Cl. Wind 67 D4
Wells La. Ascot 120 A3
Welsh La. Swal 139 D1
Welshman's Rd. Silc 136 A3
Welwick Cl. Winn 87 F1
Welwyn Ave. Felt 71 F1
Wendan Rd. Newb 130 C4
Wendover Dr. Camb 152 B2
Wendover Pl. Stai 96 B2
Wendover Rd. Bou E 3 D3
Wendover Rd. Burn 41 D4
Wendover Rd. Slough 41 D4
Wendover Rd. Stai 96 B2
Wendover Way. Read 84 B4
Wenlock Edge. Char 61 D2
Wenlock Way. That 106 B1
Wensley Cl. Twyf 61 E3
Wensley Rd. Read 85 F3
Wensleydale Dr. Camb 152 B3
Wentworth Ave. Burl 119 E4
Wentworth Ave. Read 113 E4
Wentworth Ave. Slough 22 A1
Wentworth Cl. Ashf 98 A2
Wentworth Cl. Brac 142 C3
Wentworth Cl. Yate 149 E3
Wentworth Cres. Maid 39 E3
Wentworth Ct. Newb 105 D1
Wentworth Dr. Vir W 122 A2
Wentworth Way. Burl 119 E4
Wescott Rd. Woki 116 B3
Wesley Dr. Eng G 96 A1
Wessex Cl. Hung 100 B3
Wessex Gdns. Twyf 61 F2
Wessex Rd. Bou E 3 D1
Wessex Rd. Harn 70 C2
Wessex Way. Maid 39 D2
Wessons Hill. Cook 19 E4
West Cl. Ashf 97 F2
West Cl. Medm 17 E4
West Cres. Wind 66 C3
West Dean. Maid 39 F4
West Dr. Read 84 C3
West Dr. Sonn 60 C1
West Dr. Went 121 F1
West Dr. Went 122 A1
West End Ct. Sto P 22 C2
West End La. Hart 71 E4
West End La. Sto P 22 C2
West End Rd. Silc 136 C3
West Fryerne. Yate 149 E4
West Green Ct. Read 85 F3
West Green. Yate 149 D4
West Hill. Read 86 A3
West Mead. Maid 19 F1
West Mills. Newb 104 C2
West Point. Slough 41 E3
West Ramp. Harm 71 D3
West Rd. Camb 151 E3
West Rd. Felt 98 B4
West Rd. Maid 39 F4
West Ridge. Bou E 3 D2
West Sq. Iver 44 C4
West St. Hen-O-T 15 E1
West St. Maid 39 F4
West St. Mar 1 B1
West St. Newb 104 C2
West St. Read 86 A4
West View. Felt 98 B4
West View. Pease 50 B4
West Way. Shepp 125 E2
Westacott Way. Bur G 38 B2
Westborough Ct. Maid 39 E3
Westborough Rd. Maid 39 E3
Westbourne Rd. Felt 98 C3
Westbourne Rd. Sand 150 C4
Westbourne Rd. Stai 97 D1
Westbourne Terr. Read 85 E4
Westbrook Cl. Hung 100 B3
Westbrook Gdns. Brac 118 B4
Westbrook Green. Blew 11 F4
Westbrook Rd. Read 58 B1
Westbrook Rd. Stai 96 C2
Westbrook St. Blew 11 F4
Westbrook. Holy 40 C1
Westbury Cl. Crow 143 D3
Westbury Cl. Shepp 125 D2
Westbury La. Pur O T 57 D3
Westcombe Cl. Brac 118 C1
Westcote Rd. Read 85 E3
Westcotts Green. New G 91 F1
Westcroft. Slough 22 A1
Westdene Cres. Caver 58 C2
Westerdale Dr. Camb 152 A2
Westerdale. That 106 B2
Western Ave. Chert 124 A3
Western Ave. Hen-O-T 35 F4
Western Ave. Newb 104 C2
Western Ave. Stai 123 D3
Western Ave. Wood 60 C1
Western Cl. Chert 124 A3
Western Dr. Bou E 3 F3
Western Dr. Shepp 125 E2
Western Elms Ave. Read 85 F4
Western End. Newb 104 C1
Western Oaks. Read 57 F1
Western Perimeter Rd. Harm 70 A2
Western Perimeter Rd. Stan 70 A2
Western Rd. Brac 117 F4
Western Rd. Hen-O-T 35 F4
Western Rd. Read 85 F3
Westfield Cotts. Medm 16 C3
Westfield Cres. Shipl 36 A2
Westfield Cres. That 106 A2
Westfield Rd. Camb 151 D1
Westfield Rd. Caver 59 D1
Westfield Rd. Chol 13 E4
Westfield Rd. Maid 39 D4
Westfield Rd. Slough 22 A1
Westfield Rd. That 106 A3
Westfield Rd. Winn 88 A1
Westfield Way. Newb 104 C1
Westfields. Comp 31 E2
Westgate Cres. Slough 41 F3
Westgate Rd. Newb 104 C1
Westhatch Cnr. New G 91 E3
Westhatch La. New G 91 E3
Westhope Rd. Mar 1 C2
Westland Cl. Stan 70 C1
Westland. That 106 A2
Westlands Ave. Read 86 C1
Westlands Ave. Slough 41 E4
Westlands Cl. Slough 41 E4
Westlands Rd. Newb 131 D4
Westley Mill. Binf 90 C4
Westley Mill. Holy 63 F1
Westlyn Rd. Silc 135 F1
Westmacott Dr. Felt 98 C4
Westmead Dr. Newb 130 C4
Westmead. Wind 67 D2
Westminster Way. Wood 87 E1
Westmorland Cl. Woki 115 E3
Westmorland Dr. Camb 152 A2
Westmorland Dr. New G 91 F1
Westmorland Rd. Maid 39 E3
Weston Gr. Bags 145 F1
Weston Rd. Slough 41 F4
Westonbirt Dr. Caver 58 C2
Westons. Beed 51 E4
Westridge Ave. Pur O T 57 E3
Westview Dr. Twyf 61 F3
Westward Rd. Woki 115 F4
Westwates Cl. Brac 118 B4
Westway. Gori 34 B4
Westwood Glen. Read 57 E1
Westwood Green. Cook 19 F3
Westwood Rd. Mar 1 B1
Westwood Rd. Newb 105 E1
Westwood Rd. Read 57 E1
Westwood Rd. Windl 146 C3
Westwood Row. Read 57 E1
Wetherby Cl. Caver 59 E3
Wethered Dr. Burn 41 D4
Wethered Rd. Mar 1 B1
Wetton Pl. Eng G 96 A2
Wexham Park La. Iver H 23 E1
Wexham Park La. Sto P 23 E1
Wexham Rd. Slough 43 D3
Wexham St. Sto P 23 D2
Wexham Woods. Slough 43 E4
Wey Ave. Chert 124 A3
Wey Cl. Camb 151 D3
Weybridge Mead. Yate 149 F4
Weycrofts. Brac 90 C1
Weymead Cl. Chert 124 B1
Whaley Rd. Woki 116 B4
Wharf La. Bou E 3 D2
Wharf La. Hen-O-T 15 F1
Wharf Rd. Newb 105 D2
Wharf Rd. Wray 95 E4
Wharf St. Newb 105 D2
Wharf The. Newb 105 D2
Wharfdale Rd. Winn 88 A2
Wharfside. Padw 109 E2
Whatley Green. Brac 118 A2
Whatmore Cl. Stan 70 A1
Wheatash Rd. Chert 124 A1
Wheatbutts Meadow. Eton 41 F1
Wheatfield Cl. Maid 39 D2
Wheatfields Rd. Shin 113 F3
Wheatlands Cl. Read 84 C2
Wheatlands La. Ham M 130 A3
Wheatlands Rd. Slough 43 E2
Wheatley Cl. Read 86 C1
Wheatley. Brac 117 F2
Wheatsheaf La. Newb 105 D2
Wheatsheaf La. Stai 96 C1
Wheble Dr. Wood 87 E4
Wheeler Cl. Bur C 111 D2
Wheelers Green Way. That 106 C1
Wheelton Cl. Winn 87 F2
Whins Cl. Camb 151 D2
Whins Dr. Camb 151 D2
Whinshill Ct. Went 121 D1
Whistler Gr. Sand 150 B3
Whistley Cl. Brac 118 C3
Whitamore Row. Hen-O-T 35 F4
Whitby Dr. Read 86 B3
Whitby Green. Caver 59 E3
Whitby Rd. Slough 42 B3
Whitchurch Cl. Maid 19 F2
Whitchurch Rd. Pangb 56 B3
White Bridge Cl. Felt 71 F1
White City. Crow 143 E3
White Cl. Herm 78 C3
White Cl. Slough 42 B3
White Gates. Wick 75 E3
White Hart Rd. Maid 39 F4
White Hart Rd. Slough 42 B2
White Hart Row. Chert 124 A1
White Hill. Beac 3 F4
White Hill. Rem H 16 A1
White Hill. Shipl 35 D3
White Hill. Windl 146 A3
White Hill. Woo G 3 F4
White Horse La. Finch 141 E3
White Horse Rd. Wind 66 B3
White House Gdns. Yate 149 E4
White Lilies Island. Wind 67 D4
White Lion Way. Yate 149 E4
White Lodge Cl. Suth 57 D2
White Lodge. Mar B 1 B3
White Paddock. Whi Wa 39 D1
White Rd. Chil 10 B4
White Rd. Sand 150 C3
White Rock. Maid 20 A1
White Shoot. Blew 12 A3
White's La. Been 109 D4
Whitebeam Cl. Woki 115 E2
Whiteford Rd. Slough 42 C4
Whitegates La. Read 87 D4
Whitehall Dr. Arbo 140 C4
Whitehall Farm La. Vir W 122 C3
Whitehall La. Eng G 95 F1
Whitehall La. Wray 69 D1
Whitehill Cl. Mar B 1 B3
Whitehill Pl. Vir W 122 C2
Whitehill Rd. Camb 151 E4
Whitehills Green. Gori 34 B3
Whiteknights Rd. Read 86 C3
Whitelands Dr. Burl 119 E4
Whitelands Rd. That 106 B2
Whiteley. Wind 66 C4
Whitemoor La. Upp B 54 C3
Whitepit La. Fla H 3 E4
Whites Hill. Sulhd 110 C3
Whites La. Datch 68 A4
Whitestone Cl. Winn 87 F2
Whitewalls Cl. Comp 31 F3
Whiteways Ct. Stai 97 D1
Whitley Cl. Stan 70 C1
Whitley Park La. Read 86 B2
Whitley Rd. Yate 149 E2
Whitley St. Read 86 A3
Whitley Wood La. Read 113 E4
Whitley Wood Rd. Read 113 E4
Whitmoor Rd. Bags 145 F1
Whitmore Cl. Sand 143 E1
Whitmore La. Sunn 121 D2
Whitstone Gdns. Read 86 B1
Whittaker Rd. Slough 21 F1
Whittenham Cl. Slough 43 D3
Whittle Cl. Crow 143 D1
Whittle Cl. Woki 141 F4
Whittle Parkway. Slough 41 E4
Whitton Cl. Brac 118 C3
Whitton Cl. Winn 87 E1
Whitworth Rd. Bark 141 D4
Whurley Way. Maid 19 F1
Whynstones Rd. Ascot 120 A2
Whyteladyes La. Cook 19 F3
Wick Hill La. Woki 142 A3
Wick La. Eng G 94 C1
Wick Rd. Eng G 95 D1
Wick's Green. Binf 90 A2
Wickford Way. Read 113 F4
Wickham Cl. Bags 145 F3
Wickham La. Eng G 96 A1
Wickham Rd. Camb 151 F4
Wickham Rd. Winn 87 F1
Wickham Vale. Brac 117 F2
Widbrook Rd. Maid 20 A2
Widecombe Pl. Read 86 A1
Widecroft Rd. Iver 44 C4
Widmere La. Mar B 1 A4
Wield Ct. Winn 87 F1
Wiggett Gr. Binf 90 B1
Wigmore La. Read 58 A1
Wigmore La. Read 58 B1
Wigmore La. Thea 83 E1
Wigmore Rd. Tad 134 C1
Wilberforce Way. Brac 118 B2
Wilcox Gdns. Stai 124 C3
Wild Briar. Woki 141 F4
Wild Cl. Winn 114 B4
Wildcroft Dr. Woki 116 A1
Wilder Ave. Pangb 56 C3
Wilderness Ct. Read 87 D2
Wilderness Rd. Camb 151 F1
Wilderness Rd. Read 87 D2
Wilders Cl. Brac 91 D1
Wilders Cl. Camb 151 F2
Wildgreen N. Slough 44 A1
Wildgreen S. Slough 44 A1
Wildridings Rd. Brac 118 A3
Wildridings Sq. Brac 118 A3
Wildwood Dr. Tad 134 B1
Wildwood Gdns. Yate 149 E2
Wilford Rd. Slough 43 F1
Wilfred Way. That 107 D2
Wilfrids Wood Cl. Bou E 3 D3
Willats Cl. Chert 124 A2
William Cl. That 106 B1
William Ellis Cl. Old W 68 A1
William Slim Wood. Burl 92 A1
William St. Read 85 F4
William St. Slough 42 C3
William St. Wind 67 E3
Williant Cl. Whi Wa 38 C1
Willington Cl. Camb 151 D3
Willoners. Slough 42 A4
Willoughby Rd. Brac 117 F3
Willoughby Rd. Slough 44 A2
Willow Cl. Bur C 111 D3
Willow Cl. Fla H 3 E3
Willow Cl. Iver 69 E4
Willow Cl. Newb 104 C1
Willow Ct. Camb 151 E1
Willow Dr. Brac 118 B4
Willow Dr. Maid 40 A1
Willow Dr. Twyf 61 E3
Willow Gdns. Read 86 C1
Willow Green. West E 153 F3
Willow La. Black 150 B2
Willow La. Wray 36 B2
Willow Park. Sto P 23 D3
Willow Pl. Eton 67 E4
Willow Rd. Newt 131 F1
Willow Rd. Stan 69 F3
Willow St. Read 86 A3
Willow Tree Glade. Bur C 84 B2
Willow Way. Sand 142 C1
Willow Wlk. Chert 124 A1
Willow Wlk. Eng G 95 E2
Willowbrook Rd. Stan 97 F3
Willowbrook. Eton 42 B1
Willowdale. Woki 141 F4
Willowford. Yate 149 E3
Willowmead Cl. Mar 1 C2
Willowmead Cl. Newb 130 B3
Willowmead Gdns. Mar 1 C2
Willowmead Rd. Mar 1 C2
Willowmead Sq. Mar 1 C2
Willowmead. Stai 124 A4
Willows End. Sand 150 A4
Willows La. Bou E 3 D2
Willows The. Caver 59 D1
Willows The. Light 146 B1
Willowside. Wood 60 C1
Willson Rd. Eng G 95 D2
Wilmington Cl. Wood 87 F4
Wilmot Cl. Binf 90 B1
Wilmot Rd. Burn 21 D1
Wilmot Way. Camb 151 F2
Wilmot Wlk. Newb 130 B3
Wilmott Cl. Winn 88 A1
Wilsford Cl. Read 113 F4
Wilson Ave. Hen-O-T 35 F4
Wilson Cl. Comp 31 F2
Wilson Ct. Winn 88 A1
Wilson Rd. Read 85 E4
Wilton Cl. Harm 70 B4
Wilton Cres. Wind 66 B2
Wilton Rd. Camb 151 D2
Wilton Rd. Read 85 E4
Wiltshire Ave. Crow 143 D3
Wiltshire Ave. Slough 22 B1
Wiltshire Dr. Woki 116 B4
Wiltshire Gr. New G 91 F1
Wiltshire Rd. Mar 1 C2
Wiltshire Rd. Woki 116 B4
Wiltshire Wlk. Read 84 A3
Wilwood Rd. Brac 117 F4
Wilwyne Cl. Caver 59 E2
Wimbledon Cl. Camb 144 C1
Wimbledon Rd. Camb 144 C1
Wimblington Dr. Winn 114 B4
Wimborne Gdns. Read 58 A1
Wimbushes. Woki 141 E3
Winbury Ct. Maid 39 F4
Wincanton Rd. Read 113 E4
Winch Cl. Binf 90 B2
Winchbottom La. Lit M 2 A3
Winchcombe Rd. Newb 105 D1
Winchcombe Rd. Twyf 61 F2
Winchester Cl. Stan 69 F3
Winchester Dr. Maid 39 D2
Winchester Rd. Harl 71 F4
Winchester Rd. Read 86 A2
Winchester Way. Black 150 B3
Winchgrove Rd. Brac 91 D1
Winchstone Cl. Stai 124 C3
Wincroft Rd. Caver 58 C3
Windermere Cl. Felt 98 C4
Windermere Cl. Read 88 B2
Windermere Cl. Stai 96 A1
Windermere Rd. Light 146 A1
Windermere Rd. Read 86 B2
Windermere Way. Slough 41 E4
Windermere Way. That 106 A2
Winding Wood Dr. Camb 152 A2
Windle Cl. Windl 146 B2
Windlebrook Green. Brac 118 A4
Windlesham Ct. Windl 146 B4
Windlesham Rd. Brac 117 F4
Windlesham Rd. West E 153 F4
Windmill Ave. Woki 115 F4
Windmill Cl. Stai 98 C1
Windmill Cl. Wind 67 D3
Windmill Cl. Woki 115 F4
Windmill Cnr. Mort 137 D3
Windmill Field. Windl 146 B2
Windmill La. Buck 108 A3
Windmill La. Wool 108 A3
Windmill Rd W. Stai 125 F4
Windmill Rd. Brac 118 A4
Windmill Rd. Cook 19 F3
Windmill Rd. Fulm 23 E4
Windmill Rd. Mort 137 D3
Windmill Rd. Slough 42 B3
Windmill Rd. Stai 125 F4
Windrush Ave. Slough 44 A2
Windrush Hts. Sand 150 A4
Windrush Way. Maid 39 F4
Windrush Way. Read 85 D4
Windsor Dr. Ashf 97 E2
Windsor Hill. Bou E 3 F3
Windsor La. Burn 21 E1
Windsor Park Rd. Harl 71 F4
Windsor Rd. Ascot 120 A4
Windsor Rd. Datch 68 A4
Windsor Rd. Eng G 95 F3
Windsor Rd. Holy 40 B1
Windsor Rd. Maid 40 B1
Windsor Rd. Oak G 40 B1
Windsor Rd. Oak G 40 B1
Windsor Rd. Slough 42 C2
Windsor Rd. Sto P 23 D4
Windsor Rd. Wray 68 C1
Windsor Ride. Sand 151 D4
Windsor Ride. Woki 142 A4
Windsor Rise. Newb 131 E4
Windsor St. Chert 124 A2
Windsor Way. Read 84 A2
Wing Cl. Mar 1 B1
Wingate Rd. Wood 87 F3
Wingfield Gdns. Camb 152 B2
Wingrove Rd. Read 85 E3
Winkfield Cl. Woki 116 A2
Winkfield La. Wink 92 B4
Winkfield Rd. Ascot 120 A4
Winkfield Row. Burl 92 A2
Winkfield St. Burl 92 B3
Winnersh Gate. Winn 88 B1
Winnersh Gr. Winn 88 B1
Winscombe. Brac 117 F2
Winser Dr. Read 85 E3
Winston Cl. Shin 113 E1
Winston Way. Pur O T 57 D3
Winston Way. That 105 F2
Winter Hill. Cook 2 B1
Winter Hill. Cook 19 D2
Winter Hill. Cook 19 D4
Winter Hill. Maid 19 D2
Winterbourne Rd. Box 76 C2
Winterbourne Rd. Wint 76 C2
Winterton Dr. Newb 104 B3
Winton Cres. Yate 149 E3
Winton Rd. Read 113 E4
Wintoun Path. Slough 21 F1
Wintringham Way. Pur O T 57 E3
Winvale. Slough 42 C2
Winwood. Slough 43 E4
Wise's Firs. Sulhd 110 B2
Wishmoor Cl. Camb 151 F4
Wishmoor Rd. Camb 151 F4
Wispington Cl. Winn 87 E1
Wistaria La. Yate 149 E3
Wisteria Cl. Woki 115 F3
Wiston Terr. Read 86 A4
Witcham Cl. Winn 114 B4
Withey Cl. Wind 66 C3
Witheygate Ave. Stai 97 D1
Withy Cl. Light 146 B1
Withy Cl. Read 84 B3
Withy Croft. Slough 43 F4
Withybed La. Kint 101 F2
Wittenham Ave. Read 57 D3
Wittenham Rd. Brac 118 C4
Woburn Cl. Camb 152 A1
Woburn Cl. Caver 58 C2
Wokingham Rd. Brac 117 F4
Wokingham Rd. Hurst 88 C4
Wokingham Rd. Read 87 E2
Wokingham Rd. Sand 142 C1
Wolf La. Wind 66 C2
Wolseley St. Read 86 A3
Wolsey Rd. Ashf 97 F2

Wolsey Rd. Caver

Wolsey Rd. Caver 59 D1
Wolsingham Way. That 106 B1
Wondesford Dale. Binf 90 B2
Wooburn Manor Park. Bou E ... 3 F3
Wooburn Mews. Bou E 3 F3
Wood Cl. Wind 67 E2
Wood End. Crow 142 C2
Wood Green Cl. Read 85 F4
Wood La. Arbo 114 C2
Wood La. Binf 90 B1
Wood La. Iver 44 B4
Wood La. Slough 42 A2
Wood Moor. Finch 141 F1
Wood Rd. Camb 151 D1
Wood Rd. Stai 125 D3
Wood Ridge. Newb 130 C4
Woodberry Cl. Caver 59 D2
Woodbine Cl. Sand 150 B4
Woodbine Cl. Winn 87 E1
Woodbine La. Newt 130 C1
Woodbourne Cl. Yate 149 E3
Woodbridge Rd. Black 150 A3
Woodbridge Rd. Read 84 A3
Woodbury. Lamb 25 E1
Woodby Dr. Sunn 120 C1
Woodcote Rd. Caver 58 C2
Woodcote Rd. Sou S 14 B2
Woodcote Way. Caver 58 B3
Woodcote. Maid 39 E3
Woodend Cl. Burl 119 F4
Woodend Dr. Ascot 120 A2
Woodenhill. Brac 117 F1
Woodfield Dr. Maid 39 D3
Woodfield Way. Thea 83 F2
Woodford Cl. Caver 58 C2
Woodford Green. Brac 118 C3
Woodford Way. Slough 22 A1
Woodhall La. Windl 146 C4
Woodhaw. Stai 96 A2
Woodhouse La. Head 133 E1
Woodhouse St. Binf 90 C1
Woodhouse St. Brac 117 F4
Woodhurst La. Woki 115 F4
Woodhurst Rd. Maid 20 A1
Woodies Cl. Binf 90 B1
Woodland Ave. Slough 42 B3
Woodland Ave. Wind 66 C2
Woodland Ave. Woki 115 F4
Woodland Cl. Mar 1 C2

Woodland Cres. Brac 91 E1
Woodland Dr. Read 84 B4
Woodland Way. Mar 1 C2
Woodlands Ave. Bur C 111 D2
Woodlands Ave. Wood 87 E4
Woodlands Busn Park. Maid ... 39 D1
Woodlands Cl. Ascot 119 F2
Woodlands Cl. Black 150 C1
Woodlands Cl. Herm 78 C3
Woodlands Ct. Crow 143 F1
Woodlands Gr. Caver 59 F2
Woodlands La. Windl 146 C2
Woodlands Parade. Ashf 98 B1
Woodlands Park Ave. Whi Wa 39 D1
Woodlands Park Rd. Maid 39 D2
Woodlands Park Rd. Whi Wa . 39 D2
Woodlands Rd E. Vir W 122 B3
Woodlands Rd W. Vir W 122 B3
Woodlands Rd. Camb 151 D3
Woodlands Rd. Shipl 35 F2
Woodlands Rd. Tad 134 B1
Woodlands Rd. Vir W 122 B3
Woodlands Ride. Ascot 120 A2
Woodlands The. Woki 115 E2
Woodlands Wlk. Black 150 C1
Woodlands. Yate 149 E2
Woodlee Cl. Vir W 122 B4
Woodley Green. Wood 87 F4
Woodman Cl. Read 113 E3
Woodman's La. Bur C 110 C2
Woodmancott Cl. Brac 118 C2
Woodmere Cl. Read 87 D1
Woodmere. Brac 118 C3
Woodmoor End. Cook 20 A4
Woodpecker Cl. Twyf 61 F2
Woodridge Cl. Brac 118 B3
Woodrow Dr. Woki 116 C3
Woods Rd. Caver 59 F2
Woodsend Cl. Read 113 E4
Woodshore Cl. Vir W 122 A2
Woodside Ave. Fla H 3 E4
Woodside Cl. Buck 107 E3
Woodside Cl. Woki 141 F4
Woodside La. Wink 93 E2
Woodside Rd. Ascot 93 D1
Woodside Way. Read 113 E4
Woodside Way. Vir W 122 A3
Woodside. Black 150 B2
Woodside. Fla H 3 E3

Woodside. Newb 130 B4
Woodside. Sand 150 C4
Woodstock Ave. Slough 43 C4
Woodstock Cl. Maid 19 F1
Woodstock St. Read 86 C4
Woodthorpe Rd. Ashf 97 E2
Woodthorpe Rd. Stai 97 E2
Woodview Rd. Pangb 56 B3
Woodville Cl. Black 150 A3
Woodward Cl. Winn 88 B1
Woodway Rd. Blew 12 A4
Woodway. Camb 151 D3
Woodwaye. Wood 87 E4
Woodyer Cl. Wood 87 F3
Woolacombe Dr. Read 86 C1
Woolford Cl. Burl 92 B1
Woolhampton Hill. Wool 108 B2
Woolhampton Way. Brac 118 B2
Woosehill La. Woki 115 F3
Woosehill La. Woki 115 F4
Woosehill. Woki 115 F3
Wootton Cl. Read 84 B4
Wootton Dr. Woo G 3 F4
Wootton Rd. Hen-O-T 35 E4
Wootton Way. Maid 39 E3
Worcester Cl. Maid 39 E2
Worcester Cl. Read 85 D3
Worcester Dr. Ashf 98 A2
Wordsworth Ave. Yate 149 D2
Wordsworth Ct. Caver 59 E4
Wordsworth Rd. Slough 21 E1
Wordsworth Rd. That 106 B2
Wordsworth. Brac 117 F2
Worlds End Hill. Brac 118 C2
Worple Ave. Stai 97 D1
Worple Rd. Stai 97 D1
Worple The. Wray 68 C1
Worrall Way. Read 113 F4
Worster Rd. Cook 19 F3
Worton Dr. Read 113 D4
Wrabness Way. Stai 124 A4
Wraysbury Rd. Stai 96 B3
Wraysbury Rd. Wray 96 B3
Wren Cl. Bur C 111 D2
Wren Cl. Woki 115 F3
Wren Cl. Yate 149 D3
Wren Ct. Slough 44 A2
Wren's Ave. Ashf 98 B2
Wrenfield Dr. Caver 58 C3

Wrensfield. Mar 1 B1
Wrenswood Cl. Read 113 D4
Wright Cl. Wood 88 A4
Wright. Oak G 66 B2
Wroxham Rd. Wood 87 E4
Wroxham. Brac 117 F2
Wurford Dr. That 106 C2
Wyatt Rd. Stai 97 D2
Wyatt Rd. Wind 66 B2
Wychcotes. Caver 58 C2
Wychelm Rd. Light 153 E4
Wychelm Rd. Shin 113 F3
Wychwood Ave. Brac 118 C3
Wychwood Cl. Read 86 C1
Wychwood Cres. Read 86 C2
Wychwood Pl. Camb 145 D1
Wychwood Pl. Camb 152 A4
Wycombe La. Woo G 3 F4
Wycombe Rd. Mar 1 C2
Wycombe Rd. Mar B 1 C3
Wye Cl. Ashf 98 A2
Wye Cl. Read 84 C3
Wye Rd. Woo G 3 F4
Wykeham Cl. Harm 71 D4
Wykeham Rd. Read 87 D3
Wylam. Brac 117 F2
Wylands Rd. Slough 44 A1
Wyld Court Hill. Hamp N 53 E3
Wymers Cl. Burn 21 D2
Wymers Wood Rd. Burn 21 D2
Wyncote Cl. Read 86 C1
Wyndale Cl. Hen-O-T 15 F1
Wyndham Cl. Yate 149 E4
Wyndham Cres. Burn 21 D2
Wyndham Cres. Wood 60 B1
Wyndham Rd. Newb 105 E3
Wynford Cl. Read 85 E2
Wynnstay Gdns. Mar B 1 C3
Wynsham Way. Windl 146 A3
Wyre Ct. Sulh 57 E2
Wyres Dale. Brac 118 C1
Wythe Mead. Binf 90 A1
Wyvern Cl. Brac 118 A3

Yale Cl. Crow 143 F1
Yard Mead. Eng G 96 A3
Yardley. Brac 117 F2
Yarnold Cl. Woki 116 C4
Yarnton Cl. Caver 59 E3

Zinzan St. Read

Yateley Dr. Yate 149 D1
Yateley Rd. Sand 149 F4
Yattendon La. Asham 54 B1
Yattendon La. Yatt 54 B1
Yattendon Rd. Herm 79 D4
Yaverland Dr. Bags 145 E1
Ye Meads. Tapl 40 C3
Yelverton Rd. Read 86 B2
Yeomans La. Newt 131 D1
Yeomans Way. Camb 151 F3
Yeosfield. Swal 139 E2
Yeoveney Cl. Stan 96 B3
Yeovil Rd. Burn 41 F4
Yeovil Rd. Sand 143 F1
Yew Cl. Woki 115 F3
Yew Gate. Newb 104 C3
Yew La. Read 85 F3
Yew Tree Cl. Maid 39 F4
Yew Tree Ct. Gori 34 B3
Yew Tree Rd. Slough 43 D2
Yew Tree Rise. Read 84 B3
Yew Tree Wlk. Camb 151 F1
Yewhurst Cl. Twyf 61 E3
Yewtrees. Stai 123 E3
Yield Hall La. Read 86 A4
Yield Hall Pl. Read 86 A4
Yockley Cl. Camb 152 B2
Yoreham Cl. Winn 87 F1
York Ave. Slough 42 B4
York Ave. Wind 67 D3
York Cl. Newb 105 D1
York Cl. Binf 90 B2
York Rd. Camb 151 E4
York Rd. Hen-O-T 15 E1
York Rd. Hung 100 B2
York Rd. Maid 40 A4
York Rd. Mar 1 B1
York Rd. Newb 105 D1
York Rd. Read 59 D1
York Rd. Wind 67 D3
York Way. Sand 150 A4
Yorktown Rd. Sand 150 B4
Youlden Cl. Camb 152 A3
Youlden Dr. Camb 152 A3

Zealand Ave. Harm 70 C4
Zinnia Cl. Woki 115 E4
Zinzan St. Read 85 F4

O|S ORDNANCE SURVEY
STREET ATLASES

The Ordnance Survey / Philip's County Street Atlases provide unique and definitive mapping of entire counties

Counties available

- ◆ Berkshire
- ◆ Buckinghamshire
- ◆ East Essex
- ◆ West Essex
- ◆ North Hampshire
- ◆ South Hampshire
- ◆ Hertfordshire
- ◆ East Kent
- ◆ West Kent
- ◆ Nottinghamshire
- ◆ Oxfordshire
- ◆ Surrey
- ◆ East Sussex
- ◆ West Sussex
- ◆ Warwickshire

The County Street Atlases are revised and updated on a regular basis and new titles are added to the series. Many counties are now available in full-size hardback and softback editions as well as handy pocket-size versions.

The series is available from all good bookshops or by mail order direct from the publisher. However, the order form opposite may not reflect the complete range of titles available so it is advisable to check by telephone before placing your order. Payment can be made by credit card or cheque/postal order in the following ways:

By phone *Phone your order through on our special Credit Card Hotline on 0933 410511. Speak to our customer service team during office hours (9am to 5pm) or leave a message on the answering machine, quoting CSA94, your full credit card number plus expiry date and your full name and address*

By post *Simply fill out the order form opposite (you may photocopy it) and send it to:*
Cash Sales Department, Reed Book Services, PO Box 5, Rushden, Northants, NN10 6YX

STREET ATLASES

Registered office: Michelin House, 81 Fulham Road, London SW3 6RB. Registered in England No 1974080

CSA94

	Hardback £12.99	Softback £8.99	Pocket £4.99	
Berkshire	£ ___.__ ISBN 0-540-05992-7	£ ___.__ ISBN 0-540-05993-5	£ ___.__ ISBN 0-540-05994-3	£ ___.__
Buckinghamshire	£ ___.__ ISBN 0-540-05989-7	£ ___.__ ISBN 0-540-05990-0	£ ___.__ ISBN 0-540-05991-9	£ ___.__
East Essex	£ ___.__ ISBN 0-540-05848-3	£ ___.__ ISBN 0-540-05866-1	£ ___.__ ISBN 0-540-05850-5	£ ___.__
West Essex	£ ___.__ ISBN 0-540-05849-1	£ ___.__ ISBN 0-540-05867-X	£ ___.__ ISBN 0-540-05851-3	£ ___.__
North Hampshire	£ ___.__ ISBN 0-540-05852-1	£ ___.__ ISBN 0-540-05853-X	£ ___.__ ISBN 0-540-05854-8	£ ___.__
South Hampshire	£ ___.__ ISBN 0-540-05855-6	£ ___.__ ISBN 0-540-05856-4	£ ___.__ ISBN 0-540-05857-2	£ ___.__
Hertfordshire	£ ___.__ ISBN 0-540-05995-1	£ ___.__ ISBN 0-540-05996-X	£ ___.__ ISBN 0-540-05997-8	£ ___.__
East Kent	£ ___.__ ISBN 0-540-06026-7	£ ___.__ ISBN 0-540-06027-5	£ ___.__ ISBN 0-540-06028-3	£ ___.__
West Kent	£ ___.__ ISBN 0-540-06029-1	£ ___.__ ISBN 0-540-06031-3	£ ___.__ ISBN 0-540-06030-5	£ ___.__
Nottinghamshire	£ ___.__ ISBN 0-540-05858-0	£ ___.__ ISBN 0-540-05859-9	£ ___.__ ISBN 0-540-05860-2	£ ___.__
Oxfordshire	£ ___.__ ISBN 0-540-05986-2	£ ___.__ ISBN 0-540-05987-0	£ ___.__ ISBN 0-540-05988-9	£ ___.__
Surrey	£ ___.__ ISBN 0-540-05983-8	£ ___.__ ISBN 0-540-05984-6	£ ___.__ ISBN 0-540-05985-4	£ ___.__
East Sussex	£ ___.__ ISBN 0-540-05875-0	£ ___.__ ISBN 0-540-05874-2	£ ___.__ ISBN 0-540-05873-4	£ ___.__
West Sussex	£ ___.__ ISBN 0-540-05876-9	£ ___.__ ISBN 0-540-05877-7	£ ___.__ ISBN 0-540-05878-5	£ ___.__
Warwickshire	£10.99 £ ___.__ ISBN 0-540-05642-1			£ ___.__

I enclose a cheque/postal order for £ ___.__ made payable to **Reed Book Services** or please debit my ◄ Access ◄ American Express ◄ Visa account by £ ___.__

Name ___

Address ___

Postcode ___

Account number ⬭⬭⬭⬭ ⬭⬭⬭⬭ ⬭⬭⬭⬭ ⬭⬭⬭⬭

Expiry date ⬭⬭ ⬭⬭

Signature ___

◯ Please tick this box if you do not wish your name to be used by other carefully selected organisations that may wish to send you information about other products and services

◆ **Free postage and packing** ◆ *All available titles will normally be dispatched within 5 working days of receipt of order, but please allow up to 28 days for delivery.*